CLYMER®
YAMAHA
IT125-490 • 1976-1986

CLYMER®

P.O. Box 12901, Overland Park, Kansas 66282-2901

Copyright ©1987 Penton Business Media Inc.

FIRST EDITION
First Printing March, 1981
Second Printing September, 1981

SECOND EDITION
Revised by Ron Wright to include 1981 models
First Printing June, 1983

THIRD EDITION
Revised by Ron Wright to include 1982-1983 models
First Printing June, 1984
Second Printing January, 1986

FOURTH EDITION
Revised by Ron Wright to include 1984-1986 models
First Printing June, 1987
Second Printing November, 1988
Third Printing August, 1990
Fourth Printing June, 1992
Fifth Printing April, 1994
Sixth Printing September, 1996
Seventh Printing May, 1998
Eighth Printing July, 2000
Ninth Printing February, 2003
Tenth Printing December, 2007

Printed in U.S.A.

CLYMER and colophon are registered trademarks of Penton Business Media Inc.

ISBN-10: 0-89287-330-2

ISBN-13: 978-0-89287-330-2

COVER: *Photographed by Michael Brown Photographic Productions, Los Angeles, California. Motorcycle ridden by Tim Lunde. Helmet courtesy of Simpson Sports, Torrance, California. Riding apparel courtes of JT Racing, San Diego, California.*

TOOLS AND EQUIPMENT: *K & L Supply Co. at www.klsupply.com.*

All rights reserved. Reproduction or use, without express permission, of editorial or pictorial content, in any manner, is prohibited. No patent liability is assumed with respect to the use of the information contained herein. While every precaution has been taken in the preparation of this book, the publisher assumes no responsibility for errors or omissions. Neither is any liability assumed for damages resulting from use of the information contained herein. Publication of the servicing information in this manual does not imply approval of the manufacturers of the products covered.

All instructions and diagrams have been checked for accuracy and ease of application; however, success and safety in working with tools depend to a great extent upon individual accuracy, skill and caution. For this reason, the publishers are not able to guarantee the result of any procedure contained herein. Nor can they assume responsibility for any damage to property or injury to persons occasioned from the procedures. Persons engaging in the procedure do so entirely at their own risk.

Chapter One
General Information

Chapter Two
Troubleshooting

Chapter Three
Lubrication, Maintenance and Tune-up

Chapter Four
Engine

Chapter Five
Clutch and Transmission

Chapter Six
Fuel and Exhaust Systems

Chapter Seven
Electrical System

Chapter Eight
Front Suspension and Steering

Chapter Nine
Rear Suspension

Chapter Ten
Brakes

Chapter Eleven
Frame and Repainting

Supplement
1981 and Later Service Information

Index

Wiring Diagrams

CLYMER®

Publisher Shawn Etheridge

EDITORIAL

Managing Editor
James Grooms

Associate Editors
Rick Arens
Steven Thomas

Authors
Jay Bogart
Michael Morlan
George Parise
Mark Rolling
Ed Scott
Ron Wright

Technical Illustrators
Steve Amos
Errol McCarthy
Mitzi McCarthy
Bob Meyer

Group Production Manager
Dylan Goodwin

Production Manager
Greg Araujo

Senior Production Editor
Darin Watson

Production Editors
Holly McComas
Adriane Roberts

Production Designer
Jason Hale

MARKETING/SALES AND ADMINISTRATION

Sales Managers
Justin Henton
Matt Tusken

Marketing and Sales Representative
Erin Gribbin

Director, Operations–Books
Ron Rogers

Customer Service Manager
Terri Cannon

Customer Service Account Specialist
Courtney Hollars

Customer Service Representatives
Dinah Bunnell
April LeBlond

Warehouse & Inventory Manager
Leah Hicks

P.O. Box 12901, Overland Park, KS 66282-2901 • 800-262-1954 • 913-967-1719

More information available at *clymer.com*

CONTENTS

QUICK REFERENCE DATA XI

CHAPTER ONE
GENERAL INFORMATION 1

Manual organization
Service hints
Torque specifications
Safety first
Special tips
Parts replacement
Expendable supplies
What year is it?
Serial numbers
Basic hand tools
Tune-up and troubleshooting tools
Fasteners
Mechanic's tips

CHAPTER TWO
TROUBLESHOOTING 17

Operating requirements
Troubleshooting instruments
Emergency troubleshooting
Engine starting
Engine performance
Engine noises
Excessive vibration
Two-stroke pressure testing
Front suspension and steering
Brake problems

CHAPTER THREE
LUBRICATION, MAINTENANCE, AND TUNE-UP 22

Pre-checks
Tires and wheels
Lubricants
Cleaning solvent
Periodic lubrication
Periodic maintenance
Engine tune-up
Storage

CHAPTER FOUR
ENGINE 63

Engine principles
Engine lubrication
Engine cooling
Servicing engine in frame
Engine
Cylinder head
Cylinder
Piston, piston pin, and piston rings
Break-in procedure
Magneto
Reed valve assembly
Compression release (IT400C only)
Crankcase and crankshaft
Kickstarter
Service and adjustment

CHAPTER FIVE
CLUTCH AND TRANSMISSION 118

    Clutch
    Clutch cable
    Clutch release (push lever) mechanism
    External shift mechanism
    Transmission and internal shift mechanism

CHAPTER SIX
FUEL AND EXHAUST SYSTEMS 166

    Air cleaner
    Carburetor operation
    Carburetor service
    Carburetor adjustments
    Fuel shutoff valve
    Fuel tank
    Fuel filter
    Exhaust system
    Exhaust system decarbonizing
    Exhaust system repair

CHAPTER SEVEN
ELECTRICAL SYSTEM 182

    Capacitor discharge ignition
    Spark plug
    Magneto
    Ignition coil
    Engine kill switch
    Lighting system
    Speedometer housing
    Wiring diagrams

CHAPTER EIGHT
FRONT SUSPENSION AND STEERING 195

    Front wheel
    Front hub
    Wheels
    Tire changing
    Tire repairs
    Handlebar
    Steering head
    Front fork

CHAPTER NINE
REAR SUSPENSION 222

    Rear wheel
    Rear hub
    Drive sprocket
    Drive chain
    Wheel balancing
    Tire changing and tire repairs
    Rear swing arm
    Rear suspension
        (DeCarbon monocross system)
    Rear suspension (monocross type)

CHAPTER TEN
BRAKES 261

    Front brake
    Rear brake
    Front brake cable
    Rear brake pedal assembly

CHAPTER ELEVEN
FRAME AND REPAINTING 272

    Kickstand (side stand)
    Footpegs
    Frame

SUPPLEMENT
1981 AND LATER SERVICE INFORMATION 275

INDEX 331

WIRING DIAGRAMS .... end of book

CLYMER®
YAMAHA
IT125-490 • 1976-1986

QUICK REFERENCE DATA

MODEL INFORMATION

MODEL:_____ YEAR:_____

VIN NUMBER:_____

ENGINE SERIAL NUMBER:_____

CARBURETOR SERIAL NUMBER OR I.D. MARK:_____

RECOMMENDED LUBRICANTS AND FUEL

Engine oil	Yamaha Yamalube "R"; Shell Super M; Castrol R30
Transmission oil	SAE 10W/30 "SE" motor oil
Front forks	SAE 10W/20, SAE 15, SAE 10 or special fork oil
Air filter	SAE 10W/30 motor oil
Drive chain	Chainlube or 10W/30 motor oil
Control cables	Cable lube or 10W/30 motor oil
Control lever pivots	10W/30 motor oil
Steering head, wheel bearings, swing arm	Medium weight wheel bearing grease (waterproof type)
Brake cam	Lithium base
Fuel	Premium grade–research octane 90 or higher
Brake fluid	DOT 3

DRIVE CHAIN SLACK

Model	in.	mm
IT490K, L	3/4-3/16	20-30
IT465H, J	7/16-5/8	10-15
IT425G	1 9/16-2	40-50
IT400E, F	1 9/16-2	40-50
IT400C, D	2 1/8-2 3/8	55-60
IT250K	3/4-1 3/16	20-30
IT250H, J	7/16-5/8	10-15
IT250E, F, G	1 9/16-2	40-50
IT250D	2 1/8-2 3/8	55-60
IT200	1 3/16- 1 3/8	30-35
IT175J, K	1 3/16-1 3/8	30-35
IT175G, H	7/16-5/6	10-15
IT175E, F	1 9/16-2	40-50
IT175D	2 1/8-2 3/8	55-60
IT125G, H	1 9/16- 1 13/16	40-45

TIRE INFLATION PRESSURE

Tire Size	Air Pressure
Front	
3.00-21 -4PR	14 psi (1.0 kg/cm²)
	12.8 psi (0.9 kg/cm²) IT125G only
Rear	
4.10-18 -4PR	17 psi (1.2 kg/cm²)
4.50-18 -4PR	15 psi (1.1 kg/cm²)

FUEL CAPACITIES

Model	U.S. gal.	Liters
IT490K, L	3.6	13.5
IT465	3.4	13.0
IT425	3.2	12.0
IT400	3.2	12.0
IT250K	3.6	13.5
IT250D, E, F, G, H, J	3.4	13.0
IT200	2.9	11.0
IT175G, H, J, K	2.9	11.0
IT175D, E, F	2.5	9.5
IT125	2.2	8.5

TRANSMISSION OIL CAPACITY

Model	Drain/refill	Rebuild
IT490K, L	750 cc	800 cc
IT465J	750 cc	800 cc
IT465H	650 cc	700 cc
IT425G	800 cc	850 cc
IT400D, E, F	1,050-1,150 cc	1,150-1,250 cc
IT400C	950 cc	1,000 cc
IT250H, J, K	750 cc	800 cc
IT250G	800 cc	850 cc
IT250D, E, F	1,050-1,150 c	1,150-1,250 cc
IT200L	700 cc	800 cc
IT200N, S	700 cc	750 cc
IT175G, H, J, K	600 cc	700 cc
IT175D, E, F	650 cc	750 cc
IT125G, H	600-700 cc	700-800 cc

SPARK PLUG TYPE AND GAP

Model	Type	Gap in.	Gap mm
IT490K, L	Champion N-3C	0.028-0.031	0.7-0.8
IT465H, J	Champion N-3	0.024-0.028	0.6-0.7
IT425G	Champion N-3	0.024-0.028	0.6-0.7
IT400C, D, E, F	Champion N-3G	0.024-0.028	0.6-0.7
IT250K	Champion N-86	0.020-0.024	0.5-0.6
IT250D, E, F, G, H, J	Champion N-2G	0.024-0.028	0.6-0.7
IT200	Champion N-86	0.020-0.024	0.5-0.6
IT175J, K	Champion N-86	0.020-0.024	0.5-0.6
IT175H	Champion N-2G	0.028	0.7
IT175G	Champion N-59G	0.024-0.028	0.6-0.7
IT175D, E, F	Champion N-2G	0.024-0.031	0.6-0.8
IT125G, H	Champion N-2G	0.024-0.031	0.6-0.8

NOTE: If you own a 1981 or later model, first check the Supplement at the back of the book for any new service information.

CHAPTER ONE

GENERAL INFORMATION

This detailed, comprehensive manual covers the Yamaha IT series monoshock trails bikes from 1976 on. Chapters One through Twelve contain general information on all models and specific information on 1976-1980 models. The supplement at the end of the book contains information on 1981 and later models that differs from earlier years.

The expert text gives complete information on maintenance, tune-up, repair, overhaul and performance improvement. Hundreds of photos and drawings guide you through every step. The book includes all you need to keep your Yamaha in top condition.

A shop manual is a reference. You want to be able to find information fast. As in all Clymer books, this one is designed with you in mind. All chapters are thumb tabbed. Important items are extensively indexed at the rear of the book. All procedures, tables, photos, etc., in this manual assume that the reader may be working on the bike or using this manual for the first time. Finally, all the most frequently used specifications and capacities are summarized in the *Quick Reference Data* pages at the front of the book.

Keep the book handy in your tool box or tow vehicle. It may help you to better understand how your IT runs, lower repair and maintenance costs, and generally improve your satisfaction with your bike.

Refer to **Figure 1A** and **Figure 1B** for locations of the major controls. **Table 1** and **Table 2** are at the end of this chapter.

MANUAL ORGANIZATION

All dimensions and capacities are expressed in English units familiar to U.S. mechanics as well as in metric units.

This chapter provides general information and discusses equipment and tools useful both for preventive maintenance and troubleshooting.

Chapter Two provides methods and suggestions for quick and accurate diagnosis and repair of problems. Troubleshooting procedures discuss typical symptoms and logical methods to pinpoint the trouble.

Chapter Three explains all periodic lubrication and routine maintenance necessary to keep your Yamaha IT running well. Chapter Three also includes recommended tune-up procedures, eliminating the need to constantly consult chapters on the various assemblies.

Subsequent chapters describe specific systems such as the engine, clutch, transmission, fuel, exhaust, suspension and brakes. Each chapter provides disassembly, repair and assembly procedures in simple step-by-step form. If a repair is impractical for a home mechanic, it is so indicated. It is usually faster and less expensive to take such repairs to a dealer or competent repair shop. Specifications concerning a particular system

CHAPTER ONE

MAJOR CONTROLS AND COMPONENTS
1. Headlight
2. Speedometer/odometer
3. Fuel/oil fill cap
4. Clutch lever
5. Headlight switch
6. Foot peg
7. Exhaust silencer
8. Gearshift lever
9. Side stand
10. Drive chain adjuster

are included at the end of the appropriate chapter.

Some of the procedures in this manual specify special tools. In all cases, the tool is illustrated either in actual use or alone. Well-equipped mechanics may find they can substitute similar tools already on hand or can fabricate their own.

The terms NOTE, CAUTION and WARNING have a specific meaning in this manual. A NOTE provides additional information to make a step or procedure easier or clearer. Disregarding a NOTE could cause inconvience, but would not cause damage or personal injury.

A CAUTION emphasizes areas where equipment damage could result. Disregarding a CAUTION could cause permanent mechanical damage; however, personal injury is unlikely.

A WARNING emphasizes areas where personal injury or even death could result from negligence. Mechanical damage may also occur. WARNINGS *are to be taken seriously.* In some cases, serious injury or death has resulted from disregarding similar warnings.

Throughout this manual keep in mind 2 conventions. "Front" refers to the front of the bike. The front of any component, such as the engine, is the end which faces toward the front of the bike. The "left-" and "right-hand" side refer to the position of the parts as viewed by a rider sitting on the seat facing forward. For example, the throttle grip is on the right-hand

GENERAL INFORMATION

11. Taillight
12. Choke knob or lever
13. Fuel shutoff valve
14. Throttle grip
15. Front brake lever
16. Air filter
17. Rear brake pedal
18. Kickstarter crank
19. Transmission/ clutch oil fill cap

side. These rules are simple, but even experienced mechanics occasionally become disoriented.

SERVICE HINTS

Most of the service procedures covered are straightforward and can be performed by anyone reasonably handy with tools. It is suggested, however, that you consider your own capabilities carefully before attempting any operation involving major disassembly of the engine.

Some operations, for example, require the use of a press. It would be wiser to have these performed by a shop equipped for such work, rather than to try to do the job yourself with makeshift equipment. Other procedures require precise measurements. Unless you have the skills and equipment required, it would be better to have a qualified repair shop make the measurements for you.

There are many items available that can be used on your hands before and after working on your bike. A little preparation prior to getting "all greased up" will help cleaning up later.

Before starting out, work Vaseline, soap or a product like Pro-Tek (**Figure 2**) onto your forearms, into your hands and under your fingernails and cuticles. This will make cleanup a lot easier.

For cleanup, use a waterless hand soap like Sta-Lube and then finish up with powdered Boraxo and a fingernail brush.

Repairs go much faster and easier if your bike is clean before you begin work. There are special cleaners like Gunk or Bel-Ray Degreaser (**Figure 3**) for washing the engine and related parts. Just brush or spray on the cleaning solution, let it stand, then rinse it away with a garden hose. Clean all oily or greasy parts with cleaning solvent as you remove them.

> *WARNING*
> *Never use gasoline as a cleaning agent. It presents an extreme fire hazard. Be sure to work in a well-ventilated area when using cleaning solvent. Keep a fire extinguisher, rated for gasoline fires, handy in any case.*

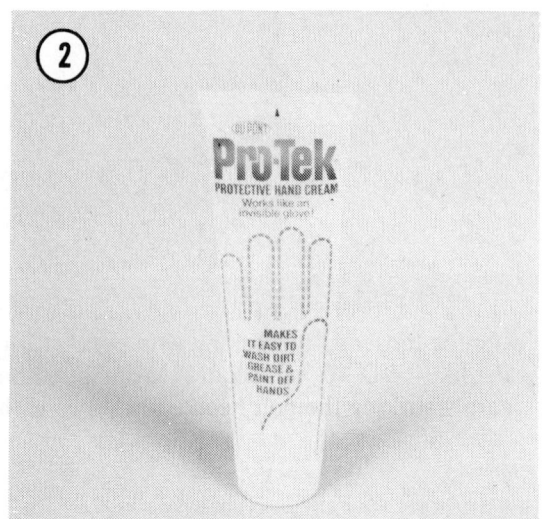

Special tools are required for some repair procedures. These may be purchased at a dealer, rented from a tool rental dealer or fabricated by a mechanic or machinist (often at a considerable savings).

Much of the labor charged for repairs made by dealers is for the removal and disassembly of other parts to reach the defective unit. It is frequently possible to perform the preliminary operations yourself and then take the defective unit in to the dealer for repair at considerable savings.

Once you have decided to tackle the job yourself, read the entire section in this manual which pertains to it, making sure you have identified the proper one. Study the illustrations and text until you have a good idea of what is involved in completing the job satisfactorily. If special tools are required, make arrangements to get them before you start. It is frustrating and time-consuming to get partly into a job and then be unable to complete it.

Simple wiring checks can be easily made at home; but knowledge of electronics is almost a necessity for performing tests with complicated electronic testing gear.

During disassembly of parts keep a few general cautions in mind. Force is rarely needed to get things apart. If parts are a tight fit, like a bearing in a case, there is usually a tool designed to separate them. Never use a screwdriver to pry apart parts with machined

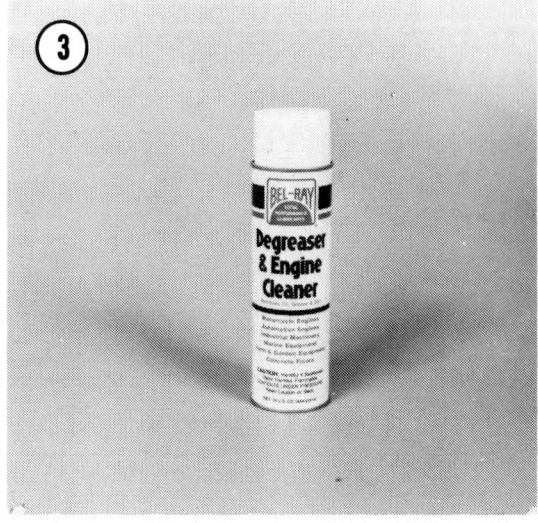

surfaces such as crankcase halves. You will mar the surfaces and end up with leaks.

Make diagrams (or take a Polaroid picture) wherever similar-appearing parts are found. For instance, crankcase bolts are often not the same length. You may think you can remember where everything came from—but mistakes are costly. There is also the possibility you may be sidetracked and not return to work for days or even weeks—in which interval carefully laid out parts may have become disturbed.

Tag all similar internal parts for location and mark all mating parts for position. Record number and thickness of any shims as they are

GENERAL INFORMATION

removed. Small parts such as bolts can be identified by placing them in plastic sandwich bags. Seal and label them with masking tape.

Wiring should be tagged with masking tape and marked as each wire is removed. Again do not rely on memory alone.

Protect finished surfaces from physical damage or corrosion. Keep gasoline off painted surfaces.

Frozen or very tight bolts and screws can often be loosened by soaking with penetrating oil, like WD-40 or Liquid Wrench, then sharply striking the bolt head a few times with a hammer and punch (or screwdriver for screws). Avoid heat unless absolutely necessary, since it may melt, warp or remove the temper from many parts.

No parts, except those assembled with a press fit, require unusual force during assembly. If a part is hard to remove or install, find out why before proceeding.

Cover all openings after removing parts to keep dirt, small tools, etc., from falling in.

When assembling 2 parts, start all fasteners, then tighten evenly.

Wiring connections and brake shoes should be kept clean and free of grease and oil.

When assembling parts, be sure all shims and washers are replaced exactly as they came out.

Whenever a rotating part butts against a stationary part, look for a shim or washer. Use new gaskets if there is any doubt about the condition of the old ones. A thin coat of oil on gaskets may help them seal effectively.

Heavy grease can be used to hold small parts in place if they tend to fall out during assembly. However, keep grease and oil away from electrical and brake components.

High spots may be sanded off a piston with sandpaper, but fine emery cloth and oil will do a much more professional job.

Carbon can be removed from the head, the piston crown and the exhaust port with a dull screwdriver. *Do not* scratch either surface. Wipe off the surface with a clean cloth when finished.

A carburetor is best cleaned by disassembling it and soaking the parts in a commercial carburetor cleaner. Never soak gaskets and rubber parts in these cleaners. Never use wire to clean out jets and air passages; they are easily damaged. Use compressed air to blow out the carburetor only if the float(s) has been removed first.

A baby bottle makes a good measuring device for adding oil to the transmission and front forks. Get one that is graduated in ounces and cubic centimeters. After it has been used for this purpose, do not let a small child drink out of it as there will always be an oil residue in it.

Take your time and do the job right. Do not forget that a newly rebuilt engine must be broken in the same as a new one. Keep the rpm within the limits given in your owner's manual when you get back in the dirt.

TORQUE SPECIFICATIONS

Torque specifications throughout this manual are given in foot-pounds (ft.-lb.) and Newton meters (N•m). Newton meters are being adopted in place of meter-kilograms (mkg) in accordance with the International Modernized Metric System. Tool manufacturers are beginning to introduce torque wrenches calibrated in Newton meters and Sears has a Craftsman line calibrated in both values.

Existing torque wrenches, calibrated in meter-kilograms, can be used by performing a simple conversion. All you have to do is move the decimal point one place to the right; e.g. 4.7 mkg = 47 N•m. This conversion is sufficient for use in this manual even though the exact mathematical conversion is 3.5 mkg = 34.3 N•m.

SAFETY FIRST

Professional mechanics can work for years and never sustain a serious injury. If you observe a few rules of common sense and safety, you can enjoy many hours servicing your own machine. If you ignore these rules you can hurt yourself or damage the bike.

1. Never use gasoline as a cleaning solvent.
2. Never smoke or use a torch in the vicinity of flammable liquids such as cleaning solvent in open containers.

3. If welding or brazing is required on the machine, remove the fuel tank and monoshock to a safe distance, at least 50 feet away.
4. Use the proper sized wrenches to avoid damage to nuts and injury to yourself.
5. When loosening a tight or stuck nut, be guided by what would happen if the wrench should slip. Be careful; protect yourself accordingly.
6. Keep your work area clean and uncluttered.
7. Wear safety goggles during all operations involving drilling, grinding or use of a cold chisel.
8. Never use worn tools.
9. Keep a fire extinguisher handy and be sure it is rated for gasoline and electrical fires.

SPECIAL TIPS

Competition machines are subjected to loads and wear far beyond those encountered in normal dirt riding. One race may take as much out of a machine as several days of trail riding. Because of the extreme demands placed on a racing machine, several points should be kept in mind when performing service and repair. The following items are general suggestions that may improve the overall life of the machine and help avoid costly failures.
1. Use a locking compound such as Loctite Lock N' Seal No. 2114 (blue Loctite) on all bolts and nuts, even though they are secured with lockwashers. This type of Loctite does not harden completely and allows easy removal of the bolt or nut. A screw or bolt lost from an engine cover or bearing retainer could easily cause serious and expensive damage before its loss is noticed.

When applying Loctite, use a small amount. If too much is used, it can work its way down the threads and stick parts together not meant to be stuck.

Keep a tube of Loctite in your tool box; when used properly it is cheap insurance.
2. Use a hammer-driven impact driver tool to remove and install all screws, particularly engine cover screws. These tools help prevent the rounding off of screw heads and ensure a tight installation.

3. When straightening out the "fold over" type lockwasher (usually used on the clutch nut), if possible, use a wide blade chisel such as an old and dull wood chisel. Such a tool provides a better purchase on the folded tab, making straightening out easier.
4. When installing the "fold-over" type lockwasher always use a new washer if possible. If a new washer is not available always fold-over a part of the washer that has not been previously folded.

Reusing the same fold may cause the washer to break, resulting in the loss of its locking ability and also resulting in a loose piece of metal adrift in the engine.

When folding the washer over, start the fold with a screwdriver and finish it with a pair of pliers. If a punch is used to make the fold, the fold may be too sharp, thereby increasing the chances of the washer breaking under stress.

These washers are relatively inexpensive and it is suggested that you keep several of each size in your tool box for field repairs.
5. When replacing missing or broken fasteners (bolts, nuts and screws), especially on the engine or frame components, always use Yamaha replacement parts. They are specially hardened for each application. The wrong 25-cent bolt could easily cause many dollars worth of serious damage, not to mention rider injury.
6. When installing gaskets in the engine, always use Yamaha replacement gaskets *without* sealer, unless designated. These gaskets are designed to swell when they come in contact with oil. Gasket sealer will prevent the gaskets from swelling as intended, which can result in oil leaks. These Yamaha gaskets are also cut from material of the precise thickness needed. Installation of a too thick or too thin gasket in a critical area could cause engine damage.

PARTS REPLACEMENT

Yamaha makes frequent changes during a model year—some minor, some relatively major. When you order parts from the dealer or other parts distributor, always order by engine and frame number. Write the numbers down and carry them with you. Compare new

GENERAL INFORMATION

parts to old before purchasing them. If they are not alike, have the parts manager explain the difference to you.

EXPENDABLE SUPPLIES

Certain expendable supplies are also required. These include grease, oil, gasket cement, wiping rags, and cleaning solvent. Ask your dealer for the special locking compounds, silicone lubricants and lube products (**Figure 4**) which make motorcycle maintenance simpler and easier. Cleaning solvent is available at some service stations.

WHAT YEAR IS IT?

It's not easy to tell one year from the other. External changes throughout the years by the factory have been relatively minor. After the bike has been thrashed around on the trials circuit for a few years and modifications have been made by a previous owner on the suspension or fuel tank, you may be left guessing as to what year it is.

The only *positive* way to correctly identify the specific year of the engine and chassis is with the factory serial numbers. Refer to the following section for their specific location. **Table 1** is a comprehensive list of the IT125-IT425 series monoshock trials motorcycles. This table includes the engine and chassis serial numbers from the beginning to the end of production for each year that that particular model was produced.

Remember that the engine may have been swapped in the frame and may not be from the same year. Always use the engine serial number for engine parts and the chassis serial number for chassis related components.

SERIAL NUMBERS

You must know the model serial number for registration purposes and when ordering replacement parts.

The frame serial number is stamped on the right-hand side of the steering head (**Figure 5**). The engine number is located on the top rear section of the engine (**Figure 6**).

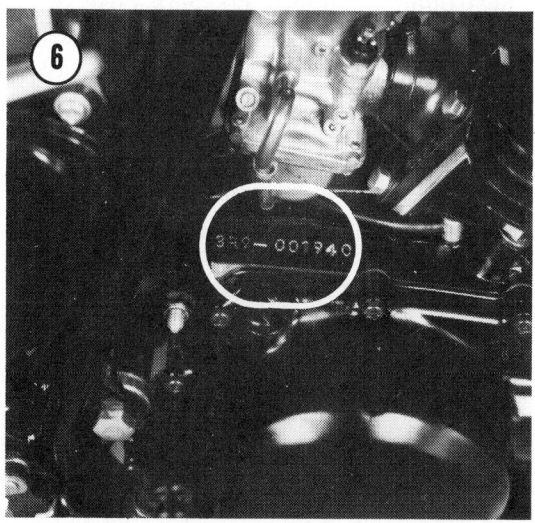

BASIC HAND TOOLS

A number of tools are required to maintain a bike in top competitive condition. You may already have some around for other work like home or car repairs. There are also tools made especially for motorcycle repairs; these you will have to purchase. In any case, a wide variety of quality tools will make motorcycle repairs more effective and easier.

Top quality tools are essential; they are also more economical in the long run. If you are now starting to build your tool collection, stay away from the "advertised specials" featured at some parts houses, discount stores and chain drug stores. These are usually a poor grade tool that can be sold cheaply and that is exactly what they are—*cheap*. They are usually made of inferior material and are thick, heavy and clumsy. Their rough finish makes them difficult to clean and they usually don't last very long. This doesn't mean that you have to run out and buy Snap-On or Proto tools. They are for the professional mechanics who use them 8 hours a day and are usually too expensive for the weekend home mechanic. The Craftsman line from Sears is a good all-around line of tools and will last you a lifetime if you take care of them. Also be careful when lending tools to "friends"—make sure they return them promptly; if not, your collection will soon disappear.

Quality tools are made of alloy steel and are heat-treated for greater strength. They are lighter and better balanced than cheap ones. Their surface is smooth, making them a pleasure to work with and easy to clean. The initial cost of good quality tools may be more but it is cheaper in the long run. Don't try to buy everything in all sizes in the beginning; do it a little at a time until you have the necessary tools.

Keep your tools clean and in a tool box. Keep them organized with the sockets and related drives together and the open-end and box wrenches together, etc. After using a tool, wipe off dirt and grease with a clean cloth and replace the tool in its correct place. Doing this will save a lot of time you would have spent trying to find a socket buried in a bunch of clutch parts.

The following tools are required to perform virtually any repair job on a motorcycle. Each tool is described and the recommended size given for starting a tool collection. **Table 2** includes all the tools that should be on hand for simple home or trials competition event repairs and/or major overhaul. Additional tools and some duplications may be added as you become more familiar with the bike. Almost all bikes (with the exception of the U.S. built Harley and some English bikes) use metric size bolts and nuts—so if you are starting your collection now, buy metric sizes.

Screwdrivers

The screwdriver is a very basic tool, but if used improperly it will do more damage than good. The slot on a screw has a definite dimension and shape. A screwdriver must be selected to conform with that shape. Use a small screwdriver for small screws and a large one for large screws or the screw head will be damaged.

Two basic types of screwdriver are required to repair the bike—a common screwdriver and the Phillips screwdriver.

Screwdrivers are available in sets which often include an assortment of common and Phillips blades. If you buy them individually, buy at least the following:

a. Common screwdriver—5/16 x 6 in. blade
b. Common screwdriver—3/8 x 12 in. blade
c. Phillips screwdriver—size 2 tip, 6 in. blade

Use screwdrivers only for driving screws. Never use a screwdiver for prying or chiseling. Do not try to remove a Phillips or Allen head screw with a common screwdriver; you can damage the head so that the proper tool will be unable to remove it.

Keep screwdrivers in the proper condition and they will last longer and perform better. Always keep the tip of a common screwdriver in good condition. **Figure 7** shows how to grind the tip to the proper shape if it becomes damaged. Note the parallel sides of the tip.

GENERAL INFORMATION

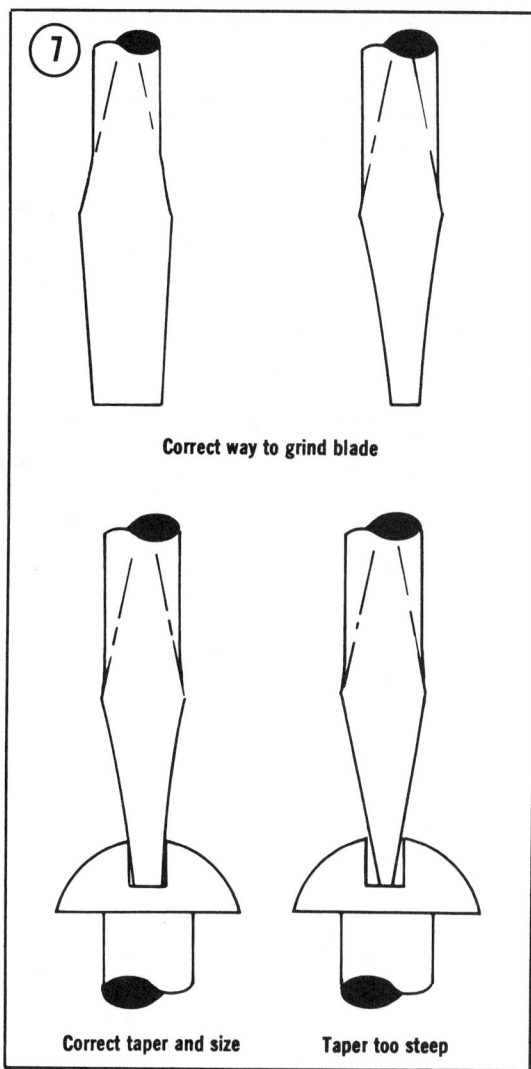

Correct way to grind blade

Correct taper and size   Taper too steep

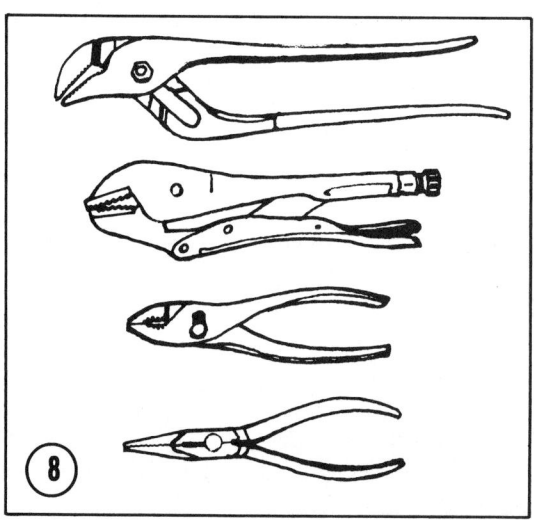

Pliers

Pliers come in a wide range of types and sizes. Pliers are useful for cutting, bending and crimping. They should never be used to cut hardened objects or to turn bolts or nuts. **Figure 8** shows several pliers useful in motorcycle repairs.

Each type of pliers has a specialized function. Gas pliers are general purpose pliers and are used mainly for holding things and for bending. Vise Grips are used as pliers or to hold objects very tight like a vise. Needlenose pliers are used to hold or bend small objects. Channel lock pliers can be adjusted to hold various sizes of objects; the jaws remain parallel to grip around objects such as pipe or tubing. There are many more types of pliers. The ones described here are most suitable for motorcycle repairs.

Box and Open-end Wrenches

Box and open-end wrenches are available in sets or separately in a variety of sizes. See **Figure 9** and **Figure 10**. The size number stamped near the end refers to the distance between 2 parallel flats on the hex head bolt or

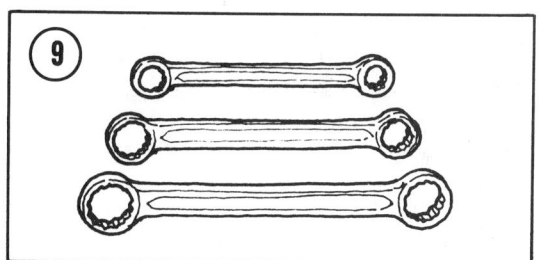

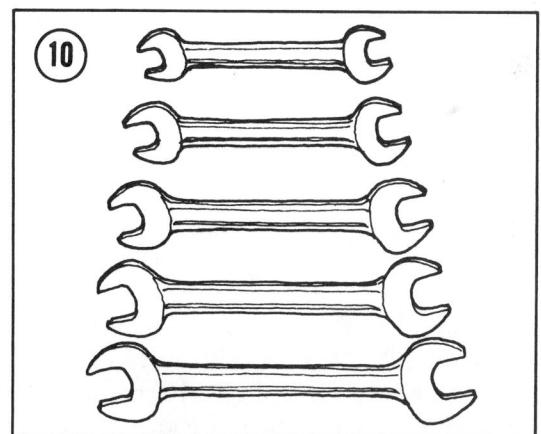

nut. They are available in metric and inch sizes. You will need metric for the IT.

A set covering 6-20 mm (plus a 32 and 34 mm) is adequate for service on the bike.

Box wrenches are usually superior to open-end wrenches. Open-end wrenches grip the nut on only 2 flats. Unless it fits well, it may slip and round off the points on the nut. The box wrench grips all 6 flats. Both 6-point and 12-point openings on box wrenches are available. The 6-point gives superior holding power; the 12-point allows a shorter swing.

Combination wrenches which are open on one side and boxed on the other are also available. Both ends are the same size.

Adjustable (Crescent) Wrenches

An adjustable wrench (also called crescent wrench) can be adjusted to fit nearly any nut or bolt head. See **Figure 11**. However, it can loosen and slip, causing damage to the nut and maybe to your knuckles. Use an adjustable wrench only when other wrenches are not available.

Crescent wrenches come in sizes ranging from 4-18 in. overall. A 6 or 8 in. wrench is recommended as an all-purpose wrench.

Socket Wrenches

This type is undoubtedly the fastest, safest and most convenient to use. See **Figure 12**. Sockets which attach to a ratchet handle are available with 6-point or 12-point openings and 1/4, 3/8 and 3/4 inch drives. The drive size indicates the size of the square hole which mates with the ratchet handle. Sockets are available in metric and inch sizes. You will need metric for the IT.

Strap Wrench

This tool, designed for removal of an automotive spin-on oil filter, is very handy for holding the magneto rotor to keep it from turning while removing and installing the securing nut. See **Figure 13**.

Torque Wrench

A torque wrench is used with a socket to measure how tight a nut or bolt is installed.

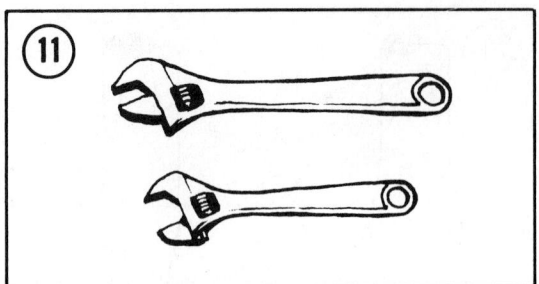

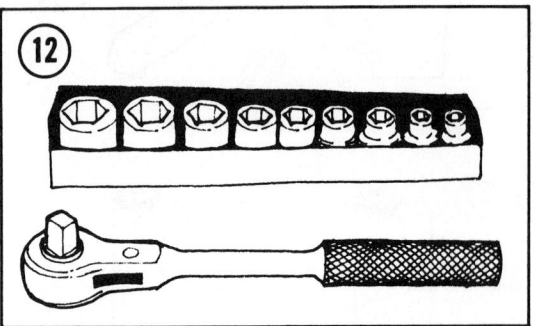

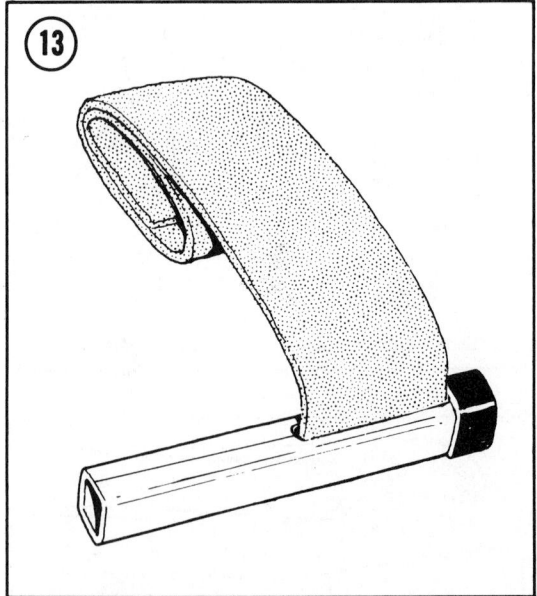

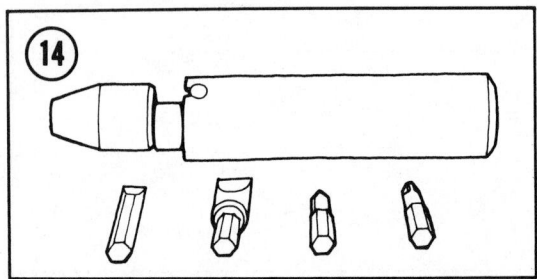

GENERAL INFORMATION

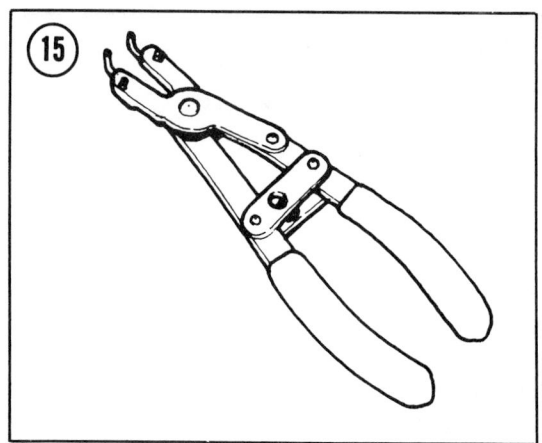

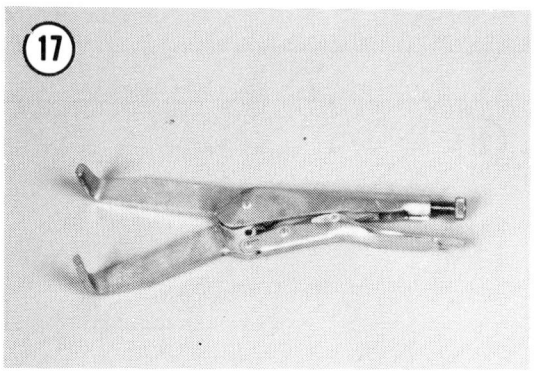

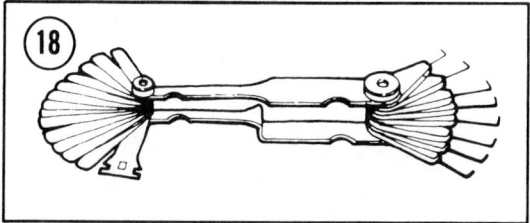

They come in a wide price range and with either 3/8 or 1/2 in. square drive. The drive size indicates the size of the square drive which mates with the socket. You will need one that measures 1-100 ft.-lb. (0-140 N•m).

Impact Driver

This tool might have been designed with the motorcycle in mind. See **Figure 14**. It makes removal of engine and clutch parts easy and eliminates damage to bolts and screw slots. Good ones are available at large hardware or auto parts stores.

Circlip Pliers

Circlip pliers (sometimes referred to as snap-ring pliers) are necessary to remove the circlips used on the transmission shaft assemblies. See **Figure 15**. Most come with a variety of size tips.

Hammers

The correct hammer is necessary for motorcycle repairs. Use only a hammer with a face (or head) of rubber or plastic or the soft-faced type that is filled with buckshot (**Figure 16**). These are sometimes necessary in engine teardowns. *Never*—repeat never—use a metal-faced hammer on the bike as severe damage will result in most cases. You can always produce the same amount of force with a soft-faced hammer.

The Grabbit

This special tool (**Figure 17**) is very useful as a holding tool especially in the removal and installation of the drive sprocket nut and clutch nut. It is called the Grabbit (part No. 969103) and is available from Joe Bolger Products, Inc., Summer Street, Barre, MA 01005.

Ignition Gauge

This tool has both flat and wire measuring gauges and is used to measure contact breaker point gap and spark plug gap. See **Figure 18**.

Good ones are available at most auto or motorcycle supply stores. Get one calibrated in millimeters.

Tire Levers

These are used to remove or install motorcycle tires. Check the working end of the tool before use and remove any burrs. Never use a screwdriver in place of a tire lever; refer to Chapter Eight for its use.

Spoke Wrench

This special wrench is used to tighten spokes (**Figure 19**). It is available at most motorcycle supply shops.

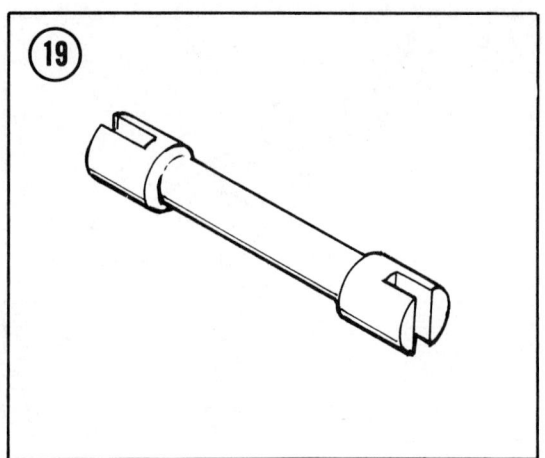

Other Special Tools

A few other special tools may be required for major service. These are described in the appropriate chapters and are available either from Yamaha dealers or other manufacturers as indicated.

TUNE-UP AND TROUBLESHOOTING TOOLS

Multimeter or VOM

This instrument (**Figure 20**) is invaluable for electrical system troubleshooting and service. A few of its functions may be duplicated by homemade test equipment, but for the serious biker it is a must. Its uses are described in the applicable sections of the book. Multimeters are available at electronic hobbyist stores and mail order outlets.

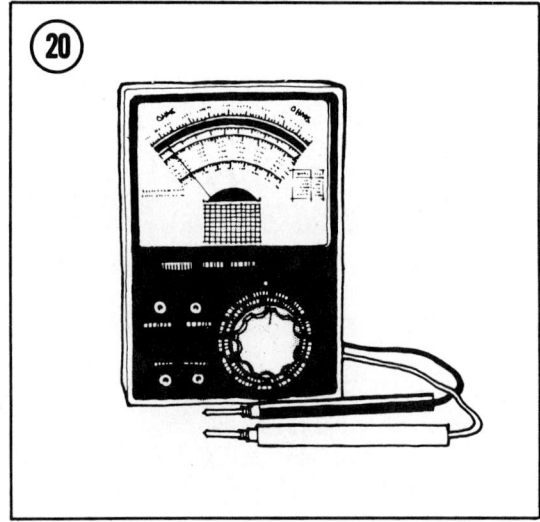

Timing Gauge (Dial Indicator)

This device is used to precisely locate the position of the piston before top dead center to achieve the most accurate ignition timing. The instrument is screwed into the spark plug hole and indicates inches and/or millimeters.

The tool shown in **Figure 21** is available from most dealers and mail order houses. Less expensive tools, which use a vernier scale instead of a dial indicator, are also available.

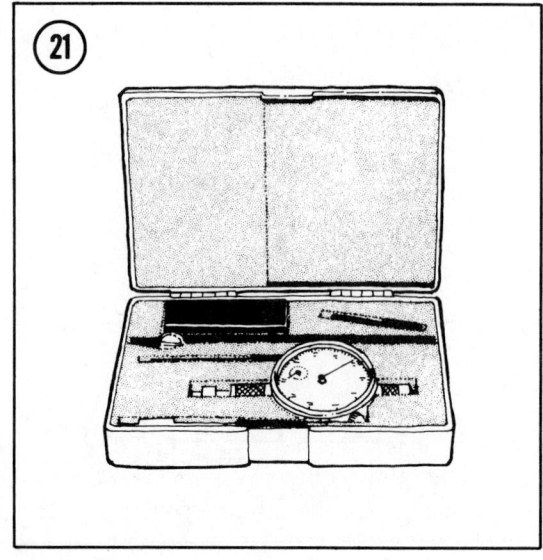

GENERAL INFORMATION

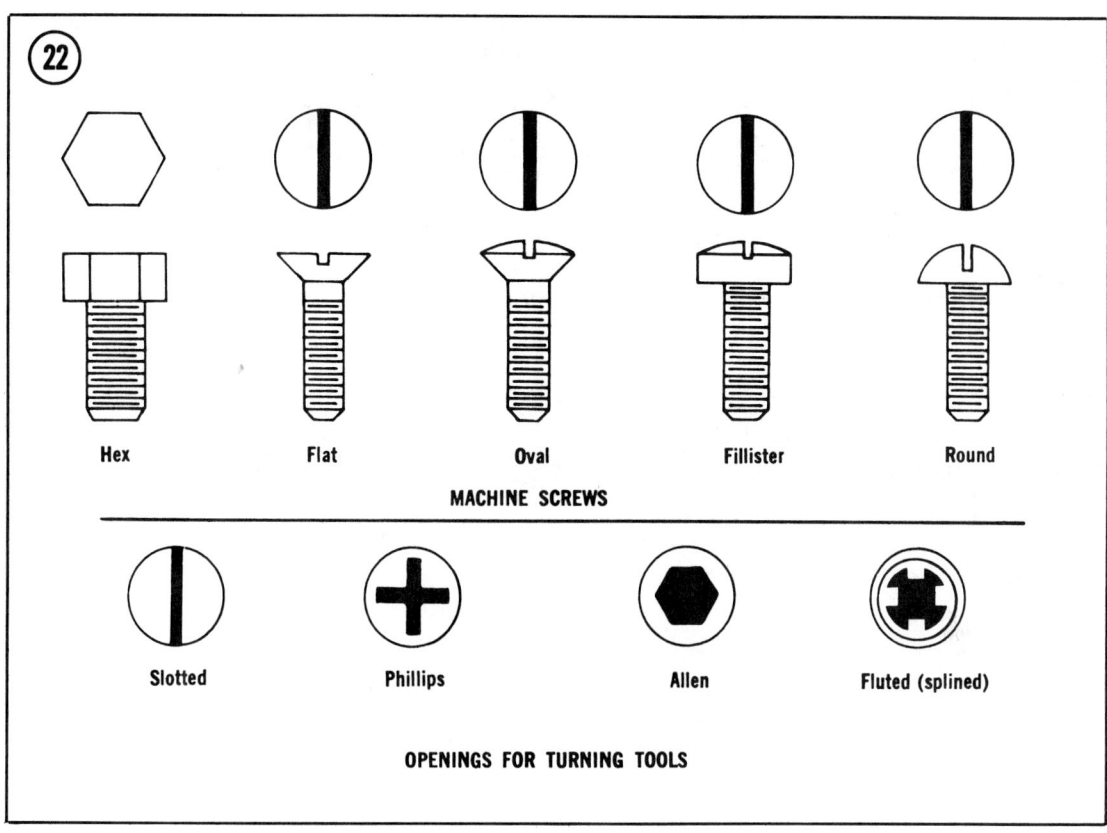

FASTENERS

In order to better understand and select basic hand tools, a knowledge of various fasteners used on the bike is important. This knowledge will also aid in selecting replacements when fasteners are damaged or corroded beyond use.

NOTE
When replacing a bolt and fastener, always use Yamaha replacement bolts, etc., especially on engine and suspension components. They are specially hardened for each application. The wrong 50 cent bolt could easily cause many dollars worth of damage not to mention rider injury.

Threads

Nuts, bolts and screws are manufactured in a wide range of thread patterns. To join a nut and bolt, it is necessary that the diameter of the bolt and the diameter of the hole in the nut be the same. It is equally important that the threads on both be properly matched.

The best way to ensure that the threads on the 2 fasteners are the same is to turn the nut on the bolt with fingers only. If much force is needed, check the thread condition on both fasteners. If thread condition is good (not stripped), but the fasteners jam, the threads are not compatible. Take the fasteners to a motorcycle dealer for proper mates.

Most fasteners are cut so that a fastener must be turned *clockwise* to tighten it. These are called right-hand threads. Some components have left-hand threads; they must be turned *counterclockwise* to tighten them.

NOTE
When replacing threaded components, rely on your dealer's experience; take the old part in for replacement.

Machine Screws

There are many different types of machine screws. **Figure 22** shows a number of screw heads requiring different types of turning tools. Heads are also designed to protrude above the metal (round) or to be slightly recessed in the metal (flat).

When replacing a damaged screw, take it to a dealer. Match the head type, diameter and threads exactly. In addition, match the type of metal used. For example, if the old screw is chrome plated, the new one should be chrome plated to resist corrosion and rust.

Bolts

Commonly called bolts, the technical name for these fasteners is cap screws. They are specified by diameter and thread pitch, e.g., M14 x 1 specifies a bolt 14 mm in diameter with a thread pitch of 1 mm. The measurement across 2 flats on the head of the bolt indicates the proper wrench size to use.

When replacing damaged bolts, follow the same advice given for machine screws.

Nuts

Nuts are manufactured in a variety of types and sizes. Most nuts on bikes are hexagonal (6-sided) and fit on bolts, screws and studs with the same diameter and thread pitch.

Figure 23 shows several nuts usually found on bikes. The common nut (A) is normally used with a lockwasher. The locknut (B) has a nylon insert which prevents the nut from loosening and does not require a lockwasher. To indicate the size of the nut, manufacturers specify the diameter of the opening and the thread pitch, e.g., M14 x 1 indicates a 14 mm opening and a 1 mm thread pitch.

This is, of course, the same as for bolts, but with no length dimension given. In addition, the measurement across 2 flats on the nut indicates the proper wrench size to be used.

When replacing a damaged nut, take it to a dealer. Match the type, diameter and threads exactly.

Washers

There are 2 major types of washers—flat washers and lockwashers. Flat washers are simple discs with a hole cut to fit a screw or bolt. Lockwashers are designed to prevent a fastener from working loose, due to vibration, expansion and contraction. **Figure 24** shows

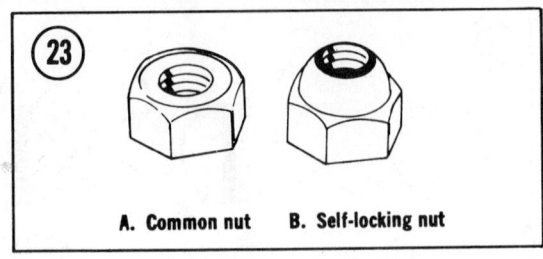
A. Common nut   B. Self-locking nut

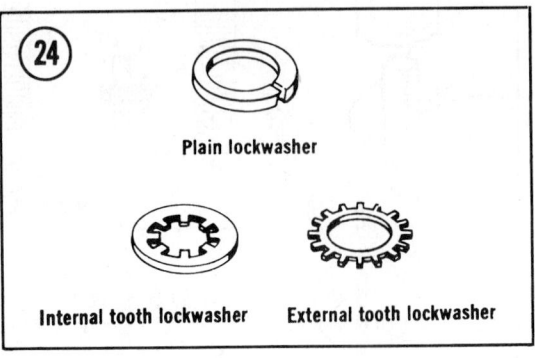
Plain lockwasher

Internal tooth lockwasher   External tooth lockwasher

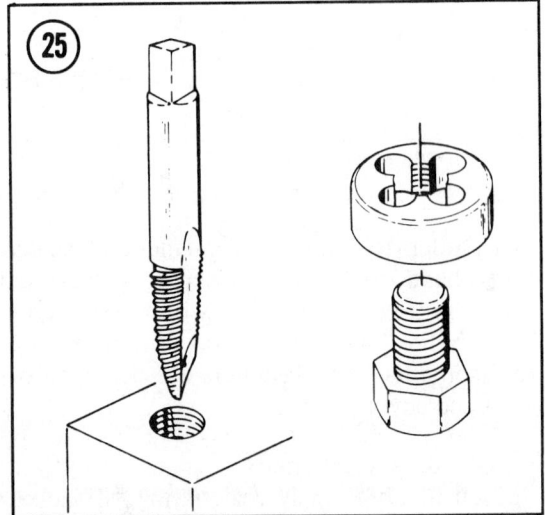

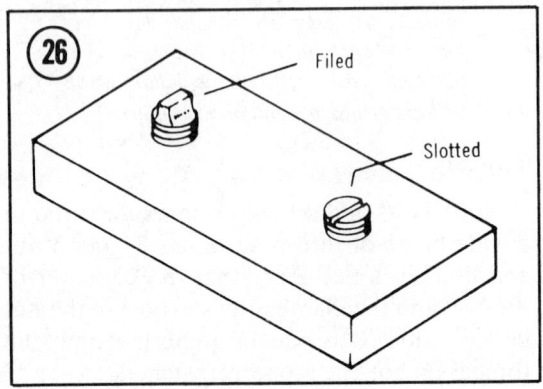
Filed
Slotted

GENERAL INFORMATION

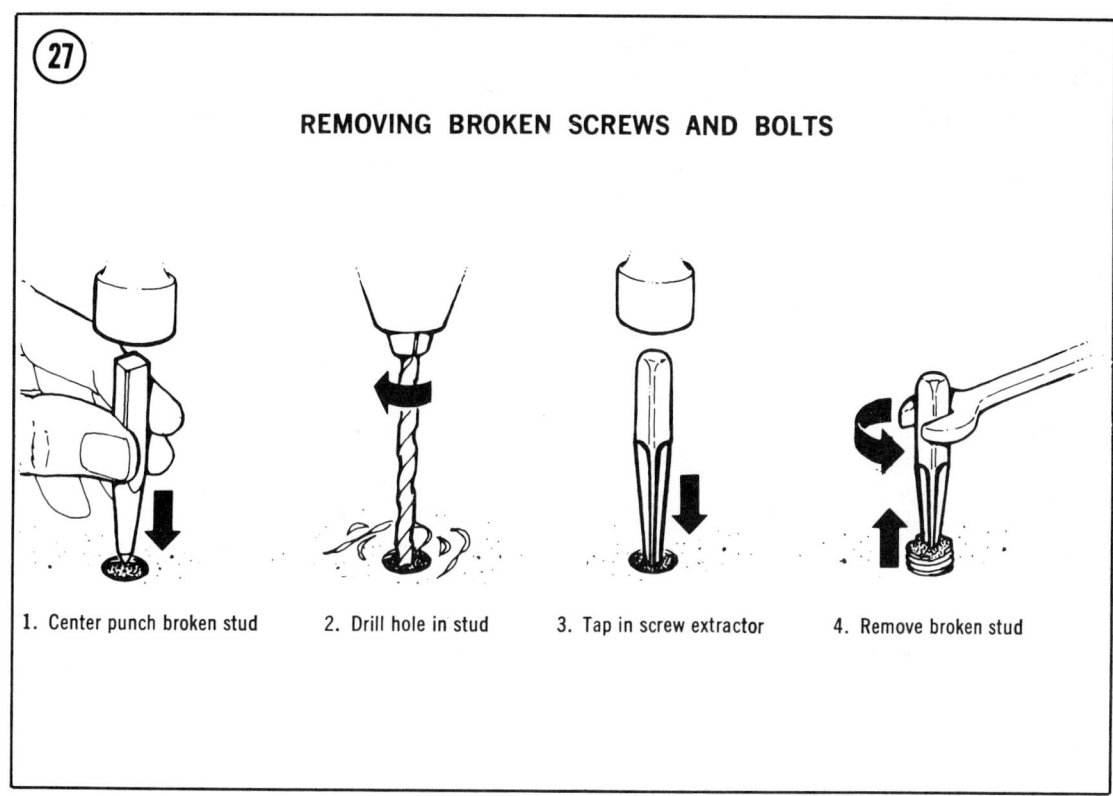

27. REMOVING BROKEN SCREWS AND BOLTS
1. Center punch broken stud
2. Drill hole in stud
3. Tap in screw extractor
4. Remove broken stud

several washers. Note that flat washers are often used between lockwashers and a fastener to act as a smooth bearing surface. This permits the fastener to be turned easily with a tool.

MECHANIC'S TIPS

Removing Frozen Nuts and Screws

When a fastener rusts and cannot be removed, several methods may be used to loosen it. First, apply penetrating oil such as Liquid Wrench or WD-40 (available at any hardware or auto supply store). Apply it liberally. Rap the fastener several times with a small hammer; do not hit it hard enough to cause damage.

For frozen screws, apply penetrating oil as described, then insert a screwdriver in the slot and rap the top of the screwdriver with a hammer. This loosens the rust so the screw can be removed in the normal way. If the screw head is too chewed up to use a screwdriver, grip the head with Vise Grip pliers and twist the screw out.

Remedying Stripped Threads

Occasionally, threads are stripped through carelessness or impact damage. Often the threads can be cleaned up by running a tap (for internal threads on nuts) or die (for internal threads on bolts) through threads. See **Figure 25**.

Removing Broken Screws or Bolts

When the head breaks off a screw or bolt, several methods are available for removing the remaining portion.

If a large portion of the remainder projects out, try gripping it with Vise Grips. If the projecting portion is too small, try filing it to fit a wrench or cut a slot in it to fit a screwdriver. See **Figure 26**.

If the head breaks off flush, try using a screw extractor. To do this, centerpunch the exact center of the remaining portion of the screw or bolt. Drill a small hole in the screw and tap the extractor into the hole. Back the screw out with a wrench on the extractor. See **Figure 27**.

CHAPTER ONE

Table 1 ENGINE AND CHASSIS NUMBERS

Model Number and Year	Engine Serial No. (Start to End)	Frame Serial No. (Start to End)
IT425G 1980	3R8-000101-on	3R8-000101-on
IT400F 1979	2X8-000101-N.A.	2X8-000101-N.A.
IT400E 1978	1W6-100101-103010	1W6-100101-103010
IT400D 1977	1W6-000101-003540	1W6-000101-003540
IT400C 1976	510-200101-205196	510-200101-205196
IT250G 1980	3R7-000101-	3R4-000101
IT250F 1979	2X7-000101-N.A.	2X7-000101-N.A.
IT250E 1978	2K9-000101-003179	2K9-000101-003179
IT250D 1977	1W5-000101-002480	1W5-000101-002480
IT175G 1980	3R6-000101-on	3R6-000101-on
IT175F 1979	2W6-000101-N.A.	2W6-000101-N.A.
IT175E 1978	1W2-020101-031100	1W2-020101-031100
IT175D 1977	1W2-000101-010428	1W2-000101-010428
IT125G 1980*	3R9-000101-on	3R9-000101-on

*First year of production.
N.A.: Information not available.

Table 2 WORKSHOP TOOLS

Tool	Size or Specifications
Screwdriver	
Common	5/16 x 8 in. blade
Common	3/8 x 12 in. blade
Phillips	Size 2 tip. 6 in. overall
Pliers	
Gas pliers	6 in. overall
Vise Grips	10 in. overall
Needle nose	6 in. overall
Channel lock	12 in. overall
Snap ring	—
Wrenches	
Box-end set	6-20, 32 and 34 mm
Open-end set	6-20, 32 and 34 mm
Crescent (adjustable)	6 and 12 in. overall
Socket set	1/2 in. drive ratchet with 6-20, 32 and 34 mm
Spoke wrench	—
Other special tools	
Strap wrench	—
Impact driver	1/2 in. drive with assorted tips
Torque wrench	1/2 in. drive—0-100 ft.-lb.
Tire levers	For motorcycle tires
Ignition gauge	—
Spoke wrench	—

> **NOTE:** If you own a 1981 or later model, first check the Supplement at the back of the book for any new service information.

CHAPTER TWO

TROUBLESHOOTING

Diagnosing mechanical problems is relatively simple if you use orderly procedures and keep a few basic principles in mind.

The troubleshooting procedures in this chapter analyze typical symptoms and show logical methods of isolating causes. These are not the only methods. There may be several ways to solve a problem, but only a systematic, methodical approach can guarantee success.

Never assume anything. Do not overlook the obvious. If you are riding along and the engine suddenly quits, check the easiest, most accessible problems first. Is there gasoline in the tank? Is the fuel shutoff valve in the ON position? Has the spark plug wire fallen off?

If nothing obvious turns up in a quick check, look a little further. Learning to recognize and describe symptoms will make repairs easier for you or a mechanic at the shop. Describe problems accurately and fully. Saying that "it won't run" isn't the same as saying "it quit climbing a hill and won't start," or that it "sat in my garage for 3 months and then wouldn't start."

Gather as many symptoms together as possible to aid in diagnosis. Note whether the engine lost power gradually or all at once, what color smoke (if any) came from the exhaust and so on. Remember that the more complicated a machine is, the easier it is to troubleshoot because symptoms point to specific problems.

After the symptoms are defined, areas which could cause the problems are tested and analyzed. Guessing at the cause of a problem may provide the solution, but it can easily lead to frustration, wasted time and a series of expensive, unnecessary parts replacements.

You do not need fancy equipment or complicated test gear to determine whether repairs can be attempted at home. A few simple checks could save a large repair bill and time lost while the bike sits in a dealer's service department. On the other hand, be realistic and don't attempt repairs beyond your abilities. Service departments tend to charge a lot for putting together a disassembled engine that may have been abused. Some dealers won't even take on such a job—so use common sense and don't get in over your head.

OPERATING REQUIREMENTS

An engine needs 3 basics to run properly; correct fuel/air mixture, compression and a spark at the correct time. If one or more are missing, the engine just won't run. The electrical system is the weakest link of the 3 basics. More problems result from electrical breakdowns than from any other source. Keep that in mind before you begin tampering with carburetor adjustments and the like.

If the bike has been sitting for any length of time and refuses to start, check and clean the spark plug and then look to the gasoline delivery system. This includes the fuel tank, fuel shutoff valve and fuel line to the carburetor. Gasoline deposits may have formed and gummed up the carburetor jets and air passages. Gasoline tends to lose its fire-power after standing for long periods. Condensation may contaminate it with water. Drain old gas and try starting with a fresh tankful.

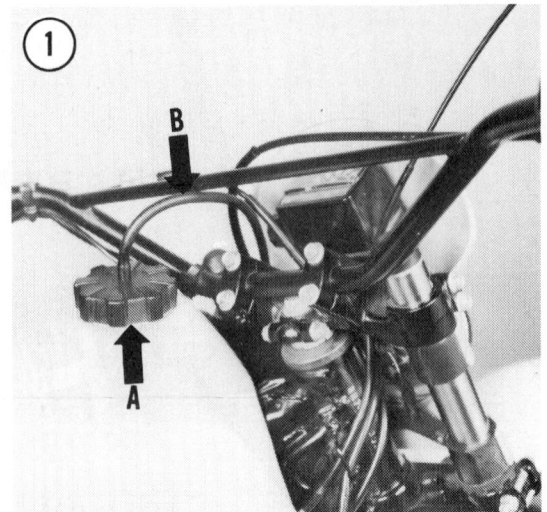

TROUBLESHOOTING INSTRUMENTS

Chapter One lists the instruments needed and detailed instructions on their use.

EMERGENCY TROUBLESHOOTING

When the IT is difficult to start or won't start at all, it does not help to wear out your leg stomping on the kickstarter. Check for obvious problems even before getting out your tools. Go down the following list step by step. Do each one; you may be embarrassed to find your kill switch is stuck in the ON position, but that is better than wearing out your leg. If it still will not start, refer to the appropriate troubleshooting procedure which follows in this chapter.

1. Is there fuel in the tank? Remove the filler cap (A, **Figure 1**) and rock the bike. Listen for fuel sloshing around. Also check that the vent tube (B, **Figure 1**) is not clogged. Remove and blow it out.

WARNING
Do not use an open flame to check in the tank. A serious explosion is certain to result.

2. Is the fuel/oil mixture correct? If there is any doubt, drain the tank and refill with the correct fuel/oil mixture.
3. Is the fuel shutoff valve in the ON position (**Figure 2**)?
4. Make sure the kill switch is not stuck in the ON position.
5. Is the spark plug wire on tight (**Figure 3**)?
6. Is the choke (**Figure 4**) in the right position? The lever type should be pushed *down* or the knob type pulled *out* for a cold engine and the opposite for a warm engine.

ENGINE STARTING

An engine that refuses to start or is difficult to start is very frustrating. More often than not, the problem is very minor and can be found with a simple and logical troubleshooting approach.

TROUBLESHOOTING

The following items show a beginning point from which to isolate engine starting problems.

Engine Fails to Start

Perform the following spark test to determine if ignition system is operating properly.
1. Remove the spark plug.
2. Connect the spark plug wire and connector to the spark plug and touch the spark plug base to a good ground like the engine cylinder head. Position the spark plug so you can see the electrode.

3. Crank the engine over with the kickstarter. A fat blue spark should be evident across the spark plug electrode.

WARNING
Do not hold the spark plug, wire or connector or a serious electrical shock may result.

4. If the spark is good, check for one or more of the following possible malfunctions:
   a. Obstructed fuel line
   b. Leaking head or cylinder base gasket.
5. If spark is not good, check for one or more of the following:
   a. Weak ignition coil
   b. Weak CDI unit
   c. Loose electrical connections
   d. Ignition coil ground wire—it may be loose or broken.

Engine Is Difficult to Start

Check for one or more of the following possible malfunctions:
   a. Fouled spark plug
   b. Improperly adjusted choke
   c. Contaminated fuel system
   d. Improperly adjusted carburetor
   e. Weak ignition coil
   f. Weak CDI unit
   g. Incorrect ignition coil
   h. Poor compression.

Engine Will Not Crank

Check for one or more of the following possible malfunctions:
   a. Defective kickstarter
   b. Seized piston
   c. Seized crankshaft bearings
   d. Broken connecting rod.

ENGINE PERFORMANCE

In the following check list, it is assumed that the engine runs, but is not operating at peak performance. This will serve as a starting point from which to isolate a performance malfunction.

The possible causes for each malfunction are listed in a logical sequence and in order of probability.

Engine Will Not Idle

a. Carburetor incorrectly adjusted
b. Fouled or improperly gapped spark plug
c. Head gasket leaking
d. Fuel mixture incorrect
e. Obstructed fuel line or fuel shutoff valve.

Engine Misses at High Speed

a. Fouled or improperly gapped spark plug
b. Improper ignition timing
c. Improper carburetor main jet selection
d. Weak ignition coil
e. Obstructed fuel line or fuel shutoff valve.

Engine Overheating

a. Too lean a fuel/oil mixture—incorrect carburetor adjustment or jet selection
b. Improper ignition timing
c. Improper spark plug heat range
d. Intake system or crankcase air leak
e. Damaged or blocked cooling fins.

Smoky Exhaust and Engine Runs Roughly

a. Carburetor adjustment incorrect—mixture too rich
b. Incorrect fuel/oil mixture
c. Choke not operating correctly
d. Water or other contaminants in fuel
e. Clogged fuel line
f. Clogged air filter element.

Engine Loses Power

a. Carburetor incorrectly adjusted
b. Engine overheating
c. Improper ignition timing
d. Incorrectly gapped spark plug
e. Weak ignition coil
f. Weak CDI unit
g. Obstructed muffler
h. Dragging brake(s).

Engine Lacks Acceleration

a. Carburetor mixture too lean
b. Clogged fuel line
c. Incorrect fuel/oil mixture
d. Improper ignition timing
e. Dragging brake(s).

ENGINE NOISES

1. *Knocking or pinging during acceleration*—Caused by using a lower octane fuel than recommended. May also be caused by poor fuel. Pinging can also be caused by a spark plug of the wrong heat range. Refer to *Correct Spark Plug Heat Range* in Chapter Three.

2. *Slapping or rattling noises at low speed or during acceleration*—May be caused by piston slap, i.e., excessive piston to cylinder wall clearance.

3. *Knocking or rapping while decelerating*—Usually caused by excessive rod bearing clearance.

4. *Persistent knocking and vibration*—Usually caused by excessive main bearing clearance.

5. *Rapid on-off squeal*—Compression leak around cylinder head gasket or spark plug.

EXCESSIVE VIBRATION

This can be difficult to find without disassembling the engine. Usually this is caused by loose engine mounting hardware. High speed vibration may be due to out-of-round or out-of-balance tire(s).

TWO-STROKE PRESSURE TESTING

Many owners of 2-stroke bikes are plagued by hard starting and generally poor running for which there seems to be no cause. Carburetion and ignition may be good and a compression test may show that all is well in the engine's upper end.

What a compression test does not show is lack of primary compression. The crankcase in a 2-stroke engine must be alternately under pressure and vacuum. After the piston closes the intake port, further downward movement of the piston causes the entrapped mixture to be pressurized so that it can rush quickly into the cylinder when the scavenging ports are opened. Upward piston movement creates a slight vacuum in the crankcase, enabling fuel/air mixture to be drawn in from the carburetor.

If crankcase seals or cylinder gaskets leak, the crankcase cannot hold pressure or vacuum

TROUBLESHOOTING

and proper engine operation becomes impossible. Any other source of leakage such as a defective cylinder base gasket or porous or cracked crankcase castings will result in the same conditions.

It is possible, however, to test for and isolate engine pressure leaks. The test is simple but does require elaborate equipment. Briefly, what is done is to seal off all natural engine openings, then apply air pressure. If the engine does not hold air, a leak or leaks is indicated. Then it is only necessary to locate and repair all leaks.

The following procedure describes a typical pressure test.
1. Remove the carburetor.
2. Install the pressure adapter and its gasket in place of the carburetor.
3. Block off the exhaust port, using suitable adapters and fittings.
4. Connect the pressurizing bulb and gauge to the pressure fitting installed where the carburetor was, then squeeze the bulb until the gauge indicates approximately 9 lb.
5. Observe the pressure gauge. If the engine is in good condition, pressure should not drop more than 1 psi in several minutes. Any pressure loss of more than 1 psi in 1 minute indicates serious sealing problems.

Before condemning the engine, first be sure that there are no leaks in the test equipment itself. Then go over the entire engine carefully.

Large leaks can be heard; smaller ones can be found by going over every possible leakage source with a small brush and liquid soap solution. The following are possible leakage points:
  a. Crankshaft seals
  b. Spark plug
  c. Cylinder head joint
  d. Cylinder base joint
  e. Carburetor base joint
  f. Crankcase joint.

FRONT SUSPENSION AND STEERING

Poor handling may be caused by improper front or rear tire pressure, a damaged or bent frame or front steering components, worn front shock absorbers, worn wheel bearings or dragging brakes. Also check front end alignment as described in Chapter Eight.

BRAKE PROBLEMS

Sticking brakes may be caused by worn or weak return springs, improper cable adjustment or dry pivot and cam bushings. Grabbing brakes may be caused by greasy linings which must be replaced. Brake grab may also be due to an out-of-round drum. Glazed linings will cause loss of stopping power.

NOTE: If you own a 1981 or later model, first check the Supplement at the back of the book for any new service information.

CHAPTER THREE

LUBRICATION, MAINTENANCE, AND TUNE-UP

If this is your first experience with a motorcycle, you should become acquainted with products that are available in auto or motorcycle parts and supply stores. Look into the tune-up tools and parts and check out the different lubricants such as 2-stroke motor oil, fork oil, locking compounds and greases (**Figure 1**). Also check engine degreasers, like Gunk or Bel-Ray Degreaser, for cleaning your engine prior to working on it or after each event.

The more you get involved in your Yamaha the more you will want to work on it. Start out by doing simple tune-up, lubrication and maintenance. Tackle more involved jobs as you gain experience.

The Yamaha IT trials bike is a relatively simple machine but to gain the utmost in safety, performance and useful life from it, it is necessary to make periodic inspections and adjustments. It frequently happens that minor problems are found during such inspections that are simple and inexpensive to correct at the time, but which could lead to major problems if not corrected.

This chapter explains lubrication, maintenance and tune-up procedures required for the IT. **Table 1** is a suggested maintenance schedule (**Tables 1-14** are located at the end of this chapter). However, each owner will have to determine individual maintenance requirements based on the type and frequency of use that each machine is subjected to. Full-time trials competition each weekend naturally requires a much more stringent maintenance schedule than occasional trail or sport riding.

NOTE
Due to the number of models and years covered in this book, be sure to follow the correct procedures and specifications for your specific model and year. Also use the correct quantity and type of fluid as indicated in the tables.

LUBRICATION, MAINTENANCE, AND TUNE-UP

PRE-CHECKS

The following checks should be performed prior to each event or before the first ride of the day.
1. Inspect all fuel lines and fittings for wetness (leaks).
2. Make sure the fuel tank is full and has the correct fuel/oil mixture; refer to **Table 2**.
3. Make sure the air cleaner is clean and that the cover is securely in place.
4. Check the clutch/transmission oil level.
5. Check the operation of the clutch and adjust if necessary.
6. Check that the accelerator and brake levers operate properly with no binding.
7. Inspect the condition of the front and rear suspension; make sure it has a good solid feel with no looseness.
8. Check the condition of the drive chain for wear and correct tension.
9. Check tire pressure. Refer to **Table 3**.
10. Check the exhaust system for damage.
11. Check the tightness of all fasteners, especially engine mounting hardware.

TIRES AND WHEELS

Tire Pressure

Tire pressure should be checked and adjusted to maintain the smoothness of the tire, good traction and handling, and to get the maximum life out of the tire. A simple, accurate gauge (**Figure 2**) can be purchased for a few dollars and should be carried in your tool box. The appropriate tire pressures are shown in **Table 3**.

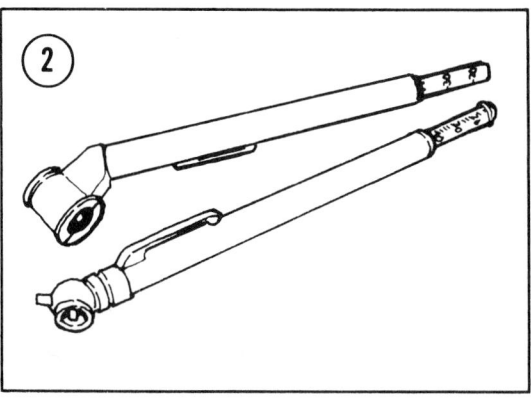

Tire Inspection

The tires take a lot of punishment due to the variety of terrain they are subject to. Inspect them periodically for excessive wear, cuts, abrasions, etc. If you find a nail or other object in the tire, mark its location with a light crayon prior to removing it. This will help locate the hole for repair. Refer to Chapter Eight for tire changing and repair information.

Wheel Spoke Tension

Tap each spoke with a wrench. The higher the pitch of sound it makes, the tighter the spoke. The lower the sound frequency, the looser the spoke. A "ping" is good; a "klunk" says the spoke is too loose.

If one or more spokes are loose, tighten them as described under *Wheels* in Chapter Eight.

Rim Inspection

Frequently inspect the condition of the wheel rims. If a rim has been damaged it might have been enough to knock it out of alignment. Improper wheel alignment can cause severe vibration and result in an unsafe riding condition.

LUBRICANTS

Oil

Oil is graded according to its viscosity, which is an indication of how thick it is. The Society of Automotive Engineers (SAE) system distinguishes oil viscosity by numbers. Thick oils have higher viscosity numbers than thin oils. For example, an SAE 5 oil is a thin oil while an SAE 90 oil is relatively thick.

Grease

A good quality grease (preferably waterproof) should be used for many of the parts on the IT; refer to **Figure 3**. Water does not wash grease off parts as easily as it washes off oil. In addition, grease maintains its lubricating qualities better than oil on long and strenuous events. In a pinch, though, the wrong lubricant is better than none at all. Correct the situation as soon as possible.

CLEANING SOLVENT

A number of solvents can be used to remove old dirt, grease and oil. Kerosene is readily available and comparatively inexpensive. Another inexpensive solvent similar to kerosene is ordinary diesel fuel. Both of these solvents have a very high-temperature flash point and can be used safely in any adequately ventilated area away from open flames.

WARNING
Never use gasoline*. Gasoline is extremely volatile and contains tremendously destructive potential energy. The slightest spark from metal parts accidently hitting or a tool slipping could cause a fatal explosion.*

PERIODIC LUBRICATION

Refer to **Figure 4** for lubrication points.

Engine Lubrication

WARNING
Serious fire hazards always exist around gasoline. Do not allow any smoking in areas where fuel is being mixed or while refueling your machine. Always have a fire extinguisher rated for gasoline and electrical fires within reach, just to play it safe.

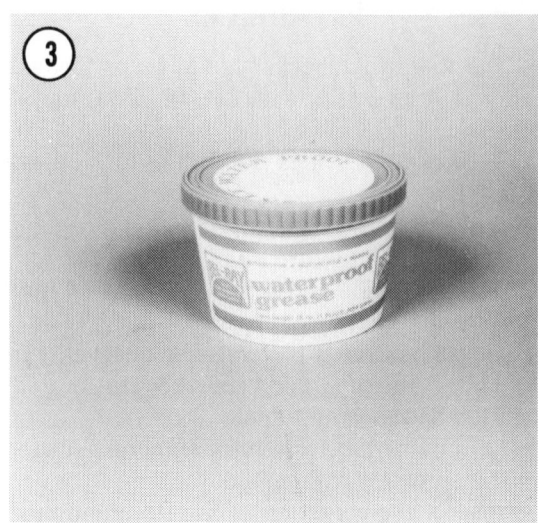

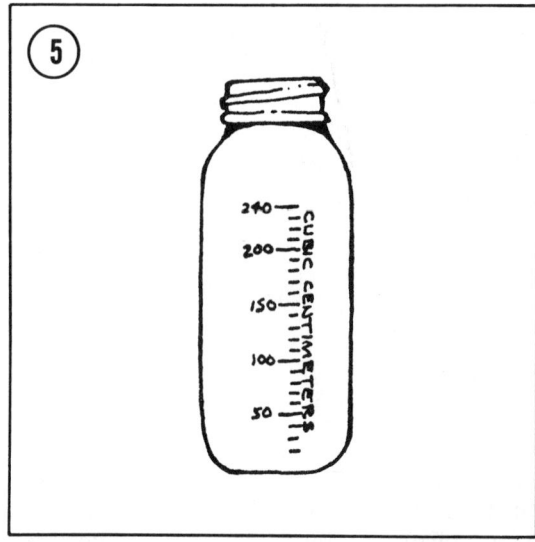

The engine in all IT models is lubricated by oil mixed with gasoline. The correct fuel/oil ratio is listed in **Table 2**. Refer to **Table 4** for recommended oils and fuels. Mix the oil and gasoline thoroughly in a separate, clean, sealable container larger than the quantity being mixed to allow room for agitation. Always measure the quantities exactly. Fuel capacity for the various models is given in **Table 5**. Use a good grade of premium fuel rated at 90+ octane.

Use a baby bottle (**Figure 5**) with graduations in both fluid ounces (oz.) and cubic centimeters (cc) on the side.

Pour the required amount of oil into the mixing container and add approximately 1/2 the required amount of gasoline. Agitate the mixture thoroughly, then add the remaining fuel and agitate again until all is mixed well.

NOTE
Always mix a fresh amount of fuel the morning of the trials event or ride; do not mix more than you will use that day. Do not keep any fuel overnight; dispose of any excess properly.

To avoid any contaminants entering into the fuel system, use a funnel with a filter when pouring the fuel into the bike's tank.

LUBRICATION, MAINTENANCE, AND TUNE-UP

LUBRICATION POINTS

1. Speedometer gear housin
2. Front forks
3. Control cables
4. Throttle grip
5. Drive chain
6. Front brake camshaft
7. Front wheel bearings
8. Steering head bearings
9. Clutch/transmission oil
10. Side stand pivot point
11. Rear brake camshaft
12. Rear wheel bearings

CHAPTER THREE

Transmission Oil Checking and Changing

Proper operation and long service for the clutch and transmission require clean oil. Oil should be changed at the intervals indicated in **Table 1**. Check oil level frequently and add any oil necessary to maintain the correct level. Refer to **Table 6** for oil capacities for the various models.

Try to use the same brand of oil; do not mix 2 brand types at the same time as they all vary slightly in their composition. The use of oil additives is not recommended as it may cause clutch slippage.

Checking

1. Start the engine and let it warm up approximately 2-3 minutes. Shut it off.
2. Place the bike in an upright position; place a small piece of wood under the kickstand.
3. Unscrew the oil level screw (A, **Figure 6**). If any oil runs out, the level is correct. If not, oil must be added.
4. To add oil, remove the oil fill cap (B, **Figure 6**) and add oil until it just begins to run out the screw hole.
5. Install the oil fill cap and oil level screw.

Changing

To drain the oil you will need the following (**Figure 7**):
   a. Drain pan
   b. Funnel
   c. Can opener or pour spout
   d. 1 quart of oil

There are a number of ways to discard the old oil safely. The easiest way is to pour it from the drain pan into a half gallon plastic bleach or milk bottle. Tighten the cap and place it in your household trash.

> *NOTE*
> *Never dispose of motor oil in the trash, on the ground, or down a storm drain. Many service stations accept used motor oil and waste haulers provide curbside used motor oil collection. Do not combine other fluids with motor oil to be recycled. To locate a recycler, contact the American Petroleum Institute (API) at www.recycleoil.org.*

1. Start the engine and let it reach operating temperature.
2. Shut it off and place a drain pan under the engine.

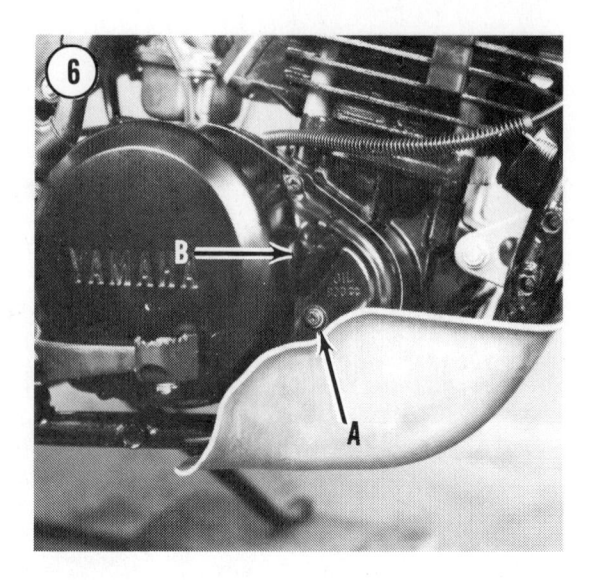

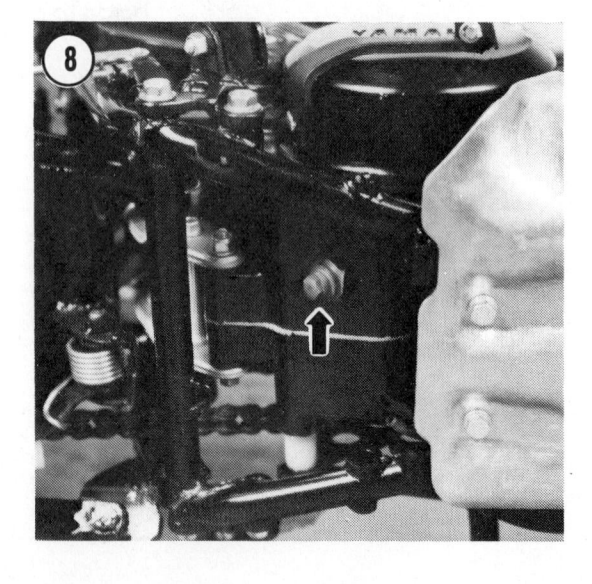

LUBRICATION, MAINTENANCE, AND TUNE-UP

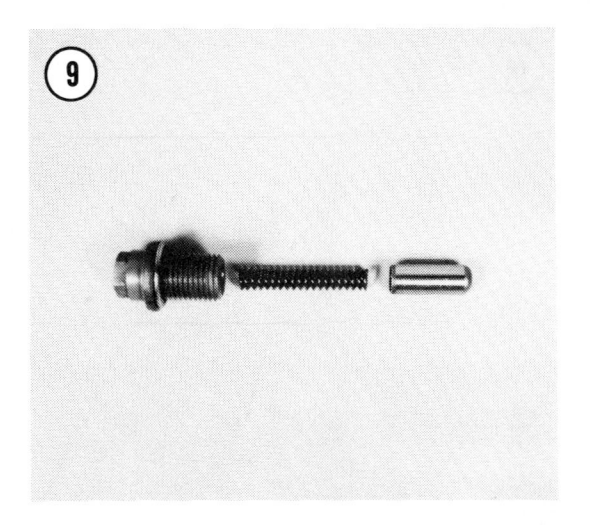

3. Remove the drain plug (**Figure 8**). Remove the oil fill cap (B, **Figure 6**); this will speed up the flow of oil.

NOTE
*On some models the drain plug is also the transmission shift drum neutral locator (containing a spring and cam stopper). See **Figure 9**. Make sure these parts are not lost in the drain pan.*

4. Let it drain for at least 15-20 minutes.
5. Inspect the condition of the sealing washer on the drain plug. Replace it if its condition is in doubt.
6. Install the drain plug (reassemble the transmission shift drum neutral locator on models so equipped). Tighten it securely.
7. Fill the transmission (**Figure 10**) with the correct weight and quantity oil. Refer to **Table 6**.
8. Screw in the oil fill cap and start the engine; let it idle for 2-3 minutes. Check for leaks.
9. Turn the engine off and check for correct oil level; adjust as necessary.

Front Fork Oil Change

The following procedure describes how to change the fork oil with the forks installed in the frame. The forks can be removed and disassembled if the fork oil is really contaminated and you want to flush out the fork assembly. Refer to *Front Forks* in Chapter Eight.

The fork oil should be changed at the intervals described in **Table 1**. If it becomes contaminated with dirt or water, change it immediately.

WARNING
Release the fork air pressure gradually. If released too fast, oil will spurt out with the air. Protect your eyes and clothing accordingly.

1. On models with air assist forks, remove the upper black protective cap (**Figure 11**) on the top of the fork tube. Remove the dust cap; use a small slot-head screwdriver or similar tool and expel all air pressure in the fork.

CHAPTER THREE

2. On models with air assist forks, remove the top fork cap assembly.

3. On models without air assist, remove the fork top cap (**Figure 12**).

> *NOTE*
> *Remove the fork cap slowly as the fork spring is under pressure and will push itself out when the fork cap is removed.*

4. Remove the spacer, spring seat and fork spring.

5. Place a drain pan under the drain screw (**Figure 13**) and remove the screw. Allow the oil to drain for at least 5 minutes. *Never reuse the oil.*

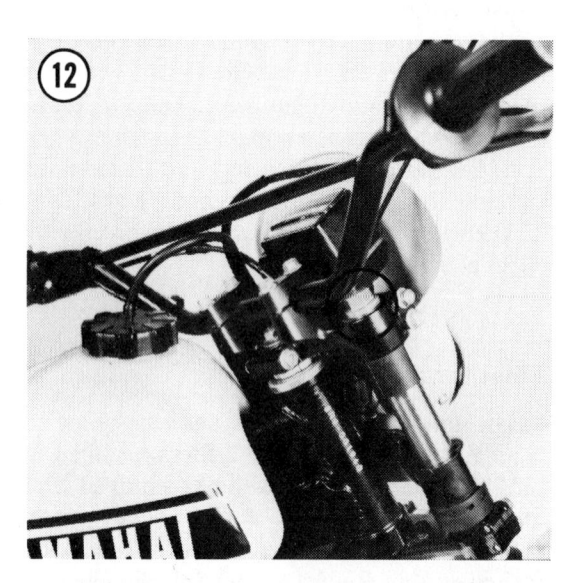

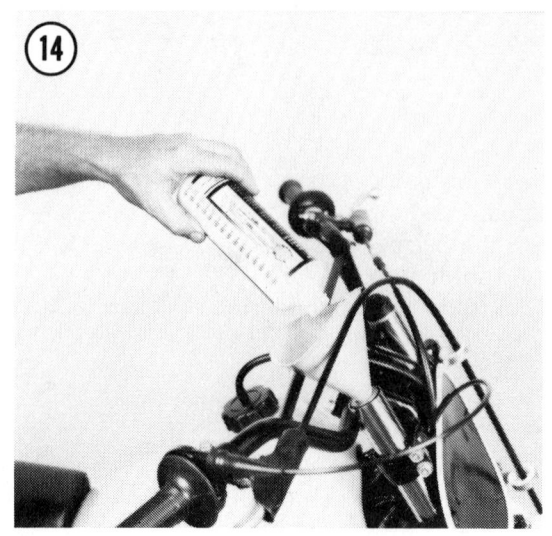

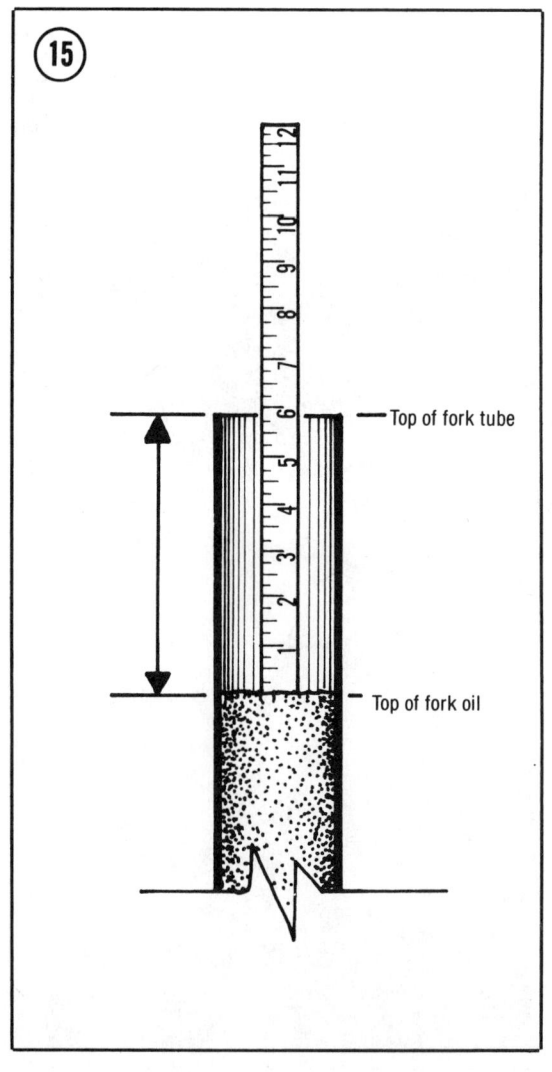

LUBRICATION, MAINTENANCE, AND TUNE-UP

CAUTION
Do not allow the fork oil to come in contact with any of the brake components.

6. With both of the bike's wheels on the ground and the front brake applied, push down on the handlebar grips to work the forks up and down. Continue until all oil is expelled.
7. Inspect the condition of the gasket on the drain screw; replace it if necessary. Install the drain screw.
8. Repeat Steps 1-7 for the other fork.
9. Fill each fork with the specified weight and quantity fork oil (**Figure 14**).

NOTE
*On models IT425, IT250 and IT175 since 1980, after pouring in the oil, measure the distance from the top of the fork tube to the top of the oil with the forks fully bottomed. Refer to **Table 7** and **Figure 15**. To assure a precise oil level you may want to invest in S & W Products Fork Oil Level Adjuster*

Kit shown in **Figure 16**. Follow the manufacturer's simple and easy-to-use instructions and you will end up with the same oil level in each fork leg.

NOTE
The weight of the oil can vary according to your own preference and the conditions of the trials course (lighter weight for less damping and heavier for more damping action). Always add the specified amount of oil.

10. Inspect the condition of the O-ring seal on the top cap; replace if necessary.

11. Install the fork spring(s), spring seat and spacer (**Figure 17**). Install the fork top cap while pushing down on the spring. Start the fork cap slowly and don't cross thread it. Tighten it to the torque specification listed in **Table 8**.

12. After assembling each fork tube, slowly pump the forks several times to expel air from

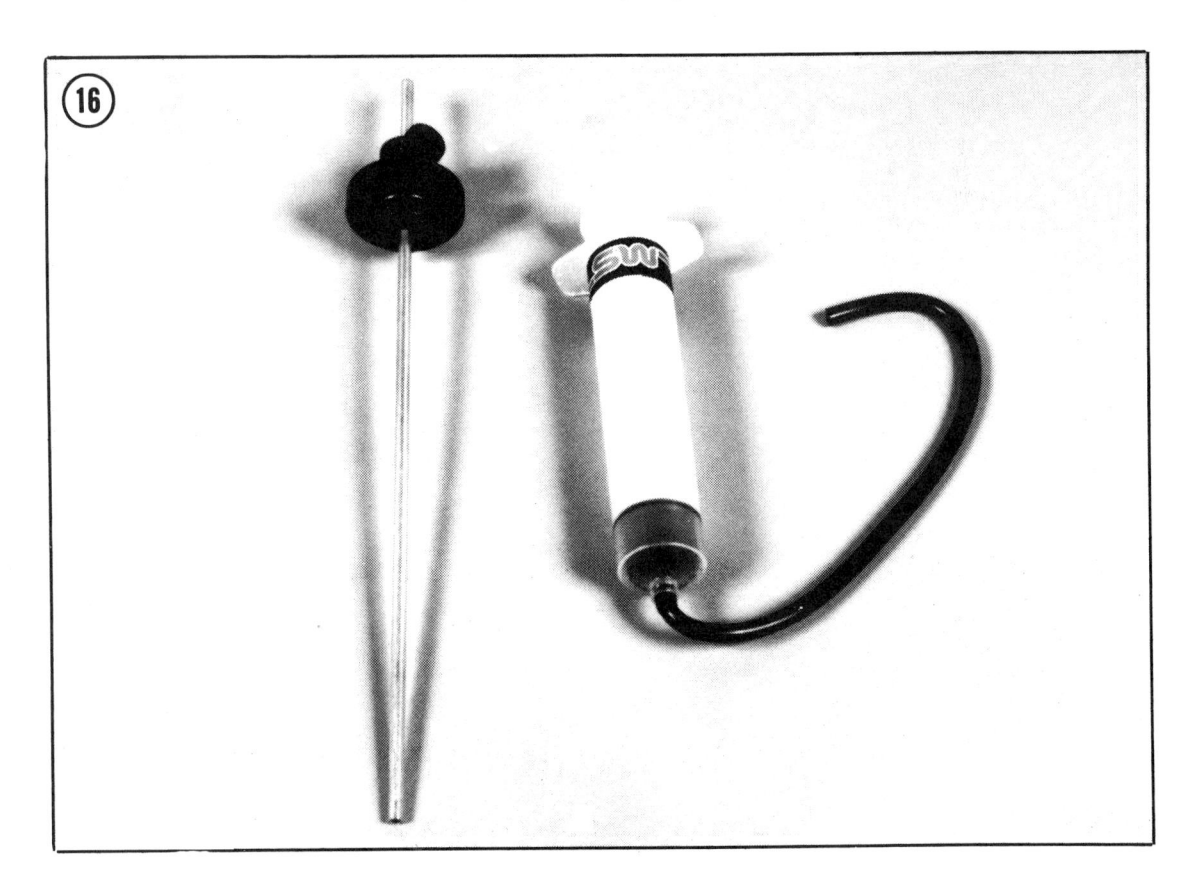

the upper and lower fork chambers and to distribute the oil.

13. On models with air assist forks, inflate each fork tube to the correct air pressure as indicated in **Table 9**. Refer to *Front Fork Air Pressure* following.

14. Road test the bike and check for leaks.

Front Fork Air Pressure (On Models So Equipped)

For proper damping action of the front forks the air pressure must be maintained at the correct pressure and both forks must have the same pressure.

1. Place wood blocks or a milk crate under the frame to elevate the front wheel off the ground. There must be no weight on the front wheel.
2. Remove the black rubber cap (**Figure 11**).
3. Remove the dust cap.
4. Use a small manual air pump like the S & W Mini-Pump. Attach it to the air fitting on top of each fork (**Figure 18**) and inflate to the inflation pressure as shown in **Table 9**. **Figure 18** is shown on a Yamaha YZ400; the setup is the same for the IT series.

> *CAUTION*
> *Never use a high-pressure air supply to pressurize the forks. Never exceed the maximum allowable air pressure of 36 psi (2.5 kg/cm^2) or the oil seal will be damaged. The air pressure difference between the 2 forks should be 1.4 psi (0.1 kg/cm^2) or less.*

> *CAUTION*
> *Use only compressed air or nitrogen—do not use any other type of compressed gas as an explosion may result. Never heat the front forks with a torch or place them near an open flame or extreme heat.*

5. Install the dust cap and black rubber cap.

Drive Chain

Clean and lubricate the drive chain at intervals described in **Table 1** or more frequently if desired. A properly maintained chain will provide maximum service life and reliability.

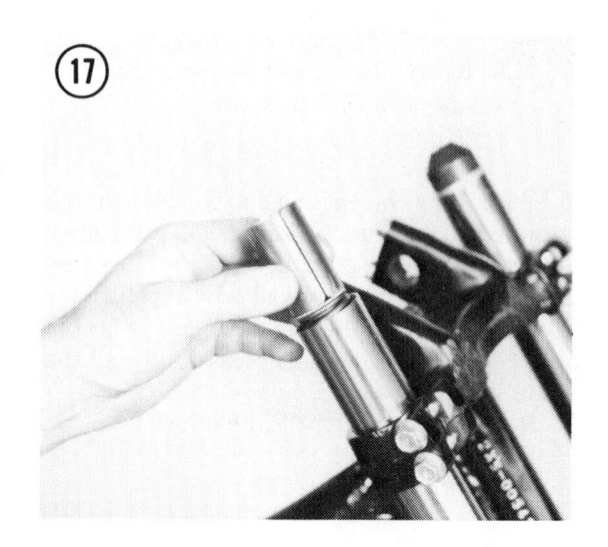

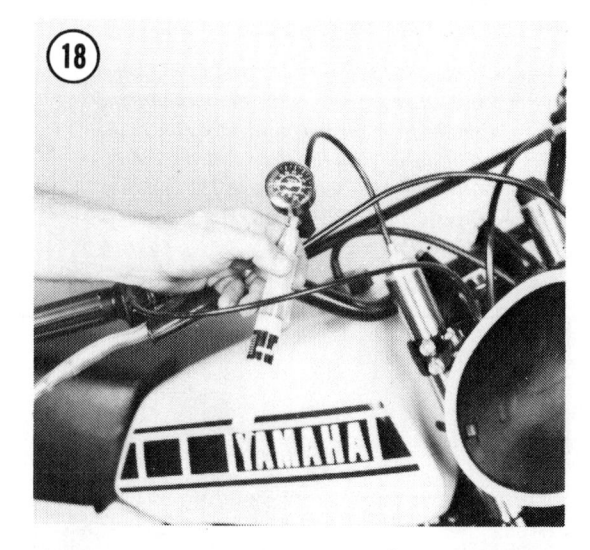

LUBRICATION, MAINTENANCE, AND TUNE-UP

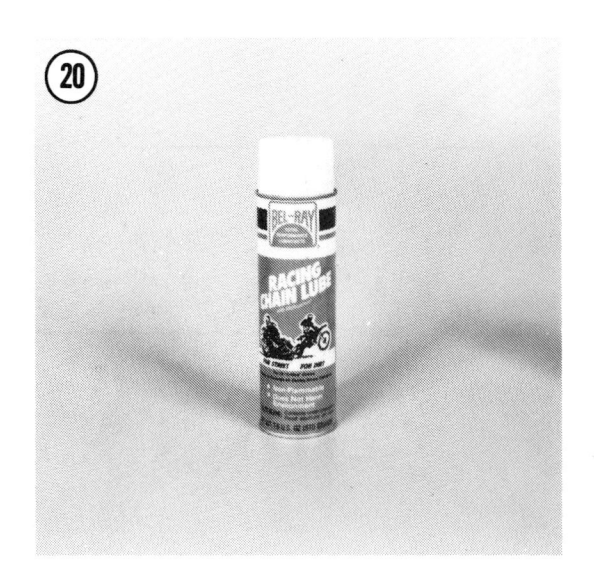

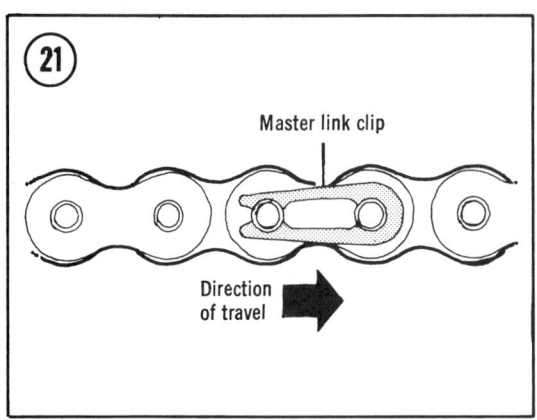

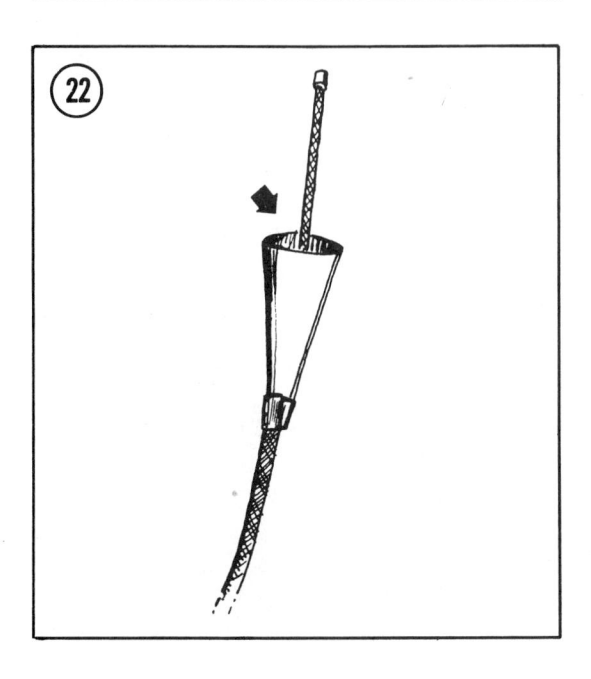

1. Disconnect the master link (**Figure 19**) and remove the chain from the motorcycle.
2. Immerse the chain in a pan of cleaning solvent and allow it to soak for about half an hour. Move it around and flex it during this period so that the dirt between the pins and rollers may work its way out.
3. Scrub the rollers and side plates with a stiff brush and rinse away loosened dirt. Rinse it a couple of times to make sure all dirt and grit are washed out. Hang up the chain and allow it to thoroughly dry.
4. Lubricate the chain with a good grade of chain lubricant (**Figure 20**), carefully following the manufacturer's instructions. If a chain lubricant isn't available use 10W/30 motor oil.
5. Reinstall the chain on the motorcycle. Use a new master link clip and install it so that the closed end of the clip is facing the direction of chain travel (**Figure 21**).

WARNING
Always check the master link clip after the bike has been rolled backwards such as when unloading it from a truck or trailer. The master link clip may have snagged on the chain guide or tensioner and become disengaged. Obviously, losing a chain while riding can cause a serious spill, not to mention the chain damage which may occur.

Control Cables

The control cables should be lubricated at intervals as described in **Table 1**. They should also be inspected at this time for fraying, and the cable sheath should be checked for chafing. The cables are relatively inexpensive and should be replaced when found to be faulty.

The control cables can be lubricated either with oil or with any of the popular cable lubricants and a cable lubricator. The first method requires more time and the complete lubrication of the entire cable is less certain.

CAUTION
Never use a graphite cable lubricant to lubricate the throttle cable. The graphite will work its way through the cable and into the carburetor. The graphite will then cause abnormal

slide-to-carburetor bore wear. Replacement of the carburetor could become necessary. A graphite lubricant, however, works well on brake and clutch cables.

Oil method

1. Disconnect the cables from the clutch lever and the throttle grip assembly.
2. Make a cone of stiff paper and tape it to the end of the cable sheath (**Figure 22**).
3. Hold the cable upright and pour a small amount of light oil (SAE 10W/30) into the cone. Work the cable in and out of the sheath for several minutes to help the oil work its way down to the end of the cable.

NOTE
To avoid a mess, place a shop cloth at the end of the cable to catch the oil as it runs out.

4. Remove the cone, reconnect the cable and adjust the cable(s) as described in this chapter.

NOTE
While the throttle housing is separated, apply a light coat of grease to the metal surfaces of the grip assembly and to the handlebar.

Lubricator Method

1. Disconnect the cables from the clutch lever and the throttle grip assembly.
2. Attach a lubricator following the manufacturer's instructions.
3. Insert the nozzle of the lubricant can in the lubricator, press the button on the can and hold it down until the lubricant begins to flow out of the other end of the cable.

NOTE
Place a shop cloth at the end of the cable(s) to catch all excess lubricant that will flow out.

4. Remove the lubricator, reconnect the cable(s) and adjust the cable(s) as described in this chapter.

Miscellaneous Lubrication Points

Lubricate the clutch lever (**Figure 23**), front brake lever (**Figure 24**), rear brake pedal pivot point (**Figure 25**), and the side stand pivot point (**Figure 26**).

LUBRICATION, MAINTENANCE, AND TUNE-UP

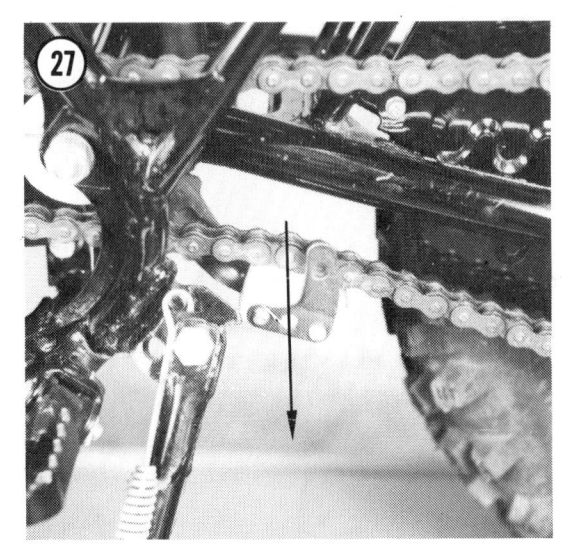

PERIODIC MAINTENANCE

Front Fork Air Pressure

Refer to *Front Fork Air Pressure* in *Periodic Lubrication* in this chapter.

Monoshock Adjustment

Refer to *Monoshock Adjustments* in Chapter Nine for complete details.

Drive Chain Adjustment

The drive chain should be checked and adjusted prior to each event or weekend ride.
1. Place the bike on the sidestand.

> *NOTE*
> *This adjustment must be made with the bike vertical, with both wheels on the ground, and **without a rider sitting on it**.*

2A. On all models except IT175G, push the chain tensioner (**Figure 27**) down. The free movement of the chain is measured on the *upper run* for IT125 models and on the *lower run* for all other models. Free movement should be as specified in **Table 10**. See **Figure 28**.

> *NOTE*
> *The dimensions given in **Table 10** for models IT400D and C, IT250D and IT175D are different than those listed in the original Factory Owner's Service Manual. The dimension was changed according to a Factory Technical Bulletin due to increased rear wheel travel.*

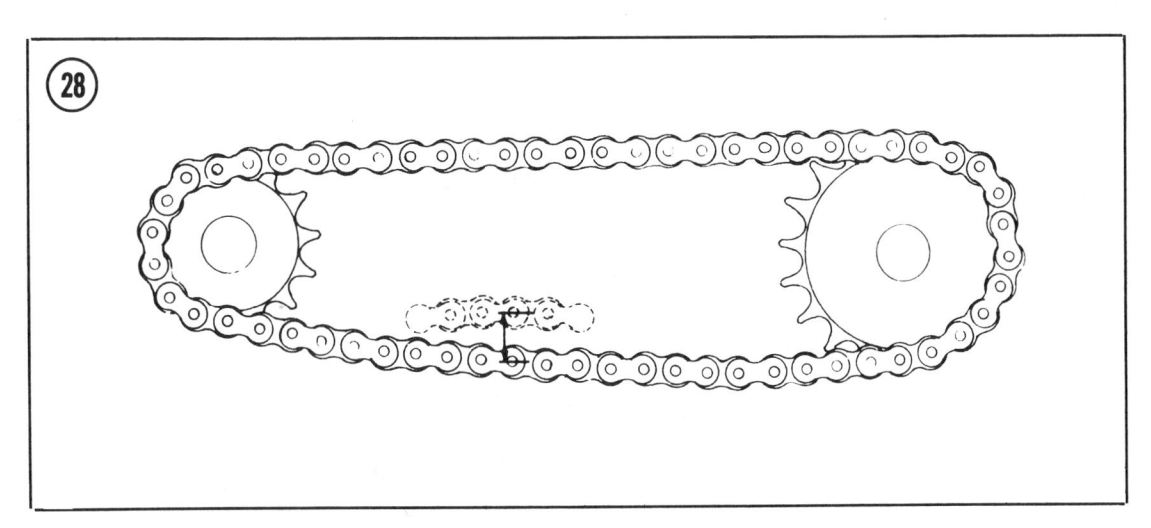

2B. On model IT175G, the free movement is measured on the *upper run* of the chain (**Figure 29**). This model is not equipped with a chain tensioner.

3. To adjust, remove the cotter pin (on models so equipped) and loosen the rear axle nut (**Figure 30**).

4. Move the snail chain adjusters (A, **Figure 31**) until the correct slack is achieved. Be sure that the marks on both adjusters align with the same marks on each side of the swing arm (B, **Figure 31**). Make sure the notch on the adjuster is seated completely on the pin.

NOTE
Rotate the rear wheel to move the chain to another position and recheck the adjustment; chains rarely wear or stretch evenly and, as a result, the free play will not remain constant over the entire chain. If the chain cannot be adjusted within these limits, it is excessively worn and stretched and should be replaced.

5. Sight along the top of the drive chain from the rear sprocket to see that it is correctly aligned. It should leave the top of the rear sprocket in a straight line (A, **Figure 32**). If it is cocked to one side or the other (B and C, **Figure 32**) the wheel is incorrectly aligned and must be corrected. Refer to Step 4.

6. Tighten the rear axle nut to the torque specification in **Table 11**. On models so equipped, install a new cotter pin.

NOTE
Always install a new cotter pin; never reuse an old one.

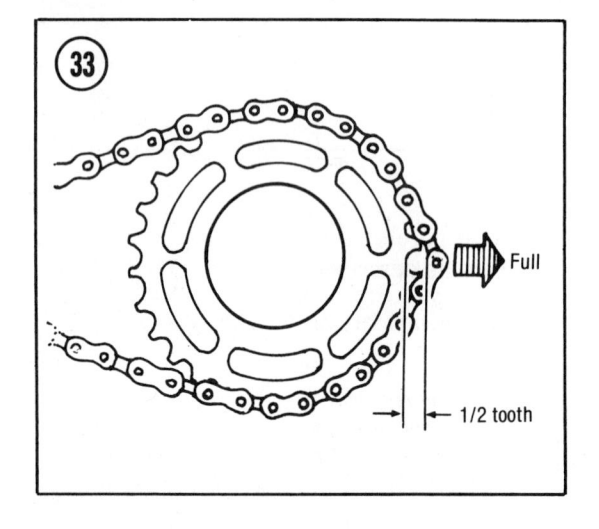

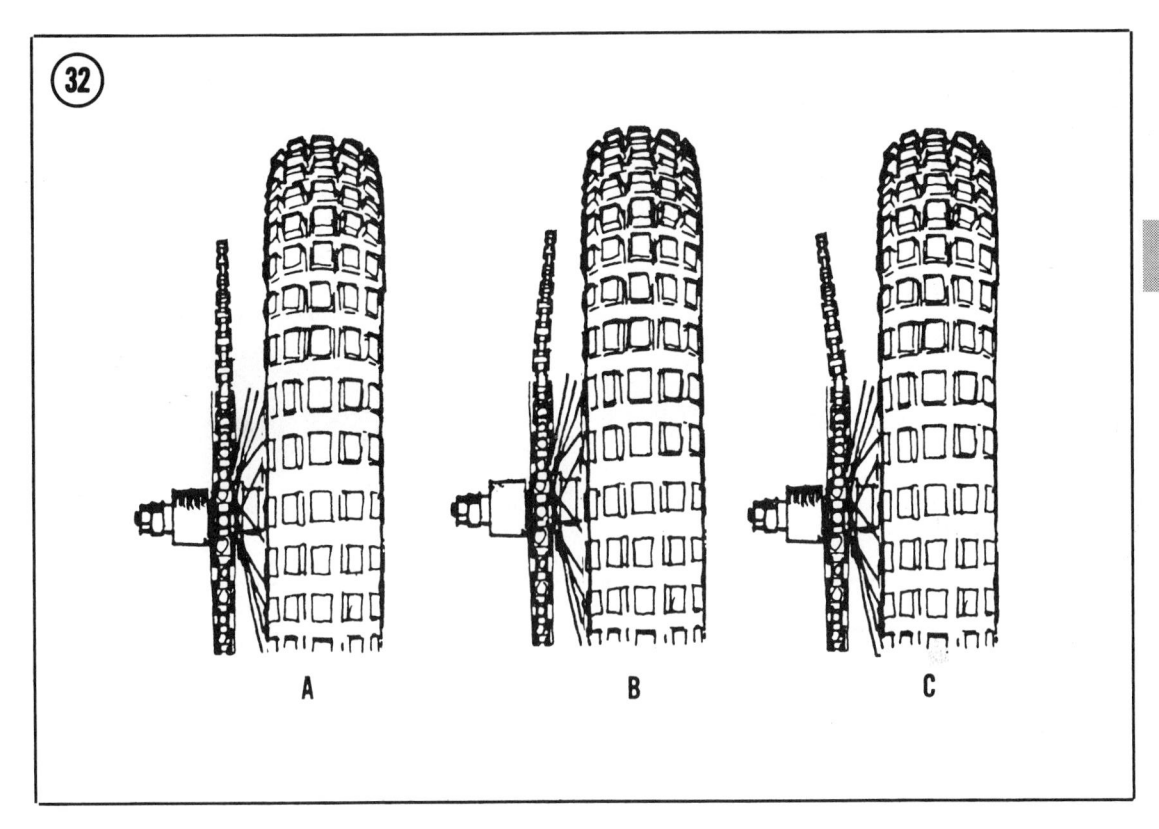

LUBRICATION, MAINTENANCE, AND TUNE-UP

1/2 the length of the sprocket teeth (**Figure 33**) it has stretched and must be further inspected as described in the following.

1. Remove the drive chain and clean it as described under *Drive Chain Lubrication* in this chapter.
2. After cleaning the chain, examine it carefully for wear or damage. If any signs are visible, replace the chain.
3. Lay the chain alongside a ruler (**Figure 34**), compress the links together, then stretch them apart. If more than 1/4 in. (6.3 mm) of movement is possible, replace the chain as it is too worn to be used again.

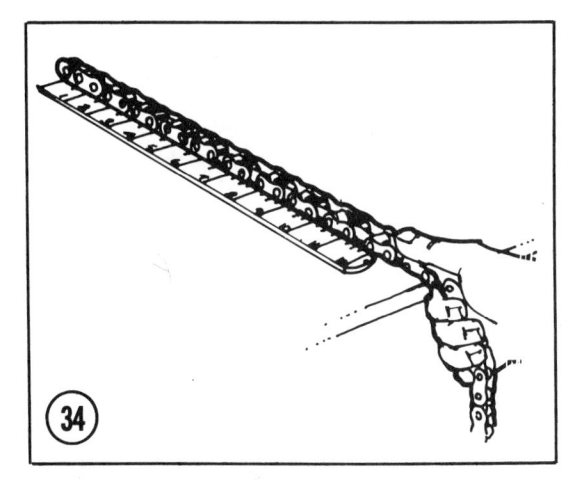

7. After the drive chain has been adjusted, the rear brake pedal free play must be adjusted as described in this chapter.

NOTE
*Refer to **Table 12** for replacement chain type and number.*

CAUTION
*Always check both sprockets (**Figure 35**) every time the chain is removed. If any wear is visible on the teeth, replace the sprocket(s). Never install a new chain over worn sprockets or a worn chain over new sprockets.*

Drive Chain Inspection

NOTE
Prior to removing the drive chain from the bike, pull back on the chain with your fingers at the driven sprocket. If the chain can be pulled away from the sprocket by

35

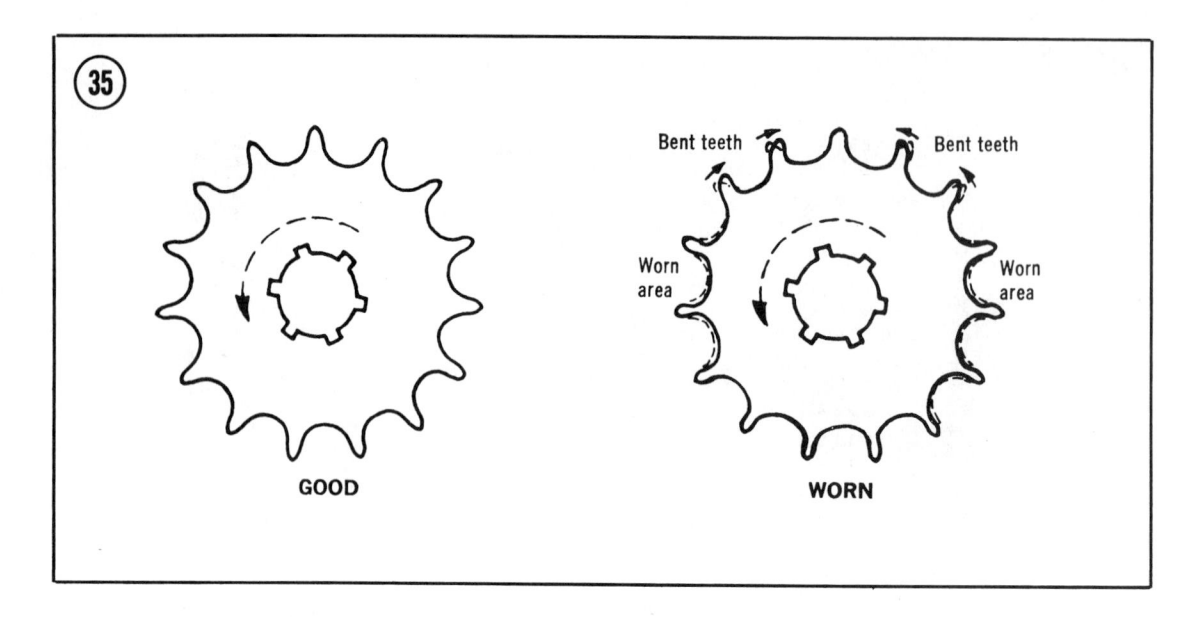

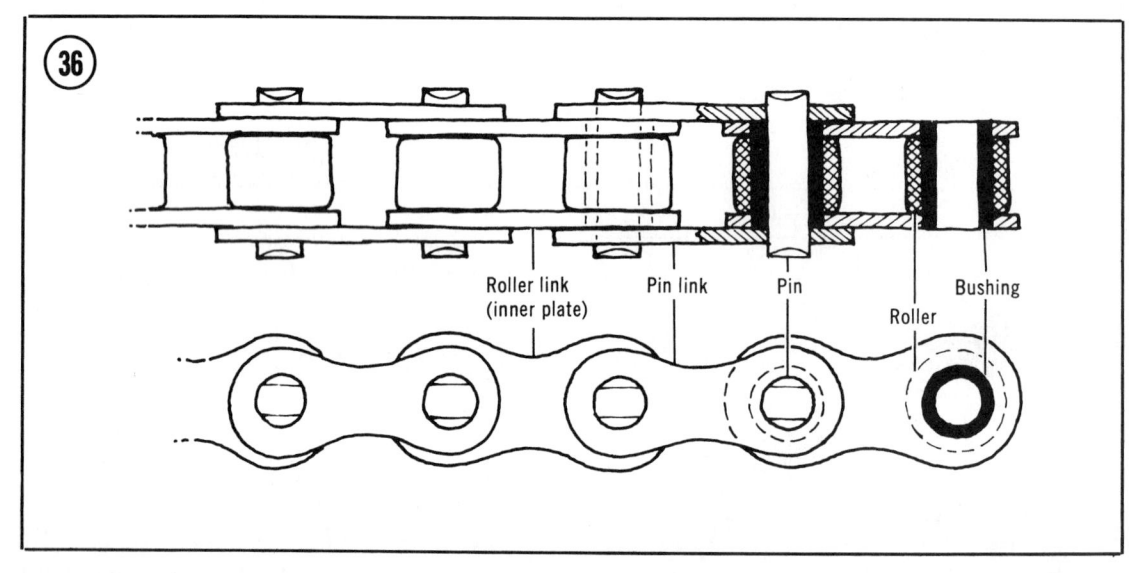

GOOD   WORN

Bent teeth — Worn area

36

Roller link (inner plate) — Pin link — Pin — Roller — Bushing

4. Check the inner faces of the inner plates (**Figure 36**). They should be lightly polished on both sides. If they show considerable wear on both sides, the sprockets are not aligned. Adjust alignment as described under Steps 4 and 5 of *Drive Chain Adjustment* in this chapter.
5. Lubricate the drive chain with a good grade of chain lubricant (**Figure 20**) following the manufacturer's instructions. If a lubricant is not available use 10W/30 motor oil.
6. Reinstall the chain as described under *Drive Chain Lubrication* in this chapter.
7. Adjust the rear brake pedal free play as described in this chapter.

Drive Chain Guard and Roller Replacement

The drive chain guard and rollers should be inspected and replaced as necessary. It is a good idea to inspect them prior to each event. A chain that is too loosely adjusted will cause excessive wear and may cause damage to the rear swing arm.

1. On some models the chain guard on the swing arm pivot shaft is removed simply by pulling it off to the rear (it has a diagonal cut in it, as shown in **Figure 37**). Install it by spreading it partially open and slipping it onto

LUBRICATION, MAINTENANCE, AND TUNE-UP

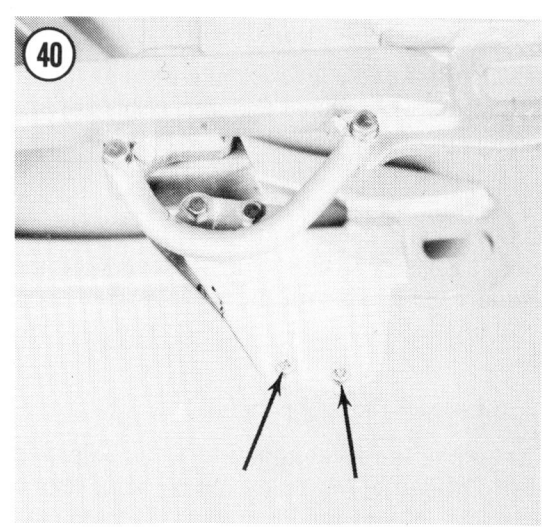

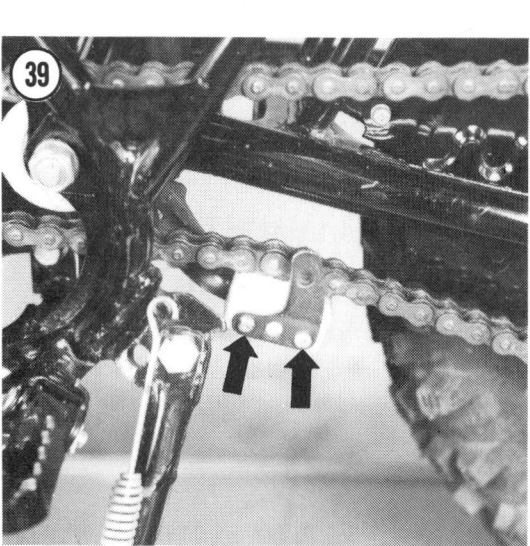

the swing arm. Spin it around a couple of times to make sure it is seated correctly. On other models it is necessary to partially remove the rear swing arm for chain guard removal (**Figure 38**); refer to Chapter Nine.

2. Remove the screws (**Figure 39**) securing the rubbing block on the drive chain tensioner and remove it. Install a new rubbing block and tighten the screws securely.

3. Remove the bolt and nut securing the chain roller(s) and remove them. Install new roller(s) and tighten the bolts securely.

4. On models with an aluminum swing arm, remove the screws (**Figure 40**) securing the chain guard to the rear of the swing arm and remove the guard. Install a new guard and tighten the screws securely.

NOTE
*Prior to installing the new chain guard, make sure the metal backing plate behind the chain guard is not bent. If bent, it must be straightened or replaced as it will cause the chain to wear prematurely. Remove the bolts (**Figure 41**) securing it, remove the plate and straighten or replace with a new one. Figure 41 is shown with the swing arm removed for clarity; it is not necessary to remove it to perform this step.*

5. On models with an aluminum swing arm, remove the screws (**Figure 42**) securing the rubbing block on top of the swing arm and remove the block. Install a new rubbing block and tighten the screws securely.

CHAPTER THREE

Front Brake Lever Adjustment

The front brake lever should be adjusted to suit your own personal preference, but should maintain a minimum cable slack of 0.2-0.32 in. (5-8 mm); refer to **Figure 43**. The brake lever should travel this amount before the brake shoes come in contact with the drum, but must not be adjusted so closely that the brake shoes contact the drum with the lever relaxed. The primary adjustment should be made at the hand lever.

1. Slide back the rubber boot.

2. Loosen the locknut and turn the adjusting barrel (**Figure 44**) in or out to achieve the correct amount of free play. Tighten the locknut.

3. Because of normal brake wear, this adjustment will eventually be "used up." It is then necessary to loosen the locknut and screw the adjusting barrel all the way in toward the hand grip. Tighten the locknut.

4. At the adjuster on the brake panel, loosen the locknut and turn the adjuster nut (**Figure 45**) until the brake lever can be used once again for the fine adjustment. Be sure to tighten the locknut.

5. If proper adjustment cannot be achieved by the use of these adjustment points the cable has stretched and must be replaced; refer to Chapter Ten.

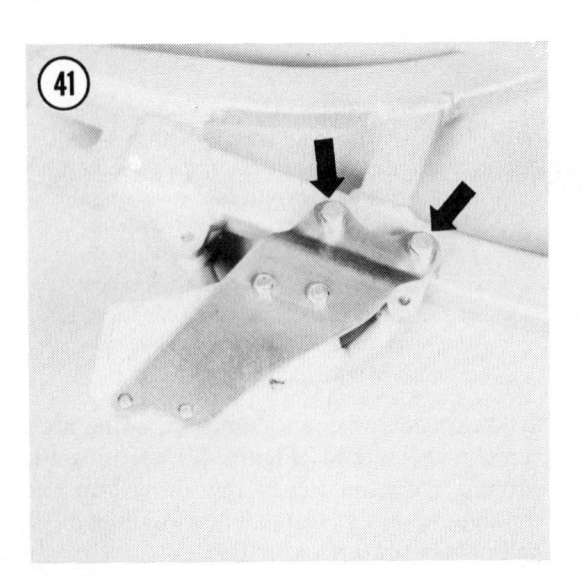

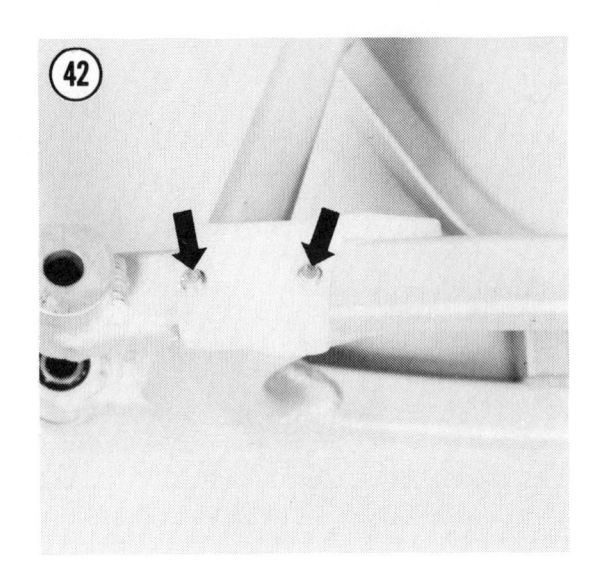

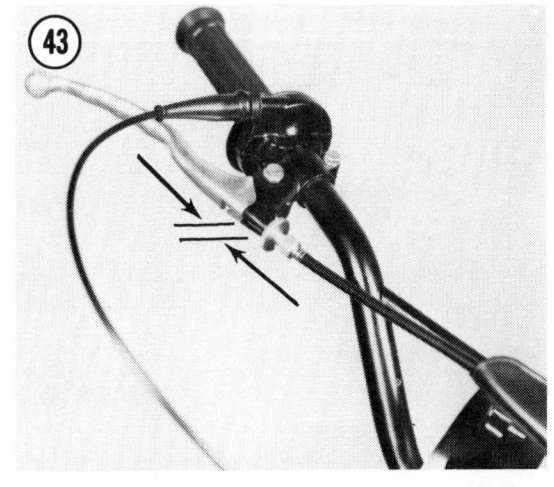

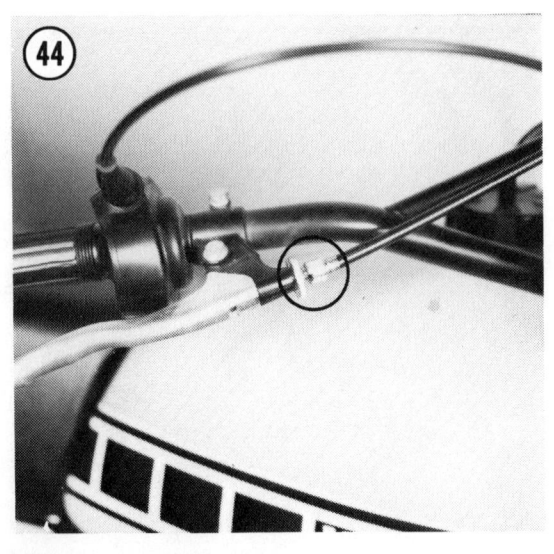

LUBRICATION, MAINTENANCE, AND TUNE-UP

Rear Brake Pedal Height Adjustment

The position of the pedal should be adjusted to your own personal preference.
1. Place the bike on the side stand.
2. Check that the brake pedal is in the at-rest position.
3. To change height position, loosen the locknut and turn the adjuster (**Figure 46**). Looking at the adjuster head, turn it *clockwise* to lower the pedal and *counterclockwise* to raise the pedal.
4. Tighten the locknut and adjust the pedal free play as described in the following procedure.

Rear Brake Pedal Free Play

Adjust the brake pedal to the desired height as described earlier. Turn the adjustment nut on the end of the brake rod (**Figure 47**) until the pedal has 0.8-1.2 in. (20-30 mm) of free play (**Figure 48**). Free play is the distance the pedal travels from the at-rest position to the applied position when the pedal is lightly depressed by hand.

Rotate the rear wheel and check for brake drag. Also operate the pedal several times to make sure it returns to the at-rest position immediately after release.

Clutch Mechanism Adjustment

The clutch should be adjusted at the intervals indicated in **Table 1**.

1. Drain the transmission oil as described under *Transmission Oil—Checking and Draining* in this chapter.

2. On all models except IT175G, remove the skidplate, rear brake pedal, right-hand foot peg and right-hand crankcase cover (**Figure 49**).

3. On model IT175G, remove the skidplate, left-hand footpeg, shift lever and left-hand crankcase cover.

4. Completely loosen the locknut on the clutch cable inline adjuster and screw in the adjuster (A, **Figure 50**) until it is tight.

5. Loosen the locknut on the hand lever and screw the adjuster barrel (B, **Figure 50**) in all the way.

6. Loosen the clutch mechanism locknut (A, **Figure 51**).

7. On all models except the IT175G, push the push lever (**Figure 52**) toward the front of the engine until it stops. Hold it in this position and turn the adjuster (B, **Figure 51**) in until the center of the push lever aligns with the match mark on the crankcase (**Figure 53**).

8. On model IT175G, turn the cable inline adjuster (A, **Figure 50**) until the edge of the push lever and the mark on the crankcase align. Tighten the inline adjuster locknut. Turn the mechanism adjuster (B, **Figure 51**) clockwise until resistance is felt, then back the mechanism adjuster out (counterclockwise) 1/4 turn and tighten the locknut (A, **Figure 51**).

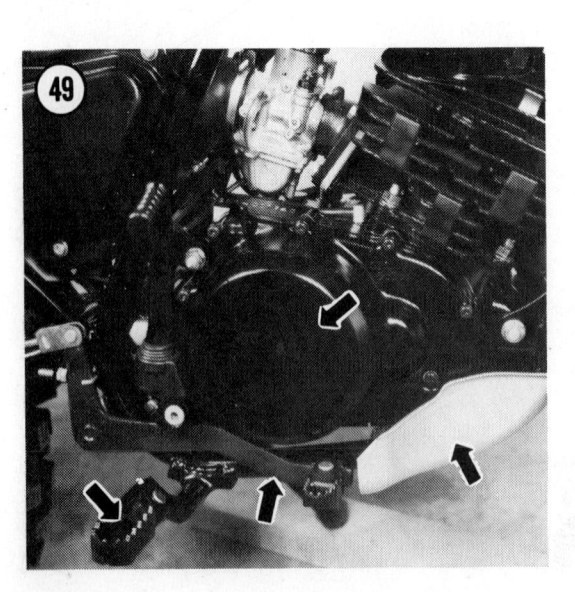

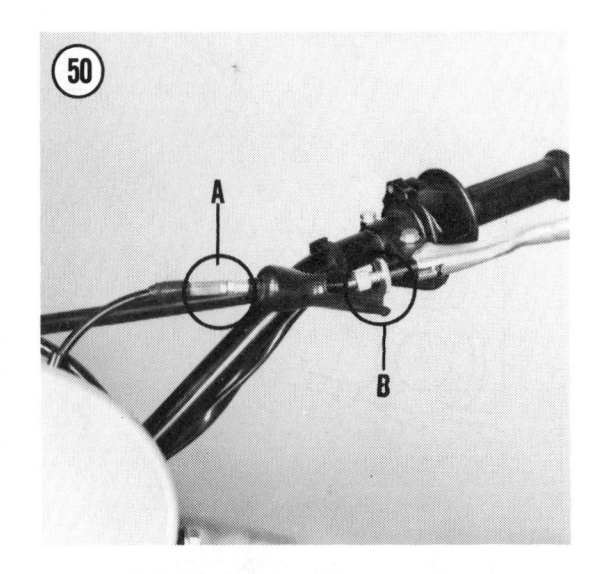

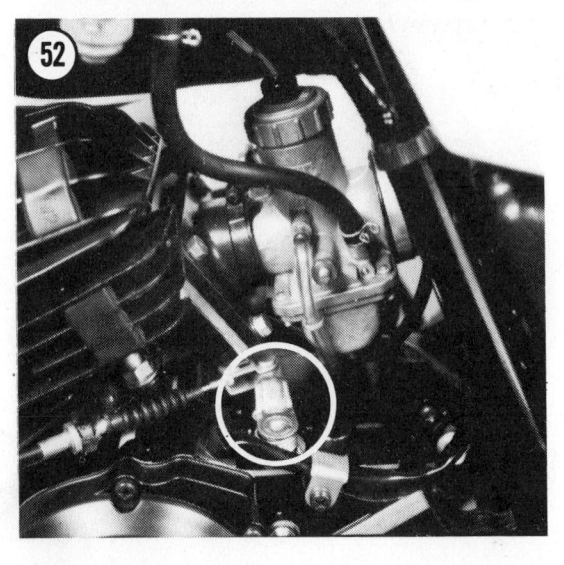

LUBRICATION, MAINTENANCE, AND TUNE-UP

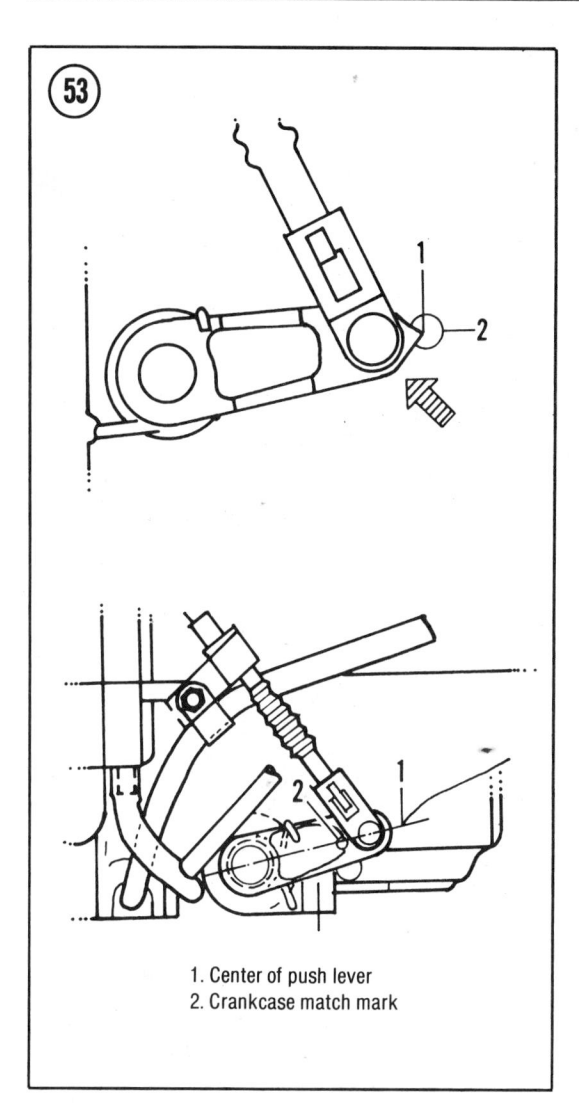

9. On all models except IT175G, install the right-hand crankcase cover, rear brake lever, left-hand footpeg and skidplate.

10. On model IT175G, install the left-hand crankcase cover, shift lever, left-hand foot peg and skidplate.

11. On all models, refill the transmission with the correct quantity and type oil as described in this chapter.

Clutch Lever Free Play Adjustment

Clutch lever free play should be adjusted according to rider preference but a minimum cable slack of 0.08-0.12 in. (2-3 mm) should be maintained; refer to **Figure 54**.

1. Adjust the clutch mechanism first as previously described.

2. Loosen the locknut and turn the adjusting barrel (**Figure 55**) in or out to obtain the correct amount of free play. Tighten the locknut.

NOTE
There are 2 adjustment locations on the cable, one on the hand lever and the cable length adjuster. Either or both of these adjusters can be used for this procedure.

3. If the proper amount of clutch cable free play cannot be achieved using both adjustment

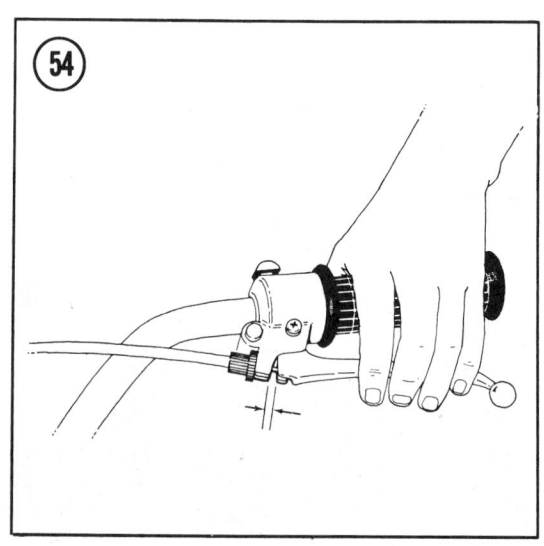

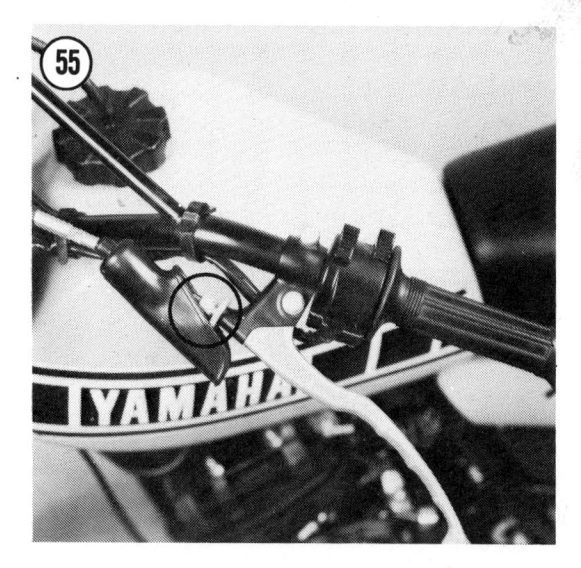

53
1. Center of push lever
2. Crankcase match mark

54

55

points, the cable has stretched to the point that it needs replacing. Refer to *Clutch Cable Removal/Installation* in Chapter Five for the complete procedure.

Throttle Adjustment and Operation

The throttle grip should have 0.12-0.20 in. (3-5 mm) rotational free play at the grip flange (**Figure 56**). If adjustment is necessary, loosen the locknut (A, **Figure 57**) and turn the adjuster (B, **Figure 57**) on top of the carburetor in or out to achieve proper free play rotation. Tighten the locknut (A).

Check the throttle cable from grip to carburetor. Make sure it is not kinked or chafed. Replace as necessary.

Make sure the throttle grip rotates freely from a fully closed to fully open position. Check with the handlebar at center, at full right and at full left. If necessary, remove the throttle grip and apply a lithium base grease to it.

Air Cleaner

The air cleaner element should be removed, cleaned and re-oiled at intervals indicated in **Table 1**.

The air cleaner removes dust and abrasive particles from the air before the air enters the carburetor and engine. Very fine particles that may enter into the engine will cause rapid wear to the piston rings, cylinder and bearings and may clog small passages in the carburetor. Never run the IT without the air cleaner element installed.

Proper air cleaner servicing can do more to ensure long service from your engine than any other single item.

It is a good idea to have a second air cleaner element on hand and ready to be installed, to replace the first unit between events.

Servicing

NOTE
Due to the number of models covered in this book, the following is a basic procedure using one model as a guide. Removal of side plates and any additional panels will vary slightly on each model.

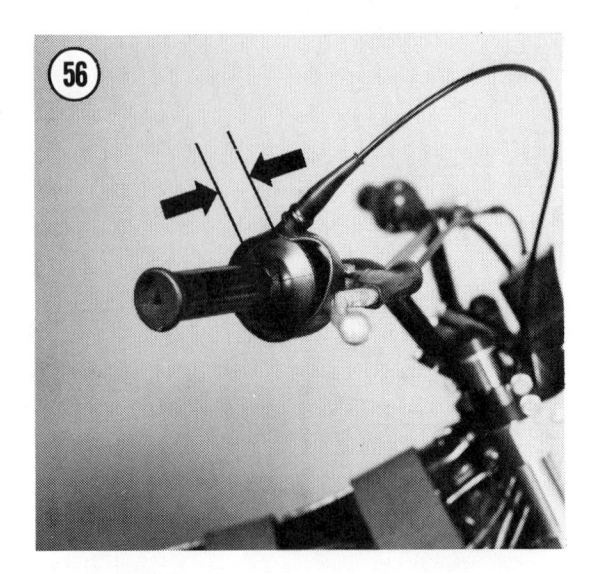

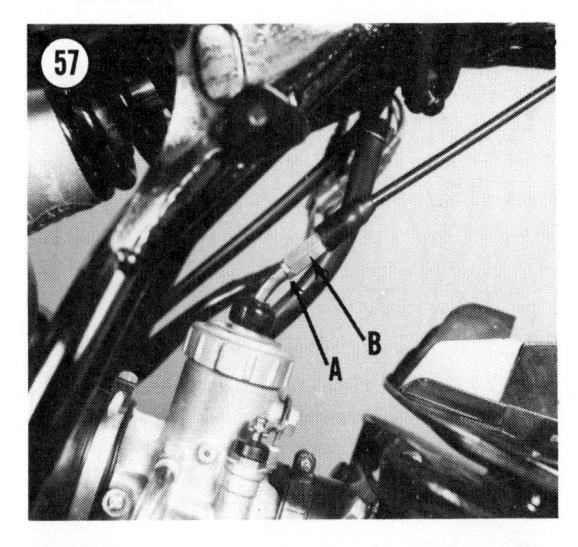

LUBRICATION, MAINTENANCE, AND TUNE-UP

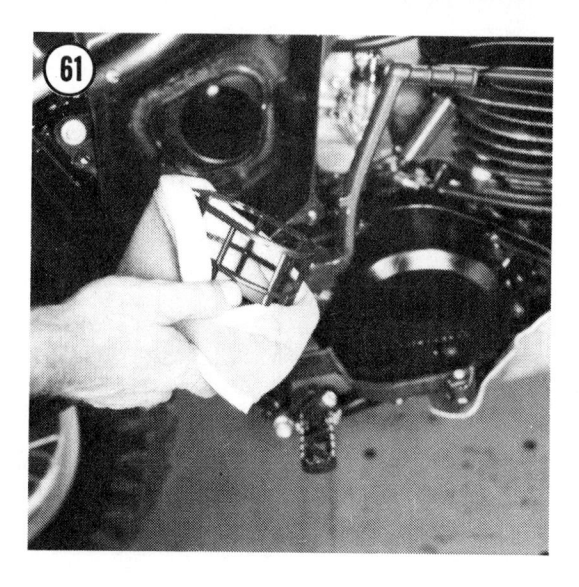

1. Remove the side number plate (**Figure 58**).
2. Remove the screw(s) securing the cover (**Figure 59**) and remove it.
3. Pull the element (**Figure 60**) out of the air box.
4. Separate the element from the holder (**Figure 61**).
5. Clean the element gently in cleaning solvent until all dirt is removed. Thoroughly dry in a clean shop cloth until all solvent residue is removed. Let it dry for about one hour.

NOTE
Inspect the element; if it is torn or broken in any area it should be replaced. Do not run with a damaged element as it may allow dirt to enter the engine.

6. Pour a small amount of 30W engine oil or air filter oil (**Figure 62**) onto the element and work it thoroughly into the porous foam material. Do not oversaturate the element as too much oil will restrict air flow. The element will be discolored by the oil and should have an even color indicating that the oil is distributed evenly. Let it dry for another hour prior to installation. If installed too soon, the chemical carrier in the special filter oil will be drawn into the engine and may cause damage.
7. Wipe out the interior of the air box (**Figure 63**) with a shop rag and cleaning solvent. Make sure the drain plug in the bottom of the air box is clean and open.

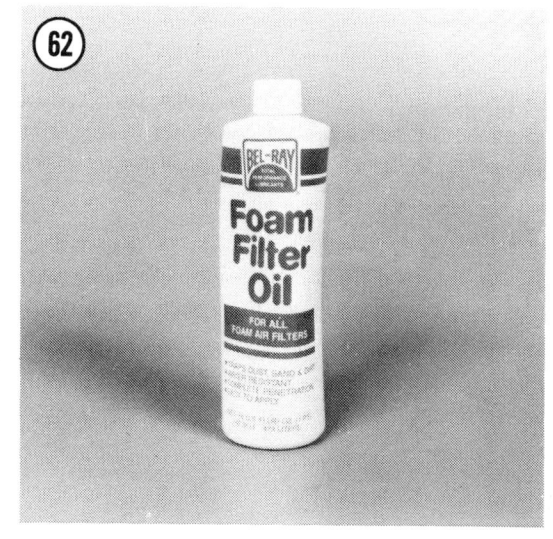

8. Install the element onto the holder. Apply a light coat of wheel bearing grease to the sealing edges (**Figure 64**) of the element to provide a good airtight seal between the element and the air box.

9. Install the element assembly into the air box. Make sure it seats properly against the air box.

CAUTION
An improperly installed air cleaner element will allow dirt and grit to enter the carburetor and engine, causing expensive engine damage.

10. Install any holders and install the cover.

NOTE
On models with an airtight cover, inspect the sealing edge (Figure 65) of the cover. If it is damaged in any way, it must be replaced.

Fuel Line Inspection

Inspect the condition of the fuel line from the fuel tank to the carburetor (**Figure 66**). If it is cracked or starting to deteriorate it must be replaced. Make sure the small hose clamps are in place and holding securely. Also make sure that the overflow tubes are in place (**Figure 67**).

WARNING
A damaged or deteriorated fuel line presents a very dangerous fire hazard to both the rider and the machine if fuel should spill onto a hot engine or exhaust pipe.

LUBRICATION, MAINTENANCE, AND TUNE-UP

Wheel Bearings

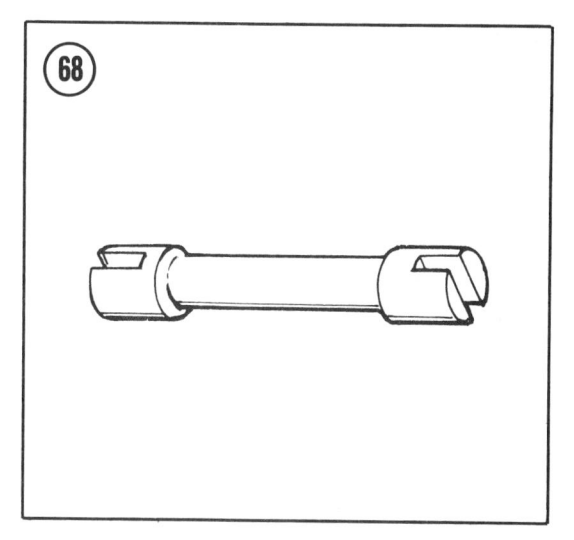

The wheel bearings should be checked as indicated in **Table 1** or after crossing small rivers or creeks. Refer to Chapters Eight and Nine for complete service procedures.

Steering Head Adjustment Check

The steering head is fitted with either roller bearings or loose ball bearings, depending on the model. It should be checked prior to each event or weekend ride.

Place the bike up on wood blocks or a milk crate so that the front wheel is off the ground.

Hold onto the front fork tubes and gently rock the fork assembly back and forth. If you can feel looseness refer to *Steering Head Adjustment* in Chapter Eight.

Wheel Hubs, Rims and Spokes

Check wheel hubs and rims for bends and other signs of damage. Check both wheels for broken or bent spokes. Replace damaged or broken spokes as described under *Wheels* in Chapter Eight. Pluck each spoke with your finger like a guitar string or tap each one lightly with a small hammer. All spokes should emit the same sound. A spoke that is too tight will have a higher pitch than the others; one that is too loose will have a lower pitch. If only one or two spokes are slightly out of adjustment, adjust them with a spoke wrench made for this purpose (**Figure 68**). If more are affected, the wheel should be removed and trued. Refer to *Spoke Adjustment* in Chapter Eight.

Front Suspension Check

1. Apply the front brake and pump the forks up and down as vigorously as possible. Check for smooth operation and look for any oil leaks.
2. Make sure the upper and lower fork bridge bolts (**Figure 69**) are tight.
3. Make sure the front axle nut is tight and the cotter pin is in place (**Figure 70**).

CAUTION
If any of the previously mentioned bolts and nuts are loose, refer to Chapter Eight for correct procedures and torque specifications.

Rear Suspension Check

1. Place wooden blocks or a milk crate under the engine to raise the rear wheel off the ground.
2. Push hard on the rear wheel (sideways) to check for side play in the rear swing arm bushings. Remove the blocks from under the engine.
3. Check that the mounting bolts (or pins) securing the monoshock to the swing arm (**Figure 71** and **Figure 72**) are tight.
4. Make sure the rear axle nut is tight and the cotter pin is in place (**Figure 73**) on models so equipped.

CAUTION
If any of the previously mentioned nuts are loose, refer to Chapter Nine for correct procedures and torque specifications.

Nuts, Bolts and Other Fasteners

Constant vibration can loosen many of the fasteners on the motorcycle. Check the tightness of all fasteners, especially those on:
   a. Engine mounting hardware
   b. Engine crankcase covers
   c. Handlebar and front forks
   d. Gearshift lever
   e. Kickstarter lever
   f. Brake pedal and lever
   g. Exhaust system.

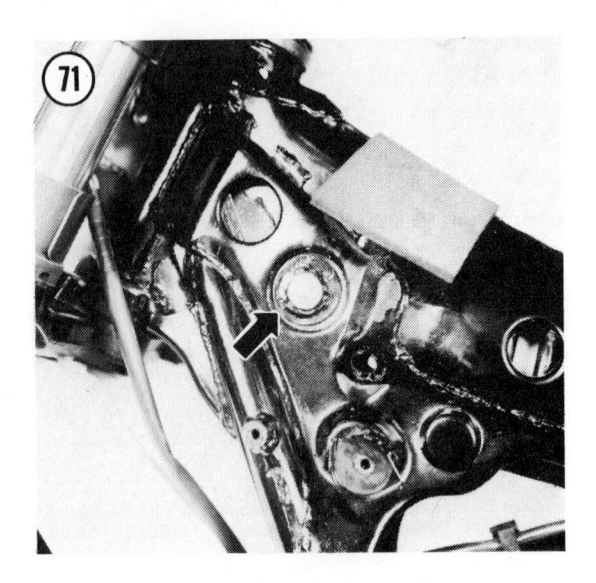

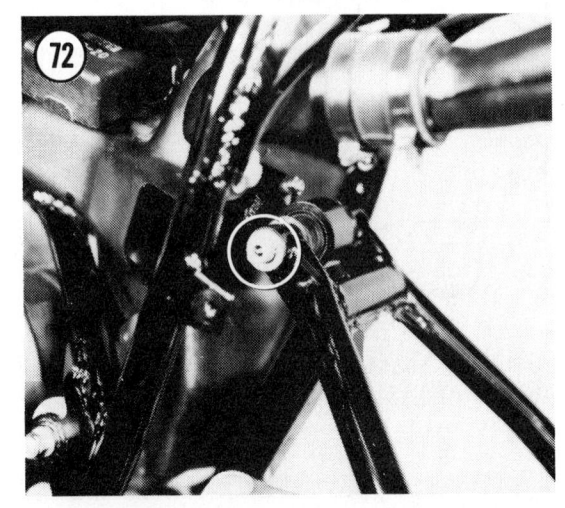

LUBRICATION, MAINTENANCE, AND TUNE-UP

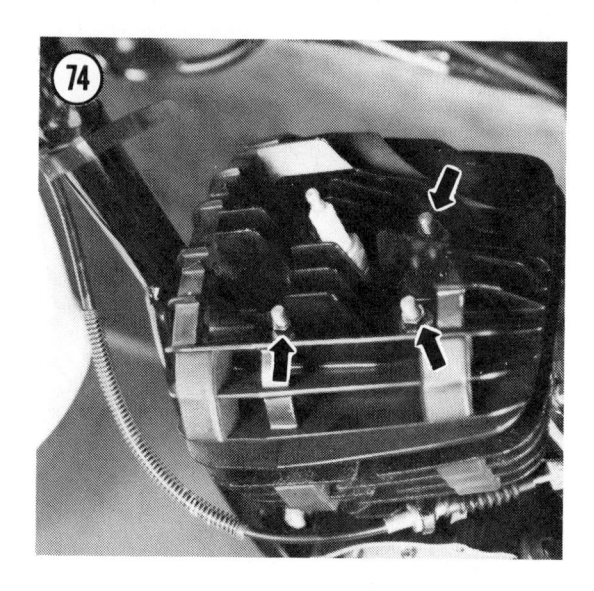

ENGINE TUNE-UP

The number of definitions of the term "tune-up" is probably equal to the number of people defining it. For the purposes of this book, a tune-up is general adjustment and maintenance to ensure peak engine performance.

The following paragraphs discuss each facet of a proper tune-up. These should be performed in the order given. Unless otherwise specified, the engine should be thoroughly cool before starting any tune-up procedure.

Have the new parts on hand before you begin.

To perform a tune-up on your IT, you will need the following tools and equipment:
   a. 14 mm spark plug wrench
   b. Socket wrench and assorted sockets
   c. Phillips head screwdriver
   d. Allen wrench (some models only)
   e. Spark plug wire feeler gauge and gapper tool
   f. Dial indicator
   g. Flywheel puller.

Cylinder Head Nuts

The engine must be at room temperature for this procedure.

1. Place support blocks under the frame to hold the bike securely.
2. Remove the seat.
3. Turn the fuel shutoff valve to the OFF position and remove the fuel line to the carburetor.
4. Remove the fuel tank.
5. Tighten the cylinder head nuts equally in a crisscross pattern to 18 ft.-lb. (25 N•m); refer to **Figure 74**. Some models have one bolt in place of one of the nuts; tighten to the same torque value.

Leave the seat and fuel tank off for the next procedures.

Correct Spark Plug Heat Range

Spark plugs are available in various heat ranges, hotter or colder than the plugs originally installed at the factory.

Select plugs of the heat range designed for the loads and conditions under which the IT will be run. Use of incorrect heat ranges can cause a seized piston, scored cylinder wall or damaged piston crown.

In general, use a hot plug for low speeds and low temperatures. Use a cold plug for high speeds, high engine loads, and high temperatures. The plug should operate hot enough to burn off unwanted deposits, but not so hot that it is damaged or causes preignition. A spark plug of the correct heat range will show a light tan color on the portion of the insulator within the cylinder after the plug has been in service.

The reach (length) of a plug is also important. A longer than normal plug could interfere with the piston, causing permanent and severe damage; refer to **Figure 75**.

The standard heat range spark plugs for the various models are listed in **Table 13**.

Spark Plug Removal/Cleaning

1. Grasp the spark plug lead as near the plug as possible and pull it off the plug. If it is stuck to the plug, twist it slightly to break it loose.
2. Blow away any dirt that has accumulated in the spark plug well.

CAUTION
The dirt could fall into the cylinder when the plug is removed, causing serious engine damage.

3. Remove the spark plug with a 14 mm spark plug wrench.

NOTE
If the plug is difficult to remove, apply penetrating oil, like WD-40 or Liquid Wrench, around the base of the plug and let it soak in about 10-20 minutes.

4. Inspect the plug carefully. Look for a broken center porcelain, excessively eroded electrodes and excessive carbon or oil fouling. If deposits are light, the plug may be cleaned in solvent with a wire brush or cleaned in a special spark plug sandblast cleaner. Regap the plug as explained in the following section.

Gapping and Installing the Plug

A new spark plug should be carefully gapped to ensure a reliable, consistant spark. You must use a special spark plug gapping tool and a wire feeler gauge.

1. Remove the new spark plug from the box. Screw on the small piece that is loose in the box (**Figure 76**).

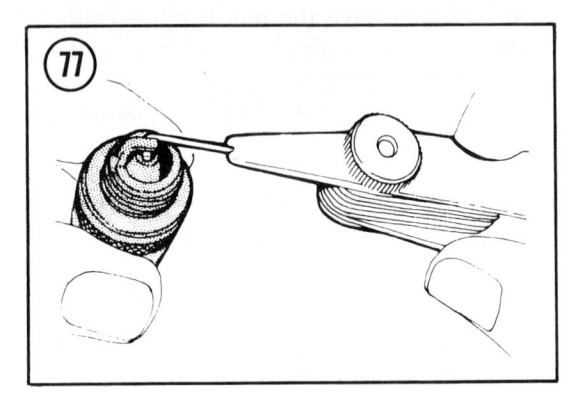

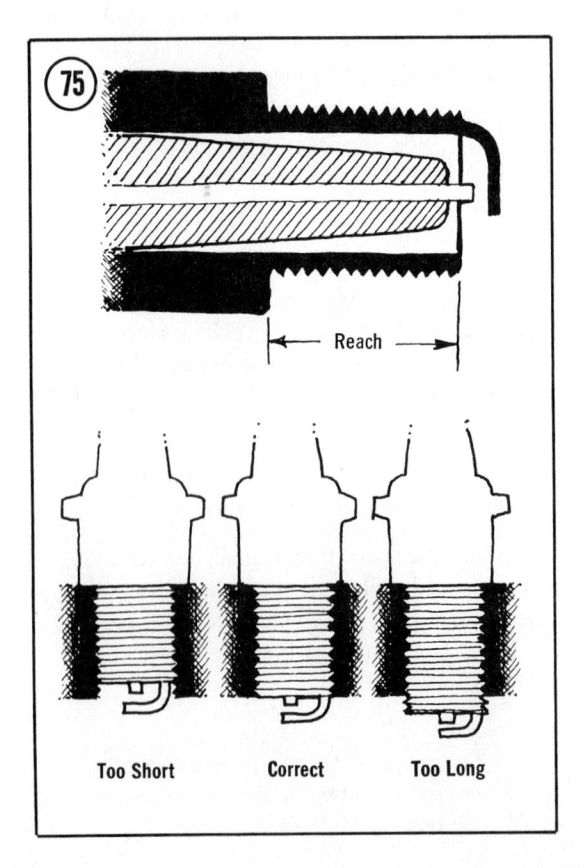

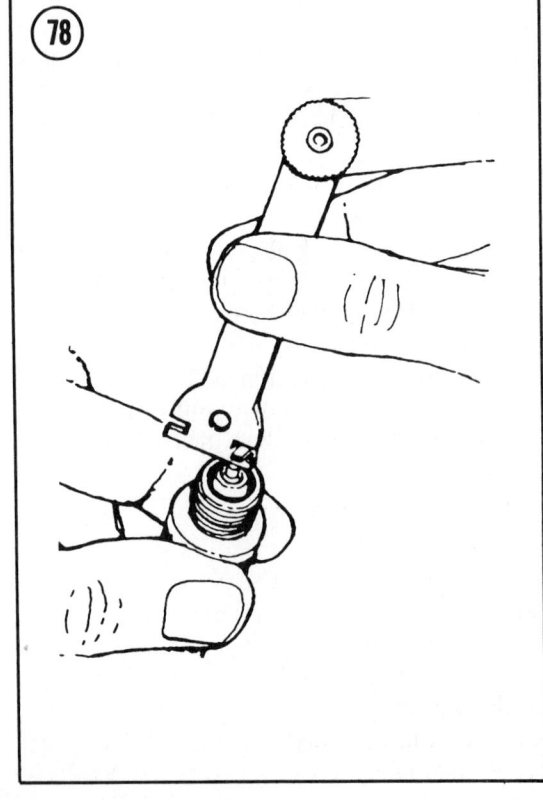

LUBRICATION, MAINTENANCE, AND TUNE-UP

2. Insert a wire feeler gauge between the center and side electrode (**Figure 77**). The correct gap is listed in **Table 13**. If the gap is correct, you will feel a slight drag as you pull the wire through. If there is no drag, or the gauge won't pass through, bend the side electrode with a gapping tool (**Figure 78**) to set the proper gap.
3. Put a small drop of oil on the threads of the spark plug.
4. Screw the spark plug in by hand until it seats. Very little effort is required. If force is necessary, you have the plug cross-threaded; unscrew it and try again.
5. Use a spark plug wrench and tighten the plug an additional 1/4 to 1/2 turn after the gasket has made contact with the head. If you are installing an old, regapped plug and reusing the old gasket, only tighten an additional 1/4 turn.

NOTE
Do not overtighten. This will only squash the gasket and destroy its sealing ability.

6. Install the spark plug wire; make sure it is on tight.

Reading Spark Plugs

Much information about engine and spark plug performance can be determined by careful examination of the spark plug. This information is only valid after performing the following steps.
1. Ride the bike a short distance at full throttle in any gear.
2. Turn off the kill switch before closing the throttle and simultaneously pull in the clutch or shift to NEUTRAL; coast and brake to a stop.
3. Remove the spark plug and examine it. Compare it to **Figure 79**.

If the insulator is white or burned, the plug is too hot and should be replaced with a colder one.

A too-cold plug will have sooty or oily deposits.

If the plug has a light tan or gray colored deposit and no abnormal gap wear or electrode erosion is evident, the plug and the engine are running properly.

If the plug exhibits a black insulator tip, a damp and oily film over the firing end and a carbon layer over the entire nose it is oil fouled. An oil fouled plug can be cleaned, but it is better to replace it.

Ignition Timing

The Yamaha IT bikes are equipped with a capacitor discharge ignition (CDI) without breaker points. This greatly simplifies ignition timing and makes the ignition system much less susceptable to failures caused by dirt and moisture.

Since there are no components to wear, adjusting the ignition timing is only necessary after the engine has been reassembled or if the base plate screws have worked loose.

The static timing procedure used for some models requires the use of a special tool called a dial indicator (**Figure 80**). These can be purchased from either a Yamaha dealer, motorcycle or auto supply store or mail order supply house. A dial indicator, dial indicator tool stand and gauge needle are needed.

NOTE
Before starting this procedure, check all electrical connections related to the ignition system. Make sure all connections are tight and free of corrosion and that all ground connections are tight.

Dynamic timing–all models since 1980 (except IT175)

1. Start the engine and let it reach normal operating temperature. Stop the engine.
2. Remove the screws securing the ignition cover and remove it (**Figure 81**).
3. Connect a portable tachometer (**Figure 82**) and timing light (**Figure 83**) to the engine following the manufacturers' instructions.

CAUTION
*The exhaust system is **hot**; protect yourself accordingly!*

4. Restart the engine and let it idle.

CHAPTER THREE

SPARK PLUG CONDITION

NORMAL
- Identified by light tan or gray deposits on the firing tip.
- Can be cleaned.

GAP BRIDGED
- Identified by deposit buildup closing gap between electrodes.
- Caused by oil or carbon fouling. If deposits are not excessive, the plug can be cleaned.

OIL FOULED
- Identified by wet black deposits on the insulator shell bore and electrodes.
- Caused by excessive oil entering combustion chamber through worn rings and pistons, excessive clearance between valve guides and stems, or worn or loose bearings. Can be cleaned. If engine is not repaired, use a hotter plug.

CARBON FOULED
- Identified by black, dry fluffy carbon deposits on insulator tips, exposed shell surfaces and electrodes.
- Caused by too cold a plug, weak ignition, dirty air cleaner, too rich a fuel mixture, or excessive idling. Can be cleaned.

LEAD FOULED
- Identified by dark gray, black, yellow, or tan deposits or a fused glazed coating on the insulator tip.
- Caused by highly leaded gasoline. Can be cleaned.

WORN
- Identified by severely eroded or worn electrodes.
- Caused by normal wear. Should be replaced.

FUSED SPOT DEPOSIT
- Identified by melted or spotty deposits resembling bubbles or blisters.
- Caused by sudden acceleration. Can be cleaned.

OVERHEATING
- Identified by a white or light gray insulator with small black or gray brown spots and with bluish-burnt appearance of electrodes.
- Caused by engine overheating, wrong type of fuel, loose spark plugs, too hot a plug, or incorrect ignition timing. Replace the plug.

PREIGNITION
- Identified by melted electrodes and possibly blistered insulator. Metallic deposits on insulator indicate engine damage.
- Caused by wrong type of fuel, incorrect ignition timing or advance, too hot a plug, burned valves, or engine overheating. Replace the plug.

LUBRICATION, MAINTENANCE, AND TUNE-UP

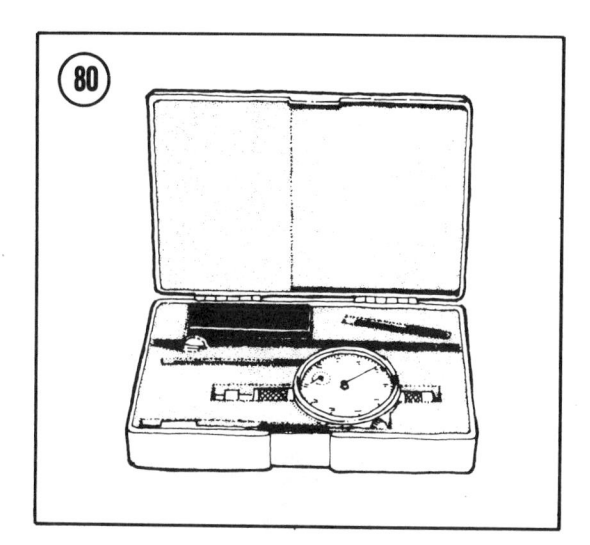

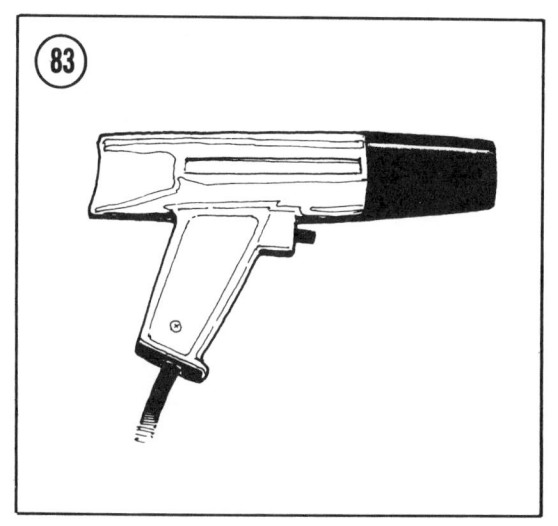

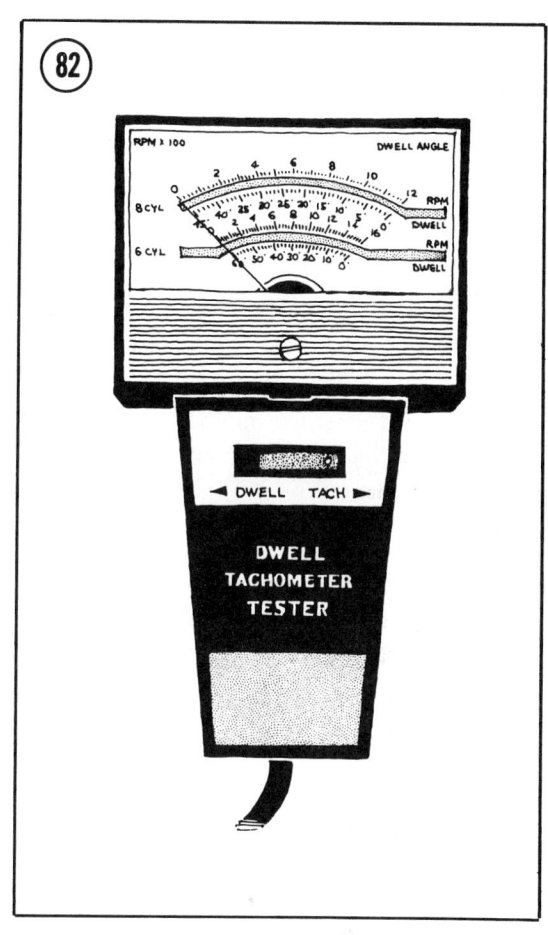

5. Adjust the idle speed if necessary as described under *Carburetor Idle Speed Adjustment* in this chapter. Idle speed should be:

    a. IT425: 2,500 rpm
    b. IT250: 5,000 rpm
    c. IT125: 2,000 rpm

6. Shine the timing light on the timing marks on the magneto flywheel. The timing is correct if the magneto flywheel mark aligns with the fixed mark on the crankcase (**Figure 84**).

7. If timing is incorrect, stop the engine and remove the magneto rotor as described under *Magneto Removal/Installation* in Chapter Four.

8. Loosen the screws (A, **Figure 85**) securing the base plate and rotate it until the mark on the base plate aligns with the mark on the crankcase (B, **Figure 85**). Tighten the screws

securely, making sure the base plate does not move while doing this.

9. Install the magneto rotor and repeat Steps 4, 5 and 6.

10. If necessary repeat Steps 4-8 until timing is correct.

11. Disconnect the timing light and portable tachometer.

12. Install the ignition cover and gasket.

Static timing–all 1976-1979 models and IT175 since 1980

1. Remove the front muffler assembly as described under *Muffler Assembly Removal/Installation* in Chapter Six.

2. Remove the spark plug.

3. Remove the gearshift lever (**Figure 86**).

4. Remove the screws securing the ignition cover (**Figure 87**) and remove it and the gasket.

5. Install the dial indicator assembly (**Figure 88**) into the spark plug hole.

6. Rotate the magneto rotor until the piston is at top dead center (TDC). Tighten the set screw on the dial indicator to secure it properly in the cylinder head.

7. Align the zero on the dial gauge face exactly with the gauge needle. Rotate the rotor back and forth to be sure that the gauge does not go past zero. Readjust if necessary.

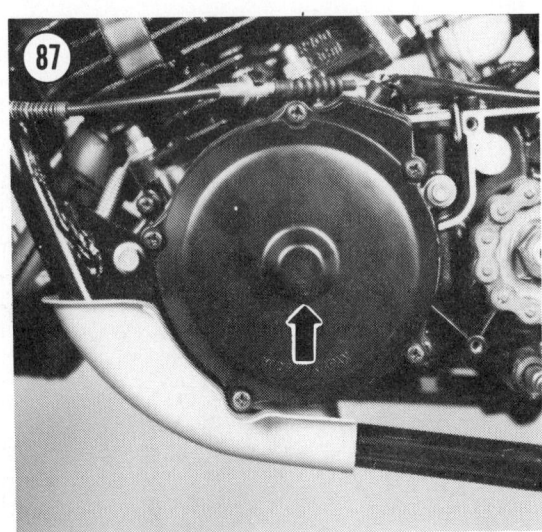

LUBRICATION, MAINTENANCE, AND TUNE-UP

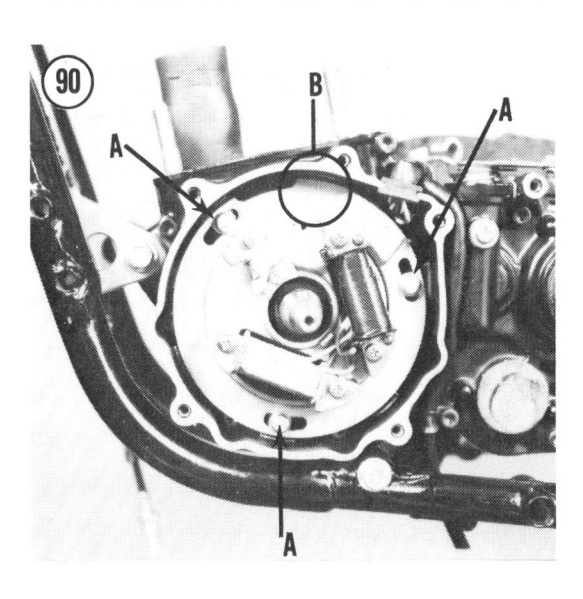

8. Starting at TDC rotate the magneto rotor *clockwise* until the dial reads the dimension given in **Table 14** for your specific model.
9. Check that the timing mark on the magneto rotor aligns with the fixed mark on the crankcase (**Figure 89**).
10. If timing is incorrect, remove the magneto rotor as described under *Magneto Removal/Installation* in Chapter Four.
11. Loosen the screws (A, **Figure 90**) securing the base plate and rotate it until the marks on the base plate align with the mark on the crankcase (B, **Figure 90**). Tighten the screws securely, making sure the base plate does not move while doing this.
12. Install the magneto rotor and repeat Steps 8 and 9.
13. If necessary repeat Steps 10 and 11 until timing is correct.
14. Unscrew the dial indicator assembly and install the spark plug.
15. Install the ignition cover and gasket, gearshift lever and muffler assembly.

Idle Speed Adjustment

The air cleaner must be cleaned before starting this procedure or the results will be inaccurate.

1. Turn the pilot air screw (**Figure 91**) in until it *lightly* seats.
2. Back it out the following number of turns:
    a. IT425G: 1-1/2 turns
    b. IT400F: 2-1/4 turns

c. IT400E, D: 1-1/4 turns
   d. IT400C: 1.0 turn
   e. IT250G, F: 1-1/2 turns
   f. IT250E, D: 1.0 turn
   g. IT175G, F: 1-1/4 turns
   h. IT175E, D: 1-1/2 turns
   i. IT125G: 1-3/4 turns.
3. Start the engine and let it reach normal operating temperature.
4. Loosen the locknut and turn the idle stop screw (**Figure 92**) in or out to achieve the desired idle speed. This speed should be set to your own personal preference.
5. Turn the pilot air screw in or out to achieve the highest possible engine rpm.
6. Turn the idle stop screw in or out again to achieve the desired idle speed. Tighten the locknut (**Figure 92**).

WARNING
With the engine idling, move the handlebar from side to side. If idle speed increases during this movement, the throttle cable may need adjusting or may be incorrectly routed through the frame. Correct this problem immediately. Do not ride the bike in this unsafe condition.

7. After this adjustment is completed, test ride the bike. Throttle response from idle should be rapid and without any hesitation. If there is any hesitation, turn the pilot air screw in or out in 1/4 turn increments until this problem is solved.

Decarbonizing

The carbon deposits should be removed from the piston, cylinder head, exhaust port and muffler as indicated in **Table 1**. If they are not cleaned off they will cause preignition (ping), overheating and high fuel consumption.

Engine Decarbonizing

1. Remove the cylinder head and cylinder as described under *Cylinder Removal/Installation* in Chapter Four.
2. Gently scrape off carbon deposits from the top of the piston and cylinder head (**Figure 93**) with a dull screwdriver or the end of a hacksaw blade (**Figure 94**). Do not scratch the surface.

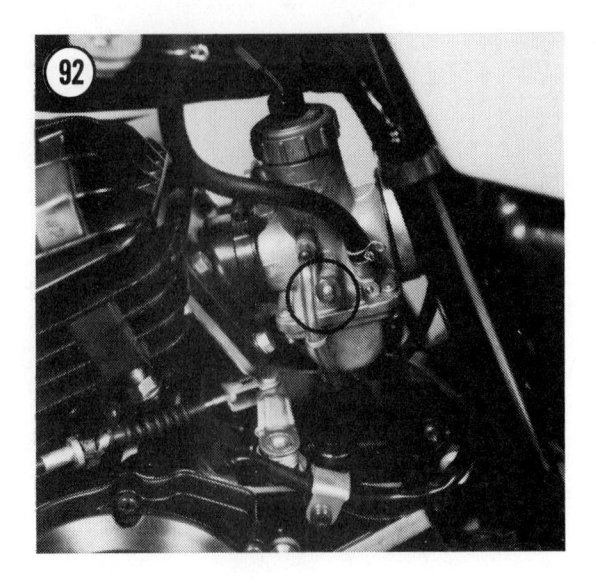

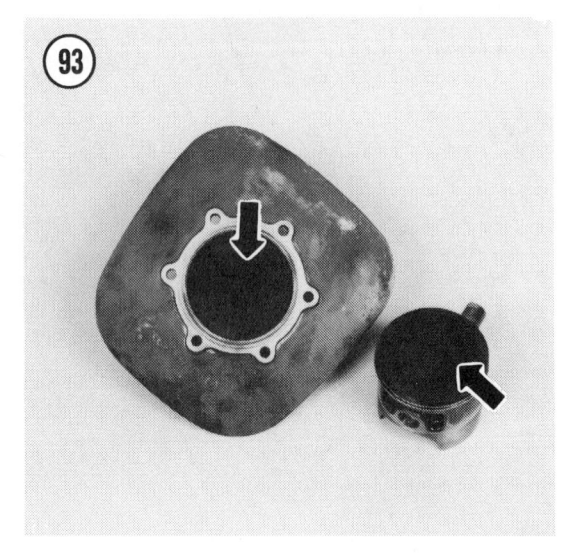

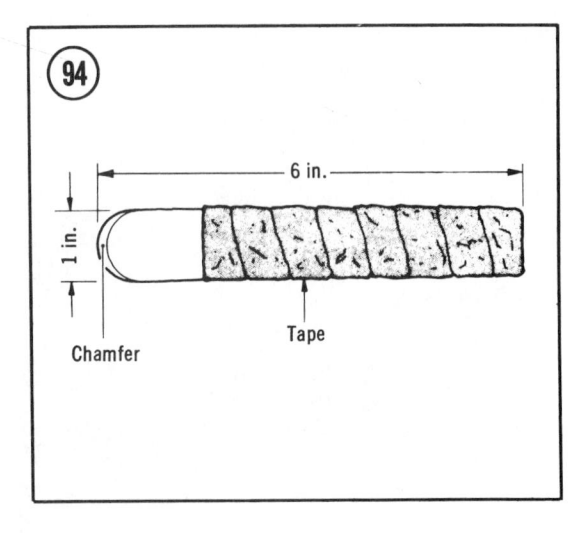

LUBRICATION, MAINTENANCE, AND TUNE-UP

2. Gently scrape off carbon deposits from the interior of the head pipe where it attaches to the cylinder.
3. Clean out the rest of the interior of the expansion chamber by running a piece of used motorcycle drive chain around in it. Another way to clean the area is with a length of wire cable with one end frayed held in an electric drill. Run the wire around in the front portion a couple of times. Shake out all loose carbon. Also tap on the outer shell of the exhaust pipe assembly with a plastic mallet to break loose any additional carbon.
4. Blow out the expansion chamber with compressed air.
5. Remove the end of the silencer (**Figure 96**). Clean out its interior with a wire brush and blow out all residue.
6. Visually inspect the entire exhaust pipe assembly, especially in the many areas of welds, for cracks or other damage. Replace if necessary.
7. Install the assembly.

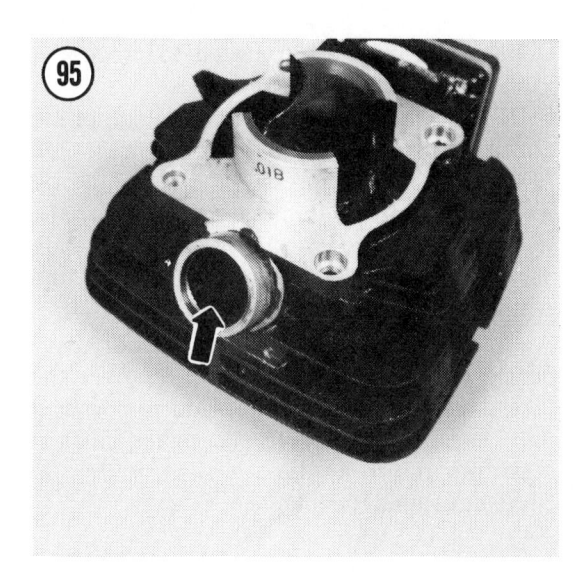

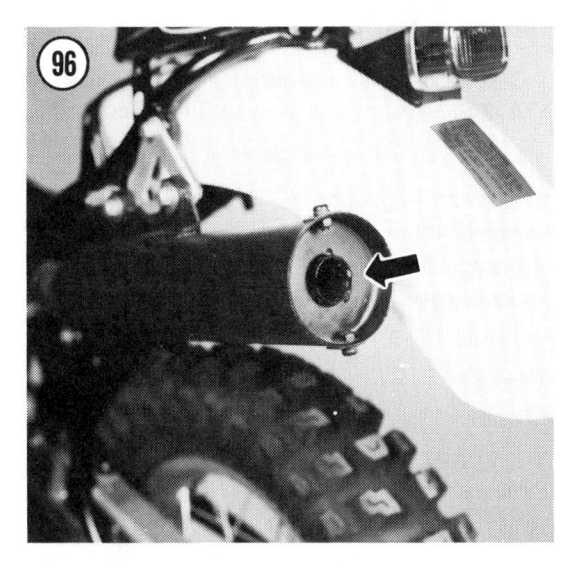

Stuff a shop cloth into the opening in the crankcase to keep any residue from entering it.
3. Wipe the surfaces clean with a cloth dipped in cleaning solvent.
4. Scrape off the carbon in the exhaust port (**Figure 95**) with a dull screwdriver or the end of a hacksaw blade (**Figure 94**). Do not scratch the surface.
5. Install the cylinder and cylinder head.

Exhaust System Decarbonizing

1. Remove the exhaust pipe assembly as described under *Exhaust System Removal/Installation* in Chapter Six.

STORAGE

Several months of inactivity can cause serious problems and a general deterioration of the IT's condition. This is especially true in areas of weather extremes. During the winter months it is advisable to specially prepare the bike for lay-up.

Selecting a Storage Area

Most cyclists store their bikes in their home garages. If you do not have a home garage, facilities suitable for long-term motorcycle storage are readily available for rent or lease in most areas. In selecting a building, consider the following points.
1. The storage area must be dry, free from dampness and excessive humidity. Heating is not necessary, but the building should be well-insulated to minimize extreme temperature variations.
2. Buildings with large window areas should be avoided or such windows should be masked if direct sunlight can fall on the bike. This is also a good security measure.

3. Buildings in industrial areas, where factories are liable to emit corrosive fumes, are not desirable nor are facilities near bodies of salt water.

4. The area should be selected to minimize the possibility of loss from fire, theft or vandalism. The area should be fully insured, perhaps with a package covering fire, theft, vandalism, weather and liability. The advice of your insurance agent should be solicited in these matters. The building should be fireproof and items such as the security of doors and windows, alarm facility and proximity of police should be considered.

Preparing Bike for Storage

Careful preparation will minimize deterioration and make it easier to restore the bike to service later. Use the following procedure.

1. Wash the bike completely. Make certain to remove all dirt in all the hard-to-reach parts like the cooling fins on the head and cylinder. Completely dry all parts of the bike to remove all moisture. Wax all painted and polished surfaces, including any chromed areas.

2. Run the bike for about 20-30 minutes to warm up the oil in the clutch and transmission. Drain the oil, regardless of the time since the last oil change. Refill with the normal quantity and type of oil.

3. Drain all gasoline from the fuel tank, the interconnecting hose and the carburetor. Leave the fuel shutoff valve in the ON position. As an alternative, a fuel preservative may be added to the fuel. This preservative is available from many motorcycle shops and marine equipment suppliers.

4. Lubricate the drive chain and control cables; refer to specific procedures in this chapter.

5. Remove the spark plug and add about one teaspoon of SAE 10W/30 motor oil into the cylinder. Reinstall the spark plug and, without starting the engine, turn it over to distribute the oil to the cylinder walls and piston. Depress the engine kill switch to prevent it from starting during this procedure.

6. Tape or tie a plastic bag over the end of the muffler to prevent the entry of moisture.

7. Check the tire pressure, inflate to the correct pressure and move the bike to the storage area. Place it securely on a milk crate or wood blocks with both wheels off the ground.

8. Cover the bike with a tarp, blanket or heavy plastic drop cloth. Place this cover over the bike mainly as a dust cover—do not wrap it tightly, especially any plastic material, as it may trap moisture. Leave room for air to circulate around the bike.

Inspection During Storage

Try to inspect the bike weekly while in storage. Any deterioration should be corrected as soon as possible. For example, if corrosion of bright metal parts is observed, cover them with a light coat of grease or silicone spray after a thorough polishing.

Turn the engine over a couple of times—don't start it; use the kickstarter and hold the kill switch ON. Pump the front forks to keep the seals lubricated.

Restoring Bike to Service

A bike that has been properly prepared and stored in a suitable area requires only light maintenance to restore it to service. It is advisable, however, to perform a tune-up.

1. Before removing the bike from the storage area, reinflate the tires to the correct pressures. Air loss during storage may have nearly flattened the tires and moving the bike can cause damage to tires, tubes and rims.

WARNING
During the next step, place a metal container under the carburetor to catch all fuel or it will create a real fire danger if allowed to drain onto the bike and the floor. Dispose of the fuel properly.

LUBRICATION, MAINTENANCE, AND TUNE-UP

2. When the bike is brought to the work area, drain the fuel tank if fuel preservative was used. Turn the fuel shutoff valve to the OFF position and refill the fuel tank with the correct fuel/oil mixture. Remove the main jet cover on the base of the carburetor, turn the fuel shutoff valve to the ON position and allow several cups of fuel to pass through the fuel system. Turn the fuel shutoff valve to the OFF position and install the main jet cover.

3. Remove the spark plug and squirt a small amount of fuel into the cylinder to help remove the oil coating.

4. Install a fresh spark plug and start up the engine.

5. Perform the standard tune-up as described earlier in this chapter.

6. Check the operation of the engine kill switch. Oxidation of the switch contacts during storage may make it inoperative.

7. Clean and test ride the motorcycle.

WARNING
If any type of preservative (Armor All or equivalent) has been applied to the tire treads, be sure the tires are well "scrubbed-in" prior to any fast riding or cornering on a hard surface. If not, they will slip right out from under you.

Tables are on the following pages.

Table 1 MAINTENANCE SCHEDULE*

Piston	
Clean and inspect	Every event
Replace	As required
Piston rings	
Replace	Every 900 miles (1,500 km)
Cylinder head	
Inspect	Every event
Clean and retighten	Every event
Cylinder	
Clean and inspect	Every event
Retighten	Every event
Crankshaft main bearing	
Inspect	Every event (900 mi./1,500 km)
Replace	As required
Piston wrist pin	
Inspect	Every event
Replace	As required
Magneto rotor nut	
Retighten	Every 3rd event
Kickstarter idle gear	
Inspect and replace	As required
Clutch	
Adjust and replace	As required
Transmission	
Change oil	Every event (300 mi./500 km)
Inspect gears and shift forks	As required
Exhaust system	
Inspect	Every event
Decarbonize	As required
Carburetor	
Inspect and adjust	Every event
Clean and retighten	Every 300 mi. (500 km)
Fuel shutoff valve	
Clean	Every event
Air filter	
Clean and oil	Every event
Replace	As required
Spark plug	
Inspect and clean	Every event
Replace	As required
CDI connections	
Inspect electrical connections	Every event
Drive chain	
Clean and lubricate	Every event
Check tension and alignment	Every event
Replace	As required
Chain guards and rollers	
Inspect and replace	As required
Frame	
Clean and inspect	Every event

(continued)

LUBRICATION, MAINTENANCE, AND TUNE-UP

Table 1 MAINTENANCE SCHEDULE* (continued)

Front fork	
Change oil	Every event
Replace oil seal	As required
Check and adjust air pressure	Every event
Monoshock	
Inspect and adjust	Every event
Lubricate	Every event
Steering head	
Inspect adjustment	Every event
Clean and lubricate	Every 2nd event
Replace bearings	As required
Swing arm	
Inspect	Every event
Lubricate	Every 900 mi. (1,500 km)
Wheels and tires	
Check pressure, runout, and spoke tension	Every event
Inspect wheel bearings	Every event
Replace wheel bearings	As required
Throttle control	
Lubricate	Every event
Control cables	
Check routing and connections	Every event
Inspect and lubricate	Every event
Clutch and brake hand lever pivot points	
Lubricate	Every event
Retighten	Every event
Brakes	
Clean, inspect, adjust	Every event
Replace linings	As required
Miscellaneous bolts and fasteners	
Inspect and tighten	Every race

*This Yamaha Factory maintenance schedule should be considered as a guide to general maintenance and lubrication intervals. Harder than normal use and exposure to mud, water, sand, high humidity, etc. will naturally dictate more frequent attention to most maintenance items.

Table 2 CORRECT FUEL/OIL MIXTURE

Initial break-in oil (either a new bike or rebuilt engine)	12:1 to 16:1
Normal mixture/premium gasoline	20:1

Table 3 TIRE INFLATION PRESSURE

Tire Size	Air Pressure
Front	
3.00-21 -4PR	14 psi (1.0 kg/cm^2)
	12.8 psi (0.9 kg/cm^2) IT125G only
Rear	
4.10-18 -4PR	17 psi (1.2 kg/cm^2)
4.50-18 -4PR	15 psi (1.1 kg/cm^2)

Table 4 RECOMMENDED LUBRICANTS AND FUEL

Engine oil	Yamaha Yamalube "R"
	Shell Super M
	Castrol R30
Transmission oil	SAE 10W/30 "SE" motor oil
Front forks	SAE20W, SAE15, SAE10, or special fork oil
Air filter	SAE10W/30 motor oil
Drive chain	Chain lube or 10W/30 motor oil
Control cables	Cable lube or 10W/30 motor oil
Control lever pivots	10W/30 motor oil
Steering head, wheel bearings, swing arm	Medium weight wheel bearing grease (waterproof type)
Brake cam	Lithium base
Fuel	Premium grade — research octane 90 or higher

Table 5 FUEL CAPACITIES

Model	U.S. Gal.	Liters
IT425	3.2	12.0
IT400	3.2	12.0
IT250	3.2	12.0
IT175G	2.9	11.0
IT175F, E, D	2.5	9.5
IT125	2.2	8.5

Table 6 TRANSMISSION OIL CAPACITY

Model	Drain/Refill	Rebuild
IT425G	800 cc	850 cc
IT400F, E, D	1,050-1,150 cc	1,150-1,250 cc
IT400C	950 cc	1,000 cc
IT250G	800 cc	850 cc
IT250F, E, D	1,050-1,150 cc	1,150-1,250 cc
IT175G	600 cc	700 cc
IT175F, E, D	650 cc	750 cc
IT125G	600-700 cc	700-800 cc

Table 7 FRONT FORK OIL CAPACITY AND MEASUREMENT

Model	Capacity oz. (cc)	Measurement in. (mm)
IT425G	10.8 (319)	7.20 (183)
IT400F	10.0 (296)	*
IT400E, D	8.4 (250)	*
IT400C	8.3 (246)	*
IT250G	10.8 (319)	7.20 (183)
IT250F	10.01 (296)	*
IT250E, D	8.4 (250)	*
IT175G	10.7 (317)	7.30 (185)
IT175F	9.0 (268)	*
IT175E, D	8.8 (262)	*
IT125G	5.5 (163)	*

*Dimensions do not apply to these models

LUBRICATION, MAINTENANCE, AND TUNE-UP

Table 8 FRONT FORK CAP TORQUE SPECIFICATIONS

Model	Foot-Pounds (ft.-lb.)	Newton Meters (N•m)
IT425G	18	25
IT400F, E, D, C	18	25
IT250G	18	25
IT250F, E, D	18	25
IT175G	16.5	23
IT175F, E, D	14.5	20
IT125G	16	23

Table 9 FRONT FORK AIR PRESSURE

Model	Psi	Kg/cm²
IT400G	12.8	0.9
IT400F, E, D	12.8	0.9
IT400C	*	*
IT250G, F, E, D	12.8	0.9
IT175G	0	0
IT175F, E, D	*	*
IT125G	*	*

*Does not apply to these models

Table 10 DRIVE CHAIN SLACK

Model	Inches	Millimeters
IT425G	1.6-2.0	40-50
IT400F, E	1.6-2.0	40-50
IT400D, C	2.2-2.6	55-60
IT250G	1.6-2.0	40-50
IT250F, E	1.6-2.0	40-50
IT250D	2.2-2.6	55-60
IT175G	0.4-0.6	10-15
IT175F, E	1.6-2.0	40-50
IT175D	2.2-2.6	55-60
IT125G	**1.6-1.8**	**40-45**

Table 11 REAR AXLE NUT TORQUE SPECIFICATIONS

Model	Foot-pounds (ft.-lb.)	Newton Meters (N•m)
IT425G	58	80
IT400F	58	80
IT400E, D, C	65	90
IT250G, F	58	80
IT250E, D	65	90
IT175G	68	85
IT175F, E	60	85
IT175D	72	100
IT125G	60	85

CHAPTER THREE

Table 12 DRIVE CHAIN REPLACEMENT NUMBERS

Model	Type	Number of Links
IT425G	DK 520 S	101
IT400F	DK 520 DS	101
IT400E, D	DK 520 TR	105
IT400C	DK 520 T	104
IT250G	DK 520 S	101
IT250F	DK 520 DS	101
IT250E, D	DK 520 TR	103
IT175G	DK 520 DS	100
IT175F	DK 520 TR	95
IT175E	DK 520 T	95
IT175D	DK 520 TR	93
IT125G	DK 520 DS	100

Table 13 SPARK PLUG TYPE AND GAP

Model	Type	Gap In.	(mm)
IT425G	Champion N-3	0.024-0.028	(0.6-0.7)
IT400F, E, D, C	Champion N-3G	0.024-0.028	(0.6-0.7)
IT250 (all)	Champion N-2G	0.024-0.028	(0.6-0.7)
IT175G	Champion N-59G	0.024-0.028	(0.6-0.7)
IT175F, E, D	Champion N-2G	0.024-0.028	(0.6-0.7)
IT125G	Champion N-2G	0.024-0.031	(0.6-0.8)

Table 14 TIMING DIMENSIONS (WITH DIAL INDICATOR)

Model	Inches*	Millimeters*
IT425G	Does not apply	(check dynamically)
IT400F	0.122	3.1
IT400E, D, C	0.106	2.7
IT250G, F, E, D	0.090	2.3
IT175G	0.102	2.6
IT175F	0.118	3.0
IT175E, D	0.091	2.3
IT125G	0.102	2.6

*All dimensions taken at Before Top Dead Center (BTDC).

NOTE: If you own a 1981 or later model, first check the Supplement at the back of the book for any new service information.

CHAPTER FOUR

ENGINE

The engines covered in this manual for the IT series range from the IT125 to the IT425. This chapter contains information for removal, inspection, service and reassembly of the engine. Although the clutch and transmission are located within the engine they are covered in Chapter Five to simplify this material.

Service procedures for the different models are basically the same except for splitting and disassembling the crankcases. Where it would be too confusing to cover all models in one procedure, the different types or models are covered separately. When differences occur within one procedure they are identified.

Prior to removing the engine or any major assembly, clean the entire engine and frame with a good grade commercial degreaser like Gunk or Bel-Ray Degreaser (**Figure 1**). It is easier to work on a clean engine and you will do a better job.

Make certain that you have all the necessary tools available, especially any special tool(s), and purchase replacement parts prior to disassembly. Make sure you have a clean place to work.

It is a good idea to identify and mark parts as they are removed to help during assembly and installation. Clean all parts thoroughly upon removal, then place them in trays or boxes with their associated mounting hardware. Do not rely on memory alone as it may be days or weeks before you complete the job.

Throughout the text there is frequent mention of the right-hand and left-hand side of the engine. This refers to the engine as it sits in the bike's frame, not as it sits on your workbench.

Refer to **Table 1** for engine specifications and **Table 2** for torque values. **Tables 1-3** are at the end of this chapter.

ENGINE PRINCIPLES

Figure 2 explains how the engine works. This will be helpful when troubleshooting or repairing the engine.

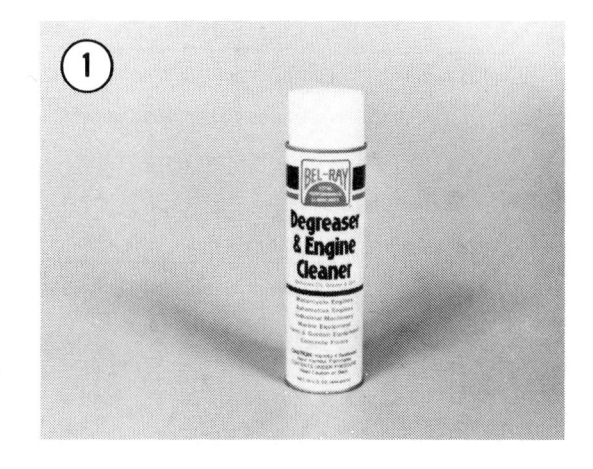

2-STROKE OPERATING PRINCIPLES

The crankshaft in this discussion is rotating in a clockwise direction.

As the piston travels downward, it uncovers the exhaust port (A) allowing the exhaust gases, that are under pressure, to leave the cylinder. A fresh fuel/air charge, which has been compressed slightly, travels from the crankcase into the cylinder through the transfer port (B). Since this charge enters under pressure, it also helps to push out the exhaust gases.

While the crankshaft continues to rotate, the piston moves upward, covering the transfer (B) and exhaust (A) ports. The piston is now compressing the new fuel/air mixture and creating a low pressure area in the crankcase at the same time. As the piston continues to travel, it uncovers the intake port (C). A fresh fuel/air charge, from the carburetor (D), is drawn into the crankcase through the intake port, because of the low pressure within it.

Now, as the piston almost reaches the top of its travel, the spark plug fires, thus igniting the compressed fuel/air mixture. The piston continues to top dead center (TDC) and is pushed downward by the expanding gases.

As the piston travels down, the exhaust gases leave the cylinder and the complete cycle starts all over again.

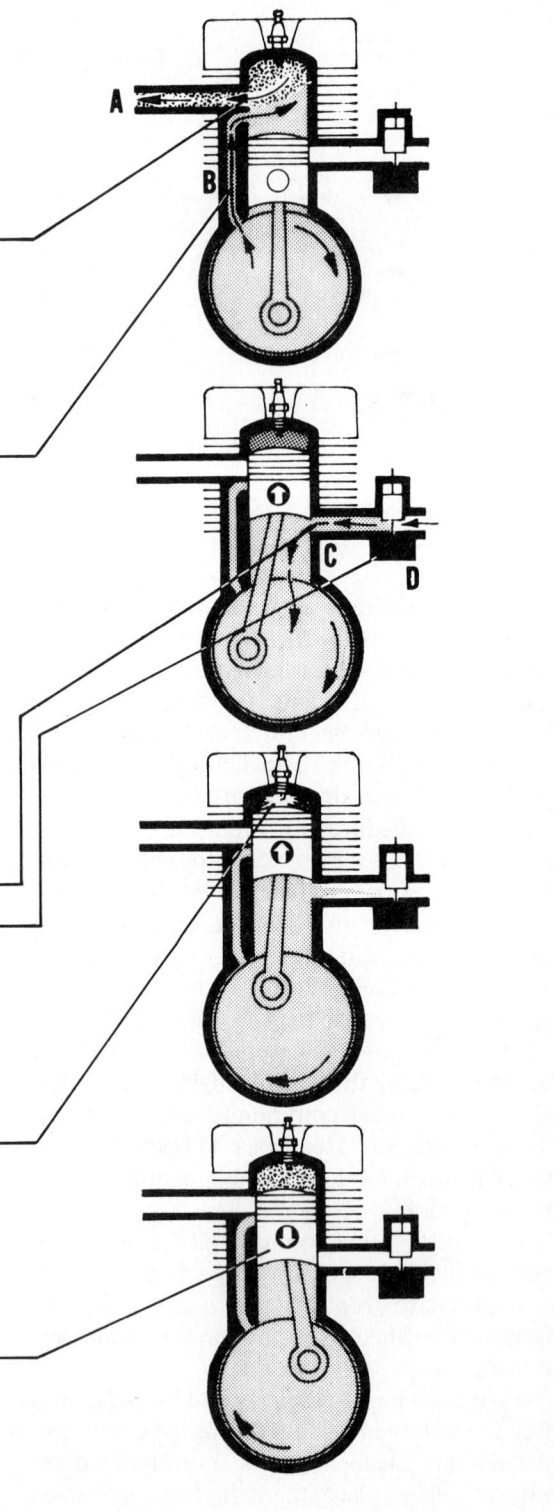

ENGINE

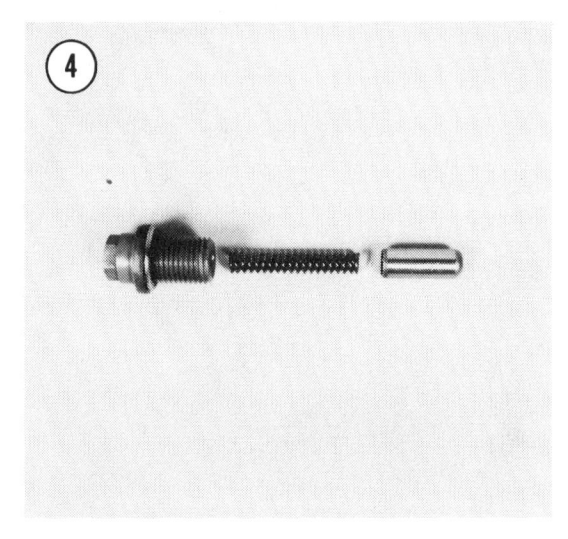

ENGINE LUBRICATION

Lubrication for the engine is provided by the fuel/oil mixture used to power the engine. There is no oil supply in the crankcase as it would be drawn into the cylinder and foul the spark plug. There is sufficient oil in the mixture to lubricate both the crankshaft bearings and the cylinder. The clutch and transmission have their own oil supply.

ENGINE COOLING

Cooling is provided by air passing over the cooling fins on the engine cylinder head and cylinder. It is very important to keep these fins free from buildup of dirt, oil, grease and other foreign matter. Brush out the fins with a whisk broom or small stiff paint brush.

CAUTION
Remember, these fins are thin in order to dissipate heat and may be damaged if struck too hard.

SERVICING ENGINE IN FRAME

The following components can be serviced while the engine is mounted in the frame (the bike's frame is a great holding fixture—especially when breaking loose stubborn bolts and nuts):

a. Cylinder head
b. Cylinder
c. Piston
d. Carburetor
e. Magneto
f. Clutch

ENGINE

Removal/Installation

1. Place a drain pan under the drain plug (**Figure 3**) for the clutch/transmission oil and remove it. Allow the oil to completely drain. Follow the procedure in Chapter Three.

NOTE
*On some models the drain plug is also the shift drum neutral locator. Don't lose the parts (**Figure 4**) in the oil drain pan.*

2. Remove the bolts securing the skid plate (**Figure 5**) and remove it.

3. Place a milk crate or wood block(s) under the frame to support the bike securely.

4. Turn the fuel shutoff valve to the OFF position and remove the fuel line to the carburetor.

5. Remove the seat and both side covers (**Figure 6**).

6. Remove the bolts (A, **Figure 7**) securing the front of the fuel tank. Pull up and unhook the strap (B, **Figure 7**) securing the rear of the tank. Pull the fuel fill cap vent tube (C, **Figure 7**) free from the steering head area. Pull the tank to the rear and remove it.

7. Remove the exhaust system (A, **Figure 8**) as described under *Exhaust System Removal/Installation* in Chapter Six.

8. Remove the carburetor (B, **Figure 8**) as described under *Carburetor Removal/Installation* in Chapter Six.

9. Remove the gearshift lever (A, **Figure 9**), drive sprocket cover (B, **Figure 9**) and left-hand footpeg.

10. Remove the right-hand footpeg and the rear brake pedal assembly.

11. Remove the kickstarter lever.

12. Remove the master link (**Figure 10**) on the drive chain and remove the chain.

13. Remove the clutch assembly as described under *Clutch Removal/Installation* in Chapter Five.

NOTE
If you are only removing the engine assembly and do not intend to disassemble it, do not perform Steps 13-15; proceed to Step 16.

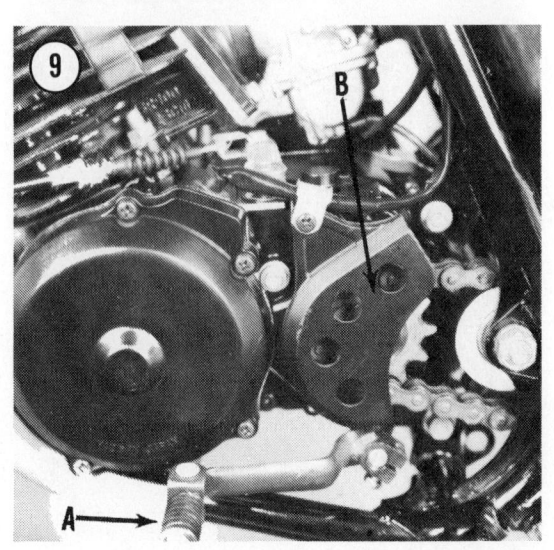

ENGINE

⑩

14. Remove the magneto as described under *Magneto Removal/Installation* in Chapter Seven.

15. Remove the cylinder head, cylinder and piston as described in this chapter.

16. On all models except IT175 since 1980, remove the engine mounting bolts and nuts (**Figure 11**) and remove the crankcase assembly.

NOTE
Reinstall the rear long mounting bolt to keep the rear swing arm in place.

⑪

17. On model IT175 since 1980, remove the engine mounting bolts and nuts (**Figure 12**) and remove the crankcase assembly.

NOTE
*After the engine has been removed, reinstall the rear long mounting bolt in one side and a long drift or socket extension in the other side of the rear swing arm pivot (**Figure 13**). This will keep the rear swing arm in place.*

18. On all models except IT175 since 1980, inspect the condition of the rear engine mounting bracket. This part takes a lot of engine torque and will wear and become loose in the area indicated in **Figure 14**. Replace the assembly if it is worn or loose.

19. Install by reversing these removal steps.

⑫

⑬

20. Fill the clutch/transmission with the correct type and quantity oil; refer to Chapter Three.

21. Adjust the clutch, drive chain and rear brake pedal as described in Chapter Three.

22. Start the engine and check for leaks.

CYLINDER HEAD

Removal/Installation

CAUTION
To prevent any warpage and damage, remove the cylinder head only when the engine is at room temperature.

1. Remove the seat, side covers and fuel tank.

2. Disconnect the spark plug wire and remove the spark plug (**Figure 15**).

3. Remove the exhaust system as described under *Exhaust System Removal/Installation* in Chapter Six.

4. Remove the nuts and washers or bolts (**Figure 16**) securing the cylinder head in a crisscross pattern. The number of nuts varies from 4 to 6 among the different models.

5. Loosen the head by tapping around the perimeter with a rubber or plastic mallet. If necessary, *gently* pry the head loose with a broad tipped screwdriver.

CAUTION
Remember, the cooling fins are fragile and may be damaged if tapped or pried on too hard. Never use a metal hammer.

NOTE
Sometimes it is possible to loosen the head with engine compression. Rotate the engine with the kickstarter (reinstall the spark plug). As the piston reaches TDC on the compression stroke, it will pop the head loose.

6. Remove the cylinder head by pulling it straight up and off the cylinder studs.

7. Remove the cylinder head gasket and discard it.

8. Clean the cylinder head as described under *Engine Decarbonizing* Chapter Three.

9. Install the cylinder head gasket.

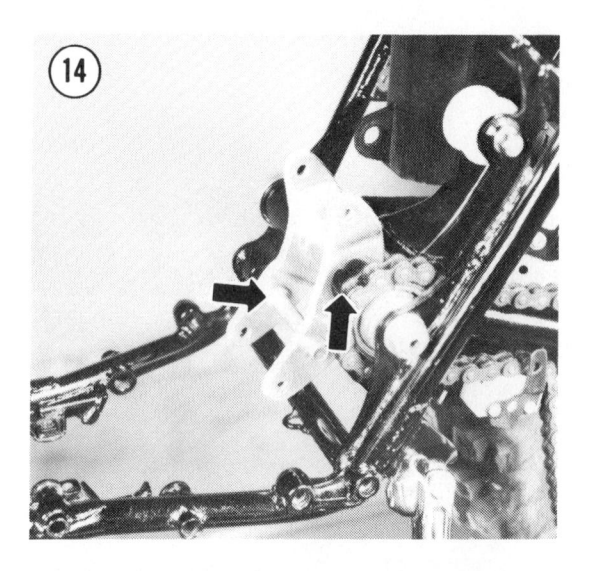

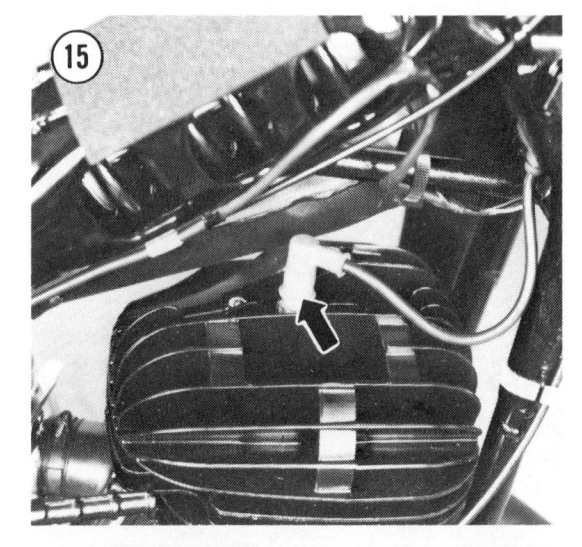

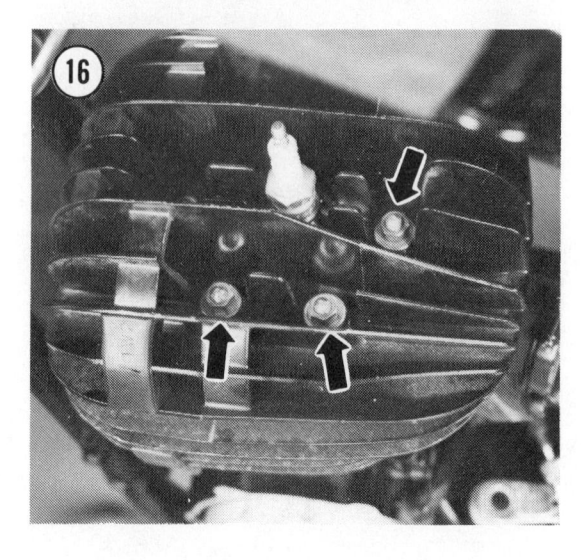

ENGINE

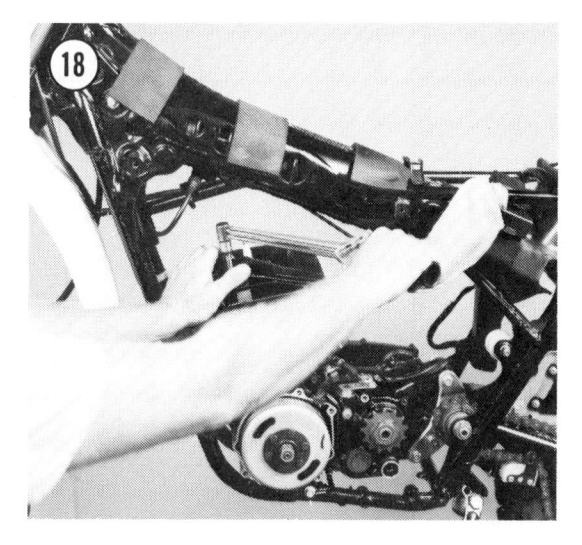

NOTE
*Install the head gasket with the point or projection (**Figure 17**) facing forward.*

10. Install the cylinder head and secure it with the washers and nuts. Screw the nuts on finger-tight.

11. Tighten the nuts or bolts (**Figure 18**) in a crisscross pattern to the torque values in **Table 2** at the end of this chapter.

12. Install all items which were removed.

CYLINDER

Removal

1. Remove the cylinder head as described under *Cylinder Head Removal/Installation* in this chapter.

2. Remove the carburetor as described under *Carburetor Removal/Installation* in Chapter Six.

3. Remove the special long inner nuts (**Figure 19**) or outer nuts (**Figure 20**). The type of nut varies with each model. Loosen and remove them in a crisscross pattern.

NOTE
On models IT250D and IT400D, there are sealing washers under each of these special long nuts—don't lose them as they must be reinstalled.

4. Loosen the cylinder by tapping around the perimeter with a rubber or plastic mallet. If

CHAPTER FOUR

necessary, *gently* pry the cylinder loose with a broad-tipped screwdriver.

NOTE
On model IT400C, disconnect the compression release mechanism actuator cable from the cylinder and tie it up out of the way.

5. Rotate the engine so the piston is at the bottom of its stroke. Pull the cylinder straight up and off the crankcase studs and piston.

CAUTION
Remember, the cooling fins are fragile and may be damaged if tapped or pried on too hard. Do not use a metal hammer.

6. Remove the cylinder base gasket and discard it. Install a piston holding fixture under the piston (**Figure 21**) to protect the piston skirt from damage. This fixture may be purchased or may be a homemade unit of wood. See **Figure 22**.

Inspection

The following procedure requires the use of highly specialized and expensive measuring instruments. If such equipment is not readily available, have the measurements performed by a dealer or machine shop.

Measure the cylinder bore with a cylinder gauge (**Figure 23**) or inside micrometer at the points shown in **Figure 24**.

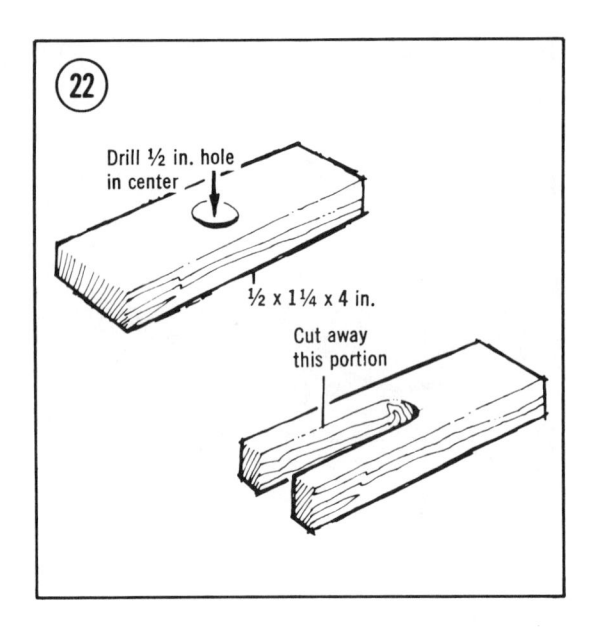

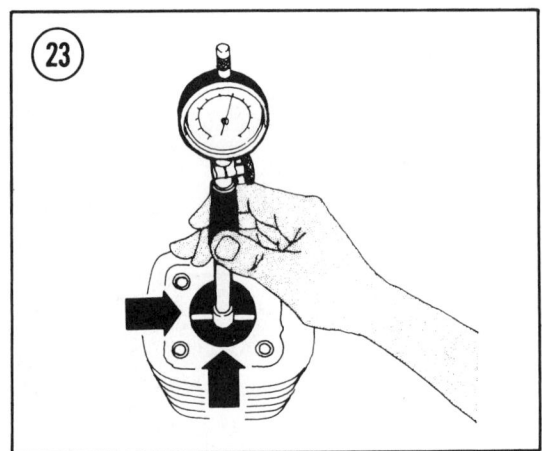

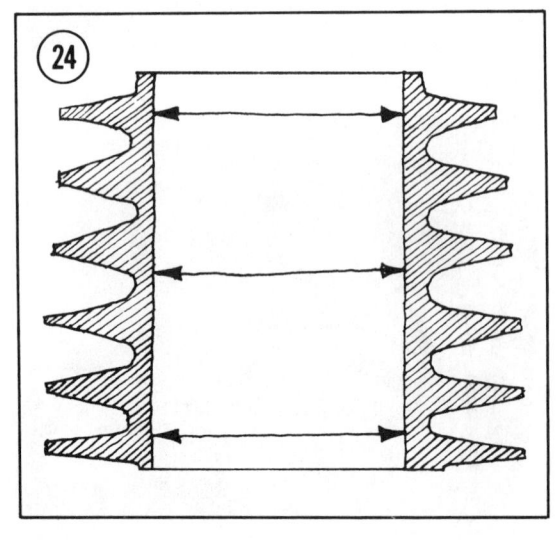

ENGINE

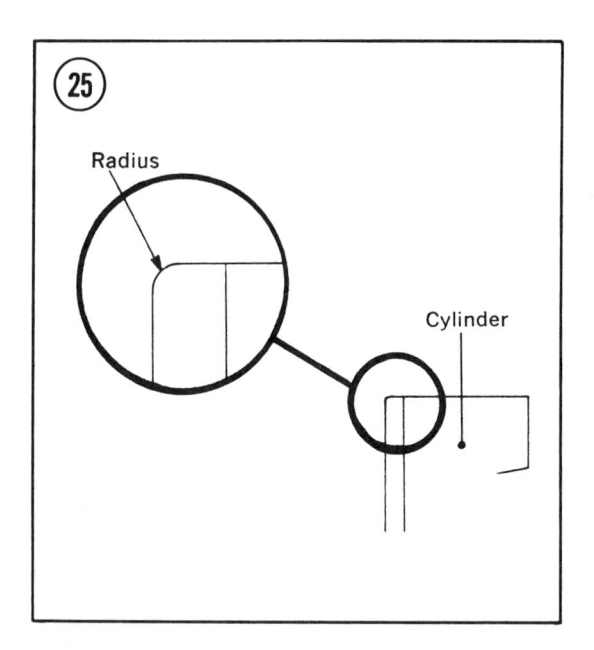

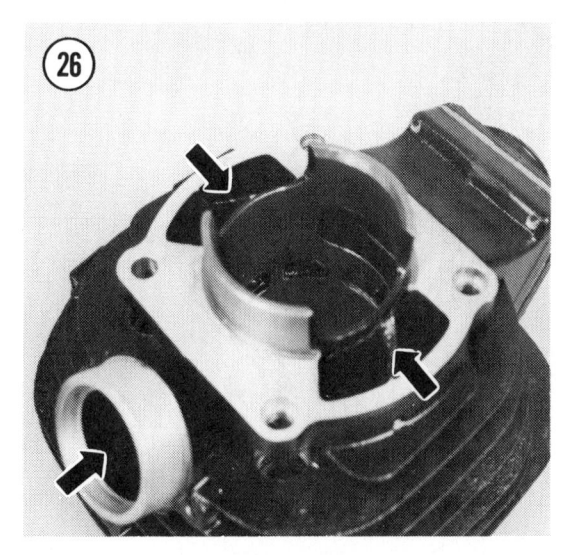

Measure in 2 axes—in line with the wrist pin and at 90° to the pin. If the taper or out-of-round is 0.04 in. (0.01 mm) or greater, the cylinder must be rebored to the next oversize and a new piston installed.

NOTE
The new piston should be obtained before the cylinder is bored so that the piston can be measured; slight manufacturing tolerances must be taken into account to determine the actual size and working clearance indicated in **Table 1**.

After the cylinder has been bored, the edges of the ports must be radiused with a fine file or grinder to prevent them from snagging the rings (**Figure 25**).

Inspect the condition of the transfer ports and the exhaust port (**Figure 26**). Clean the exhaust port as described under *Engine Decarbonizing* in Chapter Three.

Remove and inspect the reed valve as described under *Reed Valve Assembly* in this chapter.

Installation

1. Check that the top surface of the crankcase and the bottom surface of the cylinder are clean prior to installation.
2. Install a new base gasket and the 2 locating dowels (**Figure 27**).

NOTE
*The locating dowels are located on the centerline of the crankcase on the IT175G (**Figure 28**) or on the studs (**Figure 29**) on all other models.*

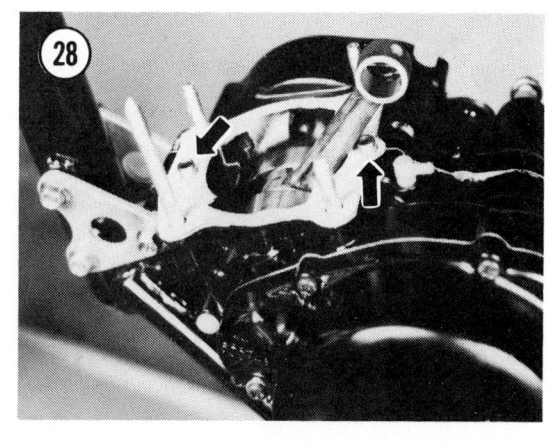

3. Make sure the end gaps of the piston rings are lined up with the locating pins in the ring grooves (A, **Figure 30**). Lightly oil the piston rings and the inside of the cylinder bore. Rotate the crankshaft to bring the piston in contact with the piston holding fixture (B, **Figure 30**).
4. Start the cylinder down over the piston *with the exhaust port facing forward.* See **Figure 31**.
5. Compress each ring with your fingers as the cylinder starts to slide over it.

NOTE
Make sure the rings are still properly aligned with the locating pins in the piston.

6. Slide the cylinder down until it bottoms on the piston holding fixture.
7. Remove the piston holding fixture and slide the cylinder into place on the crankcase.

CAUTION
On models IT250D and IT400D, make sure the sealing washers are put in place under the special long nuts. If not installed, the nuts will bottom out on the crankcase studs and the cylinder will not seal properly. This will cause an air leak which will result in poor engine performance, leaning out of the fuel/air mixture and severe damage to the engine.

8. Install the special long inner nuts (A, **Figure 32**) and outer nuts (B, **Figure 32**). The

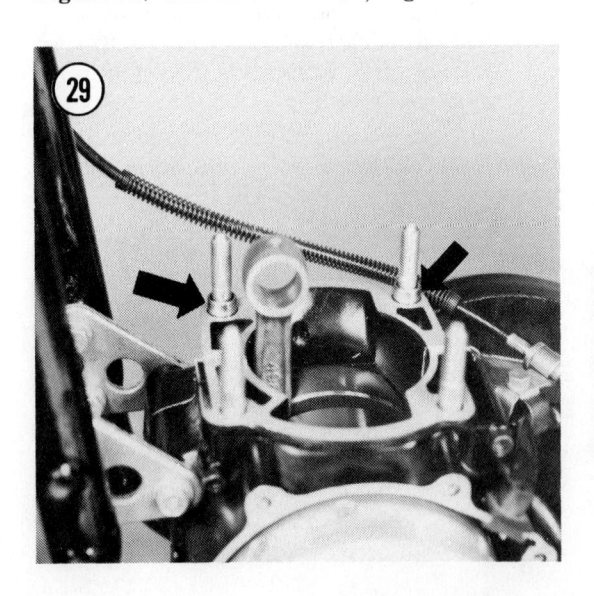

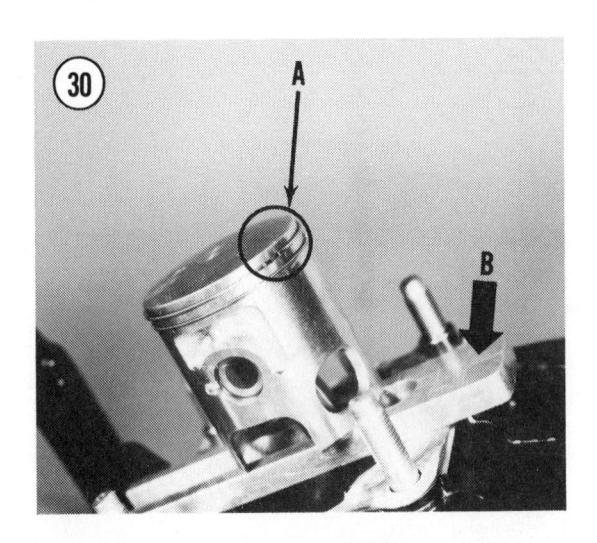

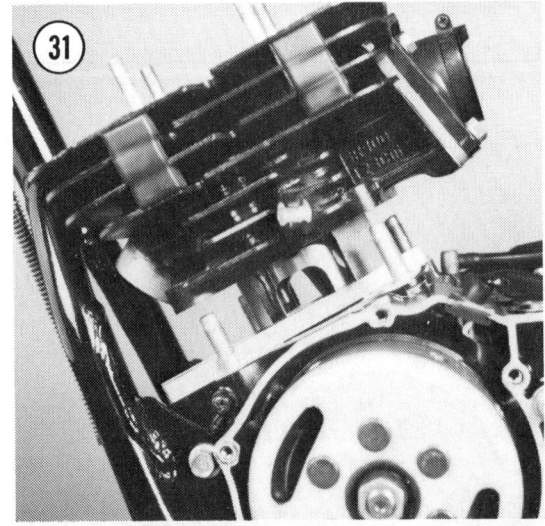

ENGINE

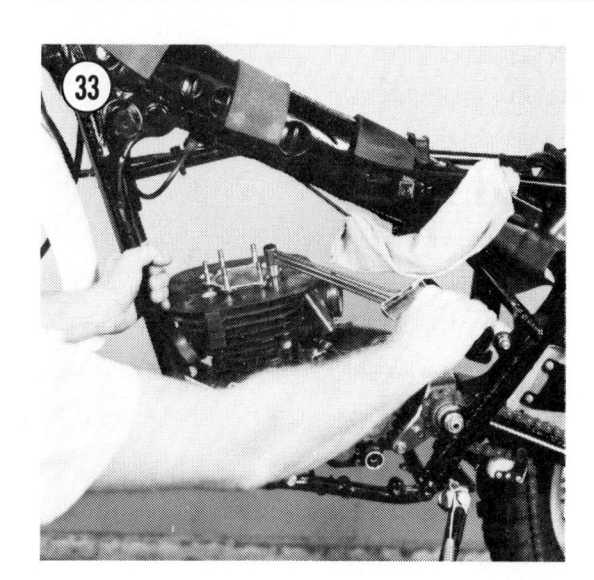

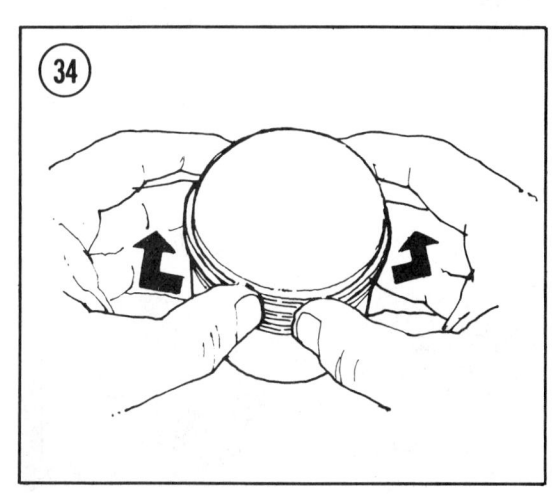

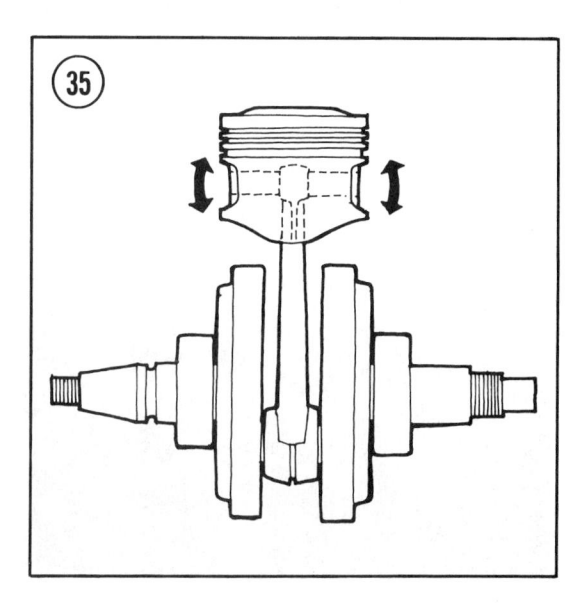

type of nut varies with each model. Tighten them in a crisscross pattern (**Figure 33**) to the torque values in **Table 2** at the end of this chapter.

9. On model IT400C, attach the compression release mechanism actuator cable. Adjust it as described under *Compression Release* in this chapter.

10. Install the cylinder head as described under *Cylinder Head Removal/Installation* in this chapter.

11. Install the carburetor as described under *Carburetor Removal/Installation* in Chapter Six.

12. Follow the *Break-in Procedure* in this chapter if the cylinder was rebored or honed or if a new piston or piston rings were installed.

PISTON, PISTON PIN AND PISTON RINGS

The piston used in the IT series is made of an aluminum alloy. The piston pin is a precision fit and is held in place by a clip at each end. A caged needle bearing is used on the small end of the connecting rod.

The piston can be removed with the engine in the frame.

Piston Removal

1. Remove the cylinder head and cylinder as described under *Cylinder Removal* in this chapter.

2. Remove the top ring by spreading the ends with your thumbs just enough to slide the ring up over the piston (**Figure 34**). Repeat for the other ring.

3. Before removing the piston, hold the rod tightly and rock the piston as shown in **Figure 35**. Any rocking motion (do not confuse with the normal sliding motion) indicates wear on the piston pin, needle bearing or piston pin bore (more likely a combination of all three).

NOTE
Wrap a clean shop cloth under the piston so that the piston pin clip will not fall into the crankcase.

4. Remove the clips from each side of the piston pin bore (**Figure 36**) with a small screwdriver or scribe. Hold your thumb over

one edge of the clip when removing it to prevent it from springing out.

5. Use a proper size wooden dowel or socket extension and push out the piston pin.

CAUTION
Be careful when removing the pin to avoid damaging the connecting rod needle bearing. If it is necessary to gently tap the pin to remove it, be sure that the piston is properly supported so that lateral shock is not transmitted to either connecting rod bearing.

6. If the piston pin is difficult to remove, heat the piston and pin with a butane torch. The pin will probably push right out. Heat the piston to only about 140°F (60°C), i.e., until it is too warm to touch, but not excessively hot. If the pin is still difficult to push out, use a homemade tool as shown in **Figure 37**.
7. Lift the piston off the connecting rod.
8. Remove the needle bearing from the connecting rod (**Figure 38**).
9. If the piston is going to be left off for some time, place a piece of foam insulation tube (**Figure 39**) over the end of the rod to protect it.

Inspection

1. Clean the needle bearing in solvent and dry it thoroughly. Use a magnifying glass and inspect the condition of the bearing cage for

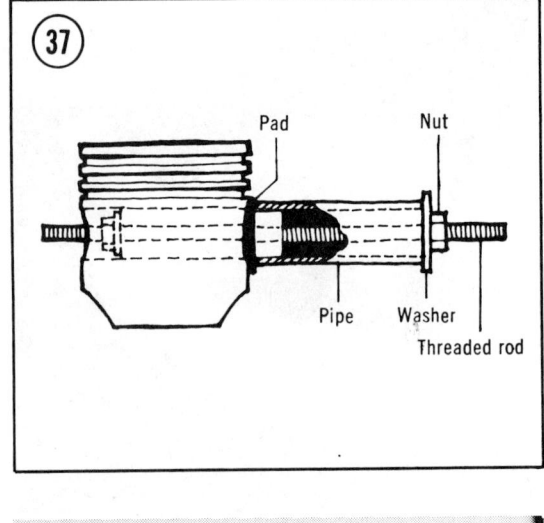

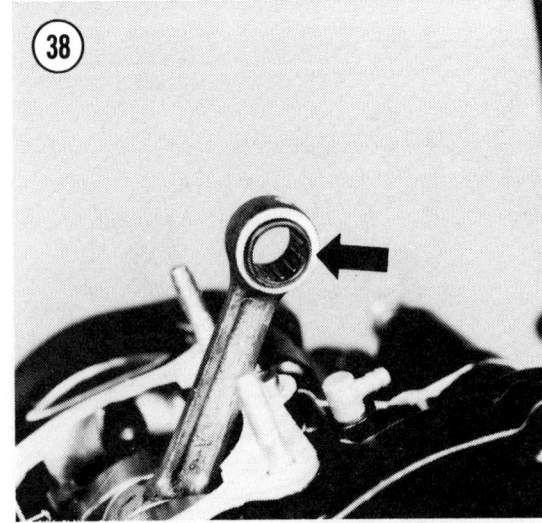

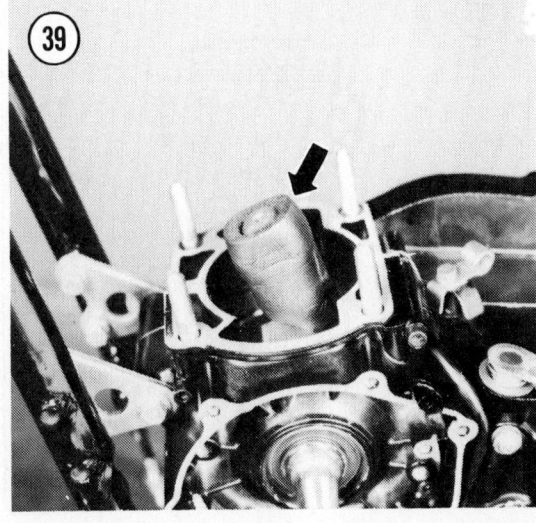

ENGINE

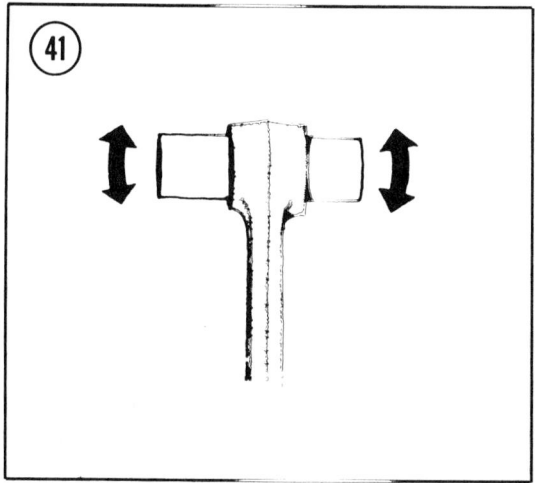

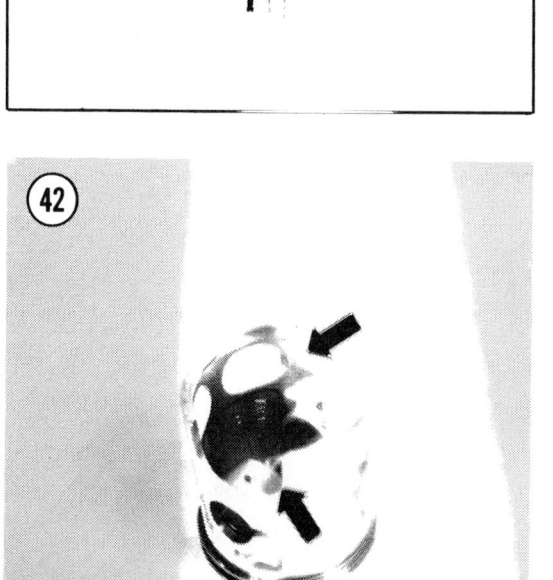

cracks at the corners of the needle slots (**Figure 40**) and inspect the needles themselves for cracking. If any cracks are found, the bearing must be replaced.

2. Wipe the bore in the connecting rod with a clean rag and check it for galling, scratches or any other signs of wear or damage. If any of these conditions exist, replace as described under *Crankshaft and Crankcase* in this chapter.

3. Oil the needle bearing and pin and install them in the connecting rod. Slowly rotate the pin and check for radial and axial play (**Figure 41**). If any play exists, the pin and bearing should be replaced, providing the rod bore is in good condition. If the condition of the rod bore is in question, the old pin and bearing can be checked with a new connecting rod.

4. Carefully check the piston for cracks at the top edge of the transfer cutaways (**Figure 42**) and replace it if any are found. Check the piston skirt (**Figure 43**) for brown varnish buildup. More than a slight amount is an indication of worn or sticking rings which should be replaced.

5. Check the piston skirt for galling and abrasion which may have been caused by piston seizure. If light galling is present, smooth the affected area with No. 400 emery paper and oil or a fine oilstone. However, if galling is severe or if the piston is deeply scored, replace it.

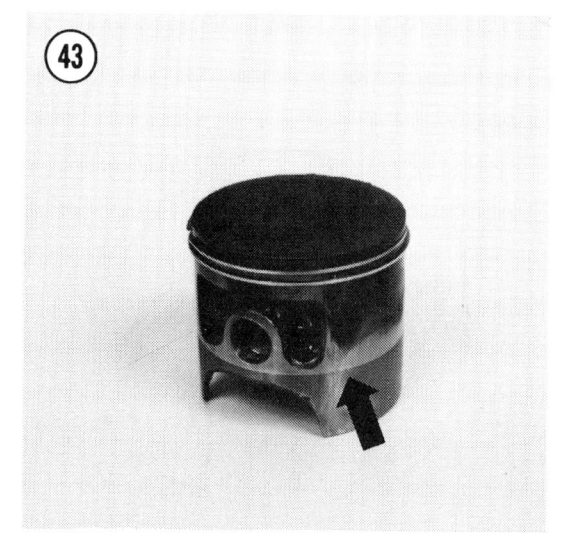

CHAPTER FOUR

6. Measure each ring for wear as shown in **Figure 44**. Place each ring, one at a time, into the cylinder and push it in about 3/4 in. (20 mm) with the crown of the piston to ensure that the ring is square in the cylinder bore. Measure the gap with a flat feeler gauge and compare to dimensions in **Table 1**. If the gap is greater than specified, the rings should be replaced. When installing new rings, measure their end gap in the same manner as for old ones. If the gap is less than specified, carefully file the ends with a fine cut file (**Figure 45**) until the gap is correct.

7. Carefully remove all carbon buildup from the ring grooves. Inspect the grooves carefully for burrs, nicks or broken and cracked lands. Recondition or replace the piston if necessary.

8. Roll each ring around its piston groove as shown in **Figure 46** to check for binding. Minor binding may be cleaned up with a fine cut file.

9. Measure the side clearance of each ring in its groove with a flat feeler gauge (**Figure 47**) and compare to dimensions given in **Table 1**. If the clearance is greater than specified, the rings must be replaced. If the clearance is still excessive with new rings, the piston must also be replaced.

10. Measure the outside diameter of the piston across the skirt (**Figure 48**) at right angles to the piston pin. Because the piston skirt on most models is cut away for the intake passageway, use **Table 3** to determine the distance up from the bottom of the piston skirt at which to measure (**Figure 49**).

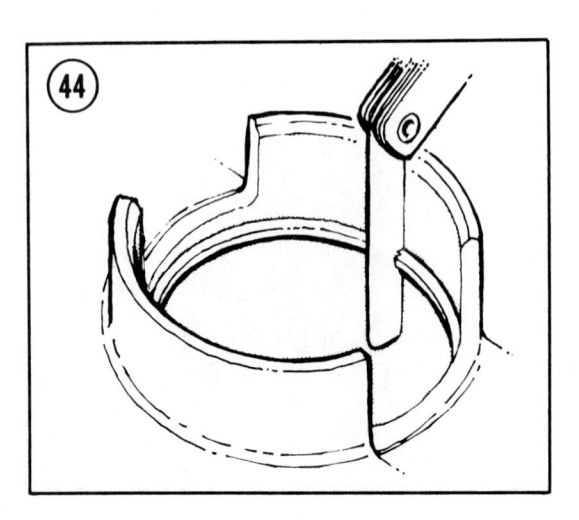

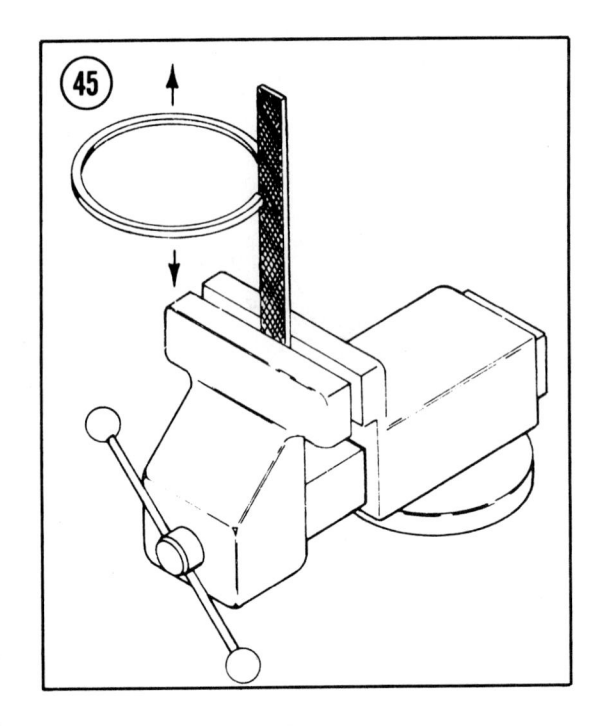

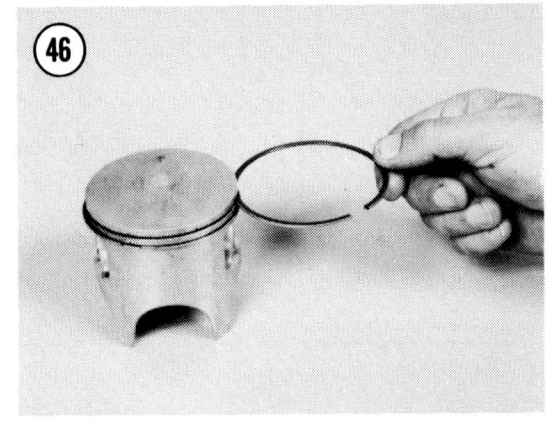

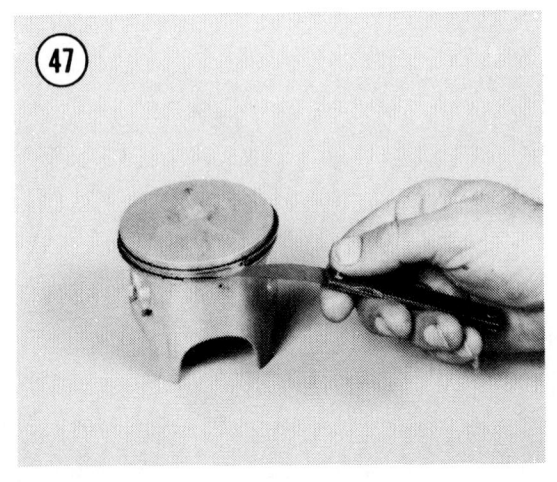

ENGINE

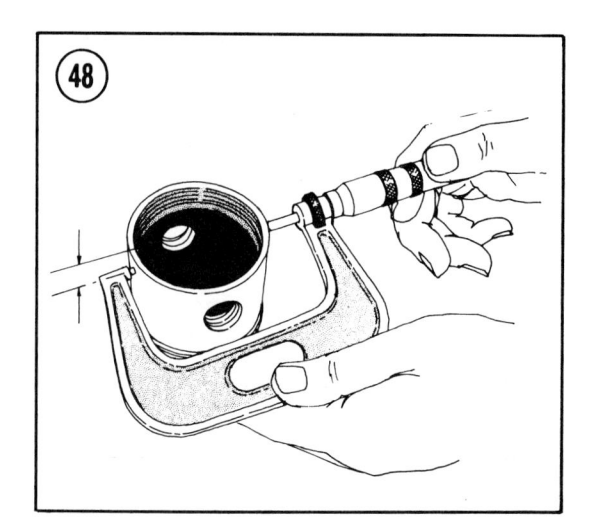

NOTE
*Do not measure from one of the intake fingers to the exhaust skirt (**Figure 50**) as the piston will appear to be undersize. This measurement point is not correct due to the way the piston is ground during manufacturing.*

11. The measurement taken in Step 10 is to be used with the cylinder dimension taken in *Cylinder Inspection* in this chapter to establish the piston clearance.

12. Piston clearance is the difference between the maximum piston diameter and the minimum cylinder diameter. For a run-in (used) piston and cylinder, subtract the dimension of the piston from the cylinder dimension. If the clearance exceeds the dimension in **Table 1**, the cylinder should be rebored to the next oversize and a new piston installed.

13. To establish a final overbore dimension with a new piston, add the piston skirt measurement to the specified clearance. This will determine the dimension for the cylinder overbore size.

Piston Installation

1. Lightly oil the needle bearing with assembly oil (**Figure 51**) and install it in the connecting rod (**Figure 52**).

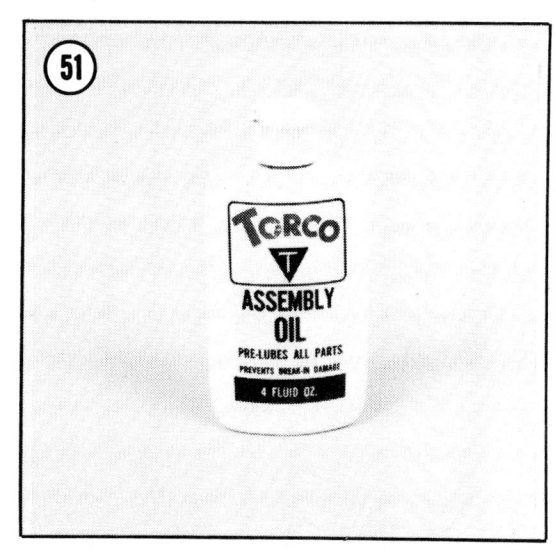

2. Oil the wrist pin and install it in the piston until its end extends slightly beyond the inside of the boss (**Figure 53**).

3. Place the piston over the connecting rod with the arrow on the piston crown pointing forward (**Figure 54**). Line up the pin with the bearing and push the pin into the piston until it is even with the piston pin clip grooves.

CAUTION
If it is necessary to tap the piston pin into the connecting rod, do so gently with a block of wood or a soft-faced hammer. Make sure you support the piston to prevent the lateral shock from being transmitted to the lower connecting rod bearing.

4. Install new piston pin clips in the ends of the pin boss. Make sure they are seated in the grooves.

NOTE
*Install the clips with the gap away from the cutout in the piston (**Figure 55**) on models equipped with this type of piston.*

5. Check the installation by rocking the piston back and forth around the pin axis and from side to side along the axis. It should rotate freely back and forth but not from side to side.

6. Install the piston rings—first the bottom one, then the top—by carefully spreading the ends of the ring with your thumbs and slipping

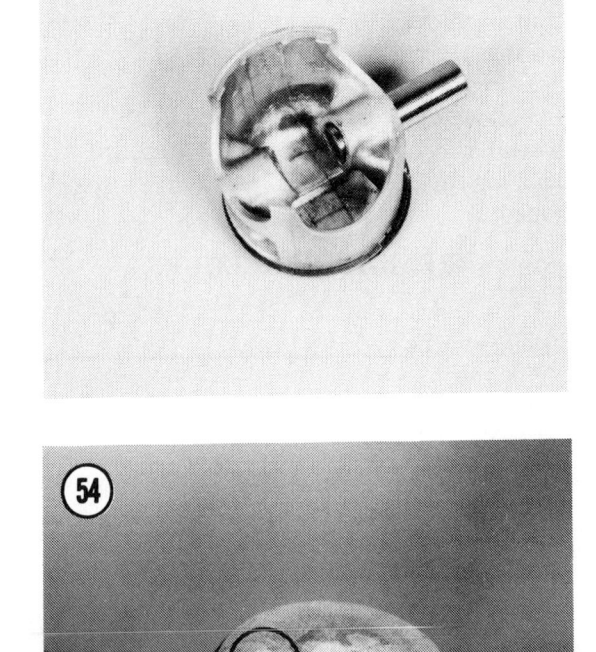

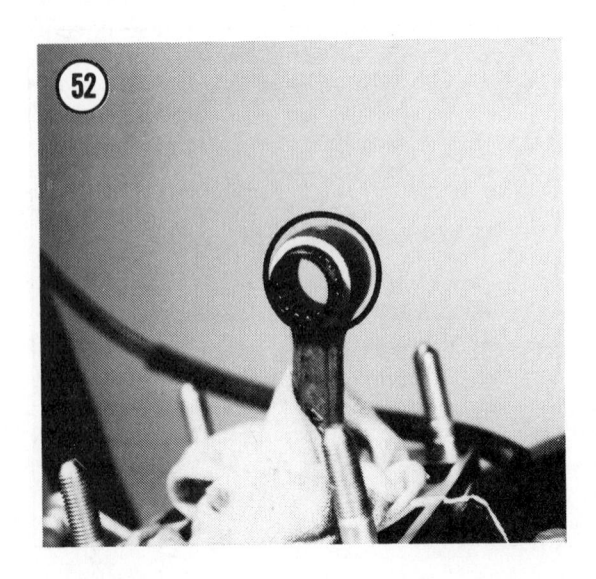

ENGINE

the ring over the top of the piston. Make sure that the marks on the piston rings are toward the top of the piston.

7. Make sure the rings are seated completely in their grooves all the way around the piston and that the ends are aligned with the locating pins (**Figure 56**).

8. Follow the *Break-in Procedure* in this chapter if a new piston or piston rings have been installed or if the cylinder was rebored or honed.

BREAK-IN PROCEDURE

If the rings were replaced, a new piston installed or the cylinder rebored or honed, the engine must be run in at moderate speeds and loads for no less than 2 hours. Don't exceed 75 percent of normal allowable rpm during run-in. After the first half hour, remove the spark plug and check its condition. The electrode should be dry and clean and the color of the insulation should be light to medium tan. If the insulator is white (indicating a too lean fuel/air mixture) or if it is dark and oily (indicating a too rich fuel/air mixture ratio), correct the condition with a main jet change; both incorrect conditions produce excessive engine heat and can lead to damage to the rings, piston and cylinder before they have had a chance to seat in.

NOTE
*When breaking in a rebuilt engine, don't forget to use an oil/fuel mixture ratio recommended for new engines. See **Table 2**, Chapter Three for ratio recommendations.*

Refer to Chapter Three for further information on how to read a spark plug and to Chapter Six for carburetor jet change.

MAGNETO

Removal/Installation

Refer to *Magneto* in Chapter Seven for complete details on magneto removal, inspection and installation.

REED VALVE ASSEMBLY

All IT engines are equipped with a power reed valve assembly that is installed in the intake port of the cylinder. The smallest displacement engine (IT125) has 2 reeds per side for a total of 4. The larger displacement engines (IT175 through IT425) have 3 reeds per side for a total of 6.

Particular care must be taken when handling and repairing the reed valve assembly. A malfunctioning reed valve will cause severe performance loss as well as contribute to early engine failure due to a too lean mixture.

Removal/Installation

1. Remove the cylinder head and cylinder as described under *Cylinder Removal/Installation* in this chapter.
2. Remove the Allen head (**Figure 57**) or hex head bolts (**Figure 58**) securing the reed valve assembly to the cylinder.
3. Carefully remove the reed valve assembly from the cylinder. If the assembly is difficult to remove, use a drift or broad-tipped screwdriver and gently tap the side of the assembly to help break it loose from the gasket and cylinder.

CHAPTER FOUR

4. Inspect as described in the following procedure.

5. Install a new gasket (**Figure 59**) and insert the reed valve assembly into the cylinder (**Figure 60**). The assembly can be installed with either end up.

6. Install the rubber intake manifold with the carburetor locating notch (**Figure 61**) facing *up*. Tighten the bolts securely.

Inspection

Refer to **Figure 62** for basic reed valve construction. Stainless steel reeds (a) open the inlet port in response to crankcase pressure changes, allowing the fuel/air mixture to enter. They then close, allowing the crankcase to pressurize. The reed stop (d) are the stops or limiters of the reeds which prevent them from opening too far.

1. Carefully examine the reed valve assembly (**Figure 63**) for visible signs of wear, distortion or damage.
2. If reed stops are not equally spaced from the reed plate, pad the jaws of a wide-jaw pair of pliers and gently bend reed stops as necessary.
3. Remove the screws (**Figure 64**) securing the reed stop to the reed body. Be careful that the screwdriver does not slip off and damage the reed plate.
4. Carefully examine the reed plate, reed stop and gasket. Check for signs of cracks, metal fatigue, distortion or foreign matter damage.

ENGINE

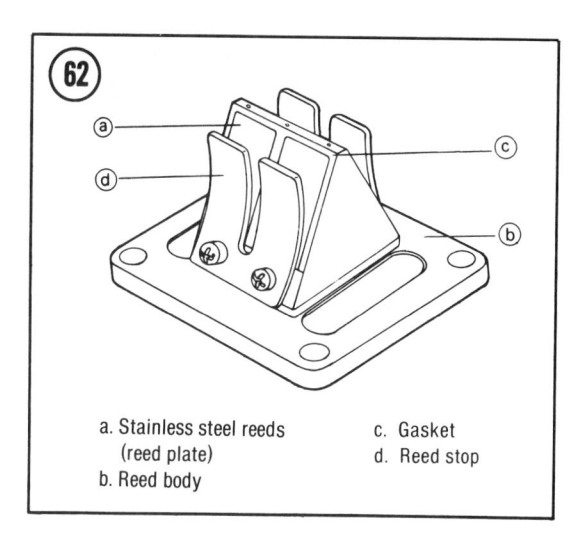

Figure 62
a. Stainless steel reeds (reed plate)
b. Reed body
c. Gasket
d. Reed stop

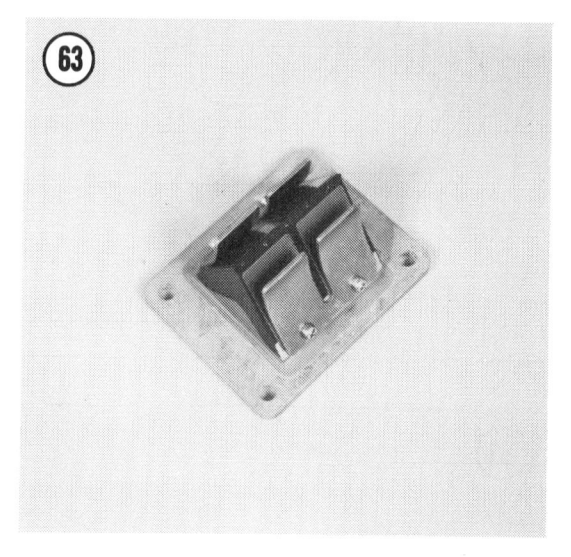

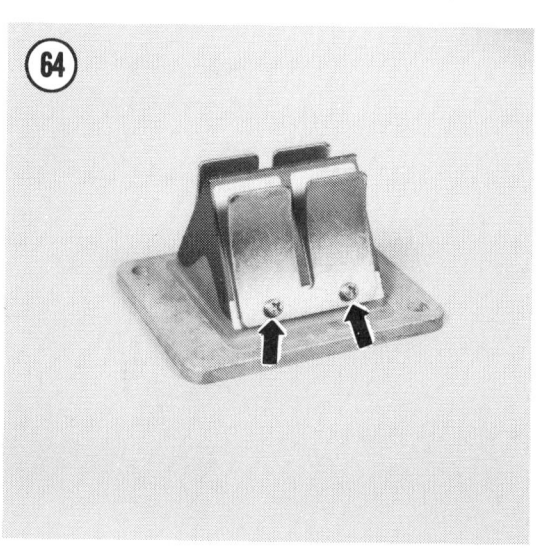

Pay particular attention to the rubber gasket seal. The reed stops and reed plates are available as replacement parts but if the rubber gasket seal is damaged the entire assembly must be replaced.

5. Reassemble the unit. Install the reed plate and reed stop with the cut-off corner (**Figure 65**) in the lower right-hand corner. Apply Loctite Lock N' Seal to the screw threads prior to installation and tighten the screws to 5-6 ft.-lb. (7-8 N•m).

NOTE
Make sure that all parts are clean and free of any small dirt particles or lint from a shop cloth as they may cause distortion in the reed plate.

6. Reinstall the reed valve assembly as previously described.

COMPRESSION RELEASE (IT400C ONLY)

The IT400C is equipped with a compression release mechanism to ease starting the engine with the kickstarter. When the kickstarter is depressed the compression release valve is opened via a cable mechanism. Refer to **Figure 66** and **Figure 67** for operation and mechanism components.

In order for it to function properly, it must be adjusted to provide for full lever travel

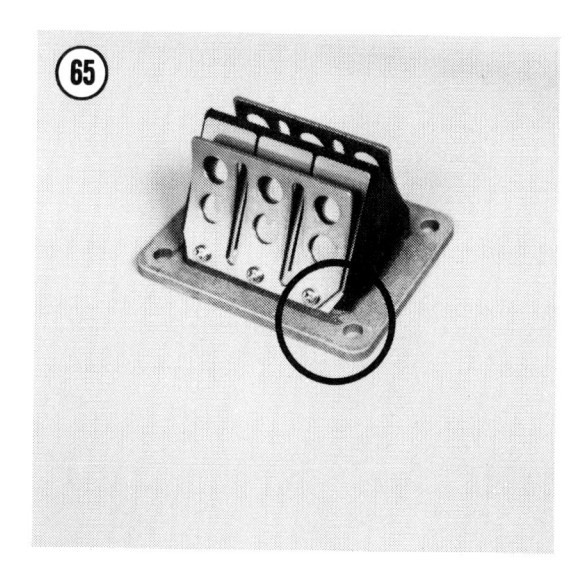

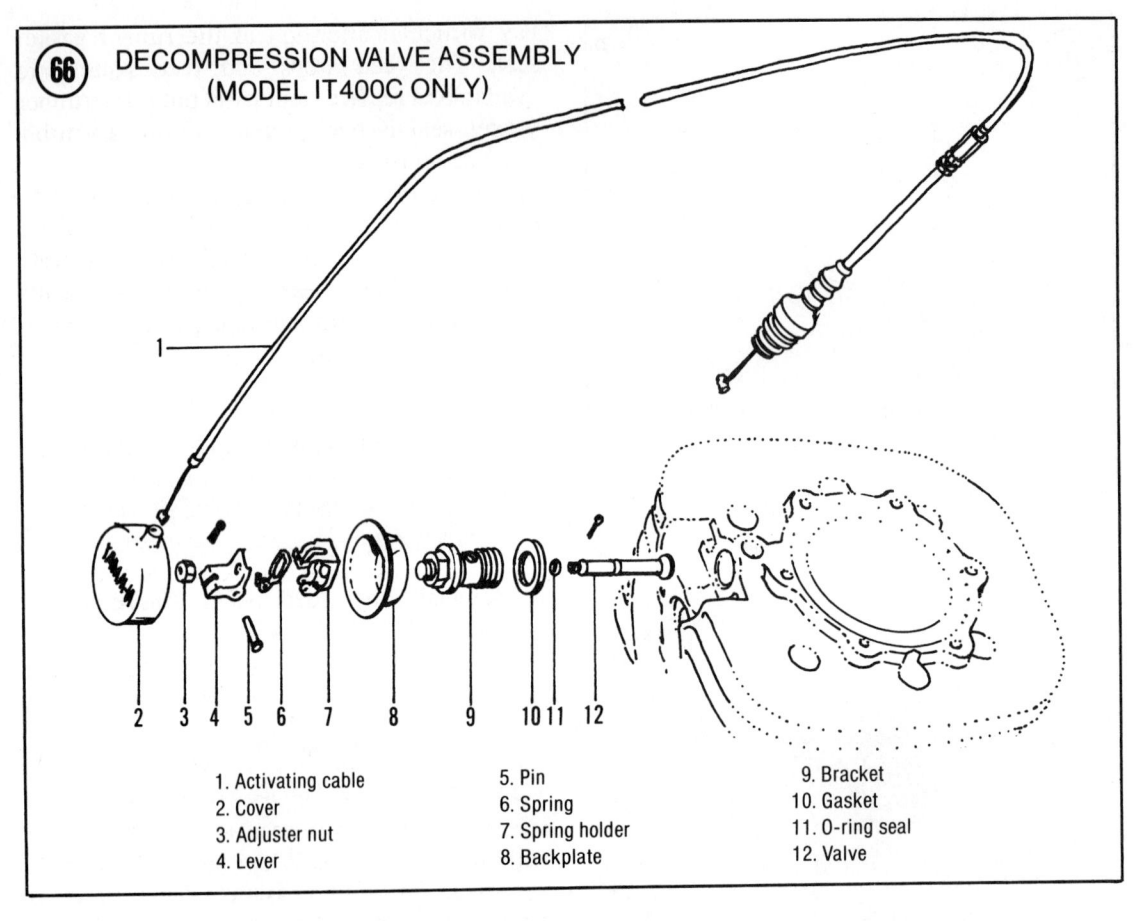

CHAPTER FOUR

66 DECOMPRESSION VALVE ASSEMBLY (MODEL IT400C ONLY)

1. Activating cable
2. Cover
3. Adjuster nut
4. Lever
5. Pin
6. Spring
7. Spring holder
8. Backplate
9. Bracket
10. Gasket
11. O-ring seal
12. Valve

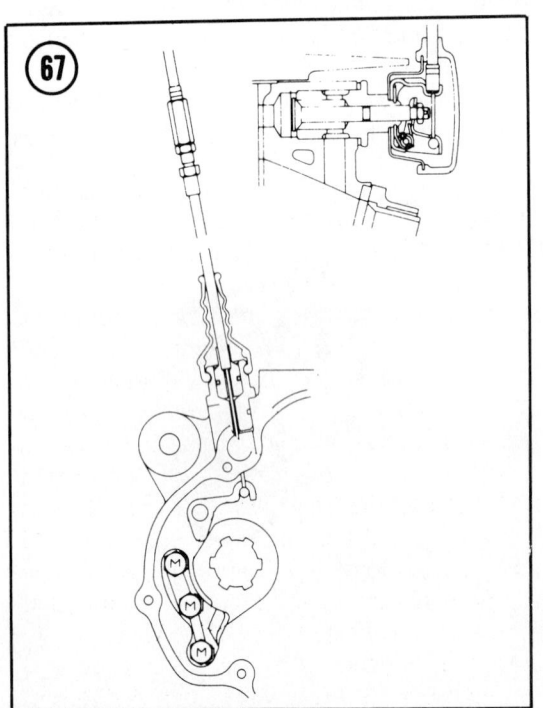

67

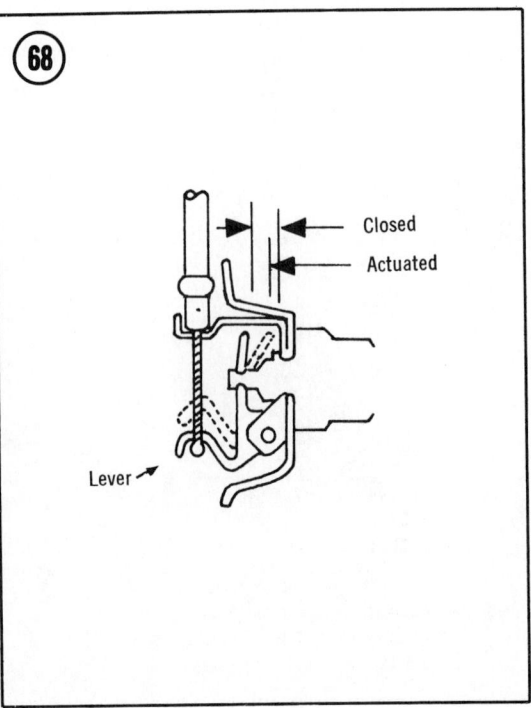

68

Closed
Actuated
Lever

ENGINE

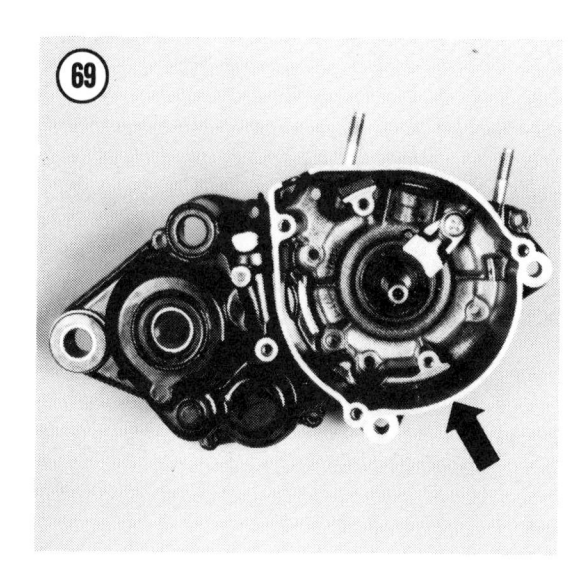

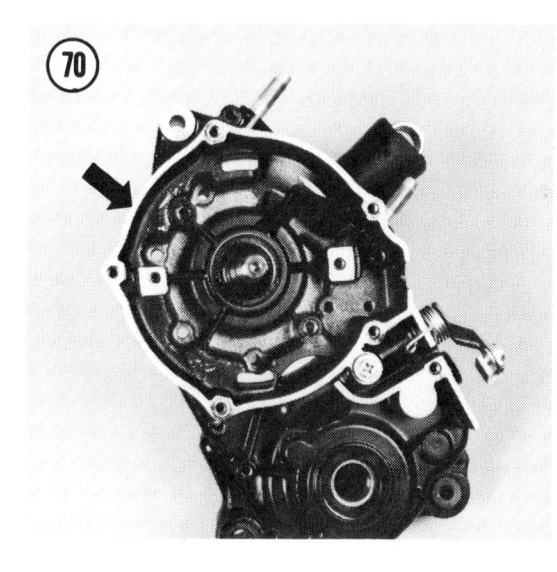

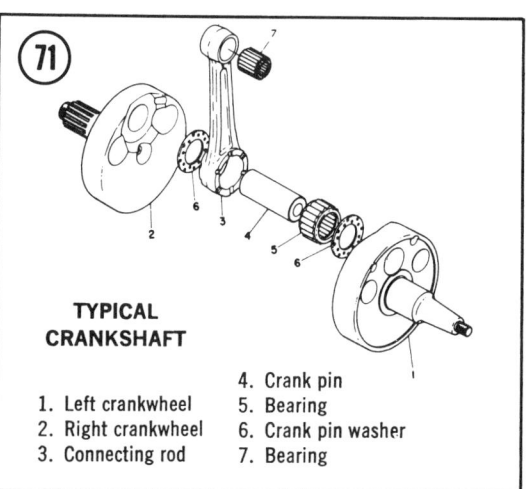

(Figure 68). When the compression release mechanism is in the *release* or engine starting position, the end of the lever must come to within 0.020 in. (0.5 mm) of the back plate, but it must not touch it.

If adjustment is necessary, remove the cover and loosen the adjuster locknut. Turn the adjuster until the correct amount of clearance is obtained. Tighten the locknut and recheck the clearance.

CRANKCASE AND CRANKSHAFT

Disassembly of the crankcase—splitting the cases—and removal of the crankshaft assembly require that the engine be removed from the frame. However, the cylinder head, cylinder and all other attached assemblies should be removed while the engine is still in the frame.

The crankcase is made in 2 halves of precision diecast aluminum alloy and is of the "thin-walled" type. To avoid damage do not hammer or pry on any of the interior or exterior projected walls (**Figure 69** and **Figure 70**). These areas are easily damaged. They are assembled without a gasket; only gasket cement is used as a sealer. Dowel pins align the crankcase halves when they are bolted together.

The crankshaft assembly is made up of 2 full-circle flywheels pressed together on a hollow crankpin. The connecting rod big end bearing on the crankpin is a needle bearing assembly (**Figure 71**). The crankshaft assembly is supported in 2 ball bearing in the crankcase. Service to the crankshaft is limited to removal and replacement.

The procedure which follows is presented as a complete, step-by-step, major lower end rebuild that should be followed if an engine is to be completely reconditioned. However, if you're replacing a part that you know is defective, the disassembly should be carried out only until the failed part is accessible; there is no need to disassemble the engine beyond that point so long as you know the remaining components are in good condition and that they were not affected by the failed part.

In the 5 years that the IT has been a "monoshocker" there have been 4 different

TYPICAL CRANKSHAFT

1. Left crankwheel
2. Right crankwheel
3. Connecting rod
4. Crank pin
5. Bearing
6. Crank pin washer
7. Bearing

basic engines. The upper end is basically the same on all with the exception of a larger cylinder, piston and cylinder head. The lower end is different in all models. The kickstarter, shift mechanism (external and internal) and transmission are all different in some way. Because of this, crankcase disassembly and assembly are covered in different procedures and are placed into groups (Type I, II, III and IV). Inspection and bearing and oil seal replacement are basically the same on all models and are covered in one procedure. Variations between different models are identified where they occur.

Crankcase Disassembly (Type I)

The Type I crankcase is found in the following models:
IT425G
IT400F
IT250G, F

1. Remove all exterior engine assemblies as described in this chapter and other related chapters.

NOTE
Drain the clutch/transmission oil as described in Chapter Three.

2. Straighten the tab on the drive sprocket lockwasher.
3. Unscrew the locknut and remove it and the lockwasher (**Figure 72**).

ENGINE

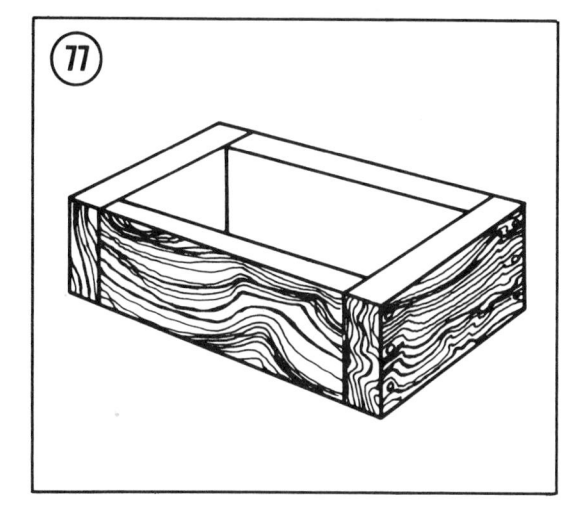

4. Remove the drive sprocket (**Figure 73**) and collar (**Figure 74**).

5. Remove the shift drum external plug (**Figure 75**), circlip and flat washer (**Figure 76**).

6. Loosen all bolts securing the crankcase halves together by one-quarter turn. To prevent warpage, loosen them in a crisscross pattern. It is easier to loosen tight screws with the engine still in the frame.

7. Remove the engine from the frame as described under *Engine Removal/Installation* in this chapter.

NOTE
*Set the engine on 2 wood blocks or fabricate a holding fixture of 2 x 4 inch wood as shown in **Figure 77**.*

8. Remove all bolts loosened in Step 6; refer to **Figure 78**. Be sure to remove all of them.

NOTE
To ease assembly, draw the case outline on cardboard, then punch holes to correspond with screw locations. Insert the screws in their appropriate locations. Also record the position of any clips that hold electrical wires or drain tubes.

9. Unscrew the clutch/transmission drain plug and neutral locator (**Figure 79**). Don't lose the spring and plunger within it.

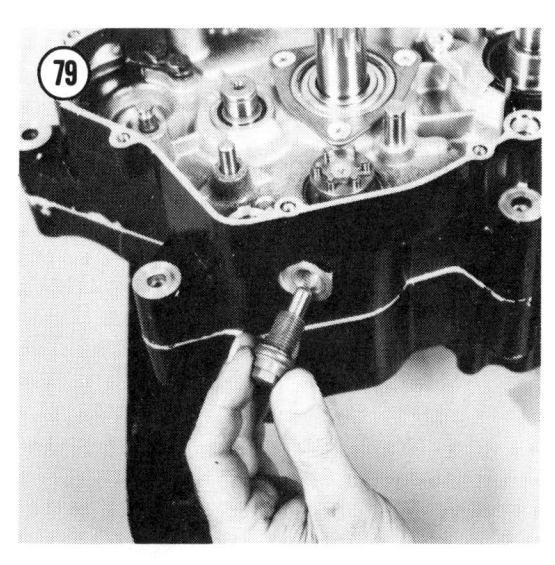

81

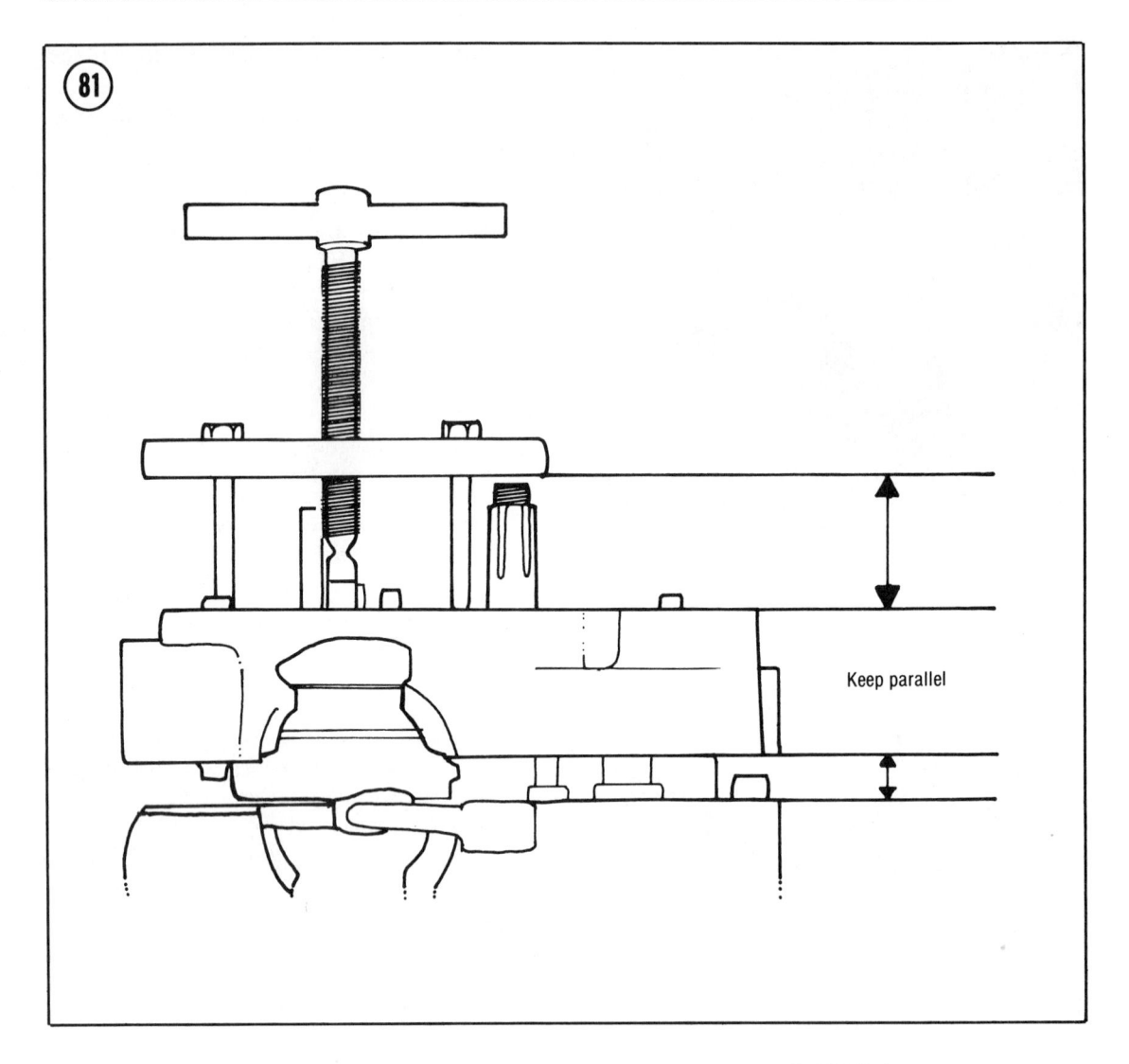

Keep parallel

CAUTION
*Perform the next step directly over and close to the workbench as the crankcase halves may easily separate. **Do not** hammer on the crankcase halves or they will be damaged.*

10. Hold onto the right-hand crankcase and studs and tap on the right-hand end of the crankshaft and transmission shaft with a plastic or rubber mallet until the crankshaft and crankcase separate.

11. If the crankcase and crankshaft will not separate using the method in Step 10, proceed with the following method using a special puller.

CAUTION
*Crankcase separation requires only hand pressure on the puller screw. If extreme pressure seems to be needed during the following steps or if both halves will not remain parallel, **stop immediately**. Check for crankcase screws not removed, or any part that is still attached or for transmission shafts hung up in a bearing. Relieve puller pressure immediately.*

12. Remove the crankcase oil seal retainer (A, **Figure 80**) and the plug (B, **Figure 80**).
13. Install the crankcase separating tool (Yamaha part No. 90890-01135) into the right-hand crankcase. Tighten the securing bolts into the crankcase, making sure the tool body is parallel with the crankcase. If

ENGINE

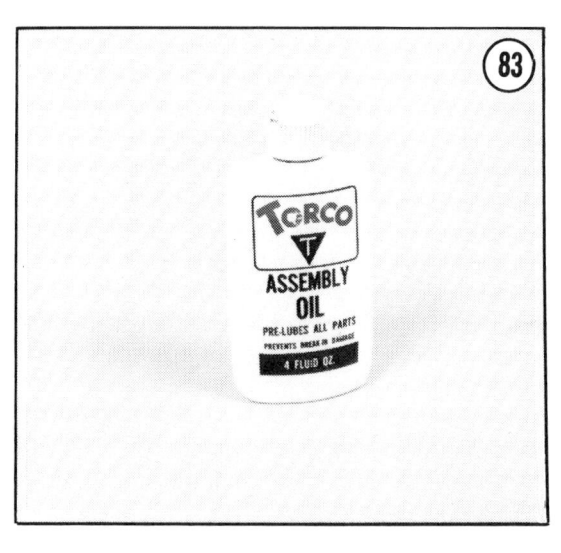

necessary, back out one of the bolts until the tool is parallel.

14. Screw the puller *clockwise* until both cases begin to separate.

CAUTION
*While tightening the puller make sure the body is kept parallel to the crankcase surface (**Figure 81**). or it will put an uneven stress on the case halves and damage them.*

15. Use a plastic or rubber mallet and gently tap the crankcase half and transmission shaft to help during separation.

NOTE
Never pry between case halves. Doing so may result in oil leaks requiring replacement of the case halves.

16. Don't lose the 2 locating dowels if they came out of the case. They do not have to be removed from the case if they are secure.

17. Unscrew the crankcase separator tool and reinstall the crankcase plug.

18. The transmission assemblies and the crankshaft assemblies will usually stay in the left-hand crankcase half. Lift up and carefully remove *only* the transmission, shift drum and shift fork assemblies (**Figure 82**).

19. Do not remove the crankshaft assembly from the left-hand crankcase half. This operation should be entrusted to a Yamaha dealer who can remove it and install a new one if necessary.

20. Inspect the crankcase halves and crankshaft as described under *Crankcase and Crankshaft Inspection—All Models* later in this chapter.

Crankcase Assembly (Type I)

1. Apply assembly oil (**Figure 83**) to the inner race of all bearings (**Figure 84**) in both crankcase halves.

2. Install the transmission assemblies, shift shafts and shift drum in the right-hand crankcase half and lightly oil all shaft ends (A, **Figure 85**). Refer to Chapter Five for the correct procedure for your specific model.

NOTE

Do not *install the shift drum neutral locator at this time. The spring pressure will push the shift drum over just enough to misalign the free end of the drum from the bearing in the right-hand crankcase during assembly.*

NOTE

Set the crankcase half assembly on 2 wood blocks or the wood holding fixture shown in the disassembly procedure.

4. Apply a light coat of non-hardening liquid gasket as shown in **Figure 86** (Yamabond No. 4, 4-Three Bond or equivalent) to the mating surfaces of both crankcase halves. Install the 2 locating dowels (B, **Figure 85**) if they were removed.

NOTE

Make sure the mating surfaces are clean and free of all old gasket material to make sure you get a leak-free seal.

5. Set the upper crankcase half over the one on the blocks. Push it down squarely into place until it reaches the crankshaft bearing (**Figure 87**); there is usually about 1/2 inch left to go.

6. Lightly tap the case halves together with a plastic or rubber mallet (**Figure 88**) until they seat.

CAUTION

Crankcase halves should fit together without force. If the crankcase halves do

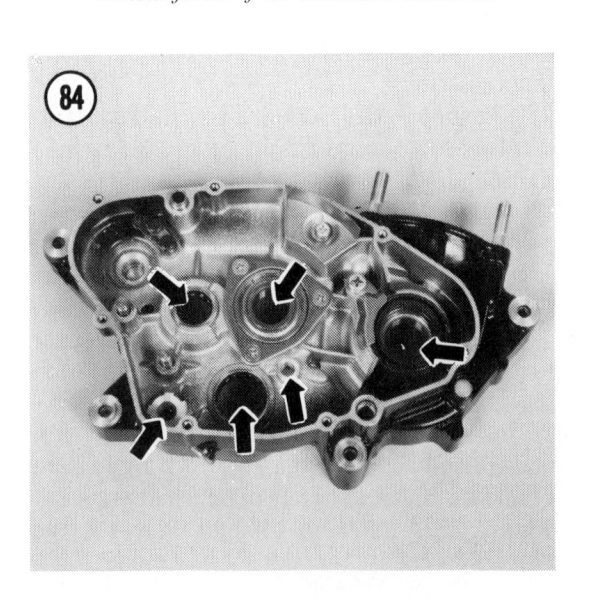

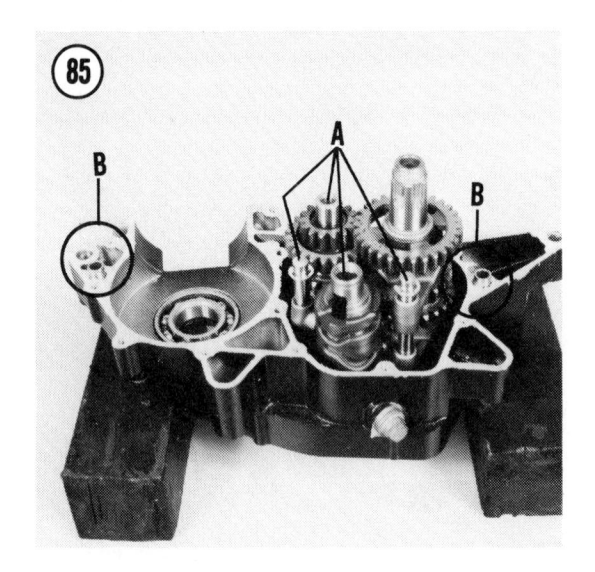

ENGINE

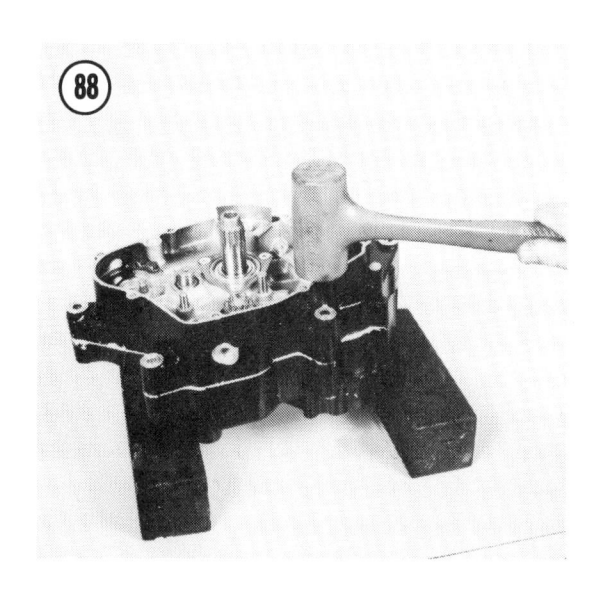

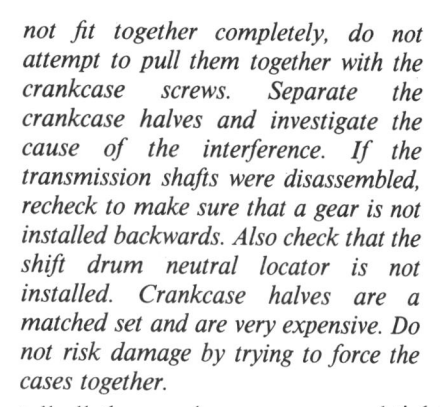

(88)

not fit together completely, do not attempt to pull them together with the crankcase screws. Separate the crankcase halves and investigate the cause of the interference. If the transmission shafts were disassembled, recheck to make sure that a gear is not installed backwards. Also check that the shift drum neutral locator is not installed. Crankcase halves are a matched set and are very expensive. Do not risk damage by trying to force the cases together.

7. Install all the crankcase screws and tighten only finger-tight. Place any clips (**Figure 89**) under the screws in the locations recorded in Step 8, *Removal*.

8. Securely tighten the screws in 2 stages in a crisscross pattern until they are firmly hand-tight.

9. After the crankcase halves are completely assembled, rotate the crankshaft and transmission shafts to make sure there is no binding. If any is present, disassemble the crankcase and correct the problem.

10. Install the engine in the frame and tighten the mounting bolts and nuts to the torque values in **Table 2**.

11. Push on the right-hand end of the shift drum and install the washer and circlip (**Figure 90**). Without pushing on the shift drum it is impossible to correctly install the circlip. Install the shift drum external plug (**Figure 91**).

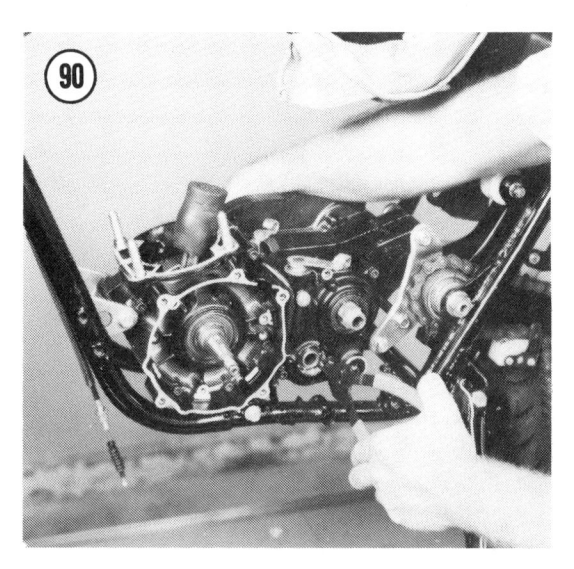

12. Install the clutch/transmission drain plug, and neutral locator, spring and plunger.
13. Install the collar, drive sprocket and a new lockwasher. Install a new lockwasher after at least the second removal or when the lockwasher begins to look like the one in **Figure 92**.
14. Attach a "Grabbit" to the drive sprocket (**Figure 93**) and tighten the nut to the torque value in **Table 2**.
15. Bend up the tab on the lockwasher (**Figure 94**).
16. Install all exterior engine assemblies as described in this chapter and other related chapters.

Crankcase Disassembly (Type II)

The Type II crankcase is found in the following models:
IT400E, D, C
IT250E, D

1. Remove all exterior engine assemblies as described in this chapter and other related chapters.

NOTE
Drain the clutch/transmission oil as described in Chapter Three.

2. Straighten the tab on the drive sprocket lockwasher.
3. Unscrew the locknut and remove it and the lockwasher.
4. Remove the drive sprocket and collar.
5. Remove the shift drum external plug (A, **Figure 95**), circlip and flat washer.
6. Loosen all bolts securing the crankcase halves together by one-quarter turn. To prevent warpage, loosen them in a crisscross pattern. It is easier to loosen tight screws with the engine still in the frame.
7. Remove the engine from the frame as described under *Engine Removal/Installation* in this chapter.

NOTE
*Set the engine on 2 wood blocks or fabricate a holding fixture of 2 x 4 inch wood as shown in **Figure 77**.*

8. Remove all bolts loosened in Step 6; refer to **Figure 96**. Be sure to remove all of them.

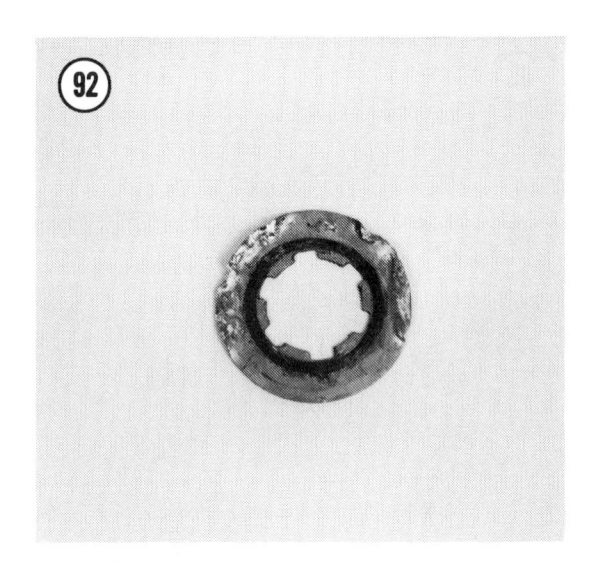

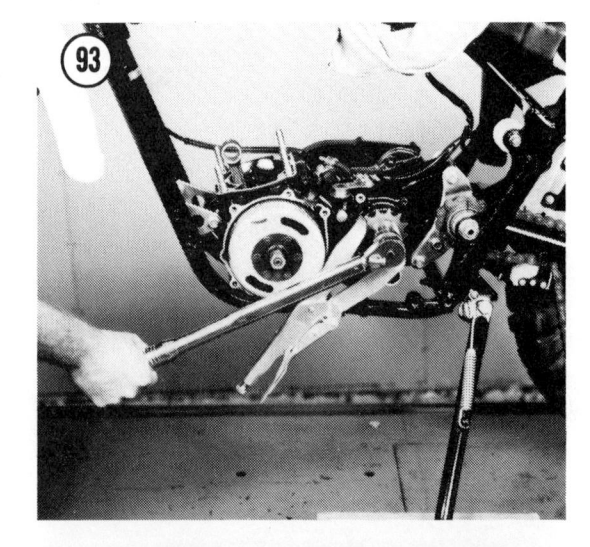

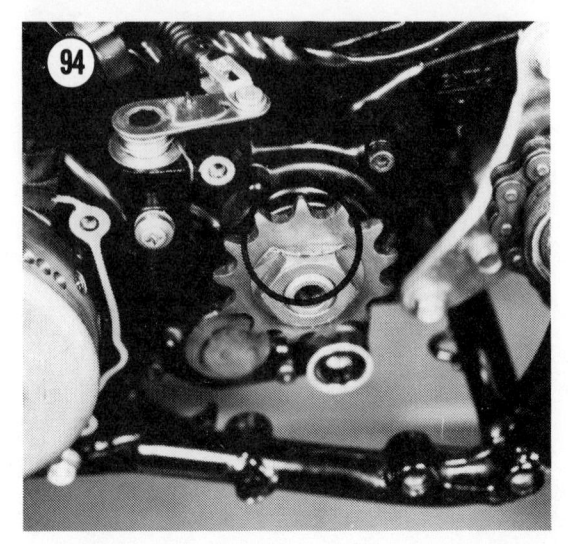

ENGINE

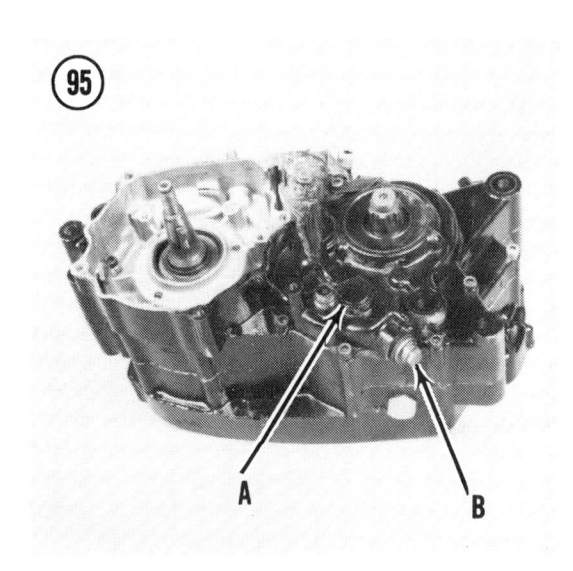

NOTE
To ease assembly, draw the case outline on cardboard, then punch holes to correspond with screw locations. Insert the screws in their appropriate locations. Also record the position of any clips that hold electrical wires or drain tubes.

9. Unscrew the shift drum neutral locator (B, **Figure 95**). Don't lose the spring and plunger within it.

CAUTION
*Perform the next step directly over and close to the workbench as the crankcase halves may easily separate. **Do not** hammer on the crankcase halves or they will be damaged.*

10. Hold onto the right-hand crankcase and studs and tap on the right-hand end of the crankshaft and transmission shaft with a plastic or rubber mallet until the crankshaft and crankcase separate.

11. If the crankcase and crankshaft will not separate using the method in Step 10, proceed with the following method using a special puller.

CAUTION
*Crankcase separation requires only hand pressure on the puller screw. If extreme pressure seems to be needed during the following steps or if both halves will not remain parallel, **stop immediately**. Check for crankcase screws not removed, for any part that is still attached or for transmission shafts hung up in a bearing. Relieve puller pressure immediately.*

12. Remove both crankcase oil seal retainers (**Figure 97**).

13. Install the crankcase separating tool (Yamaha part No. 90890-01135) into the right-hand crankcase. Tighten the securing bolts into the crankcase, making sure the tool body is parallel with the crankcase. If necessary, back out one of the bolts until the tool is parallel.

14. Screw the puller *clockwise* until both cases begin to separate.

CAUTION
*While tightening the puller make sure the body is kept parallel to the crankcase surface (**Figure 81**). Otherwise it will put an uneven stress on the case halves and may damage them.*

15. Use a plastic or rubber mallet and gently tap the crankcase half and transmission shaft to help during separation.

NOTE
Never pry between case halves. Doing so may result in oil leaks requiring replacement of the case halves.

16. Don't lose the 2 locating dowels if they came out of the case. They do not have to be removed from the case if they are secure.
17. Unscrew the crankcase separator tool and reinstall the crankcase oil seal retainers.
18. The transmission assemblies and the crankshaft assemblies will usually stay in the left-hand case half. Lift up and carefully remove the transmission, shift drum and shift fork assemblies (**Figure 98**).
19. Do not remove the crankshaft assembly from the left-hand crankcase half. This operation should be entrusted to a Yamaha dealer who can remove it and install a new one if necessary.
20. Inspect the crankcase halves and crankshaft as described under *Crankcase and Crankshaft Inspection—All Models* later in this chapter.

Crankcase Assembly (Type II)

1. Apply assembly oil (**Figure 83**) to the inner race of all bearings in both crankcase halves.
2. Install the transmission assemblies, shift shafts and shift drum in the left-hand crankcase half and lightly oil all shaft ends (**Figure 98**). Refer to Chapter Five for the correct procedure for your specific model.

NOTE
***Do not** install the shift drum neutral locator at this time. The spring pressure will push the shift drum over just enough to misalign the free end of the drum from the bearing in the right-hand crankcase during assembly.*

NOTE
Set the crankcase half assembly on 2 wood blocks or the wood holding fixture shown in the disassembly procedure.

3. Apply a light coat of non-hardening liquid gasket (Yamabond No. 4, 4-Three Bond or equivalent) to the mating surfaces of both crankcase halves. Install the 2 locating dowels if they were removed.

NOTE
Make sure the mating surfaces are clean and free of all old gasket material to make sure you get a leak free seal.

4. Set the upper crankcase half over the one on the blocks. Push it down squarely into place until it reaches the crankshaft bearing. There is usually about 1/2 inch left to go.
5. Lightly tap the case halves together with a plastic or rubber mallet (**Figure 99**) until they seat.

CAUTION
Crankcase halves should fit together without force. If the crankcase halves do not fit together completely, do not attempt to pull them together with the crankcase screws. Separate the crankcase halves and investigate the cause of the interference. If the transmission shafts were disassembled, recheck to make sure that a gear is not installed backwards. Also check that the shift drum neutral locator is not installed. Crankcase halves are a matched set and are very expensive. Do not risk damage by trying to force the cases together.

6. Install all the crankcase screws and tighten only finger-tight. Place any clips under the screws in the locations recorded in Step 8, *Removal*.
7. Securely tighten the screws in 2 stages in a crisscross pattern until they are firmly hand tight.
8. After the crankcase halves are completely assembled, rotate the crankshaft and transmission shafts to make sure there is no binding. If any is present, disassemble the crankcase and correct the problem.
9. Install the engine in the frame and tighten the mounting bolts and nuts to the torque values in **Table 2**.

ENGINE

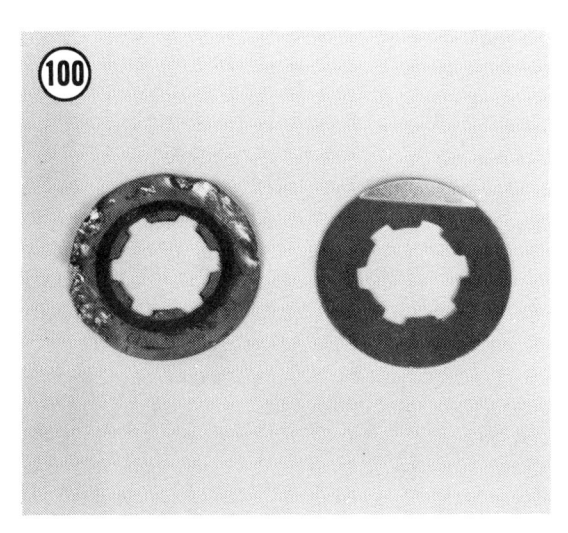

10. Push on the right-hand end of the shift drum and install the washer and circlip. Without pushing on the shift drum it is impossible to correctly install the circlip. Install the shift drum external plug (A, **Figure 95**).

11. Install the shift drum neutral locator (B, **Figure 95**), spring, and plunger.

12. Install the collar, drive sprocket and a new lockwasher. Install a new lockwasher after at least the second removal or when the lockwasher begins to look like the one on the left in **Figure 100**.

13. Attach a "Grabbit" to the drive sprocket (**Figure 93**) and tighten the nut to the torque value in **Table 2**.

NOTE
Figure 93 is shown on a Type I engine—the application is the same for Type II.

14. Bend up the tab on the lockwasher.

15. Install all exterior engine assemblies as described in this chapter and other related chapters.

Crankcase Disassembly (Type III)

The Type III crankcase is found on the following model:
IT175G

1. Remove all exterior engine assemblies as described in this chapter and other related chapters.

NOTE
Drain the clutch/transmission oil as described in Chapter Three.

2. Straightening the tab on the drive sprocket lockwasher.

3. Unscrew the locknut and remove it and the lockwasher (**Figure 101**).

4. Remove the drive sprocket and collar.

5. Loosen all bolts securing the crankcase halves together one-quarter turn. To prevent warpage, loosen them in a crisscross pattern. It is easier to loosen tight screws with the engine still in the frame.

6. Remove the engine from the frame as described under *Engine Removal/Installation* in this chapter.

NOTE
Set the engine on 2 wood blocks or fabricate a holding fixture of 2 X 4 inch wood as shown in Figure 102.

7. Remove all bolts loosened in Step 5; refer to **Figure 103**. Be sure to remove all of them.

NOTE
To ease assembly, draw the case outline on cardboard, then punch holes to correspond with screw locations. Insert the screws in their appropriate locations. Also record the position of any clips that hold electrical wires or drain tubes.

CAUTION
Perform the next step directly over and close to the workbench as the crankcase halves may easily separate. Do not hammer on the crankcase halves or they will be damaged.

8. Hold onto the left-hand crankcase or studs and tap on the left-hand end of the crankshaft and transmission shaft with a plastic or rubber mallet until the crankshaft and crankcase separate.

9. If the crankcase and crankshaft will not separate using the method in Step 8, proceed with the following method using a special puller.

CAUTION
Crankcase separation requires only hand pressure on the puller screw. If extreme

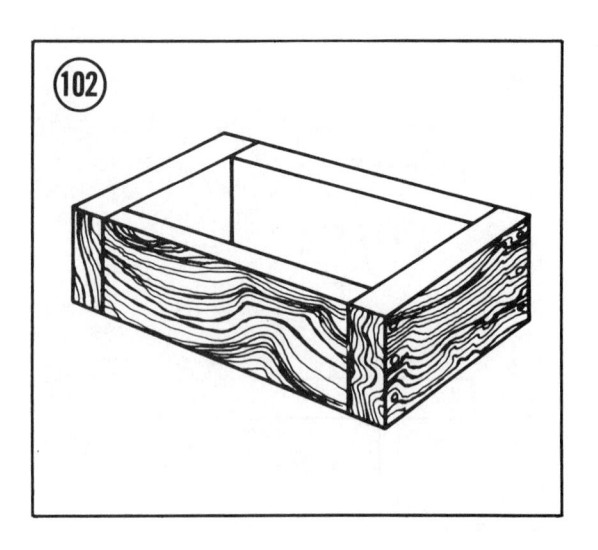

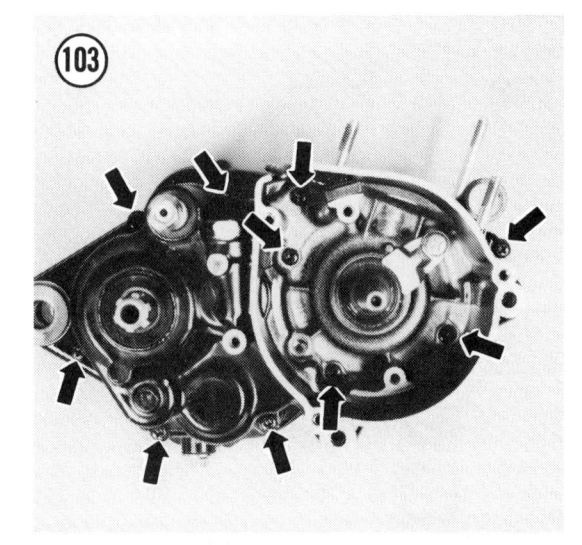

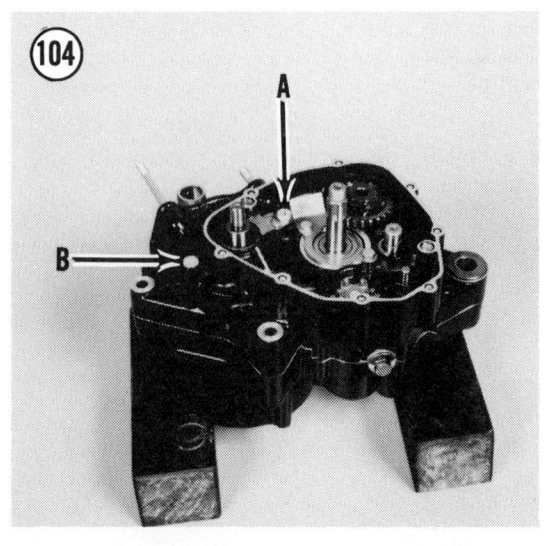

ENGINE

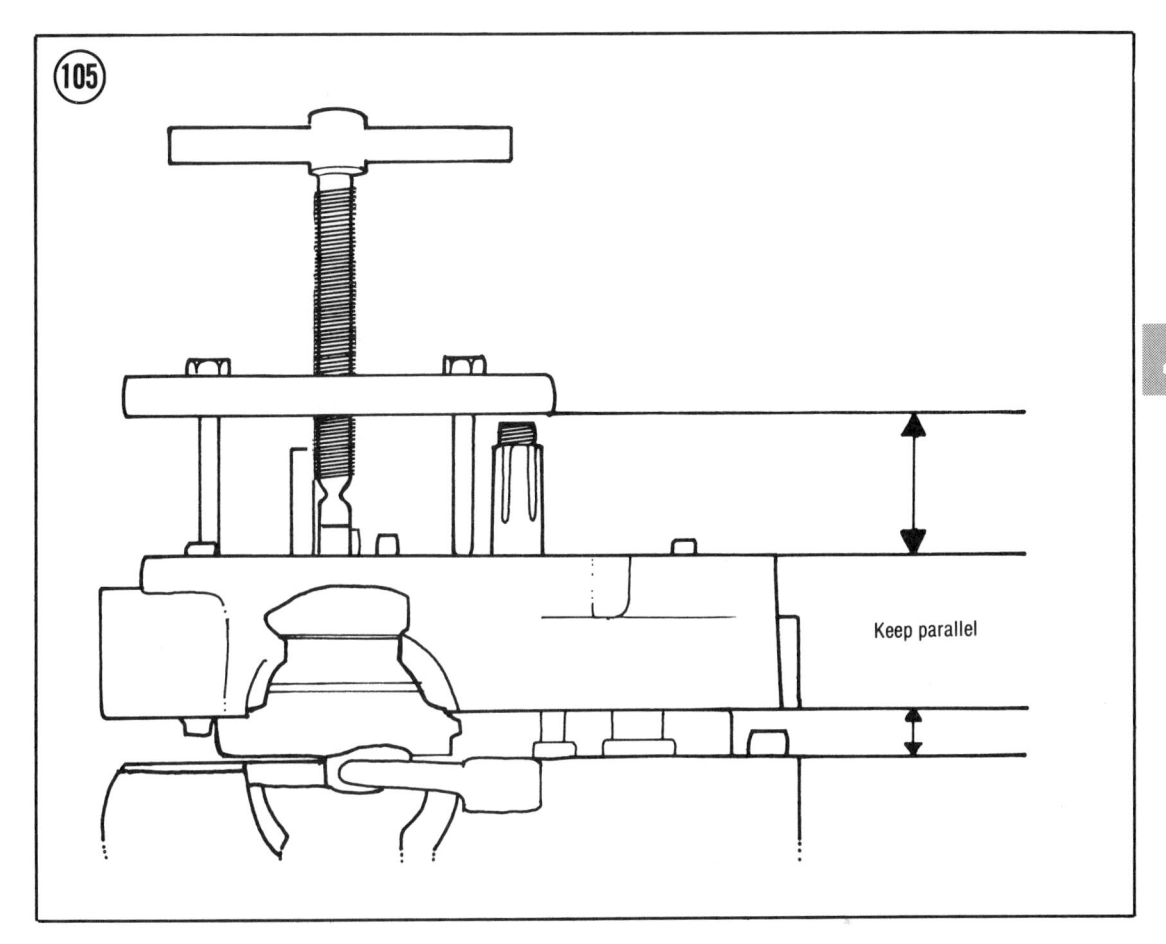

(105)

Keep parallel

*pressure seems to be needed during the following steps or if both halves will not remain parallel, **stop immediately**. Check for crankcase screws not removed, for any part that is still attached, and for transmission shafts hung up in a bearing. Relieve puller pressure immediately.*

10. Remove the crankcase oil seal retainer (A, **Figure 104**) and the plug (B, **Figure 104**).
11. Install the crankcase separating tool, (Yamaha part No. 90890-01135) into the right-hand crankcase. Tighten the securing bolts into the crankcase, making sure the tool body is parallel with the crankcase. If necessary, back out one of the bolts until the tool is parallel.
12. Screw the puller *clockwise* until both cases begin to separate.

CAUTION
*While tightening the puller make sure the body is kept parallel to the crankcase surface (**Figure 105**). Otherwise it will put an uneven stress on the case halves and damage them.*

13. Use a plastic or rubber mallet and gently tap the crankcase half and transmission shaft to help during separation.

NOTE
Never pry between case halves. Doing so may result in oil leaks requiring replacement of the case halves.

14. Don't lose the 2 locating dowels if they came out of the case. They do not have to be removed from the case if they are secure.
15. Unscrew the crankcase separator tool and reinstall the crankcase plug.
16. The transmission assemblies and the crankshaft assemblies will usually stay in the right-hand case half. Lift up and carefully remove the transmission, shift drum and shift fork assemblies (**Figure 106**).

17. Remove the kickstarter assembly from the left-hand crankcase; refer to the correct procedure at the end of this chapter.

18. Do not remove the crankshaft assembly (**Figure 107**) from the right-hand crankcase. This operation should be entrusted to a Yamaha dealer who can remove it and install a new one if necessary.

19. Inspect the crankcase halves and crankshaft as described under *Crankcase and Crankshaft Inspection—All Models* later in this chapter.

Crankcase Assembly (Type III)

1. Apply assembly oil (**Figure 108**) to the inner race of all bearings (**Figure 109**) in both crankcase halves.
2. Install the kickstarter assembly in the left-hand crankcase half. Refer to the kickstarter procedure at the end of this chapter for your specific model.
3. Install the transmission assemblies, shift shafts, and shift drum in the right-hand crankcase half and lightly oil all shaft ends (A, **Figure 110**). Refer to Chapter Five for the correct procedure for your specific model.

NOTE
Set the crankcase half assembly on 2 wood blocks or the wood holding fixture shown in the disassembly procedure.

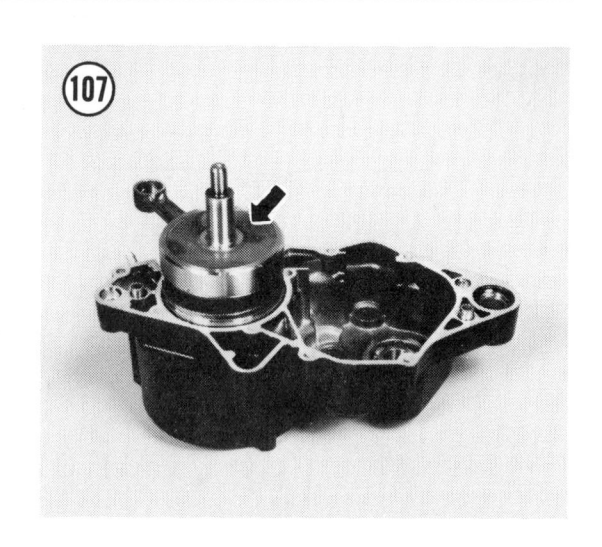

ENGINE

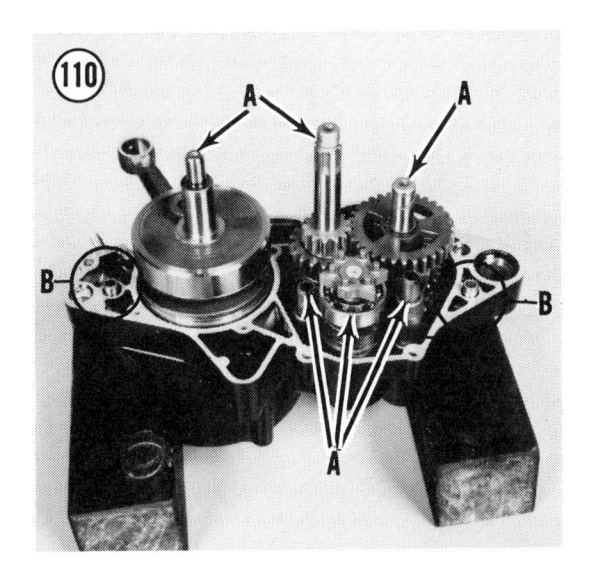

4. Apply a light coat of non-hardening liquid gasket shown in **Figure 111** (Yamabond No. 4, 4-Three Bond or equivalent) to the mating surfaces of both crankcase halves. Install the 2 locating dowels (B, **Figure 110**) if they were removed.

NOTE
Make sure the mating surfaces are clean and free of all old gasket material to make sure you get a leak free seal.

5. Set the upper crankcase half over the one on the blocks. Push it down squarely into place until it reaches the crankshaft bearing. There is usually with about 1/2 inch left to go.

6. Lightly tap the case halves together with a plastic or rubber mallet until they seat.

CAUTION
Crankcase halves should fit together without force. If the crankcase halves do not fit together completely, do not attempt to pull them together with the crankcase screws. Separate the crankcase halves and investigate the cause of the interference. If the transmission shafts were disassembled, recheck to make sure that a gear is not installed backwards. Crankcase halves are a matched set and are very expensive. Do not risk damage by trying to force the cases together.

7. Install all the crankcase screws and tighten only finger-tight.

8. Securely tighten the screws in 2 stages in a crisscross pattern until they are firmly hand-tight.

9. After the crankcase halves are completely assembled, rotate the crankshaft and transmission shafts to make sure there is no binding. If any is present, disassemble the crankcase and correct the problem.

10. Install the engine in the frame and tighten the mounting bolts and nuts to the torque values in **Table 2**.

11. Install the collar (**Figure 112**), drive sprocket and a new lockwasher (**Figure 101**). Install a new lockwasher after at least the second removal or when the lockwasher begins to look like the one in **Figure 113**.

12. Attach a "Grabbit" to the drive sprocket (**Figure 114**) and tighten the nut to the torque value in **Table 2**.

13. Bend up the tab on the lockwasher.
14. Install all exterior engine assemblies as described in this chapter and other related chapters.

Crankcase Disassembly (Type IV)

The Type IV crankcase is found in the following models:
IT175F, E, D
IT125G, F

1. Remove all exterior engine assemblies as described in this chapter and other related chapters.

NOTE
Drain the clutch/transmission oil as described in Chapter Three.

2. Straighten the tab on the drive sprocket lockwasher.
3. Unscrew the locknut and remove it and the lockwasher.
4. Remove the drive sprocket and collar.
5. Loosen all bolts securing the crankcase halves together by one-quarter turn. To prevent warpage, loosen them in a crisscross pattern. It is easier to loosen tight screws with the engine still in the frame.
6. Remove the engine from the frame as described under *Engine Removal/Installation* in this chapter.

NOTE
Set the engine on 2 wood blocks or fabricate a holding fixture of 2 X 4 inch wood as shown in Figure 102.

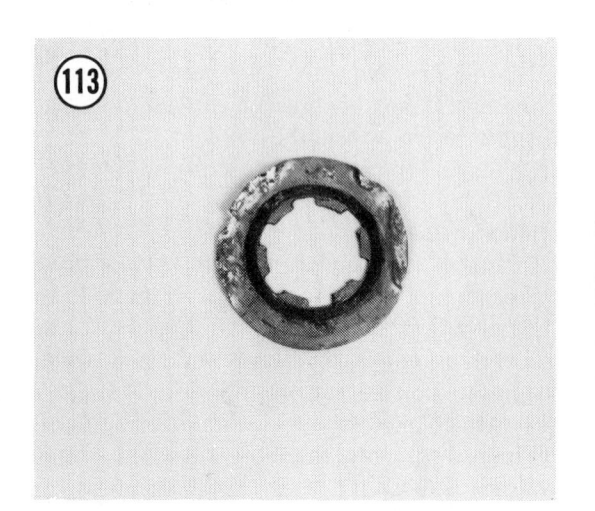

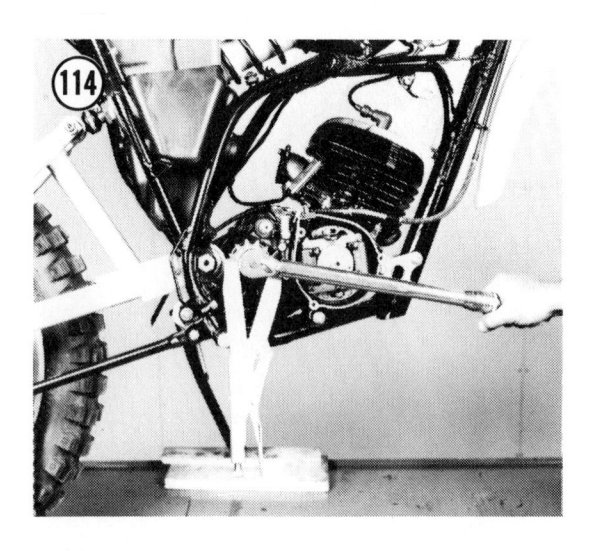

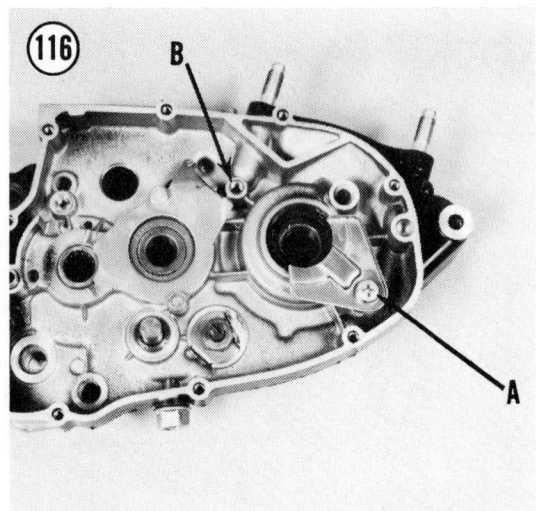

ENGINE

7. Remove all bolts loosened in Step 5; refer to **Figure 115**. Be sure to remove all of them.

NOTE
To ease assembly, draw the case outline on cardboard, then punch holes to correspond with screw locations. Insert the screws in their appropriate locations.

CAUTION
*Perform the next step directly over and close to the workbench as the crankcase halves may easily separate. **Do not** hammer on the crankcase halves as they will be damaged.*

8. Hold onto the right-hand crankcase or studs and tap on the right-hand end of the crankshaft and transmission shaft with a plastic or rubber mallet until the crankshaft and crankcase separate.

9. If the crankcase and crankshaft will not separate using the method in Step 8, proceed with the following method using a special puller.

CAUTION
*Crankcase separation requires only hand pressure on the puller screw. If extreme pressure seems to be needed during the following steps or if both halves will not remain parallel, **stop immediately**. Check for crankcase screws not removed, for any part that is still attached, and for transmission shafts hung up in a bearing. Relieve puller pressure immediately.*

10. Remove the crankcase oil seal retainer (A, **Figure 116**).

11. Install the crankcase separating tool, (Yamaha part No. 90890-01135) into the right-hand crankcase. Use the threaded hole (B, **Figure 116**). Tighten the securing bolts into the crankcase, making sure the tool body is parallel with the crankcase. If necessary, back out one of the bolts until the tool is parallel.

NOTE
***Figure 116** is shown with the crankcase disassembled for clarity.*

12. Screw the puller *clockwise* until both cases begin to separate.

CAUTION
*While tightening the puller make sure the body is kept parallel to the crankcase surface (**Figure 105**). Otherwise it will put an uneven stress on the case halves and damage them.*

13. Use a plastic or rubber mallet and gently tap the crankcase half and transmission shaft to help during separation.

NOTE
Never pry between case halves. Doing so may result in oil leaks requiring replacement of the case halves.

14. Don't lose the 2 locating dowels if they came out of the case. They do not have to be removed from the case if they are secure.

15. Unscrew the crankcase separator tool and reinstall the crankcase plug.

16. The transmission assemblies and the crankshaft assemblies will usually stay in the left-hand case half. Remove the upper rear engine mount spacer assembly. Lift up and carefully remove the transmission and shift fork assemblies.

17. Refer to Chapter Five for the correct procedure and remove the shift drum assembly.

18. Do not remove the crankshaft assembly from the left-hand crankcase. This operation should be entrusted to a Yamaha dealer who can remove it and install a new one if necessary.

19. Inspect the crankcase halves and crankshaft as described under *Crankcase and Crankshaft Inspection—All Models* later in this chapter.

Crankcase Assembly (Type IV)

1. Apply assembly oil (**Figure 108**) to the inner race of all bearings in both crankcase halves (**Figure 117**).

2. Install the transmission assemblies, shift shafts and shift drum in the right-hand

crankcase half and lightly oil all shaft ends (**Figure 118**). Refer to Chapter Five for the correct procedure for your specific model.

> *NOTE*
> *Set the crankcase half assembly on 2 wood blocks or the wood holding fixture shown in the disassembly procedure.*

3. Make sure the large dowel pin is in place (**Figure 119**) in the right-hand crankcase and install the upper rear engine mount spacer assembly (**Figure 120**).

> *NOTE*
> *Make sure the O-ring seals are in good condition; replace if necessary.*

4. Apply a light coat of non-hardening liquid gasket (Yamabond No. 4, 4-Three Bond or equivalent) to the mating surfaces of both crankcase halves.

> *NOTE*
> *Make sure the mating surfaces are clean and free of all old gasket material to make sure you get a leak free seal.*

5. Install the small dowel pin (**Figure 121**) at the front if it was removed.
6. Set the left-hand crankcase half over the one on the blocks. Push it down squarely into place until it reaches the crankshaft bearing. There is usually about 1/2 inch left to go; refer to **Figure 122**.

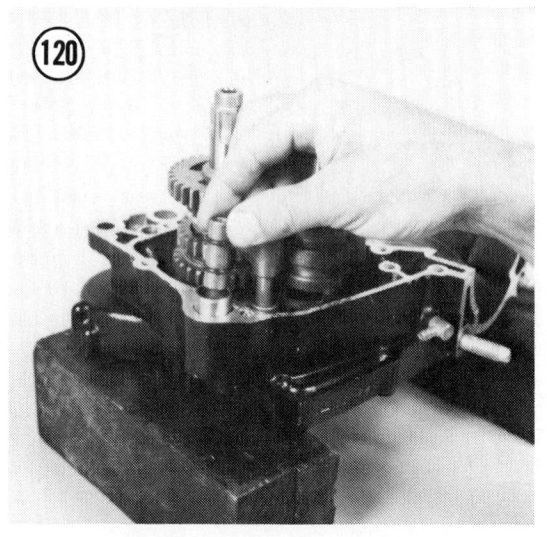

ENGINE

7. Lightly tap the case halves together with a plastic or rubber mallet until they seat.

CAUTION
Crankcase halves should fit together without force. If the crankcase halves do not fit together completely, do not attempt to pull them together with the crankcase screws. Separate the crankcase halves and investigate the cause of the interference. If the transmission shafts were disassembled, recheck to make sure that a gear is not installed backwards. Crankcase halves are a matched set and are very expensive. Do not risk damage by trying to force the cases together.

8. Install all the crankcase screws and tighten only finger-tight.
9. Securely tighten the screws in 2 stages in a crisscross pattern until they are firmly hand-tight.
10. After the crankcase halves are completely assembled, rotate the crankshaft and transmission shafts to make sure there is no binding. If any is present, disassemble the crankcase and correct the problem.
11. Install the engine in the frame and tighten the mounting bolts and nuts to the torque values in **Table 2**.
12. Install the collar (**Figure 123**), drive sprocket, and new lockwasher. Install a new lockwasher after at least the second removal or when the lockwasher begins to look like the one on the left in **Figure 124**.

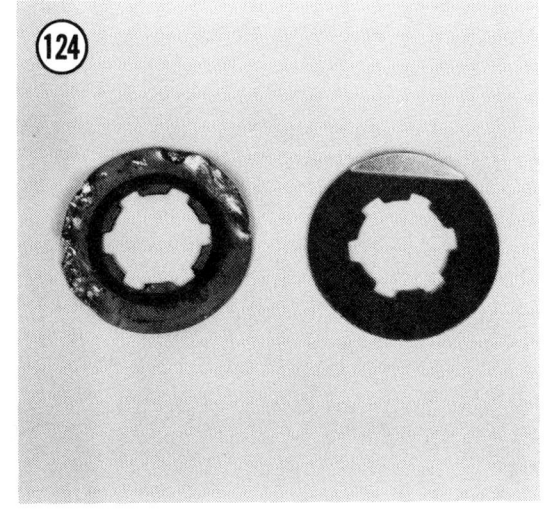

13. Attach a "Grabbit" to the drive sprocket (**Figure 125**) and tighten the nut to the torque value in **Table 2**.

14. Bend up the tab on the lockwasher (**Figure 126**).

15. Install all exterior engine assemblies as described in this chapter and other related chapters.

Crankcase and Crankshaft Inspection—All Models

The crankcases in the 4 different engine groups (Type I, II, III and IV) are all different in some way but the inspection procedure is basically the same for all. The following procedure will cover all models and the figures will represent components from the different models.

1. Clean both crankcase halves inside and out with cleaning solvent. Thoroughly dry with compressed air and wipe off with a clean shop cloth. Be sure to remove all traces of old gasket sealer from all mating surfaces.

2. Check the crankshaft main bearings (**Figure 127**) for roughness, pitting, galling and play by rotating them slowly by hand. If any roughness or play can be felt in the bearing it must be replaced. Refer to *Bearing and Oil Seal Replacement* in this chapter.

NOTE
The bearing in the crankcase can be inspected with the crankshaft still installed

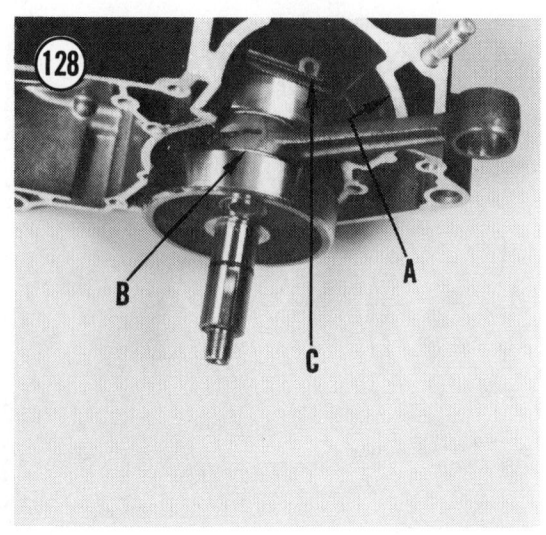

ENGINE

*by turning the crankshaft by hand (hold to the connecting rod to prevent damage to the surrounding crankcase opening—A, **Figure 128**). If this bearing is OK, apply a liberal coating of 2-stroke oil to the connecting rod big end (B, **Figure 128**) and into the crankshaft bearing delivery hole (C, **Figure 128**). Make sure that this bearing is well lubricated as it was washed in solvent and not exposed for thorough drying.*

3. Inspect the condition of all the other bearings (**Figure 129**) for the transmission and shift drum as described in the previous step. Replace as necessary.

4. Carefully inspect the cases for cracks and fractures, especially in the lower areas (**Figure 130**); they are vulnerable to rock damage. Also check the areas around the stiffening ribs, around bearing bosses and threaded holes (**Figure 131**). If any are found, have them repaired by a shop specializing in the repair of precision aluminum castings or replace them.

5. Check the condition of the connecting rod big end bearing by grasping the rod in one hand and lifting up on it. With the heel of your other hand, rap sharply on the top of the rod. A sharp metallic sound, such as a click, is an indication that the bearing or crankpin or both are worn and the crankshaft assembly should be replaced.

6. Check the connecting rod to crankshaft side clearance with a flat feeler gauge (**Figure 132**).

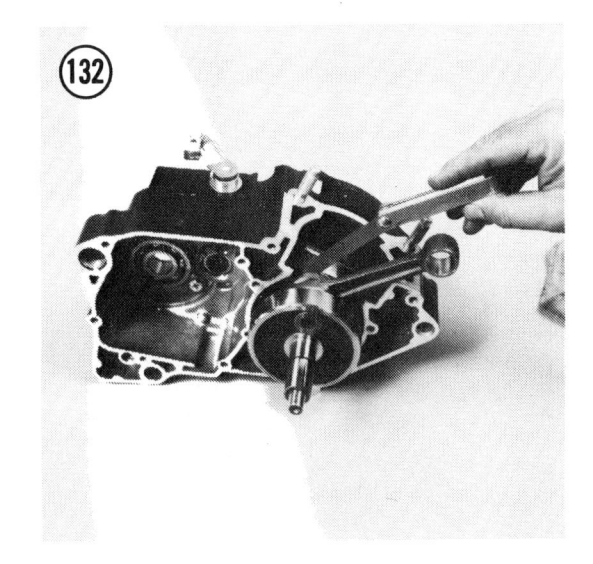

Compare to dimensions given in **Table 1**. If the clearance is greater than specified the crankshaft assembly must be replaced.

NOTE
Other inspections of the crankshaft assembly involve accurate measuring equipment and should be entrusted to a Yamaha dealer or competent machine shop. The crankshaft assembly operates under severe stress and dimensional tolerances are critical. If any are off by the slightest amount it may cause a considerable amount of damage or destruction of the engine. The crankshaft assembly must be replaced as a unit as it cannot be serviced without the aid of a 10-12 ton (9,000-11,000 kilogram) capacity press, holding fixtures and crankshaft jig.

7. Inspect the condition of the filler plugs in the crankshaft counterwheels (**Figure 133**) on models balanced this way. If they have holes in them or are damaged they should be replaced as this would in effect increase the area of the crankcase volume, lowering the compression ratio. This operation is best left to a Yamaha dealer.

8. Remove all oil seals—they should be replaced each time the crankcase is disassembled. Refer to *Bearing and Oil Seal Replacement* in this chapter.

ENGINE

Bearing and Oil Seal Replacement

1. Prior to removing the bearings, the oil seals should be removed. Remove the screw securing the oil seal retainer (**Figure 134**) on the crankshaft and remove the retainer.

2. Pry out the oil seals with a small screwdriver, taking care not to damage the crankcase bore. If the seals are old and difficult to remove, heat the cases as described in Step 4 and use an awl to punch a small hole in the steel backing of the seal. Install a small sheet metal screw part way into the seal and pull the seal out with a pair of pliers.

CAUTION
Do not install the screw too deep or it may contact and damage the bearing behind it.

3. Remove the screws securing the bearing retainers (**Figure 135** and **Figure 136**) and remove them and the retainers.

4. The bearings are installed with a slight interference fit. The crankcase must be heated in an oven to a temperature of about 212°F (100°C). An easy way to check the temperature is to drop tiny drops of water on the case; if they sizzle and evaporate immediately, the temperature is correct. Heat only one case at a time.

CAUTION
Do not heat the cases with a torch (propane or acetylene); never bring a flame into contact with the bearing or case. The direct heat will destroy the case hardening of the bearing and will likely cause warpage of the case.

5. Remove the case from the oven and hold onto the 2 crankcase studs with a kitchen pot holder, heavy gloves or heavy shop cloths — *it is hot*.

6. Remove the oil seals if not already removed (see Step 2).

7. Hold the crankcase with the bearing side down and tap it squarely on a piece of soft wood. Continue to tap until the bearing(s) fall out. Repeat for the other half.

CAUTION
Be sure to tap the crankcase squarely on the piece of wood. Avoid damaging the seal surface of the crankcase.

8. If the bearings are difficult to remove, they can be gently tapped out with a socket or piece of pipe the same size as the bearing outer race.

NOTE
If the bearings or seals are difficult to remove or install, don't take a chance on expensive damage. Have the work performed by a Yamaha dealer or competent machine shop.

9. While heating up the crankcase halves, place the new bearings in a freezer if possible. Chilling them will slightly reduce their overall diameter while the hot crankcase is slightly larger due to heat expansion. This will make installation much easier.

10. While the crankcase is still hot, press each new bearing into place in the crankcase by hand until it seats completely. Do not hammer it in. If the bearing will not seat, remove it and cool it again. Reheat the crankcase and install the bearing again.

11. Oil seals are best installed with a special tool available from a Yamaha dealer or motorcycle supply store. However, a proper size socket or piece of pipe can be substituted. Make sure that the bearings and seals are not cocked in the hole and that they are seated properly.

KICKSTARTER

The kickstarters for the different engines are all basically the same but all have different components and are assembled differently. They are divided into different groups and given a type designation which relates to different models. With the exception of the Type IV, all can be removed without splitting the crankcase.

The Type I kickstarter (**Figure 137**) is found on the following models:
   IT425G
   IT250G, F
   IT400F

The Type II kickstarter (**Figure 138**) is found on the following models:
   IT400E, D
   IT250F, E, D

The Type III kickstarter (**Figure 139**) is found on the following model:
   IT400C

CHAPTER FOUR

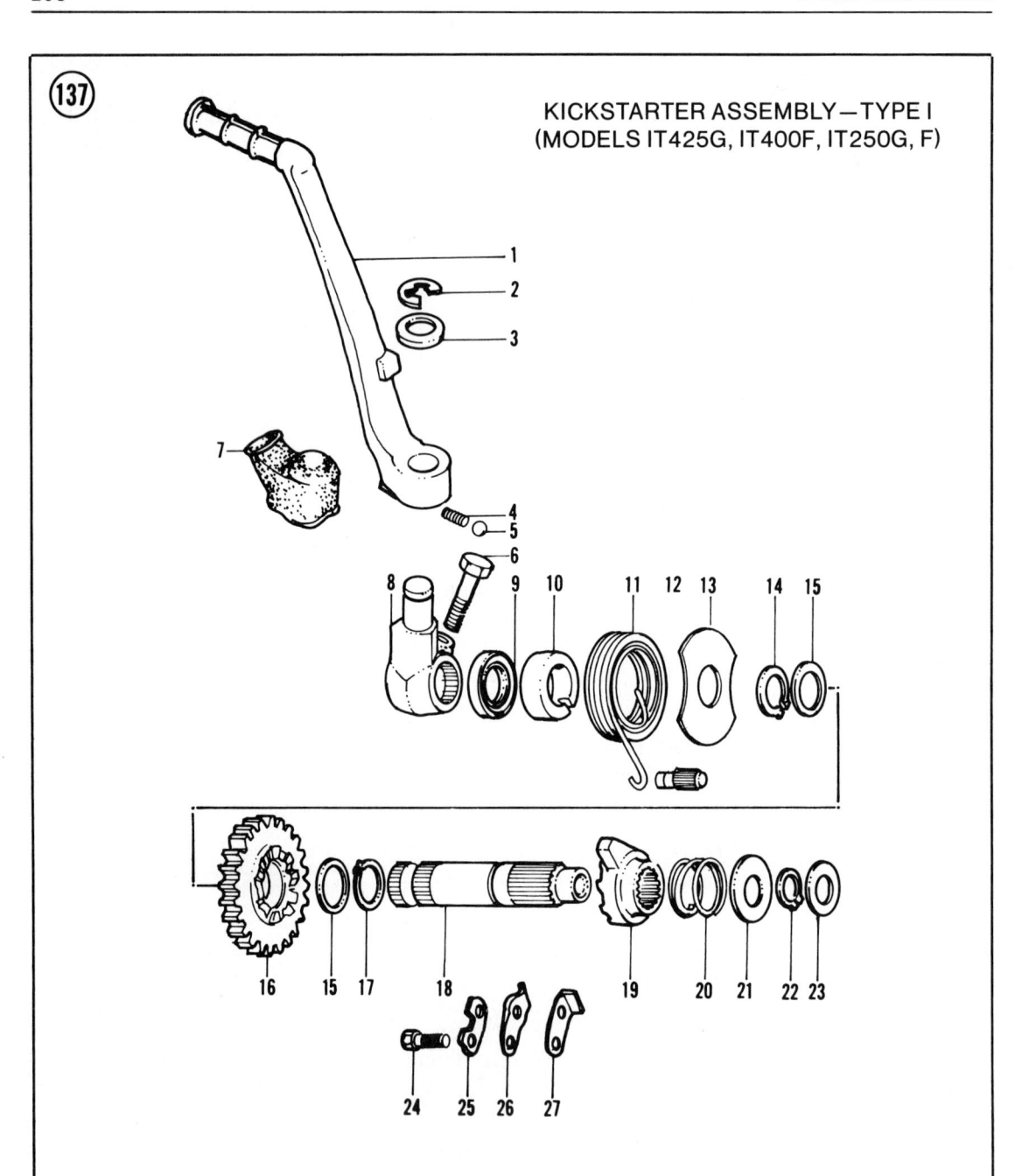

KICKSTARTER ASSEMBLY—TYPE I
(MODELS IT425G, IT400F, IT250G, F)

1. Crank
2. E-clip
3. Washer
4. Spring
5. Ball
6. Bolt
7. Rubber boot
8. Pivot boss
9. Oil seal
10. Collar
11. Kickstarter return spring
12. Stopper pin
13. Spring cover
14. Circlip
15. Shim
16. Ratchet gear
17. Circlip
18. Shaft
19. Kickstarter ratchet
20. Ratchet spring
21. Spring cover
22. Circlip
23. Washer
24. Bolt
25. Lockwasher
26. Ratchet wheel guide
27. Stopper plate

ENGINE

**KICKSTARTER ASSEMBLY—TYPE II
(MODELS IT400E, D, IT250F, E, D)**

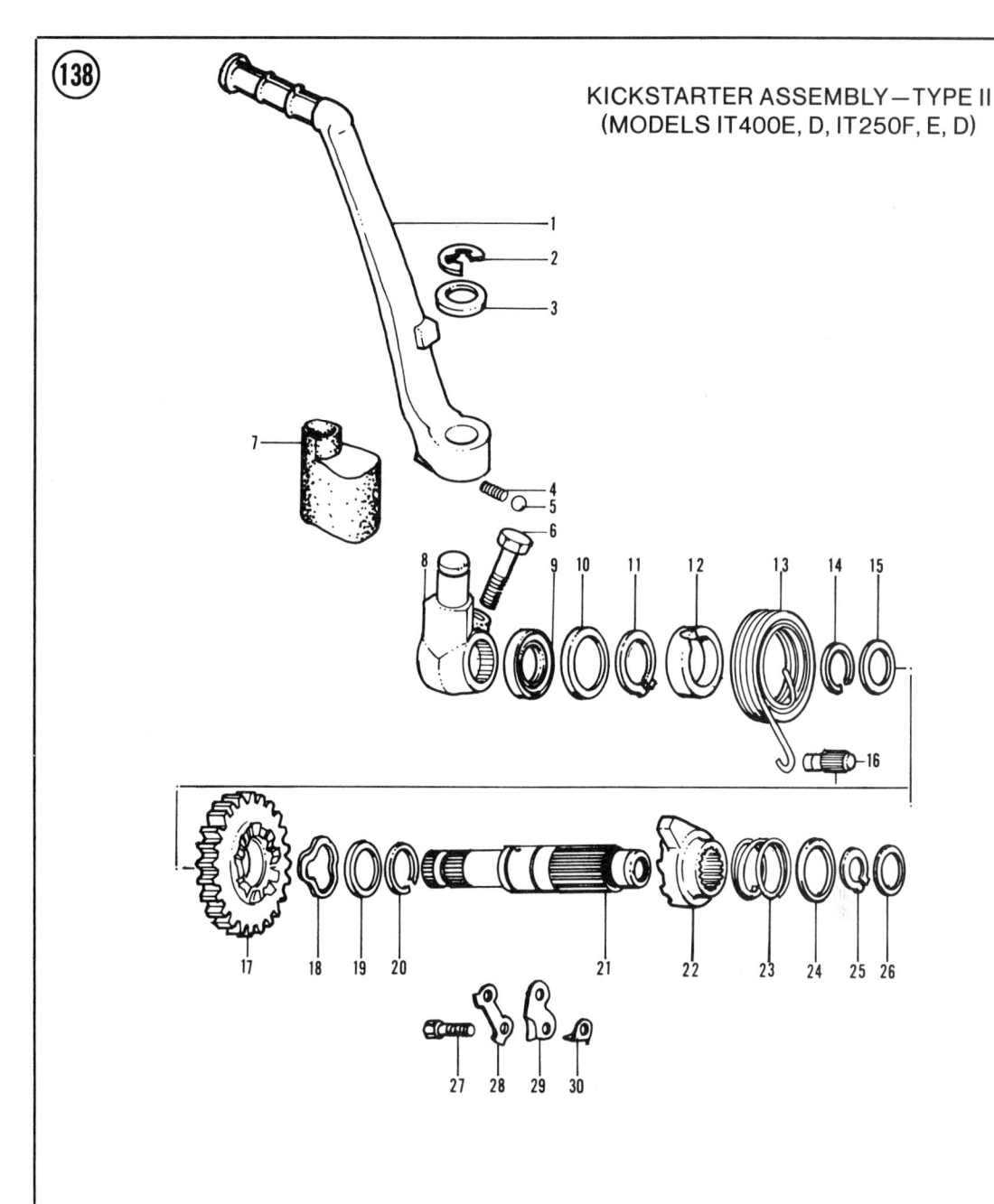

1. Crank
2. E-clip
3. Washer
4. Spring
5. Ball
6. Bolt
7. Rubber boot
8. Pivot boss
9. Oil seal
10. Washer
11. Circlip
12. Collar
13. Kickstarter return spring
14. Washer
15. Circlip
16. Stopper pin
17. Ratchet gear
18. Wave washer
19. Washer
20. Circlip
21. Shaft
22. Kickstarter ratchet
23. Ratchet spring
24. Washer
25. Circlip
26. Washer
27. Bolt
28. Lockwasher
29. Ratchet wheel guide
30. Stopper plate

CHAPTER FOUR

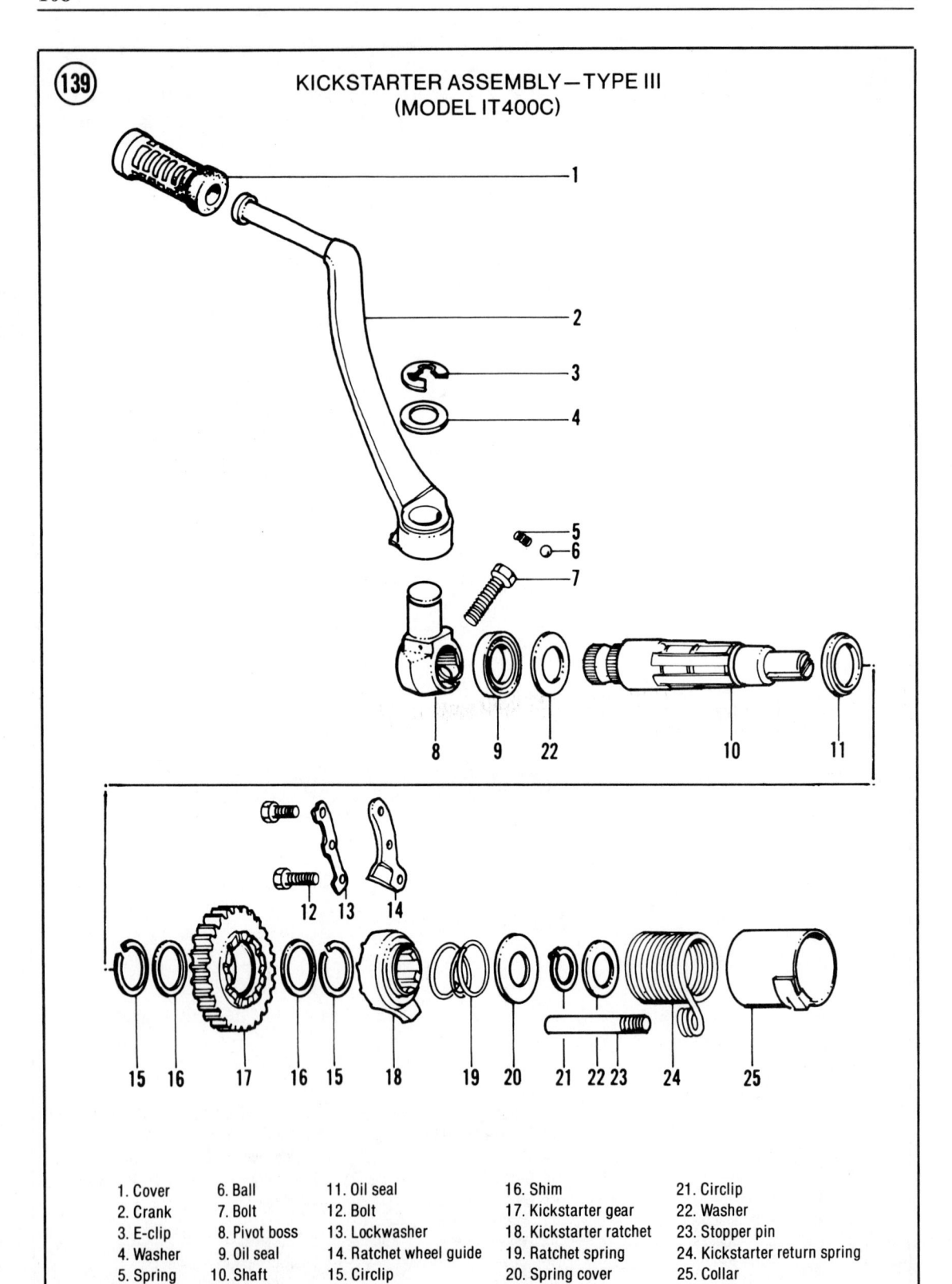

KICKSTARTER ASSEMBLY — TYPE III (MODEL IT400C)

1. Cover
2. Crank
3. E-clip
4. Washer
5. Spring
6. Ball
7. Bolt
8. Pivot boss
9. Oil seal
10. Shaft
11. Oil seal
12. Bolt
13. Lockwasher
14. Ratchet wheel guide
15. Circlip
16. Shim
17. Kickstarter gear
18. Kickstarter ratchet
19. Ratchet spring
20. Spring cover
21. Circlip
22. Washer
23. Stopper pin
24. Kickstarter return spring
25. Collar

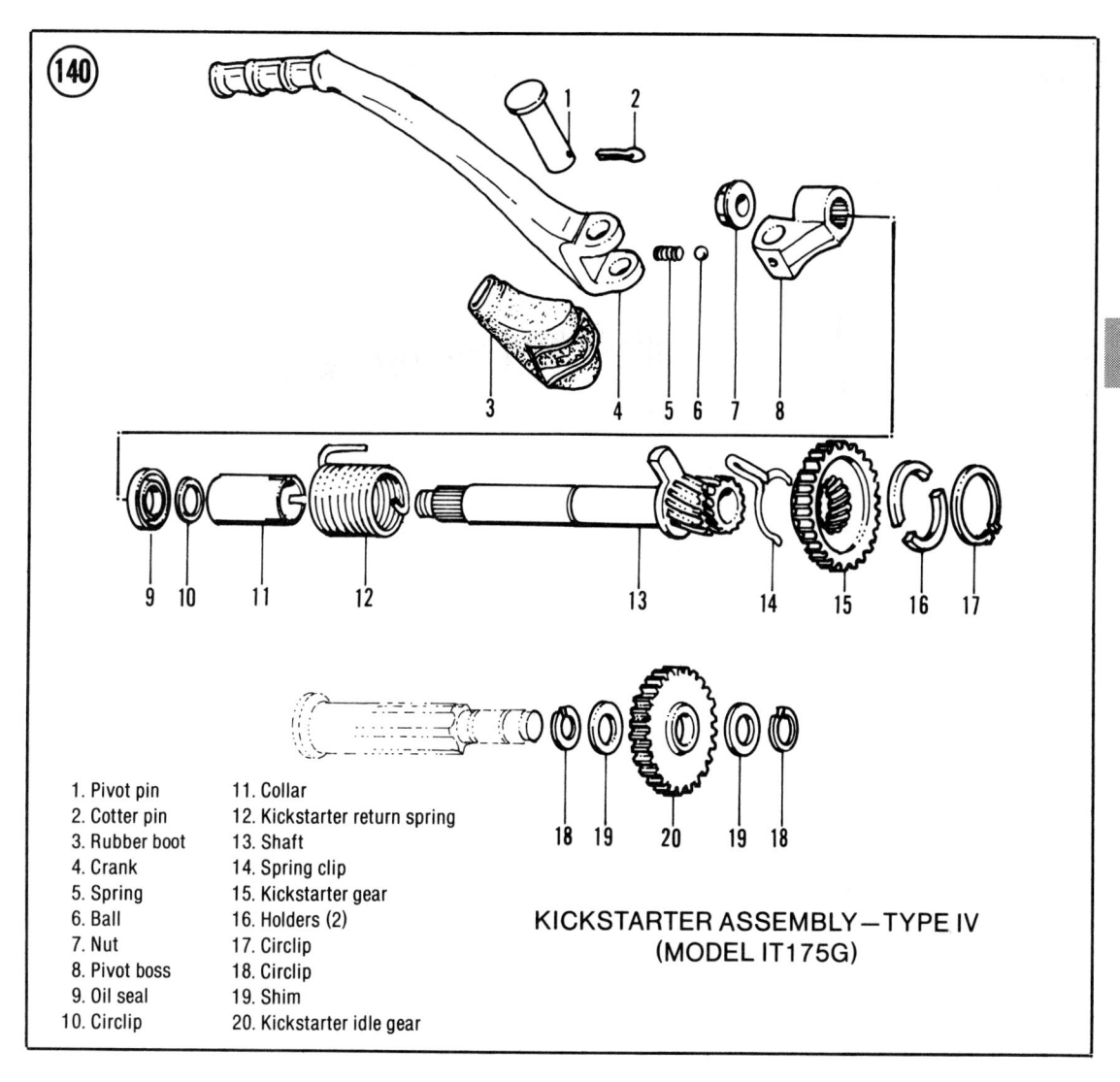

ENGINE

Figure 140: KICKSTARTER ASSEMBLY—TYPE IV (MODEL IT175G)

1. Pivot pin
2. Cotter pin
3. Rubber boot
4. Crank
5. Spring
6. Ball
7. Nut
8. Pivot boss
9. Oil seal
10. Circlip
11. Collar
12. Kickstarter return spring
13. Shaft
14. Spring clip
15. Kickstarter gear
16. Holders (2)
17. Circlip
18. Circlip
19. Shim
20. Kickstarter idle gear

The Type IV kickstarter (**Figure 140**) is found on the following model:
IT175G

The Type V kickstarter (**Figure 141**) is found on the following models:
IT175F, E, D
IT125G

The following procedures on a Type I (external type) and Type IV (internal type within the crankcase) represent typical kickstarter removal, inspection and installation sequences. Minor variations exist between models. Pay particular attention to the location and positioning of spacers, washers and springs to make assembly easier.

Removal (Type I, II, III and V)

NOTE
A Type I is used to illustrate this procedure. As previously mentioned, there are variations among the different models.

1. Remove the clutch assembly as described under *Clutch Removal/Installation*.
2. Remove the kickstarter return spring from the pin (A, **Figure 142**) and pull the assembly from the crankcase (B, **Figure 142**).

NOTE
Don't lose the thin shim on the inside end of the shaft. Sometimes it will stick in the depression in the crankcase.

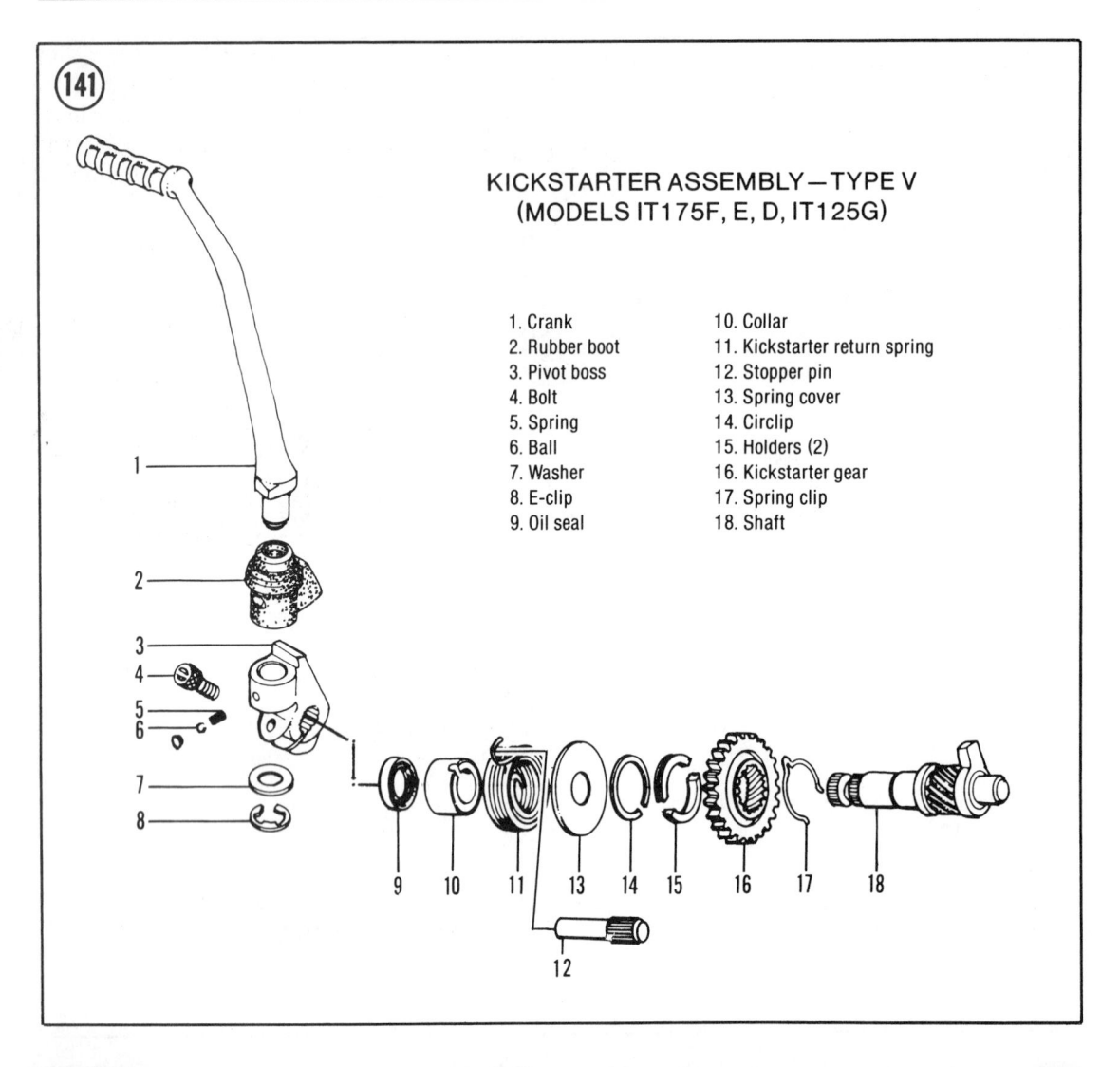

CHAPTER FOUR

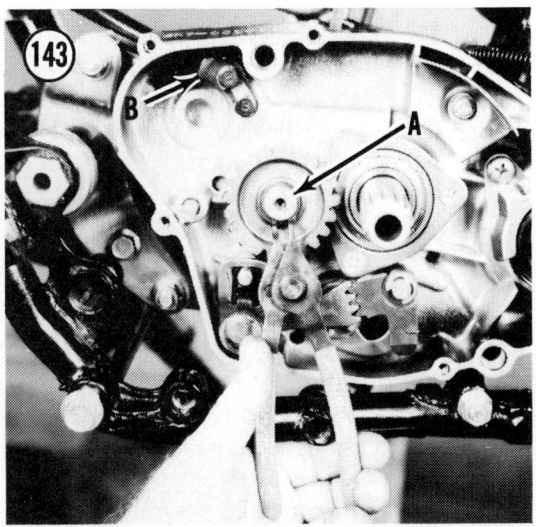

**KICKSTARTER ASSEMBLY—TYPE V
(MODELS IT175F, E, D, IT125G)**

1. Crank
2. Rubber boot
3. Pivot boss
4. Bolt
5. Spring
6. Ball
7. Washer
8. E-clip
9. Oil seal
10. Collar
11. Kickstarter return spring
12. Stopper pin
13. Spring cover
14. Circlip
15. Holders (2)
16. Kickstarter gear
17. Spring clip
18. Shaft

ENGINE

3. On Type V kickstarters, remove the spring end from the hole in the crankcase rib.
4. Remove the circlip and shim (A, **Figure 143**) securing the kickstarter idle gear and remove the gear and the shim behind it (**Figure 144**).

Disassembly/Inspection/Assembly (Type I, II, III and V)

1. Remove the collar, return spring and spring cover (**Figure 145**).
2. Turn the shaft over and remove the circlip, spring cover and spring (**Figure 146**).
3. Slide off the kickstarter ratchet (**Figure 147**).
4. Remove the circlip (A, **Figure 148**) and slide off the ratchet gear (B, **Figure 148**).

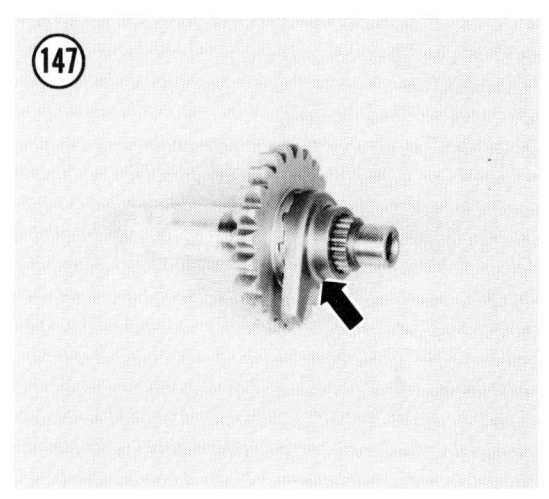

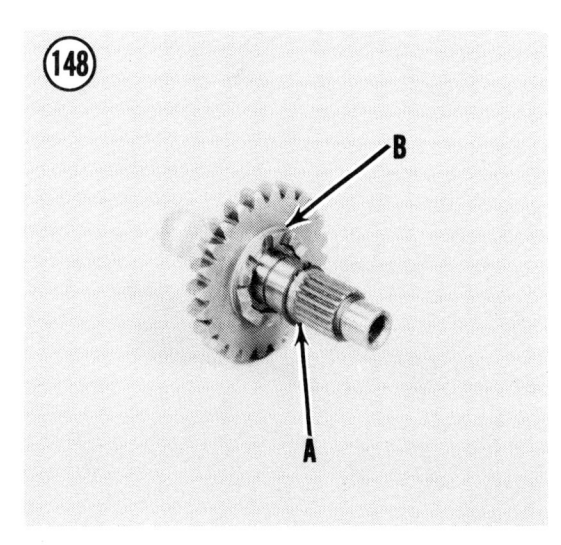

5. Check for broken, chipped or missing teeth on the gear; replace if necessary.
6. Make sure the ratchet gear operates properly and smoothly on the shaft.
7. Check all parts for uneven wear; replace any that are questionable.
8. Apply assembly oil to the sliding surfaces of all parts.
9. Slide on the ratchet gear and install the circlip.
10. Install the kickstarter ratchet; align the punch mark (A, **Figure 149**) on the shaft with the straight portion of the kickstarter ratchet (B, **Figure 149**). This is necessary to maintain the proper spring-to-ratchet relationship.
11. Install the ratchet spring, spring cover and circlip.

Installation
(Type I, II, III and V)

Refer to **Figure 150** for correct placement of components.
1. Install the inner shim (**Figure 151**) behind the kickstarter idle gear and install the idle gear.
2. Install the kickstarter idle gear and outer shim (**Figure 152**).
3. Install the circlip (A, **Figure 143**).
4. Install the shim (**Figure 153**) on the end of the shaft and install the assembled kickstarter unit into the crankcase.

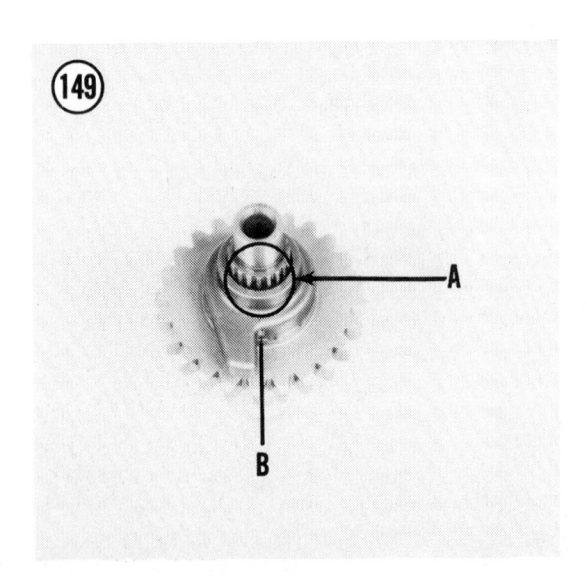

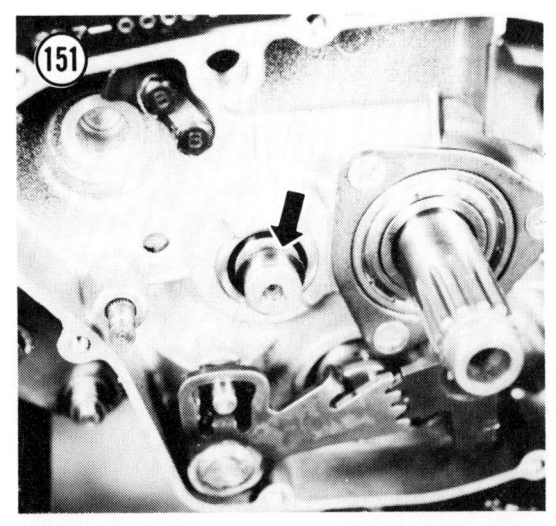

ENGINE

NOTE
*Make sure the flat surface on the kickstarter ratchet is engaged behind the stopper plate that is attached to the crankcase (B, **Figure 143**).*

5. Pull the return spring into position with Vise Grips and place it on the stopper (A, **Figure 142**).

WARNING
The spring is under pressure during this part of the procedure; protect yourself accordingly.

6. On a Type V kickstarter assembly, make sure the projection on the spring clip (**Figure 154**) is engaged into the notch in the crankcase (**Figure 155**). The spring hook goes into an opening in the edge of the crankcase rib (**Figure 156**).

7. Install the clutch assembly as described under *Clutch Removal/Installation* in Chapter Five.

Removal/Disassembly (Type IV)

1. Remove the engine as described under *Engine Removal/Installation* in this chapter.
2. Disassemble the crankcase as described under *Crankcase Disassembly/Assembly* in this chapter.
3. Remove the circlip securing the holders (A, **Figure 157**) and remove them and the

kickstarter gear (B, **Figure 157**) and spring clip (C, **Figure 157**).
4. From the inside, remove the circlip securing the collar (**Figure 158**).
5. Using Vise Grips carefully pull the return spring up and out of the hole in the crankcase.
6. Slide off the return spring and collar from the inside of the crankcase and withdraw the shaft from the outside.

Inspection (Type IV)

1. Check for broken, chipped or missing teeth on the gear; replace if necessary. Refer to A, **Figure 159**.
2. Make sure the spirals within the kickstarter gear and on the outside of the shaft are in good condition with no burrs or rough spots; replace if necessary.
3. Check all parts for uneven wear (B, **Figure 159**); replace any that are questionable.
4. Apply assembly oil to the sliding surfaces of all parts.

Assembly/Installation (Type IV)

1. Insert the shaft from the outside and position the shaft so that the hole faces up (**Figure 160**).
2. Install the return spring and insert the inside hook of the spring into the hole in the shaft (A, **Figure 161**).
3. Slide on the spacer. Align the slot in the spacer (B, **Figure 161**) with the inside hook of the return spring and push the spacer all the way in.
4. Pull up on the outside hook of the return spring with Vise Grips and install the hook in the hole in the crankcase (**Figure 162**).
5. Install the circlip (**Figure 158**).
6. On the outside, slide on the spring clip and kickstarter gear.
7. Install the 2 holders and secure them with the circlip (A, **Figure 157**).
8. Assemble the crankcase halves and install the engine.

SERVICE AND ADJUSTMENT

When the engine has been assembled and installed in the bike, walk around the bike and thoroughly double check all work. Do not be in a hurry to ride the bike. You have invested alot of time, energy and money so far so don't waste it by forgetting some little item that may cost additional time and money. *Thoroughly* check and recheck all components, systems and controls on the bike. Make sure all cables are correctly routed, adjusted and secured and all bolts and nuts properly tightened. Position all electrical wires away from the exhaust system and control levers.

Refer to Chapter Three and perform all maintenance and lubrication procedures including all related adjustments.

This little time spent will prevent a lot of frustration and save not only time but money as well.

ENGINE

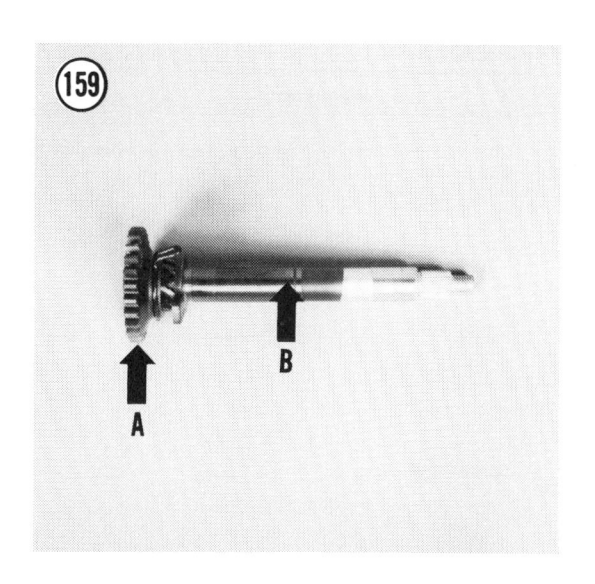

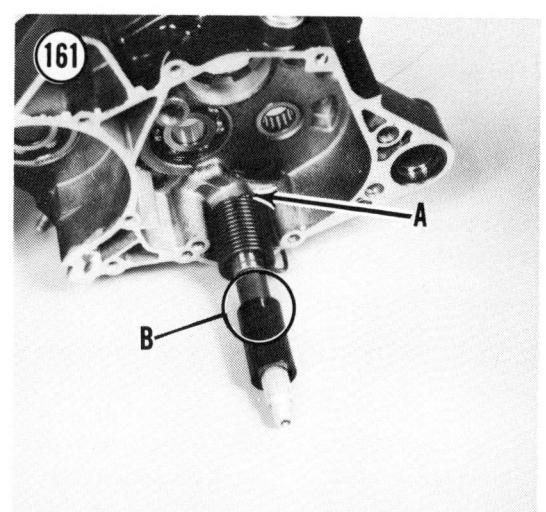

Tables are on the following pages.

Table 1 ENGINE SPECIFICATIONS

Item	Specifications	Wear Limit
Cylinder		
Bore and stroke		
IT425	3.35 x 2.93 in. (85 x 75 mm)	—
IT400	3.35 x 2.76 in. (85 x 70 mm)	—
IT250	2.8 x 2.5 in. (70 x 64 mm)	—
IT175	2.60 x 1.97 in. (66 x 50 mm)	—
IT125	2.2 x 1.97 in. (56 x 50 mm)	
Bore		
IT425	3.346 in. (85 mm)	3.35 in. (85.1 mm)
IT400	3.346 in. (85 mm)	3.35 in. (85.1 mm)
IT250	2.75 in. (70 mm)	2.76 in. (70.1 mm)
IT175	2.598 in. (66.0 mm)	2.602 in. (66.1 mm)
IT125	2.204 in. (50.0 mm)	2.205 in. (56.02 mm)
Taper limit	—	0.003 in. (0.08 mm)
Out-of-round	—	0.002 in. (0.05 mm)
Piston		
Piston/cylinder clearance		
IT425	0.0020-0.0023 in. (0.050-0.060 mm)	—
IT400	0.0020-0.0022 in. (0.050-0.055 mm)	—
IT250	0.0018-0.0020 in. (0.045-0.050 mm)	—
IT175	0.0020-0.0022 in. (0.050-0.055 mm)	—
IT125	0.0018-0.0020 in. (0.045-0.050 mm)	—
Piston rings (top and second)		
Ring end gap		
IT425	0.016-0.022 in. (0.4-0.55 mm)	—
IT400	0.012-0.020 in. (0.3-0.5 mm)	—
IT250	0.012-0.020 in. (0.3-0.5 mm)	—
IT175	0.008-0.016 in. (0.2-0.4 mm)	—
IT125	0.012-0.019 in. (0.3-0.5 mm)	—
Ring side clearance		
All models	—	0.004 in. (0.1 mm)
Crankshaft		
Deflection	—	0.0012 in. (0.03 mm)
Big end side clearance	—	
IT425, IT400, IT250		0.010-0.030 in. (0.25-0.75 mm)
IT175, IT125		0.008-0.028 in. (0.20-0.70 mm)

ENGINE

Table 2 ENGINE TORQUE SPECIFICATIONS

Item	Foot-pounds (Ft.-lb.)	Newton Meters (N•m)
Cylinder head	18	25
Cylinder nuts	22-25	30-35
Clutch nut		
IT425, IT400, IT250	55	75
IT175	36	50
IT125	40	55
Drive sprocket		
IT425, IT400, IT250	18-22	25-30
IT175G	22	30
IT175F, E, D	43-46	60-65
IT125	40	55
Magneto		
IT425G, IT400F	30	40
IT400E, D, C	58	80
IT250G, IT250F	30	40
IT250D, E	58	80
IT175G	50	75
IT175F, E, D	36	50
IT125	50	70

Table 3 PISTON MEASUREMENT LOCATION*

Model	Inches	Millimeters
IT425G	0.40	10
IT400E, D, C	0.40	10
IT250	0.40	10
IT175G	0.71	18
IT175F, E, D	0.40	10
IT125G	0.40	10

*Indicates dimension up from the bottom of the piston skirt at right angles to the wrist pin.

NOTE: If you own a 1981 or later model, first check the Supplement at the back of the book for any new service information.

CHAPTER FIVE

CLUTCH AND TRANSMISSION

This chapter contains procedures for removal, inspection and installation of the clutch, transmission and shift mechanism (external and internal). There is basically one type of clutch mechanism, 2 transmissions (5-speed and 6-speed) and a variety of shift mechanisms used on the various IT models. Be sure to follow the correct procedure for your specific model.

CLUTCH

The clutch used on the IT is a wet multiplate type immersed in the oil supply it shares with the transmission. The clutch boss is splined to the transmission main shaft and the clutch housing can rotate freely on the main shaft. The clutch housing is geared to the primary drive gear attached to the crankshaft.

The clutch release mechanism is mounted within the top of the crankcase on the side opposite the clutch mechanism. The mechanism consists of a push lever assembly which is operated by the clutch cable. Pulling the clutch lever and cable pivots the push lever that in turn pushes the clutch pushrod. This actuates the pressure plate and disengages the clutch mechanism.

The clutch assemblies used with the different engines are basically the same. Some have a different number of components (clutch plates and friction discs) and are assembled a little differently; where differences occur they are identified. Because of the minor variations pay particular attention to the location and positioning of spacers and washers to make assembly easier.

The clutch can be removed while the engine is in the frame.

Refer to **Table 1** for all clutch specifications and **Table 2** for clutch torque specifications. **Table 1** and **Table 2** are at the end of this chapter.

Figure 1 shows the clutch assembly and release mechanism for the various models.

Removal/Disassembly

NOTE
This procedure is shown with components from 2 different models, the IT250G and IT125G.

1. Remove the bolts (**Figure 2**) securing the footpeg and remove it.
2. Remove the rear brake pedal assembly as described under *Rear Brake Pedal Removal/Installation* in Chapter Ten.
3. Remove the bolts (**Figure 3**) securing the skidplate and remove it.
4. Remove the kickstarter lever (**Figure 4**).

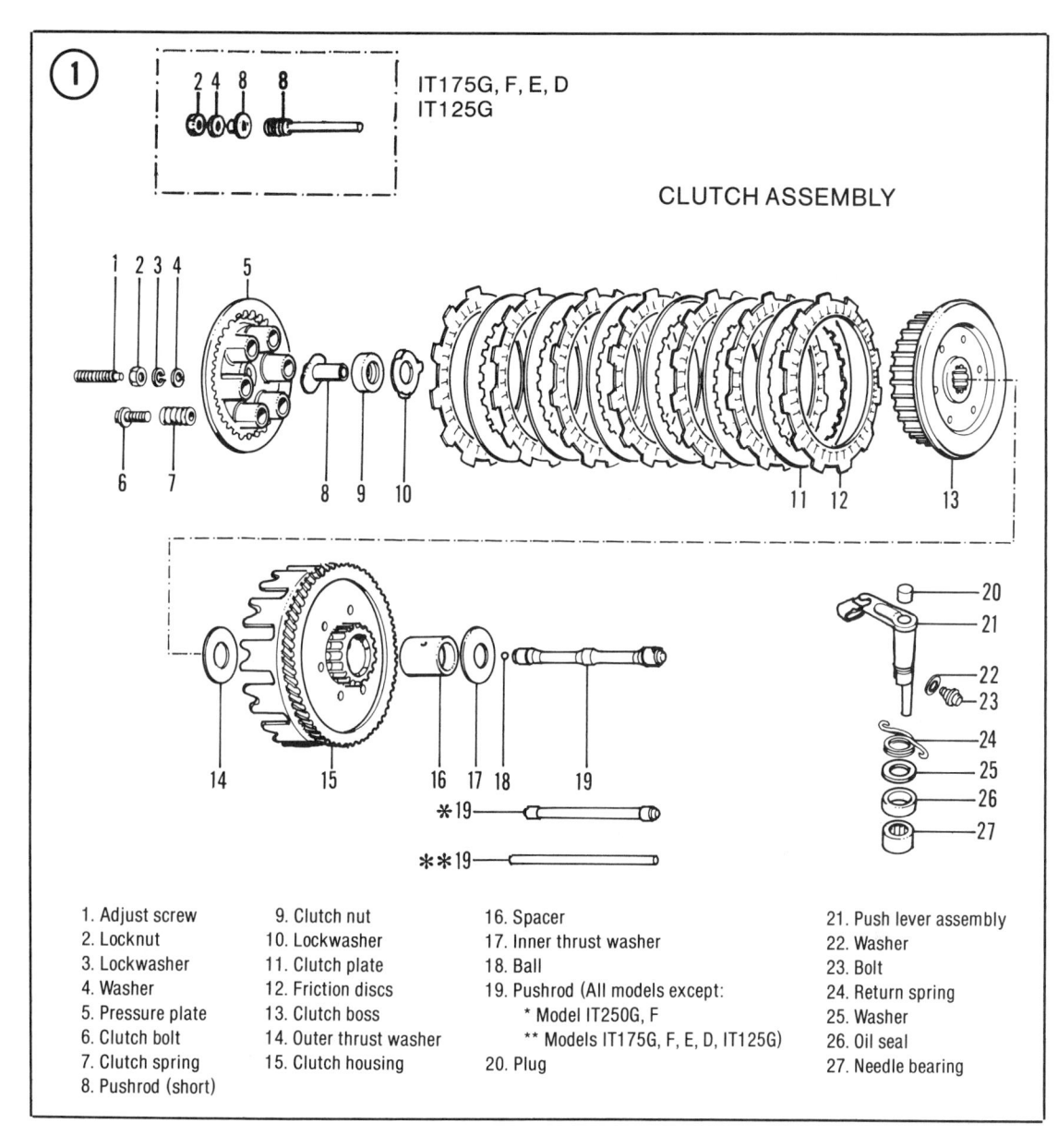

CLUTCH AND TRANSMISSION

IT175G, F, E, D
IT125G

CLUTCH ASSEMBLY

1. Adjust screw
2. Locknut
3. Lockwasher
4. Washer
5. Pressure plate
6. Clutch bolt
7. Clutch spring
8. Pushrod (short)
9. Clutch nut
10. Lockwasher
11. Clutch plate
12. Friction discs
13. Clutch boss
14. Outer thrust washer
15. Clutch housing
16. Spacer
17. Inner thrust washer
18. Ball
19. Pushrod (All models except:
   * Model IT250G, F
   ** Models IT175G, F, E, D, IT125G)
20. Plug
21. Push lever assembly
22. Washer
23. Bolt
24. Return spring
25. Washer
26. Oil seal
27. Needle bearing

CHAPTER FIVE

5. Place a milk crate or wood block(s) under the frame to support the bike securely.

6. Drain the clutch/transmission oil as described in Chapter Three.

7. Remove the screws (**Figures 5**) securing the clutch cover and remove it and the gasket. Remove and save the 2 locating dowels.

8. Using a crisscross pattern, remove the clutch bolts (**Figure 6**) securing the pressure plate.

NOTE
*If the primary drive gear is going to be removed, loosen the nut (**Figure 7**) at this time but don't remove the nut or gear. You will need the clutch housing to aid in removal. Place a broad-tipped screwdriver or aluminum wedge between the primary drive and driven gear (located on the backside of the clutch housing) to hold the gear while you loosen the nut. Don't try to use a shop cloth as the gears are bevel-cut and will cut the cloth to shreds. Also, watch your fingers—these gears are sharp, even on a well run-in bike.*

9. Remove the pressure plate and springs (**Figure 8**).

10. Remove all the clutch plates and friction discs (**Figure 9**).

11. Straighten out the locking tab on the clutch nut (**Figure 10**).

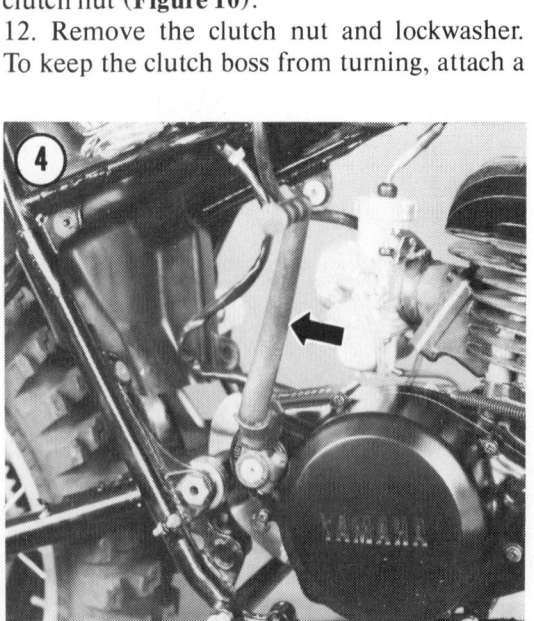

12. Remove the clutch nut and lockwasher. To keep the clutch boss from turning, attach a

CLUTCH AND TRANSMISSION

special tool like the "Grabbit" (**Figure 11**) to it.

NOTE
*The "Grabbit" is described under **Basic Hand Tools** in Chapter One.*

CAUTION
Do not insert a screwdriver or pry bar between the clutch housing and the clutch boss. The fingers on the clutch housing are fragile and can be tweaked out of alignment very easily.

13. Remove the clutch boss, steel ball and pushrod.
14. Remove the outer thrust washer (A, **Figure 12**) and the clutch housing (B, **Figure 12**).
15. Remove the spacer (**Figure 13**) and inner thrust washer (A, **Figure 14**).
16. Remove the primary drive gear nut (B, **Figure 14**) loosened in Step 8 and remove the lockwasher and gear (**Figure 15**).
17. Remove the Woodruff key and the O-ring seal on the crankshaft (**Figure 16**).

Inspection

NOTE
The following measurements apply to all models unless otherwise specified.

CHAPTER FIVE

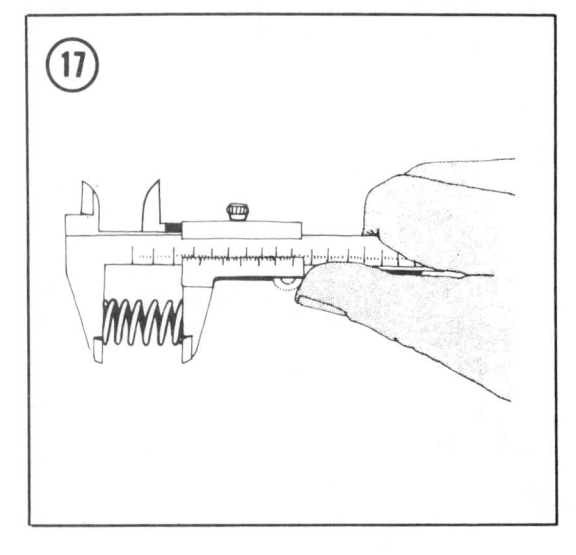

CLUTCH AND TRANSMISSION

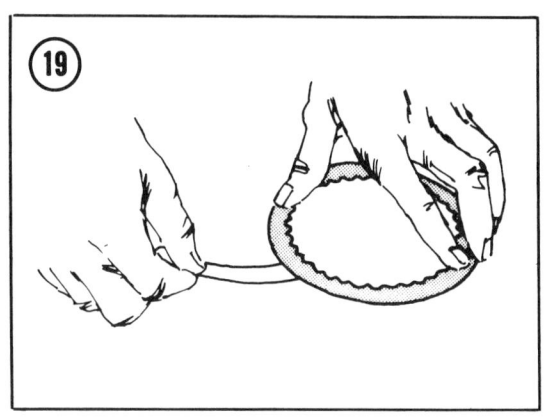

1. Clean all parts in a petroleum based solvent such as kerosene and thoroughly dry with compressed air.

2. Measure the free length of each clutch spring as shown in **Figure 17**. If any of the springs are worn to the following dimension or less, replace all springs as a set.
   a. All models except IT125G: 1.38 in. (35 mm)
   b. Model IT125G: 1.30 in. (33 mm)

3. Measure the thickness of each friction disc at several places around the disc as shown in **Figure 18**. A new friction disc measures 0.12 in. (3.0 mm). Replace any that measure 0.106 in. (2.7 mm) or less. For optimum performance, replace all discs as a set even if only a few need replacement.

4. Check the clutch plates for warpage on a surface plate such as a piece of plate glass (**Figure 19**). Replace any that are warped 0.002 in. (0.05 mm) or more. For optimum performance, replace all plates as a set even if only a few require replacement.

5. Inspect the condition of the pushrod assembly (**Figure 20**) within the pressure plate. If the end is damaged, remove the nut, spring and plate washer (**Figure 21**) and remove the assembly. Replace the assembly if damaged.

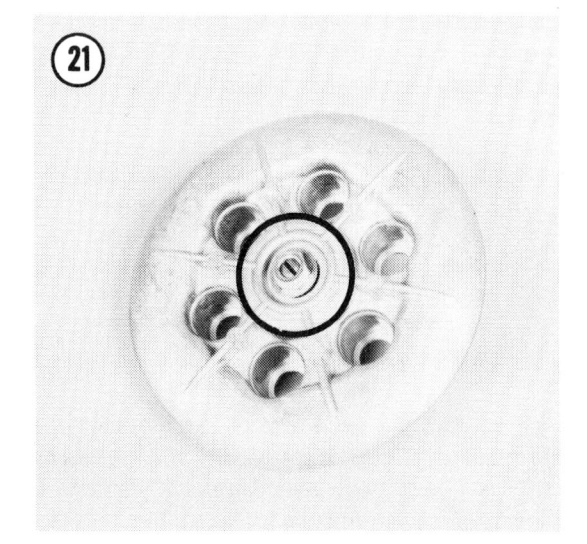

6. Inspect the condition of the grooves in the pressure plate and clutch boss (A, **Figure 22**). If either shows signs of wear or galling (**Figure 23**) it should be replaced.

7. Inspect the condition of the inner splines (B, **Figure 22**) in the clutch boss; if damaged the clutch boss should be replaced.

8. Inspect the condition of the teeth on the primary driven gear and kickstarter gear (**Figure 24**). Remove any small nicks on the gear teeth with an oilstone. If damage is severe as shown in **Figure 25** the clutch housing should be removed. This damage was caused by the primary drive gear working loose from the crankshaft.

9. Inspect the condition of the slots in the clutch housing (**Figure 26**) for cracks, nicks or galling where it comes in contact with the friction disc tabs. If any severe damage is evident (**Figure 27**), the housing must be replaced. This condition will cause erratic clutch operation.

10. Apply a light coat of oil to the clutch housing inner bushing (**Figure 28**) and insert the spacer. It should be a smooth finger-press fit and should rotate smoothly within the bushing. If rotation is rough or loose, replace either the spacer or the clutch housing.

11. Roll the clutch pushrod (**Figure 29**) on a flat surface to check for bends or damage. Examine the end that rides against the ball (**Figure 30**); if a worn depression is evident the pushrod should be replaced. This type of wear will take up some of the clutch movement adjustment.

NOTE
*The clutch pushrod varies in length and construction with the different models as shown in **Figure 1**. Also on models with 2 pushrods, the ends are bluish in color due to a manufacturing process and not due to lack of lubrication.*

12. Inspect the condition of the teeth on the primary drive gear. Remove any small nicks on the gear teeth with an oilstone. If damage is severe, the gear must be replaced.

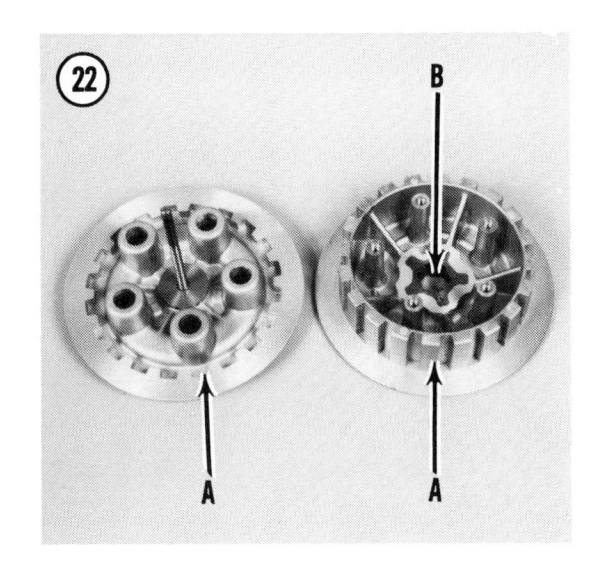

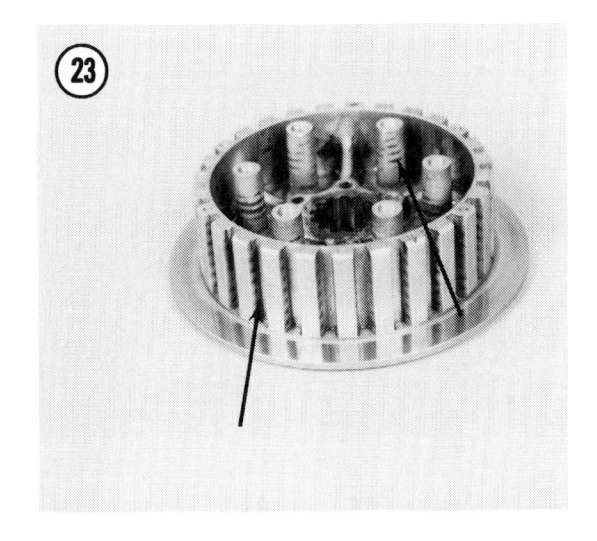

CLUTCH AND TRANSMISSION

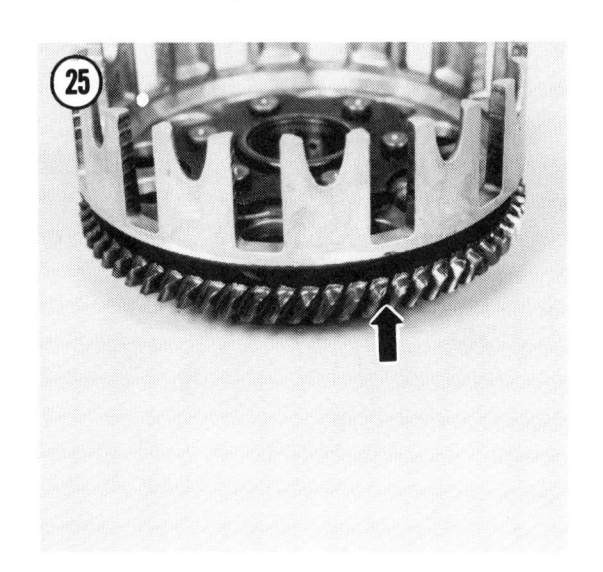

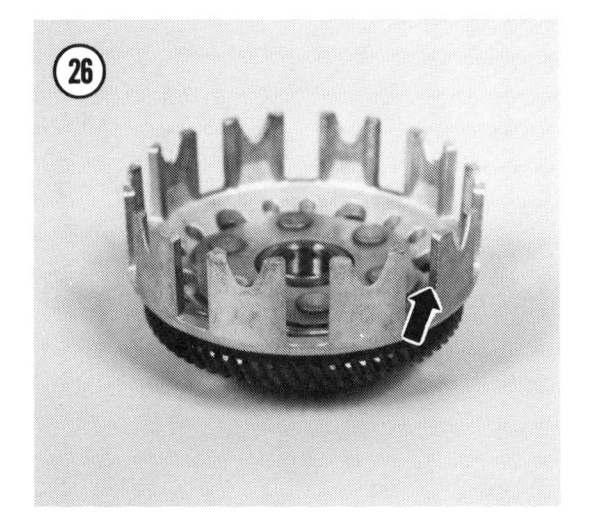

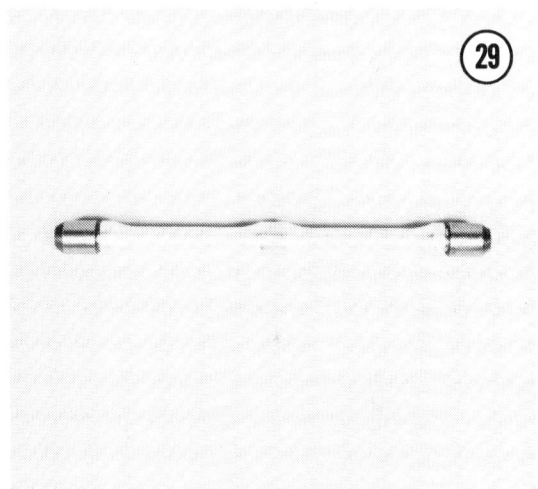

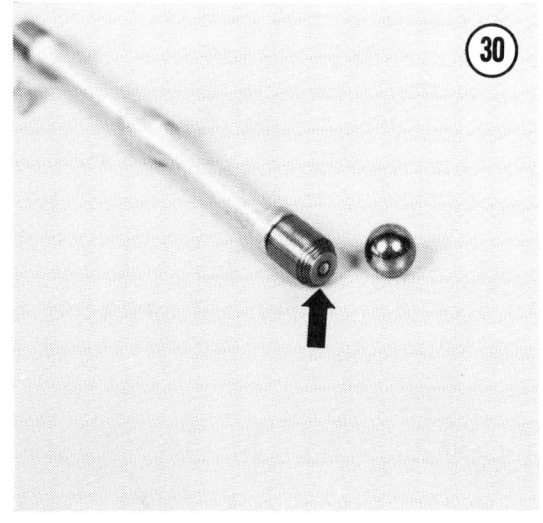

125

Assembly/Installation

1. Install a new O-ring seal on the crankshaft (**Figure 31**). Set it into place with a suitable size socket or piece of tubing (**Figure 32**). Install the Woodruff key (**Figure 33**). Make sure the key is seated correctly in the groove in the crankshaft.
2. Install the primary drive gear, lockwasher (**Figure 34**) and nut (**Figure 35**). Do not try to tighten the nut at this time.
3. Install the inner thrust washer and spacer (**Figure 36**).
4. Slide on the clutch housing and install the inner thrust washer (**Figure 37**).
5. Slide on the clutch boss and install a new lockwasher (**Figure 38**). Make sure the 3 locating tangs are installed into the holes in the clutch boss. Always replace the lockwasher at least every other time the clutch is disassembled or if it looks like the one on the left in **Figure 39**.
6. Install the clutch nut and tighten (**Figure 40**) to the torque specifications in **Table 2**. Use the "Grabbit" as described in Step 12, *Removal/Disassembly.*
7. Bend up the tab of the lockwasher onto one of the flats on the clutch nut (**Figure 41**).

CAUTION
If either friction or clutch plates have been cleaned or replaced, apply clean clutch/transmission oil to all plate surfaces before installation to avoid having the clutch lock up when used for the first time.

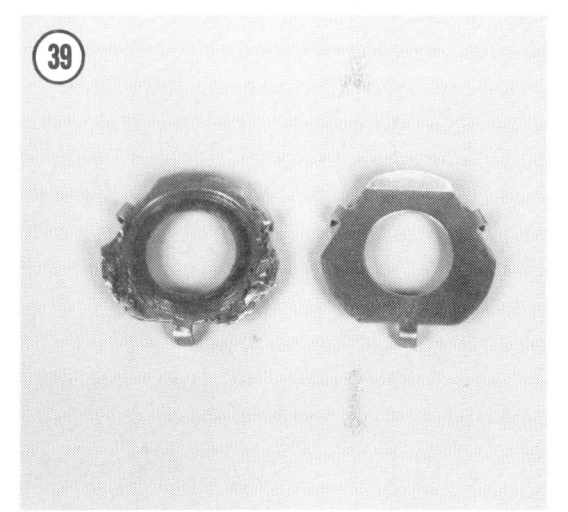

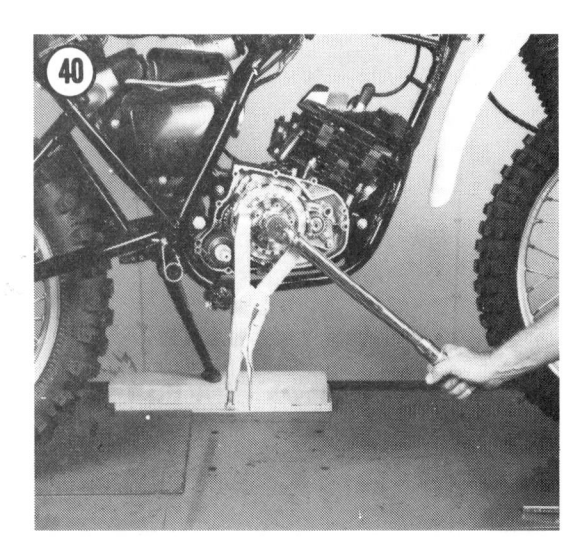

CLUTCH AND TRANSMISSION

127

8. Install a friction disc first (**Figure 42**) and then a clutch plate. Continue to install a friction disc then a clutch plate until all are installed. Refer to **Table 1** for the exact number of friction discs and clutch plates for your specific model.

9. Apply a light coat of grease to the clutch pushrod and install it (**Figure 43** or **Figure 44**).

10. Apply a light coat of grease to the ball and install it (**Figure 45**). Make sure it does not roll out.

11. On models so marked, align the arrows on the pressure plate with the arrows on the clutch boss (**Figure 46**) and install it. On models without the arrows, alignment is not necessary.

12. Install the clutch springs and bolts. Tighten the bolts (**Figure 47**) in a crisscross pattern in 2-3 stages.

13. Insert a broad tipped screwdriver or aluminum wedge between the primary drive and driven gear (located on the backside of the clutch housing) and tighten the primary drive gear nut (**Figure 48**) to the torque value in **Table 2**. Don't try to use a shop cloth to hold the gear as the gears are bevel-cut and will cut the cloth to shreds. Also, watch your fingers as these gears are sharp—even on a well run-in bike.

14. Install the 2 locating dowels and new cover gasket (**Figure 49** or **Figure 50**).

15. Install the cover and tighten all screws.

16. Install the kickstarter lever, skidplate, rear brake pedal assembly and right-hand footpeg.

17. Refill the clutch/transmission with oil as described in Chapter Three.

CLUTCH AND TRANSMISSION

129

CLUTCH CABLE

Replacement

In time the clutch cable will stretch to the point that it will have to be replaced.

1. Turn the fuel shutoff valve to the OFF position and remove the fuel line to the carburetor.
2. Remove the seat.
3. Remove the fuel tank.

NOTE
Some of the following figures are shown with the engine partially disassembled for clarity. It is not necessary to remove these components for cable replacement.

4. Pull the protective boot away from the clutch lever and loosen the locknut and adjusting barrel (**Figure 51**).
5. Slip the cable end out of the hand lever.
6. At the top of the engine, pry open the locking tab (**Figure 52**) on the top of the push lever and remove the cable end.
7. On models with the clutch release mechanism on the left-hand side, remove the bolt and clamp (**Figure 53**) securing the clutch cable to the top of the crankcase.
8. On models with the clutch release mechanism on the right-hand side, remove the cable from the clip (**Figure 54**) on the side of the cylinder.

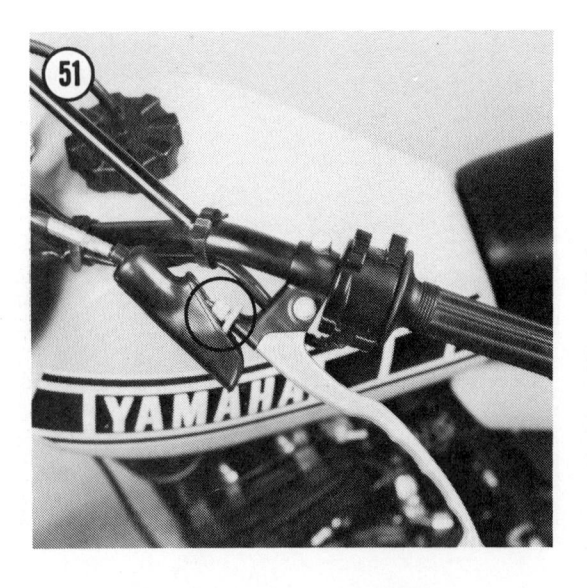

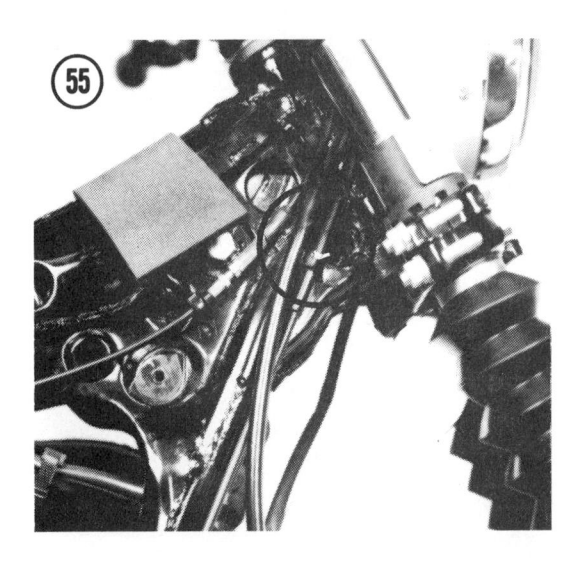

CLUTCH AND TRANSMISSION

NOTE
Prior to removing the cable make a drawing (or take a Polaroid picture) of the cable routing through the frame. It is very easy to forget after it has been removed. Replace it exactly as it was, avoiding any sharp turns.

9. Pull the cable out of any retaining clips on the frame (**Figure 55**).

10. Remove the cable and replace it with a new one.

11. Install by reversing these removal steps. Be sure to bend over the locking tab on the clutch push lever (**Figure 56**).

12. Adjust the cable as described in Chapter Three.

CLUTCH RELEASE (PUSH LEVER) MECHANISM

Removal/Installation

1. Perform Steps 4-9 under *Clutch Cable Replacement* in this chapter.

2. Remove the locating bolt (**Figure 57**) securing the release mechanism in the crankcase.

3. Withdraw the push lever and remove the washer and spring.

4. Inspect the condition of the oil seal and roller bearing in the crankcase (**Figure 58**). Rotate the bearing with your finger; make sure it rotates smoothly with no signs of wear or

damage. If the bearing has to be replaced, the crankcase must be split to gain access to it; refer to Chapter Four.

5. Install the push lever, spring and washer (**Figure 59**) into the crankcase. Install the locating bolt.

6. Install the clutch cable by reversing Steps 4-9 under *Clutch Cable Replacement* in this chapter.

EXTERNAL SHIFT MECHANISM

The external shift mechanisms for the different engines are basically the same but all have different components and are assembled differently. For the following procedures, they are divided into groups and given a type designation.

The Type I external shift mechanism is found in the following models:
IT425G
IT400F
IT250G, F

The Type II external shift mechanism is found in the following models:
IT400E, D, C
IT250E, D

The Type III external shift mechanism is found in the following model:
IT175G

The Type IV external shift mechanism is found in the following models:
IT175F, E, D
IT125G

The external shift mechanism is located on the same side of the crankcase as the clutch assembly and can be removed with the engine in the frame. To remove the shift drum and shift forks it is necessary to remove the engine and split the crankcase. This procedure is covered under *Transmission and Internal Shift Mechanism* in this chapter.

NOTE
The gearshift lever is subject to a lot of abuse under trials event competition or very hard riding. If the motorcycle has been in a hard spill, the gearshift lever may have been hit and the shaft bent. It is very hard to straighten the shaft without subjecting the crankcase to abnormal stress where the shaft enters the case.

CLUTCH AND TRANSMISSION

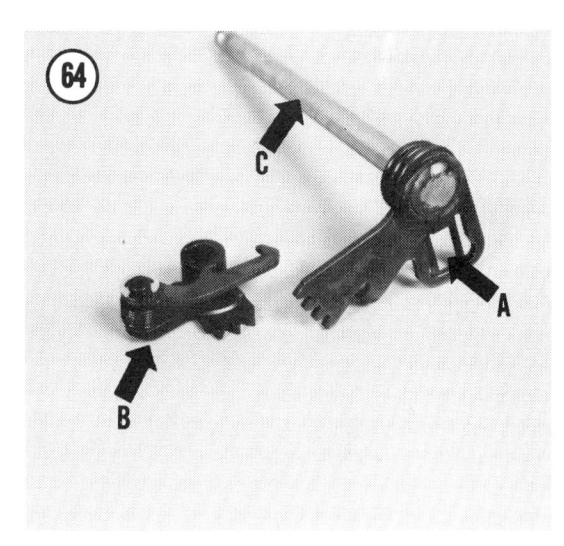

If the shaft is bent enough to prevent it from being withdrawn from the crankcase, there is little recourse but to cut the shaft off with a hacksaw very close to the crankcase. It is much cheaper in the long run to replace the shaft than risk damaging a very expensive crankcase.

The following procedures are fairly short but are kept separate to avoid any confusion between the different shift mechanism types.

Removal/Inspection/Installation (Type I)

1. Remove the clutch assembly as described under *Clutch Removal/Installation* for your specific model in this chapter.
2. Remove the gearshift lever (**Figure 60**).
3. Remove the E-clip (**Figure 61**) securing the shift pawl assembly.
4. Push down on the inner leg of the shift pawl and slide off the assembly (**Figure 62**).

NOTE
Don't lose the washer and plastic spacer on the left-hand side when the gearshift lever assembly is withdrawn.

5. Withdraw the gearshift lever assembly (**Figure 63**). See the NOTE regarding a bent shaft in the introduction to this procedure if the assembly is difficult to remove.
6. Inspect the condition of the gearshift lever return spring (A, **Figure 64**). If broken or weak it must be replaced. Use a new spacer when replacing the spring.
7. Inspect the shift pawl assembly spring (B, **Figure 64**). If broken or weak, remove the E-clip and replace the spring.
8. Inspect the gearshift lever assembly shaft (C, **Figure 64**) for bending, wear or other damage; replace if necessary.
9. Inspect the condition of the E-clip (**Figure 65**) on the backside of the shift pawl assembly. Replace if loose or worn.
10. Install the shift pawl assembly and install the E-clip.
11. Install the gearshift lever assembly. Align the index mark on the shift pawl assembly with the center of the shift lever assembly (A, **Figure 66**). Make sure the return spring is correctly positioned onto the stopper plate bolt (B, **Figure 66**).

12. Remove the drive sprocket cover.

13. Install the washer and plastic spacer (**Figure 67**) onto the shift lever shaft.

14. Install the drive sprocket cover and install the gearshift lever.

15. Install the clutch assembly as described in this chapter.

Removal/Inspection/Installation (Type II)

1. Remove the clutch assembly as described under *Clutch Removal/Installation* for your specific model in this chapter.

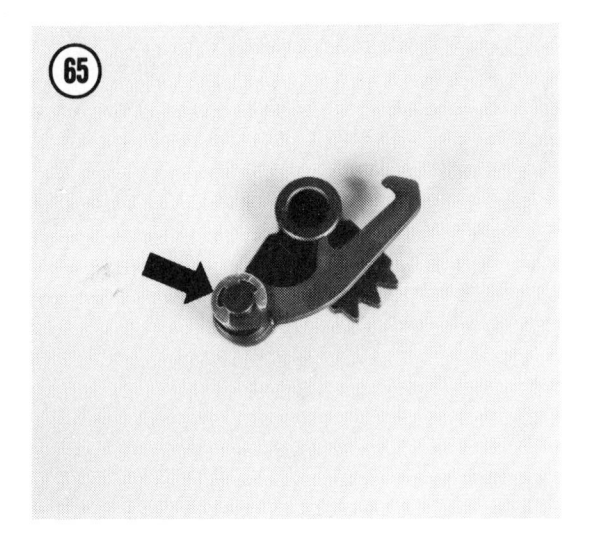

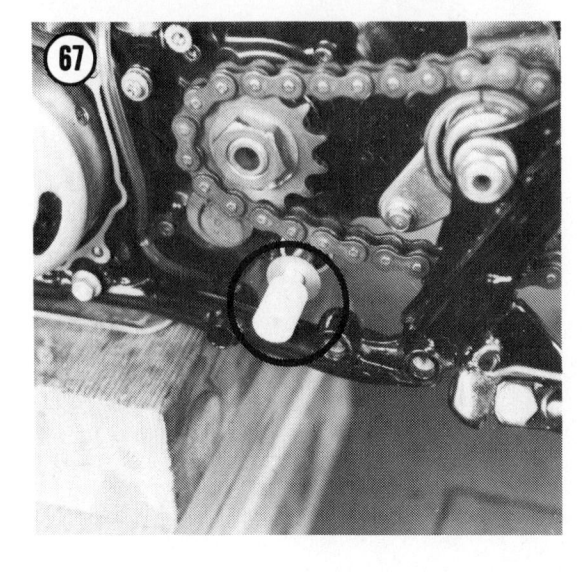

2. Remove the gearshift lever.

3. Withdraw the gearshift lever assembly (**Figure 68**). See the NOTE regarding a bent shaft in the introduction to this procedure if the assembly is difficult to remove.

4. Remove the E-clip (**Figure 69**) securing the shift pawl assembly and slide off the assembly (**Figure 70**).

5. Inspect the condition of the return spring on the shift lever assembly. If broken or weak it must be replaced. Use a new spacer when replacing the spring.

6. Inspect the shift pawl assembly spring. If broken or weak remove the E-clip and replace the spring.

7. Inspect the gearshift lever assembly shaft (**Figure 71**) for bending, wear or other damage; replace if necessary.

8. Install the shift pawl assembly and install the E-clip (**Figure 69**).

9. Install the gearshift lever assembly. Align the index mark on the shift pawl assembly with the center of the shift lever assembly (**Figure 72**). Make sure the return spring is correctly positioned onto the stopper plate bolt (**Figure 73**).

10. Install the shift lever and install the clutch assembly as described in this chapter.

Removal/Inspection/Installation (Type III)

1. Remove the clutch assembly as described under *Clutch Removal/Installation* for your specific model in this chapter.

CLUTCH AND TRANSMISSION

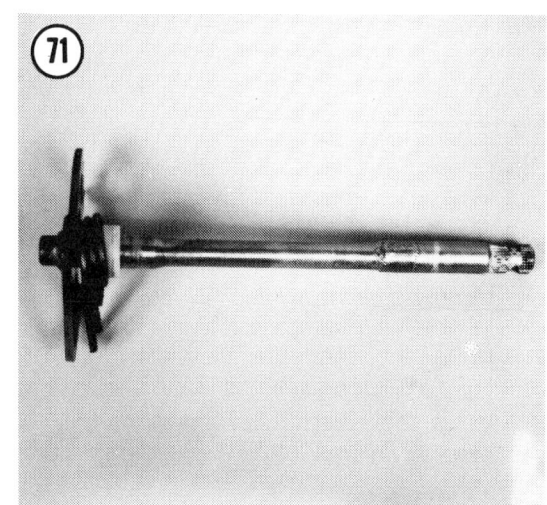

135

2. Remove the gearshift lever (**Figure 74**).

3. Withdraw the gearshift lever assembly (A, **Figure 75**). See the NOTE regarding a bent shaft in the introduction to this procedure if the assembly is difficult to remove.

4. Remove the flange bolt securing the shift pawl and spring (**Figure 76**) and remove them.

5. Remove the flat head screw (A, **Figure 77**) securing the shift cam and remove the cam and the flat key.

6. Inspect the condition of the spring. If broken or weak it must be replaced.

7. Inspect the gearshift lever assembly shaft for bending, wear or other damage; replace if necessary.

8. Install the flat key and shift cam. Apply Loctite Lock N' Seal to the threads of the flat head screw prior to installing it. Tighten it securely.

9. Install the spring (B, **Figure 77**) as shown with the lower end in the relief in the crankcase.

10. Install the shift pawl, engaging correctly it with the spring and install the flange bolt (**Figure 76**). Tighten the flange bolt securely.

11. Install the gearshift lever assembly. Make sure the return spring is correctly positioned onto the stopper plate bolt (B, **Figure 75**) and that it is engaged with the pins on the shift cam (C, **Figure 75**).

12. Install the shift lever and install the clutch assembly as described in this chapter.

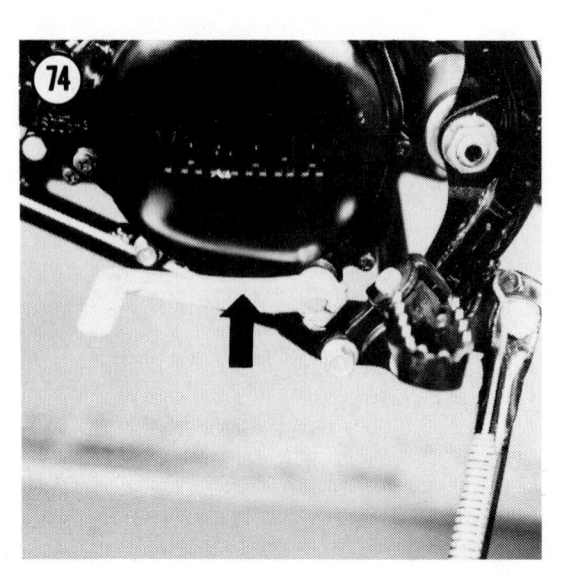

CLUTCH AND TRANSMISSION

Removal/Inspection/Installation (Type IV)

1. Remove the clutch assembly as described under *Clutch Removal/Installation* for your specific model in this chapter.
2. Remove the gearshift lever.
3. Withdraw the gearshift lever shaft (**Figure 78**). See the NOTE regarding a bent shaft in the introduction to this procedure if the assembly is difficult to remove.

NOTE
Do not lose the small bushing on the backside of the engagement finger.

4. Push up on the upper part of the shift arm (**Figure 79**) and disengage it from the shift cam. Pull the shift arm assembly out and remove it.
5. Remove the return spring (A, **Figure 80**), flange bolt (B, **Figure 80**) and shift pawl (C, **Figure 80**).
6. Remove the E-clip (**Figure 81**) and remove the washer and shift cam.
7. Remove the shift cam pin (**Figure 82**).
8. Inspect the condition of the return spring on the shift arm assembly. If broken or weak it must be replaced.

NOTE
On early production models of the IT175D there is a Factory Technical Bulletin regarding a modification to the shift lever assembly for added shifting reliability. The

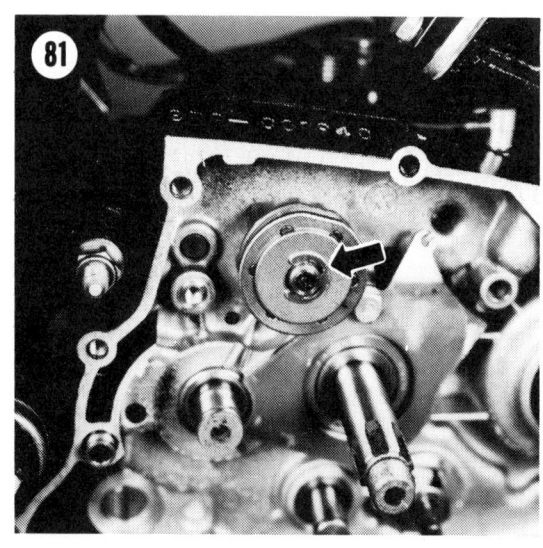

CHAPTER FIVE

window must be opened up a little at the lower right-hand corner to allow additional movement of the arm. Grind out 0.002-0.003 in. (0.5-0.7 mm) of material from this area (**Figure 83**). If you use a power grinder, work slowly so as not to remove too much material. Scribe a line on first and work down to it slowly. **Wear eye protection** if a power grinder is used. On this particular model, the alignment of the lever to the shift drum is also critical; refer to Steps 17-19. The engine serial numbers affected by this modification are as follows: 1W2-000101 to -000220, 1W2-000421 to -000740, 1W2-002501 to -003710 and 1W2-006831 to -006829. Engine serial numbers not listed have already been modified by the factory.

9. Inspect the shift pawl return spring. If broken or weak it should be replaced.
10. Inspect the gearshift lever shaft for bending, wear or other damage; replace if necessary.
11. Install the shift cam pin.
12. Install the shift cam aligning the index mark on the cam with the one on the shaft (**Figure 84**).
13. Install the washer (**Figure 85**) and the E-clip (**Figure 81**).
14. Install the shift pawl, flange bolt and return spring. Make sure the shift pawl roller is riding on the back portion of the shift cam as shown in **Figure 86**.
15. Push up on the upper part of the shift arm and push the shift arm assembly into place (**Figure 87**).
16. Shift the transmission into 1st gear. The index mark on the shift cam and upper shift arm must align (**Figure 88**) for a proper shift progression from gear to gear.
17. If they do not align, remove the shift arm assembly and straighten the locking tab on the locknut. Loosen the locknut and turn the eccentric screw (**Figure 89**) in or out for proper alignment. Reinstall the shift arm assembly and recheck alignment; repeat until correct. After alignment is correct, tighten the locknut and bend up one side of the locking tab against it.
18. Reinstall the shift arm assembly.

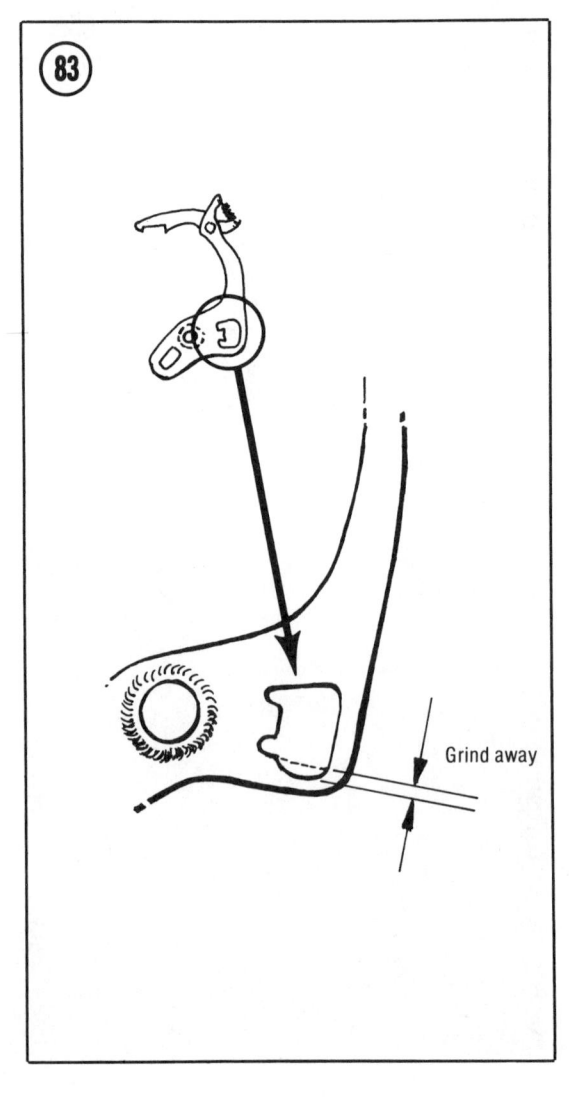

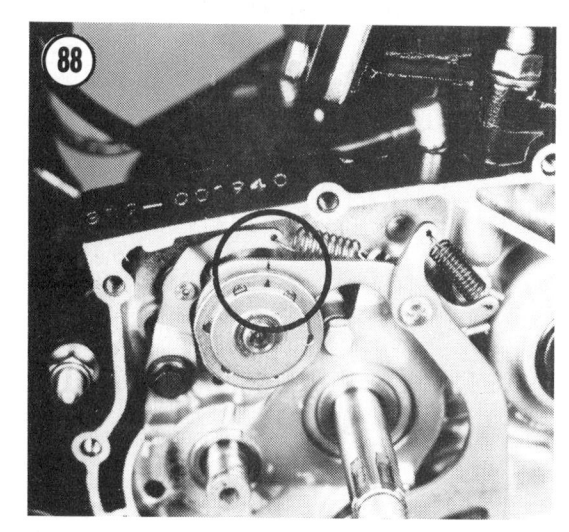

CLUTCH AND TRANSMISSION

19. Install the small bushing (**Figure 90**) into the backside of the engagement finger and install the shift lever shaft.

> *NOTE*
> *Make sure the return spring is properly engaged with the stopper bolt (eccentric screw); refer to **Figure 91**.*

20. Make sure the finger is correctly installed into the elongated slot in the shift arm assembly.
21. Install the shift lever and clutch assembly as described in this chapter.

TRANSMISSION AND INTERNAL SHIFT MECHANISM

The transmission and internal shift mechanism (shift drum and forks) are basically the same on all models. The transmission is either a 5-speed or 6-speed unit; however, there are 4 different internal shift mechanisms with major or minor differences.

To gain access to the transmission and internal shift mechanism it is necessary to remove the engine and split the crankcase. Once the crankcase has been split, removal of the transmission and shift drum and forks is a simple task of pulling the assemblies up and out of the crankcase. Installation is more complicated and is covered more completely than the removal sequence.

Because of the differences among models pay particular attention to the location of spacers, washers and bearings during disassembly. Write down the order in which parts were removed to simplify assembly and ensure the correct placement of all parts.

> *NOTE*
> *If disassembling a used, well run-in engine for the first time by yourself, pay particular attention to any additional shims that may have been added by a previous owner. These may have been added to take up the tolerance of worn components and must be reinstalled in the same position since the shims have developed a wear pattern. If new parts are going to be installed these shims may be eliminated. This is something you will have to determine upon reassembly.*

The transmission is either a 5-speed or 6-speed constant mesh type.

The 5-speed transmission (**Figure 92**) is found in the following models:
IT425G
IT400F, E, D, C

The 6-speed transmission (**Figure 93** or **Figure 94**) is found in the following models:
IT250G, F, E, D
IT175G, F, E, D
IT125G

CLUTCH AND TRANSMISSION

Fig. 92 — 5-SPEED TRANSMISSION (MODELS IT425G, IT400F, E, D, C)

1. Bearing
2. Circlip
3. Thrust washer (** not used on Models IT425G, IT400C)
4. Countershaft 1st gear
5. Countershaft 4th gear
6. Circlip
   (* not used on Model IT400C)
7. Splined washer
8. Countershaft 3rd gear
9. Countershaft 5th gear
10. Washer
    (* not used on Model IT400C)
11. Countershaft 2nd gear
12. Countershaft
13. Main shaft
14. Main shaft 4th gear
15. Main shaft 3rd gear
16. Main shaft 5th gear
17. Main shaft 2nd gear
18. Needle bearing

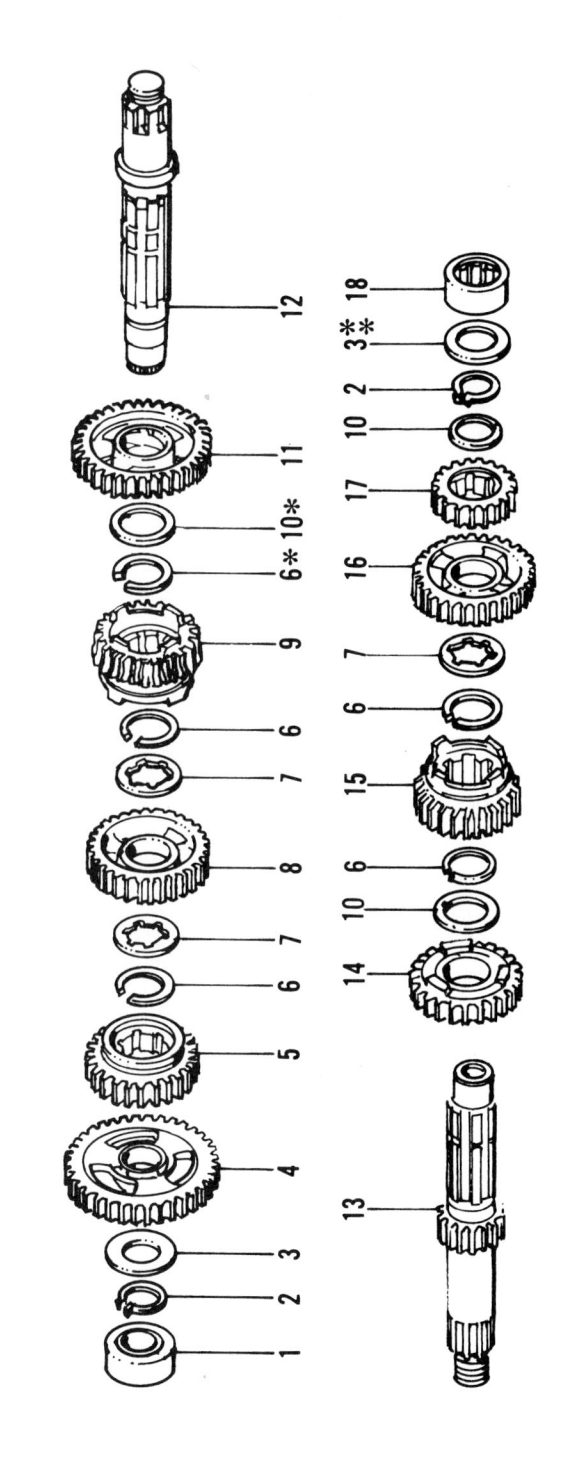

CHAPTER FIVE

6-SPEED TRANSMISSION (MODELS IT250G, G; IT175G, F, E, D; IT125G)

1. Bearing
2. Circlip
3. Thrust washer
4. Countershaft 1st gear
5. Countershaft 5th gear
6. Circlip
7. Splined washer
8. Countershaft 3rd gear
9. Countershaft 4th gear
10. Countershaft 6th gear
11. Shim
12. Countershaft 2nd gear
13. Countershaft
14. Main shaft
15. Main shaft 5th gear
16. Washer
17. Circlip
18. Main shaft 3rd/4th gear
19. Circlip
20. Washer
21. Main shaft 6th gear
22. Main shaft 2nd gear
23. Washer (not used on Models IT175G, F, E, IT125G)
24. Circlip
25. Washer (not used on Models IT175G, F, E, IT125G)
26. Needle bearing

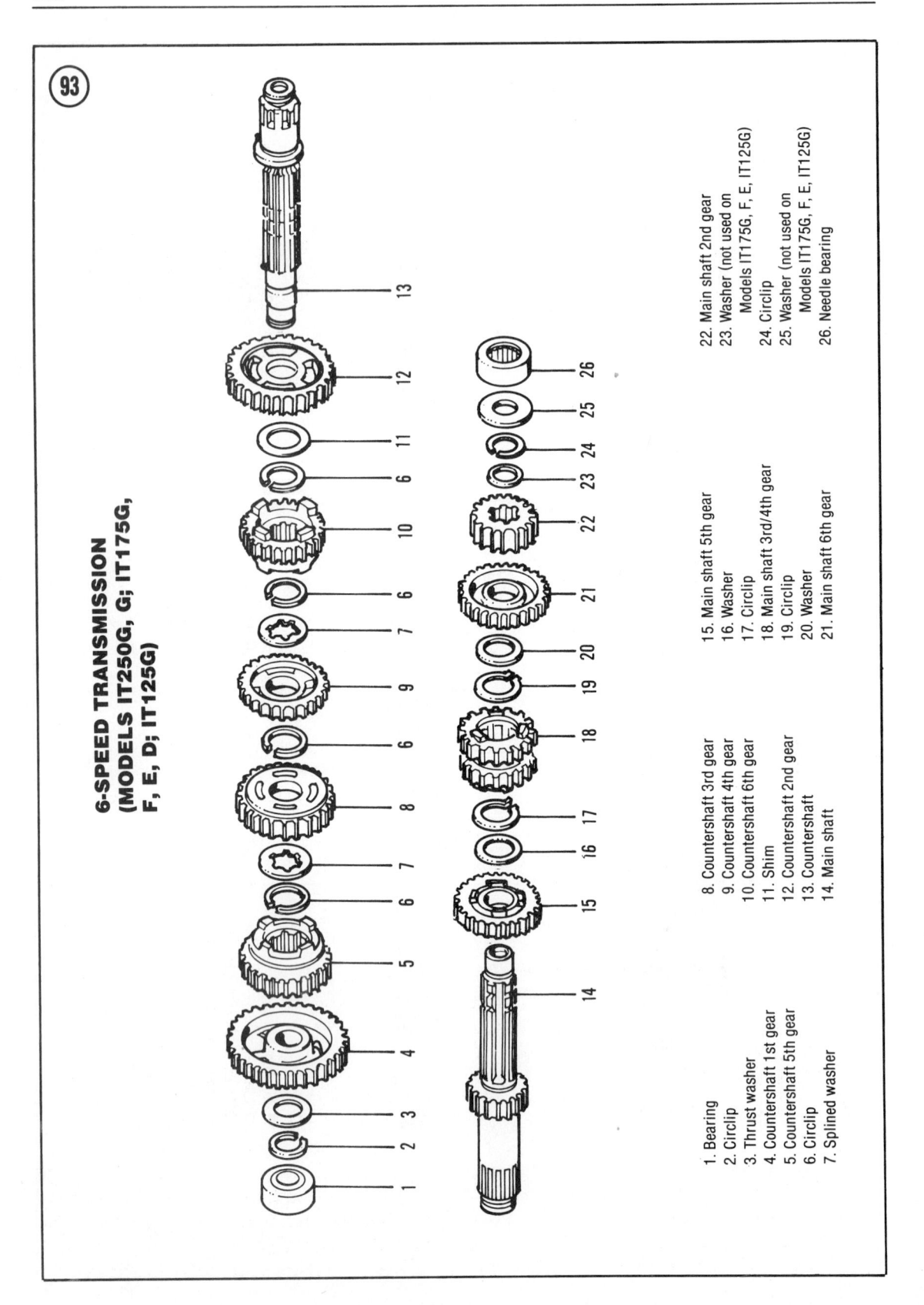

CLUTCH AND TRANSMISSION

94

**6-SPEED TRANSMISSION
(MODEL IT 250E, D)**

1. Bearing
2. Circlip
3. Thrust washer
4. Countershaft 1st gear
5. Countershaft 5th gear
6. Countershaft 3rd gear
7. Circlip
8. Countershaft 4th gear
9. Countershaft 6th gear
10. Countershaft 2nd gear
11. Countershaft
12. Main shaft 1st gear
13. Main shaft 5th gear
14. Main shaft 3rd/4th gear
15. Main shaft 6th gear
16. Main shaft 2nd gear

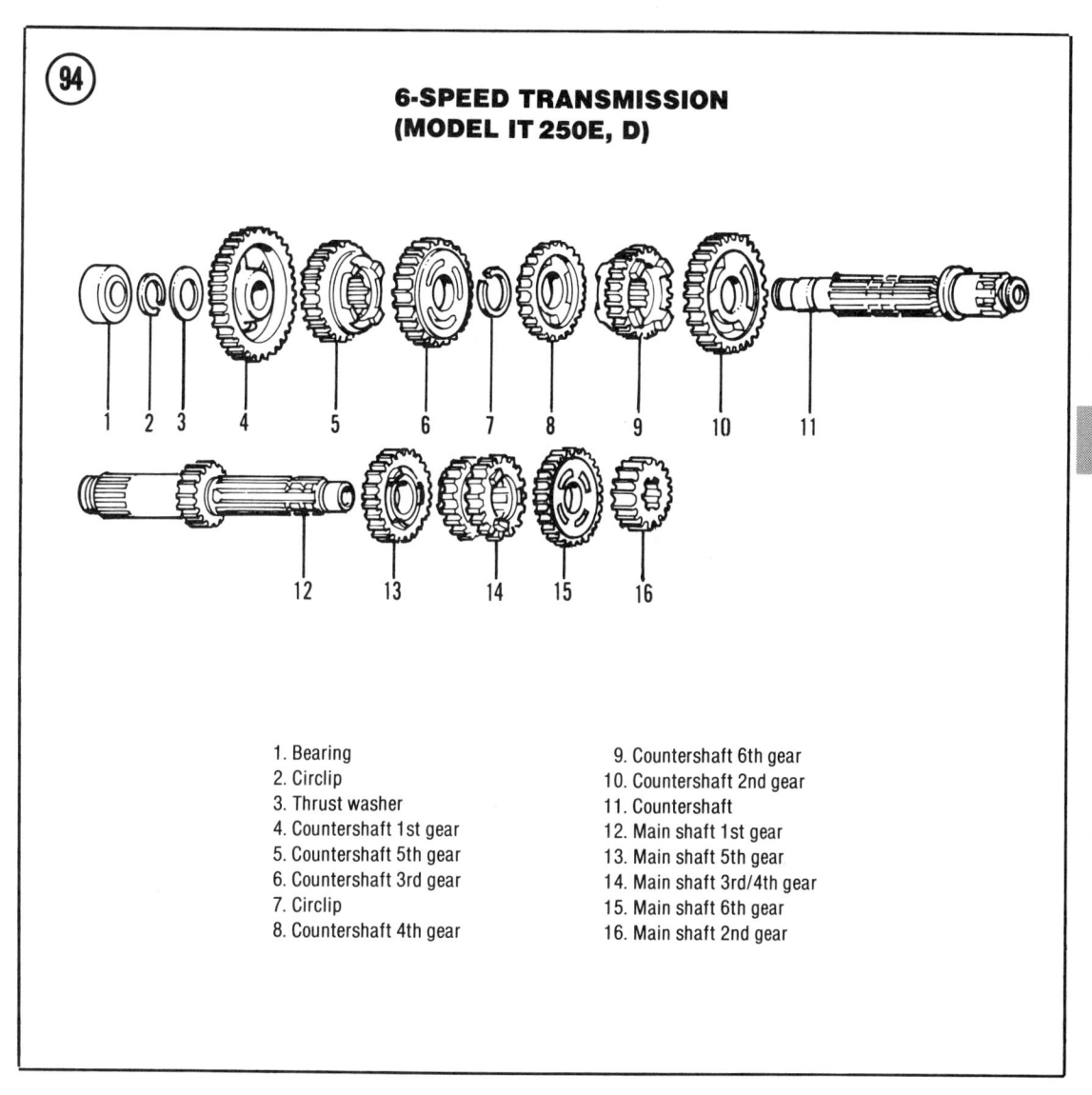

The internal shift mechanisms are basically the same but differences do occur in all models. They are separated into types that relate to different models and years.

The Type I internal shift mechanism (**Figure 95**) is found in the following models:

IT425G
IT400F
IT250G, F

The Type II internal shift mechanism (**Figure 96**) is found in the following models:
IT400E, D, C
IT250E, D

The Type III internal shift mechanism (**Figure 97**) is found in the following model:
IT175G

The Type IV internal shift mechanism (**Figure 98**) is found in the following models:
IT175F, E, D
IT125G

The following procedures cover a typical 5-speed transmission and a typical 6-speed transmission. There are variations among different models using these transmissions so pay particular attention to the location of spacers and washers during disassembly. Disassembly and inspection procedures for both the transmission and internal shift components are covered later in this chapter.

CHAPTER FIVE

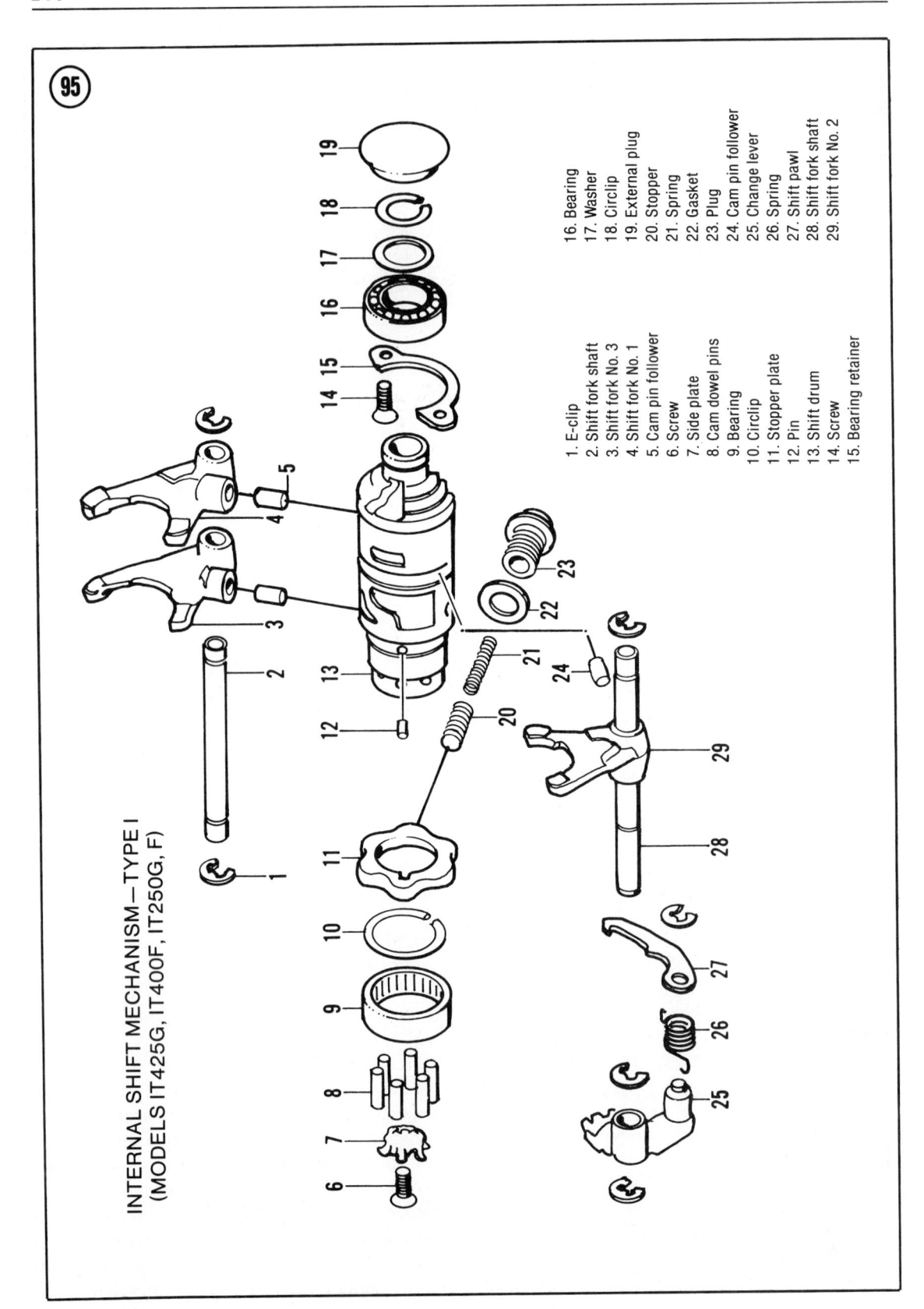

INTERNAL SHIFT MECHANISM—TYPE I (MODELS IT425G, IT400F, IT250G, F)

1. E-clip
2. Shift fork shaft
3. Shift fork No. 3
4. Shift fork No. 1
5. Cam pin follower
6. Screw
7. Side plate
8. Cam dowel pins
9. Bearing
10. Circlip
11. Stopper plate
12. Pin
13. Shift drum
14. Screw
15. Bearing retainer
16. Bearing
17. Washer
18. Circlip
19. External plug
20. Stopper
21. Spring
22. Gasket
23. Plug
24. Cam pin follower
25. Change lever
26. Spring
27. Shift pawl
28. Shift fork shaft
29. Shift fork No. 2

CLUTCH AND TRANSMISSION 145

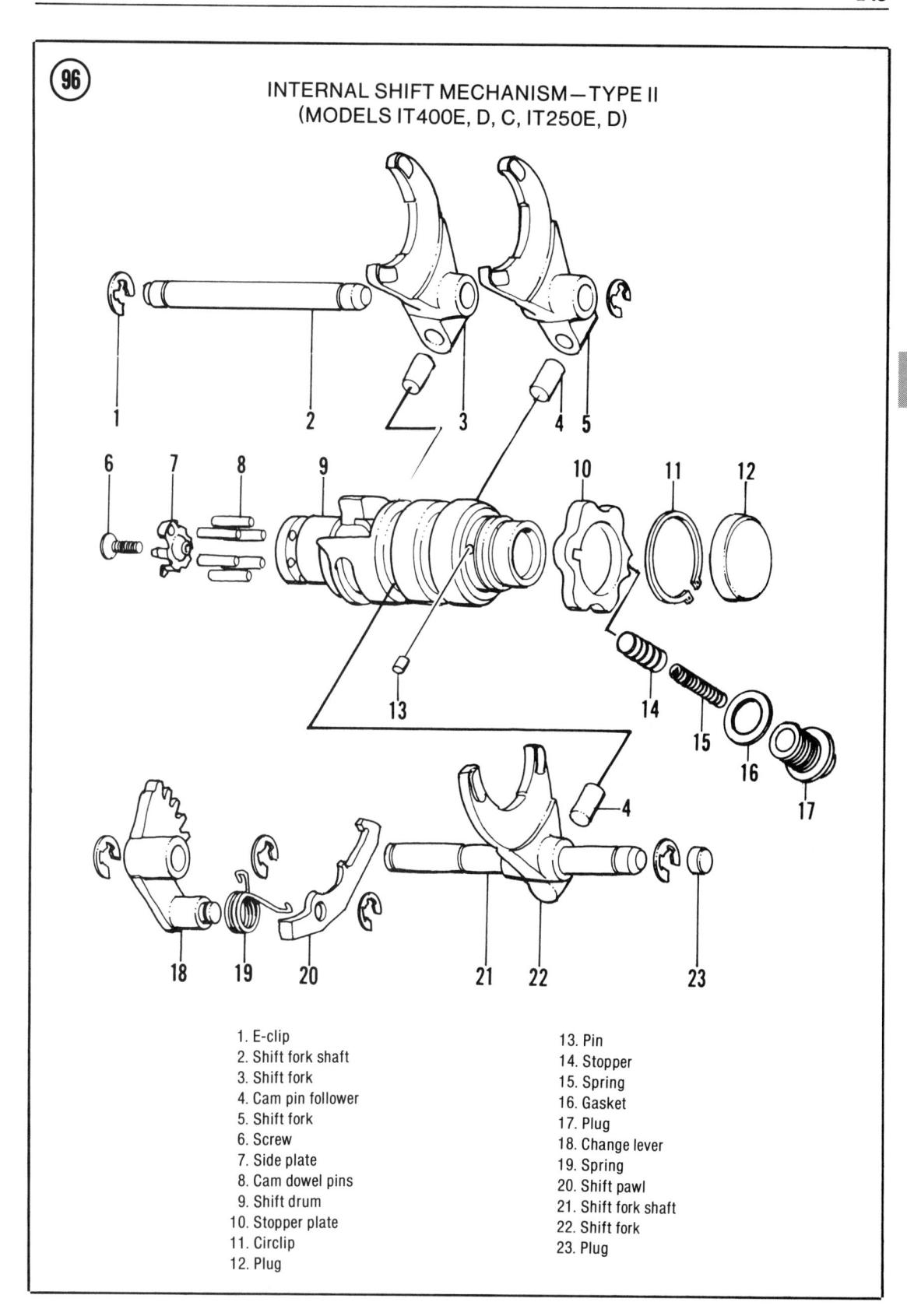

INTERNAL SHIFT MECHANISM—TYPE II
(MODELS IT400E, D, C, IT250E, D)

1. E-clip
2. Shift fork shaft
3. Shift fork
4. Cam pin follower
5. Shift fork
6. Screw
7. Side plate
8. Cam dowel pins
9. Shift drum
10. Stopper plate
11. Circlip
12. Plug
13. Pin
14. Stopper
15. Spring
16. Gasket
17. Plug
18. Change lever
19. Spring
20. Shift pawl
21. Shift fork shaft
22. Shift fork
23. Plug

CHAPTER FIVE

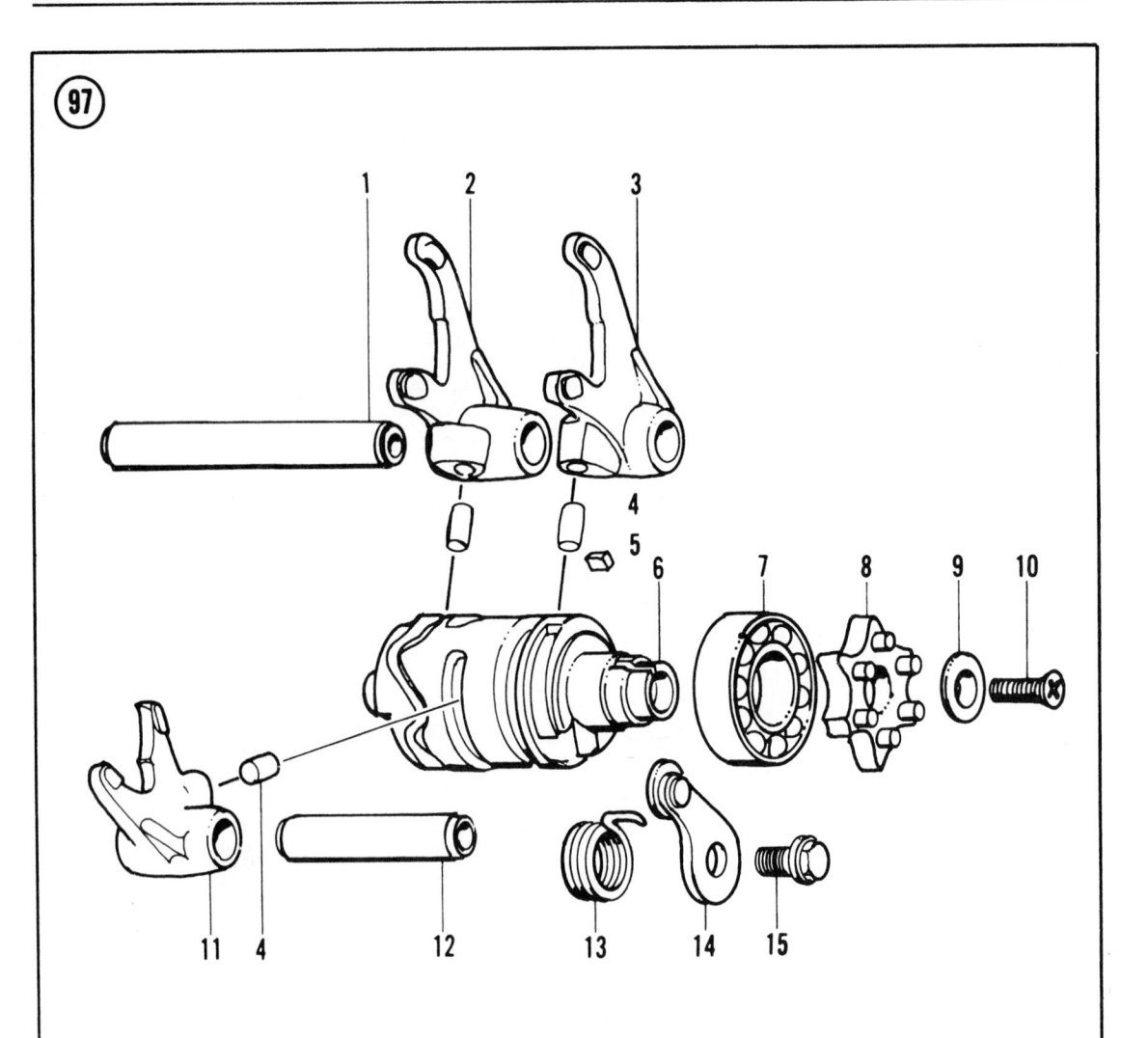

(97)

INTERNAL SHIFT MECHANISM—TYPE III
(MODEL IT175G)

1. Shift fork shaft (long)
2. Shift fork No. 3
3. Shift fork No. 1
4. Cam pin follower
5. Key
6. Shift drum
7. Bearing
8. Stopper plate
9. Washer
10. Screw
11. Shift fork No. 2
12. Shift fork shaft (short)
13. Spring
14. Shift pawl
15. Bolt

CLUTCH AND TRANSMISSION

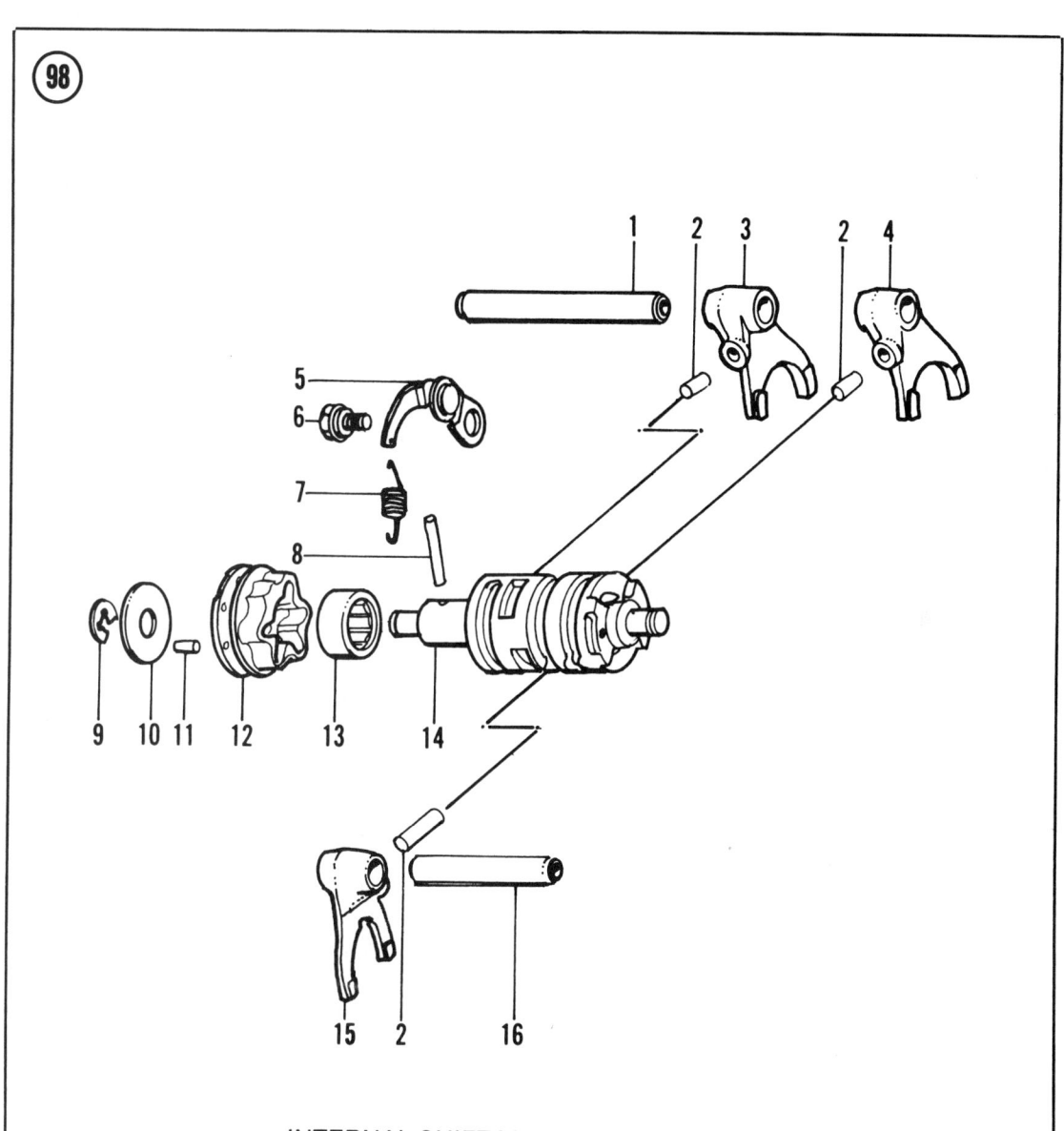

98

INTERNAL SHIFT MECHANISM—TYPE IV
(MODELS IT175F, E, D, IT125G)

1. Shift fork shaft (long)
2. Cam pin follower
3. Shift fork No. 3
4. Shift fork No. 1
5. Shift pawl
6. Bolt
7. Spring
8. Pin
9. E-clip
10. Washer
11. Dowel pin
12. Stopper pin
13. Bearing
14. Shift drum
15. Shift fork No. 2
16. Shift fork shaft (short)

5-Speed Transmission and Internal Shift Mechanism Removal/Installation

1. Remove the engine and split the crankcase as described under *Crankcase Disassembly* for your specific model.

2. Pull the shift fork shafts up just enough to free them from their bearing holes in the crankcase.

3. Pivot the shafts away from the shift drum (**Figure 99**) to allow room for shift drum removal.

4. Remove the shift drum.

5. Remove the shift forks and shafts (A, **Figure 100**) and remove both transmission assemblies (B, **Figure 100**).

6. Disassemble and inspect the shift forks and transmission assemblies as described later in this chapter.

7. Install the 2 transmission assemblies by meshing them together in their proper relationship to each other. Install them in the left-hand crankcase. Hold the washer in place on the main shaft (**Figure 101**) and make sure it is still positioned correctly after the assemblies are completely installed (**Figure 102**). After both assemblies are installed, tap on the end of both shafts with a plastic or rubber mallet to make sure they are completely seated.

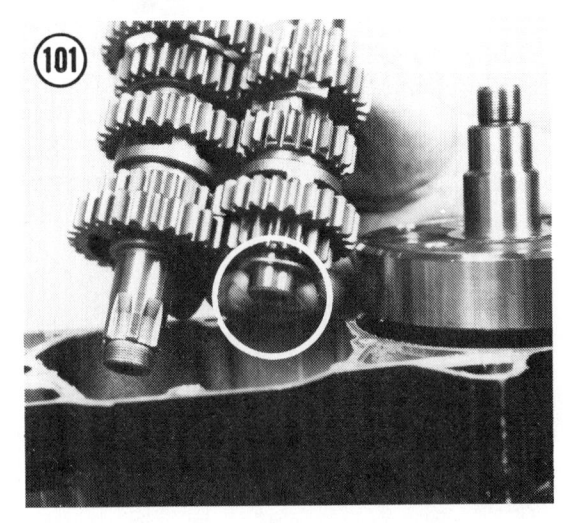

CLUTCH AND TRANSMISSION 149

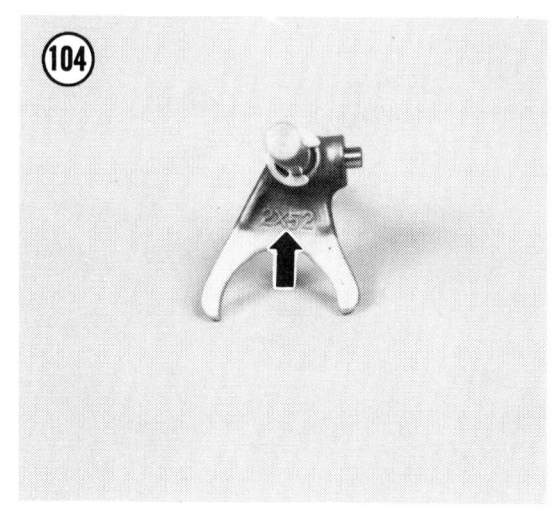

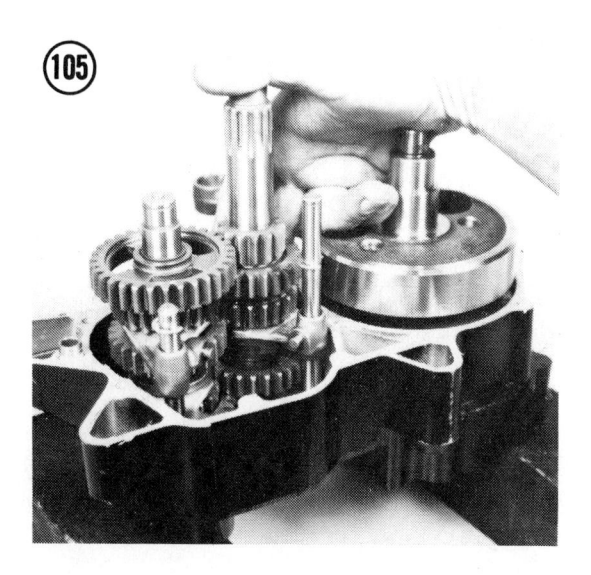

NOTE
*If the washer shown in **Figure 101** does not seat correctly it will hold the transmission shaft up a little and prevent the crankcase halves from seating completely.*

8. Install the rear shift forks and shaft. Engage the shift forks into the grooves in the gears (**Figure 103**) but *do not* insert the shift fork shaft into the bearing hole in the crankcase. Leave it pivoted away from the shift drum.

NOTE
*If the shift forks have been disassembled, make sure the identifying mark (**Figure 104**) on each fork is facing **up**.*

9. Install the front shift fork and shaft. Pull up on the gear with the shift fork groove and engage the shift fork into the groove (**Figure 105**). *Do not* insert the shift fork shaft into the bearing hole in the crankcase (**Figure 106**)—leave it pivoted away from the shift drum.

10. Coat all shift drum bearing and sliding surfaces with assembly oil and install it. Pivot each shift fork assembly into mesh with the shift drum and insert fork shafts into crankcase holes. Make sure all 3 cam pin followers are in mesh with the shift drum grooves (**Figure 107**).

11. Spin the transmission shafts and shift through the gears using the shift drum. Make sure you can shift into all gears. This is the

time to find that something may be installed incorrectly—not after the crankcase is completely assembled.

NOTE
This procedure is best done with the aid of a helper as the assemblies are loose and won't spin very easily. Have the helper spin the transmission shaft while you turn the shift drum through all the gears.

12. Assemble the crankcase as described under *Crankcase Assembly* for your specific model.

6-Speed Transmission and Internal Shift Mechanism Removal/Installation

This procedure uses 3 different models to show many of the special steps for easy removal and installation.

1. Remove the engine and split the crankcase as described under *Crankcase Disassembly* for your specific model.

2. Pull the shift fork shafts up just enough to free them from their bearing holes in the crankcase.

3. Pivot the shafts away from the shift drum (**Figure 108**) to allow room for shift drum removal.

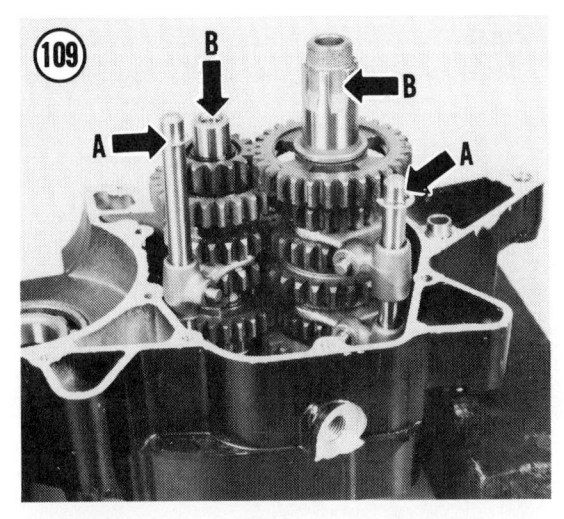

CLUTCH AND TRANSMISSION

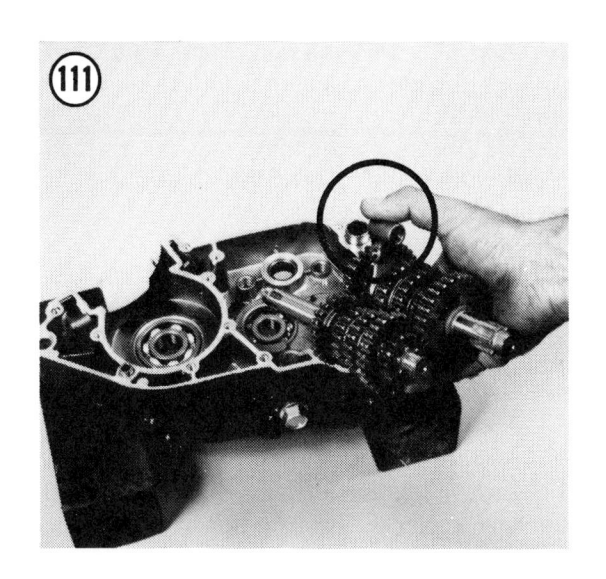

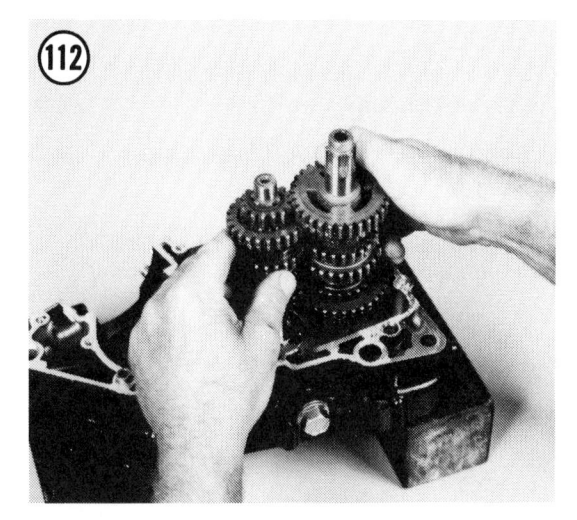

NOTE
On some later models the crankcases are smaller and do not have room to allow the the shift forks to pivot. On these models, pull the shift fork shafts up and out of the shift forks.

4. Remove the shift drum.
5. Remove the shift forks and shafts (A, **Figure 109**) and remove both transmission assemblies (B, **Figure 109**). On small-crankcase models, remove only the shift forks (**Figure 110**). The shift fork shafts have already been removed.
6. Disassemble and inspect the shift forks and transmission assemblies as described later in this chapter.
7. On the IT175, install the lower rear shift fork onto the transmission shaft (**Figure 111**) prior to installing the transmission assemblies as described in Step 8 (**Figure 112**). The surrounding area will be very tight if you try to install the fork later (**Figure 113**).
8. Install the 2 transmission assemblies by meshing them together in their proper relationship to each other. Place a rubber band around the top end (**Figure 114**) of the shafts to hold them together—*be sure to remove it after installation is complete.* After they are installed, tap on the end of both shafts with a plastic or rubber mallet (**Figure 115**) to make sure they are completely seated.

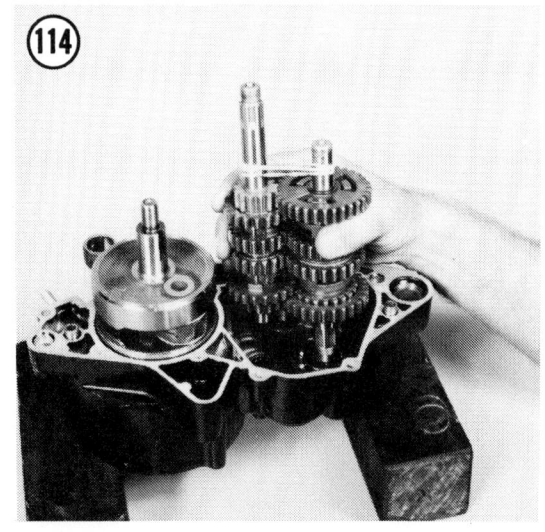

9. Install the rear shift forks and shaft. Engage the shift forks into the grooves in the gears but *do not* insert the shift fork shaft into the bearing hole in the crankcase. Leave it pivoted away from the shift drum.

NOTE
*If the shift forks have been disassembled, make sure the identifying mark (**Figure 116**) on each fork is facing **up**.*

10. Install the front shift fork and shaft (**Figure 117**). *Do not* insert the shift fork shaft into the bearing hole in the crankcase (**Figure 118**)—leave it pivoted away from the shift drum. On small-crankcase models, insert only the shift forks into their proper position (**Figure 119**). *Do not* install the shift fork shafts at this time.
11. Coat all bearing and sliding surfaces of the shift drum with assembly oil and install it. Pivot each shift fork assembly into mesh with the shift drum. On small-crankcase models, pivot the shift forks into position and then install the shift fork shafts. On the IT175 it is necessary to slightly lift up on the upper 2 gears and shift fork (**Figure 120**) to install the shift fork pin follower into the shift drum.
12. Make sure all 3 cam pin followers are in mesh with the shift drum grooves (**Figure 121**) and shafts are in crankcase holes.

13. Spin the transmission shafts and shift through the gears using the shift drum. Make sure you can shift into all gears. This is the time to find that something may be installed incorrectly—not after the crankcase is completely assembled.

NOTE
This procedure is best done with the aid of a helper as the assemblies are loose and won't spin very easily. Have the helper spin the transmission shaft while you turn the shift drum through all the gears.

14. Assemble the crankcase as described under *Crankcase Assembly* for your specific model.

Main Shaft Disassembly/Inspection/Assembly (5-Speed Transmission)

Refer to **Figure 92** for this procedure.

NOTE
*A helpful "tool" that should be used for transmission disassembly is a large egg flat (the type that restaurants get their eggs in). As you remove a part from the shaft set it in one of the depressions in the same position from which it was removed (**Figure 122**). This is an easy way to remember the correct relationship of all parts.*

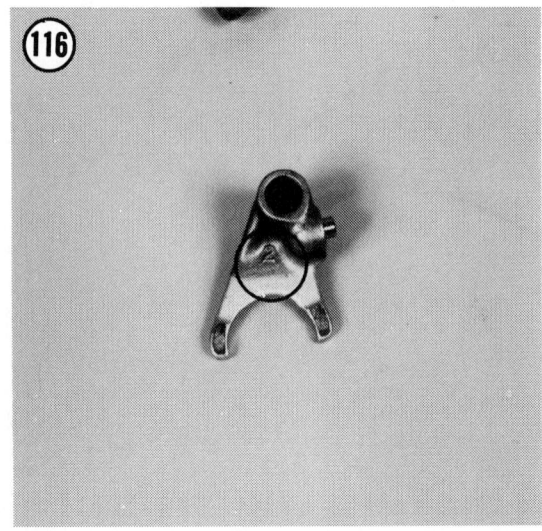

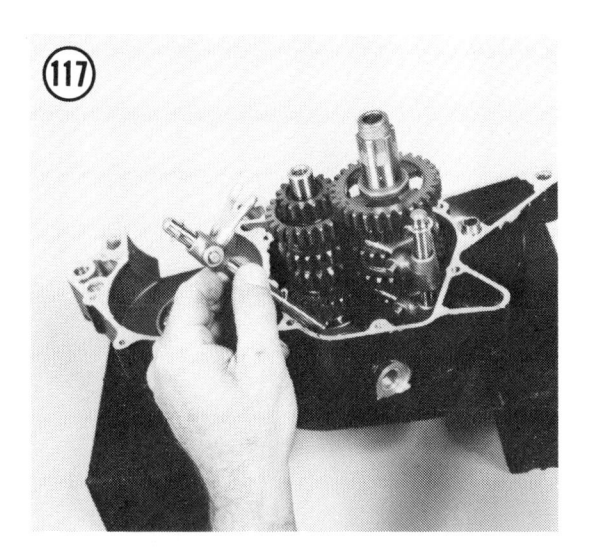

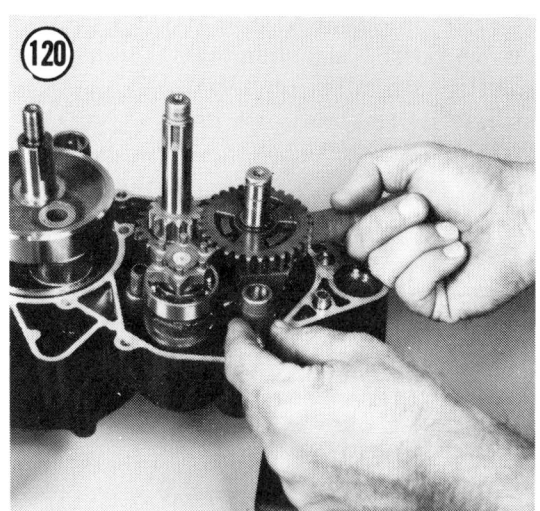

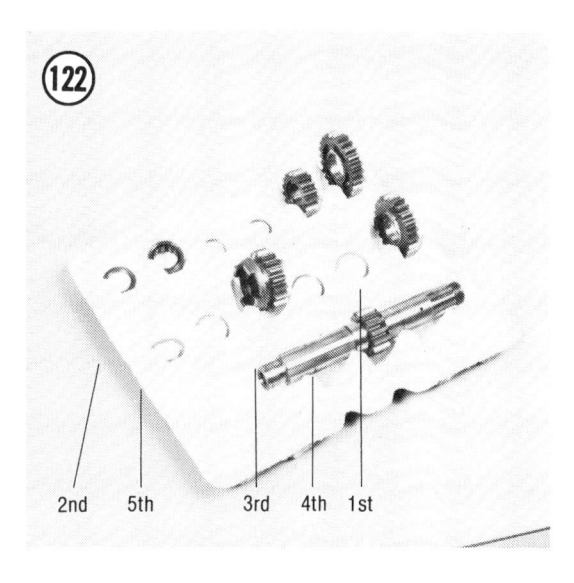

CLUTCH AND TRANSMISSION

153

(117)

(118)

(119)

(120)

(121)

(122)
2nd 5th   3rd 4th 1st

1. Place the assembled shaft into a large can or plastic bucket and thoroughly clean with solvent and a stiff brush. Dry with compressed air or let it sit on rags to drip dry.
2. Remove the roller bearing and washer.

NOTE
On IT425G and IT400C models there is no washer next to the roller bearing.

3. Remove the circlip and washer and slide off the 2nd and 5th gears.
4. Remove the splined washer, circlip and 3rd gear.
5. Remove the circlip, washer and 4th gear.
6. Check each gear for excessive wear, burrs, pitting or chipped or missing teeth. Make sure the lugs (**Figure 123**) on the gears are in good condition.

NOTE
Defective gears should be replaced. It is a good idea to replace the mating gear on the countershaft even though it may not show as much wear or damage.

7. Make sure that all gears slide smoothly on the main shaft splines.

NOTE
*It is a good idea to replace all circlips (**Figure 124**) every other time the transmission is disassembled as they take a beating in a competition machine.*

8. Slide on 4th gear and install the washer and circlip (**Figure 125**).
9. Slide on 3rd gear and install the circlip and washer (**Figure 126**).
10. Slide on 5th gear with the recessed side going on first (**Figure 127**).
11. Install 2nd gear with the recess facing outward (**Figure 128**). Install the washer and circlip (**Figure 129**).
12. Install the washer and roller bearing (**Figure 130**).

NOTE
There is no washer on IT425G and IT400C models.

13. After assembly is complete, refer to **Figure 131** for the correct placement of all

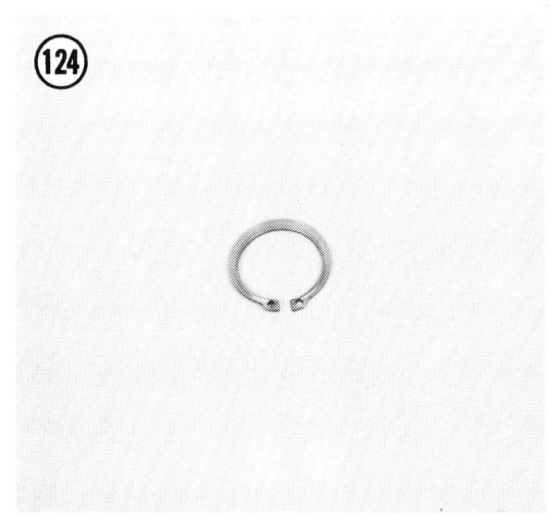

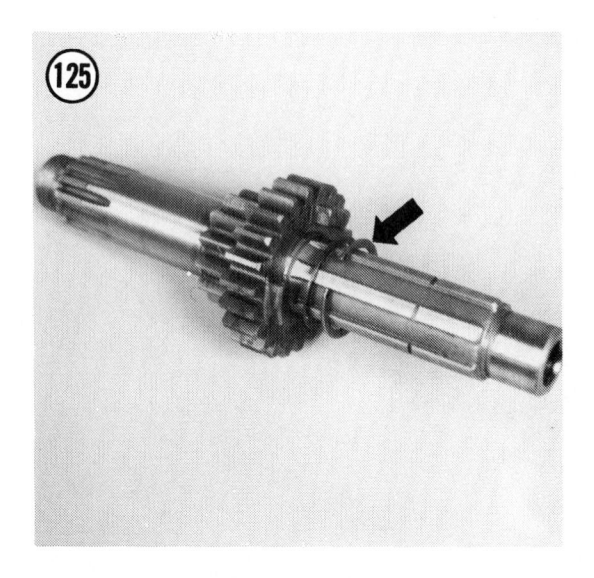

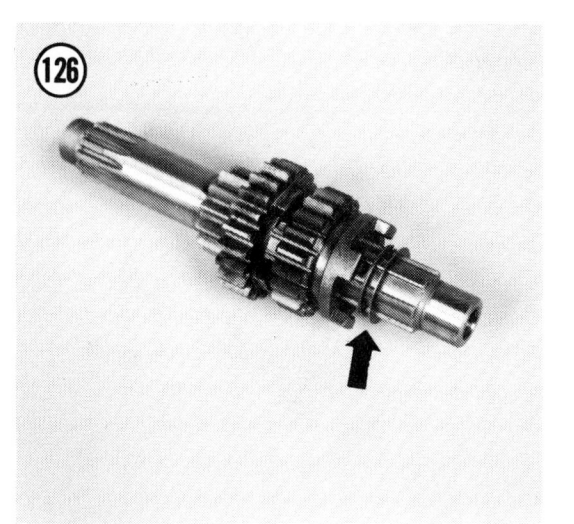

CLUTCH AND TRANSMISSION

155

gears. Make sure all circlips are seated correctly in the main shaft grooves.

Countershaft Disassembly/ Inspection/Assembly (5-Speed Transmission)

Refer to **Figure 92** for this procedure.

> *NOTE*
> *Use the large egg flat (used on the main shaft disassembly) during the countershaft disassembly (**Figure 132**). This is an easy way to remember the correct relationship of all parts.*

1. Place the assembled shaft into a large can or plastic bucket and thoroughly clean with solvent and a stiff brush. Dry with compressed air or let it sit on rags to drip dry.
2. Remove the circlip and washer and slide off the 1st and 4th gears.
3. Remove the circlip and splined washer and slide off 3rd gear.
4. Remove the splined washer and circlip and slide off 5th gear.
5. Remove the circlip, washer and 2nd gear.
6. Check each gear for excessive wear, burrs, pitting, or chipped or missing teeth. Make sure the lugs (**Figure 123**) on the gears are in good condition.

> *NOTE*
> *Defective gears should be replaced. It is a good idea to replace the mating gear on the main shaft even though it may not show as much wear or damage.*

7. Make sure that all gears slide smoothly on the countershaft splines.

> *NOTE*
> *It is a good idea to replace all circlips (**Figure 124**) every other time the transmission is disassembled as they take a beating in a competition machine.*

8. Slide on 2nd gear (flush side on first) and install the washer and circlip (**Figure 133**).
9. Slide on 5th gear and install the circlip and washer (**Figure 134**).
10. Slide on 3rd gear (recessed side on first).
11. Install the splined washer and circlip and slide on 4th gear (**Figure 135**).
12. Slide on 1st gear (**Figure 136**).
13. Install the washer and circlip (**Figure 137**).
14. After assembly is complete, refer to **Figure 138** for the correct placement of all gears. Make sure all circlips are seated corrcectly in the countershaft grooves.

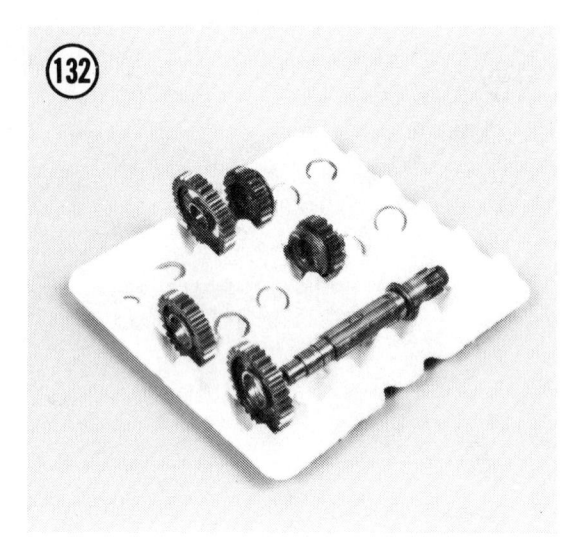

> *NOTE*
> *After both transmission shafts have been assembled, mesh the 2 assemblies together in the correct position (**Figure 139**). Check that all gears meet correctly. This is your last check prior to installing the assemblies into the crankcase; make sure they are correctly assembled.*

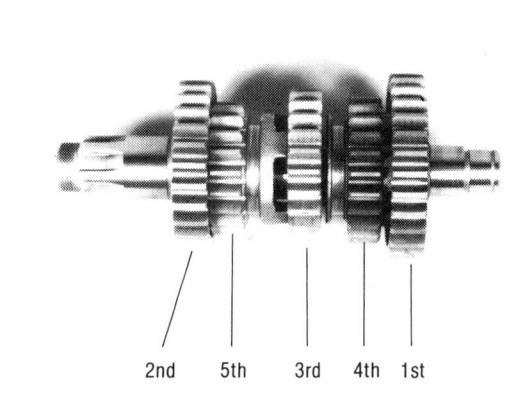

CLUTCH AND TRANSMISSION

157

2nd 5th 3rd 4th 1st

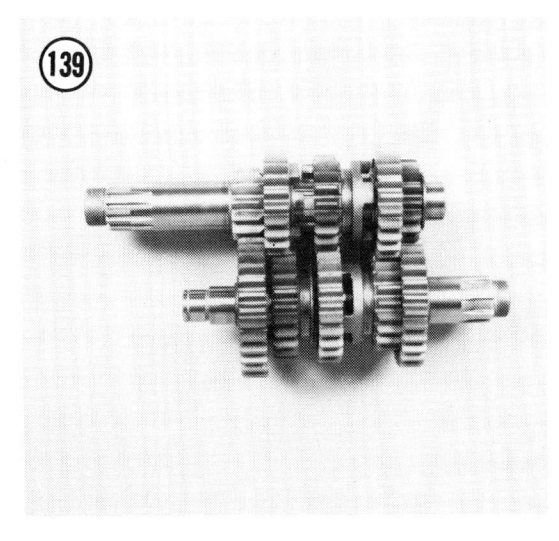

Main Shaft
Disassembly/Inspection/Assembly
(6-Speed Transmission)

Refer to **Figure 93** or **Figure 94** for this procedure. The transmission used on the IT250E (**Figure 94**) is slightly different from all other models. It uses fewer circlips and washers so pay particular attention to the location of all items during disassembly.

NOTE
*A helpful "tool" that should be used for transmission disassembly is a large egg flat (the type that restaurants get their eggs in). As you remove a part from the shaft set it in one of the depressions in the same position from which it was removed (**Figure 140**). This is an easy way to remember the correct relationship of all parts.*

1. Place the assembled shaft into a large can or plastic bucket and thoroughly clean with solvent and a stiff brush. Dry with compressed air or let it sit on rags to drip dry.
2. Remove the circlip and washer and slide off 2nd and 6th gears.

NOTE
On models IT175G, F and E and IT125G there is no washer. Just remove the circlip and slide off 2nd and 6th gears.

3. Remove the washer, circlip and the 3rd/4th combination gear.
4. Remove the circlip, washer and 5th gear.
5. Check each gear for excessive wear, burrs, pitting or chipped or missing teeth. Make sure the lugs (**Figure 141**) on the gears are in good condition.

NOTE
Defective gears should be replaced. It is a good idea to replace the mating gear on the countershaft even though it may not show as much wear or damage.

6. Make sure that all gears slide smoothly on the main shaft splines.

NOTE
*It is a good idea to replace all circlips (**Figure 142**) every other time the transmission is disassembled as they take a beating in a competition machine.*

7. Slide on 5th gear and install the washer and circlip (**Figure 143**).
8. Slide on the 3rd/4th combination gear and install the circlip and washer (**Figure 144**).

NOTE
Install this combination gear with the smaller diameter gear (3rd gear) on first, toward 5th gear.

9. Slide on 6th gear (**Figure 145**).
10. Slide on 2nd gear (**Figure 146**) and install the washer and circlip (**Figure 147**).

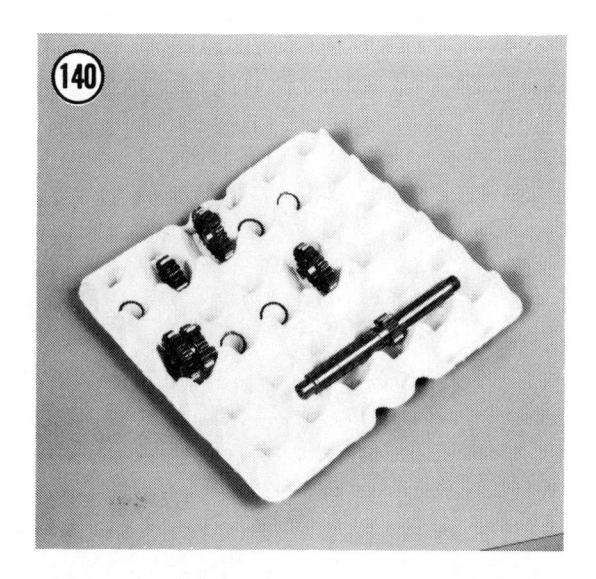

CLUTCH AND TRANSMISSION

159

11. After assembly is complete refer to **Figure 148** for the correct placement of all gears. Make sure all circlips are seated correctly in the main shaft grooves.

Countershaft Disassembly/Inspection/Assembly (6-Speed Transmission)

Refer to **Figure 93** or **Figure 94** for this procedure.

NOTE
*Use the large egg flat (used on the main shaft disassembly) during the countershaft disassembly (**Figure 149**). This is an easy way to remember the correct relationship of all parts.*

1. Place the assembled shaft into a large can or plastic bucket and thoroughly clean with solvent and a stiff brush. Dry with compressed air or let it sit on rags to drip dry.
2. Remove the circlip and washer and slide off 1st and 5th gears.
3. Remove the circlip and splined washer and slide off 3rd gear.
4. Remove the circlip and slide off 4th gear.
5. Remove the splined washer, and circlip and slide off 6th gear.
6. Remove the circlip and washer and slide off 2nd gear.
7. Check each gear for excessive wear, burrs, pitting or chipped or missing teeth. Make sure the lugs (**Figure 150**) on the gears are in good condition.

NOTE
Defective gears should be replaced. It is a good idea to replace the mating gear on the main shaft even though it may not show as much wear or damage.

8. Make sure that all gears slide smoothly on the countershaft splines.

NOTE
*It is a good idea to replace all circlips (**Figure 142**) every other time the transmission is disassembled as they take a beating in a competition machine.*

9. Slide on 2nd gear (flush side on first) and install the washer and circlip (**Figure 151**).

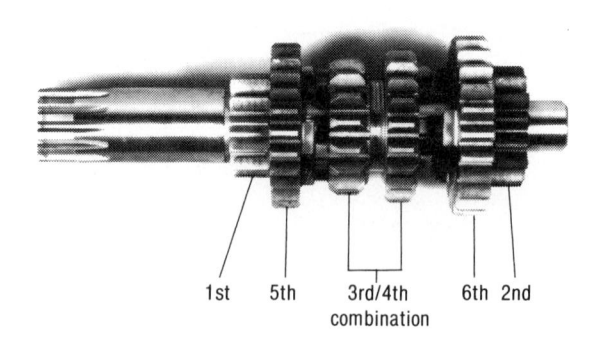

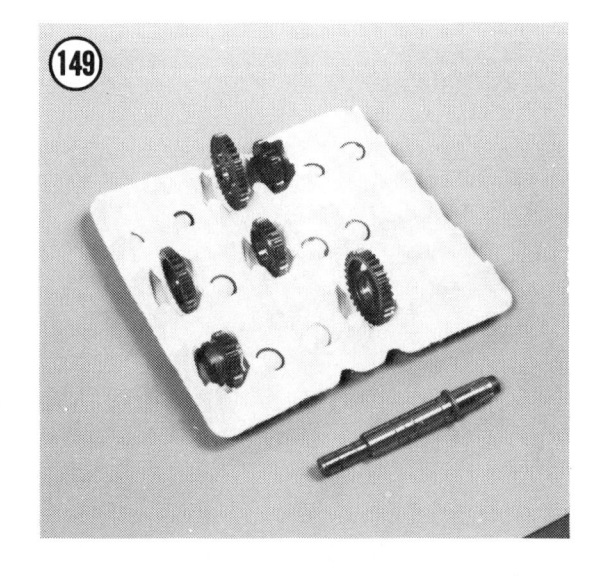

CLUTCH AND TRANSMISSION

10. Slide on 6th gear and install the circlip and washer (**Figure 152**).

11. Slide on 4th gear (recessed side on first) for the IT175; refer to **Figure 153**. On IT250 models install 4th gear as shown in **Figure 154**. On all models install the circlip.

12. Install 3rd gear (flush side on first) and install the splined washer and circlip (**Figure 155**).

13. Slide on 5th and 1st gears (**Figure 156**) and install the washer and circlip (**Figure 157**).

14. After assembly is complete, refer to **Figure 158** for the correct placement of all gears. Make sure all circlips are seated correctly in the countershaft grooves.

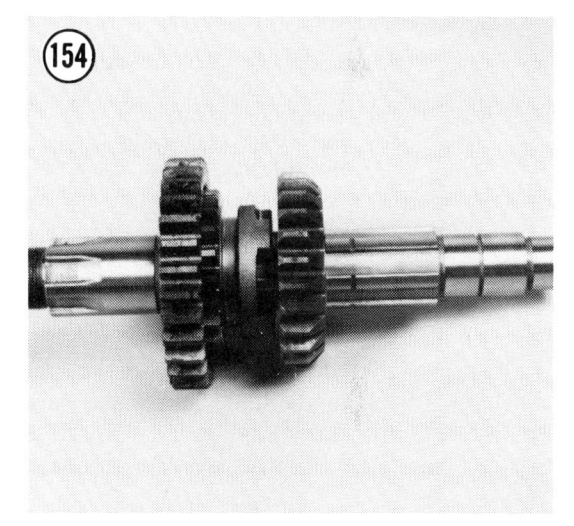

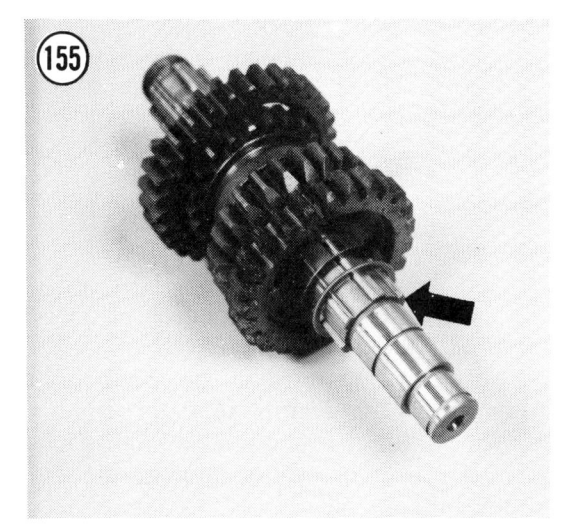

NOTE
*After both transmission shafts have been assembled, mesh the 2 assemblies together in the correct position (**Figure 159**). Check that all gears meet correctly. This is your last check prior to installing the assemblies into the crankcase; make sure they are correctly assembled.*

Internal Shift Mechanism Inspection

Refer to **Figures 95-98** for this procedure.

NOTE
*Due to the number of different internal shift mechanisms (Type 1 through IV), components from all different types are not shown in the following procedure. Prior to removal or disassembly of any of the components, lay the assembly (**Figure 160**) down on a piece of paper or cardboard and carefully trace around it. Write down the identifying marks or numbers (**Figure 161**) next to the item. Also mark where circlips, if any, are located. This will take a little extra time now but it may save some time and frustration later.*

1. Inspect each shift fork for signs of wear or cracking. Check for bending and make sure each fork slides smoothly on its respective shaft (**Figure 162**). Replace worn or damaged forks.

NOTE
*Check for any arc-shaped wear or burn marks (**Figure 163**) on the shift forks. This indicates that the shift fork has come in contact with the gear. The fork fingers are excessively worn and the fork must be replaced.*

2. Roll the shift fork shaft on a flat surface such as a piece of plate glass and check for any bending. If the shaft is bent, replace it.
3. Check the grooves in the shift drum (**Figure 164** or **Figure 165**) for wear or roughness. If any of the groove profiles have excessive wear or damage, replace the shift drum.

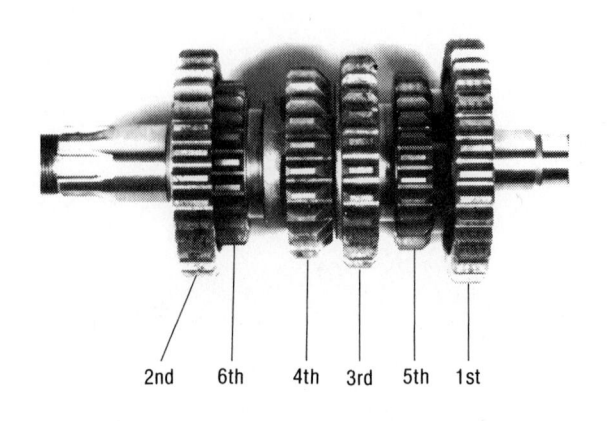

CLUTCH AND TRANSMISSION

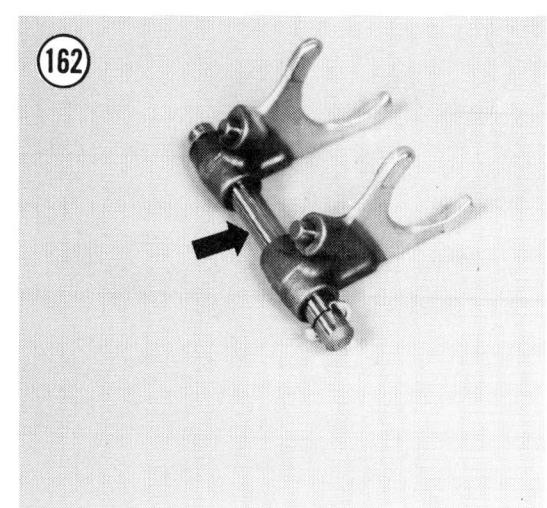

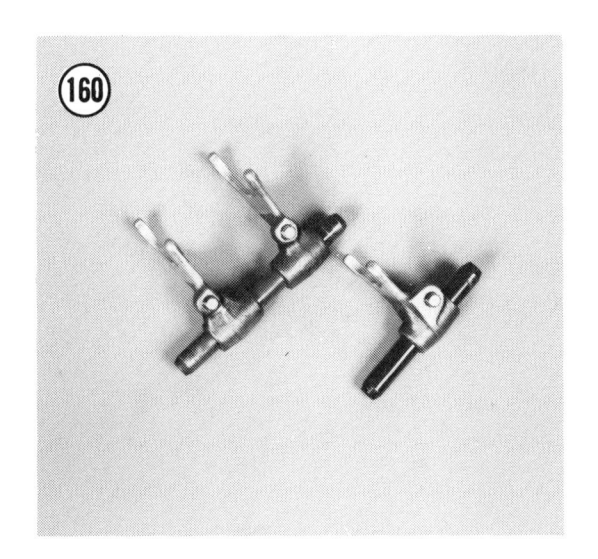

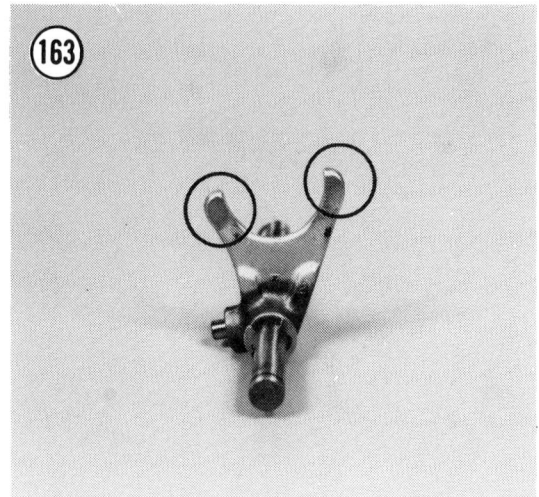

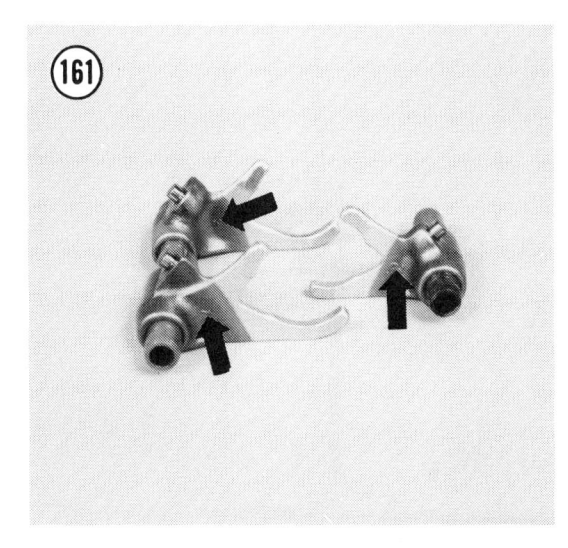

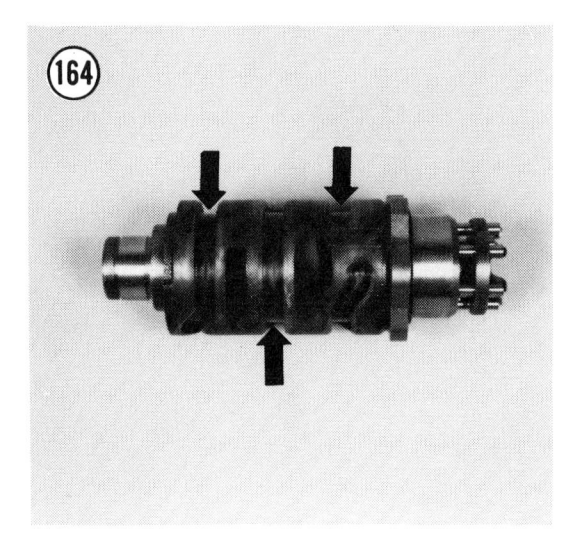

163

CHAPTER FIVE

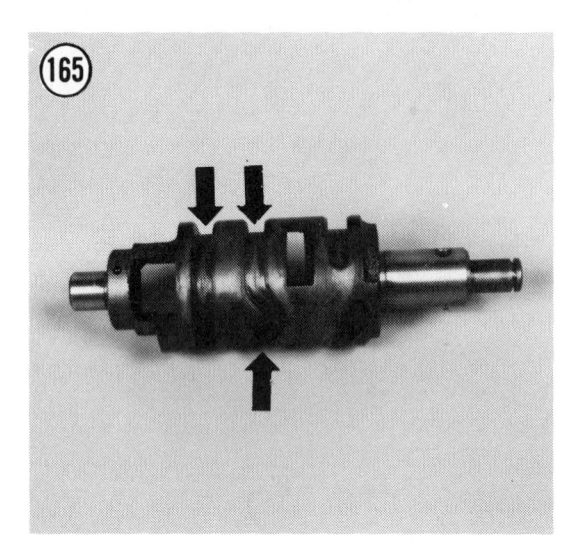

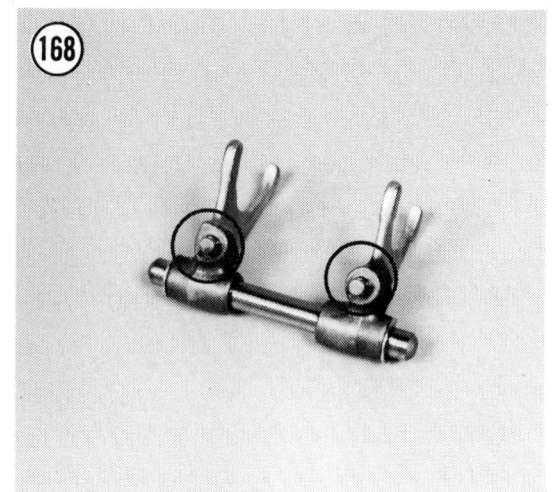

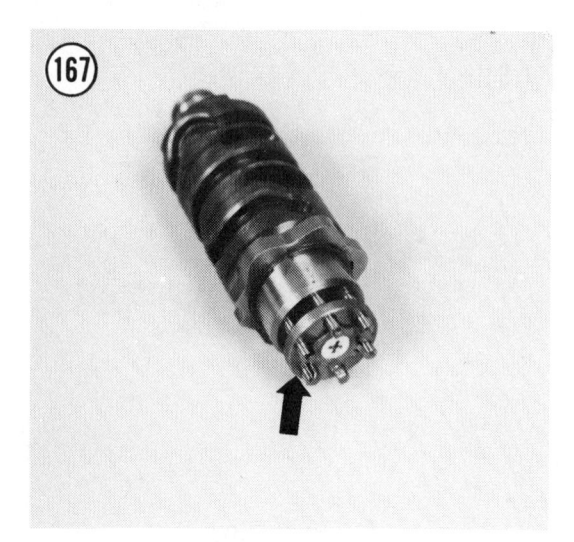

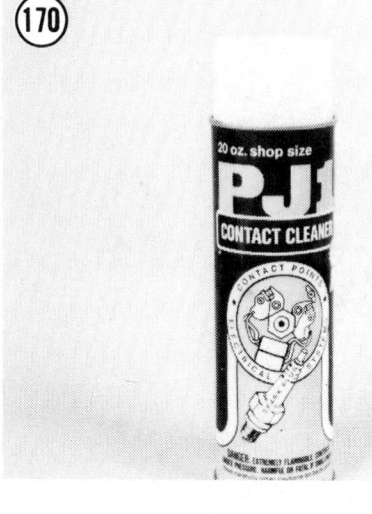

CLUTCH AND TRANSMISSION

4. On models with an integral bearing (**Figure 166**), check it for smooth operation. Make sure it spins freely with no signs of wear or damage. Replace if necessary.

5. On Type I and II, check the shift cam dowel pins (**Figure 167**) and side plate for wear, looseness or damage; replace any defective parts.

6. Check the cam pin followers (**Figures 168**) in each shift fork. They should fit snugly but not too tight. Check the end that rides in the shift drum for wear or burrs. Replace as necessary.

7. Inspect the condition of the ramps on the stopper plate (**Figure 169**) for wear or roughness. Check the tightness of the screw securing the stopper plate. If it is loose, remove the screw, washer and stopper plate. Clean the threads of the screw with a nonresidual cleaner (contact point cleaner—see **Figure 170**) and dry thoroughly. Apply Loctite Stud N' Bearing Mount to the screw threads and reinstall all components. Tighten the screw securely.

8. If shift fork assemblies have been disassembled, apply a light coat of oil to the shafts and inside bores of the fingers prior to installation.

Table 2   CLUTCH TORQUE SPECIFICATIONS

Item	Foot-pounds (ft.-lb.)	Newton Meters (N•m)
Clutch nut		
IT425G	55	72
IT400	55	72
IT250	55	72
IT175	36	50
IT125	40	55

Table 1   CLUTCH SPECIFICATIONS

Item	Standard	Wear Limit
Friction disc thickness	0.12 in. (3.0 mm)	0.006 in. (2.7 mm)
Clutch plate warpage	—	0.0020 in. (0.05 mm)
Clutch spring free length	1.42 in. (36.0 mm)	1.38 in. (35.0 mm)
Items per model	Friction disc	Clutch plates
IT425	7	6
IT400	7	6
IT250G, F	5	4
IT250E, D	6	5
IT175	6	5
IT125	5	4

> **NOTE:** If you own a 1981 or later model, first check the Supplement at the back of the book for any new service information.

CHAPTER SIX

FUEL AND EXHAUST SYSTEMS

The fuel system consists of the fuel tank, the shutoff valve, a single Mikuni carburetor and the air cleaner. There are slight differences among the various models; these are noted in the procedures.

The exhaust system consists of an exhaust pipe assembly and a silencer.

This chapter includes service procedures for all parts of the fuel system and exhaust system.

AIR CLEANER

The air cleaner must be cleaned frequently. Refer to Chapter Three for specific procedures and service intervals.

CARBURETOR OPERATION

For proper operation a gasoline engine must be supplied with fuel and air mixed in proper proportions by weight. A mixture in which there is an excess of fuel is said to be rich. A lean mixture is one which contains insufficient fuel. A properly adjusted carburetor supplies the proper mixture to the engine under all operating conditions.

Mikuni carburetors consist of several major systems. A float and float valve mechanism maintain a constant fuel level in the float bowl. The pilot system supplies fuel at low speeds. The main fuel system supplies fuel at medium and high speeds. Finally, a starter (choke) system supplies the very rich mixture needed to start a cold engine.

CARBURETOR SERVICE

Major carburetor service (removal and cleaning) should be performed after every trials event on a strictly competition bike. On a bike that is used for fun on weekends, it should be performed whenever the engine is decarbonized or when poor engine performance, hesitation and little or no response to mixture adjustment is observed. After owning and running the bike for a period of time, you will learn your own service interval.

Carburetor specifications are covered in **Table 1** at the end of this chapter.

Carburetor Removal/Installation

The Mikuni carburetors used on all of these models are basically the same. Slight differences do occur among models, so it is important to pay particular attention to the location and order of parts during disassembly.

1. Place a milk crate or wood block(s) under the engine to support it securely.
2. Turn the fuel shutoff valve to the OFF position and remove the fuel line to the carburetor.

FUEL AND EXHAUST SYSTEMS

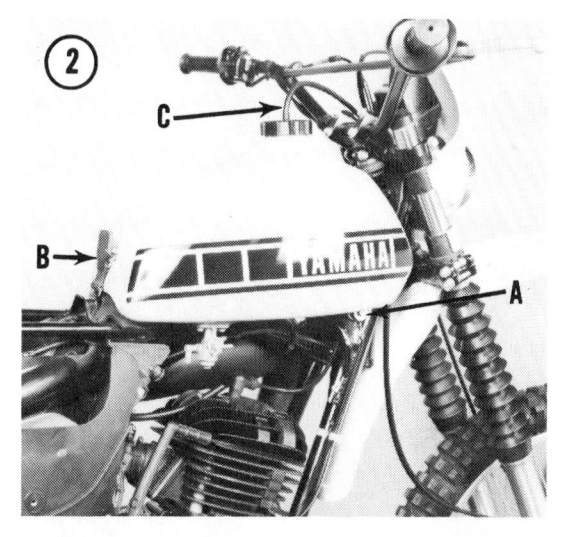

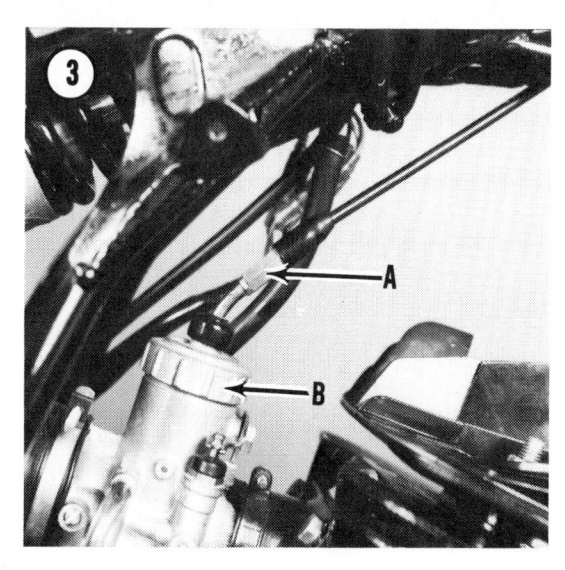

3. Remove the seat and number plates (**Figure 1**).

4. Remove the bolts (A, **Figure 2**) securing the front of the fuel tank. Pull up and unhook the strap (B, **Figure 2**) securing the rear of the tank. Pull the fuel fill cap vent tube (C, **Figure 2**) free from the steering head area. Pull the tank to the rear and remove it.

5. Loosen the locknut and adjuster on the throttle cable (A, **Figure 3**) on top of the carburetor.

NOTE
Prior to removing the top cap, thoroughly clean the area around it so no dirt will fall into the carburetor.

6. Unscrew the carburetor top cap (B, **Figure 3**) and pull the throttle valve assembly up and out of the carburetor.

NOTE
If the top cap and throttle valve assembly are not going to be removed from the throttle cable for cleaning, wrap them in a clean shop cloth or place them in a plastic bag to help keep them clean.

7. Loosen the clamping screws (**Figure 4**) on both rubber boots. Slide the clamps off away from the carburetor.

CHAPTER SIX

8. Make sure all drain tubes are free (**Figure 5**).
9. Carefully work the carburetor free from the rubber boots and remove it.
10. Take the carburetor to a workbench for disassembly and cleaning.
11. Install by reversing these removal steps. When installing the carburetor onto the engine side be sure to properly align the boss on the carburetor air horn with the groove in the rubber boot (**Figure 6**).

Disassembly/Cleaning/ Inspection/Assembly

Refer to **Figure 7** or **Figure 8** for your specific carburetor for this procedure and to **Table 1** for carburetor specifications.

All of the carburetors are basically the same although minor variations exist among different models and years. Where major differences occur they are identified.

1. Remove the screws securing the float bowl (**Figure 9**) and remove it.
2. The float arm pin (**Figure 10**) is wedged in place. Do not remove it unless you are sure the valve needle is faulty. If necessary, carefully push the pin out. Avoid damaging the posts that hold it in place. Remove the float lever, float valve needle, seat, washer and plate.

NOTE
On IT125G, carefully remove the floats from the float lever.

3. Remove the main jet (**Figure 11**).
4. Remove the main jet holder/washer (**Figure 12**) on models so equipped.
5. Remove the needle jet (**Figure 13**).
6. Unscrew the pilot jet (**Figure 14**).
7. Remove the plastic drain tubes (A, **Figure 15**), choke assembly (B, **Figure 15**), throttle adjust screw and spring (C, **Figure 15**).
8. On all models except IT125G, remove the plastic caps (A, **Figure 16**) securing the float posts and remove the floats.
9. Remove the seal in the float bowl (B, **Figure 16**).
10. Remove the float bowl plug and O-ring seal (**Figure 17**).
11. Remove the clip (**Figure 18**) securing the throttle cable in the slide assembly.
12. Remove the throttle cable from the throttle valve assembly (**Figure 19**) and remove the assembly.
13. Remove the 2 screws (**Figure 20**) securing the jet needle into the throttle valve assembly and disassemble it (**Figure 21**). If the jet needle clip is to be removed, record the position prior to removal.

NOTE
Further disassembly is neither necessary nor recommended. If throttle or choke shafts or butterflies are damaged, take the carburetor body to your dealer for replacement.

FUEL AND EXHAUST SYSTEMS

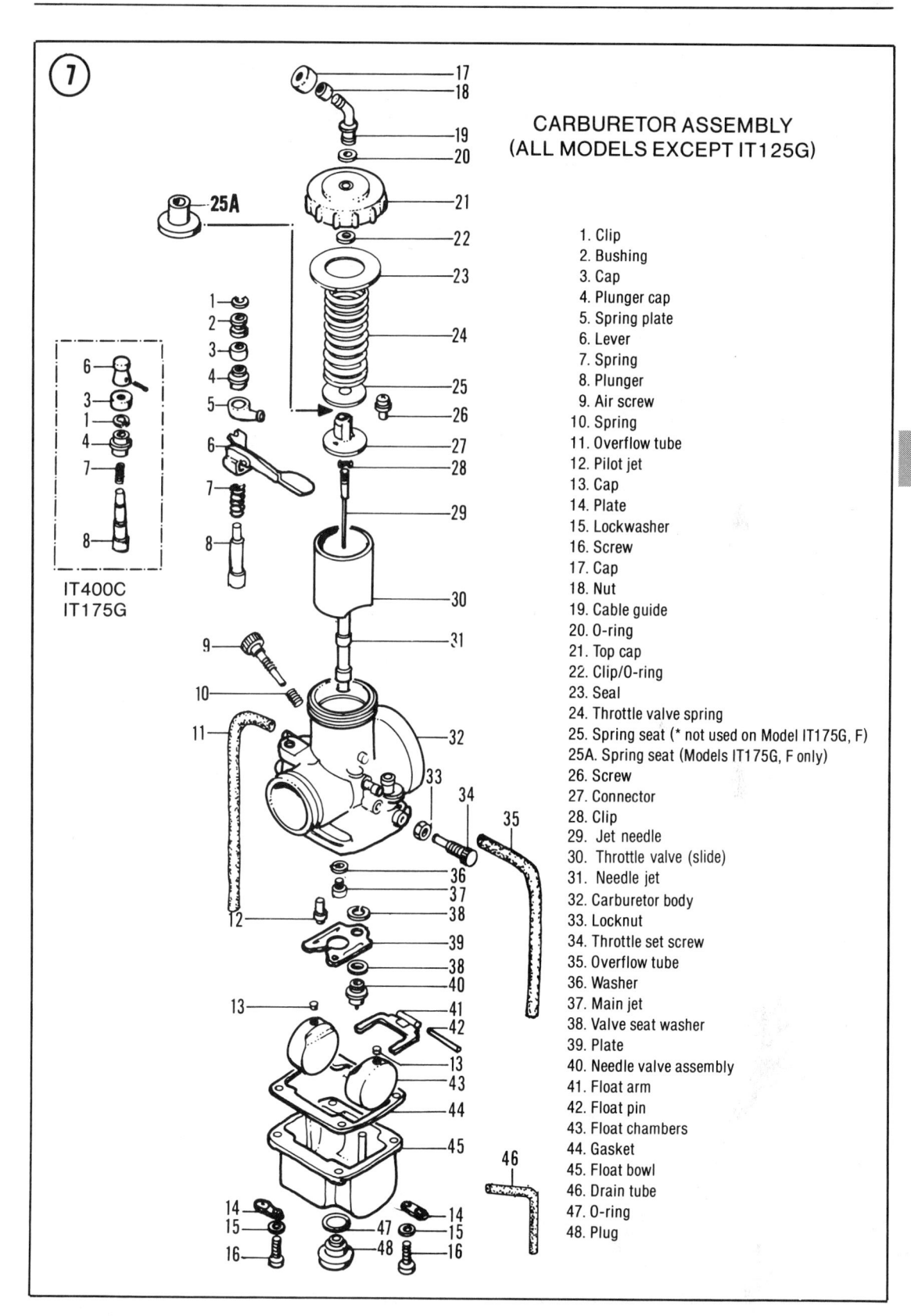

CARBURETOR ASSEMBLY (ALL MODELS EXCEPT IT125G)

1. Clip
2. Bushing
3. Cap
4. Plunger cap
5. Spring plate
6. Lever
7. Spring
8. Plunger
9. Air screw
10. Spring
11. Overflow tube
12. Pilot jet
13. Cap
14. Plate
15. Lockwasher
16. Screw
17. Cap
18. Nut
19. Cable guide
20. O-ring
21. Top cap
22. Clip/O-ring
23. Seal
24. Throttle valve spring
25. Spring seat (* not used on Model IT175G, F)
25A. Spring seat (Models IT175G, F only)
26. Screw
27. Connector
28. Clip
29. Jet needle
30. Throttle valve (slide)
31. Needle jet
32. Carburetor body
33. Locknut
34. Throttle set screw
35. Overflow tube
36. Washer
37. Main jet
38. Valve seat washer
39. Plate
40. Needle valve assembly
41. Float arm
42. Float pin
43. Float chambers
44. Gasket
45. Float bowl
46. Drain tube
47. O-ring
48. Plug

IT400C
IT175G

CHAPTER SIX

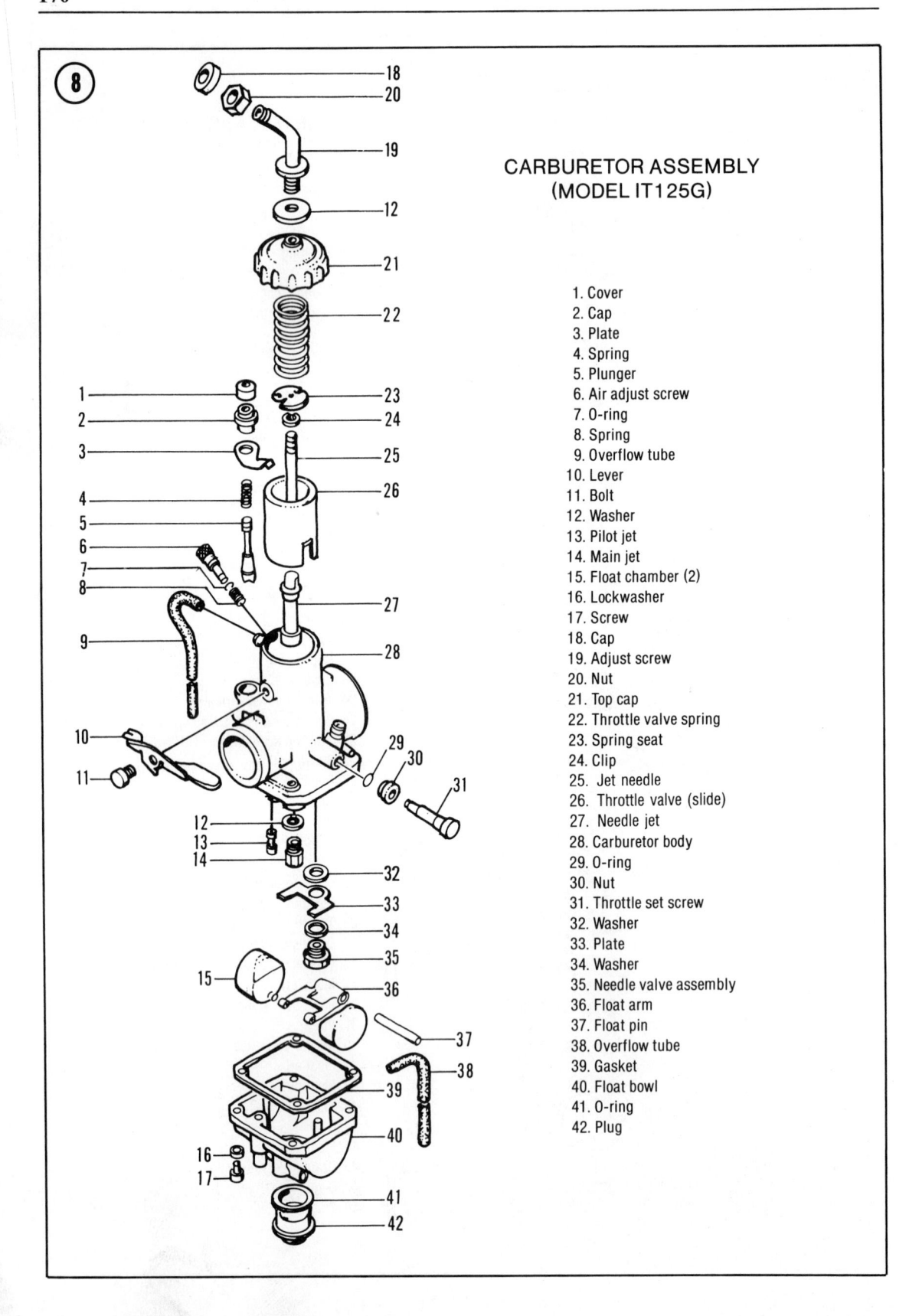

CARBURETOR ASSEMBLY (MODEL IT125G)

1. Cover
2. Cap
3. Plate
4. Spring
5. Plunger
6. Air adjust screw
7. O-ring
8. Spring
9. Overflow tube
10. Lever
11. Bolt
12. Washer
13. Pilot jet
14. Main jet
15. Float chamber (2)
16. Lockwasher
17. Screw
18. Cap
19. Adjust screw
20. Nut
21. Top cap
22. Throttle valve spring
23. Spring seat
24. Clip
25. Jet needle
26. Throttle valve (slide)
27. Needle jet
28. Carburetor body
29. O-ring
30. Nut
31. Throttle set screw
32. Washer
33. Plate
34. Washer
35. Needle valve assembly
36. Float arm
37. Float pin
38. Overflow tube
39. Gasket
40. Float bowl
41. O-ring
42. Plug

FUEL AND EXHAUST SYSTEMS

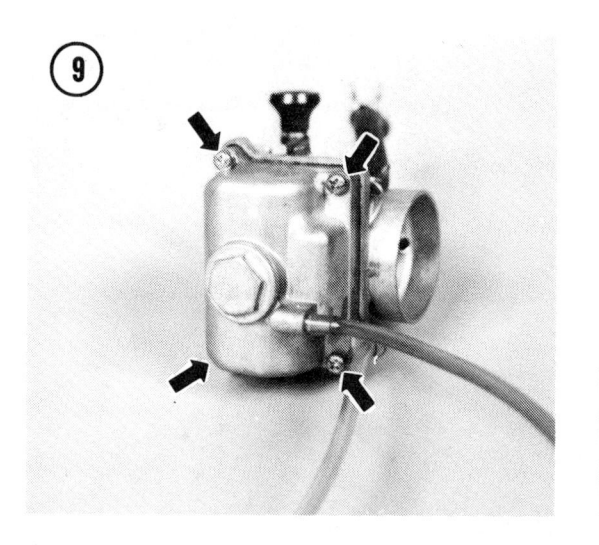

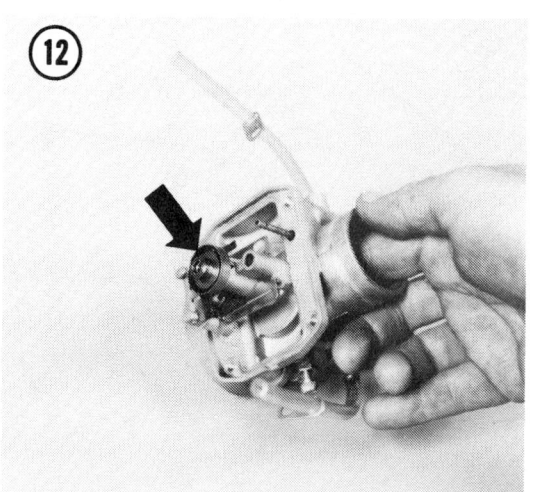

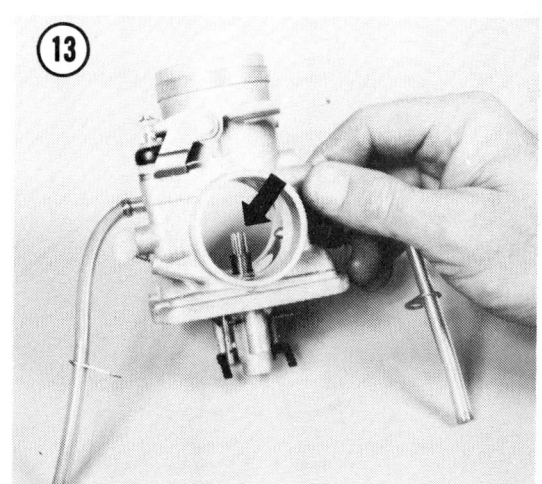

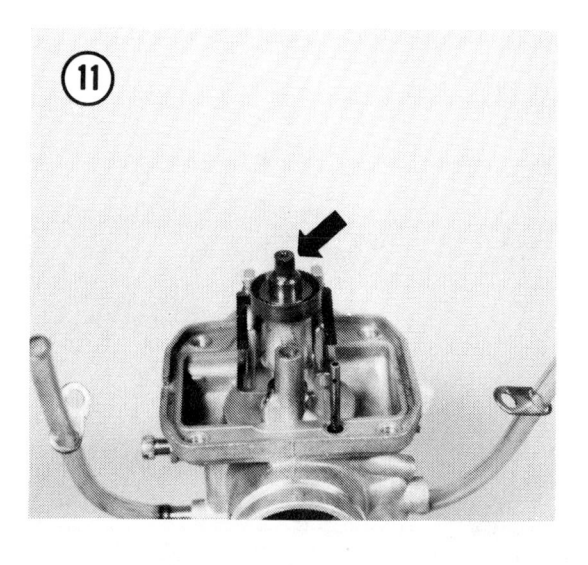

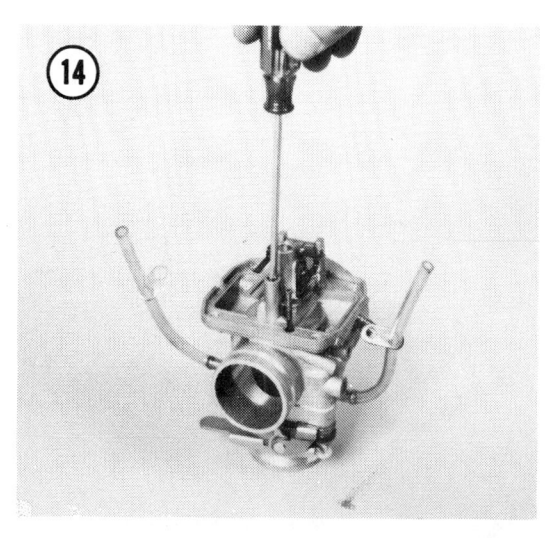

171

CHAPTER SIX

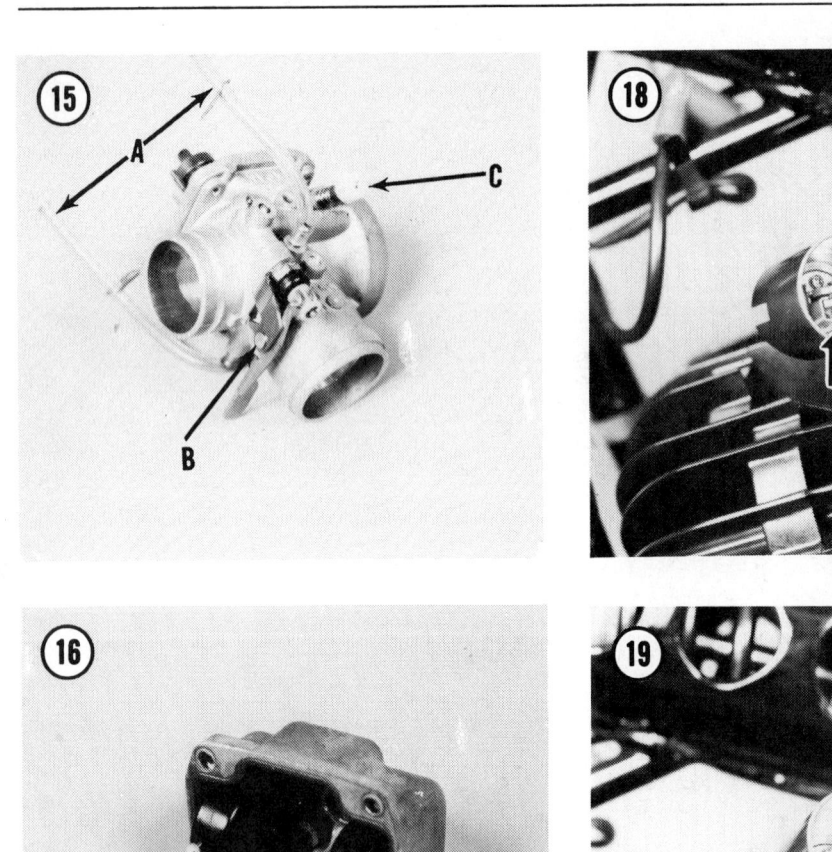

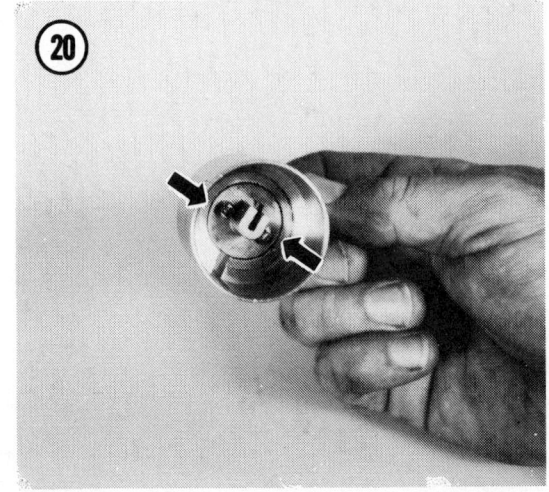

FUEL AND EXHAUST SYSTEMS

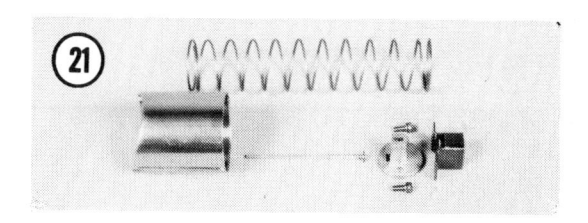

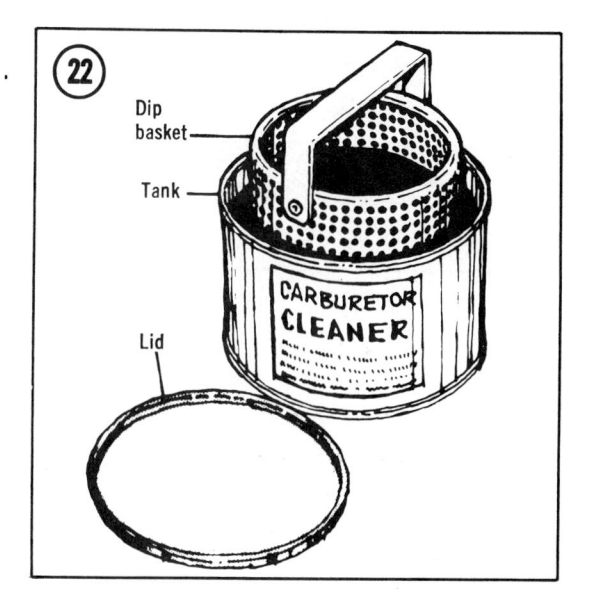

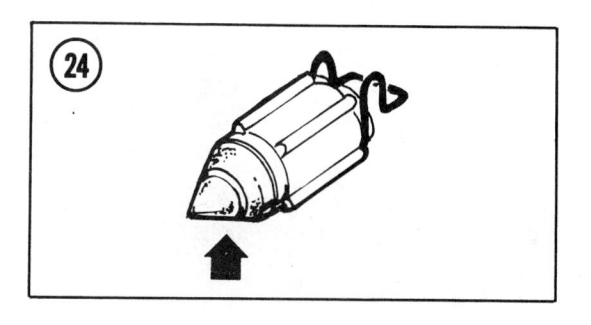

14. Clean all parts, except rubber or plastic parts, in a good grade of carburetor cleaner. This solution is available at most automotive or motorcycle supply stores in a small, resealable tank with a dip basket for just a few dollars (**Figure 22**). If it is tightly sealed when not in use, the solution will last for several cleanings. Follow the manufacturer's instructions for correct soak time (usually about 1/2 hour).

15. Remove all parts from the cleaner and blow dry with compressed air. Blow out the jets with compressed air. *Do not* use a piece of wire to clean them as minor gouges in the jet can alter flow rate and upset the fuel/air mixture.

16. Be sure to clean out the overflow tube (**Figure 23**) from both ends.

17. Inspect the condition of the end of the float valve needle (**Figure 24**) for wear or damage; replace it if necessary.

18. Inspect the condition of the O-ring seal on the float bowl plug. O-ring seals tend to become hardened after prolonged use and heat and therefore lose their ability to seal properly.

19. Be sure to install the pilot jet as shown in **Figure 25**.

20. Install the jet needle clip in the correct groove; refer to **Table 1** at the end of this chapter.

21. Check the float height and adjust if necessary. Refer to *Float Adjustment* in this chapter.

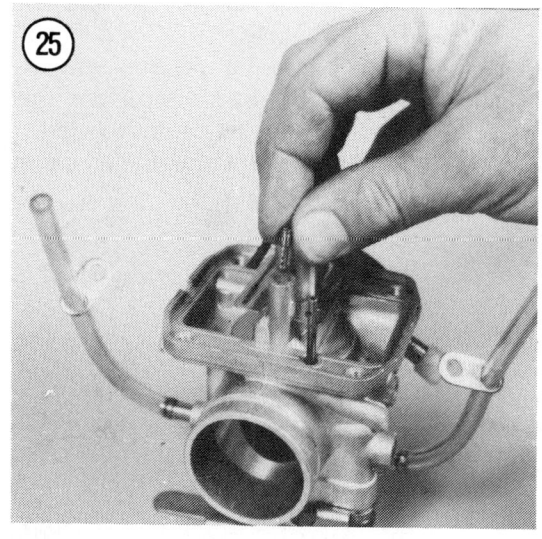

CHAPTER SIX

22. After the carburetor has been disassembled the pilot screw and the idle speed should be adjusted. Refer to *Pilot Screw and Idle Speed Adjustment* in this chapter.

CARBURETOR ADJUSTMENTS

Float Adjustment

The carburetor assembly has to be removed and partially disassembled for this adjustment.
1. Remove the carburetor as described under *Carburetor Removal/Installation* in this chapter.
2. Remove the float bowl from the main body.
3. Hold the carburetor so the float arm is just touching the float needle. Use a float level gauge (**Figure 26**) and measure the distance from the carburetor body to the float arm (**Figure 27**). Refer to **Table 1** for the correct level.
4. Adjust by carefully bending the tang on the float arm. If the float level is set too high, the result will be a rich fuel/air mixture. If it is set too low the mixture will be too lean.

NOTE
Both float chambers must be at the same height.

5. Reassemble and install the carburetor.

Jet Needle Adjustment

The position of the jet needle can be adjusted to affect the fuel/air mixture for medium throttle openings.

The top of the carburetor must be removed for this adjustment. It is easier to perform this procedure with the fuel tank removed but it can be accomplished with the fuel tank in place.

NOTE
Prior to removing the top cap, thoroughly clean the area around it so no dirt will fall into the carburetor.

1. Unscrew the carburetor top cap (**Figure 28**) and pull the throttle valve assembly up and out of the carburetor.
2. Withdraw the spring (**Figure 29**) out of the throttle valve assembly.

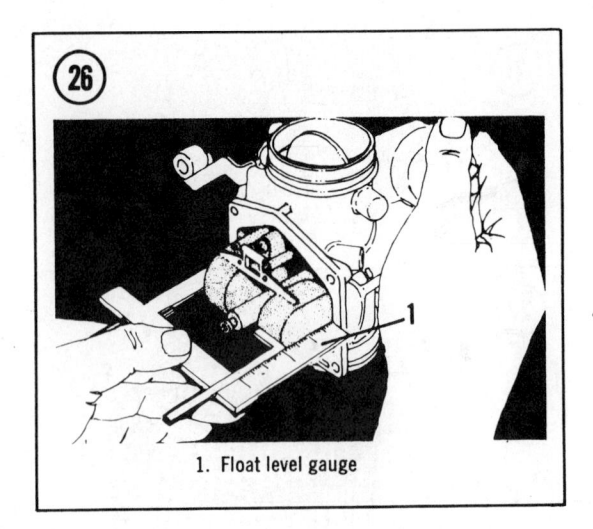

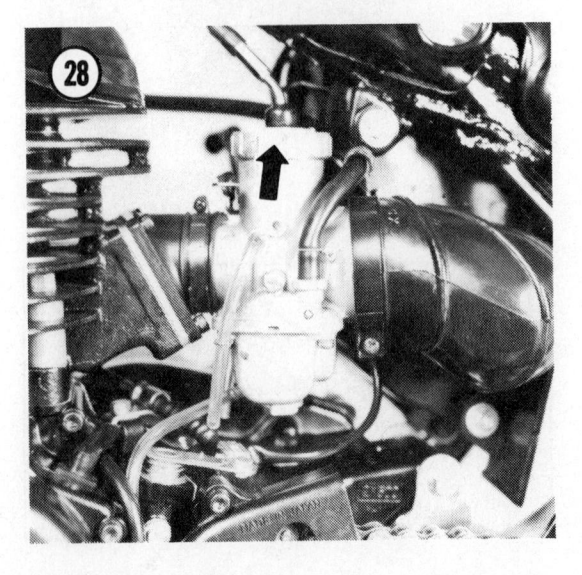

1. Float level gauge

FUEL AND EXHAUST SYSTEMS

3. Remove the clip (**Figure 30**) securing the throttle cable in place. Slide the cable out and remove the throttle valve assembly.
4. Remove the screws (**Figure 31**) securing the jet needle to the connector and remove it.
5. Slide the jet needle out of the connector and note the position of the clip. Raising the needle (lowering the clip) will enrich the mixture during mid-throttle opening, while lowering it (raising the clip) will lean the mixture; refer to **Figure 32**.
6. Refer to **Table 1** for standard clip position for all models.
7. Reassemble and install the top cap.

Pilot Screw and Idle Speed Adjustment

The air cleaner must be cleaned before starting this procedure or results will be inaccurate.

1. With the engine shut off, turn the pilot air screw (**Figure 33**) in until it *lightly* seats.
2. Back it out the following number of turns:
    a. IT425G: 1-1/2 turns
    b. IT400F: 2-1/4 turns
    c. IT400E, D: 1-1/4 turns
    d. IT400C: 1.0 turn
    e. IT250G, F: 1-1/2 turns
    f. IT250E, D: 1.0 turn
    g. IT175G, F: 1-1/4 turns
    h. IT175E, D: 1-1/2 turns
    i. IT125G: 1-3/4 turns
3. Start the engine and let it reach normal operating temperature.

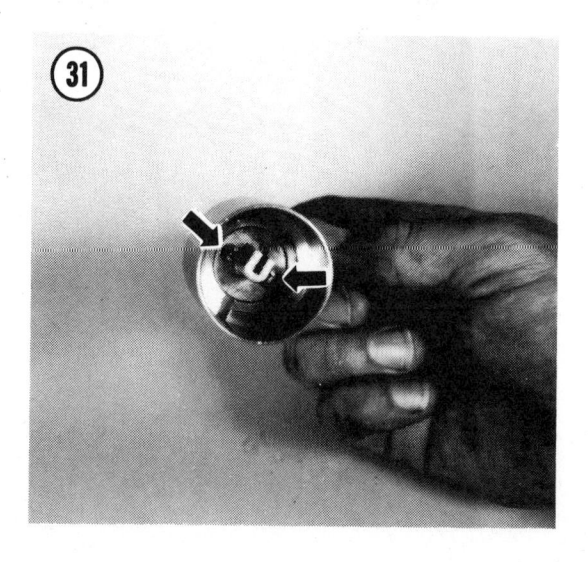

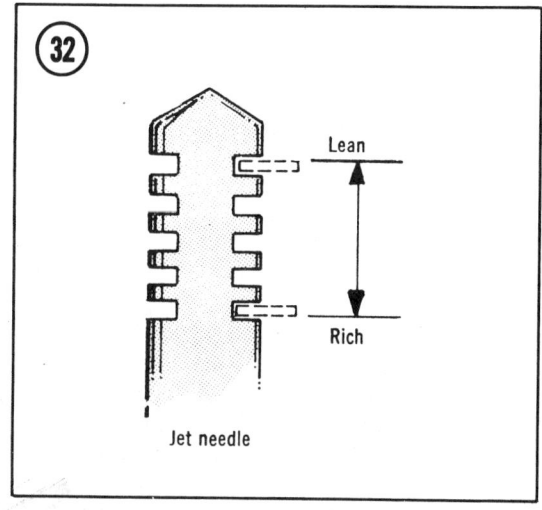

4. Loosen the locknut and turn the idle stop screw (**Figure 34**) in or out to achieve the desired idle speed. This speed should be set to your own personal preference.

5. Turn the pilot air screw in or out to achieve the highest possible engine rpm.

6. Turn the idle stop screw in or out again to achieve the desired idle speed. Tighten the locknut (**Figure 34**).

> *WARNING*
> *With the engine idling, move the handlebar from side to side. If idle speed increases during this movement, the throttle cable needs adjusting or it may be incorrectly routed through the frame. Correct this problem immediately. Do not ride the bike in this unsafe condition.*

7. After this adjustment is completed, test ride the bike. Throttle response from idle should be rapid and without any hesitation. If there is any hesitation, turn the pilot air screw in or out in 1/4 turn increments until this problem is solved.

High-altitude Adjustment (Main Jet Replacement)

If the bike is going to be raced or ridden for any sustained period in high elevations (above 5,000 ft.—1,500 m), the main jet should be changed to a one-step smaller jet. Never change the jet by more than one size at a time without test riding the bike and running a spark plug test. Refer to *Reading Spark Plugs* in Chapter Three.

The carburetor is set with the standard jet for normal sea level conditions. If the bike is run at higher altitudes or under heavy load—deep sand or mud—the main jet should be replaced with a one-step smaller size to prevent the bike from running too rich and carboning up quickly.

> *CAUTION*
> *If the bike has been rejetted for high-altitude operation (smaller jet), it must be changed back to the standard main jet if ridden at altitudes below 5,000 ft. (1,500 m). Engine overheating and piston seizure will occur if the engine runs too lean with the smaller jet.*

FUEL AND EXHAUST SYSTEMS

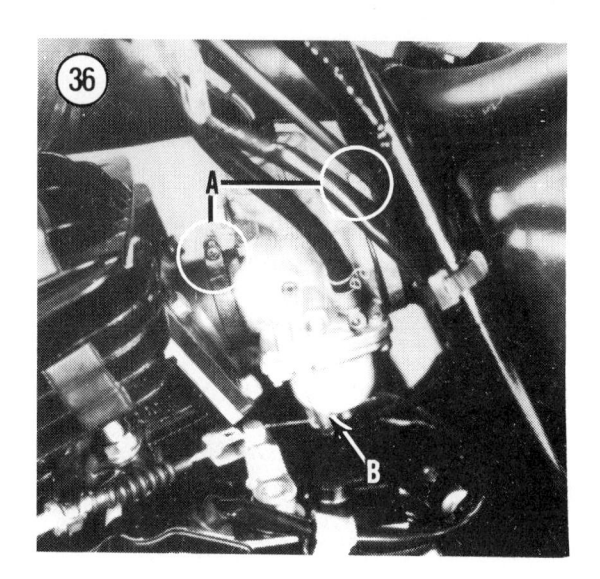

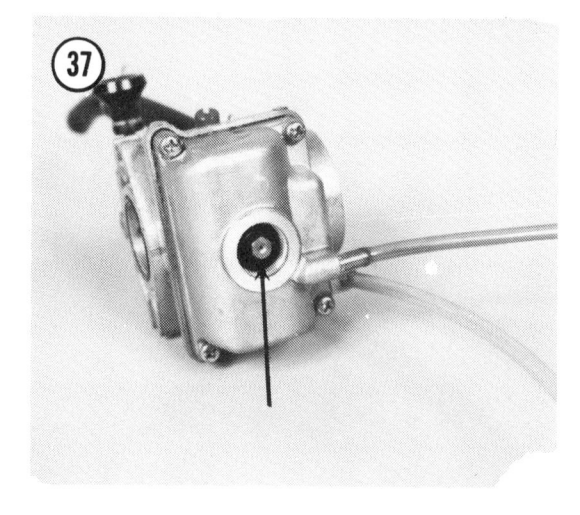

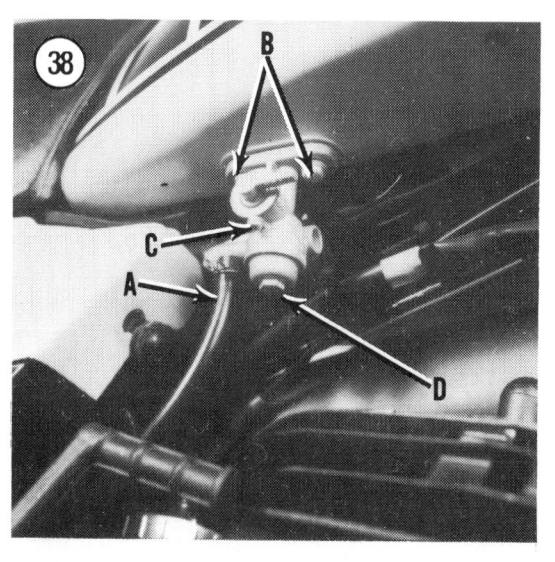

Refer to **Table 1** for standard main jet size.
1. Turn the fuel shutoff valve to the OFF position and disconnect the fuel line from the carburetor (**Figure 35**).
2. Loosen the screws on the clamping bands (A, **Figure 36**) on each side of the carburetor; pivot the carburetor to one side.

WARNING
During the next step, place a metal container under the cover to catch the fuel that will flow out. Do not let it drain out onto the engine or the bike's frame as it presents a real fire danger. **Do not perform this procedure with a hot engine.** *Dispose of the fuel properly; wipe up any that may have spilled on the bike and the floor.*

3. Loosen the main jet cover (B, **Figure 36**).
4. Remove the main jet cover.
5. The main jet (**Figure 37**) is directly under the cover; remove it and replace it with a different one—remember, change only one jet size at a time.

NOTE
Figure 37 *is shown with the carburetor partially disassembled for clarity.*

6. Install the main jet cover; tighten it securely.
7. Pivot the carburetor back to its original position; make sure it indexes into the slot in the rubber intake tube.
8. Tighten the clamping band screws and reinstall the carburetor fuel line.

FUEL SHUTOFF VALVE

Removal/Cleaning/Installation

1. Turn the fuel shutoff valve to the OFF position and remove the flexible fuel line to the carburetor (A, **Figure 38**).
2. Place the loose end into a clean, sealable, metal container. This fuel can be reused if kept clean.
3. Open the valve to the ON position and remove the fuel filler cap. This will allow air to enter the tank and speed up the flow of fuel. Drain the tank completely.

4. Remove the screws (B, **Figure 38**) securing the fuel shutoff valve to the tank and remove it.

5. After removing the valve, insert a corner of a clean shop rag into the opening in the tank to stop fuel dribbling onto the engine and frame.

6. Remove the small screw (C, **Figure 38**) below the handle and disassemble the handle. Remove the filter cup (D, **Figure 38**) and remove the filter and O-ring gasket. Clean all parts in solvent with a medium soft toothbrush, then dry them. Check the condition of the O-rings within the valve and the O-ring gasket; replace them if they are starting to deteriorate or get hard. Make sure the spring is not broken or getting soft; replace it if necessary.

7. Reassemble the valve and install it on the tank. Don't forget the O-ring gasket between the valve and the tank.

FUEL TANK

Removal/Installation

1. Place a milk crate or wood block(s) under the engine to support it securely.
2. Turn the fuel shutoff valve to the OFF position and remove the fuel line to the carburetor.
3. Remove the seat.
4. Remove the bolts (A, **Figure 39**) securing the front of the fuel tank. Pull up and unhook the strap (B, **Figure 39**) securing the rear of the tank. Pull the fuel fill cap vent tube (C, **Figure 39**) free from the steering head area. Pull the tank toward the rear and remove it.

FUEL FILTER

The IT is fitted with a small fuel filter screen in the shutoff valve. Considering the dirt and residue that is often found in today's gasoline, it is a good idea to install an inline fuel filter to help keep the carburetor clean.

A good quality inline fuel filter (A.C. part No. GF453 or equivalent) is available at most auto or motorcycle supply stores. Just cut the flexible fuel line from the fuel tank to the carburetor and install the filter. You may have to cut out a section of the fuel line the length of the filter, so the fuel line does not kink and restrict fuel flow.

EXHAUST SYSTEM

The exhaust system on a 2-stroke motorcycle engine is much more than a means of routing the exhaust gases to the rear of the bike. It's a vital performance component and frequently, because of its design, it is a vulnerable piece of equipment. Check the exhaust system for deep dents and fractures and repair them as described under *Exhaust System Repairs* at the end of this chapter. Check the expansion chamber frame mounting flanges for fractures and loose bolts and bushings. Check the cylinder mounting flange or collar for tightness. A loose headpipe connection will not only rob the engine of

FUEL AND EXHAUST SYSTEMS

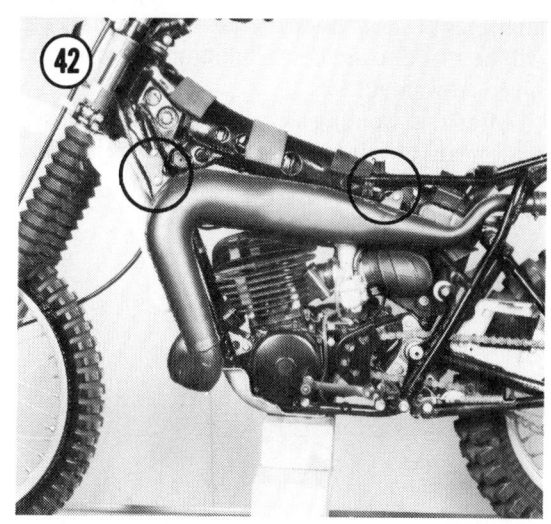

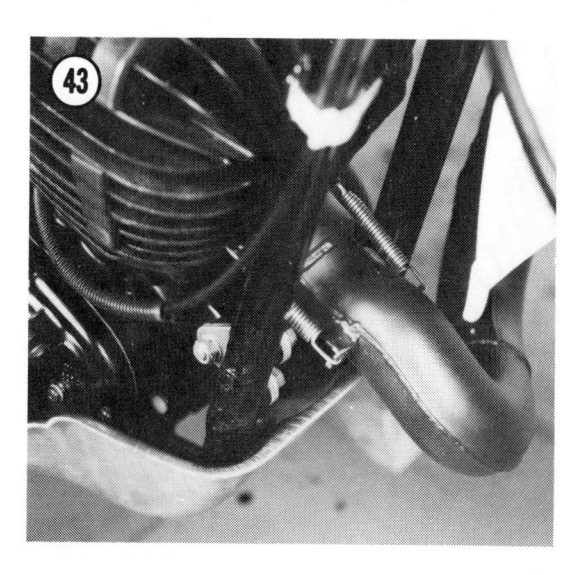

power, it could also damage the piston and cylinder.

The exhaust system on the IT consists of an exhaust pipe assembly (head pipe and expansion chamber) and a silencer. This system varies slightly with different models and years. All attachments and springs are basically the same but all models vary a little.

Removal/Installation

1. Remove the seat, the fuel tank and the side cover/number plate on the exhaust pipe side (**Figure 40**).
2. Place the bike on a milk crate or wood block(s) to support it securely.
3. Remove the springs or loosen the clamping screws (A, **Figure 41**) securing the silencer to the exhaust pipe assembly.
4. Remove the bolts and washers (B, **Figure 41**) securing the silencer to the frame and remove the silencer.
5. Loosen the bolts and washers (**Figure 42**) securing the expansion chamber to the frame.
6. Use Vise Grips and remove the springs (**Figure 43**) securing the head pipe to the cylinder exhaust port.
7. Remove the bolts and washers loosened in Step 5 and remove the exhaust pipe assembly.
8. Inspect the condition of the gaskets at all joints; replace as necessary.
9. Install the exhaust pipe assembly into position and install the frame bolts and washers only finger-tight until the head pipe springs are installed. This will minimize an exhaust leak at the cylinder.
10. Install the head pipe springs using Vise Grips. The springs on some models are under a lot of tension during installation—protect yourself accordingly. Make sure the head pipe inlet is correctly seated in the exhaust port.
11. Tighten the frame bolts securely.
12. Install the silencer and tighten the clamps securely or install the springs. Install and tighten the frame bolts securely.
13. Install the fuel tank, seat and side cover/number plate.
14. After installation is complete, make sure there are no exhaust leaks.

EXHAUST SYSTEM DECARBONIZING

Refer to Chapter Three for complete details on engine and exhaust system decarbonizing.

EXHAUST SYSTEM REPAIR

A dent in the headpipe or expansion chamber of a 2-stroke exhaust system will alter the system's flow characteristics and degrade performance. Minor damage can be easily repaired if you have welding equipment, some simple body tools and a bodyshop slide hammer.

Small Dents

1. Drill a small hole in the center of the dent. Screw the end of the slide hammer into the hole.
2. Heat the area around the dent evenly with a torch.
3. When the dent is heated to a uniform orange-red color, operate the slide hammer to raise the dent.
4. When the dent is removed, unscrew the slide hammer and weld or braze the drilled hole closed.

Large Dents

Large dents that are not crimped can be removed with heat and a slide hammer as previously described. However, several holes must be drilled along the center of the dent so that it can be pulled out evenly.

If the dent is sharply crimped along the edges, the damaged section should be cut out with a hacksaw, straightened with a body dolly and hammer and welded back into place.

Before cutting the exhaust pipe apart, scribe alignment marks over the area where the cuts will be made to aid correct alignment when the pipe is rewelded.

After the welding is completed, wire-brush and clean up all welds. Paint the entire pipe with a high-temperature paint to prevent rusting.

FUEL AND EXHAUST SYSTEMS

Table 1   CARBURETOR SPECIFICATIONS

	IT425G	IT400F	IT400E / IT400D	IT400C
Model number	VM38SS	VM38SC	VM38SC	VM38SS
I.D. mark	3R800	2X800	1W600	1K700
Main jet No.	410	370	350	340
Needle jet No.	P-8	Q-0	P-4	P-4
Pilot jet No.	60	60	60	60
Jet needle No.	6F16	6F16	6F16	6F16
Clip position	3	2	3	3
Float level	0.71 in. (18.1 mm)	0.71 in. (18.1 mm)	0.71 in. (18.1 mm)	0.71 in. (18.1 mm)

	IT250G	IT250F	IT250E	IT250D
Model number	VM36SS	VM36SC	VM36SC	VM36SC
I.D. mark	3R700	2X700	1W500	1W500
Main jet No.	350	330	360	360
Needle jet No.	P-4	P-4	P-6	P-6
Pilot jet No.	70	70	60	60
Jet needle No.	6F	6F75	6F15	6F15
Clip position	2	2	2	2
Float level	0.71 in. (18.1 mm)	0.71 in. (18.1 mm)	0.71 in. (18.1 mm)	0.71 in. (18.1 mm)

	IT175G	IT175F	IT175E	IT175D
Model number	VM32SS	VM34SS	VM34SS	VM34SS
I.D. mark	3R600	2W600	1W200	1W200
Main jet No.	210	360	360	360
Needle jet No.	P-8	P-4	P-4	P-4
Pilot jet No.	60	70	60	60
Jet needle No.	6F21	6F21	6F21	6F21
Clip position	4	4	4	4
Float level	0.92 in. (23.4 mm)	0.93 in. (23.5 mm)	0.93 in. (23.5 mm)	0.93 in. (23.5 mm)

	IT125G
Model number	VM30SS
I.D. mark	3R900
Main jet No.	200
Needle jet No.	P-4
Pilot jet No.	35
Jet needle No.	6DP19
Clip position	2
Float level	0.65 in. (16.4 mm)

NOTE: If you own a 1981 or later model, first check the Supplement at the back of the book for any new service information.

CHAPTER SEVEN

ELECTRICAL SYSTEM

The electrical system on the IT consists of an ignition and lighting circuit. Included is a magneto, CDI unit, ignition coil, spark plug, headlight, taillight and switches. The magneto is basically the same on all models. **Tables 1-2** are at the end of this chapter.

CAPACITOR DISCHARGE IGNITION

All models are equipped with a capacitor discharge ignition (CDI) system. This solid state system uses no breaker points or other moving parts.

Alternating current from the magneto is rectified to direct current and used to charge the capacitor. As the piston approaches the firing position, a pulse from the pulser coil is used to trigger the silicone controlled rectifier. The rectifier in turn allows the capacitor to discharge quickly into the primary circuit of the ignition coil, where the voltage is stepped up in the secondary circuit to a value sufficient to fire the spark plug.

CDI Precautions

Certain measures must be taken to protect the capacitor discharge system. Instantaneous damage to the semiconductors in the system will occur if the following precautions are not observed.

1. Never disconnect any of the electrical connections while the engine is running.
2. Keep all connections between the various units clean and tight. Be sure that the wiring connectors are pushed together firmly to help keep out moisture.
3. Do not substitute another type of ignition coil.
4. The CDI unit is mounted within a rubber vibration isolator. Always be sure that the isolator is in place when installing the unit.

CDI Troubleshooting

Problems with the capacitor discharge system fall into one of the following categories. See **Table 1**.
 a. Weak spark
 b. No spark

CDI Testing

Tests may be performed on the CDI unit but a good one may be damaged by someone unfamiliar with the test equipment. To be safe, have the test made by a Yamaha dealer or substitute a known good unit for a suspected one.

The CDI unit is located under the seat (**Figure 1**) or under the side number panel (**Figure 2**). This location varies slightly with different models and years.

ELECTRICAL SYSTEM

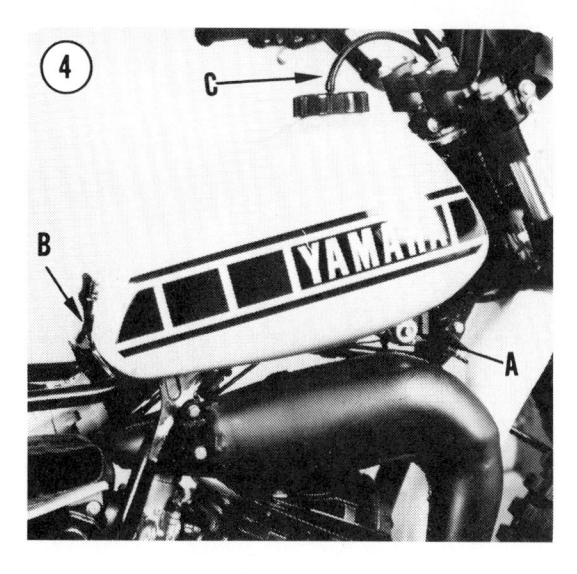

SPARK PLUG

The spark plug recommended by the factory is usually the most suitable for your machine. If riding conditions (other than trials competition) are mild, it may be advisable to go to a spark plug one step hotter than normal. Unusually severe riding conditions may require a slightly colder plug. See Chapter Three for details.

MAGNETO

The magneto generates electricity for the ignition system and lighting system. The right-hand coil is used to generate primary system current for the ignition coil. The left-hand coil generates alternating current for the headlight and taillight.

NOTE
If the headlight burns out while the engine is operating, the taillight will usually burn out due to the excess voltage in the lighting circuit. Always remember to check taillight operation after a headlight has burned out.

Rotor Removal/Installation

Refer to **Figure 3** for this procedure.
1. Place a milk crate or wood block(s) under the frame to support it securely.
2. Turn the fuel shutoff valve to the OFF position and remove the fuel line to the carburetor.
3. Remove the seat.
4. Remove the bolts (A, **Figure 4**) securing the front of the fuel tank. Pull up and unhook the strap (B, **Figure 4**) securing the rear of the tank. Pull the vent tube (C, **Figure 4**) free from the steering head area, pull the tank toward the rear and remove it.
5. Remove the shift lever (**Figure 5**).
6. Remove the screws (**Figure 6**) securing the magneto cover and remove it.

NOTE
Steps 7-15 are shown with the engine partially disassembled. It is not necessary to do so for this procedure.

CHAPTER SEVEN

MAGNETO ASSEMBLY

IT400C

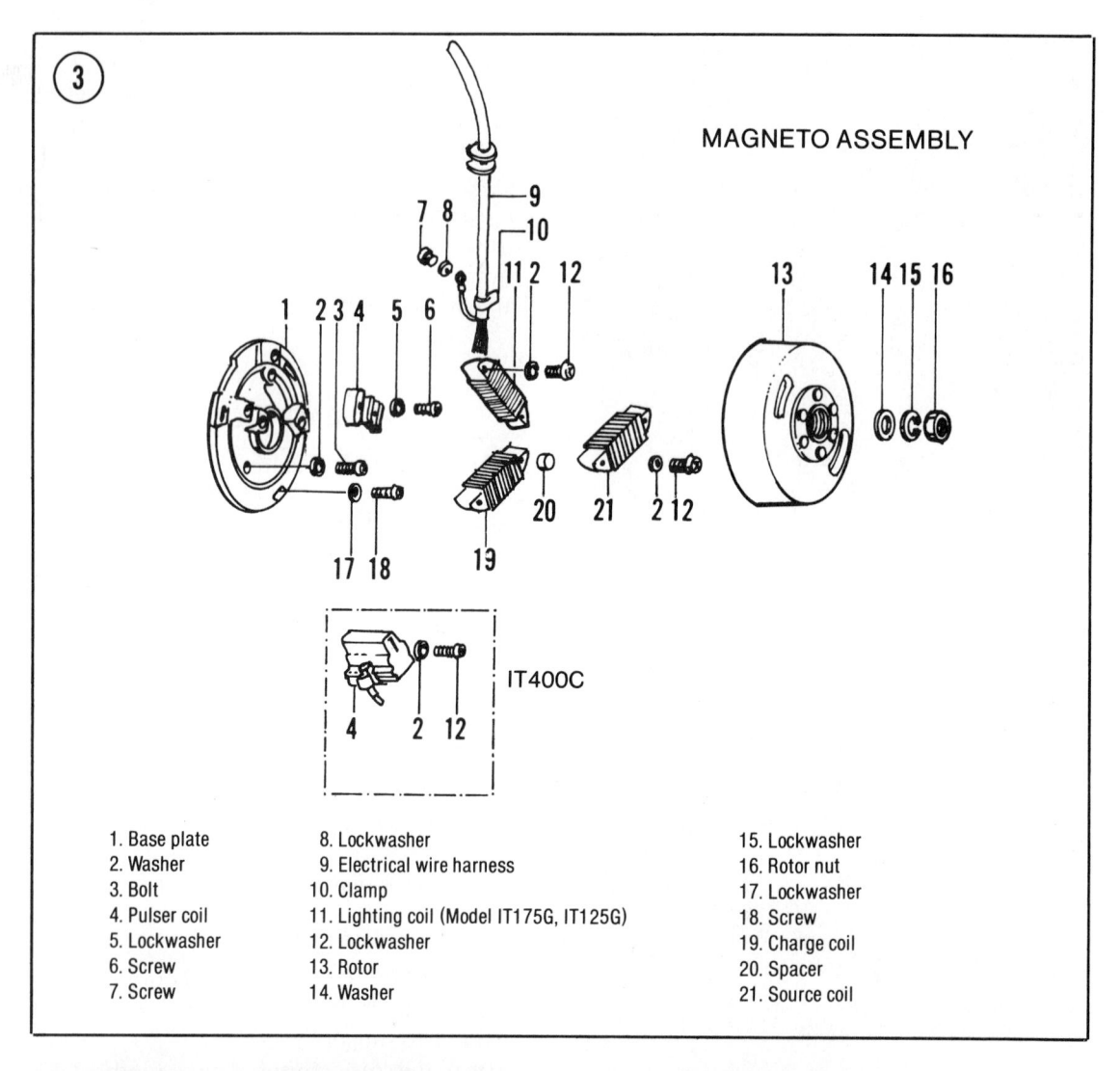

1. Base plate
2. Washer
3. Bolt
4. Pulser coil
5. Lockwasher
6. Screw
7. Screw
8. Lockwasher
9. Electrical wire harness
10. Clamp
11. Lighting coil (Model IT175G, IT125G)
12. Lockwasher
13. Rotor
14. Washer
15. Lockwasher
16. Rotor nut
17. Lockwasher
18. Screw
19. Charge coil
20. Spacer
21. Source coil

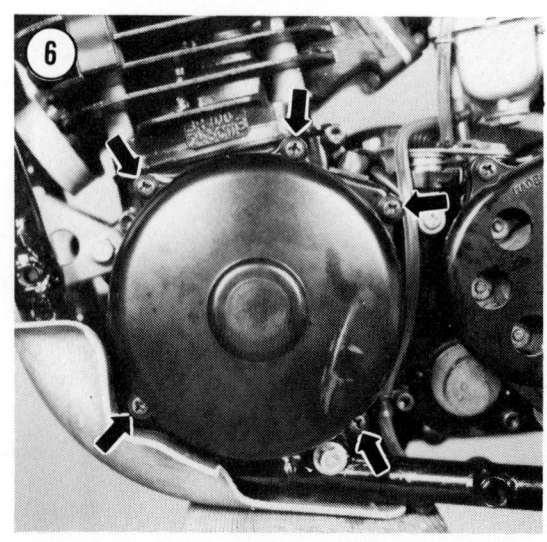

ELECTRICAL SYSTEM

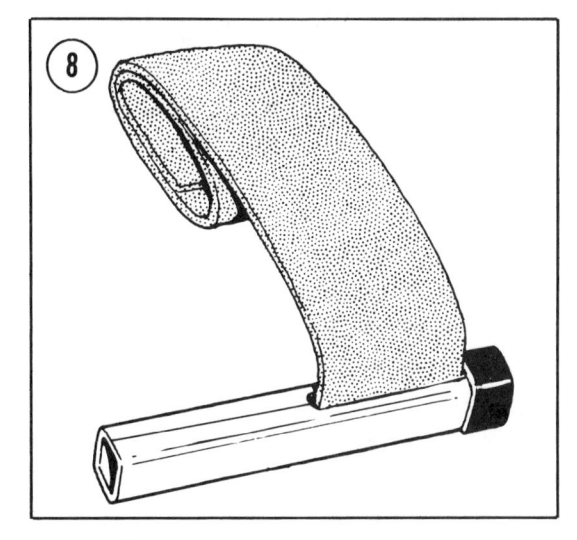

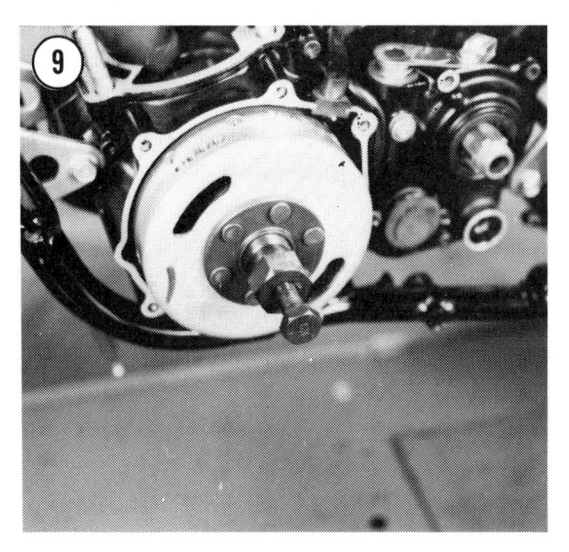

7. Remove the nut (**Figure 7**) securing the magneto rotor (flywheel) in place.

NOTE
*If necessary use a strap wrench (**Figure 8**) to keep the rotor from turning while removing the nut.*

8. Remove the lockwasher and plain washer.

9. Screw in a flywheel puller (**Figure 9**) until it stops. Use the Yamaha puller (part No. 90890-01189) or a K & N puller (part No. T-100/1) or equivalent. See **Figure 10**.

CAUTION
Don't try to remove the rotor without a puller; any attempt to do so will ultimately lead to some form of damage to the engine and/or rotor. Many aftermarket types of pullers are available from most motorcycle dealers or mail order houses. The cost for one of these pullers is about $10 and it makes an excellent addition to any mechanic's tool box. If you can't buy or borrow one, have a dealer remove the rotor.

10. Hold the puller with a wrench and gradually tighten the center bolt (**Figure 11**) until the rotor disengages from the crankshaft.

NOTE
If the rotor is difficult to remove, strike the puller center bolt with a hammer a few times. This will usually break it loose.

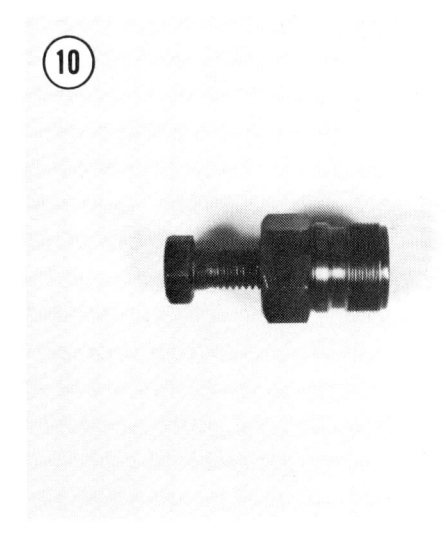

CHAPTER SEVEN

CAUTION
If normal rotor removal attempts fail, do not force the puller as the threads may be stripped out of the rotor causing expensive damage. Take it to a Yamaha dealer and have them remove it.

11. Remove the rotor and puller. Don't lose the Woodruff key on the crankshaft.

CAUTION
*Carefully inspect the inside of the rotor (**Figure 12**) for small bolts, washers or other metal "trash" that may have been picked up by the magnets. These small metal bits can cause severe damage to the magneto stator plate components.*

12. Install by reversing these removal steps, noting the following.
13. Make sure the Woodruff key (**Figure 13**) is in place on the crankshaft and align the keyway in the rotor with the key when installing the rotor.
14. Be sure to install the flat washer and lockwasher (**Figure 14**) prior to installing the rotor nut.
15. Tighten the rotor nut to torque values in **Table 2**. To keep the rotor from turning, hold it with the "Grabbit" (**Figure 15**) or a strap wrench.

NOTE
*Refer to Chapter One, **Basic Hand Tools**, for information on the "Grabbit".*

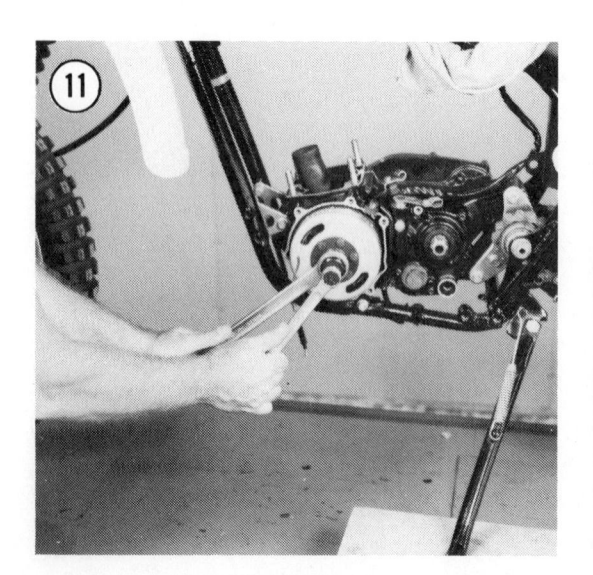

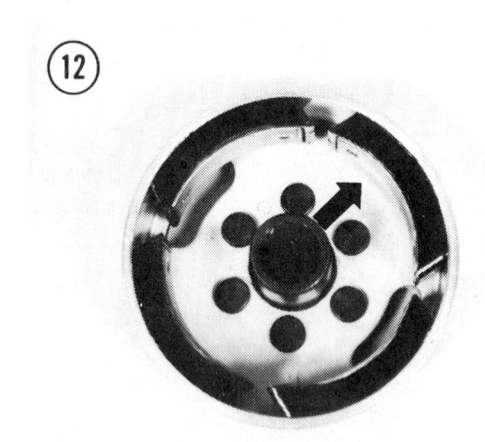

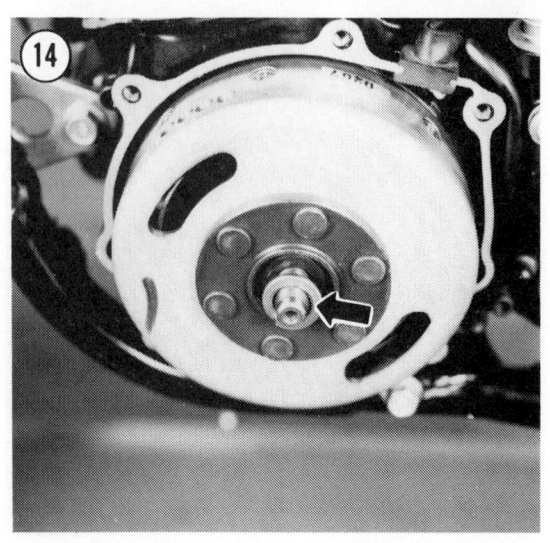

ELECTRICAL SYSTEM

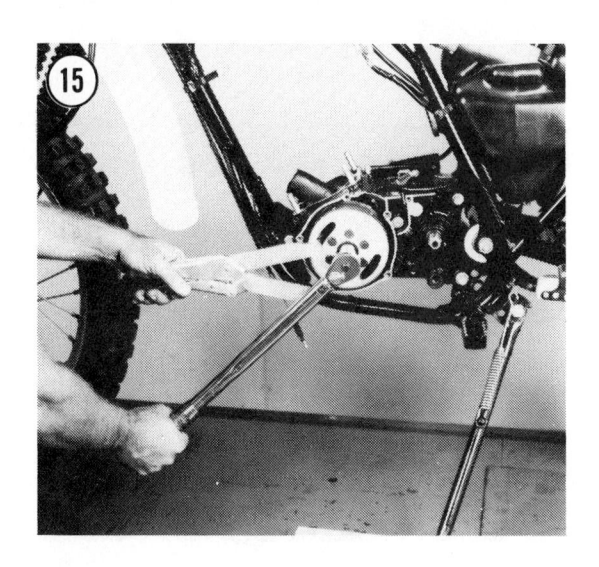

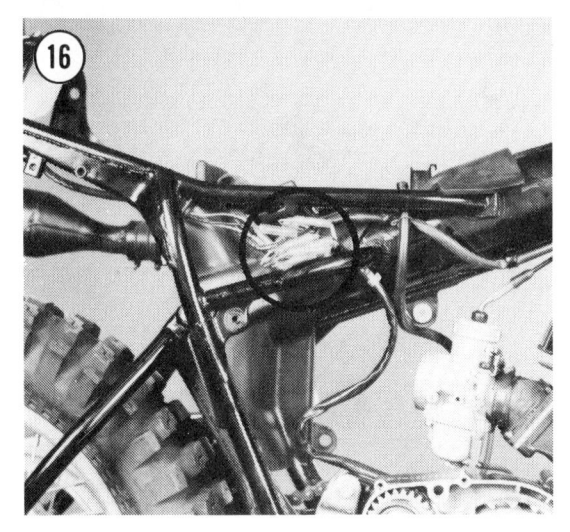

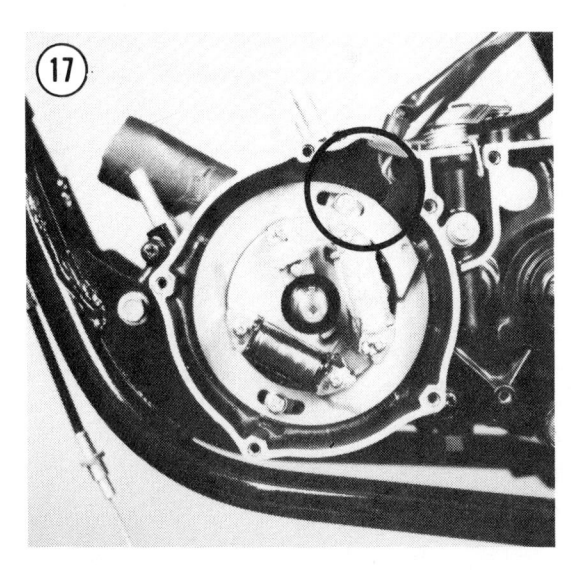

Stator Assembly Removal/Installation

1. Remove the magneto rotor as described in this chapter.
2. Disconnect the electrical wire connectors (**Figure 16**) from the magneto to the CDI unit.

NOTE
On some models is it necessary to partially remove the air cleaner assembly to gain access to the connectors.

3. Prior to removing the stator assembly, make a mark on the crankcase just above the timing mark (**Figure 17**) on the backing plate. This will assure correct ignition timing when the assembly is installed (providing it was correct prior to removal).
4. Remove the screws (**Figure 18**) securing the stator plate.
5. Carefully pull out the wiring harness with the rubber grommet from the crankcase (A, **Figure 19**) and any holding clips on the engine (B, **Figure 19**).
6. Remove the stator assembly.
7. Install by reversing these removal steps, noting the following.
8. When installing the stator assembly, align the mark made in Step 3 for preliminary ignition timing.
9. Route the electrical harness the same way it was before removal. Make sure to keep it away from the exhaust system.

10. Adjust the ignition timing as described in Chapter Three.

Charge, Lighting and Pulser Coils Replacement

1. Remove the magneto stator assembly as described in this chapter.
2. Remove the screws (**Figure 20**) securing the coils to the front of the stator plate.
3. Turn the stator plate over and disconnect the screw securing the clip and the ground connector.
4. Carefully remove the coils and wiring harness.
5. Install by reversing these removal steps.
6. Make sure all electrical connections are tight and free from corrosion. This is absolutely necessary with a CDI ignition system.

Magneto Coil Testing

Test specifications are available only for models since 1980. Pre-1980 models should be taken to a Yamaha dealer or competent specialist for testing. It is not necessary to remove the stator plate to perform the following tests. It is removed in this procedure for clarity.

Charge Coil Resistance

Use an ohmmeter set at R x 100 and check resistance between the following stator electrical terminals (**Figure 21**):

  a. High speed winding
    IT425, IT250 (red to blue): 35 ohms +/- 10%
    IT175, IT125 (red to black): 13.6 ohms +/-10%
  b. Low speed winding
    IT425 (brown to black): 240 ohms +/-10%
    IT250 (brown to green): 370 ohms +/-10%
    IT175, IT125 (black to brown): 420 ohms +/-10%

If the resistance measured does not match the specifications, the coil must be replaced.

Lighting Coil Resistance

Use an ohmmeter set at R x 1 and check resistance between the red/yellow wire

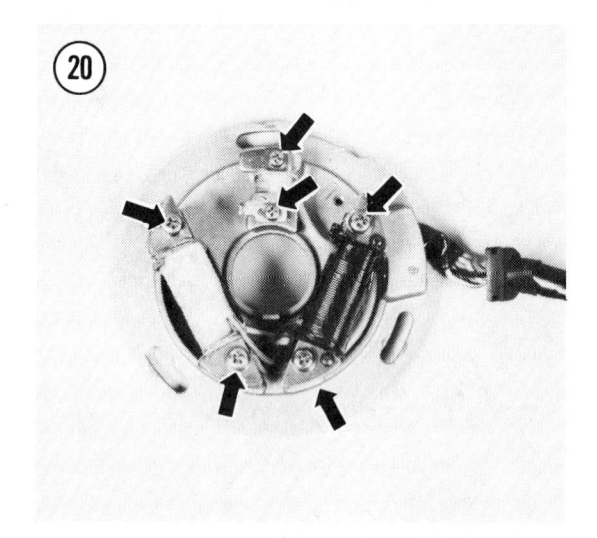

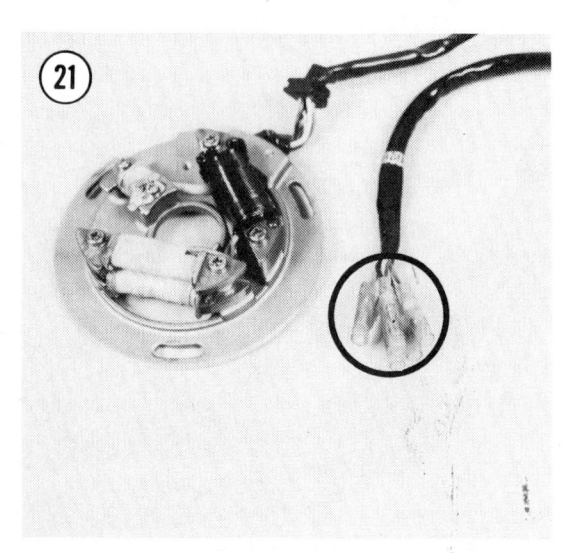

ELECTRICAL SYSTEM

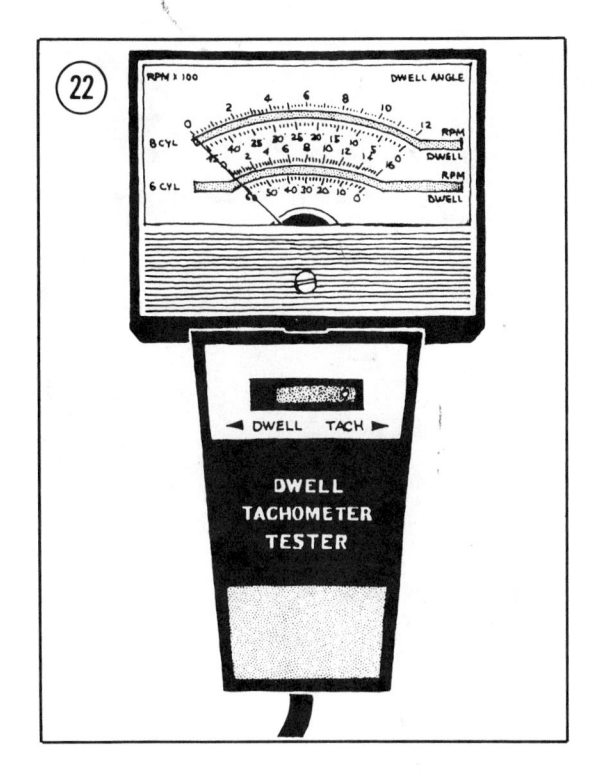

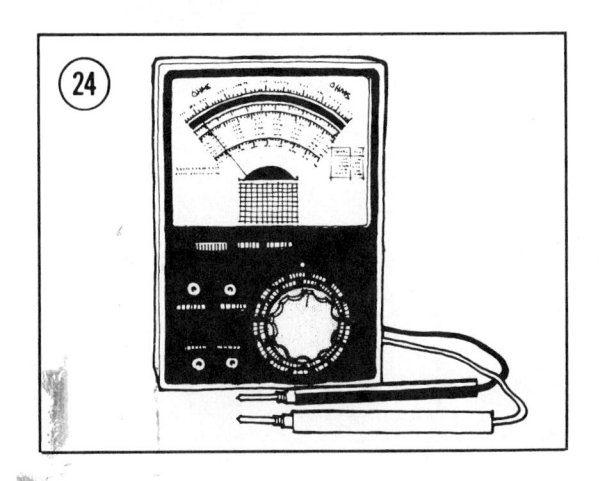

terminal and ground. Connect the positive (+) test lead to the red/yellow wire (**Figure 21**) and the negative (-) test lead to a good ground (stator plate if removed from bike or engine component if installed). The resistance should be as follows:

   a. IT425: 240 ohms +/-10%
   b. IT250: 0.43 ohms +/-10%
   c. IT175, IT125: 0.48 ohms +/-10%

If the resistance measured does not match the specifications, the coil must be replaced.

Pulser Coil Resistance

Use an ohmmeter set at R x 10 and check resistance between the white/red wire and the black wire terminals. The resistance should be as follows:

   a. IT425: 4.0 ohms +/-10%
   b. IT250: 7.5 ohms +/-10%
   c. IT175, IT125: 12.4 ohms +/-10%

If the resistance measured does not match the specifications, the coil must be replaced.

Magneto Output Test

The magneto must be assembled and installed on the engine for the following test.

1. Attach a portable tachometer (**Figure 22**) to the engine following the manufacturer's instructions.
2. Remove the screws (**Figure 23**) securing the headlight assembly (one on each side).
3. Pivot the headlight assembly out, *do not disconnect it* from the wiring harness.
4. Connect the positive (+) test lead of an AC voltmeter (**Figure 24**) into the red/yellow terminal (**Figure 25**).

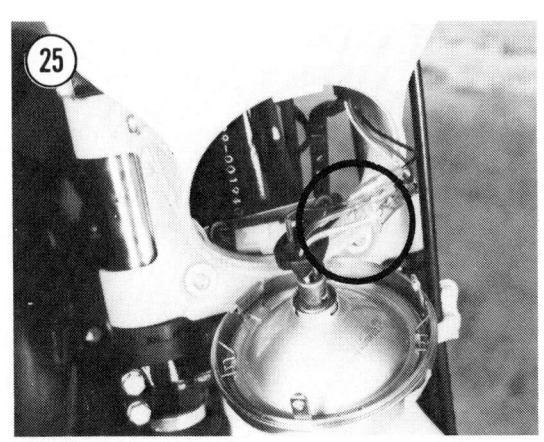

NOTE

Do not *disconnect this terminal; simply insert the test lead into the plastic protective sleeve, making sure it makes contact with the metal electrical terminal.*

5. Connect the negative (-) test lead to a good ground.
6. Start the engine and turn the lights to the ON position.
7. Check the output voltage at 2 different engine speeds. The voltage for all models should be as follows:
   a. 2,500 rpm (minimum): 5.0 volts
   b. 8,000 rpm (minimum): 7.0 volts
8. If the measured voltage is greater or less than specified, check for a bad or dirty electrical connection, damaged wires, a burned out light bulb, corroded light bulb socket or a light bulb of the incorrect wattage (usually too large). If connections are clean and tight and all lights are correct and working properly, the magneto is faulty and must be replaced.

IGNITION COIL

Removal/Installation — All Models

1. Remove the seat and fuel tank (**Figure 26**).
2. Disconnect the electrical wires from the ignition coil (**Figure 27**).
3. Remove the screws (**Figure 28**) securing the ignition coil to the frame and remove the coil.
4. Install by reversing these removal steps. Make sure all electrical connections are tight and free of corrosion.

Testing

The ignition coil is a form of transformer which develops the high voltage required to jump the spark plug gap. The only maintenance required is that of keeping the electrical connections clean and tight and occasionally checking to see that the coil is mounted securely.

If the coil condition is doubtful, there are several checks which may be made.

First, as a quick check of coil condition, disconnect the high voltage lead from the

ELECTRICAL SYSTEM

29

Secondary | Primary

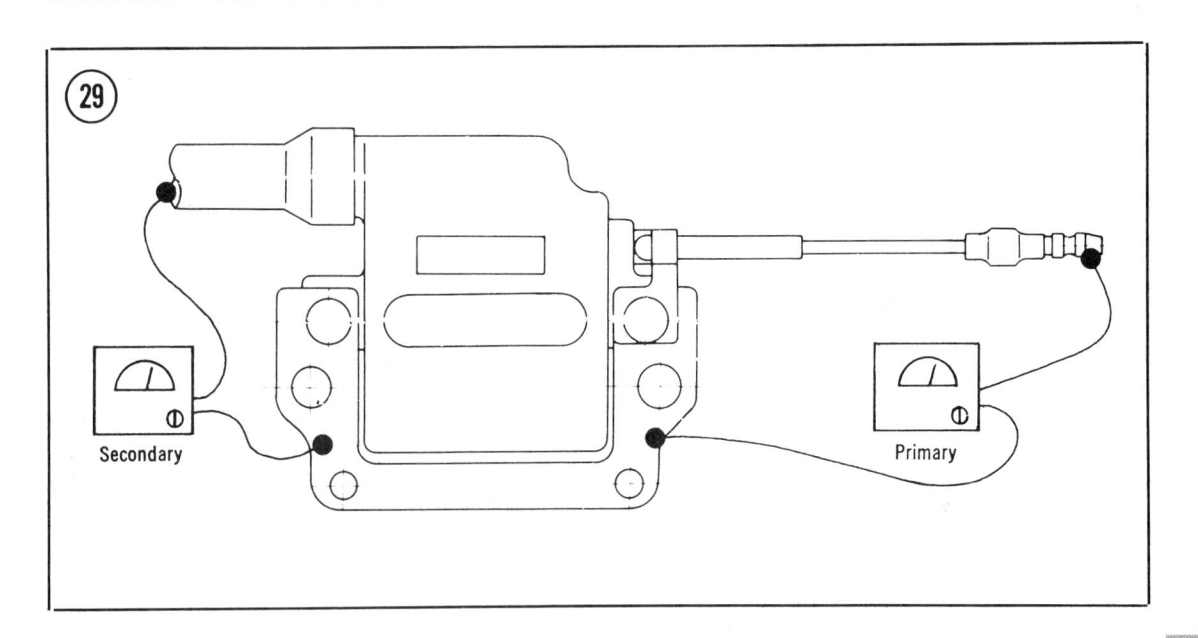

30

spark plug, then hold it about 1/4 in. (6 mm) away from the cylinder head.

WARNING
Hold the spark plug wire with an insulated screwdriver as the high voltage generated by the CDI could produce serious or fatal shocks.

Kick the engine over with the kickstarter. If a fat blue spark occurs the coil is in good condition; if not proceed as follows.

Refer to **Figure 29** for this procedure. Disconnect the ignition coil wires before testing.

1. Measure the coil primary resistance using an ohmmeter set at R x 1. Measure the resistance between the primary terminal and the mounting flange. The value should be 1.0 ohms +/- 10%.

2. Measure the secondary resistance using an ohmmeter set at R x 1,000. Measure the resistance between the secondary lead (spark plug lead) and the mounting flange. The value should be 5900 ± 15%.

3. If the coil resistance does not meet these specifications, the coil must be replaced. If the coil exhibits visible damage, it should be replaced.

ENGINE KILL SWITCH

Testing

1. Disconnect the electrical connectors from the engine kill switch (wire color black/white and black, all models).

2. Use an ohmmeter set at R x 1 and connect the 2 leads of the ohmmeter to the 2 electrical wires of the switch.

3. Push the kill switch button. If the switch is good there will be continuity (very low resistance).

4. If the needle does not move (no continuity) the switch is faulty and must be replaced. Remove the screws securing the switch (**Figure 30**) and replace it with a known good one.

LIGHTING SYSTEM

The lighting system consists only of a headlight, taillight and light switch.

If the headlight burns out while the engine is operating, the taillight will usually burn out due to the excess voltage in the lighting circuit. Always remember to check taillight operation after a headlight has been replaced.

Always use the correct wattage bulb as indicated in this section. The use of a larger wattage bulb will give a dim light and a smaller wattage bulb will burn out prematurely. If the headlight bulb burns out while the engine is running, reduce speed and replace the bulb as soon as possible.

Headlight and Number Plate Replacement

1. Remove the screws and lockwashers (**Figure 31**) securing the headlight assembly into the number plate.
2. Tilt the headlight assembly out and pull back the rubber boot (A, **Figure 32**).
3. Carefully twist the socket out of the backside of the headlight (B, **Figure 32**).
4. Remove the bulb from the headlight assembly (**Figure 33**).

> *NOTE*
> *The correct replacement bulb for all models is a 6 volt, 25W/25W bulb. Always wipe the bulb clean prior to installing it. Make sure the bulb socket is clean and free from corrosion. Clean off with fine sandpaper if necessary.*

5. If the lens assembly or the lens cover need to be replaced, remove the wire clips (C, **Figure 32**) and remove them from the trim bezel.

> *NOTE*
> *Wash off the inside and outside of the lens cover with a mild detergent and dry prior to installation.*

6. To remove the number plate, remove the screws, washers and lockwashers (**Figure 34**) securing it to the forks and remove it. While the number plate is removed, inspect the condition of the rubber dampers (**Figure 35**).

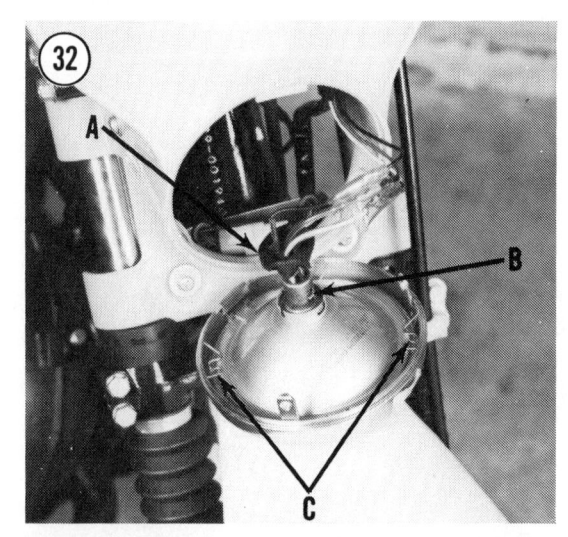

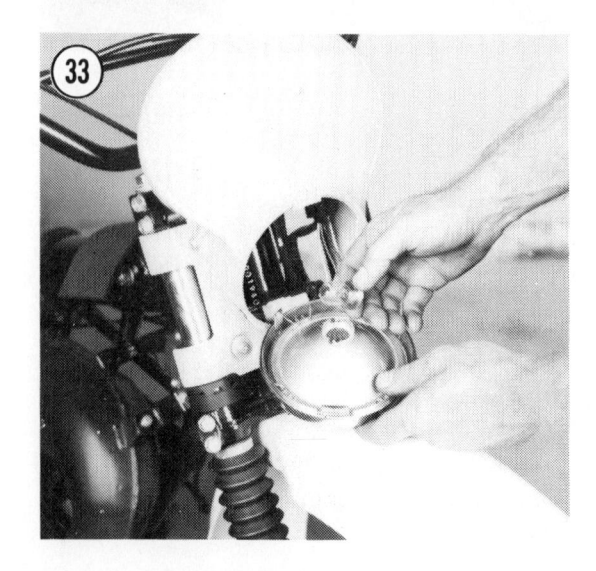

ELECTRICAL SYSTEM

If replacement is necessary, refer to *Front Fork Removal/Installation* in Chapter Eight for removal procedure.

7. Install by reversing these removal steps. Don't forget to install the washers and lockwashers with the attachment screws.

Taillight Replacement

Remove the screws securing the lens (**Figure 36**) and remove it. Wash out the inside and outside of the lens with a mild detergent and wipe dry. Replace the bulb and install the lens; do not overtighten it as the lens may crack.

NOTE
The correct replacement bulb for all models is a 6 volt, 5.3W bulb.

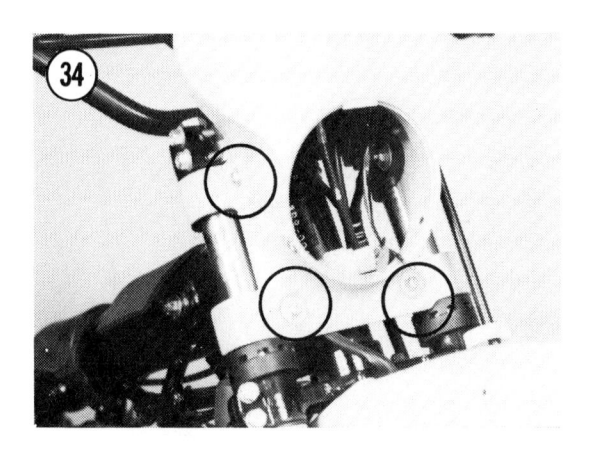

SPEEDOMETER HOUSING

Removal/Installation

1. Remove the headlight and number plate as described in this chapter.
2. Disconnect the speedometer cable (A, **Figure 37**).
3. If only the top portion is to be removed, remove the spring clips, washers and rubber dampers (B, **Figure 37**) and remove the top (C, **Figure 37**).
4. For complete removal, remove the bolts, washers and lockwashers (D, **Figure 37**).
5. Install by reversing these removal steps. Replace the rubber dampers if necessary.

WIRING DIAGRAMS

Wiring diagrams for all models are located at the end of this book.

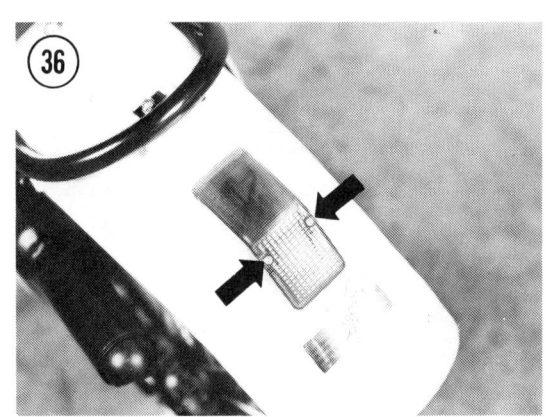

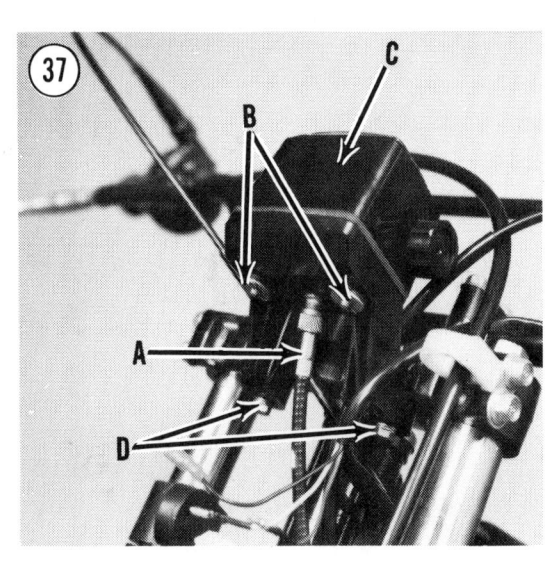

Table 1 CDI TROUBLESHOOTING

Symptoms	Probable cause
Weak spark	Poor connections (clean and retighten) High voltage leak (replace defective wire) Defective coil (replace ignition coil)
No spark	Wiring broken (replace wire) Defective ignition (replace coil) Defective pulser coil in magneto (replace coil)

Table 2 MAGNETO ROTOR NUT TORQUE SPECIFICATIONS

Model	Foot-pounds (ft.-lb.)	Newton meters (N•m)
IT425G	30	40
IT400F	30	40
IT400E, D	58	80
IT250G, F	30	40
IT250E, D	58	80
IT175G, F	50	70
IT175E, D	36	50
IT125G	50	70

> **NOTE:** If you own a 1981 or later model, first check the Supplement at the back of the book for any new service information.

CHAPTER EIGHT

FRONT SUSPENSION AND STEERING

This chapter describes repair and maintenance of the front wheel, forks and steering components.

All models are equipped with dampened telescopic forks. The dampening rate can be changed by the viscosity of the fork oil and the spring rate can be changed by replacing the original springs. Two different sets of factory springs are available for most forks in the IT series. Another variable is the addition of air pressure forks on some models. The combinations of all of these will permit you to choose the precise suspension feel for the conditions of the trials course for that day's event.

Front fork air pressure procedure and fork oil change are covered in Chapter Three.

Refer to **Table 1** for torque specifications on the front suspension. **Tables 1 and 2** are at the end of this chapter.

FRONT WHEEL

Removal

NOTE
If the brake assembly does not have to be removed for service it is not necessary to disconnect either the brake or speedometer cable (the speedometer cable enters the brake assembly only on model IT125). The brake assembly can be left partially attached to the left-hand fork leg.

1. Place a milk crate or wood block(s) under the frame to support it securely with the front wheel off the ground.
2. If the brake assembly is going to be removed, slacken the brake cable at the hand lever (**Figure 1**). Slacken the brake cable at the brake plate (A, **Figure 2**) and remove the cable end (B, **Figure 2**) from the brake arm. On model IT125, remove the speedometer cable clip and withdraw the speedometer cable (C, **Figure 2**) from the brake assembly.
3. On all models except IT125, unscrew the collar and disconnect the speedometer cable

(A, **Figure 3**) from the right-hand side of the hub.

4. Remove the cotter pin and remove the axle nut (B, **Figure 3**).

5. Remove the front axle; twist while pulling it out.

6. Carefully pull the wheel down and forward to disengage the brake panel from the boss on the front fork.

7. If the brake assembly is left in place, pivot the left-hand fork leg outward as you carefully pull the wheel forward (**Figure 4**). Leave the brake assembly partially attached to the fork leg (**Figure 5**).

Inspection

Measure the radial and axial runout of the wheel rim with a dial indicator as shown in **Figure 6**. The standard value for both radial and axial runout is 0.02 in. (0.5 mm). The maximum permissible limit on both is 0.08 in. (2 mm).

Tighten or replace any loose or bent spokes. Refer to *Spoke Adjustment* or *Spoke Inspection and Replacement* in this chapter.

Check the axle runout as described under *Front Hub Inspection* in this chapter.

Installation

1. Make sure the axle bearing surfaces of the fork sliders and the axle are free from burrs and nicks.

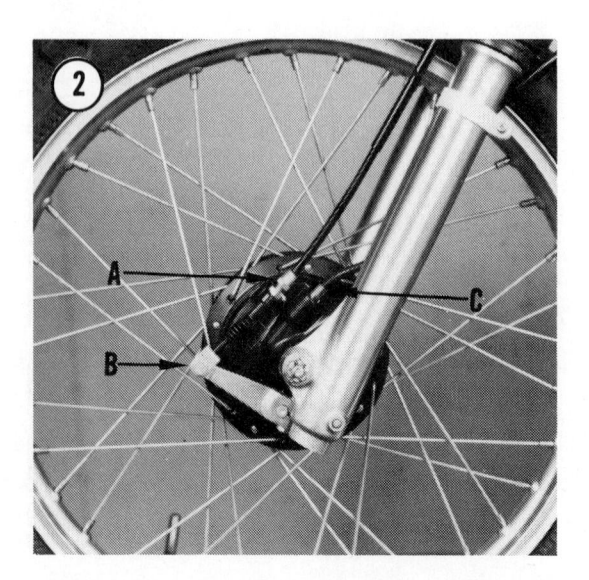

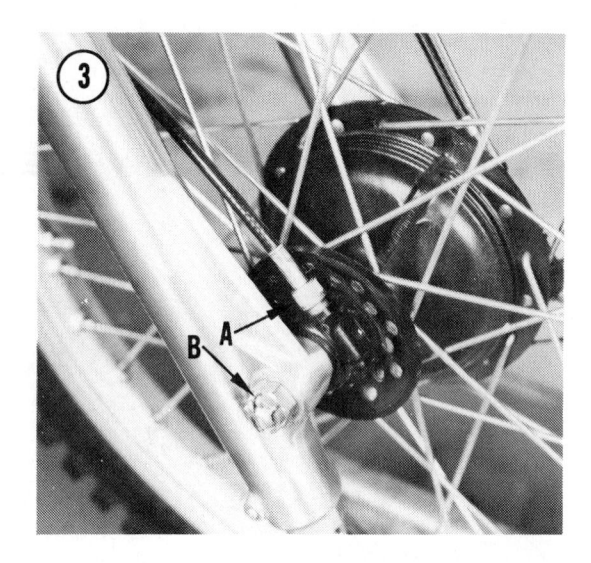

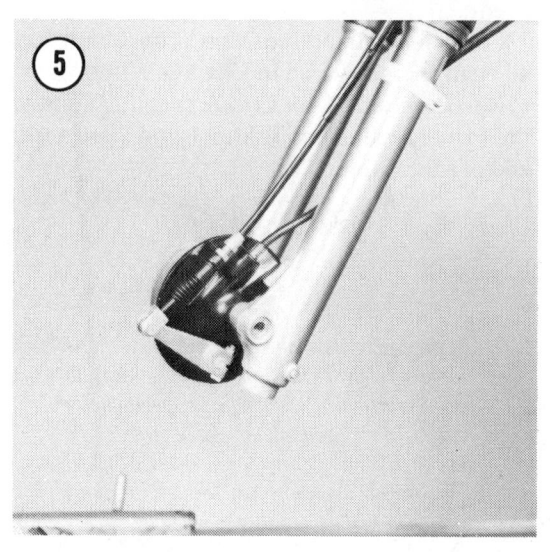

FRONT SUSPENSION AND STEERING 197

6
Dial gauge — Wheel rim

7

8

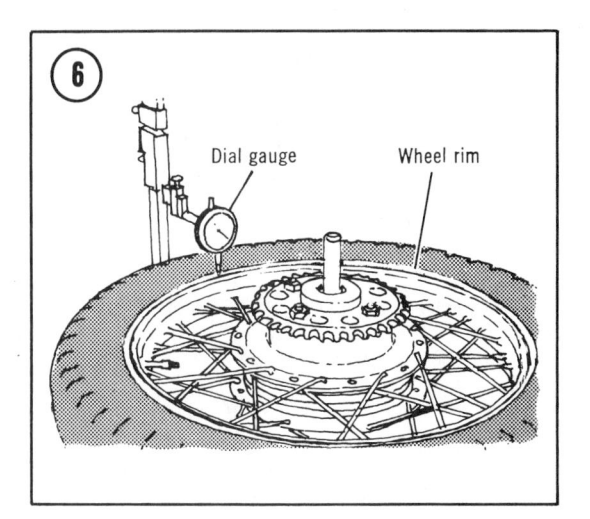

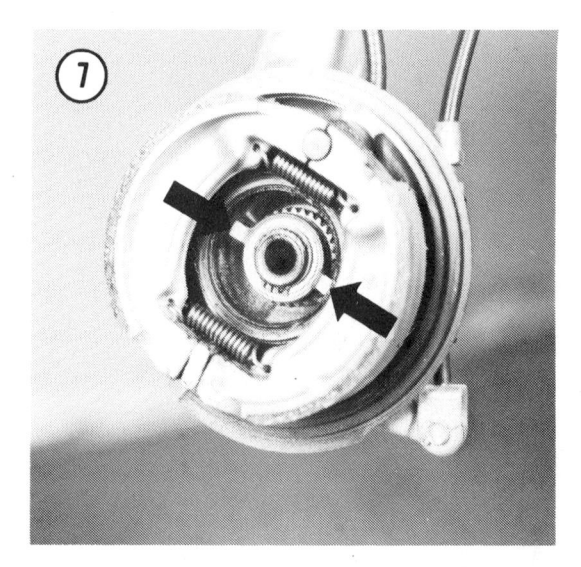

2. Clean the axle and axle holes (in fork sliders) with solvent and thoroughly dry. Make sure all surfaces the axle comes in contact with are free from dirt prior to installation.
3. Apply a light coat of grease to the axle, bearings and grease seals.
4. Position the wheel into place and insert the front axle in from the left-hand side (except on model IT125 where it is installed from the right-hand side). Make sure the tabs in the speedometer drive unit (**Figure 7**) align with the notches in the front hub.

NOTE
*Make sure the boss on the left-hand fork slider is properly engaged in the groove in the brake panel (**Figure 8**). This is necessary for proper brake operation.*

5. Tighten the axle nut to the torque value listed in **Table 1**.
6. Install a new cotter pin and bend it over completely. Never reinstall an old cotter pin as it may break and fall out.
7. If removed, attach the front brake cable and adjust the brake as described under *Front Brake Adjustment* in Chapter Three.
8. Insert the speedometer cable and attach it either with the collar or clip.

NOTE
Rotate the wheel slowly when inserting the cable so that it will engage properly.

9. After the wheel is installed, completely rotate it. Apply the brake several times to make sure that the wheel rotates freely and that the brake is operating correctly.
10. Remove the milk crate or wood blocks from under the frame.

FRONT HUB

Refer to **Figure 9** for this procedure.

Disassembly

1. Remove the front wheel as described under *Front Wheel Removal* in this chapter.

CHAPTER EIGHT

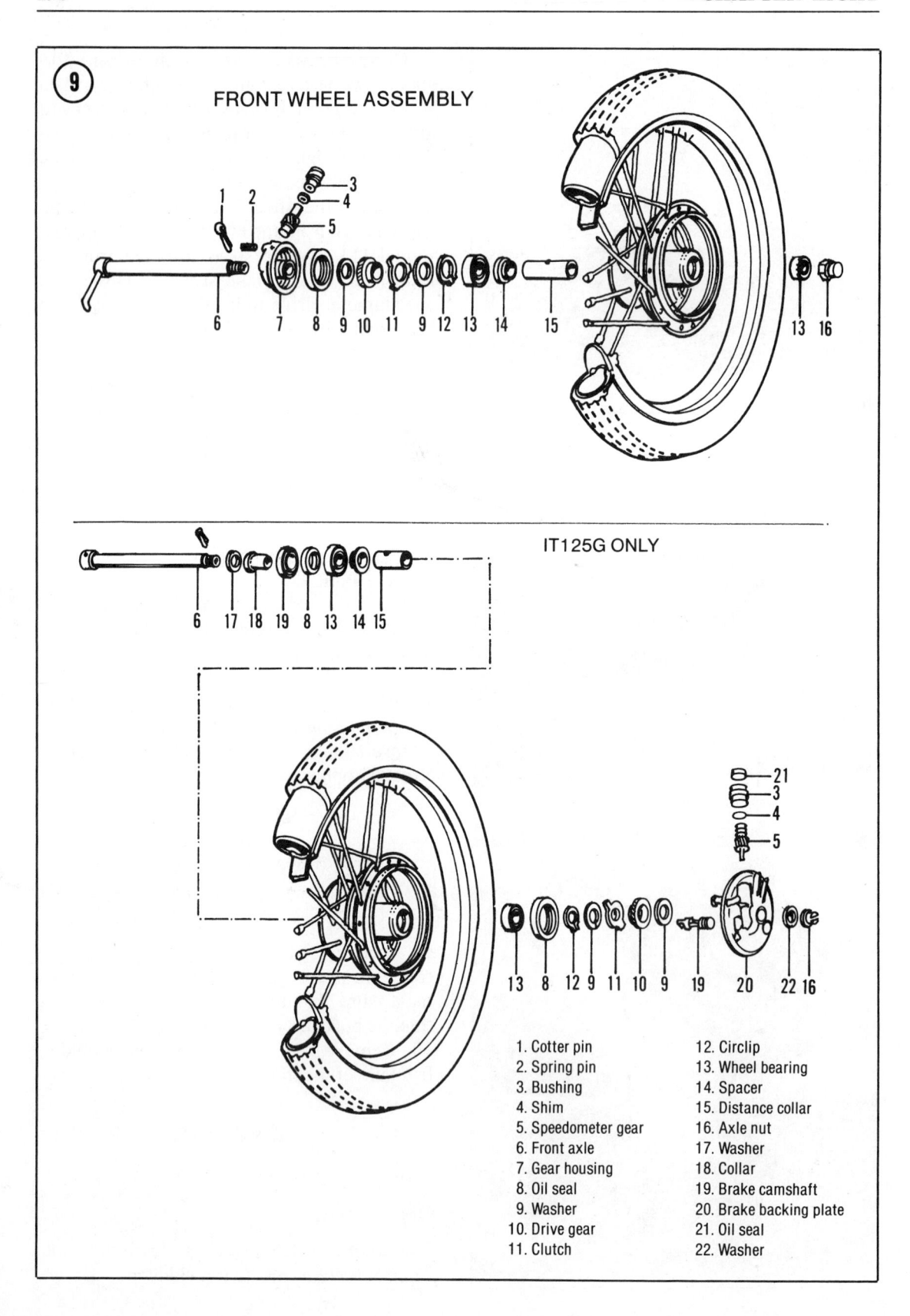

FRONT WHEEL ASSEMBLY

IT125G ONLY

1. Cotter pin
2. Spring pin
3. Bushing
4. Shim
5. Speedometer gear
6. Front axle
7. Gear housing
8. Oil seal
9. Washer
10. Drive gear
11. Clutch
12. Circlip
13. Wheel bearing
14. Spacer
15. Distance collar
16. Axle nut
17. Washer
18. Collar
19. Brake camshaft
20. Brake backing plate
21. Oil seal
22. Washer

FRONT SUSPENSION AND STEERING

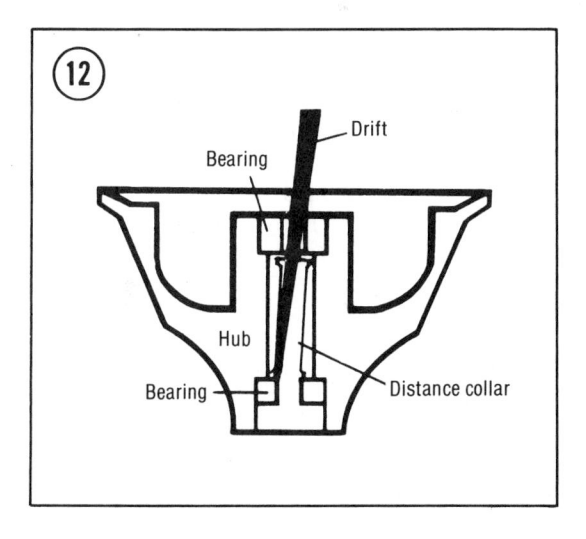

2. If still in place, pull the brake assembly straight up and out of the hub (**Figure 10**).

3. To remove the right- and left-hand bearings (**Figure 11**) and distance collar, insert a soft aluminum or brass drift into one side of the hub. Push the distance collar over to one side and place the drift on the inner race of the lower bearing (**Figure 12**). Tap the bearing out of the hub, with a hammer, working around the perimeter of the inner race.

NOTE
If the bearings are difficult to remove there is a special Yamaha tool designed to fit into the hole in the distance collar to aid in the removal.

4. Remove the distance collar and tap out the opposite bearing.

Inspection

1. Thoroughly clean out the inside of the hub with solvent and dry with compressed air or a shop cloth.

NOTE
Avoid getting any greasy solvent residue on the brake drum during this procedure. If this happens, clean it off with a clean shop cloth and lacquer thinner.

2. Do not clean sealed bearings. If non-sealed bearings are installed, thoroughly clean them in solvent and thoroughly dry with compressed air. Do not let the bearing spin while drying.

3. Turn each bearing by hand (**Figure 13**). Make sure the bearings turn smoothly.

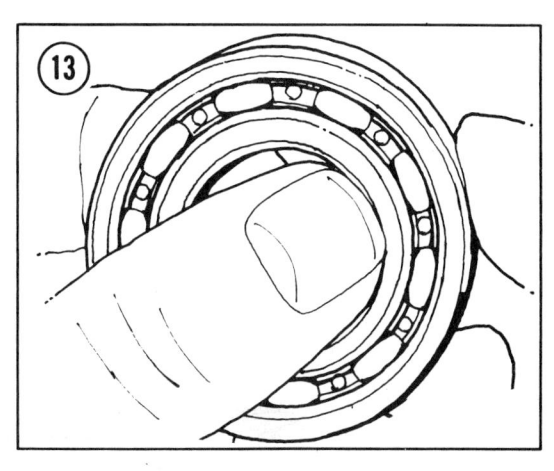

NOTE
Some axial play is normal, but radial play should be negligible. The bearing should turn smoothly.

4. On non-sealed bearings, check the balls for evidence of wear, pitting or excessive heat (bluish tint). Replace bearing if necessary; always replace as a complete set. When replacing, be sure to take your old bearings along to ensure a perfect matchup.

NOTE
Fully sealed bearings are available from many good bearing specialty shops. Fully sealed bearings provide better protection from dirt and moisture that may get into the hub.

5. Check the axle for wear and straightness. Use a V-block and dial indicators as shown in **Figure 14**. If the runout is 0.008 in. (0.2 mm) or greater, the axle should be replaced.

Assembly

1. On non-sealed bearings, pack the bearings with a good quality bearing grease. Work the grease in between the balls thoroughly. Turn the bearing by hand a couple of times to make sure the grease is distributed evenly inside the bearing.
2. Pack the wheel hub and distance collar with multipurpose grease.

CAUTION
*Install the wheel bearings with the sealed side facing out. During installation, tap the bearings squarely into place and tap on the outer race only. Use a socket (**Figure 15**) that matches the outer race diameter. Do not tap on the inner race or the bearing might be damaged. Be sure that the bearings are completely seated.*

3. Install the left-hand bearing.
4. Press in the distance collar.
5. Install the right-hand bearing.
6. Install the front wheel as described under *Front Wheel Installation* in this chapter.

WHEELS

Wheels should be inspected prior to each trials event or weekend ride in the boonies. This little time spent will help keep you in the event, or out on the trail longer.

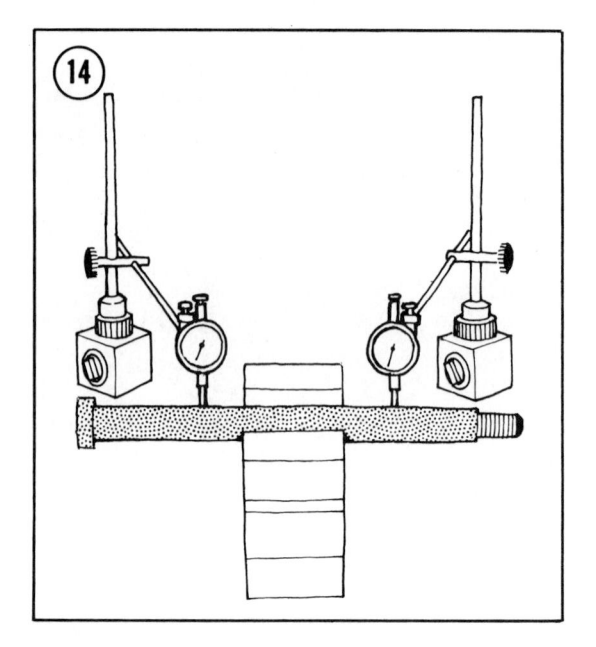

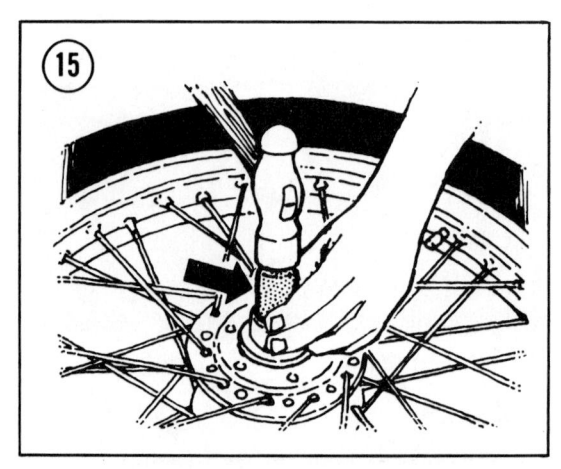

Wheel Balance

An unbalanced wheel is unsafe. Depending on the degree of unbalance and the speed of the bike, the rider may experience anything from a mild vibration to a violent shimmy and loss of control.

Balance weights are applied to the spokes on the light side of the wheel to correct the condition.

NOTE
Balance the rear wheel with the final drive sprocket assembly attached as this affects

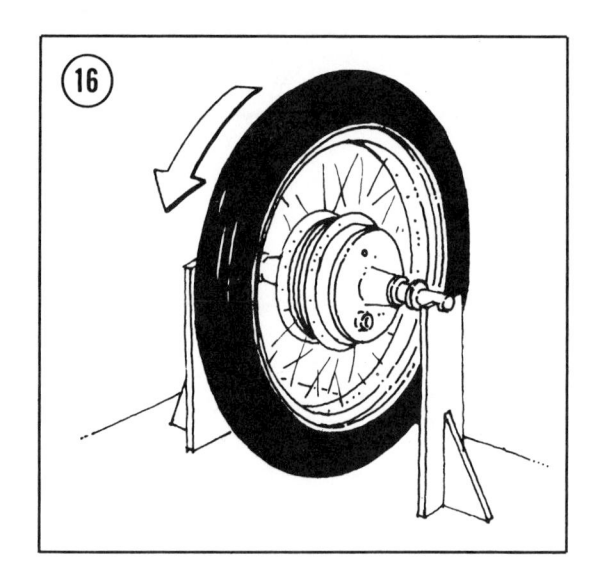

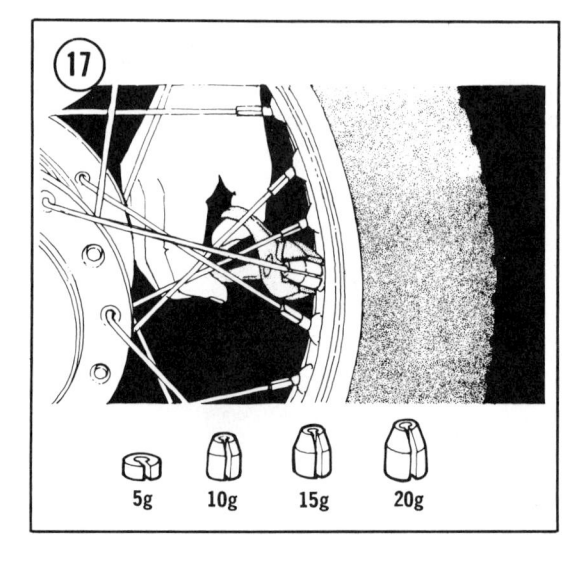

FRONT SUSPENSION AND STEERING

4. Spin the wheel several more times. If the wheel keeps coming to rest at the same point, it is out of balance.
5. Attach a weight to the upper (or light) side of the wheel on the spoke (**Figure 17**). Weights come in 4 sizes: 5, 10, 15 and 20 grams. Crimp the weight onto the spoke with ordinary gas pliers.
6. Experiment with different weights until the wheel comes to rest at a different position each time it is spun. When this happens, consider the wheel balanced and tighten the weights so they won't be thrown off.

Spoke Inspection and Replacement

Spokes loosen with use and should be checked prior to each trials event or weekend ride. The "tuning fork" method for checking spoke tightness is simple and works well. Tap each spoke with a spoke wrench or the shank of a screwdriver and listen for a tone. A tightened spoke will emit a clear, ringing tone and a loose spoke will sound flat. All the spokes in a correctly tightened wheel will emit tones of similar pitch but not necessarily the same precise tone.

Bent or stripped spokes should be replaced as soon as they are detected, as they can destruct an expensive hub. Unscrew the nipple from the spoke and depress the nipple into the rim far enough to free the end of the spoke; take care not to push the nipple all the way in. Remove the damaged spoke from the hub and use it to match a new spoke of identical length. If necessary, trim the new spoke to match the original and dress the end of the thread with a thread die. Install the new spoke in the hub and screw on the nipple; tighten it until the spoke's tone is similar to the tone of the other spokes in the wheel. Periodically check the new spoke; it will stretch and must be retightened several times before it takes its final set.

Spoke Adjustment

If all spokes appear loose, tighten all on one side of the hub, then tighten all on the other side. One-half to one turn should be sufficient; do not overtighten.

the balance. The front brake panel does not rotate with the wheel so it should be removed from the front wheel.

Before you attempt to balance the wheel, check to be sure that the wheel bearings are in good condition and properly lubricated and that the brakes do not drag. The wheel must rotate freely.
1. Remove the wheel as described under *Front Wheel Removal* or *Rear Wheel Removal* in this chapter or in Chapter Nine.
2. Mount the wheel on a fixture such as the one shown in **Figure 16** so it can rotate freely.
3. Give the wheel a spin and let it coast to a stop. Mark the tire at the lowest point.

18

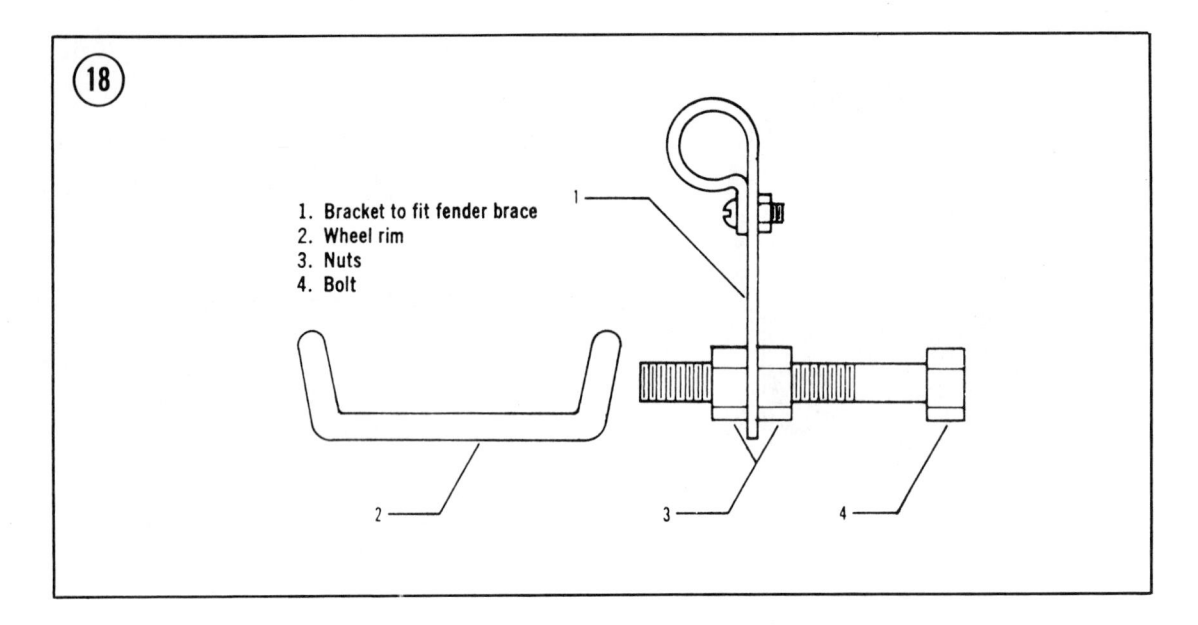

1. Bracket to fit fender brace
2. Wheel rim
3. Nuts
4. Bolt

After tightening the spokes, check rim runout to be sure you haven't pulled the rim out of shape.

One way to check rim runout is to mount a dial indicator on the front fork or swing arm, so that it bears against the rim.

If you don't have a dial indicator, improvise one as shown in **Figure 18**. Adjust the position of the bolt until it just clears the rim. Rotate the rim and note whether the clearance increases or decreases. Mark the tire with chalk or light crayon at areas that produce significantly large or small clearance. Clearance must not change by more than 0.08 in. (2 mm).

To pull the rim out, tighten spokes which terminate on the same side of the hub and loosen spokes which terminate on the opposite side of the hub (**Figure 19**). In most cases, only a slight amount of adjustment is necessary to true a rim. After adjustment, rotate the rim and make sure another area has not pulled out of true. Continue adjustment and checking until runout does not exceed 0.08 in. (2 mm).

TIRE CHANGING

Removal

1. Remove the valve core and deflate the tire.
2. Press the entire bead on both sides of the tire into the center of the rim.
3. Lubricate the beads with soapy water.

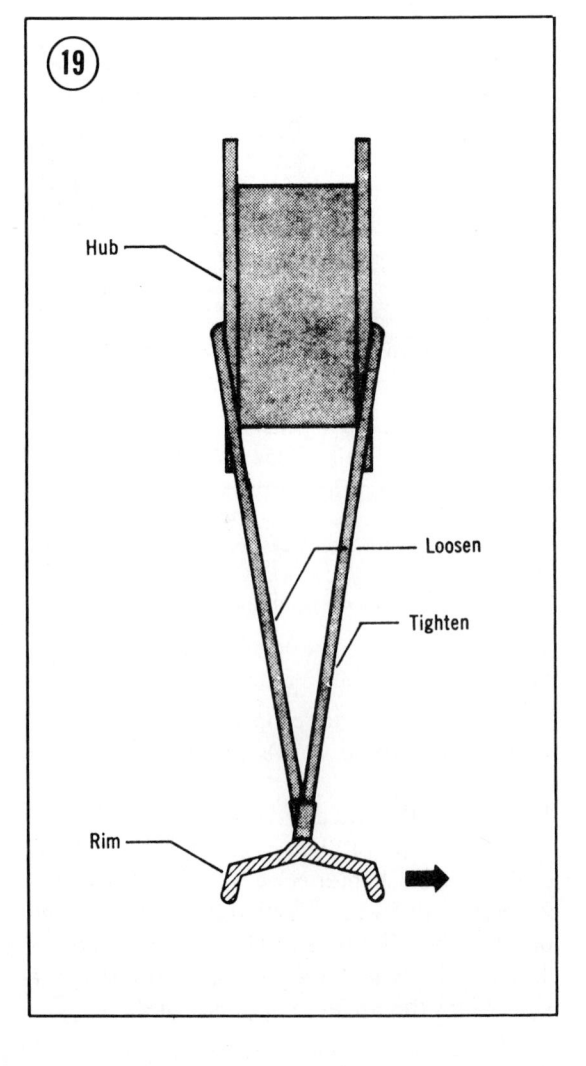

19

Hub
Loosen
Tighten
Rim

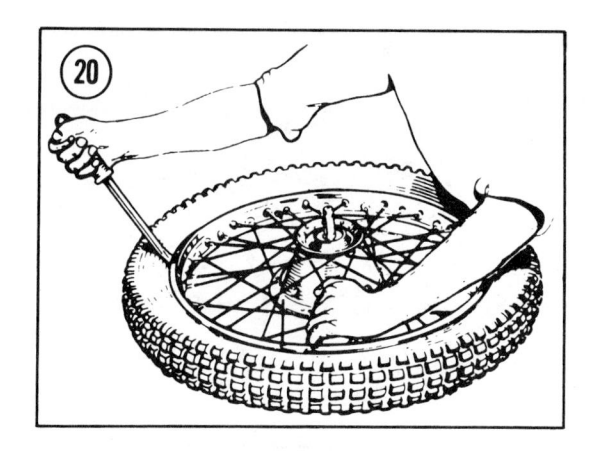

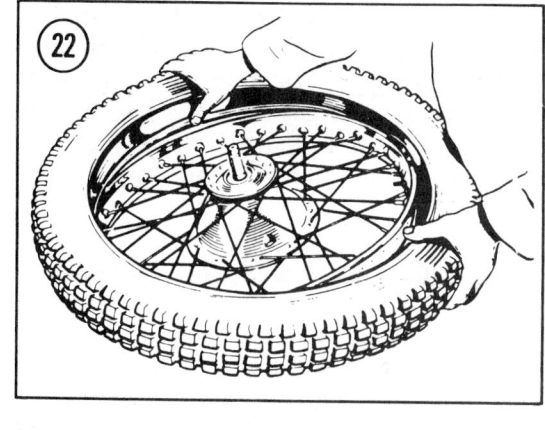

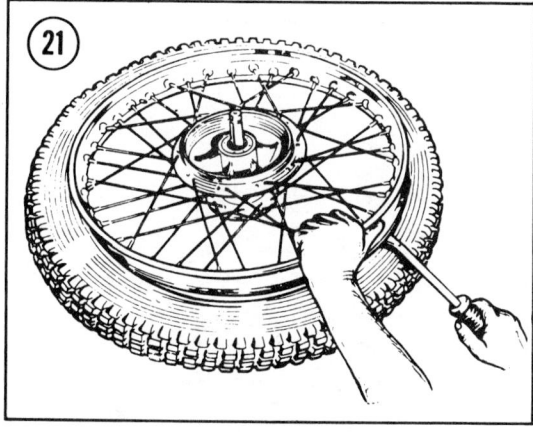

FRONT SUSPENSION AND STEERING

second bead off of the rim, working around the wheel with two tire irons as with the first bead.

Installation

1. Carefully check the tire for any damage, especially inside. On the front tire carefully check the sidewall as it is very vulnerable to damage from rocks and other sharp objects found on some trials courses.

2. A new tire may have balancing rubbers inside. These are not patches and should not be disturbed. A colored spot near the bead indicates a lighter point on the tire. This should be placed next to the valve.

3. Check that the spoke ends do not protrude through the nipples into the center of the rim where they can puncture the tube. File off any protruding spoke ends.

4. Insert the tire iron under the bead next to the valve (**Figure 20**). Force the bead on the opposite side of the tire into the center of the rim and pry the bead over the rim with the tire iron.

5. Insert a second tire iron next to the first to hold the bead over the rim. Then work around the tire with the first tire iron, prying the bead over the rim. Be careful not to pinch the inner tube with the tire irons.

6. Remove the valve from the hole in the rim and remove the tube from the tire.

NOTE
Step 7 is required only if it is necessary to completely remove the tire from the rim, such as for tire replacement.

7. Stand the tire upright. Insert the tire iron between the second bead and the side of the rim that the first bead was pried over (**Figure 21**). Force the bead on the opposite side from the tire iron into the center of the rim. Pry the

4. Be sure the rim rubber tape is in place with the rough side toward the rim.

5. Install the core into the inner tube valve. Put the tube in the tire and inflate it just enough to round it out. Too much air will make installing it in the tire difficult and too little will increase the chances of pinching the tube with the tire irons.

6. Lubricate the tire beads and rim with soapy water. Pull the tube partly out of the tire at the valve. Squeeze the beads together to hold the tube and insert the valve into the hole in the rim (**Figure 22**). The lower bead should go into the center of the rim with the upper bead outside it.

7. Press the lower bead into the rim center on each side of the valve, working around the tire

in both directions (**Figure 23**). Use a tire iron for the last few inches of the bead (**Figure 24**).

8. Press the upper bead into the rim opposite the valve. Pry the bead into the rim on both sides of the initial point with a tire iron, working around the rim to the valve (**Figure 25**).

9. Wiggle the valve to be sure the tube is not trapped under the bead. Set the valve squarely in its hole before screwing on the valve nut to hold it against the rim.

10. Check the bead on both sides of the tire for even fit around the rim. Inflate the tire slowly to seat the beads in the rim. It may be necessary to bounce the tire to complete the seating. Inflate to the required pressure. Balance the wheel as described previously.

TIRE REPAIRS

Every trials or dirt rider will eventually experience trouble with a tire or tube. Repairs and replacement are fairly simple and every rider should know the techniques.

Patching a motorcycle tube is only a temporary fix, especially on a dirt bike. The tire flexes too much and the patch could rub right off. However, a patched tire will get you back to camp where you can replace the tube with the extra one that should be carried in your tool box or tow vehicle.

Tire Repair Kits

Tire repair kits can be purchased from motorcycle dealers and some auto supply stores. When buying, specify that the kit you want is for motorcycles.

There are 2 types of tire repair kits:
 a. Hot patch
 b. Cold patch

Hot patches are stronger because they actually vulcanize to the tube, becoming part of it. However, they are far too bulky to carry for trail repairs and the strength is unnecessary for a temporary repair.

Cold patches are not vulcanized to the tube; they are simply glued to it. Though not as strong as hot patches, cold patches are still very durable. Cold patch kits are less bulky than hot and more easily applied under adverse conditions. A cold patch kit contains

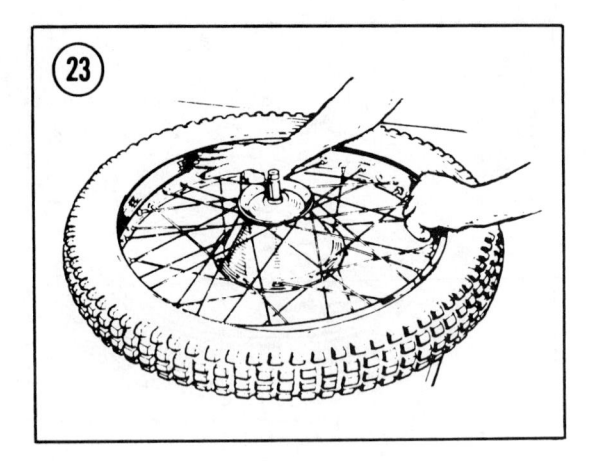

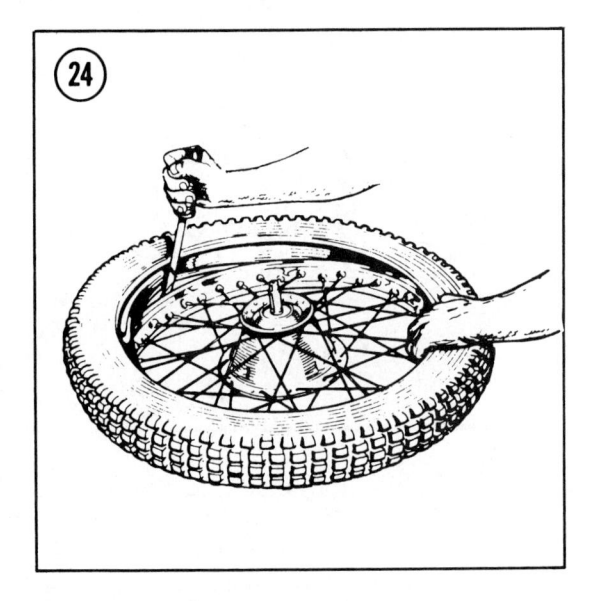

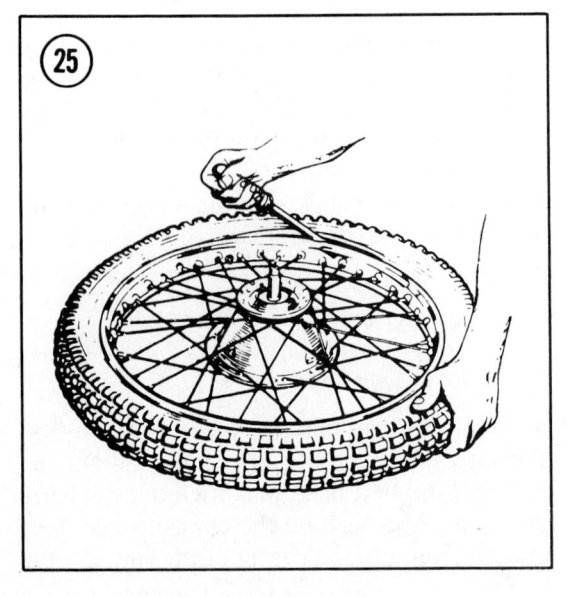

FRONT SUSPENSION AND STEERING

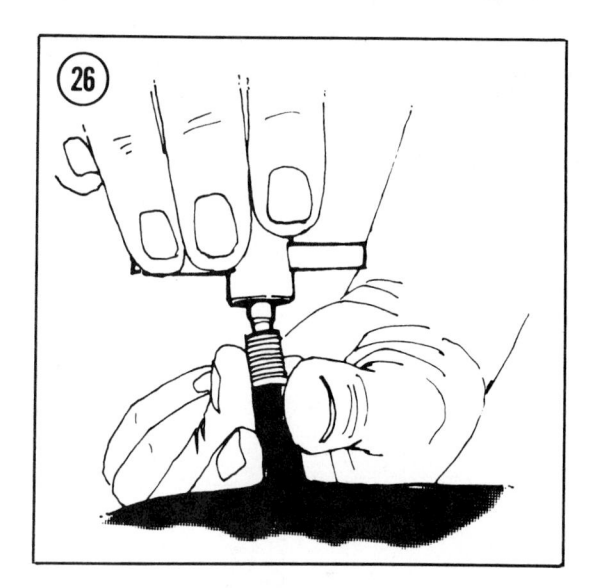

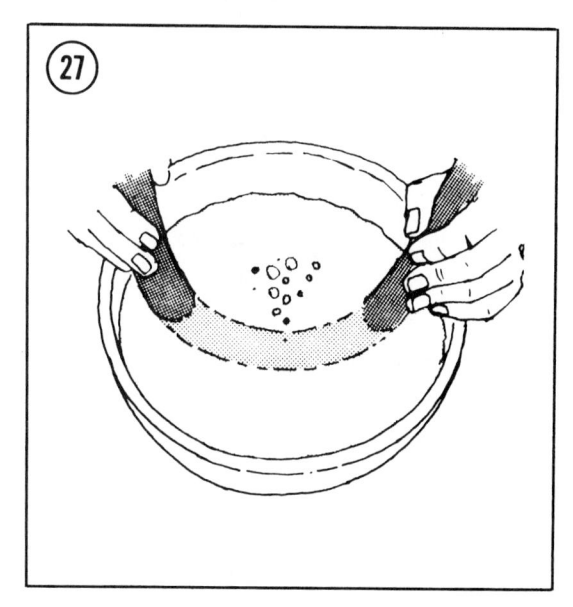

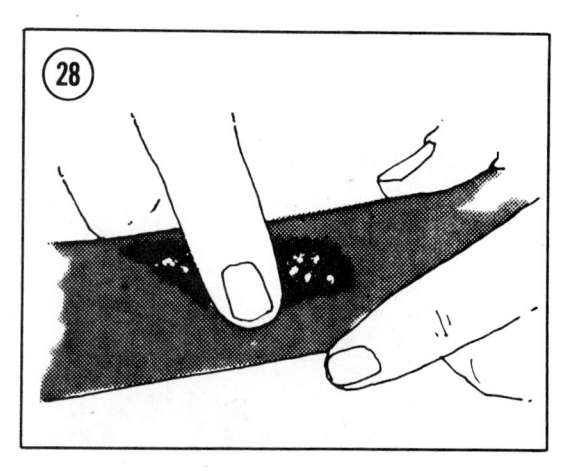

everything necessary and tucks easily in with your emergency tool kit.

Tube Inspection

1. Remove the inner tube as previously described.
2. Install the valve core into the valve stem (**Figure 26**) and inflate the tube slightly. Do not overinflate.
3. Immerse the tube in water a section at a time (**Figure 27**). Look carefully for bubbles indicating a hole. Mark each hole and continue checking until you are certain that all holes are discovered and marked. Also make sure that the valve core is not leaking; tighten it if necessary.

NOTE
*If you do not have enough water to immerse sections of the tube, try running your hand over the tube slowly and very close to the surface. If your hand is damp, it works even better. If you suspect a hole anywhere, apply some saliva to the area to verify it (**Figure 28**).*

4. Apply a cold patch using the techniques described under *Cold Patch Repair*, in this chapter.
5. Dust the patch area with talcum powder to prevent it from sticking to the tire.
6. Carefully check the inside of the tire casing for small rocks, sand or twigs which may have damaged the tube. If the inside of the tire is split, apply a patch to the area to prevent it from pinching and damaging the tube again.
7. Check the inside of the rim. Make sure the rim band is in place, with no spoke ends protruding which could puncture the tube.
8. Deflate the tube prior to installation in the tire.

Cold Patch Repairs

1. Remove the tube from the tire as previously described.
2. Roughen an area around the hole slightly larger than the patch, using a cap from the tire repair kit or a pocket knife. Do not scrape too vigorously or you may cause additional damage.

3. Apply a small quantity of special cement to the puncture and spread it evenly with your finger (**Figure 29**).

4. Allow the cement to dry until tacky—usually 30 seconds or so is sufficient.

5. Remove the backing from the patch.

> *CAUTION*
> *Do not touch the newly exposed rubber with your fingers or the patch will not stick firmly.*

6. Center the patch over the hole. Hold the patch firmly in place for about 30 seconds to allow the cement to set (**Figure 30**).

7. Dust the patched area with talcum powder to prevent sticking.

8. Install the tube as previously described.

HANDLEBAR

Removal/Installation

1. Push back the rubber boot (on models so equipped) and loosen the screws (A, **Figure 31**) securing the throttle grip assembly. Slide it off.

2. Loosen the bolts (B, **Figure 31**) clamping the front brake lever assembly and slide it off.

3. Slide off the left-hand grip (A, **Figure 32**). Remove all plastic bands securing the electrical cable to the handlebar. Loosen the screws clamping the switch housing (B, **Figure 32**) and slide it off.

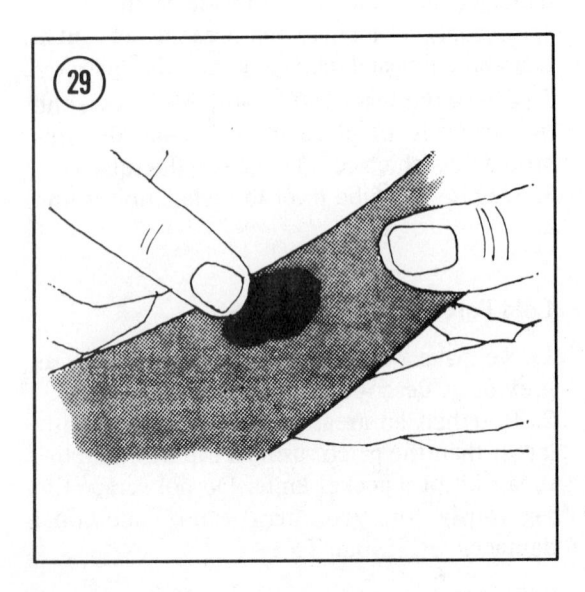

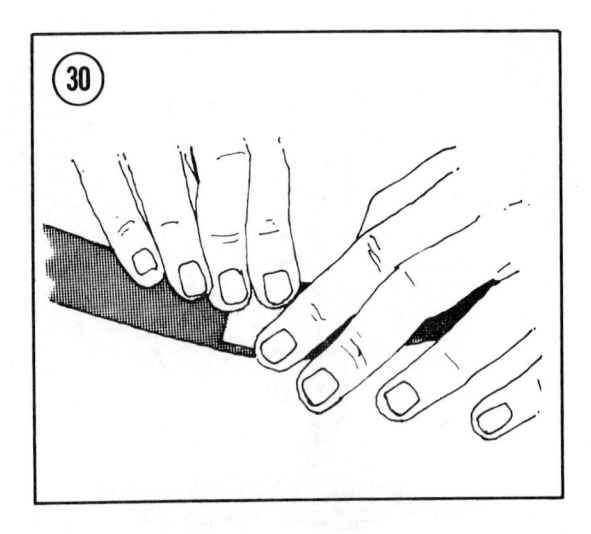

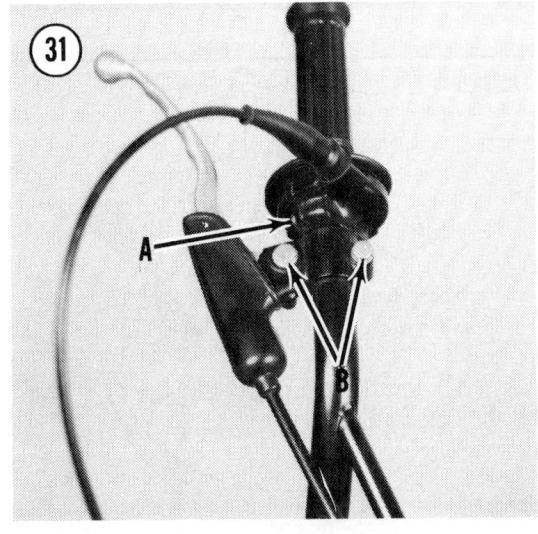

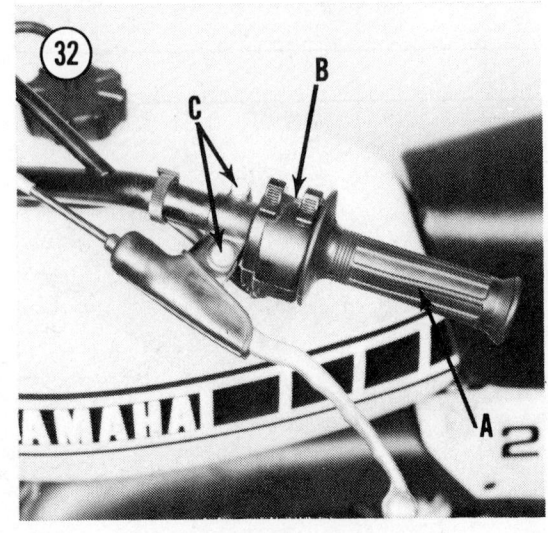

FRONT SUSPENSION AND STEERING

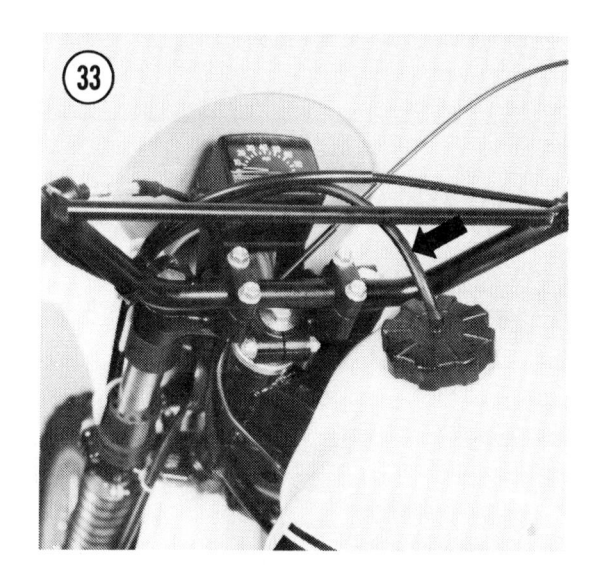

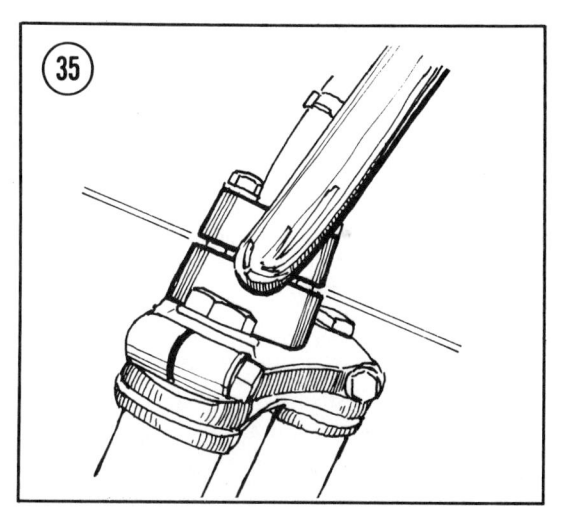

NOTE
Carefully lay the throttle assembly and cable, brake lever and cable, and switch housing over the front fender or back over the frame, so the cables do not get crimped or damaged.

4. Loosen the bolts (C, **Figure 32**) securing the clutch lever assembly and slide it off.

NOTE
Carefully lay the clutch lever assembly and cable over the front fender or back over the frame, so the cable does not get crimped or damaged.

5. Pull the fuel tank vent tube free (**Figure 33**) from the steering head area; and remove the bolts (**Figure 34**) securing the handlebar holders and remove the holders.

NOTE
***Figure 34** is shown with the fuel tank removed for clarity.*

6. Remove the handlebar.
7. Install by reversing these removal steps; note the following.
8. To maintain a good grip on the handlebar and to prevent it from slipping down, clean the knurled section of the handlbar with a wire brush. It should be kept rough so it will be held securely by the holders. The holders should also be kept clean and free of any metal that may have been gouged loose by handlebar slippage.
9. Tighten the bolts securing the handlebar to the torque specifications listed in **Table 1**. Tighten the bolts evenly to obtain an equal clearance on the holders, both front and rear (**Figure 35**).
10. Apply a light coat of multipurpose grease to the throttle grip area on the handlebar prior to installation.

WARNING
After installation is completed, make sure the brake lever does not come in contact with the throttle grip assembly when it is pulled on fully.

11. Adjust the front brake and clutch as described in Chapter Three.

STEERING HEAD

There are 2 different types of steering head assemblies used on the various models. One type uses assembled roller bearings while the other uses loose balls. Refer to **Figure 36**, **Figure 37** or **Figure 38** for this procedure.

One procedure is used to cover all models; where differences occur they are identified.

Disassembly

1. Remove the front wheel as described under *Front Wheel Removal* in this chapter.
2. Remove the handlebar as described under *Handlebar Removal/Installation* in this chapter.
3. Remove the speedometer housing as described under *Speedometer Housing Assembly Removal/Installation* in Chapter Seven.

NOTE
*Prior to removing the fork, measure the distance from the top of the fork tube to the top of the upper fork bridge (**Figure 39**); write this dimension on a piece of masking tape and attach it to the fork. This is not a standard dimension, but one derived from rider preference.*

4. Remove one fork leg as described under *Front Fork Removal/Installation* in this chapter. Leave one fork leg installed at this time.
5. Loosen the upper fork bridge pinch bolt (A, **Figure 40**).
6. Loosen the steering stem flange bolt (B, **Figure 40**).
7. Remove the remaning fork leg assembly (C, **Figure 40**).
8. Remove the upper fork bridge assembly (**Figure 41**).
9. Remove the steering head adjusting nut (**Figure 42**). Use a large drift and hammer or use the easily improvised tool shown in **Figure 43**.

NOTE
On models with loose ball bearings, have an assistant hold a large pan under the steering stem to catch the loose ball bearings while you carefully lower the steering stem.

10. Lower the steering stem assembly down and out of the steering head (**Figure 44**).

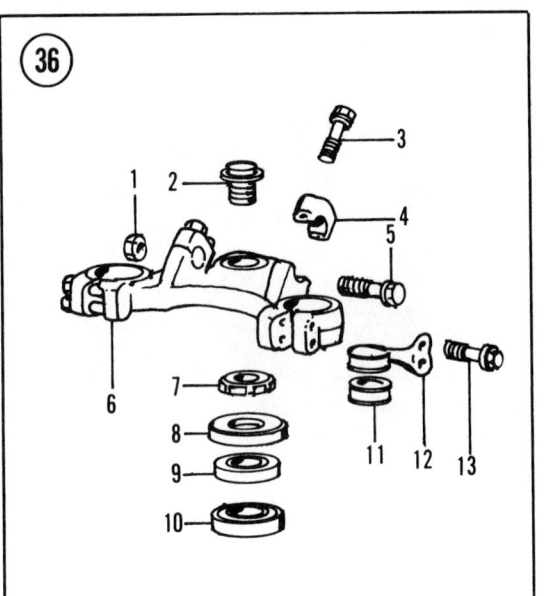

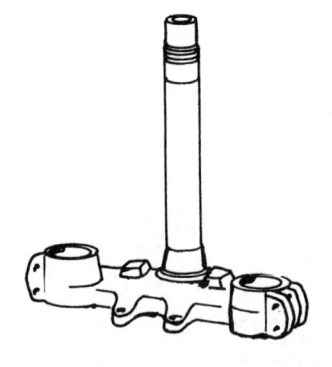

STEERING STEM ASSEMBLY (MODELS IT425G, IT400F, E, D, IT250G, F, E, D, IT175G, F, E, D)

1. Nut
2. Steering stem flange bolt
3. Bolt
4. Handlebar holder
5. Bolt
6. Upper fork bridge
7. Steering stem adjusting nut
8. Upper bearing cover
9. Upper bearing
10. Lower bearing
11. Rubber grommet
12. Guide
13. Bolt

FRONT SUSPENSION AND STEERING

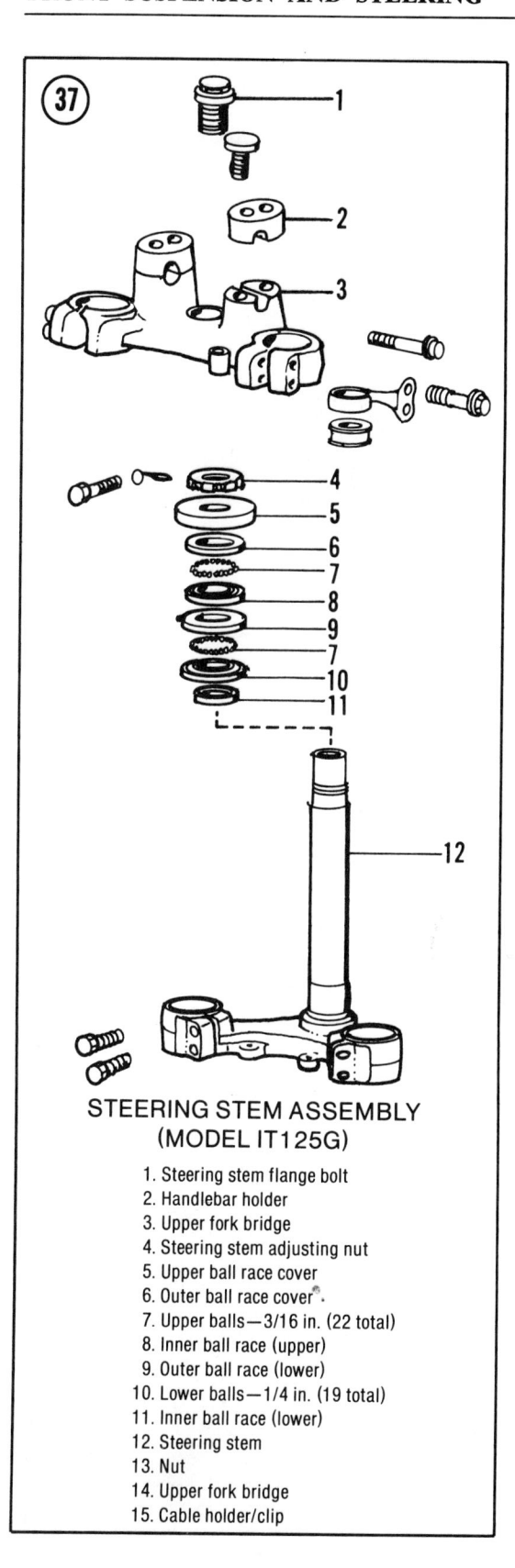

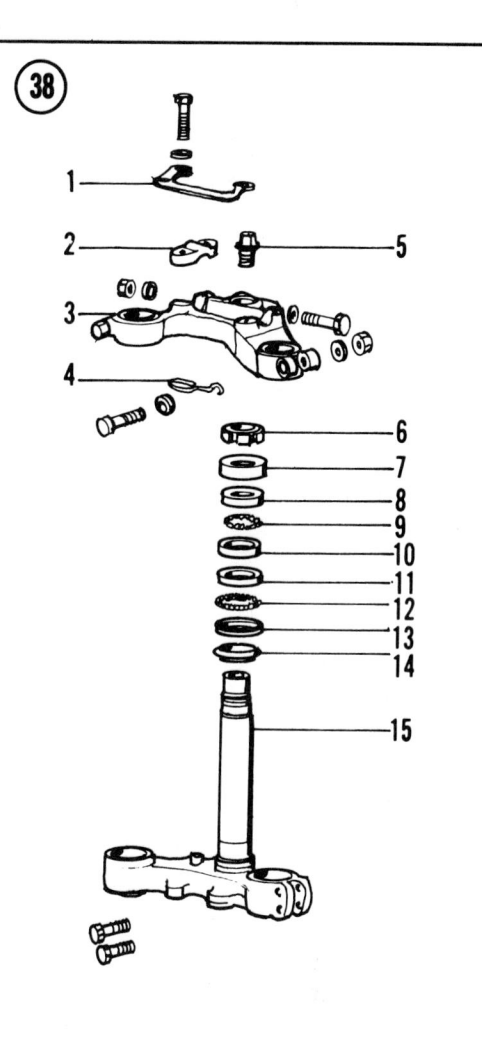

STEERING STEM ASSEMBLY (MODEL IT125G)

1. Steering stem flange bolt
2. Handlebar holder
3. Upper fork bridge
4. Steering stem adjusting nut
5. Upper ball race cover
6. Outer ball race cover
7. Upper balls—3/16 in. (22 total)
8. Inner ball race (upper)
9. Outer ball race (lower)
10. Lower balls—1/4 in. (19 total)
11. Inner ball race (lower)
12. Steering stem
13. Nut
14. Upper fork bridge
15. Cable holder/clip

STEERING STEM ASSEMBLY (MODEL IT400C)

1. Upper handlebar holder
2. Lower handlebar holder
3. Washer
4. Damper holder
5. Upper fork bridge
6. Steering stem adjusting nut
7. Washer
8. Lockwasher
9. Nut
10. Cotter pin
11. Steering stem flange bolt
12. Cable holder/clip
13. Upper bearing race cover
14. Upper and lower roller bearing assembly
15. Steering stem

210 CHAPTER EIGHT

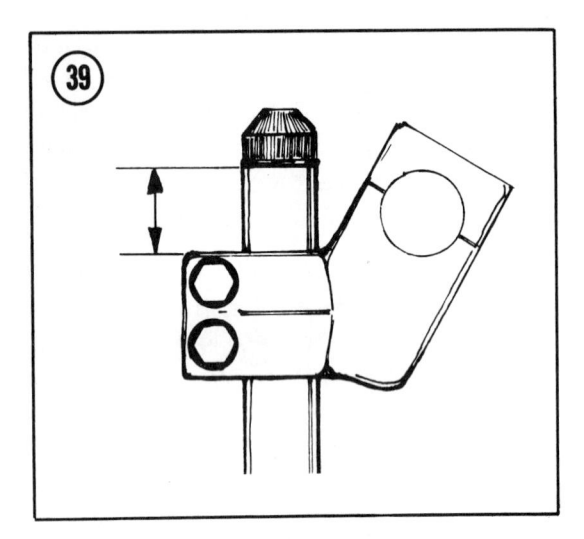

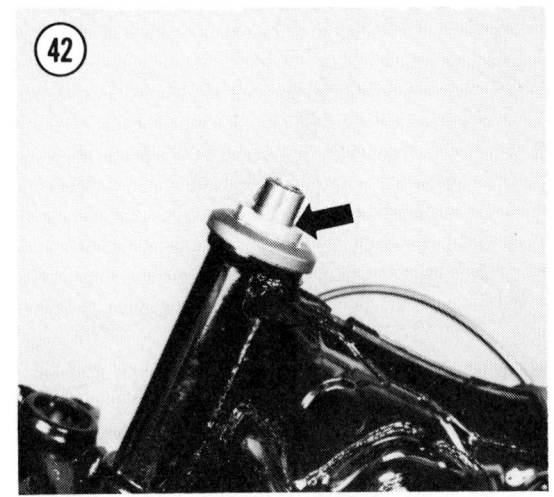

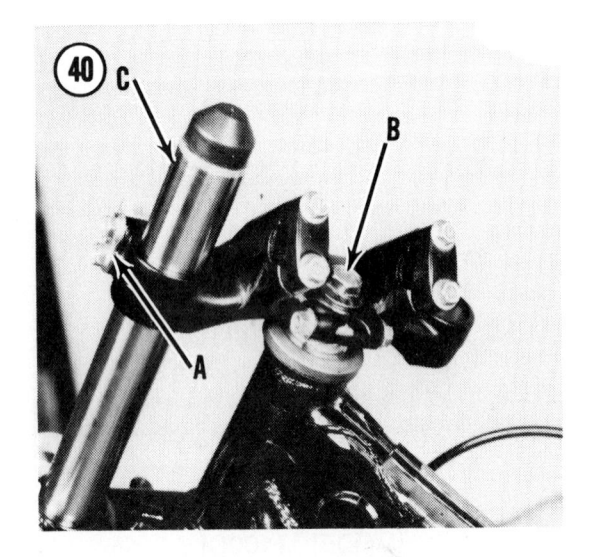

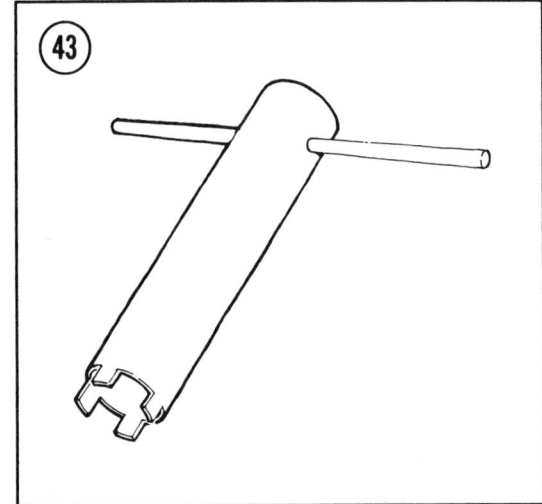

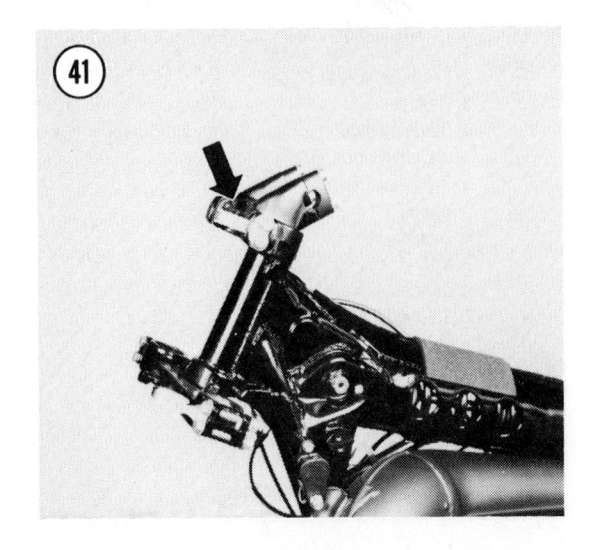

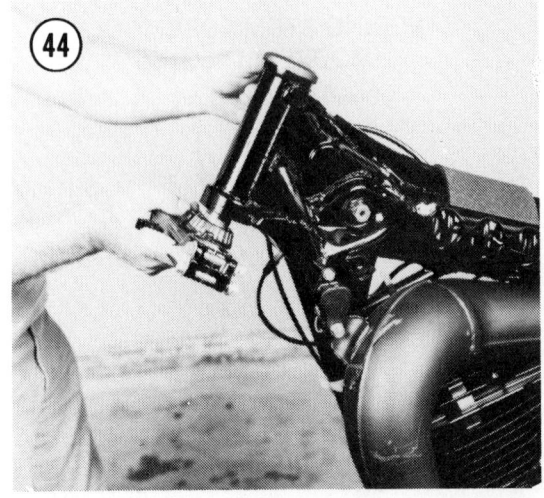

FRONT SUSPENSION AND STEERING

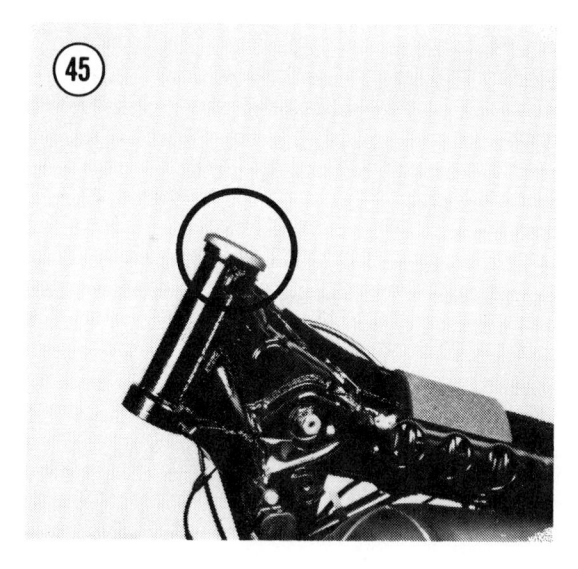

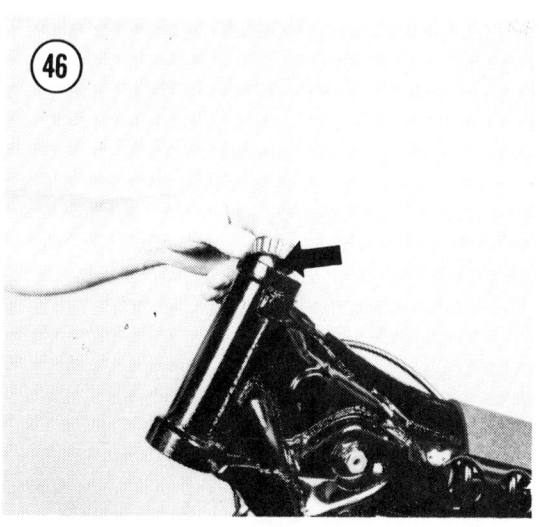

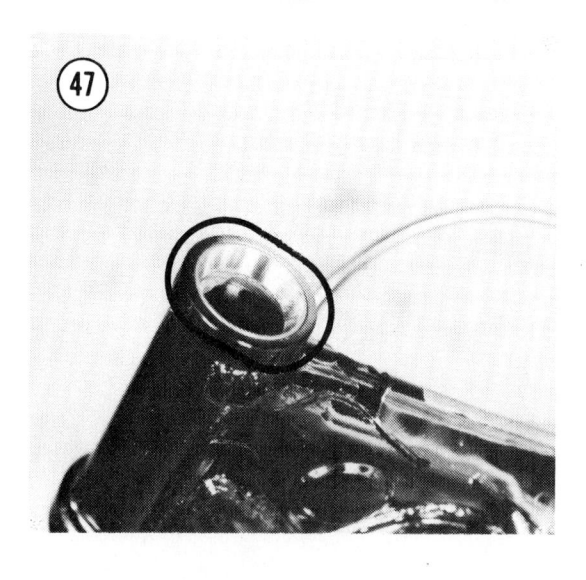

11. On models with loose ball bearings, do not intermix the balls as they are different sizes. The upper bearing has 3/16 in. balls (quantity—22) and the lower has 1/4 in. balls (quantity—19).
12. Remove the upper bearing race cover (**Figure 45**).
13. Remove the upper roller bearing assembly (**Figure 46**) or the loose ball bearings.
14. Remove the lower roller bearing assembly or the loose ball bearings.

Inspection

1. Clean the bearing races in the steering head, the steering stem races and the bearings with solvent.
2. Check the welds around the steering head for cracks and fractures. If any are found, have them repaired by a competent frame shop or welding service.
3. Check the balls or rollers for pitting, scratches or discoloration indicating wear or corrosion. Replace them in sets if any are bad.
4. Check the races (**Figure 47**) for pitting, galling, and corrosion. If any of these conditions exist, replace the races as described under *Bearing Race Replacement* in this chapter.
5. Check the steering stem for cracks and check its race for damage or wear. If this race or any race is damaged, the bearings should be replaced as a complete bearing set. Take the old races and bearings to your dealer to ensure accurate replacement.

Steering Head
Bearing Race Replacement

The headset and steering stem bearing races are pressed into place. Because they are easily bent, do not remove them unless they are worn and require replacement.

Headset race replacement

To remove the headset race, insert a hardwood stick or soft punch into the head tube (**Figure 48**) and carefully tap the race out from the inside. To get it started there is a notch in the head tube (**Figure 49**) which allows the wood or punch to get a perch on the race. After it is started, tap around the race so that neither the race nor the head tube is damaged.

CHAPTER EIGHT

To install the headset race, tap it in slowly with a block of wood, a suitable size socket or piece of pipe (**Figure 50**). Make sure they are squarely seated in the race bores before tapping them in. Tap them in until they are flush with the steering head.

NOTE
The upper and lower bearings and races are not the same size (this is true for both bearing types). Be sure that you install them at the proper ends of the head tube.

Steering stem race and grease seal replacement

To remove the steering stem race, try twisting and pulling it up by hand. If it will not come off, carefully pry it up with a screwdriver; work around in a circle, prying a little at a time. Remove the race and the grease seal on models with loose ball bearings.

On models so equipped, install the grease seal. Slide the race over the steering stem with the bearing surface pointing up. Tap the race down with a piece of hardwood; work around in a circle so the race will not be bent. Make sure it is seated squarely and is all the way down.

Steering Head Assembly

Refer to **Figure 36**, **Figure 37** or **Figure 38** for this procedure.
1. Make sure the steering head and stem races are properly seated.
2. On models with loose ball bearings, apply a coat of cold grease to the lower bearing race cone and fit 19 ball bearings around it (**Figure 51**).

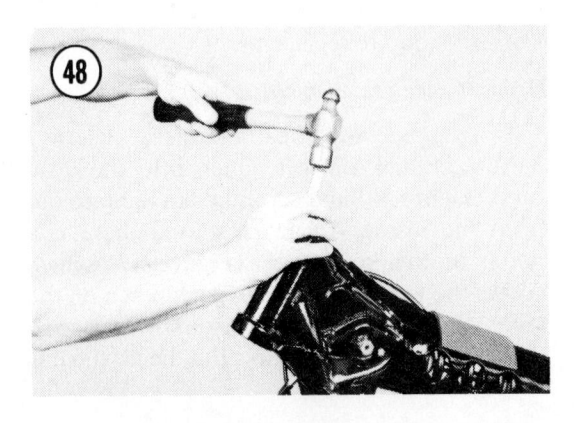

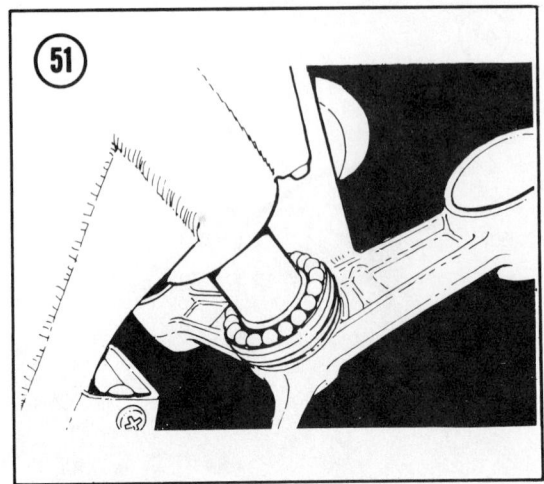

FRONT SUSPENSION AND STEERING

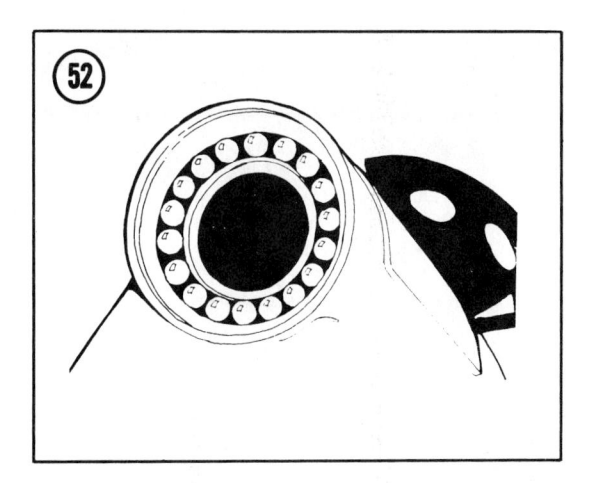

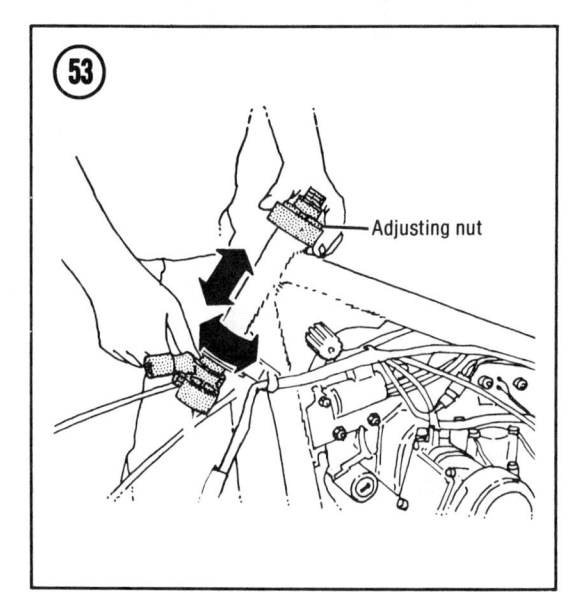

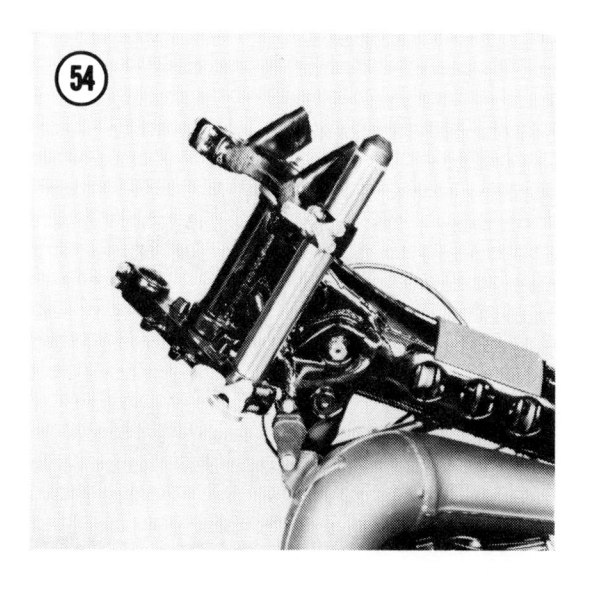

NOTE
Remember the lower balls are the larger size—1/4 in. diameter.

3. Install the lower roller bearing assembly onto the steering stem on models so equipped.
4. On models with loose ball bearings, apply a coat of cold grease to the upper bearing race cone and fit 22 ball bearings around it (**Figure 52**).

NOTE
These are the smaller ball bearings—3/16 in. diameter.

5. Install the upper roller bearing assembly into the steering head.
6. Install the steering stem into the head tube (**Figure 44**) and hold it firmly in place.
7. Install the upper bearing race cover (**Figure 45**).
8. Install the steering stem adjusting nut (**Figure 42**) and tighten it until it is snug against the upper race, then back it off 1/8 turn.

NOTE
*The adjusting nut should be just tight enough to remove horizontal and vertical play (**Figure 53**), yet loose enough so that the assembly will turn to both lock positions under its own weight after an assist.*

9. Install the upper fork bridge and steering stem flange bolt finger-tight.

NOTE
Steps 10-12 must be performed in this order to assure proper upper and lower fork bridge-to-fork alignment.

10. Slide the fork tubes into position (**Figure 54**) and tighten the lower fork bridge bolts to the torque specifications in **Table 1**.

NOTE
*Install the fork tube the original distance up from the top of the upper fork bridge; see NOTE after Step 3, **Disassembly**.*

11. Tighten the steering stem flange bolt to the torque specifications in **Table 1**.
12. Tighten the upper fork bridge bolts and pinch bolt to the torque specifications in **Table 1**.

13. Continue assembly by reversing Steps 1-4, *Steering Stem Disassembly.*
14. After a few hours of riding, the bearings have had a chance to seat; readjust the free play in the steering stem with the steering stem adjusting nut (**Figure 55**). Refer to Step 8.

Steering Stem Adjustment

If play develops in the steering system, it may only require adjustment. However, don't take a chance on it. Disassemble the stem and look for possible damage. Then reassemble and adjust as described in Step 8 of the previous procedure, *Steering Head Assembly.*

FRONT FORK

The forks on most ITs have the assist of air pressure to change handling to suit any rider and trial course terrain. There are some precautions in regard to handling these forks that differ from the ordinary oil/spring type. The following WARNINGS must be adhered to for your own safety and that of others.

> *WARNING*
> *For pressurizing the forks use only compressed air or nitrogen.* ***Do not use any other type of compressed gas*** *as an explosion may be lethal.* ***Never*** *heat the fork assembly with a torch or place it near an open flame or extreme heat as this will also result in an explosion. Always bleed off all air pressure from the forks prior to removal and disassembly.*

The front suspension uses spring-controlled, hydraulically-damped, telescopic fork plus the additional assist of air pressure on some models. Before suspecting major trouble, drain the front fork oil and refill with the proper type and quantity; refer to Chapter Three. If you still have trouble, such as poor damping, a tendency to bottom or top out or leakage around the rubber seals, follow the service procedures in this section.

To simplify fork service and to prevent the mixing of parts, the legs should be removed, serviced and installed individually.

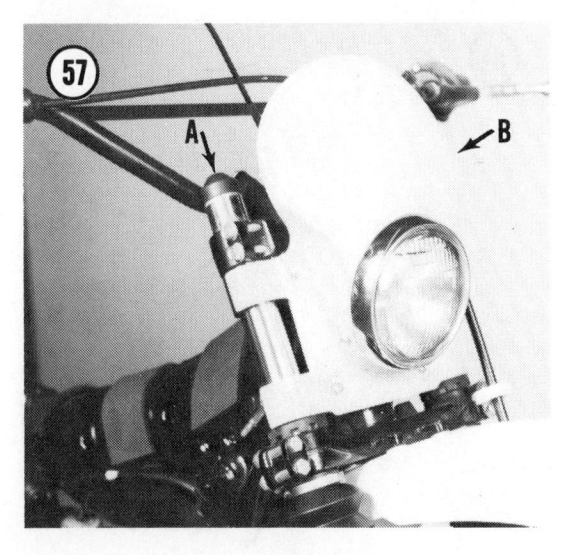

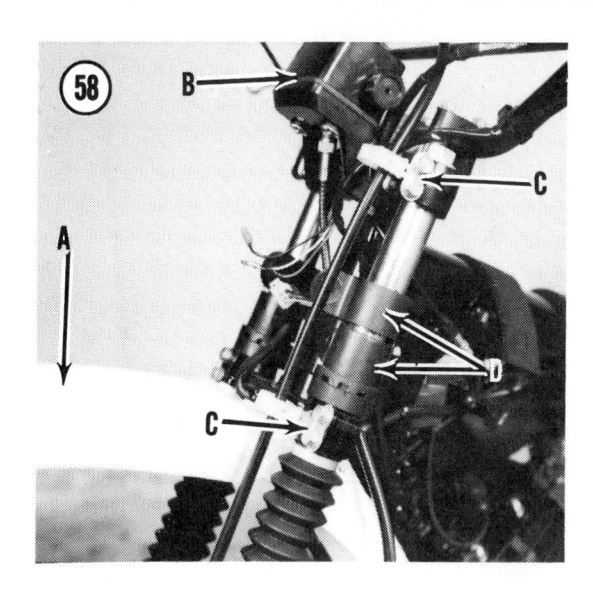

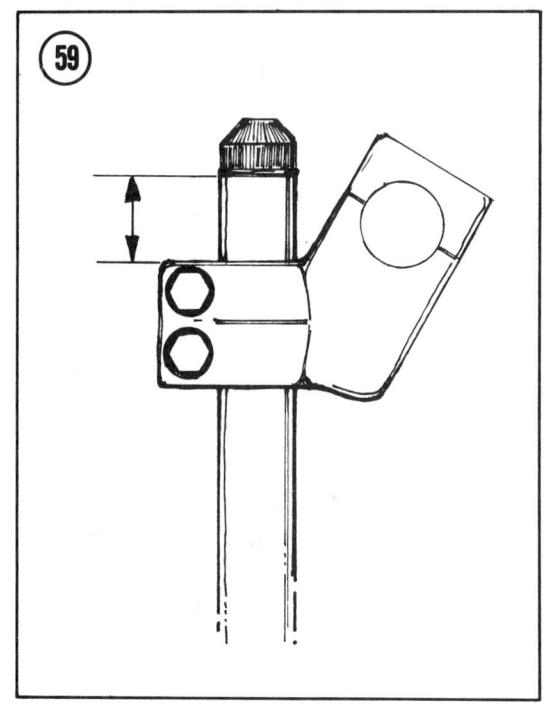

FRONT SUSPENSION AND STEERING

2. Remove the front wheel as described under *Front Wheel Removal/Installation* in this chapter.
3. On models with air assist forks, remove the top rubber cap (A, **Figure 57**). Remove the dust cap and *bleed off all air pressure* by depressing the valve stem.

> **WARNING**
> *Release the air pressure gradually. If released too fast, oil will spurt out with the air. Protect your eyes and clothing accordingly. Always bleed off all air pressure; failure to do so may cause personal injury when disassembling the fork assembly.*

4. Remove the headlight and number plate (B, **Figure 57**) as described under *Headlight and Number Plate Removal/Installation* in Chapter Seven.
5. Remove the bolts securing the front fender (A, **Figure 58**) and remove it.
6. Remove the speedometer housing (B, **Figure 58**) as described under *Speedometer Housing Assembly Removal/Installation* in Chapter Seven.
7. Loosen the top cap bolt prior to removing the fork tube.
8. Loosen the upper and lower fork bridge bolts (C, **Figure 58**).

> **NOTE**
> *Prior to removing the fork, measure the distance from the top of the fork tube to the top of the upper fork bridge (**Figure 59**); write this dimension on a piece of masking tape and attach it to the fork. This is not a standard dimension, but one derived from rider preference.*

9. Remove the fork tube. It may be necessary to slightly rotate the fork tube while pulling it down and out. As the fork tube is being removed, remove the upper and lower rubber dampers and headlight assembly mounting bracket (D, **Figure 58**).
10. Install by reversing these removal steps. Do not forget to install the rubber dampers and headlight assembly mounting bracket when installing the fork tube assemblies.
11. Install the fork tubes in the original position as noted in *Removal*, Step 8.

Removal/Installation

1. Remove the strap securing the front brake cable (A, **Figure 56**) to the left-hand fork. On model IT125G also remove the strap securing the speedometer cable (B, **Figure 56**).

> **NOTE**
> *On all other models the speedometer cable is on the right-hand side and is not retained with a strap.*

CHAPTER EIGHT

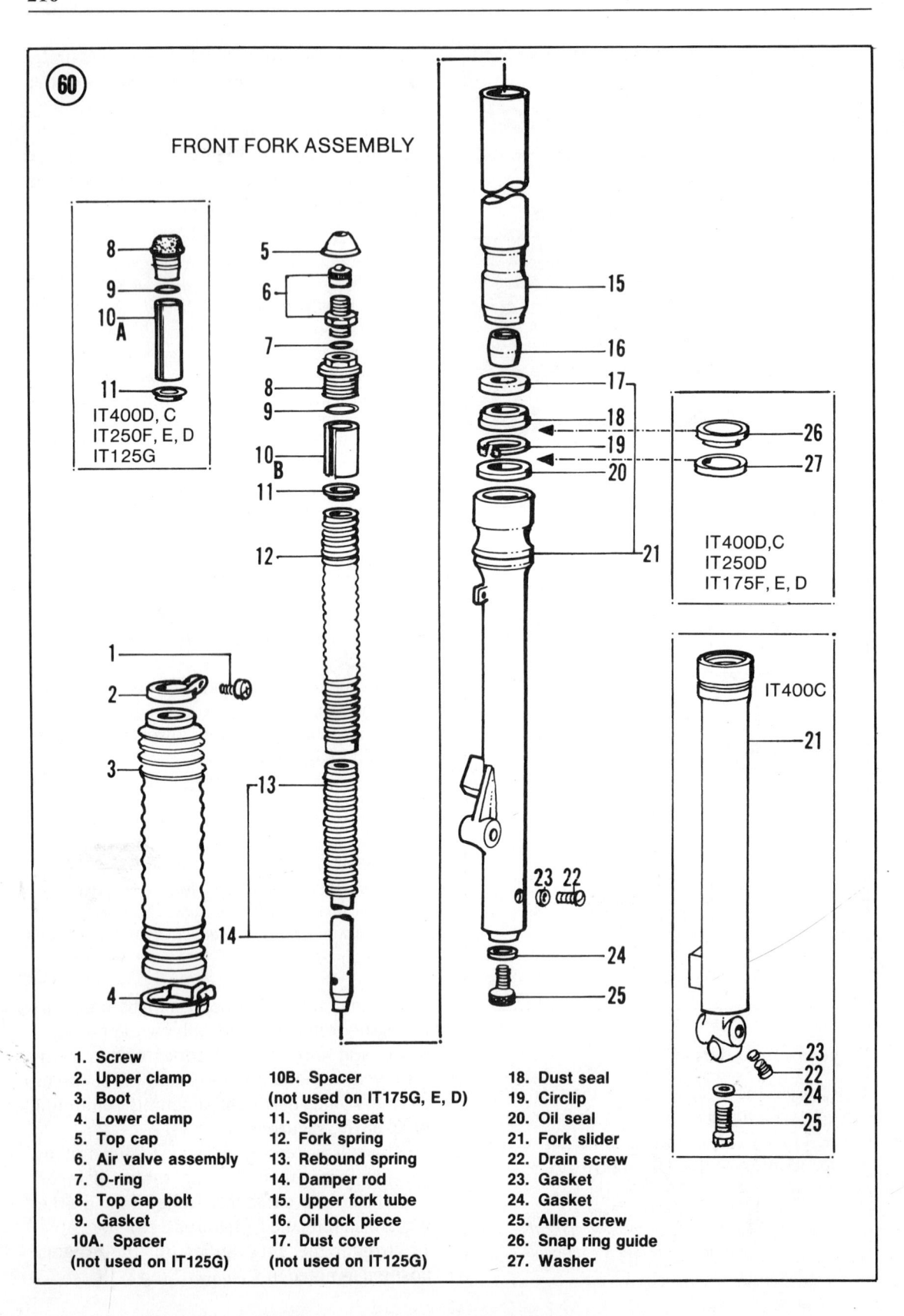

FRONT FORK ASSEMBLY

IT400D, C
IT250F, E, D
IT125G

IT400D, C
IT250D
IT175F, E, D

IT400C

1. Screw
2. Upper clamp
3. Boot
4. Lower clamp
5. Top cap
6. Air valve assembly
7. O-ring
8. Top cap bolt
9. Gasket
10A. Spacer
(not used on IT125G)
10B. Spacer
(not used on IT175G, E, D)
11. Spring seat
12. Fork spring
13. Rebound spring
14. Damper rod
15. Upper fork tube
16. Oil lock piece
17. Dust cover
(not used on IT125G)
18. Dust seal
19. Circlip
20. Oil seal
21. Fork slider
22. Drain screw
23. Gasket
24. Gasket
25. Allen screw
26. Snap ring guide
27. Washer

FRONT SUSPENSION AND STEERING

12. Tighten the bolts to the torque values in **Table 1**.

Disassembly

Refer to **Figure 60** for the following procedure. Minor variations exist among different models and years. Pay particular attention to the location and positioning of spacers, washers and springs to make sure they are assembled in the correct location. Refer to **Figure 60** during disassembly and assembly of the forks.

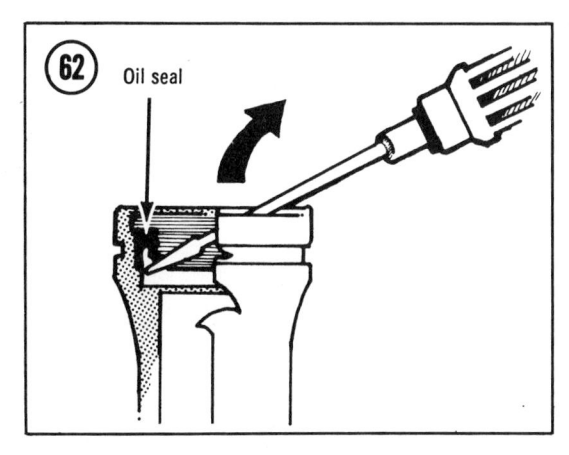

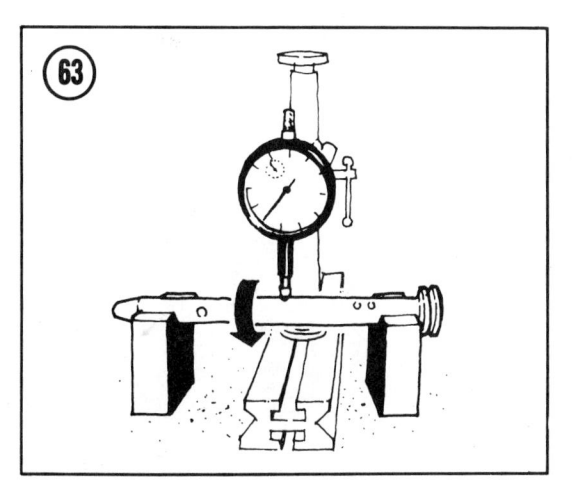

1. Hold the upper fork tube in a vise with soft jaws (**Figure 61**). Remove the top bolt and spacer and spring seat.
2. Remove the fork spring.
3. Remove the fork from the vise, pour the fork oil out and discard it. Pump the fork several times by hand to expel most of the remaining oil.
4. Clamp the slider in a vise with soft jaws.
5. Remove the Allen head screw and gasket from the bottom of the slider.

NOTE
This screw has been secured with Loctite and often is very difficult to remove because the damper rod will turn inside the slider. It sometimes can be removed with an air impact driver. If you are unable to remove it, take the fork tubes to a dealer and have them remove the screw.

6. Pull the fork tube out of the slider.
7. Remove the oil lock piece, the damper rod and the rebound spring.
8. If oil has been leaking from the top of the slider, remove the dust seal cover (not used on IT125G), dust seal, circlip and oil seal. On models IT400D and C, IT250D and IT175F, E and D, also remove the circlip guide and washer.

NOTE
It may be necessary to slightly heat the area on the slider around the oil seal prior to removal.

CAUTION
*Use a dull screwdriver blade to remove the oil seal (**Figure 62**). Do not damage the outer edge or inner surface of the slider.*

Inspection

1. Thoroughly clean all parts in solvent and dry them. Check the fork tube for signs of wear or scratches.
2. Check the damper rod for straightness. **Figure 63** shows one method. The rod should be replaced if the runout is 0.008 in. (0.2 mm) or greater.

3. Carefully check the damper rod valve and piston (**Figure 64**) for wear or damage.

4. Inspect the oil seals for scoring, nicks and loss of resiliency. Replace if their condition is questionable.

5. Check the upper fork tube for straightness. If bent or severely scratched, it should be replaced.

6. Check the lower slider for dents or exterior damage that may cause the upper fork tube to hang up during riding. Replace if necessary.

7. Measure the uncompressed length of the fork spring (not rebound spring) with a square as shown in **Figure 65**. The standard spring lengths for all models are listed in **Table 2**. Replace any spring that is about 1/2 inch or more shorter than these standard dimensions.

8. Any parts that are worn or damaged should be replaced. Simply cleaning and reinstalling unserviceable components will not improve performance of the front suspension.

Assembly

1. Coat all parts with fresh fork oil prior to installation. Install a new oil seal and circlip (**Figure 66**).

> *NOTE*
> *On models IT400D and C, IT250D and IT175F, E and D, install a washer between the oil seal and the circlip.*

2. Insert the dust seal and dust seal cover (not used on IT125G). See **Figure 67**.

> *NOTE*
> *On models IT400D and C, IT250D and IT175F, E and D, install the circlip guide, then the dust seal and dust seal cover.*

3. Install the rebound spring onto the damper rod (**Figure 68**).

4. Insert the rebound spring and the damper rod into the fork tube (**Figure 69**).

5. Temporarily install the fork spring and top cap bolt (**Figure 70**) to hold the damper rod in place.

6. Install the oil lock piece onto the damper rod (**Figure 71**) and install the upper fork assembly into the slider (**Figure 72**).

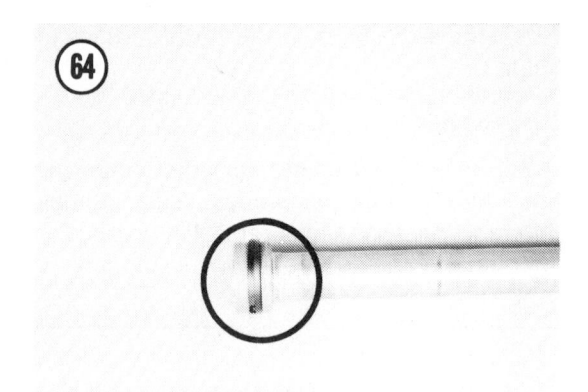

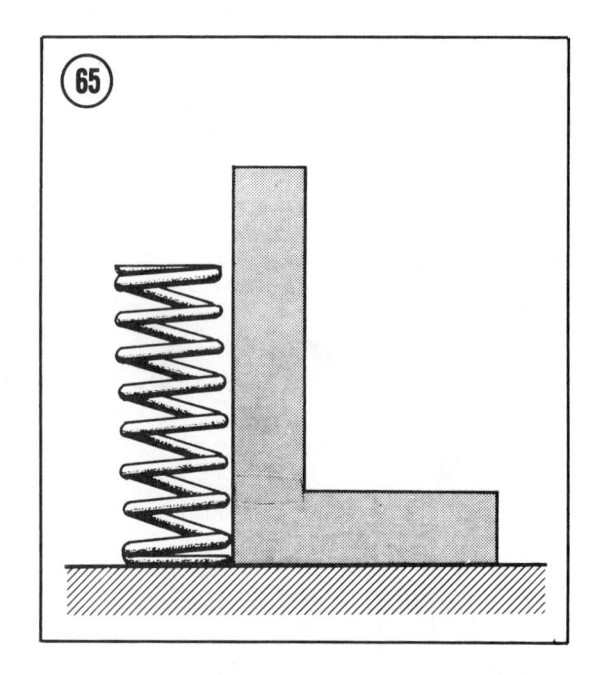

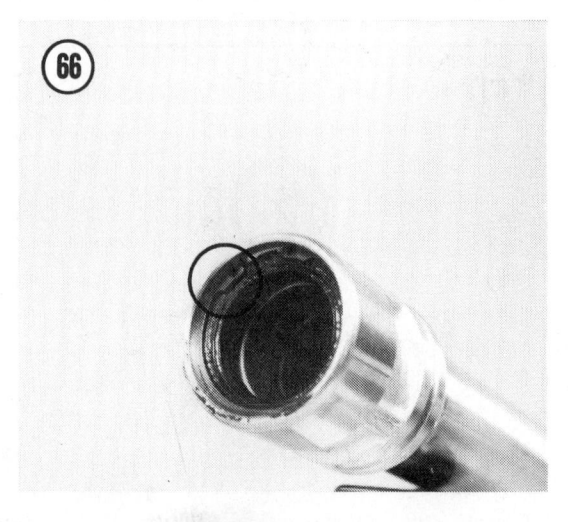

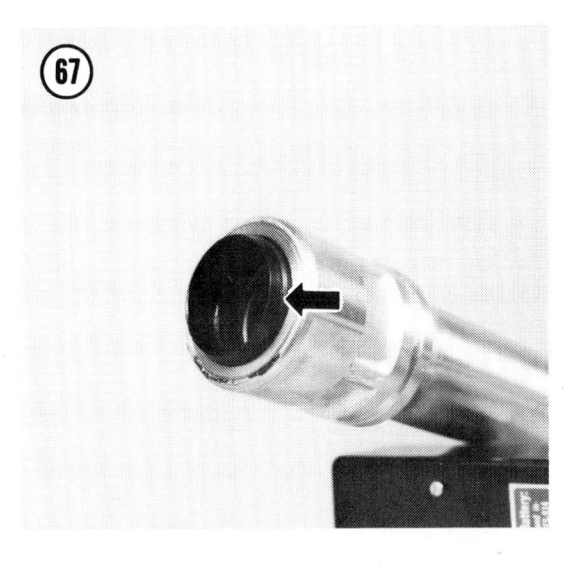

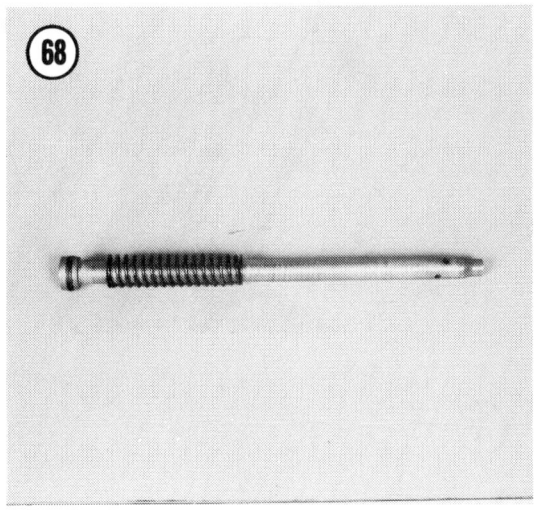

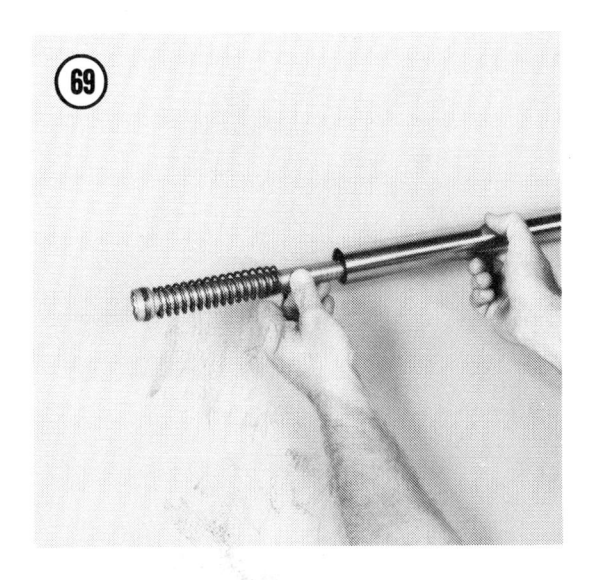

FRONT SUSPENSION AND STEERING

219

⑥⑦

⑥⑧

⑥⑨

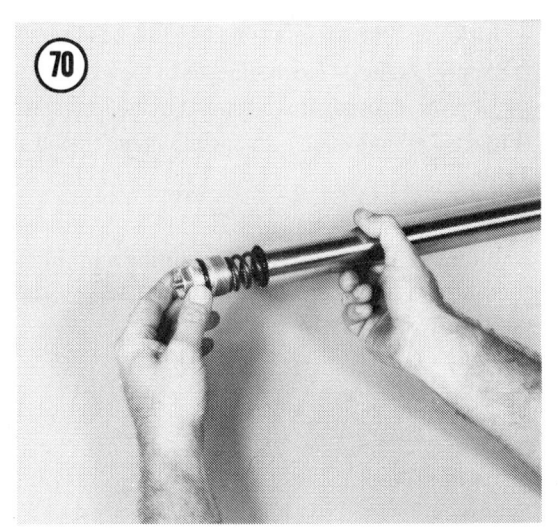

⑦⓪

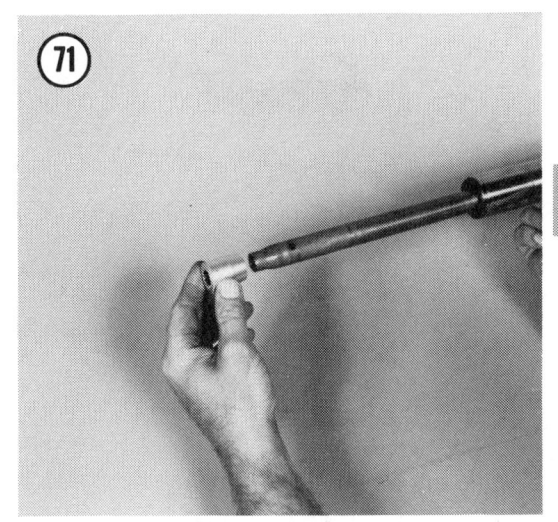

⑦①

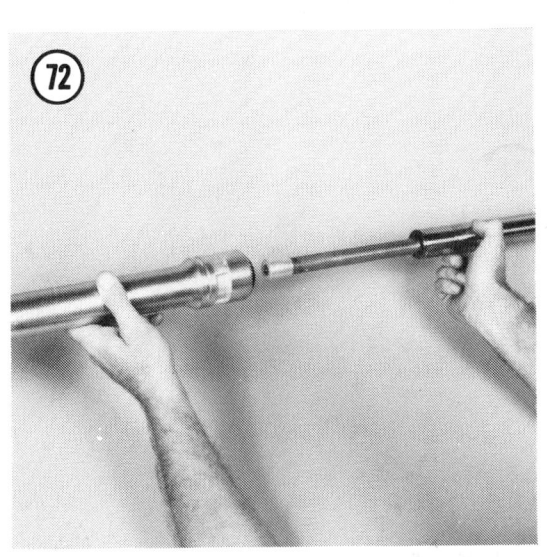

⑦②

7. Make sure the gasket is on the Allen head screw.

8. Apply Loctite 242 to the threads of the Allen head screw prior to installation. Install it in the fork slider (**Figure 73**) and tighten to specifications listed in **Table 1**.

9. Install the forks.

10. Remove the top cap bolt and spring and fill the fork tube with the correct type and quantity of fork oil; refer to Chapter Three.

11. Install the fork spring, spring seat (**Figure 74**) and spacer (**Figure 75**).

12. Inspect the condition of the O-ring seal on the top cap bolt (**Figure 76**); replace it if necessary.

13. Install the top cap bolt and tighten securely.

14. On models with air pressure assist, inflate to the correct air pressure. Refer to Chapter Three.

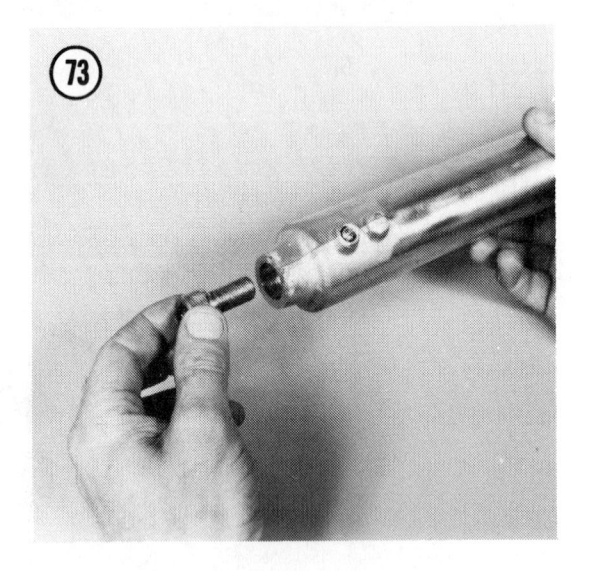

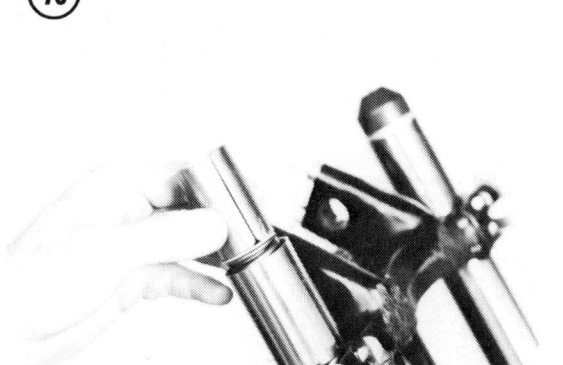

FRONT SUSPENSION AND STEERING

Table 1 FRONT SUSPENSION TORQUE SPECIFICATIONS

	IT425G IT400F, E, D	IT250 (all)	IT175 (all)	IT125G (all)
Front axle nut	43-45 (58-60)	43-45 (58-60)	60-65 (85-90)	29 (40)
Handlebar holder bolts	11-17 (15-23)	11-17 (15-23)	11-17 (15-23)	10 (14)
Fork bridge bolts upper & lower	11-17 (15-23)	11-17 (15-23)	16 (23) (IT175F, D 7-11 (11-15))	25 (35)
Steering stem bolt	68 (95) (IT400F, E 43 (60))	68 (95) (IT250F, E 43 (60))	69 (95) (IT175E, D 43 (60))	40 (55)
Steering stem pinch bolt	11-17 (15-23)	11-17 (15-23)	16 (23)	18 (24)
Fork cap bolt	18 (25)	18 (25)	14-16 (20-23)	16 (23)

NOTE: XX=ft.-lb.   (XX)=N•m

Table 2 FRONT FORK SPRING FREE LENGTH

Model	Inches	Millimeters
IT425G	23.37	593.5
IT400F	21.0	533.5
IT400E	23.84	605.5
IT400D, C	N.A.	
IT250G, F	21.0	593.5
IT250E	23.84	605.5
IT250D	N.A.	
IT175G	23.92	607.5
IT175F	18.4	468.0
IT175D, E	22.39	566.0
IT125G	23.13	587.5

N.A.: Information not available.

NOTE: If you own a 1981 or later model, first check the Supplement at the back of the book for any new service information.

CHAPTER NINE

REAR SUSPENSION

The rear suspension of the monoshock IT series is basically the same on all models. The rear swing arm is either steel or aluminum and the monoshock is nestled up in the frame backbone. There are a variety of different spring preload and damping adjustments available to suit almost any combination of rider weight and track conditions. Each adjustment procedure varies among the different models and years so be sure to follow the correct one for your specific bike.

This chapter contains repair and replacement procedures for the rear wheel and hub and rear suspension components. Service to the rear suspension consists of periodically checking bolt tightness, replacing swing arm bushings and checking the condition of the spring/gas monoshock units and replacing them as necessary.

Refer to **Table 1** for rear suspension torque specifications. **Tables 1-3** are at the end of the chapter.

REAR WHEEL

For simple removal and installation of the rear wheel see the *Quick Removal/Installation* procedure. For more complete removal and disassembly in order to service the brake or wheel bearings see *Complete Removal/Installation*.

Quick Removal/Installation
(All Models Except IT400C)

1. Place a milk crate or wood block(s) under the frame so that the rear wheel is off the ground.
2. Compress the spring and remove the brake rod from the brake lever (**Figure 1**).
3. Place the brake rod onto the hook on the swing arm (**Figure 2**).
4. On models so equipped, remove the cotter pin and loosen the axle nut (A, **Figure 3**).

REAR SUSPENSION

NOTE
*Mark the position of the chain adjuster in relation to the locator pin on the swing arm (**Figure 4**) so that the wheel can be reinstalled in the same location with the same amount of drive chain slack.*

5. Push the rear wheel forward to allow drive chain slack.
6. Pull the drive chain up and off the sprocket.
7. Remove the cotter pin from the clevis pin (B, **Figure 3**) on each side of the swing arm and remove both clevis pins.
8. Pull the wheel to the rear and remove it.
9. Install by reversing these removal steps. Locate the drive chain adjusters in the original positions as noted in Step 4. Always install new cotter pins in the clevis pins—never install an old one as it may break and fall out. Bend the end of the pin over completely.
10. Perform Steps 8, 10, and 12-15 in the *Complete Removal/Installation* procedure.

Complete Removal/Installation (All Models Except IT400C)

1. Place a milk crate or wood block(s) under the frame so that the rear wheel is off the ground.
2. Compress the spring and remove the brake rod from the brake lever (**Figure 1**).
3. Place the brake rod onto the hook on the swing arm (**Figure 2**).
4. On models so equipped, remove the cotter pin and remove the axle nut and chain adjuster (**Figure 5**). Discard the old cotter pin.

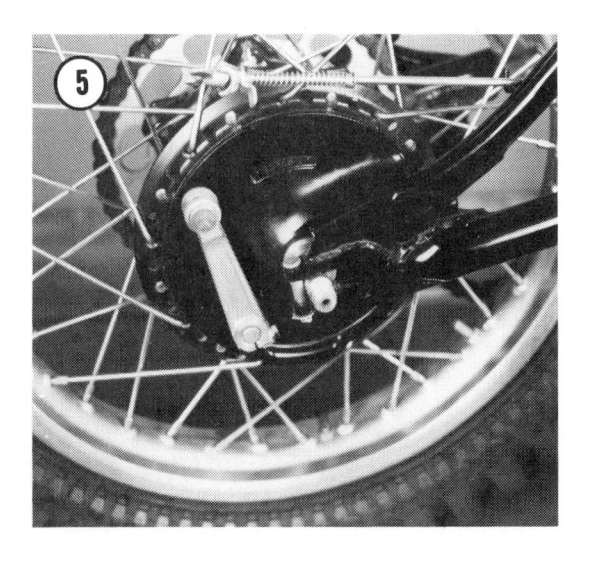

CHAPTER NINE

NOTE
*Mark the position of the chain adjuster in relation to the locator pin on the swing arm (**Figure 4**) so that the wheel can be reinstalled in the same location with the same amount of drive chain slack.*

5. Push the rear wheel forward to allow drive chain slack.
6. Pull the drive chain up and off the sprocket and withdraw the rear axle from the left-hand side (**Figure 6**).
7. Pull the wheel to the rear and remove it. Do not lose the wheel spacer on the sprocket side of the wheel.
8. Inspect the condition of the clevis pins and cotter pins (**Figure 7**). If worn or fractured they should be removed and replaced.
9. Install by reversing these removal steps; note the following. Make sure that the arm on the sprocket side of the axle is positioned correctly on top of the swing arm (**Figure 8**) prior to tightening the axle nut. Locate the drive chain adjusters in the original positions as noted in Step 4.
10. Be sure to install the axle spacer on the sprocket side of the wheel (**Figure 9**).

CAUTION
Rear wheel spacers should be periodically replaced. Frequent tightening of the rear axle nut causes the spacers to compress slightly. A compressed spacer alters swing arm to rear wheel clearance.

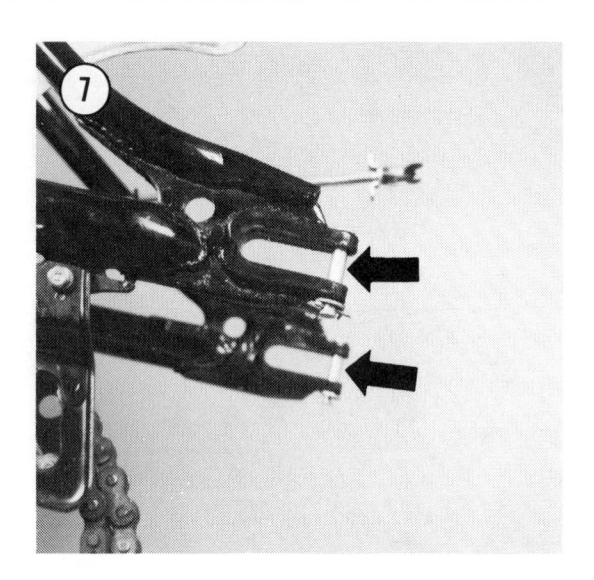

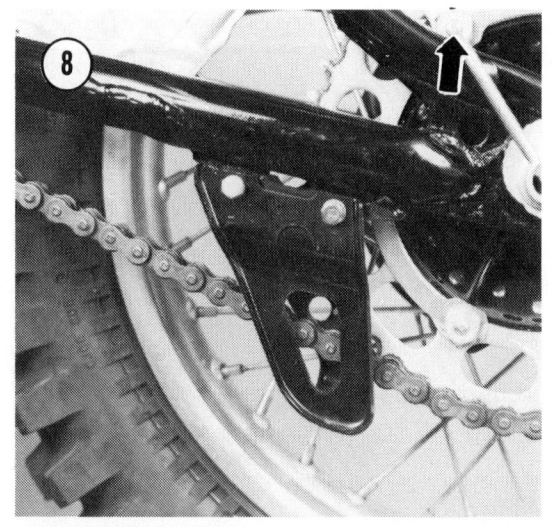

REAR SUSPENSION

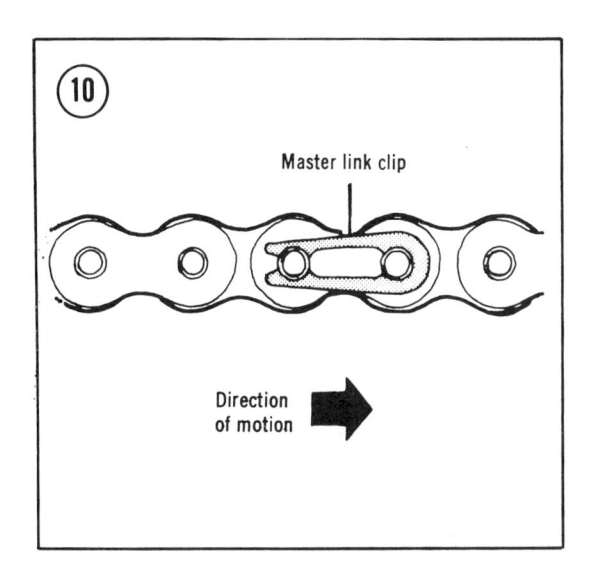

11. If the drive chain master link was removed, be sure to install a new clip with the closed end facing in the direction of chain travel (**Figure 10**).

12. Install the axle from the drive sprocket side.

13. Adjust the drive chain tension as described under *Drive Chain Adjustment* in Chapter Three.

14. Tighten the axle nut to the torque values in **Table 1**. Install a new cotter pin in the axle nut on models so equipped—never reuse an old cotter pin. Bend the cotter pin over completely.

15. After the wheel is completely installed, rotate it several times to make sure it rotates smoothly. Apply the brake several times to make sure it operates correctly.

16. Adjust the rear brake as described under *Rear Brake Pedal Adjustment* in Chapter Three.

Removal/Installation (Model IT400C)

1. Place a milk crate or wood block(s) under the frame so that the rear wheel is off the ground.

2. Unscrew the rear brake adjusting nut completely from the brake rod (**Figure 11**). Withdraw the brake rod from the brake lever and pivot it down out of the way. Reinstall the adjusting nut to avoid misplacing it.

3. Remove the bolt and nut (**Figure 12**) securing the rear brake torque link. Let it pivot down out of the way.

4. Remove the cotter pin and axle nut (**Figure 13**). Discard the old cotter pin.

5. Remove the master link (**Figure 14**) from the drive chain and remove the chain from the drive sprocket.
6. Withdraw the axle (A, **Figure 15**) from the right-hand side of the wheel. Do not lose the spacer (B, **Figure 15**).
7. Pull the wheel to the rear and remove it.
8. Leave the axle adjusters on the swing arm. If they are loose, remove them, tap the open end slightly with a hammer and reinstall on the swing arm.
9. Install by reversing these removal steps; note the following.
10. Be sure to install the axle spacer on the sprocket side of the wheel.

CAUTION
Rear wheel spacers should be periodically replaced. Frequent tightening of the rear axle nut causes the spacers to compress slightly. A compressed spacer alters swing arm to rear wheel clearance.

11. Install a new clip on the drive chain master link so that the closed end of the clip is facing the direction of chain travel (**Figure 10**).

NOTE
Install the axle adjuster onto the right-hand end of the axle prior to axle installation. Install the other adjuster prior to installing the axle nut.

12. Install the axle from the right-hand side.
13. Adjust the drive chain tension as described under *Drive Chain Adjustment* in Chapter Three.
14. Tighten the axle nut and brake torque link nut to the torque values in **Table 1** at the end of this chapter.

NOTE
Install a new cotter pin on the axle nut; never reuse an old one as it may break and fall off. Bend the cotter pin over completely.

15. After the wheel is completely installed, rotate it several times to make sure it rotates smoothly. Apply the brake several times to make sure it operates correctly.
16. Adjust the rear brake as described under *Rear Brake Pedal Adjustment* in Chapter Three.

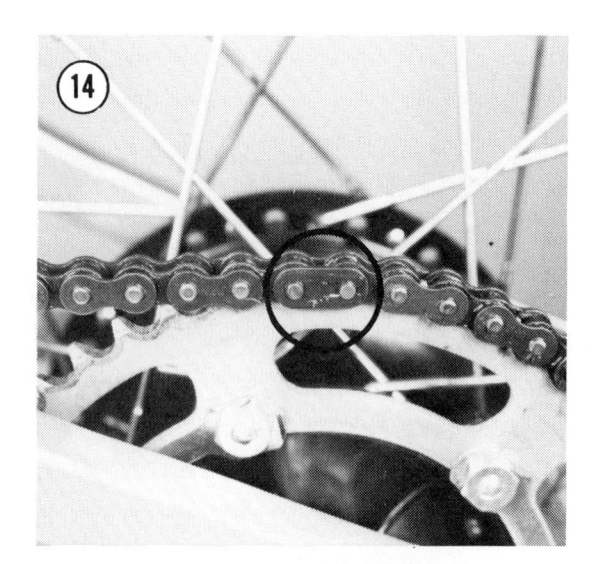

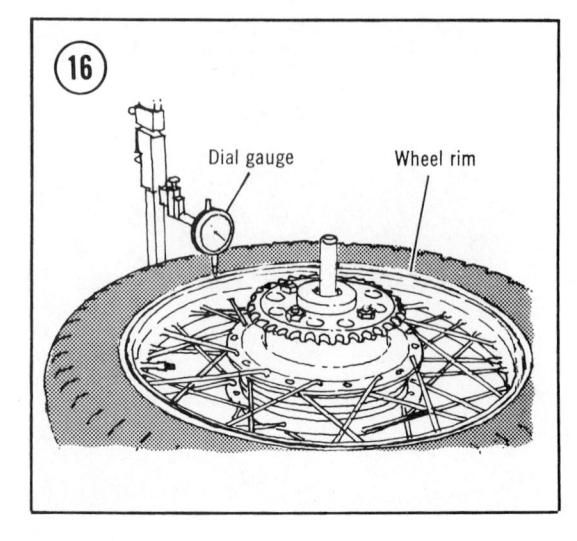

REAR SUSPENSION

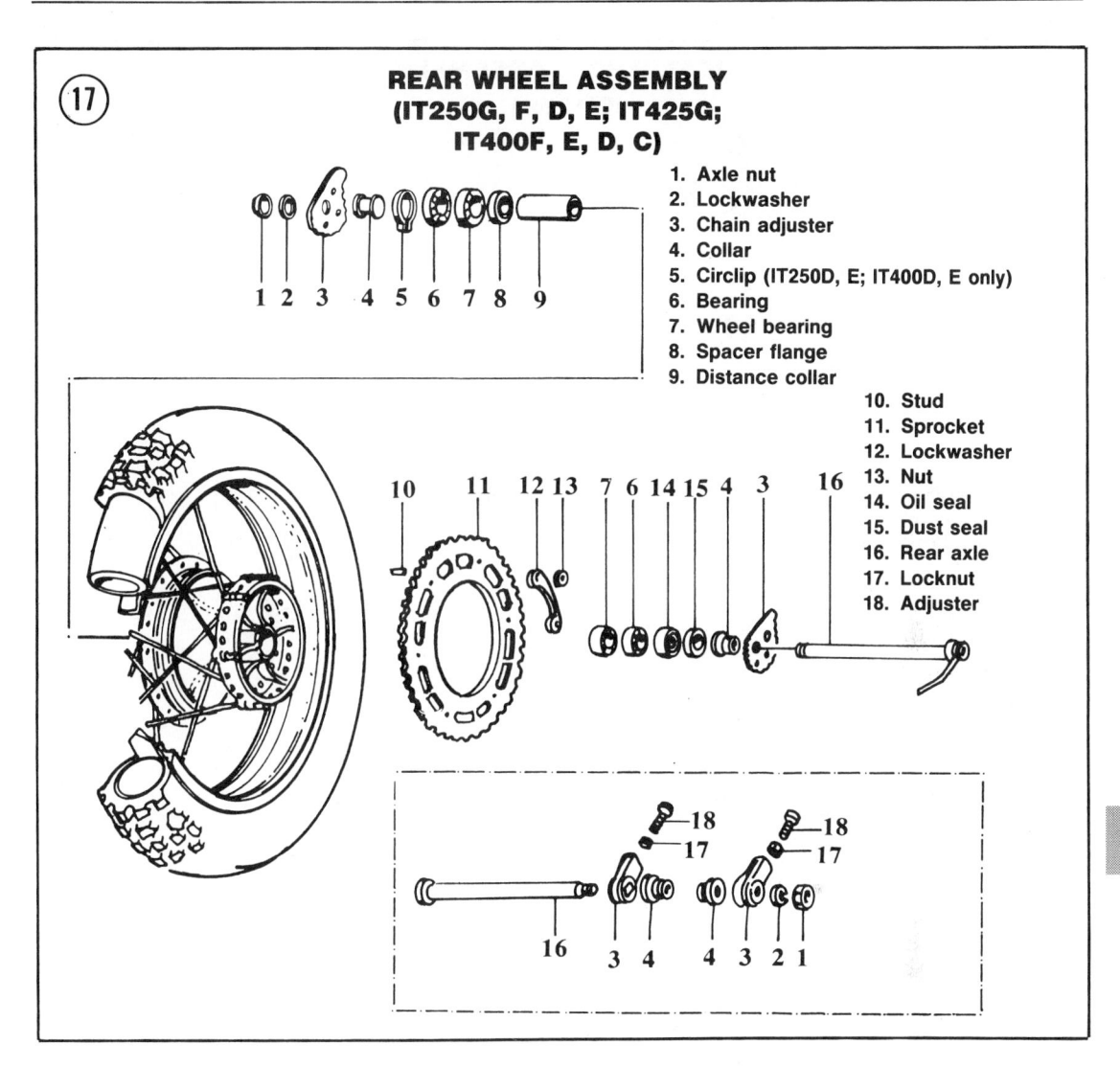

REAR WHEEL ASSEMBLY
(IT250G, F, D, E; IT425G; IT400F, E, D, C)

1. Axle nut
2. Lockwasher
3. Chain adjuster
4. Collar
5. Circlip (IT250D, E; IT400D, E only)
6. Bearing
7. Wheel bearing
8. Spacer flange
9. Distance collar
10. Stud
11. Sprocket
12. Lockwasher
13. Nut
14. Oil seal
15. Dust seal
16. Rear axle
17. Locknut
18. Adjuster

Inspection (All Models)

Measure the radial and axial runout of the wheel rim with a dial indicator as shown in **Figure 16**. The standard value for both radial and axial runout is 0.08 in. (2.0 mm).

Tighten or replace any bent or loose spokes. Refer to *Spoke Inspection and Replacement* in Chapter Eight.

Check axle runout as described under *Rear Hub Inspection* in this chapter.

REAR HUB

Refer to **Figures 17-19** for this procedure.

Disassembly

1. Remove the rear wheel as described under *Rear Wheel Removal/Installation* in this chapter.

2. Remove the axle spacers from the wheel (**Figure 20**, **Figure 21** or **Figure 22**).

3. Pull the brake assembly (**Figure 23**) straight up and out of the drum.

4. Remove the dust seal (**Figure 24**) on the side opposite the brake drum.

5. To remove the right- and left-hand bearings (**Figure 25**) and spacer, insert a soft aluminum or brass drift into one side of the hub. Push the distance collar over to one side and place the drift on the inner race of the lower bearing (**Figure 26**). Tap the bearing out of the hub with a hammer, working around the perimeter of the inner race.

228　　　　　　　　　　　　　　　　　　　　　　　　　　　　　　　　　　　CHAPTER NINE

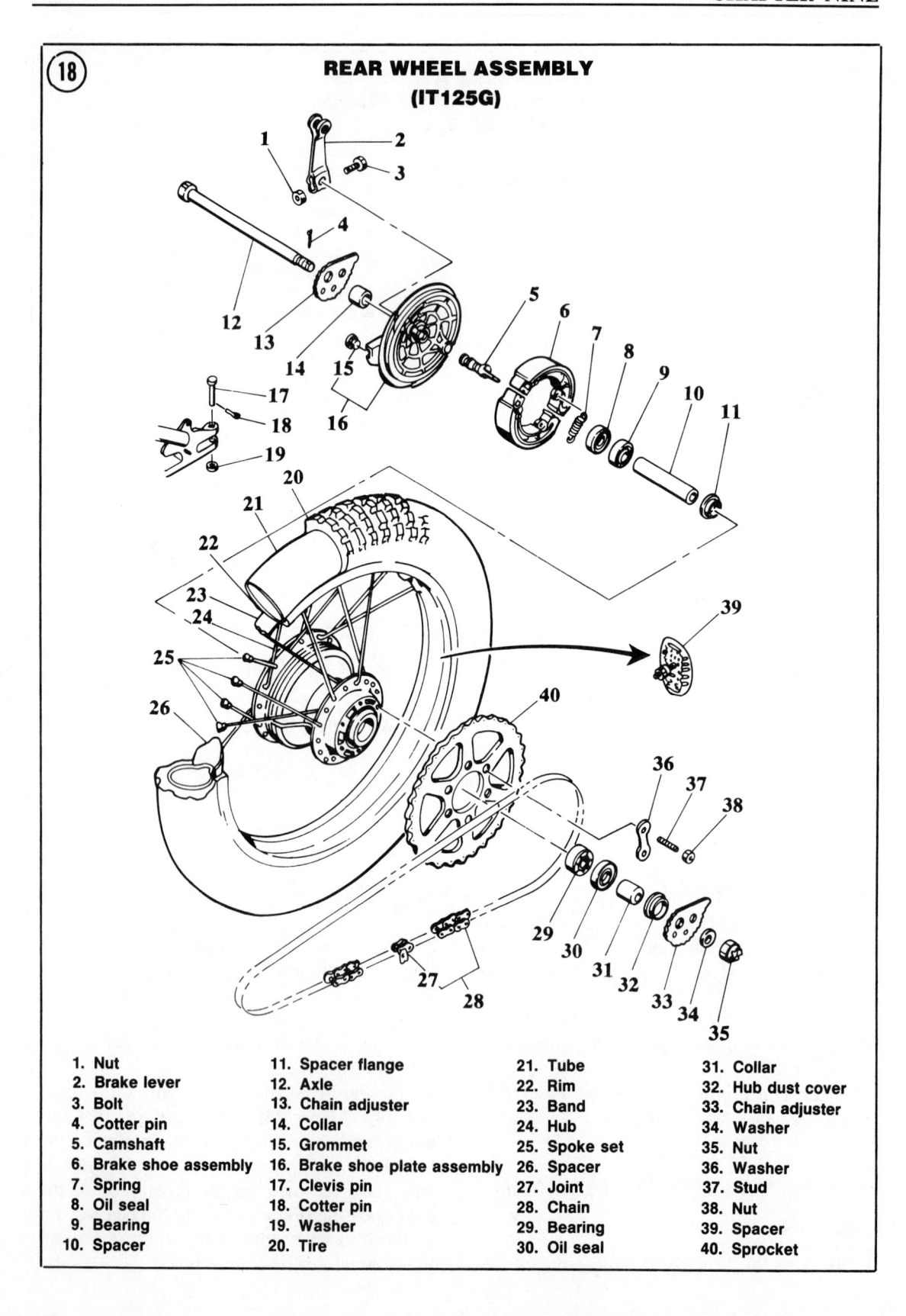

REAR WHEEL ASSEMBLY (IT125G)

1. Nut	11. Spacer flange	21. Tube	31. Collar
2. Brake lever	12. Axle	22. Rim	32. Hub dust cover
3. Bolt	13. Chain adjuster	23. Band	33. Chain adjuster
4. Cotter pin	14. Collar	24. Hub	34. Washer
5. Camshaft	15. Grommet	25. Spoke set	35. Nut
6. Brake shoe assembly	16. Brake shoe plate assembly	26. Spacer	36. Washer
7. Spring	17. Clevis pin	27. Joint	37. Stud
8. Oil seal	18. Cotter pin	28. Chain	38. Nut
9. Bearing	19. Washer	29. Bearing	39. Spacer
10. Spacer	20. Tire	30. Oil seal	40. Sprocket

REAR SUSPENSION

REAR WHEEL ASSEMBLY (IT175G)

1. Axle	11. Clevis pin	21. Band	31. Washer
2. Cotter pin	12. Cotter pin	22. Bolt	32. Nut
3. Chain adjuster	13. Lever	23. Spoke set	33. **Master link**
4. Bushing	14. Washer	24. Spacer flange	34. Drive chain
5. Brake shoe plate	15. Bolt	25. Bearing	35. Sprocket
6. Camshaft	16. Seal	26. Oil seal	36. Spacer
7. Brake shoe assembly	17. Nut	27. Hub dust cover	37. Washer
8. Spring	18. Tire	28. Collar	38. Nut
9. Bearing	19. Tube	29. Bushing	39. Clevis pin
10. Spacer	20. Rim	30. Chain adjuster	40. Cotter pin

230   CHAPTER NINE

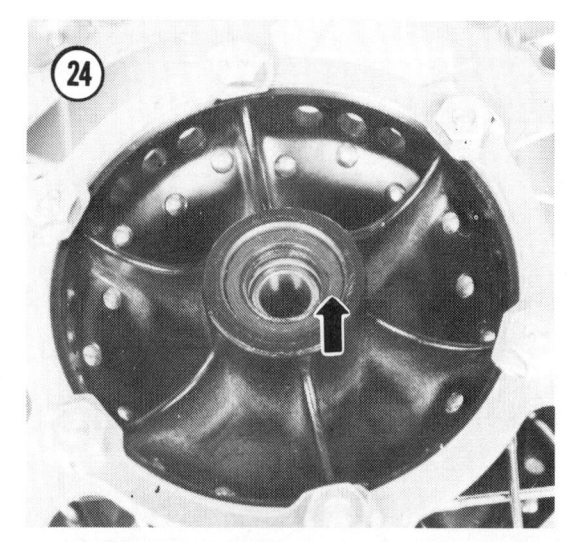

REAR SUSPENSION

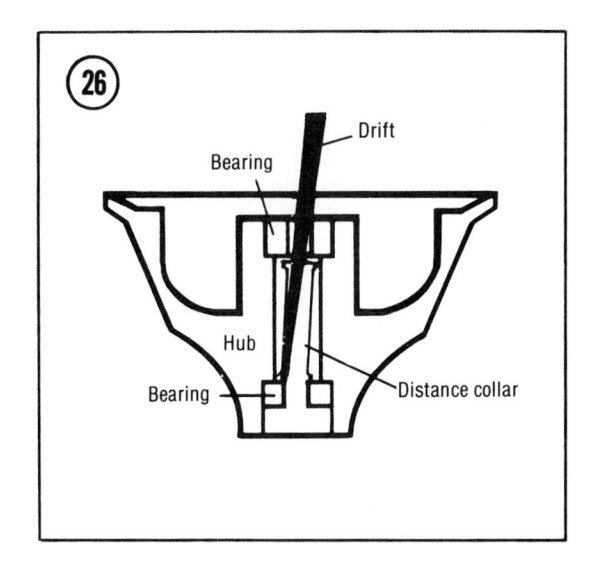

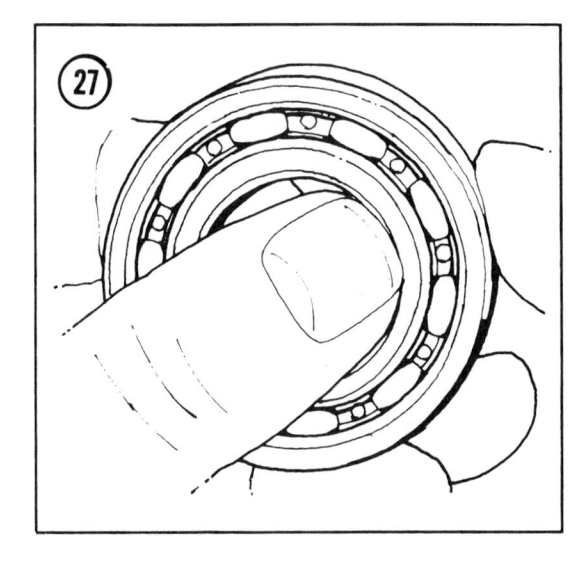

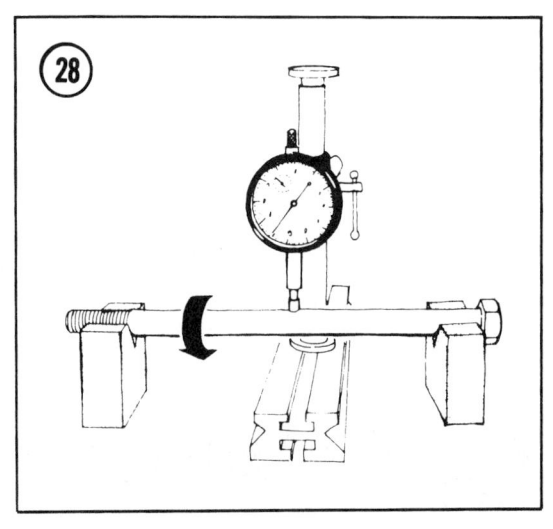

NOTE
If the bearings are difficult to remove there is a special Yamaha tool designed to fit into the hole in the distance collar to aid in the removal.

6. Remove the distance collar and tap out the opposite bearing.

Inspection

1. Thoroughly clean out the inside of the hub with solvent and dry with compressed air or a shop cloth.

NOTE
Avoid getting any greasy solvent residue on the brake drum during this procedure. If this happens, clean it off with a clean shop cloth and lacquer thinner.

2. Do not clean sealed bearings. If non-sealed bearings are installed, thoroughly dry with compressed air. Do not let the bearing spin while drying.
3. Turn each bearing by hand (**Figure 27**). Make sure the bearings turn smoothly.

NOTE
Some axial play is normal, but radial play should be negligible. The bearing should turn smoothly.

4. On non-sealed bearings, check the balls (on the non-sealed side) for evidence of wear, pitting or excessive heat (bluish tint). Replace bearings if necessary; always replace as a complete set. When replacing, be sure to take your old bearings along to ensure a perfect matchup.

NOTE
Fully sealed bearings are available from many good bearing speciality shops. Fully sealed bearings provide better protection from dirt and moisture that may get into the hub.

5. Check the axle for wear and straightness. Use V-blocks and a dial indicator as shown in **Figure 28**. If the runout is 0.008 in. (0.2 mm) or greater, the axle should be replaced.

Assembly

1. On non-sealed bearings, pack the bearings with a good quality bearing grease. Work the grease in between the balls thoroughly. Turn the bearing by hand a couple of times to make sure the grease is distributed evenly inside the bearing.
2. Pack the wheel hub with multipurpose grease.

> *CAUTION*
> *Install the wheel bearings with the sealed side facing out. Tap the bearings squarely into place and tap on the outer race only. Use a socket (Figure 29) that matches the outer race diameter. Do not tap on the inner race or the bearing might be damaged. Be sure that the bearings are completely seated.*

3. Install the left-hand bearing.
4. Press in the distance collar.
5. Install the right-hand bearing.
6. Install a new grease seal. Lubricate it with fresh multipurpose grease and tap it gently into place.
7. Install the rear wheel as described under *Rear Wheel Removal/Installation* in this chapter.

DRIVE SPROCKET

Disassembly/Assembly

The drive sprocket is held in place either with Allen head bolts or hardened hex head nuts and lockwashers. This varies with different models and years.

1. Remove the rear wheel as described under *Rear Wheel Removal/Installation* in this chapter.
2. On models with a right-hand drive chain, remove the brake panel assembly from the brake drum.
3. On models with Allen head bolts, remove the bolts (**Figure 30**) and remove the drive sprocket.
4. On models with hex head nuts, straighten the locking tabs on the lockwasher and remove the nuts and lockwashers (**Figure 31**). Remove the drive sprocket.

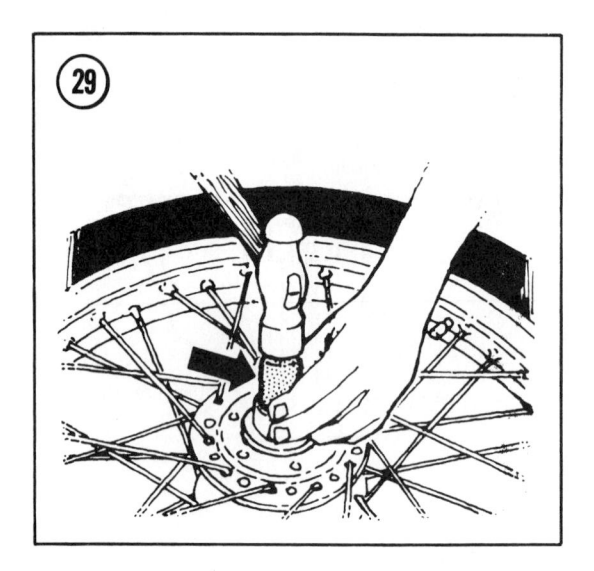

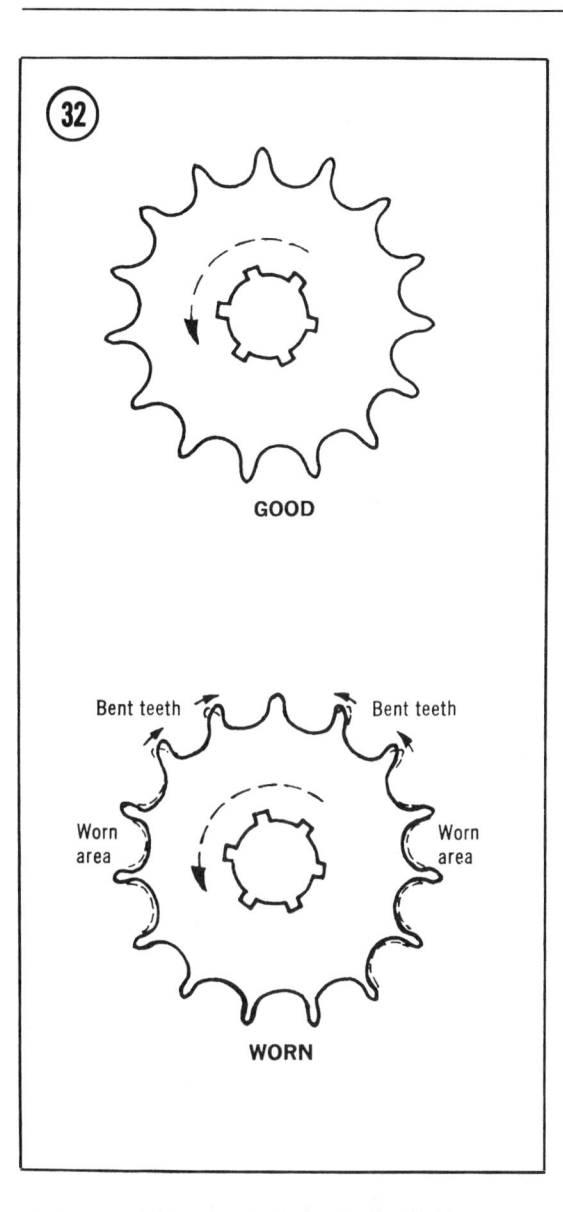

REAR SUSPENSION

5. Assemble by reversing these disassembly steps, noting the following.
6. Tighten the nuts or bolts to the torque values given in **Table 1** at the end of this chapter.
7. Install new lockwashers on models so equipped. Bend the locking tabs up.

Inspection

Inspect the condition of the teeth on the sprocket. If they are visibly worn as shown in **Figure 32**, replace the sprocket.

If the sprocket requires replacement, the drive chain is probably worn also and may need replacement. Refer to *Drive Chain Cleaning, Inspection and Lubrication* in Chapter Three for inspection instructions. Replace chain if worn.

DRIVE CHAIN

Removal/Installation

1. Place a milk crate or wood block(s) under the frame so the rear wheel is off the ground.
2. Turn the rear wheel and drive chain until the master link is accessible.
3. Remove the shift lever (**Figure 33**). Remove the bolts securing the driven sprocket cover and remove it.

NOTE
These covers vary in shape and in the amount of bolts securing them for the various models and years.

4. Remove the master link clip (**Figure 34**) and remove the master link.

5. Slowly rotate the rear wheel and pull the drive chain off the drive sprocket.
6. Install by reversing these removal steps.
7. Install a new clip on the master link so that the closed end of the clip is facing the direction of chain travel (**Figure 35**).

Service and Inspection

For service and inspection of the drive chain, refer to *Drive Chain/Cleaning, Inspection and Lubrication* in Chapter Three.

WHEEL BALANCING

Balance the rear wheel in the same manner as the front wheel. See *Wheel Balancing* in Chapter Eight.

TIRE CHANGING AND TIRE REPAIRS

Service the rear tire in the same manner as the front tire. See *Tire Changing* or *Tire Repairs* in Chapter Eight.

REAR SWING ARM

The rear swing arm is manufactured either of aluminum or steel; this varies with different models and years. Aluminum and steel swing arms are basically the same and removal and installation of both are covered in the same procedure. Disassembly, inspection and assembly are different and are covered separately.

In time, the bearings or bushings will wear beyond the service limits and will have to be replaced. The condition of the bearings or bushings can greatly affect handling performance and if worn ones are not replaced they can produce erratic and dangerous handling. Common symptoms are wheel hop, pulling to one side during acceleration and pulling to the other side during braking.

Swing Arm Removal/Installation

NOTE
This procedure is shown with both types of swing arms.

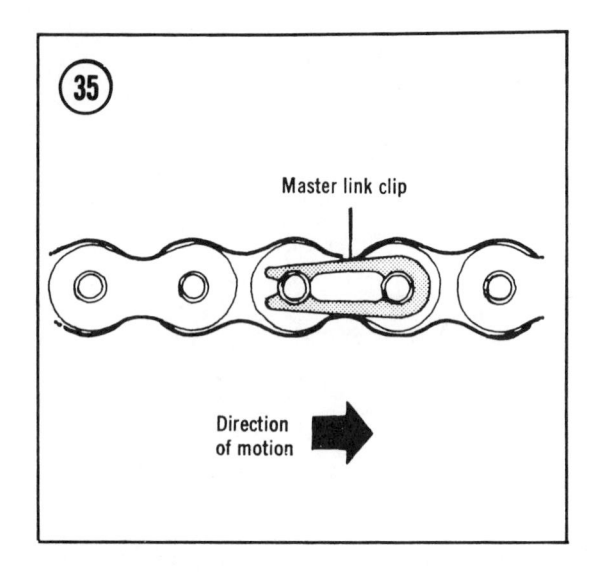

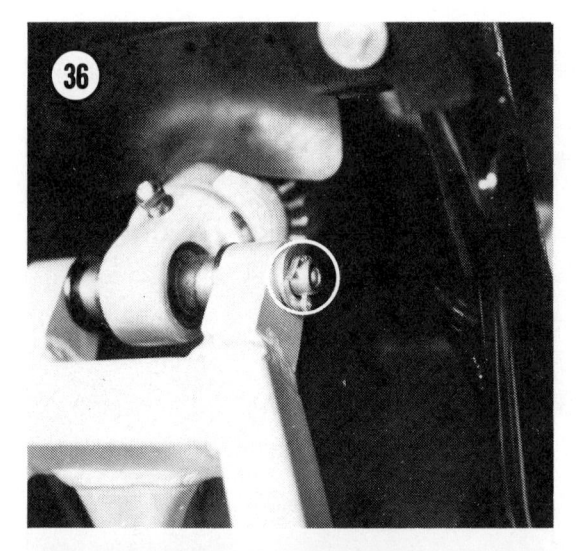

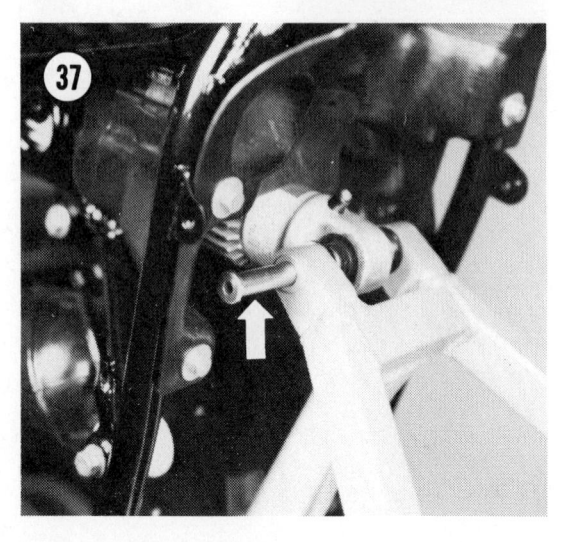

REAR SUSPENSION

1. Remove the rear wheel and drive chain as described under *Rear Wheel Removal/Installation* in this chapter.
2. Remove the cotter pin (**Figure 36**) on the end of the upper mounting pin.
3. Pull the pin out (**Figure 37**) and gently let the swing arm pivot down (**Figure 38**).

NOTE
Don't lose the cover washers on each side of the monoshock rear mount.

4. After the upper end of the swing arm is disconnected, grasp its rear end and try to move it from side to side in a horizontal arc. Maximum allowable side play is 0.04 in. (1 mm). If play is greater than this and the pivot bolt is tightened correctly, the bearings should be replaced.
5. Remove the nut and lockwasher (**Figure 39**) and withdraw the pivot bolt from the other side. It is not necessary to remove the engine to remove the swing arm.
6. Remove the swing arm assembly.
7. To install, position the swing arm into the lower mounting area. Align the holes in the swing arm with the hole in the engine rear mounting assembly. To help align the holes, insert a drift from the side opposite where the bolt is to be inserted.

NOTE
If the engine is installed it may be necessary to loosen the other engine mounting hardware to help align the swing arm holes. The lower portion of the bike's frame is very flexible and tends to move a little when major components are either removed or loosened.

8. After all holes are aligned, insert the pivot bolt and install the lockwasher and nut. Tighten the nut to the torque values in **Table 1**. Retighten engine mounting hardware if it was loosened in the previous step.
9. Install the cover washers on each side of the monoshock (**Figure 40**).

10. Apply a light coat of grease to the upper mounting pin and install it (**Figure 41**).

11. Install a new cotter pin; never reuse an old cotter pin as it may break and fall out. Hold the end of the pin with a wrench and bend over the end of the cotter pin completely (**Figure 42**).

NOTE
*Make sure that both cover washers (**Figure 43**) are installed. They are necessary to maintain the proper clearance between the monoshock and the swing arm. If they are slightly flattened out, replace them.*

12. Install the rear wheel as described under *Rear Wheel Removal/Installation* in this chapter.

Steel Swing Arm Disassembly/Inspection/Assembly

The steel rear swing arms are basically the same but differences do occur in all. They are separated into types that relate to different models and years. The main difference among the 4 types is that the Type II and IV use one long internal bushing while Type I and III have a short one at each end. Pay particular attention to the location of spacers, washers, bearings or bushings to make assembly correct and easier.

The Type I steel swing arm (**Figure 44**) is found on the following models:
  IT425G
  IT400F, E, D
  IT250G, F, E, D
  IT175F

The Type II steel swing arm (**Figure 45**) is found on the following model:
  IT125G.

The Type III steel swing arm (**Figure 46**) is found on the following models:
  IT175D, E

The Type IV steel swing arm (**Figure 47**) is found on the following model:
  IT400C

1. Remove the swing arm as described in this chapter.
2. Secure the swing arm in a vise with soft jaws.
3. Remove the chain guard/seal.

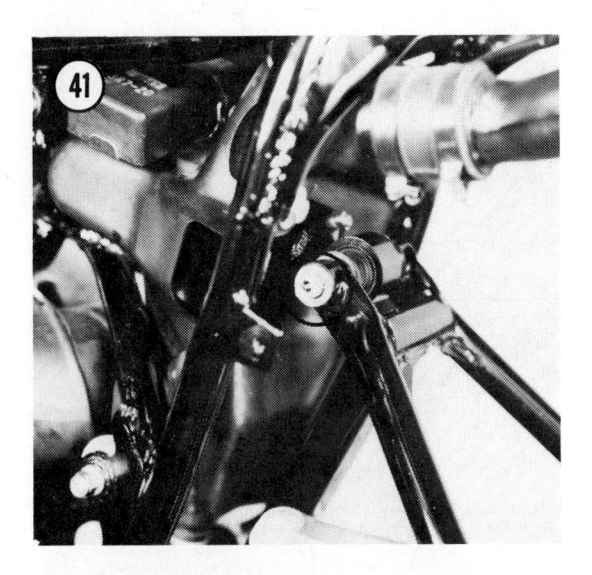

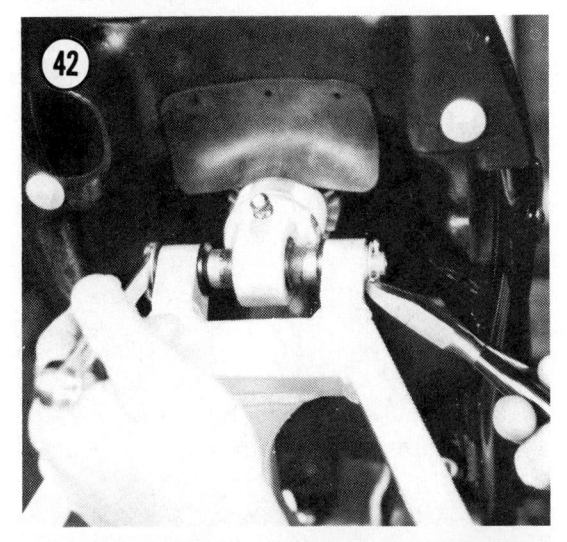

REAR SUSPENSION

TYPE 1 REAR SWING ARM ASSEMBLY (MODELS IT425G; IT400F, E, D; IT250G, F, E, D; IT175F)

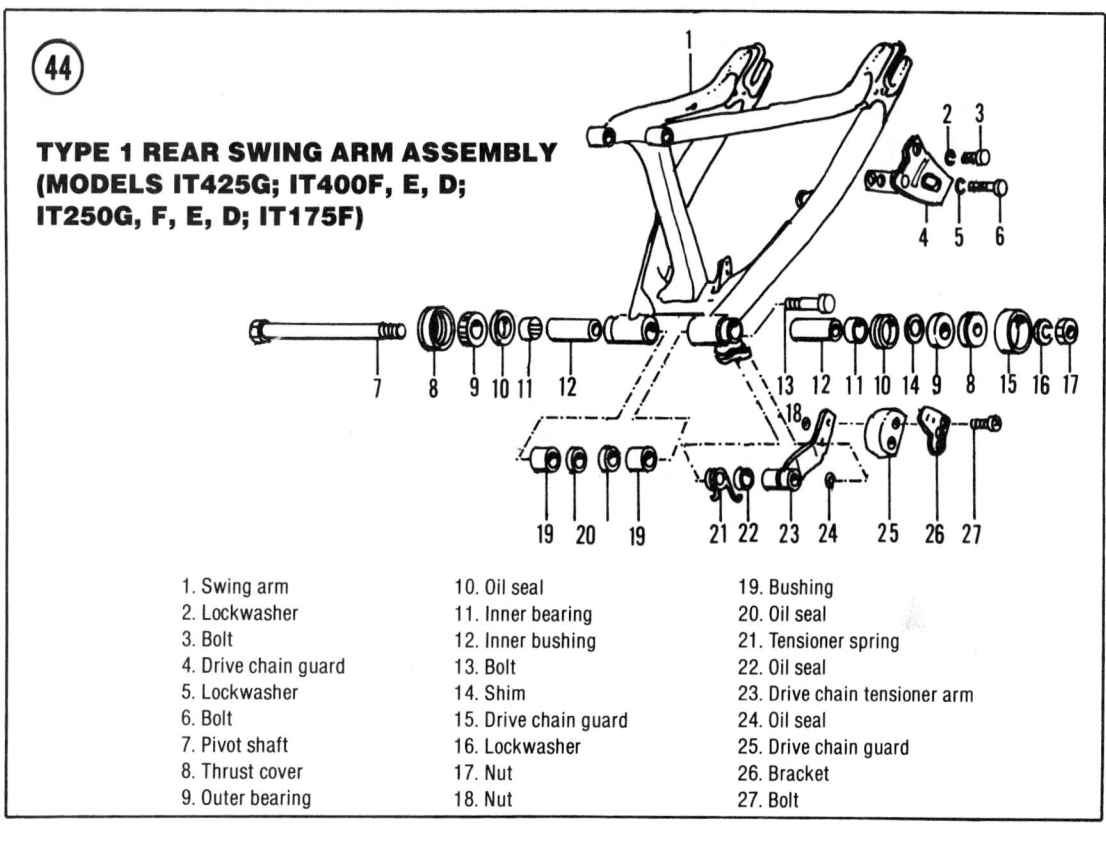

44

1. Swing arm
2. Lockwasher
3. Bolt
4. Drive chain guard
5. Lockwasher
6. Bolt
7. Pivot shaft
8. Thrust cover
9. Outer bearing
10. Oil seal
11. Inner bearing
12. Inner bushing
13. Bolt
14. Shim
15. Drive chain guard
16. Lockwasher
17. Nut
18. Nut
19. Bushing
20. Oil seal
21. Tensioner spring
22. Oil seal
23. Drive chain tensioner arm
24. Oil seal
25. Drive chain guard
26. Bracket
27. Bolt

TYPE II REAR SWING ARM ASSEMBLY (MODEL IT125G)

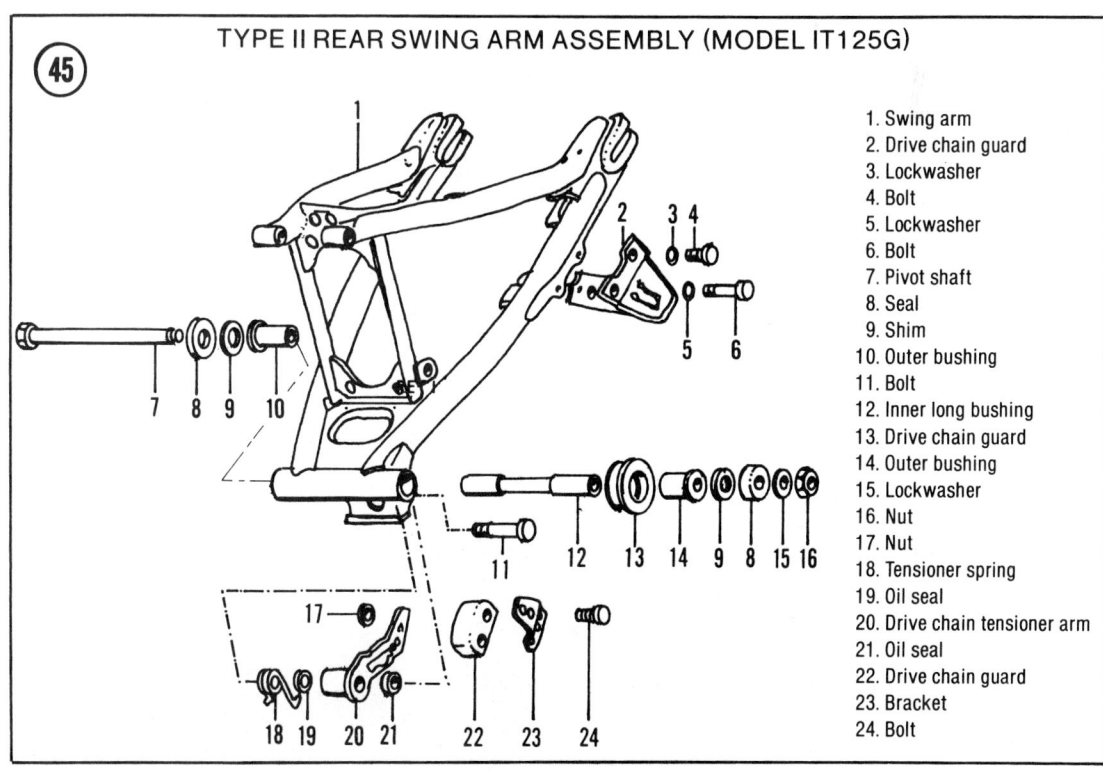

45

1. Swing arm
2. Drive chain guard
3. Lockwasher
4. Bolt
5. Lockwasher
6. Bolt
7. Pivot shaft
8. Seal
9. Shim
10. Outer bushing
11. Bolt
12. Inner long bushing
13. Drive chain guard
14. Outer bushing
15. Lockwasher
16. Nut
17. Nut
18. Tensioner spring
19. Oil seal
20. Drive chain tensioner arm
21. Oil seal
22. Drive chain guard
23. Bracket
24. Bolt

CHAPTER NINE

TYPE III REAR SWING ARM ASSEMBLY (MODEL IT175D, E)

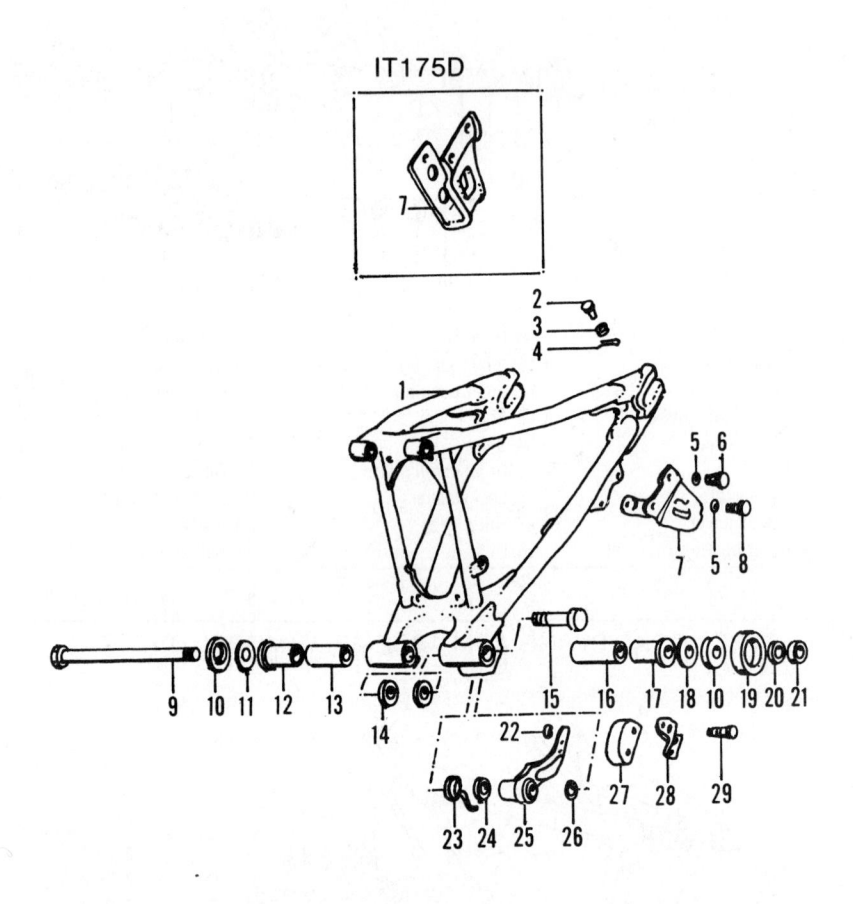

1. Swing arm
2. Bolt
3. Washer
4. Cotter pin
5. Lockwasher
6. Bolt
7. Drive chain guard
8. Bolt
9. Pivot shaft
10. Thrust cover
11. Shim
12. Outer bushing
13. Inner bushing
14. Oil seal
15. Bolt
16. Inner bushing
17. Outer bushing
18. Shim
19. Drive chain guard
20. Lockwasher
21. Nut
22. Nut
23. Tensioner spring
24. Oil seal
25. Drive chain tensioner arm
26. Oil seal
27. Drive chain guard
28. Bracket
29. Bolt

REAR SUSPENSION

239

⁴⁷ TYPE IV REAR SWING ARM ASSEMBLY (MODEL IT400C)

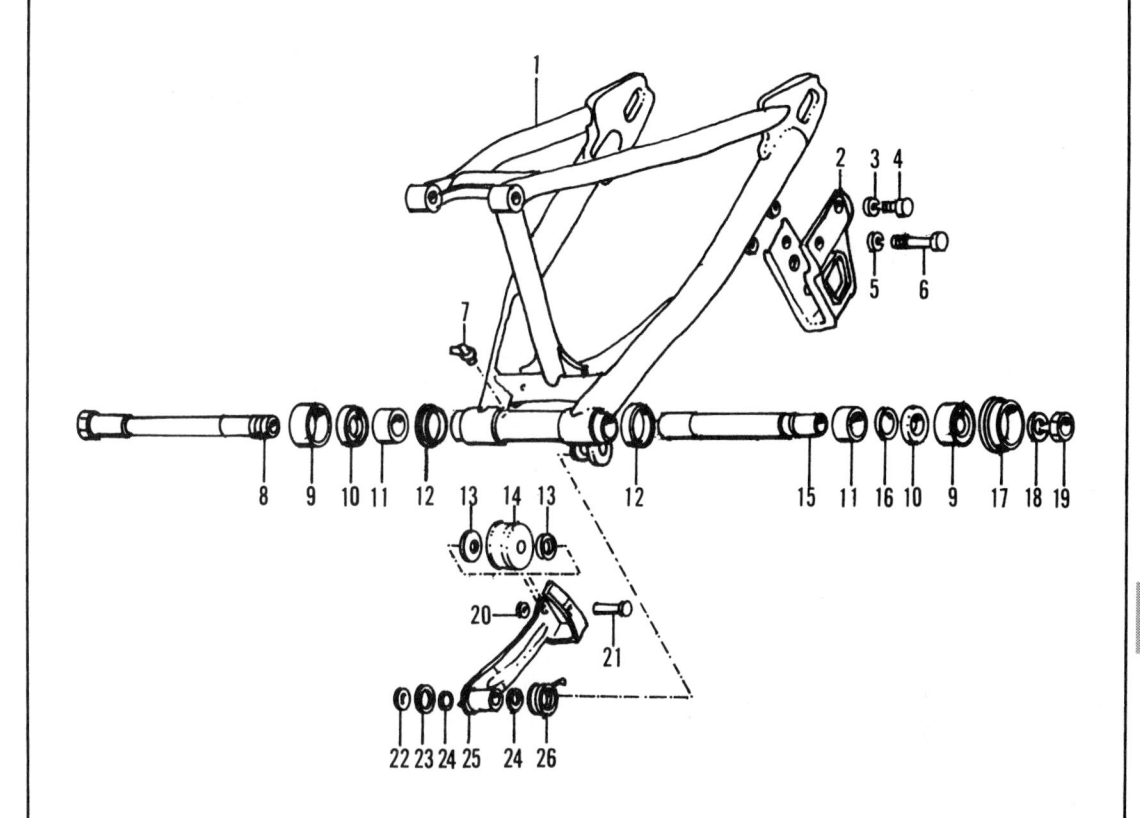

1. Swing arm
2. Drive chain guard
3. Lockwasher
4. Bolt
5. Lockwasher
6. Bolt
7. Grease fitting
8. Pivot shaft
9. Thrust cover
10. Outer bearing
11. Inner bearing
12. Oil seal
13. Washer
14. Drive chain roller
15. Inner bushing
16. Washer
17. Drive chain guard
18. Lockwasher
19. Nut
20. Washer
21. Shaft
22. E-clip
23. Washer
24. Oil seal
25. Drive chain tensioner arm
26. Tensioner spring

4. On Types II and III, remove the thrust cover/oil seal (A, **Figure 48**), the shim (B) and inner bushing (C) from each side.

NOTE
On Type II there is one long inner bushing that runs the width of the swing arm pivot.

5. On Types I and IV, remove the thrust cover, outer bearing, washer or shim, oil seal, inner bearing and bushing from each side.

NOTE
On Type IV there is one long inner bushing that runs the width of the swing arm pivot.

6. On Types I, II and III, tap out the outer bushings if they are to be replaced. Use a suitable size drift or socket and extension and carefully drive them out with a hammer.

CAUTION
Do not remove the bushings just for inspection as they are usually damaged during removal.

7. Wash all parts, including the inside of the swing arm pivot area, in solvent and thoroughly dry.
8. On Type IV, inspect the condition of the bearings. Turn the bearings by hand; make sure they rotate smoothly. If not, replace them as a set.
9. Apply a light coat of waterproof grease to all parts prior to installation.
10. Install all parts in the reverse order of disassembly. Tap new bushings into place slowly and squarely with a block of wood and hammer. Make sure that they are not cocked and that they are completely seated.

CAUTION
Never reinstall a bushing that has been removed. Removal slightly damages it so that it is no longer true to alignment. If installed, it will damage the inner bushing and create an unsafe riding condition.

11. Inspect the condition of the drive chain slider. Replace if necessary by removing the attachment bolts.

Aluminum Swing Arm Disassembly/Inspection/Assembly

The aluminum swing arm is used only on model IT175G. Refer to **Figure 49** for this procedure.
1. Remove the swing arm as described in this chapter.
2. Secure the swing arm in a vise with soft jaws.
3. Carefully remove the thrust cover (**Figure 50**).
4. Remove the oil seal, shim, washer, bearing, bushing and oil seal.
5. Tap out the inner bushings if they are to be replaced (**Figure 51**). Use a suitable size drift or socket and extension and carefully drive them out with a hammer.

CAUTION
Do not remove the bearings or bushings just for inspection as they are usually damaged during removal.

6. Wash all parts, including the inside of the swing arm pivot area, in solvent and thoroughly dry.
7. Apply a light coat of waterproof grease to all parts prior to installation. Oil the lips of the new oil seals (always replace the oil seals with new ones).
8. Install all parts in the reverse order of disassembly. Tap the bearings or bushings into

REAR SUSPENSION

49 REAR SWING ARM ASSEMBLY—ALUMINUM
(MODEL IT175G)

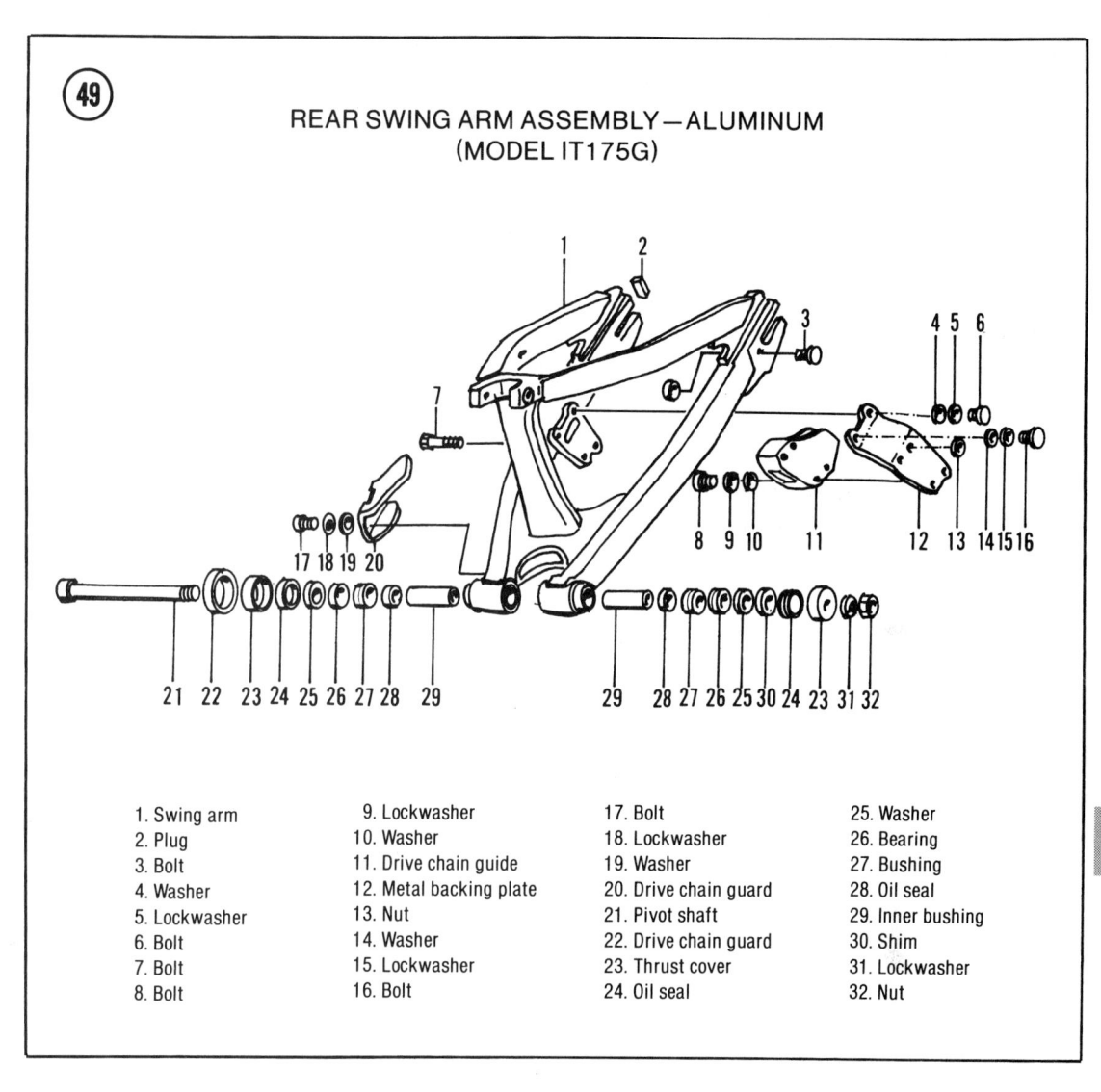

1. Swing arm
2. Plug
3. Bolt
4. Washer
5. Lockwasher
6. Bolt
7. Bolt
8. Bolt
9. Lockwasher
10. Washer
11. Drive chain guide
12. Metal backing plate
13. Nut
14. Washer
15. Lockwasher
16. Bolt
17. Bolt
18. Lockwasher
19. Washer
20. Drive chain guard
21. Pivot shaft
22. Drive chain guard
23. Thrust cover
24. Oil seal
25. Washer
26. Bearing
27. Bushing
28. Oil seal
29. Inner bushing
30. Shim
31. Lockwasher
32. Nut

50

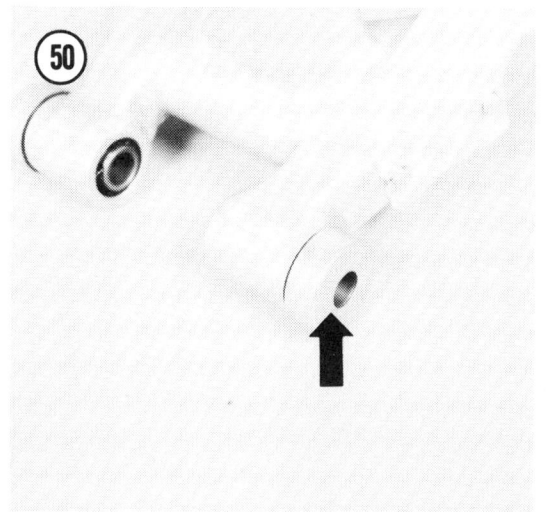

51

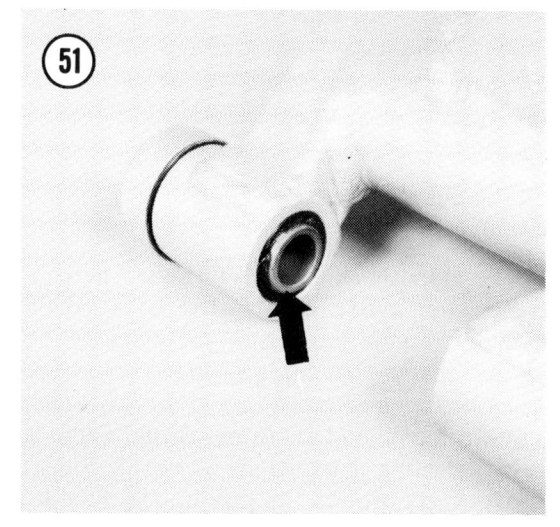

place slowly and squarely with a block of wood and hammer. Make sure they are not cocked and that they are completely seated.

> *CAUTION*
> *Never reinstall a bearing or bushing that has been removed. Removal slightly damages it so that it is no longer true to alignment. If installed, it will damage the long bushing and create an unsafe riding condition.*

9. Inspect the condition of the drive chain sliders. Replace if necessary by removing the attachment screws and/or bolts.

REAR SUSPENSION (DECARBON MONOCROSS SYSTEM)

The rear suspension on all ITs is basically the same. In 1977 the monoshock unit was improved and became the DeCarbon Monocross System. The monoshock unit is tucked up in the frame's hollow backbone under the fuel tank. On some models (since 1980) the nitrogen gas tank reservoir has been moved out from under the fuel tank and onto the side of the frame. This allows more rapid cooling to prevent shock fading.

All models offer a variety of damping and spring preload adjustments. The adjustment procedures vary with the different models and are covered separately.

Removal and installation is basically the same on all models and where differences occur they are noted.

> *NOTE*
> *The unit used on the IT400C model is substantially different from the DeCarbon type and is covered separately at the end of the chapter.*

DeCarbon Monocross System Operation

The monoshock unit is a nitrogen-charged, free-piston shock constructed of a single cylinder (**Figure 52**). Inside the cylinder are an oil chamber and gas chamber; they are separated by a free piston and O-ring which prevent the oil and gas from mixing. There is also a floating valve which allows the oil to move freely around the piston. The floating

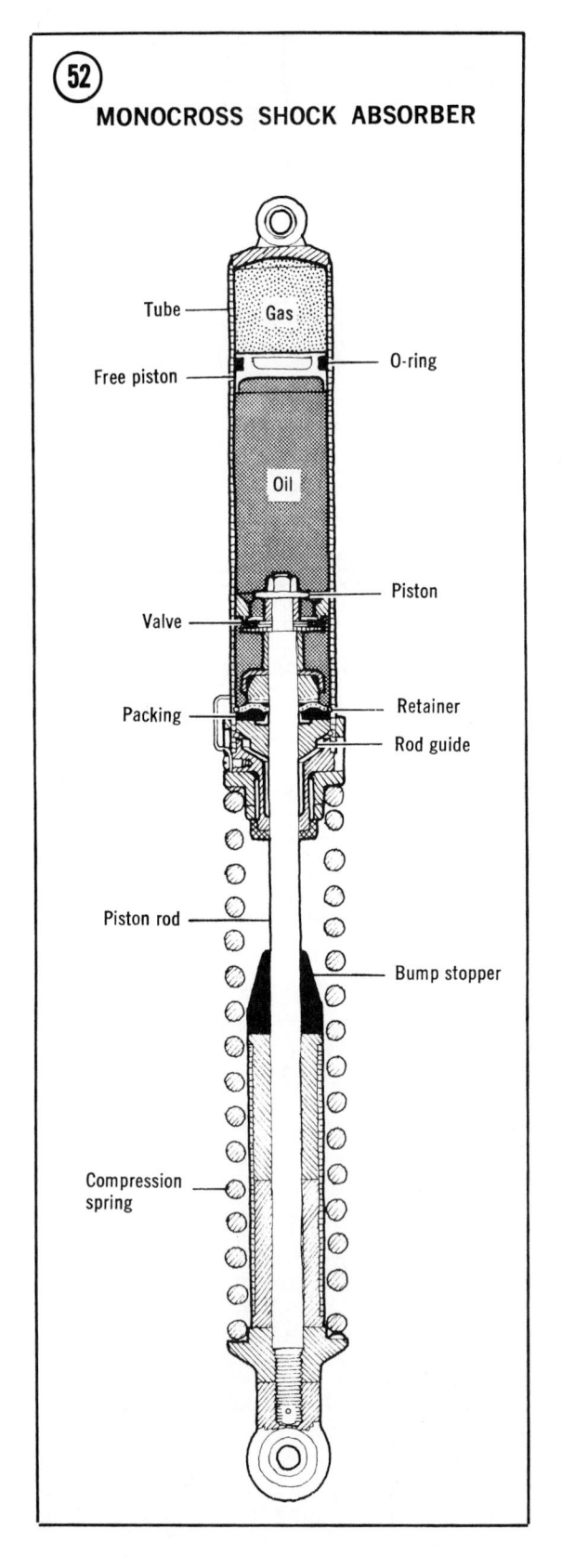

52 MONOCROSS SHOCK ABSORBER

- Tube
- Gas
- Free piston
- O-ring
- Oil
- Valve
- Piston
- Packing
- Retainer
- Rod guide
- Piston rod
- Bump stopper
- Compression spring

REAR SUSPENSION

the change in gas pressure. As the piston speed increases, the floating valve allows the oil to flow faster, creating friction and damping the stretch of the suspension. The damping amount is automatically controlled according to the speed of the piston movement.

In the compression stroke, the oil stored under the piston moves upward, compressing the nitrogen in the gas chamber. Again, as the piston moves faster, the floating valve reacts, allowing the oil to move faster, thus creating a damping force. The damping is controlled automatically by the speed of the piston.

WARNING
*The monoshock unit contains highly compressed nitrogen gas. Do not tamper with or attempt to open the damper/cylinder assembly (**Figure 53**). Do not place it near an open flame or other extreme heat. Do not weld on the frame near it. Do not dispose of the damper subassembly yourself. Take it to a Yamaha dealer where it can be deactivated and disposed of properly. Never attempt to remove the plug at the bottom of the nitrogen tank (**Figure 54**).*

Damping Adjustment—1977 and Later (Except Model IT125G)

Models With Remote Nitrogen Gas Tank

1. Remove the side cover/number plate.

NOTE
It is not necessary to remove the side cover/number plate for access but it will save a lot of cuts on the forearm from the sharp edges on the plastic.

NOTE
The following adjustment should be made one notch at a time; test ride the bike after each adjustment. Turn the adjuster until it clicks into position. There are approximately 14 notches on the stiffer side and 10 notches on the soft side.

WARNING
Do not turn the adjuster when it becomes either light or heavy to turn.

valve is an improvement over older models; it responds more quickly to changes in the pressure in the gas chamber.

NOTE
On some models since 1980, the nitrogen gas cylinder is remote from the main shock body. Operation is still basically the same except that gas cooling is more rapid.

The monoshock unit works as follows: in the stretch stroke, the oil is forced downward by

2. Using the 32 mm open end wrench provided in the owner's tool kit, turn the

adjuster (**Figure 55**) to any of the 24 steps that are available. It is not necessary to remove the shock unit to perform this adjustment.

3. To make damping stiffer, turn the adjuster *clockwise* as looking from the rear. For softer damping, turn it *counterclockwise*.

Models Without Remote Nitrogen Gas Tank

1. Remove the seat.

NOTE
On some models it is unnecessary to remove the fuel tank to gain access to the adjustment hole in the frame. Check this out prior to removing your fuel tank as instructed in Steps 2 and 3.

2. Turn the fuel shutoff valve to the OFF position and remove the fuel line to the carburetor.

3. Remove the bolts (A, **Figure 56**) securing the front of the fuel tank. Pull up and unhook the strap (B, **Figure 56**) securing the rear of the tank. Pull the vent tube (C, **Figure 56**) free from the steering head assembly. Pull the tank toward the rear and remove it.

NOTE
*This adjustment should be made one notch at a time; test ride the bike after each adjustment. Turn the adjuster until it clicks into position. There are approximately 10-12 notches on either side of the standard position. The standard position is marked wilth a paint stripe on both the shock and the adjuster (**Figure 57**).*

WARNING
*Do not turn the adjuster when it becomes either light or heavy to turn. A Yamaha Factory Bulletin was issued in reference to models IT400D, IT250D and IT175D on minimum and maximum settings. On these models only, **do not** increase damping beyond 7 clicks from the standard setting (paint stripe mark). The use of the 8th click may result in damage to the monoshock unit. Also on these models only, do not reduce to the minimum damping setting—**do not exceed past the 10th click**—from the standard setting (paint stripe mark). If set on the 11th click the adjusting collar and dowel pin may be damaged causing the monoshock to malfunction.*

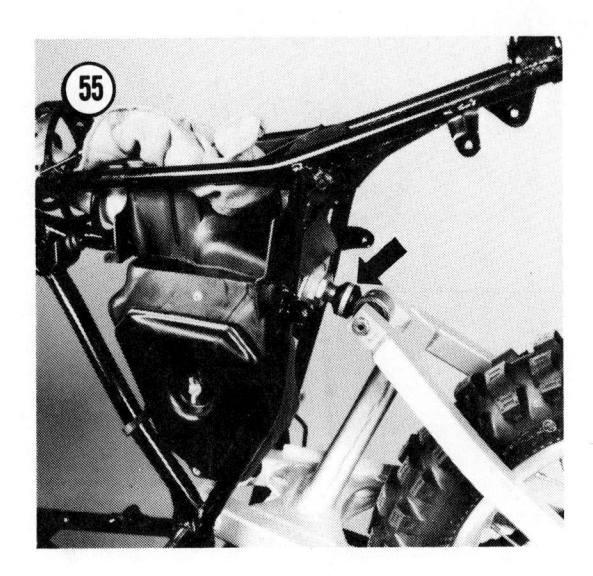

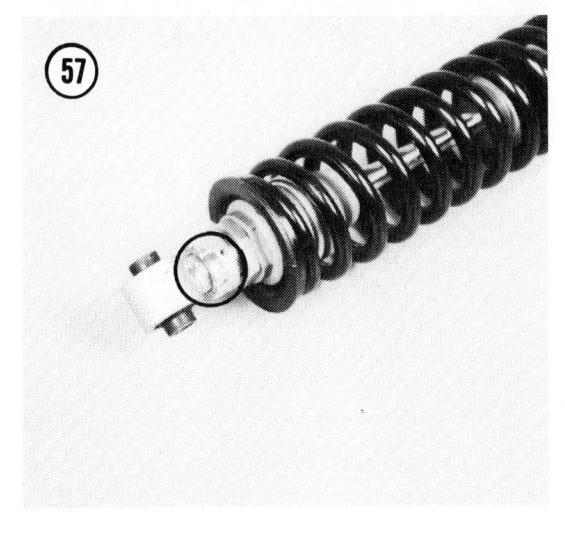

REAR SUSPENSION

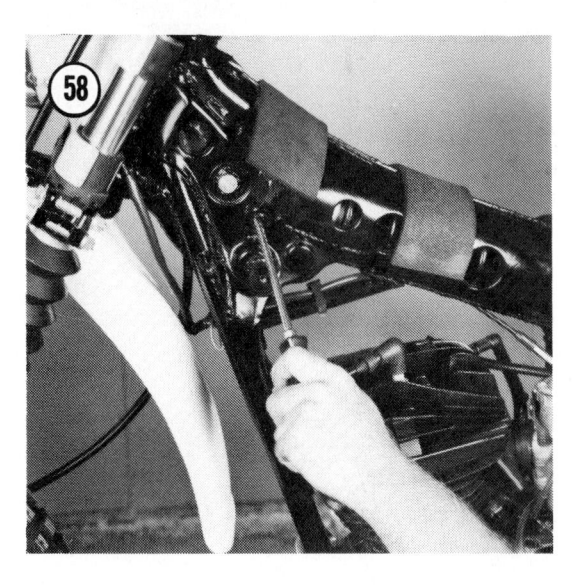

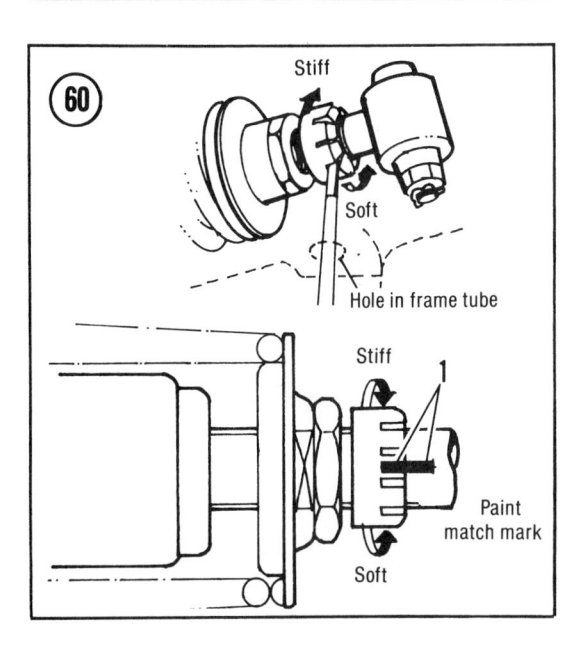

4. Insert a slotted head screwdriver through the hole in the frame (**Figure 58**). Place the blade of the screwdriver into the notches in the adjuster (**Figure 59**). Turn it in either direction as shown in **Figure 60** to achieve a stiffer or softer damping. The hole in the frame may be either on the right- or left-hand side, depending on which model you have.

5. Turn the adjuster (**Figure 59**) to any of the 20-24 steps that are available. It is not necessary to remove the shock unit to perform this adjustment. **Figure 59** is shown with it removed for clarity.

Spring Pre-load—1977 and Later (Except Model IT125G)

Models With Remote Nitrogen Gas Tank

1. Remove the side cover/number plate.

NOTE
It is not necessary to remove the side cover/number plate for access but it will save a lot of cuts on the forearm from the sharp edges on the plastic.

2. Using the 32 mm open end wrench provided in the owners tool kit, loosen the locknut and turn the adjuster (**Figure 61**). Tighten it to increase spring pre-load or loosen it to decrease.

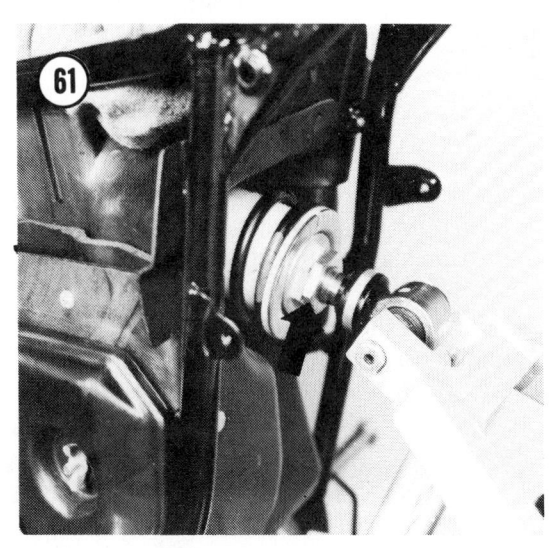

NOTE
Adjustments should be made in increments of 2 mm of spring length each time; test ride the bike after each adjustment.

3. The installed spring length (**Figure 62**) must be within the following range:
   a. Standard length–13.2 in. (335 mm).
   b. Minimum length–12.7 in. (323 mm).
   c. Maximum length–13.3 in. (338 mm).
4. After the adjustment is correct, tighten the locknut to 46 ft.-lb. (65 N•m).

Models Without Remote Nitrogen Gas Tank

1. Remove the monoshock unit as described under *Monoshock Removal/Installation* in this chapter.

2. Using the 32 mm wrench provided in the owners tool kit, loosen the locknut and turn the adjuster (**Figure 63**). Tighten it to increase spring pre-load or loosen it to decrease.

NOTE
Adjustments should be made in increments of 2 mm each time; test ride the bike after each adjustment.

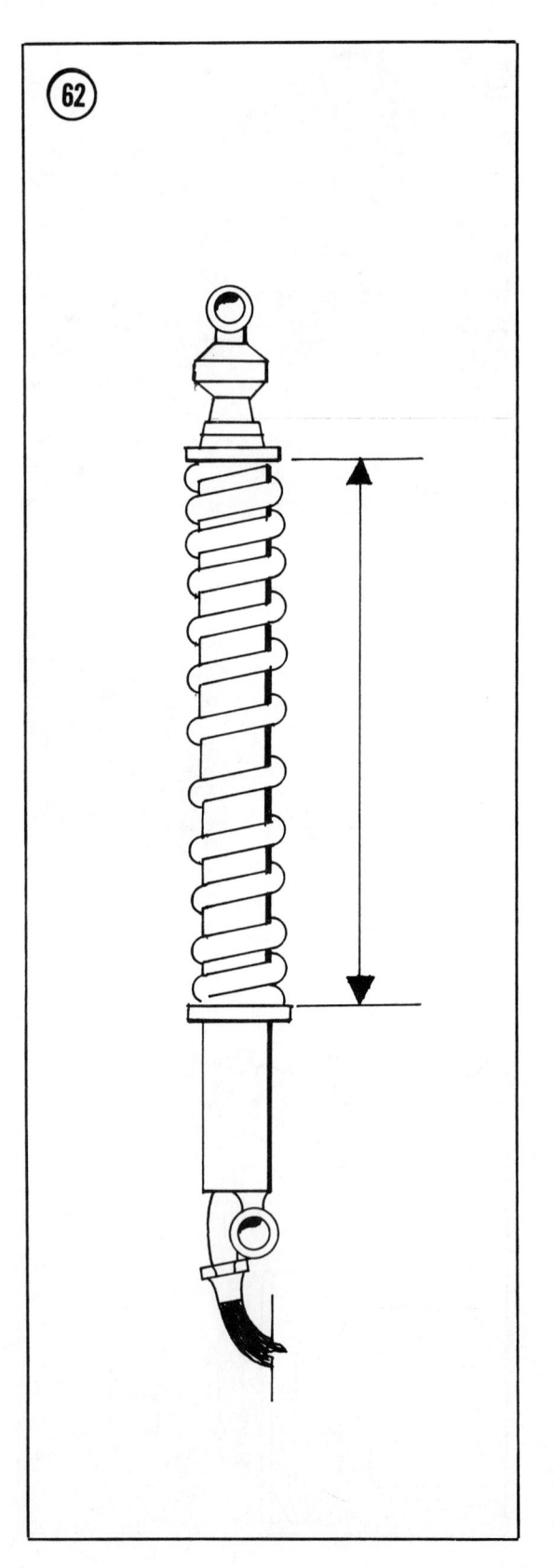

3. The installed spring length (**Figure 64**) must be within the lengths shown in **Table 2**.
4. After the adjustment is correct, tighten the locknut to 40-43 ft.-lb. (55-60 N•m).
5. Install the monoshock unit as described under *Monoshock Removal/installation* in this chapter.

Spring Pre-Load—Model IT125 Since 1980

Spring pre-load is the only adjustment available for this model's monoshock—there is no damping adjustment.
1. Remove the seat.
2. Unscrew the set screw (**Figure 65**) from the monoshock. The screw is secured to a piece of spring wire–do not remove it from this wire.

NOTE
Adjustments should be made in increments of 2 mm each time; test ride the bike after each adjustment.

REAR SUSPENSION

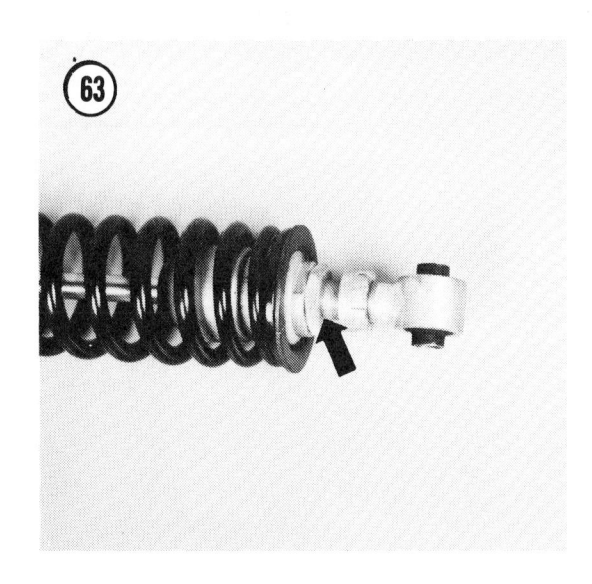

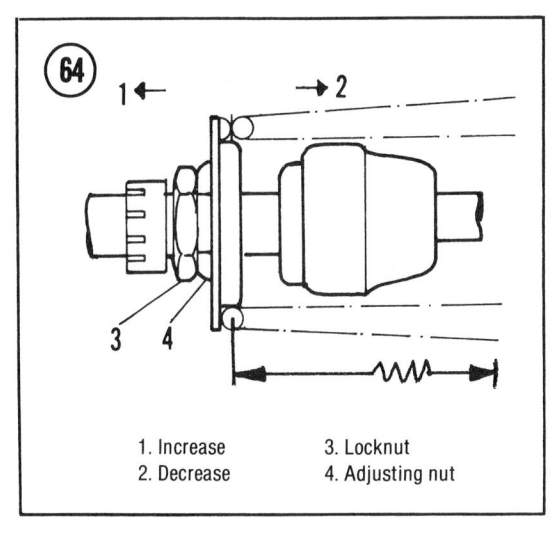

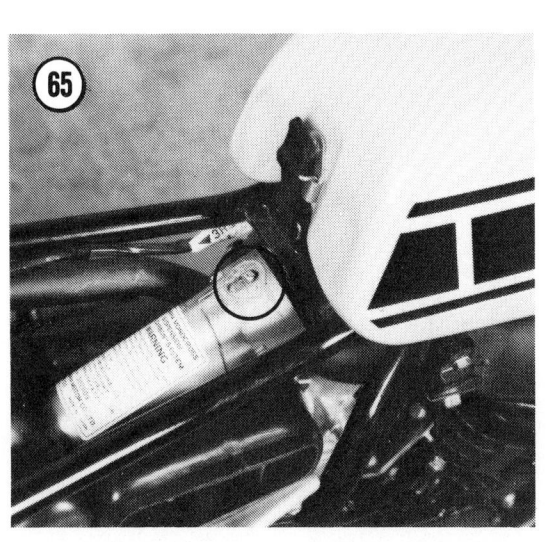

3. Use the ring nut wrench supplied in the owner's tool kit and turn the spring seat to the left-hand side to decrease spring pre-load or to the right to increase spring pre-load. Refer to **Table 3** for number of turn(s) required for each setting.

4. Install the set screw and tighten it securely.

5. Install the seat.

Monoshock Removal/Installation

Models With Remote Nitrogen Gas Tank

1. Place a milk crate or wood block(s) under the frame to lift the rear wheel off the ground by at least 10-12 inches.
2. Remove the seat.
3. Turn the fuel shutoff valve to the OFF position and remove the fuel line to the carburetor.
4. Remove the bolts (A, **Figure 66**) securing the front of the fuel tank. Pull up and unhook the strap (B, **Figure 66**) securing the rear of the tank. Pull the vent tube (C, **Figure 66**) free from the steering head assembly. Pull the tank toward the rear and remove it.
5. Remove the screw (A, **Figure 67**) securing the band to the frame. Remove the bank from the nitrogen gas tank.
6. Pull the nitrogen gas tank up and out of the rubber grommet on the frame (B, **Figure 67**).

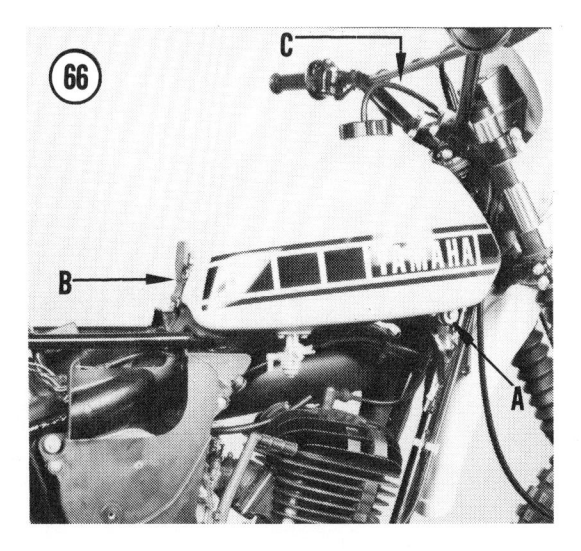

1. Increase
2. Decrease
3. Locknut
4. Adjusting nut

7. Remove the cotter pin and nut (**Figure 68**) securing the monoshock upper portion to the frame. Remove the bolt.

8. Remove the cotter pin and washer securing the monoshock lower portion to the swing arm. Remove the pin (**Figure 69**).

9. Pivot down the rear wheel and swing arm. Do not lose the 2 cover washers on each side of the monoshock.

10. Carefully withdraw the monoshock assembly out through the rear of the frame, over the rear wheel. Be careful not to damage the nitrogen gas tank and its rubber hose.

NOTE
If you cannot withdraw the monoshock over the rear wheel, either raise the bike higher or remove the rear wheel.

11. Install by reversing these removal steps, noting the following.

12. Install the cover washers on each side of the monoshock.

NOTE
Make sure that both cover washers are installed on each side of the monochock prior to inserting the pin. They are necessary to maintain the proper clearance between the monoshock and the swing arm. If they are slightly flattened out, replace them.

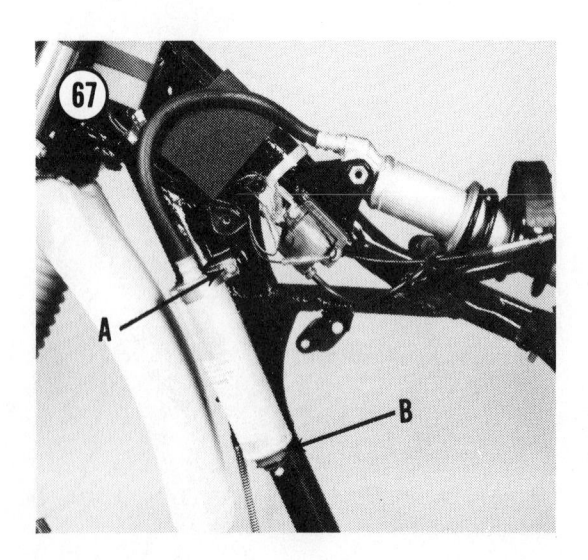

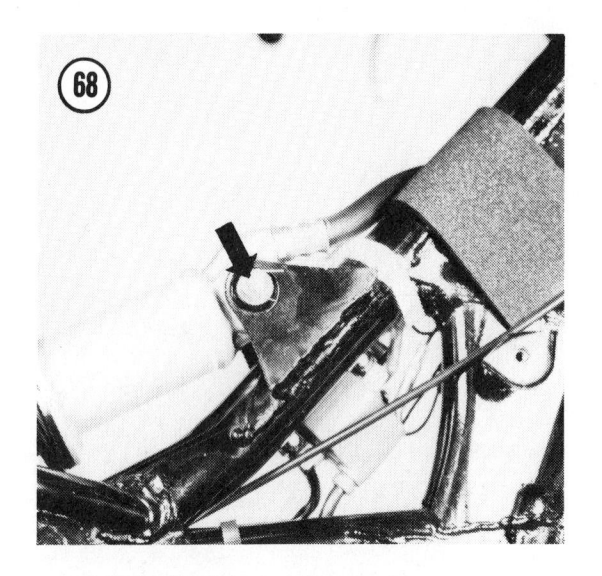

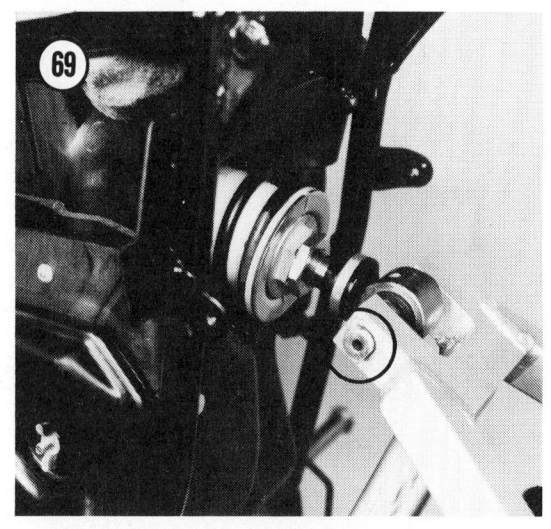

REAR SUSPENSION

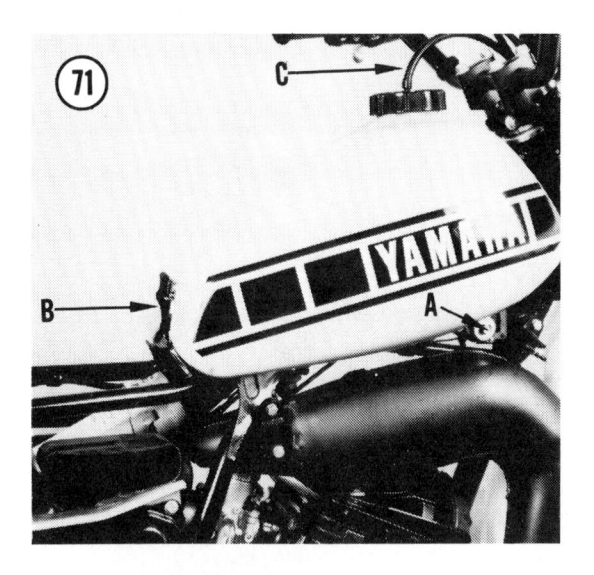

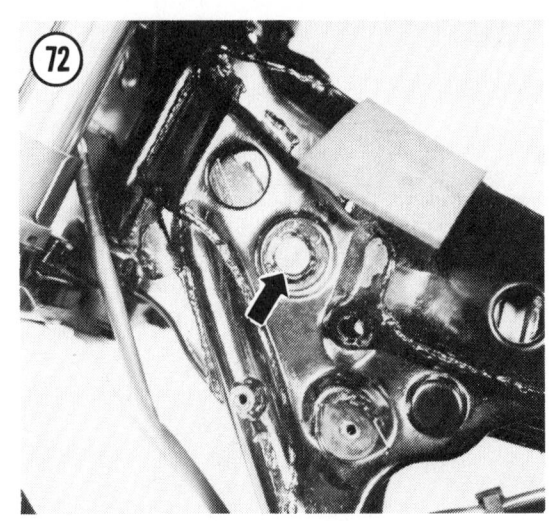

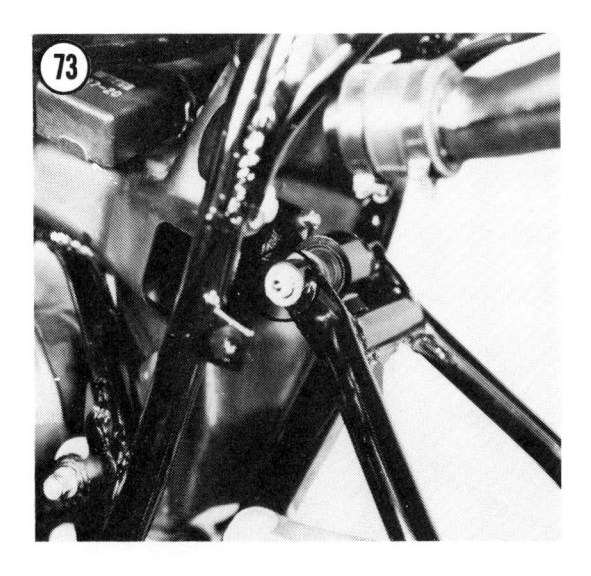

13. Apply a light coat of grease to the mounting pin (**Figure 69**) and install it from the left-hand side.

14. Install the washer and a new cotter pin (**Figure 70**)—never reuse a cotter pin as it may break and fall out. Hold the left-hand end of the pin with wrench and bend over the end of the cotter pin completely.

15. Install the bolt and nut securing the upper portion to the frame. Tighten the bolt and nut to 22 ft.-lb. (30 N•m). Install a new cotter pin—never reuse a cotter pin as it may break and fall out. Bend over the ends of all cotter pins.

16. Make sure the nitrogen gas tank is secured properly in place, with the lower end positioned in the grommet. Tighten the screw on the band securely.

Models Without Remote Nitrogen Gas Tank (1977 and Later)

Removal/Installation

1. Place a milk crate or wood block(s) under the frame to lift the rear wheel off the ground by at least 10 to 12 inches.

2. Remove the seat.

3. Turn the fuel shutoff valve to the OFF position and remove the fuel line to the carburetor.

4. Remove the bolts (A, **Figure 71**) securing the front of the fuel tank. Pull up and unhook the strap (B, **Figure 71**) securing the rear of the tank. Pull the vent tube (C, **Figure 71**) free from the steering head assembly. Pull the tank toward the rear and remove it.

5. Remove the cotter pin and nut (**Figure 72**) securing the monoshock upper portion to the frame. Remove the bolt.

6. Remove the cotter pin and washer (**Figure 73**) securing the monoshock lower portion to the swing arm. Remove the pin.

7. Pivot down the swing arm (and rear wheel). Do not lose the 2 cover washers on each side of the monoshock.

8. Carefully withdraw the monoshock assembly out through the rear of the frame over the wheel (**Figure 74**).

> *NOTE*
> *If you cannot withdraw the monoshock over the rear wheel, either raise the bike higher or remove the rear wheel as shown in **Figure 75**.*

9. Install by reversing these removal steps, noting the following.
10. Install the cover washers (**Figure 76**) on each side of the monoshock.

> *NOTE*
> *Make sure that both cover washers are installed. They are necessary to maintain the proper clearance between the monoshock and the swing arm. If they are slightly flattened out, replace them.*

11. Apply a light coat of grease to the mounting pin and install it from the left-hand side.
12. Install the washer and a new cotter pin—never reuse a cotter pin as it may break and fall out. Hold the left-hand end of the pin with a wrench and bend over the end of the cotter pin completely.
13. Install the bolt and nut securing the monoshock upper portion to the frame. Tighten the bolt and nut to 22 ft.-lb. (30 N•m). Install a new cotter pin—never reuse a cotter pin as it may break and fall out. Bend over the end of the cotter pin.

Monoshock—1977 and Later (Except IT125) Disassembly/ Inspection/Assembly

Refer to **Figure 77**, **Figure 78** or **Figure 79** for this procedure. The monoshock used in this procedure is from an IT250G. Slight variations exist among all models so pay particular attention to the location of spacers, washers and bushings to make assembly correct and easier. The spring on these monoshocks is not under the same amount of pressure as those used on a dual-shock rear suspension. Therefore a spring compression tool is not needed for disassembly.

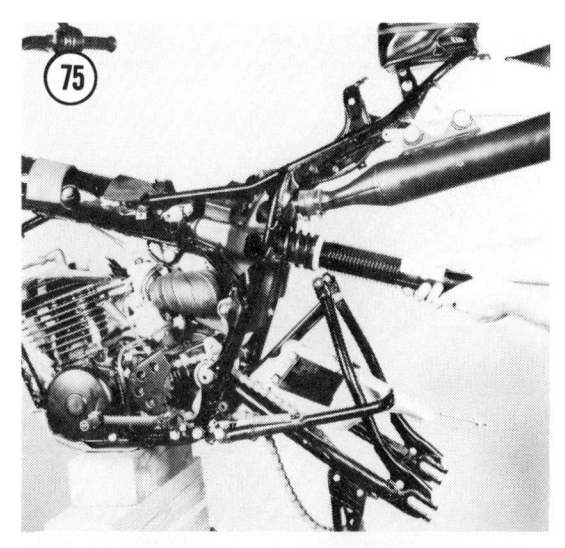

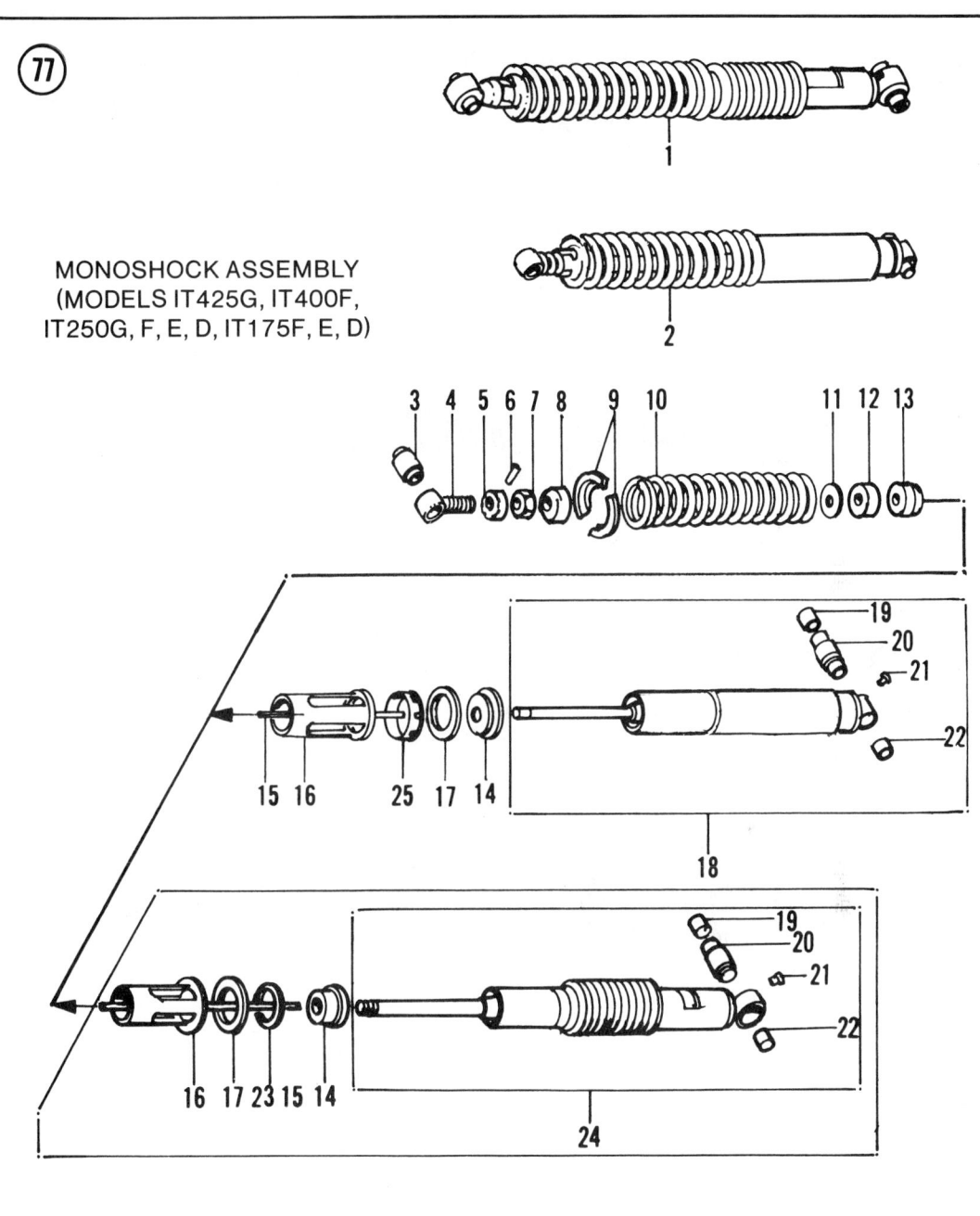

REAR SUSPENSION

MONOSHOCK ASSEMBLY (MODELS IT425G, IT400F, IT250G, F, E, D, IT175F, E, D)

1. Monoshock assembly
2. Monoshock assembly
3. Bushing
4. Frame bracket assembly
5. Adjustment nut
6. Dowel pin
7. Locknut
8. Upper spring seat
9. Spring seats (keepers)
10. Spring
11. Stopper support
12. Cover
13. Stopper
14. Case clip
15. Pushrod
16. Spring guide
17. Lower spring seat
18. Damper subassembly (Models IT400F, IT250F, IT175F, E, D)
19. Bushing
20. Bushing assembly
21. Screw
22. Bushing
23. Circlip
24. Damper subassembly (Models IT425G, IT250G)
25. Case cap

CHAPTER NINE

MONOSHOCK ASSEMBLY
(MODELS IT400E, D, IT250E, D)

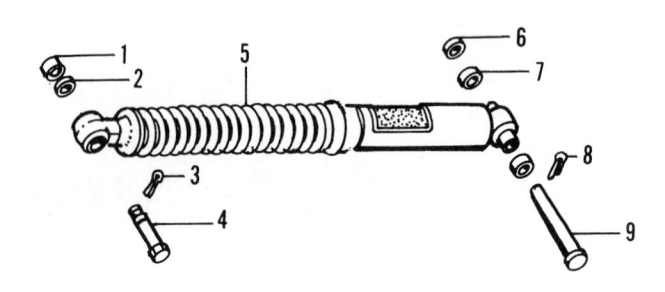

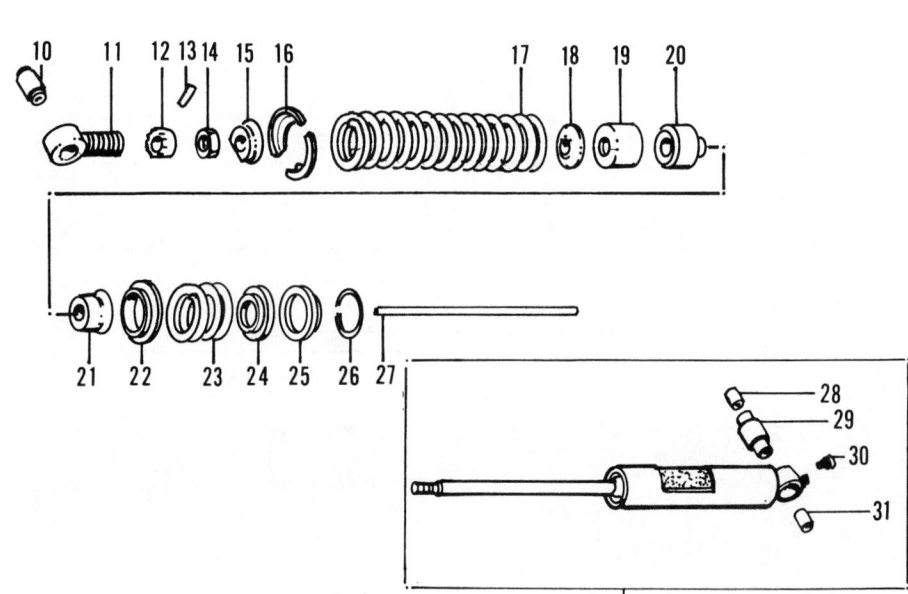

1. Nut	9. Pin	17. Spring (long)	25. Upper spring seat
2. Washer	10. Bushing assembly	18. Stopper	26. Circlip
3. Cotter pin	11. Upper bracket	19. Stopper cover	27. Pushrod
4. Bolt	12. Adjusting nut	20. Bumper stop	28. Bushing
5. Monoshock assembly	13. Dowel pin	21. Case cap	29. Bushing assembly
6. Washer	14. Locknut	22. Spring guide	30. Screw
7. Thrust cover	15. Upper spring seat	23. Spring (short)	31. Bushing
8. Cotter pin	16. Upper spring guide	24. Lower spring guide	32. Damper subassembly

REAR SUSPENSION

MONOSHOCK ASSEMBLY (MODEL IT175G)

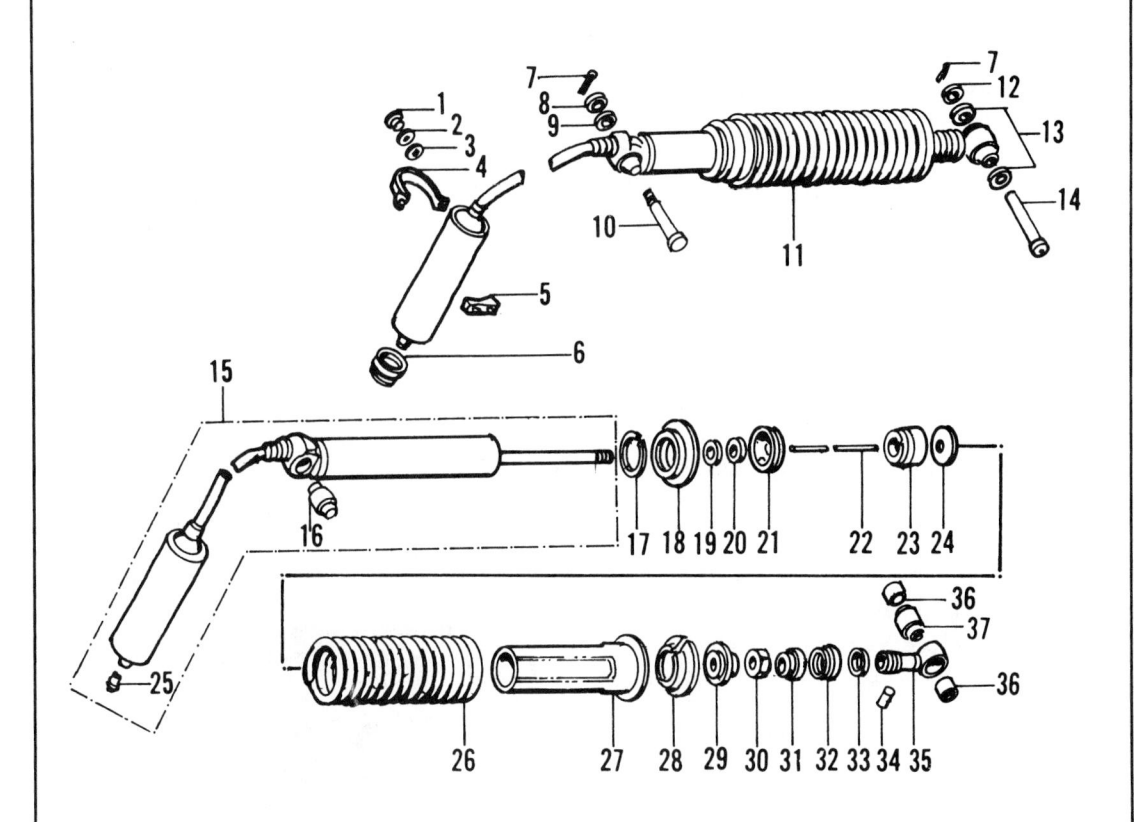

1. Screw
2. Lockwasher
3. Washer
4. Remote tank band
5. Tank damper
6. Tank grommet
7. Cotter pin
8. Nut
9. Washer
10. Bolt
11. Monoshock assembly
12. Washer
13. Thrust covers
14. Pin
15. Damper subassembly
16. Bushing
17. Circlip
18. Lower spring seat
19. Dust seal
20. Seal ring housing
21. Case cap
22. Pushrod
23. Stopper
24. Stopper support
25. Screw
26. Spring
27. Spring guide
28. Spring seats (keepers)
29. Upper spring seat
30. Pre-load locknut
31. Cover
32. Damping adjuster
33. Cover
34. Dowel pin
35. Rear bracket subassembly
36. Bushing
37. Bushing assembly

1. Remove the monoshock as described under *Monoshock Removal/Installation* in this chapter.

> *NOTE*
> *During the next steps, in order to maintain the same adjustments (damping and spring pre-load) record the number of turns of both of these adjusters as they are removed.*

2. Turn the damping adjuster (A, **Figure 80**) all the way toward the end.
3. Loosen the spring pre-load locknut and turn it and the adjuster (B, **Figure 80**) all the way toward the end.
4. As the spring pre-load adjuster is turned away from the spring the spring seats (keepers) will become loose. Remove them if they do not fall out.
5. Slide off the spring seat, spring(s) and spring guide (C, **Figure 80**).
6. Inspect the condition of the upper and lower mounting bushings (A, **Figure 81**). Replace if necessary.
7. Check the damper unit for leakage and make sure the damper rod is straight.

> *NOTE*
> *The damper unit cannot be rebuilt; it must be replaced as a unit.*

> *WARNING*
> *The monoshock unit contains highly compressed nitrogen gas. Do not tamper with or attempt to open the damper/cylinder assembly (**Figure 82**). Do not place it near an open flame or other extreme heat. Do not dispose of the damper subassembly yourself. Take it to a Yamaha dealer where it can be deactivated and disposed of properly. Never attempt to remove the plug at the bottom of the nitrogen tank (B, **Figure 81**).*

8. Install the new spring(s) making sure all parts are in their correct positions. Refer to **Figure 77**, **Figure 78** or **Figure 79**.

> *NOTE*
> *There are two optional factory springs available for this model monoshock, stiffer and the other softer than stock. The springs are color coded for easy identification. Take the bike to a Yamaha*

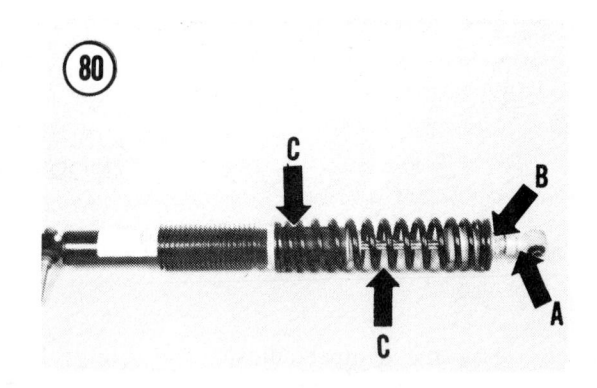

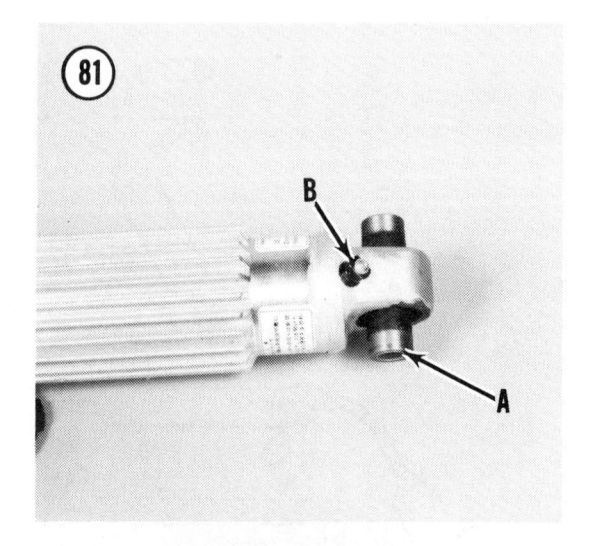

REAR SUSPENSION

dealer to choose the correct spring for your specific needs (combination of ride weight and track conditions).

9. Install the spring seats (keepers) and tighten the spring pre-load adjuster. If the original spring or a new one of the same spring rate is installed, return the adjuster to the same position as noted during disassembly. Screw in the locknut and tighten to 40-43 ft.-lb. (55-60 N•m).

10. Screw the damper adjuster to its orignal position as noted during disassembly.

NOTE
*If a new spring with a different spring rate has been installed, readjust as described under **Spring Pre-Load** and **Damping Adjustment** in this chapter.*

11. Install the monoshock as described under *Monoshock Removal/Installation* in this chapter.

Monoshock—Model IT125 Since 1980 Disassembly/Inspection/Assembly

Refer to **Figure 83** for this procedure. The springs on this monoshock are not under the same amount of pressure as those used on a dual-shock rear suspension. Therefore a spring compression tool is not needed for disassembly.

1. Remove the monoshock as described under *Monoshock Removal/Installation* in this chapter.

NOTE
During the next steps, in order to maintain the same spring pre-load adjustment record the number of turns of the adjuster as it is turned to its fully relaxed position.

2. Remove the set screw (A, **Figure 84**), leaving it attached to the spring clip retainer.
3. Relieve the spring pressure by turning the spring preload adjuster (B, **Figure 84**) all the way *counterclockwise*. This direction is established by holding onto the damper portion of the monoshock with the spring pointed away from you.
4. Remove the cotter pin (**Figure 85**) from the upper bracket.

5. Hold the spring seat (A, **Figure 86**) with a wrench and loosen the upper bracket (B, **Figure 86**).
6. Unscrew the upper bracket and spring seat from the damper rod.
7. Slide off the 2 springs, spring guide and sleeve (C, **Figure 86**).
8. Inspect the condition of the upper and lower mounting bushings; replace if necessary.
9. Check the damper unit for leakage and make sure the damper rod is straight.

NOTE
The damper unit cannot be rebuilt; it must be replaced as a unit.

WARNING
The monoshock unit contains highly compressed nitrogen gas. Do not tamper with or attempt to open the damper/cylinder assembly. Do not place it near an open flame or other extreme heat. Do not dispose of the damper sub-assembly yourself. Take it to a Yamaha dealer where it can be deactivated and disposed of properly. Never attempt to remove the plug at the bottom of the damper/cylinder.

10. Install the new springs, spring guide and sleeve. Make sure all parts are in their correct position (see **Figure 83**).
11. Screw on the spring seat and upper bracket. Tighten the upper bracket to 43 ft.-lb. (60 N•m).
12. Install a new cotter pin—never install an old cotter pin as it may break and fall out. Bend over the end of the cotter pin.
13. Return the adjuster to the original position as noted during disassembly. Screw in the set screw.
14. Turn the spring pre-load adjuster to its orignal position as noted during disassembly.
15. Install the monoshock as described under *Monoshock Removal/Installation* in this chapter.

REAR SUSPENSION (MONOCROSS TYPE)

The monocross type rear suspension on the IT400C (1976) is a very basic unit without the adjustment features later included in the

256 CHAPTER NINE

**MONOSHOCK ASSEMBLY
(MODEL IT125G)**

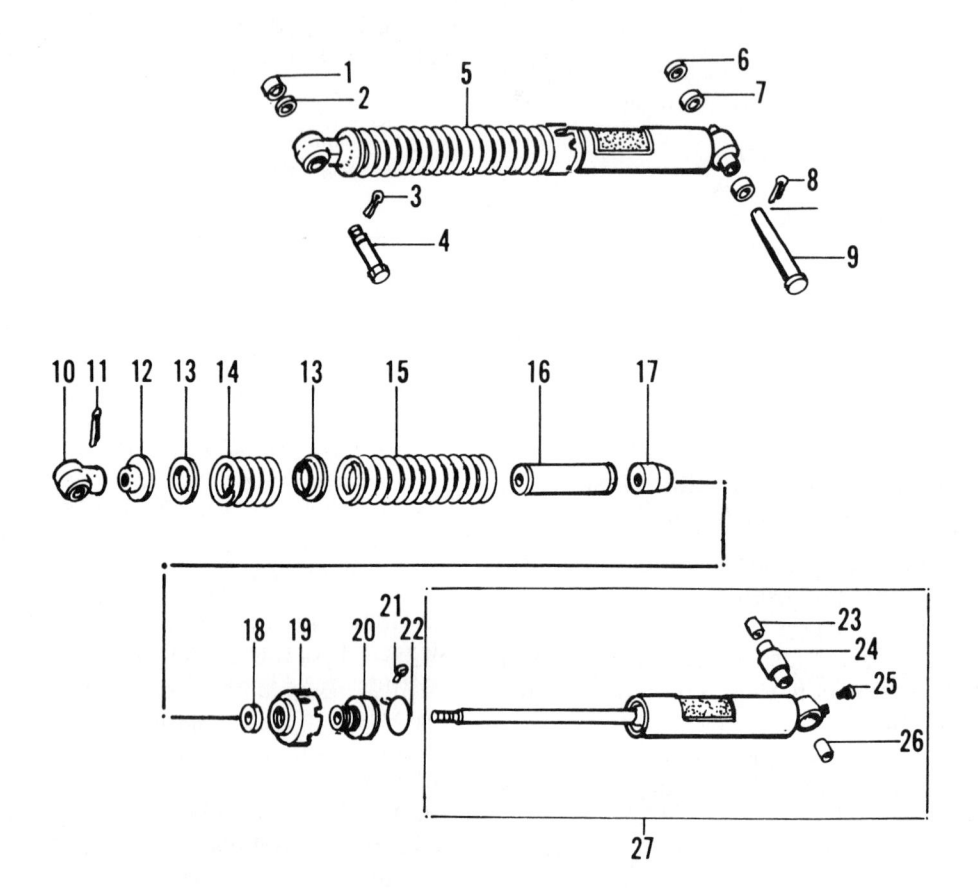

1. Nut
2. Washer
3. Cotter pin
4. Bolt
5. Monoshock assembly
6. Washer
7. Thrust cover
8. Cotter pin
9. Pin
10. Upper bracket
11. Cotter pin
12. Upper bracket
13. Spring seat/guide
14. Spring (short)
15. Spring (long)
16. Sleeve
17. Stopper
18. Inner stopper
19. Lower spring seat
20. Case cap
21. Set screw
22. Spring clip retainer
23. Bushing
24. Bushing assembly
25. Screw
26. Bushing
27. Damper subassembly

REAR SUSPENSION

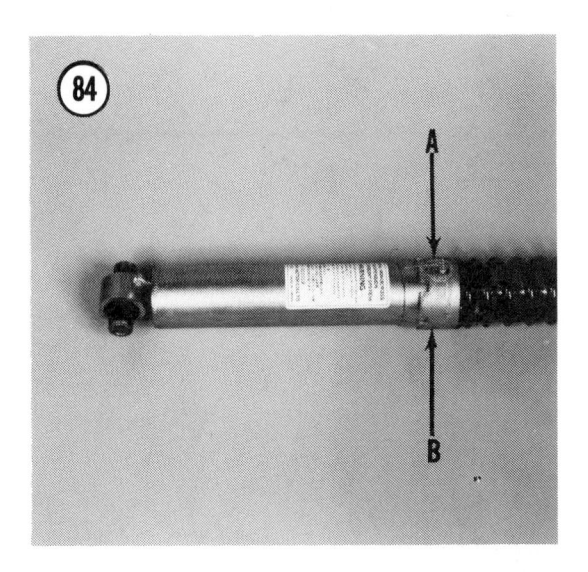

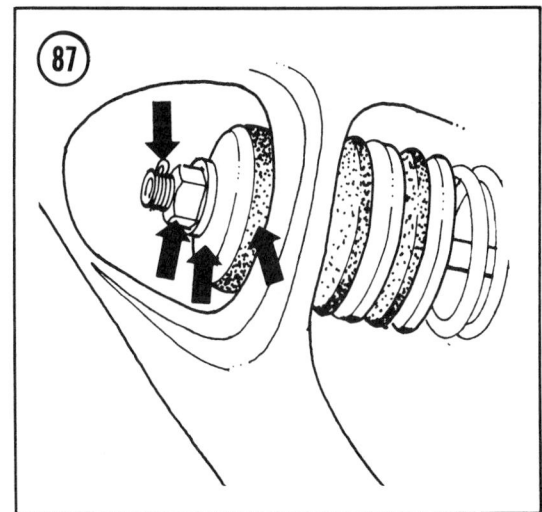

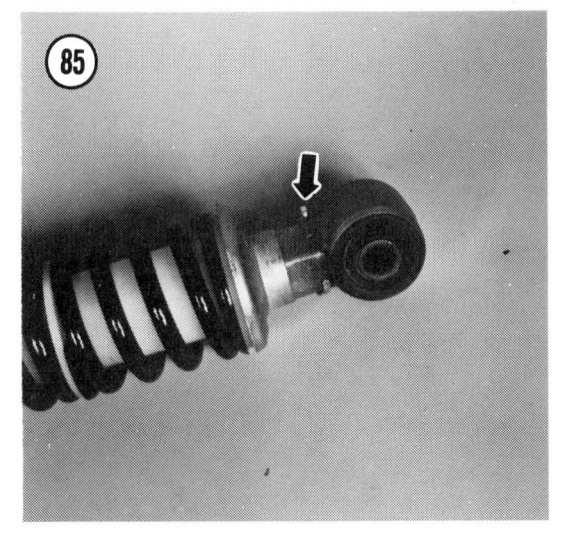

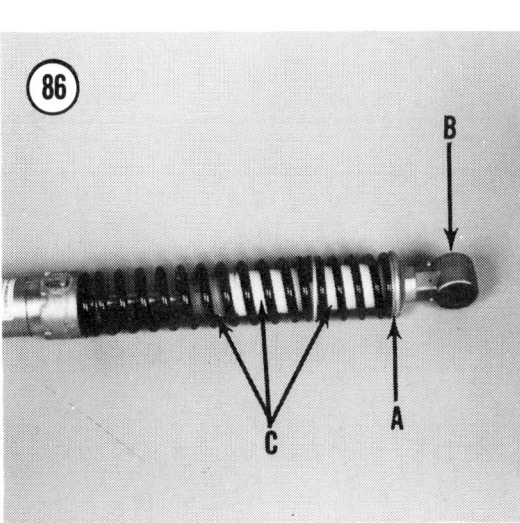

DeCarbon system. This unit has no provisions for adjusting the damping action or spring pre-load. The monoshock unit is tucked up in the frame's hollow backbone under the fuel tank.

Removal/Installation

1. Place a milk crate or wood block(s) under the frame to lift the rear wheel off the ground by at least 10 to 12 inches.
2. Remove the seat.
3. Turn the fuel shutoff valve to the OFF position and remove the fuel line to the carburetor.
4. Remove the bolt securing the rear of the fuel tank. Pull the tank toward the rear and remove it. Don't lose the 2 rubber damper pads on the frame; they will usually come off when the tank is removed.
5. Remove the cotter pin, pivot shaft nut, washer and rubber damper (**Figure 87**).
6. Remove the bolt and nut securing the membrane housing/damper unit at the rear to the swing arm. Don't lose the 2 washers.
7. Let the swing arm and rear wheel pivot down.
8. Withdraw the monoshock unit out through the rear.
9. Install by reversing these removal steps. Tighten the rear bolt and nut to 50 ft.-lb. (70 N•m) and the front nut to 14 ft.-lb. (20 N•m). Install a new cotter pin—never reuse an old

CHAPTER NINE

**MONOSHOCK ASSEMBLY
(MODEL IT400C)**

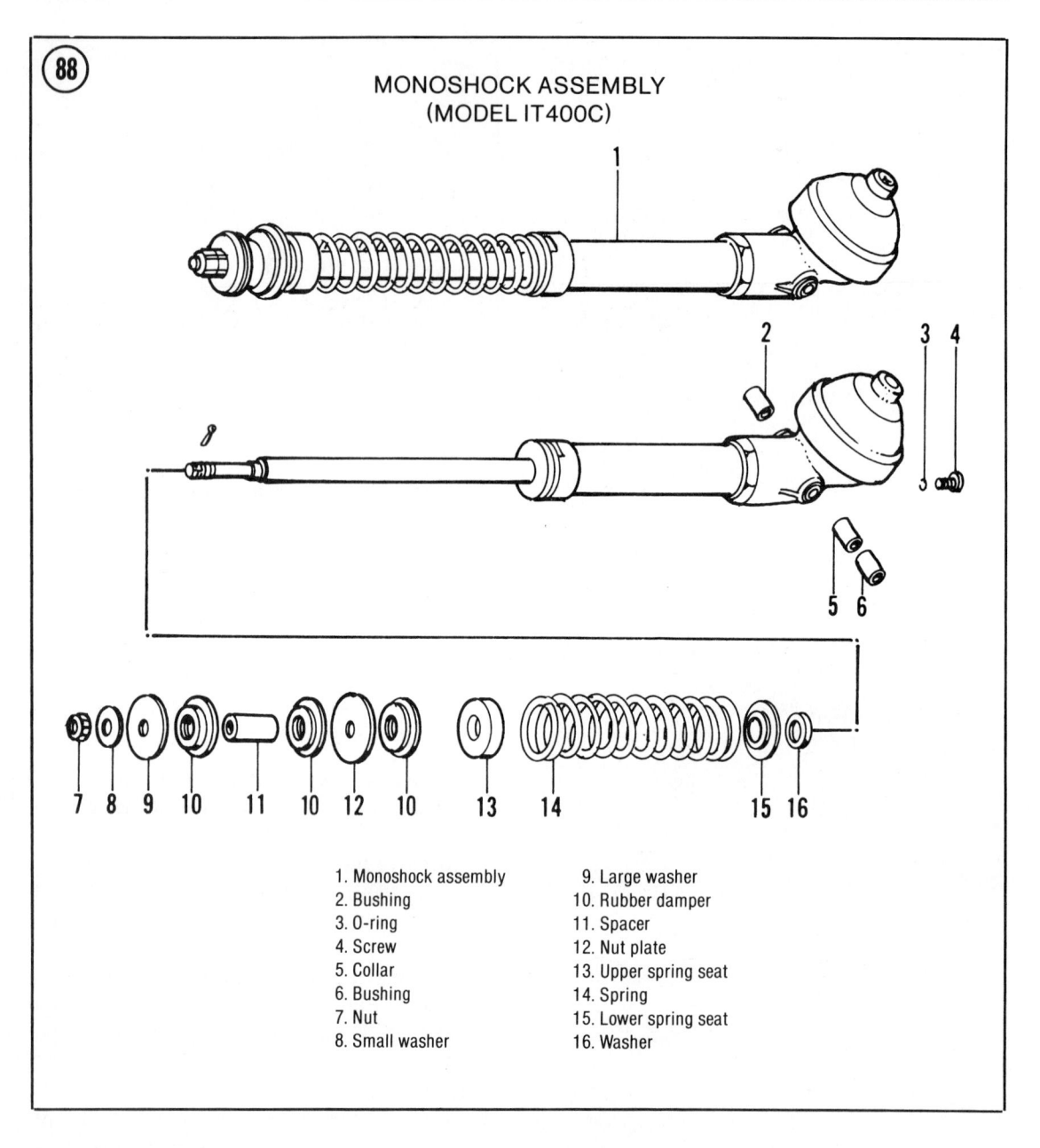

1. Monoshock assembly
2. Bushing
3. O-ring
4. Screw
5. Collar
6. Bushing
7. Nut
8. Small washer
9. Large washer
10. Rubber damper
11. Spacer
12. Nut plate
13. Upper spring seat
14. Spring
15. Lower spring seat
16. Washer

Cap case
Membrane housing damper unit
Ring unit

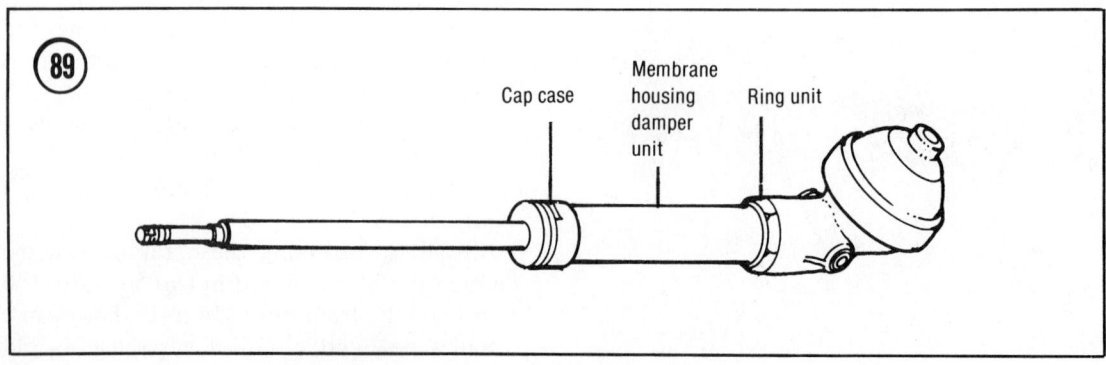

REAR SUSPENSION

one as it may break and fall out. Bend over the end of the cotter pin.

Disassembly/Inspection/Assembly

Refer to **Figure 88** for this procedure.
1. Remove the monoshock assembly as described in this chapter.
2. Place the mounting surfaces of the membrane housing/damper unit in a vise with soft jaws. Mount it so the spring end is pointed up.
3. Remove the nut (7), 2 washers (8 and 9), 2 rubber dampers (10), nutplate (12) and upper spring seat (13) from the damper rod.
4. Slide off the spring (14), lower spring seat (15) and washer (16).
5. Check the damper unit for leakage and make sure the damper rod is straight.

NOTE
The damper unit cannot be rebuilt; it must be replaced as a unit.

WARNING
The monoshock unit contains highly compressed nitrogen gas. Do not tamper with or attempt to open the membrane housing/damper unit assembly. Do not place it near an open flame or other extreme heat. Do not dispose of the damper subassembly yourself. Take it to a Yamaha dealer where it can be deactivated and disposed of properly. Never attempt to remove the plug at the bottom of the damper/cylinder.

6. Check the tightness of the 2 items shown in **Figure 89**. Loosen the ring nut and tighten the cap case to 108 ft.-lb. (150 N•m). Retighten the ring nut to 146 ft.-lb. (200 N•m). Yes, this high torque specification is correct.

NOTE
Tightening the ring nut requires a special Ring Nut Wrench. It is available from Yamaha dealers.

7. Install all items removed in Steps 3 and 4 in reverse order. Refer to **Figure 88** to make sure they are installed in the correct order.
8. Tighten the nut to 11 ft.-lb. (15 N•m).
9. Install the monoshock assembly as described in this chapter.

Tables are on the following page.

CHAPTER NINE

Table 1   REAR SUSPENSION TORQUE SPECIFICATIONS

	IT425G IT400F, E, D	IT250 (all)	IT175 (all)	IT125 (all)
Rear axle nut	58 (80)	58 (80)	60 (85) (IT175E, D 72 (100))	60 (85)
Monoshock bolt to frame	18-22 (25-30)	18-22 (25-30)	18-21* (25-30)*	18 (25)
Monoshock adjust locknut	40-43 (55-60)	40-43 (55-60)	43 (60)*	none
Swing arm pivot nut	58 (80)**	58 (80)***	60-65 (85-95)	30 (43)

*Does not apply to model IT175G
**IT400E, D: 65 (90)
***IT250E, D: 65 (90)

NOTE: XX=ft.-lb.   (XX)=N•m

Table 2   MONOSHOCK SPRING LENGTH—INSTALLED

Model	Standard	Maximum	Minimum
IT425G	11.97 (304)	12.08 (307)	11.65 (296)
IT400F	11.00 (281)	11.2 (285)	10.7 (274)
IT400E, D	10.3 (262)	10.7 (271.5)	10.1 (256.5)
IT250G	11.97 (304)	12.08 (307)	11.65 (296)
IT250F	11.00 (281)	11.2 (285)	10.7 (274)
IT250E, D	10.3 (262)	10.7 (271.5)	10.1 (256.5)
IT175G	(does not apply)		
IT175F	11.0 (280)	11.2 (285)	10.7 (274)
IT175E, D	10.3 (262)	10.7 (271.5)	10.1 (256.5)
IT125G	(does not apply)		

NOTE: XX = inches   (XX) = millimeters

**Table 3   MONOSHOCK SPRING PRE-LOAD SETTINGS
MODELS IT125 (since 1980)**

	Soft				Standard		Hard
Adjusting position	4	3	2	1	0	1	2
Number of turns	2	1½	1	½	0	½	1

> **NOTE:** If you own a 1981 or later model, first check the Supplement at the back of the book for any new service information.

CHAPTER TEN

BRAKES

Both the front and rear brakes are drum type. **Figure 1** illustrates the major components of the brake assembly. By activating the brake hand lever or foot pedal it pulls the cable or rod which in turn rotates the camshaft. This forces the brake shoes out into contact with the brake drum.

Lever and pedal free play must be maintained on both brakes to minimize brake drag and premature brake wear and maximize braking effectiveness. Refer to *Front Brake Lever Adjustment* and *Rear Brake Pedal Free Play* in Chapter Three for complete adjustment procedures.

The front brake cable must be inspected and replaced periodically as it will stretch with use until it can no longer be properly adjusted.

Brake specifications (**Table 1**) are at the end of this chapter.

FRONT BRAKE

Disassembly

Refer to **Figure 2** for this procedure.
1. Remove the front wheel as described under *Front Wheel Removal/Installation* in Chapter Eight.
2. Pull the brake assembly (**Figure 3**) straight up and out of the brake drum.

NOTE
Prior to removing the brake shoes from the backing plate, measure them as described under Inspection.

3. Remove the brake shoes from the backing plate by firmly pulling up on the center of each shoe as shown in **Figure 4**.

NOTE
Place a clean shop rag on the linings to protect them from oil and grease during removal.

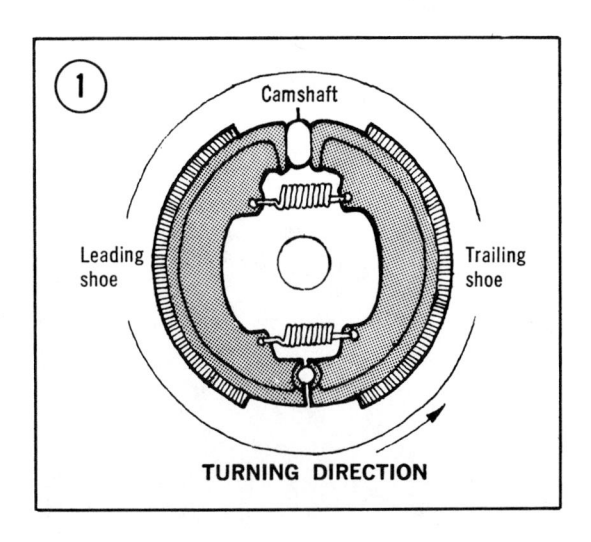

① Camshaft

Leading shoe — Trailing shoe

TURNING DIRECTION

262   CHAPTER TEN

FRONT BRAKE ASSEMBLY

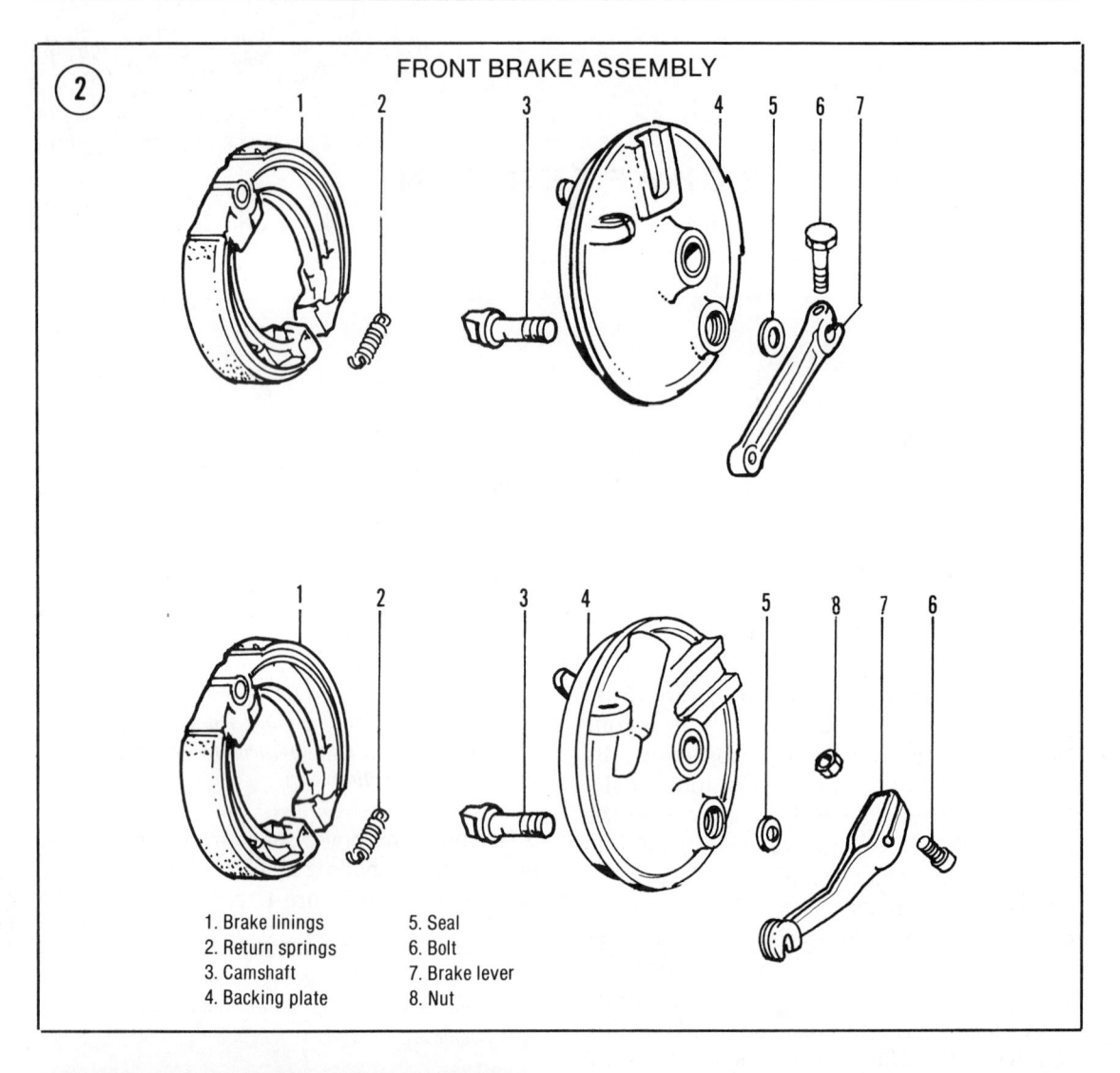

1. Brake linings
2. Return springs
3. Camshaft
4. Backing plate
5. Seal
6. Bolt
7. Brake lever
8. Nut

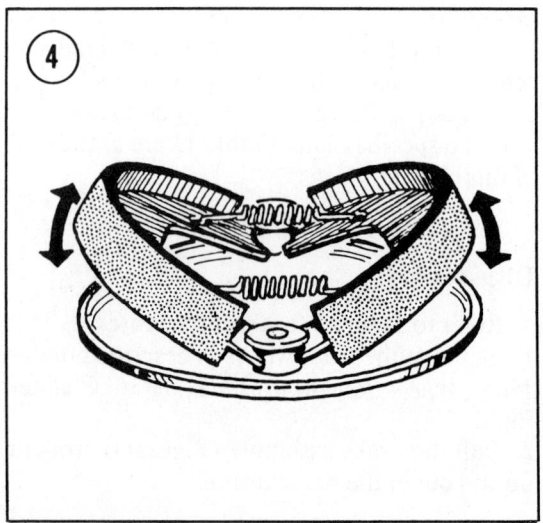

BRAKES

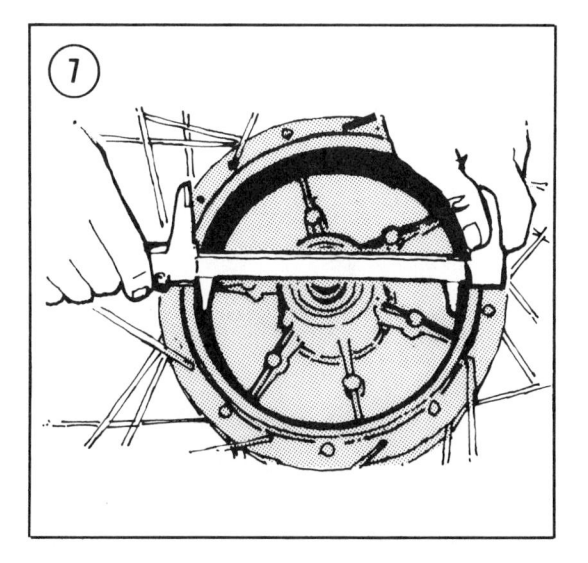

4. Remove the return springs and separate the shoes.
5. Mark the position of the cam lever to the camshaft so it can be reinstalled in the same position.
6. Loosen the bolt securing the brake lever to the cam (**Figure 5**). Remove the lever, cam seal and camshaft.

Inspection

1. Thoroughly clean and dry all parts except the linings.
2. Check the contact surface of the drum (**Figure 6**) for scoring. If there are grooves deep enough to snag a fingernail, the drum should be reground and new shoes fitted. This type of wear can be avoided to a great extent if the brakes are disassembled and thoroughly cleaned after the bike has been ridden in mud or deep sand or after each race.

NOTE
If oil or grease is on the drum surface, clean it off with a clean rag soaked in lacquer thinner — do not use any solvent that may leave an oil residue.

3. Use vernier calipers (**Figure 7**) and check the inside diameter of the drum for out-of-round or excessive wear. Refer to **Table 1** for brake specifications. Turn or replace the drum as necessary.
4. If the drum is turned, the linings will have to be replaced and the new linings arced to the new drum contour.
5. Inspect the linings for imbedded foreign material. Dirt can be removed with a stiff wire brush. Check for traces of oil or grease. If they are contaminated, they must be replaced.
6. With the linings installed on the backing plate, measure the outside diameter in the locations shown in **Figure 8** with vernier calipers. Refer to **Table 1** for brake specifications. Replace the linings if necessary.
7. Inspect the cam lobe and the pivot pin area of the shaft for wear and corrosion. Minor roughness can be removed with fine emery cloth.
8. Measure the brake shoe return springs (**Figure 9**) with vernier calipers. Refer to **Table 1** for specifications. If they are stretched,

they will not fully retract the brake shoes from the drum, resulting in a power-robbing drag on the drums and premature wear of the linings. Replace as necessary and always replace as a pair.

Assembly

1. Assemble the brake by reversing the disassembly steps. Note the following.
2. Grease the shaft(s), cam(s) and pivot post (**Figure 10**) with a light coat of molybdenum disulfide grease; avoid getting any grease on the brake plate where the linings come in contact with it.
3. When installing the brake lever onto the brake camshaft, be sure to align the two parts with the two marks made in *Disassembly* Step 5.
4. Hold the brakes shoes in a "V" formation with the return springs attached and snap them in place on the brake backing plate. Make sure they are firmly seated on it (**Figure 11**).

NOTE
If new linings are being installed, file off the leading edge of each show a little (Figure 12) so that the brake will not grab when applied.

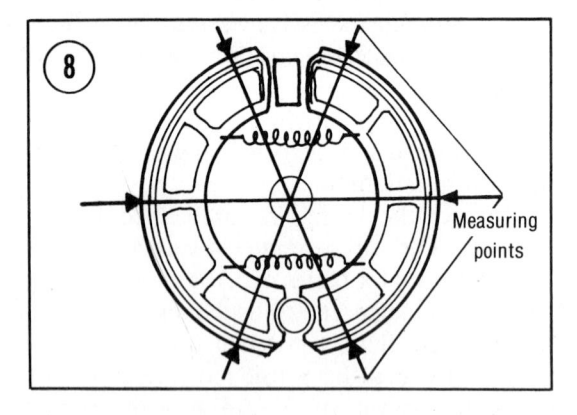

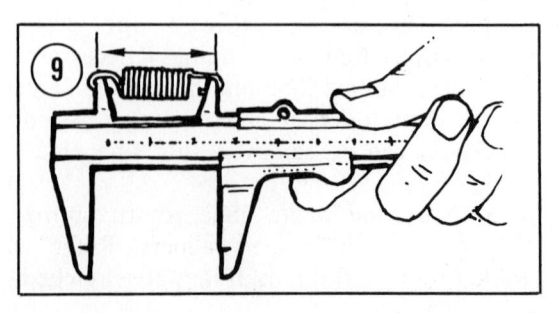

5. Install the brake panel assembly into the brake drum.
6. Install the front wheel as described under *Front Wheel Removal/Installation* in Chapter Eight.

NOTE
When installing the front wheel, be sure that the locating slot in the brake panel is engaged with the boss on the front fork leg (Figure 13). This is necessary for proper brake operation.

7. Adjust the front brake as described under *Front Brake Lever Adjustment* in Chapter Three.

REAR BRAKE

Disassembly

Refer to **Figure 14** for this procedure.

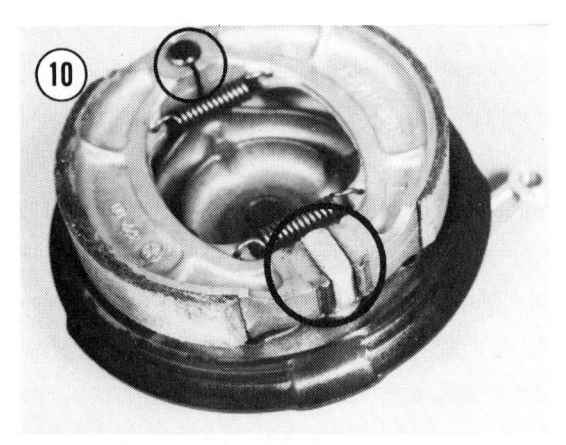

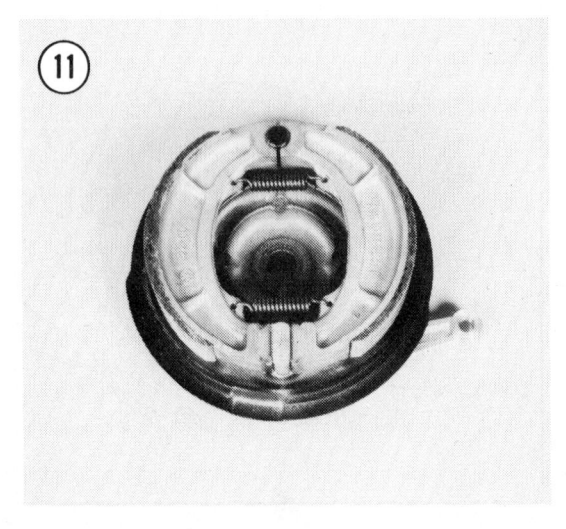

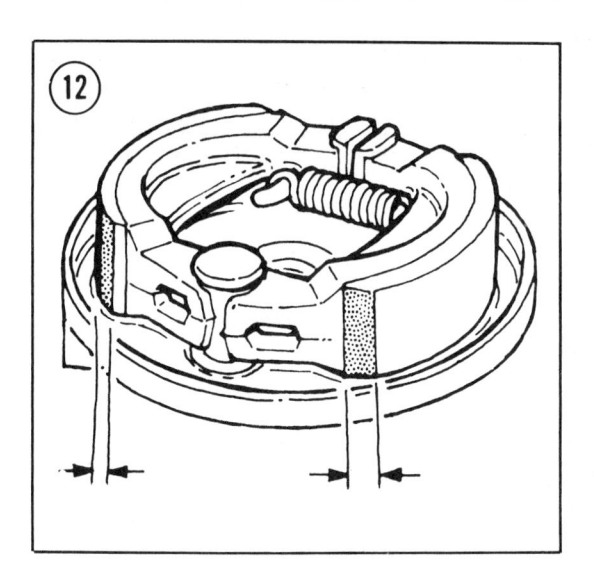

BRAKES

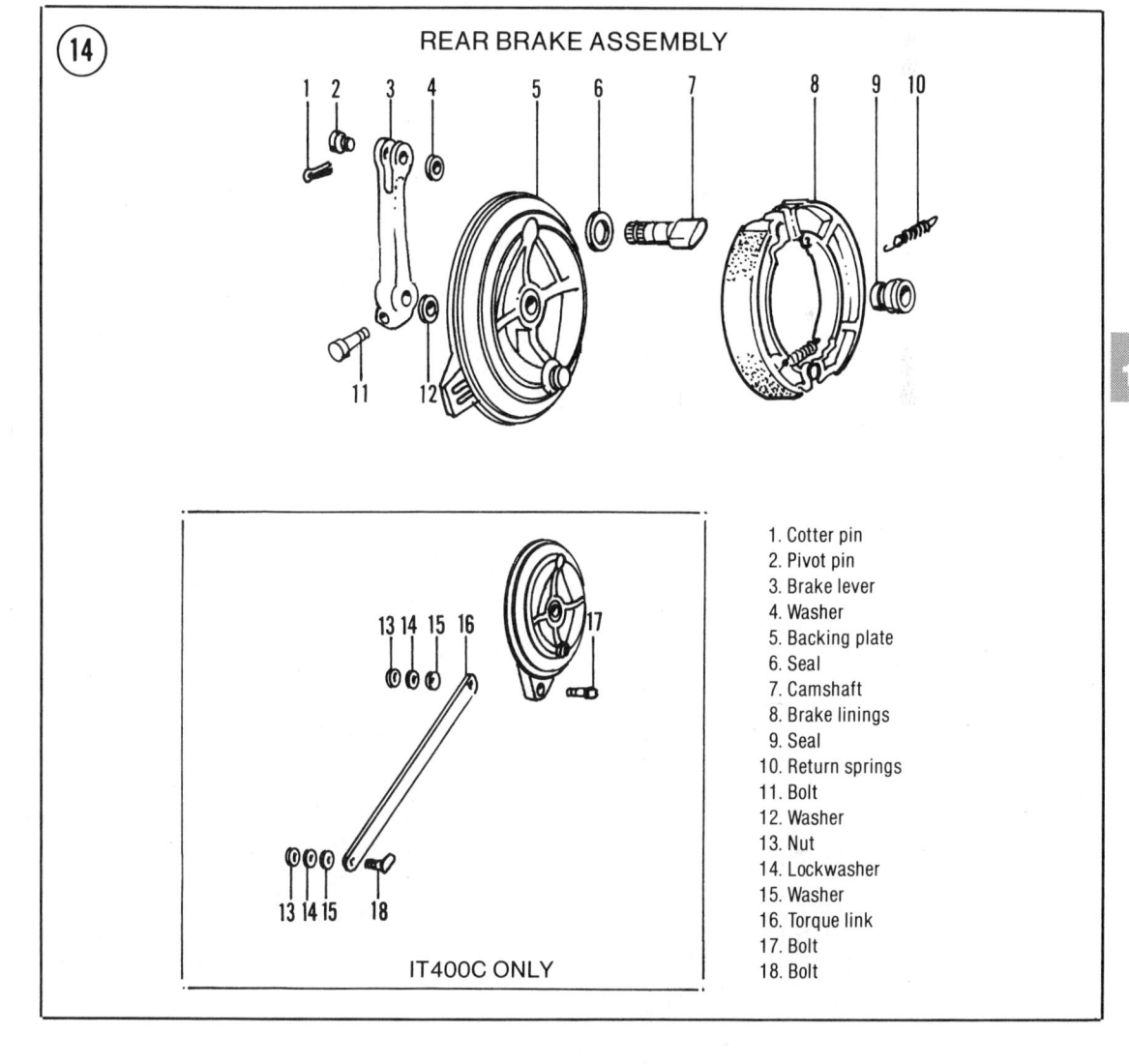

REAR BRAKE ASSEMBLY

1. Cotter pin
2. Pivot pin
3. Brake lever
4. Washer
5. Backing plate
6. Seal
7. Camshaft
8. Brake linings
9. Seal
10. Return springs
11. Bolt
12. Washer
13. Nut
14. Lockwasher
15. Washer
16. Torque link
17. Bolt
18. Bolt

IT400C ONLY

1. Remove the rear wheel as described under *Rear Wheel Removal/Installation* in Chapter Nine.
2. Pull the brake assembly (**Figure 15**) straight up and out of the brake drum.

NOTE
Prior to removing the brake shoes, measure them as described under **Inspection.**

3. Remove the brake shoes from the backing plate by firmly pulling up on the center of each shoe as shown in **Figure 16**.

NOTE
Place a clean shop rag on the linings to protect them from oil and grease during removal.

4. Remove the return springs and separate the shoes.
5. Mark the position of the cam lever to the camshaft so it can be reinstalled in the same position.
6. Loosen the bolt securing the brake lever to the cam (**Figure 17**). Remove the lever, cam seal and camshaft.

Inspection

1. Thoroughly clean and dry all parts except the linings.
2. Check the contact surface of the drum (**Figure 18**) for scoring. If there are grooves deep enough to snag a fingernail, the drum should be reground and new shoes fitted. This type of wear can be avoided to a great extent if the brakes are disassembled and thoroughly cleaned after each race or after riding in mud or deep sand.

NOTE
If oil or grease is on the drum surface, clean it off with a clean rag soaked in lacquer thinner—do not use any solvent that may leave an oil residue.

3. Use vernier calipers (**Figure 19**) and check the inside diameter of the drum for out-of-round or excessive wear. Refer to **Table 1** for brake specifications. Turn or replace the drum as necessary.

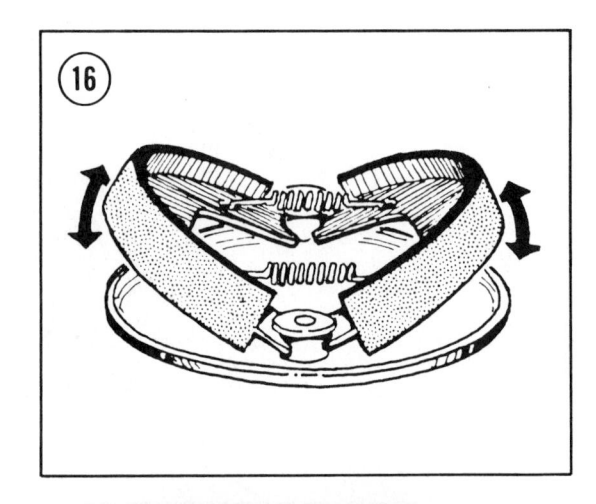

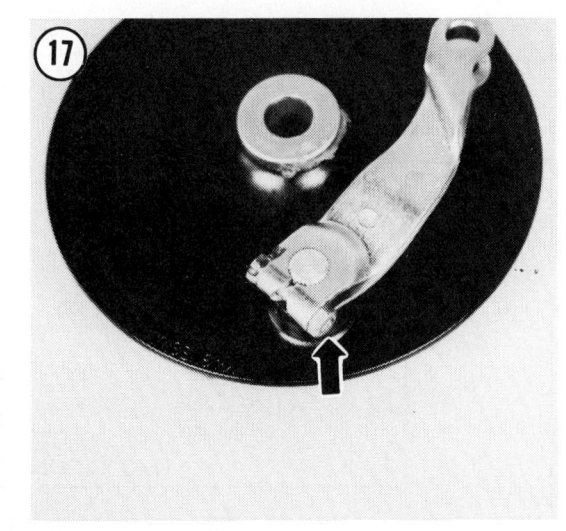

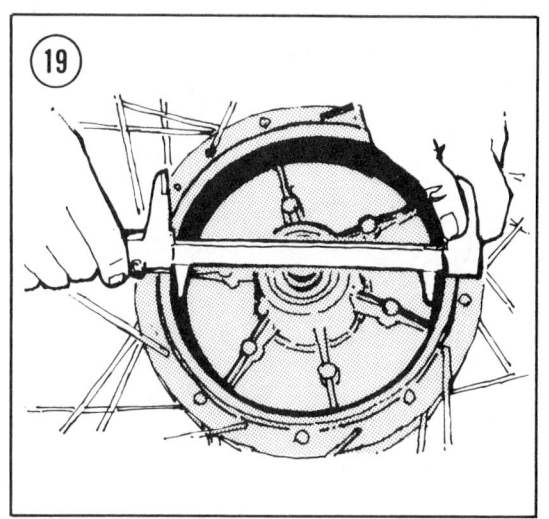

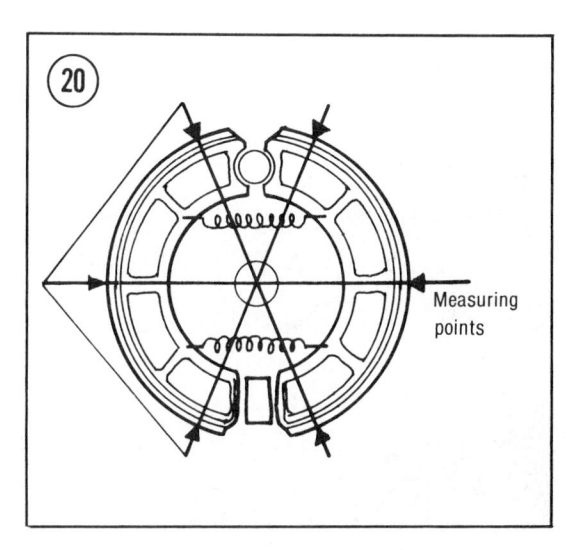

BRAKES

4. If the drum is turned, the linings will have to be replaced and the new linings arced to the new drum contour.

5. Inspect the linings for imbedded foreign material. Dirt can be removed with a stiff wire brush. Check for traces of oil or grease. If they are contaminated, they must be replaced.

6. With the linings installed on the backing plate, measure the outside diameter in the locations shown in **Figure 20** with vernier calipers. Refer to **Table 1** for brake specifications. Replace the linings if necessary.

7. Inspect the cam lobe and the pivot pin area of the shaft for wear and corrosion. Minor roughness can be removed with fine emery cloth.

8. Measure the brake shoe return springs (**Figure 21**) with vernier calipers. Refer to **Table 1** for specifications. If they are stretched, they will not fully retract the brake shoes from the drum, resulting in a power-robbing drag on the drums and premature wear of the linings. Replace as necessary and always replace as a pair.

Assembly

1. Assemble the brake by reversing the disassembly steps.
2. Grease the shaft, cam and pivot post (**Figure 22**) with a light coat of molybdenum disulfide grease; avoid getting any grease on the brake plate where the linings come in contact with it.

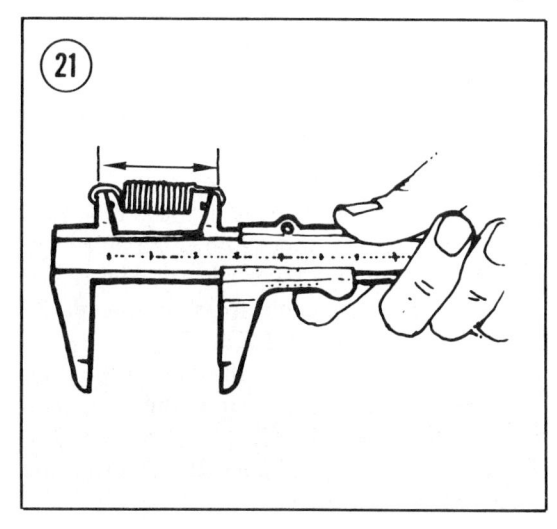

3. When installing the brake lever onto the brake camshaft, be sure to align the 2 parts with the 2 marks made in *Disassembly* Step 5.

4. Hold the brake shoes in a "V" formation with the return springs attached and snap them in place on the brake backing plate. Make sure they are firmly seated on it.

> *NOTE*
> *If new linings are being installed, file off the leading edge of each shoe a little (**Figure 23**) so that the brake will not grab when applied.*

6. Install the brake panel assembly into the brake drum.
7. Install the rear wheel as described under *Rear Wheel Removal/Installation* in Chapter Nine.
8. Adjust the rear brake as described under *Rear Brake Pedal Adjustment* in Chapter Three.

FRONT BRAKE CABLE

Brake cable adjustment should be checked periodically as the cable stretches with use and increases brake lever free play. Free play is the distance that the brake lever travels between the released position and the point when the brake shoes come in contact with the drum.

If the brake adjustment, as described in Chapter Three, can no longer be achieved the cable must be replaced.

Replacement

1. At the hand lever, loosen the locknut and turn the adjusting barrel (**Figure 24**) all the way toward the cable sheath.
2. At the brake assembly, loosen the locknut (A, **Figure 25**) and screw it all the way toward the cable sheath. Unhook the cable end from the end of the brake lever clip (B, **Figure 25**) and disconnect the cable from the receptacle on the backing plate (C, **Figure 25**).
3. Pull the hand lever all the way to the grip, remove the cable nipple from the lever and remove the cable.
4. Loosen the band (**Figure 26**) securing the cable to the front fork leg.

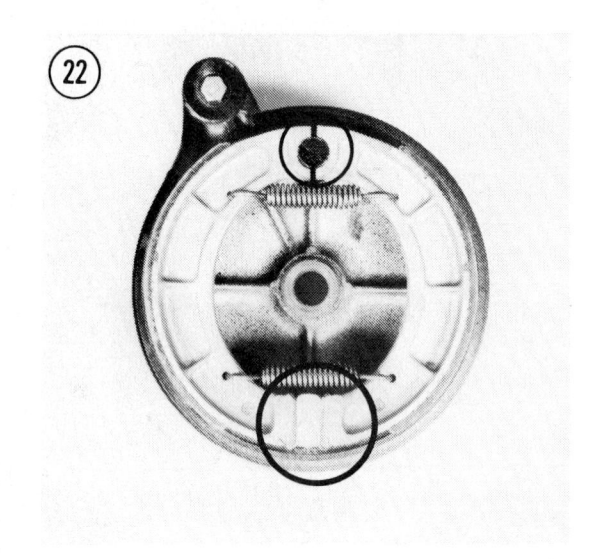

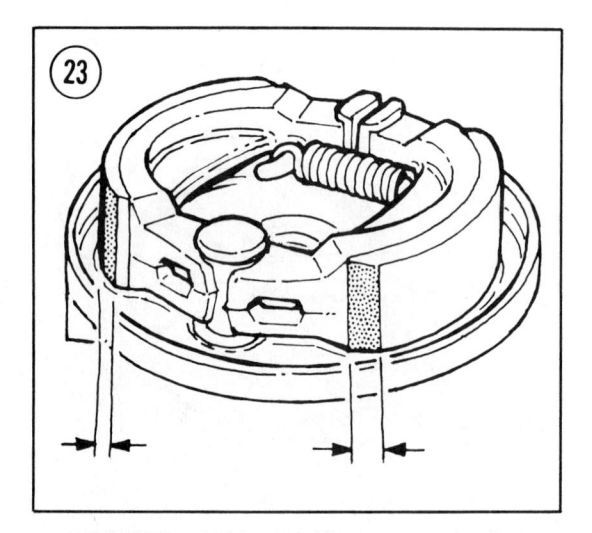

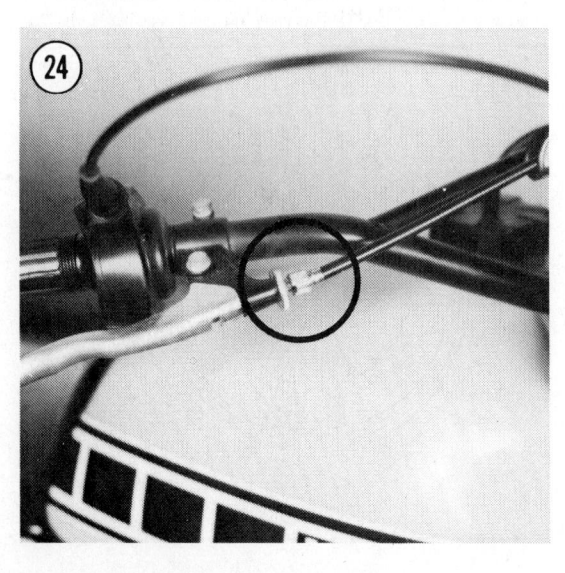

BRAKES

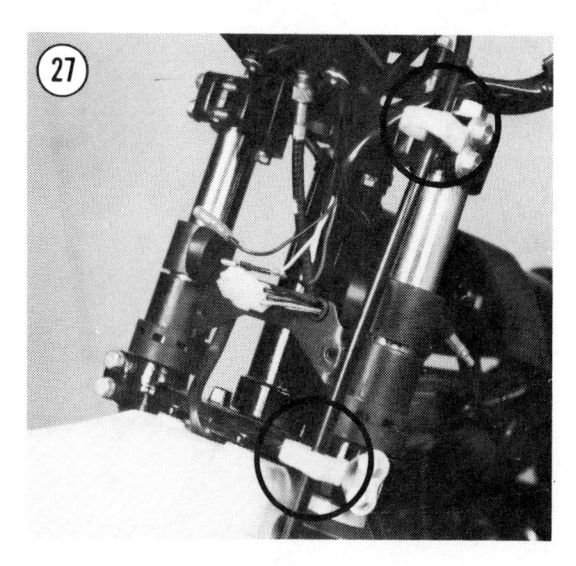

5. Withdraw the cable from the plastic holders on the front fork clamps (**Figure 27**). The number plate was removed for clarity in **Figure 27**. It does not have to be removed for cable replacement.

NOTE
Prior to removing the cable, make a drawing (or take a Polaroid picture) of the cable routing through the frame. It is very easy to forget once it has been removed. Replace it exactly as it was, avoiding any sharp turns.

6. Install by reversing these removal steps.
7. Adjust the brake as described under *Front Brake Lever Adjustment* in Chapter Three.

REAR BRAKE PEDAL ASSEMBLY

Removal/Installation

1. Place a milk crate or wood blocks under the frame to hold the bike securely in place.
2. Disconnect the rear of the brake rod from the brake lever (**Figure 28**).
3. From under the frame remove the E-clip securing the brake lever pivot arm to the frame. Pry it out of the slot with a screwdriver and hold it with your finger (**Figure 29**) as it comes out to avoid losing it.
4. On all models except IT125 carefully unhook the return spring from the hook on the frame (**Figure 30**).
5. Withdraw the pivot shaft out from the frame and remove the assembly.

NOTE
*On model IT125 disconnect the return spring from the pedal as the assembly is being removed (**Figure 31**). After the pedal assembly is removed, hook the spring onto the height adjuster screw (**Figure 32**).*

6. Install by reversing these removal steps. Apply grease to the pivot arm prior to installing it into the frame. Be sure that the return spring is properly attached.
7. Make sure that the E-clip (**Figure 33**) securing the pivot arm is correctly in place so it will not fall off.
8. Adjust the rear brake as described under *Rear Brake Pedal Free Play* in Chapter Three.

CHAPTER TEN

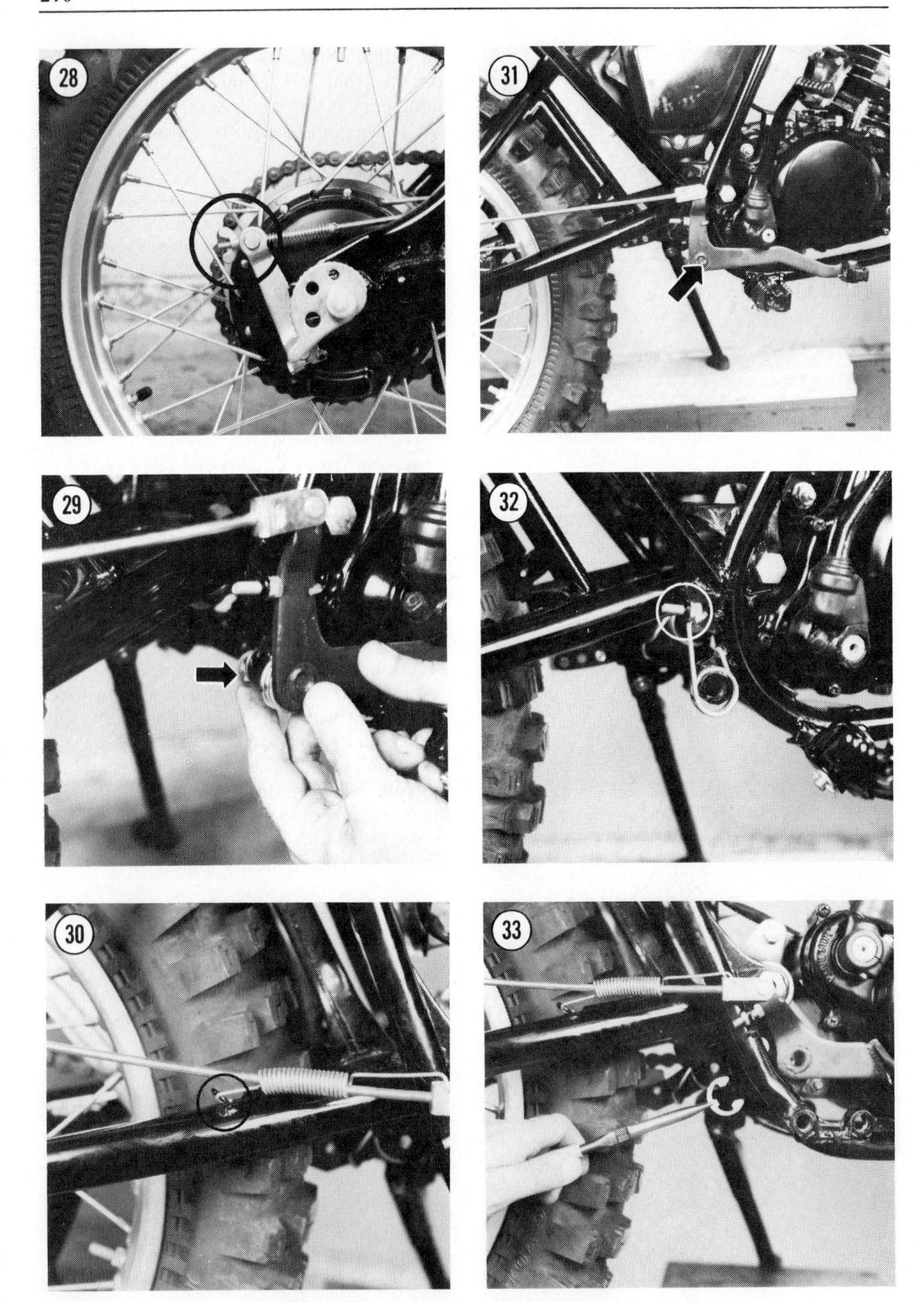

BRAKES

Table 1　BRAKE SPECIFICATIONS

Item	IT425 & IT400	IT250	IT175	IT125
Drum I.D. (new)				
Front	5.12 (130)	5.12 (130)	5.12 (130)	4.33 (110)
Rear	6.3 (160)	5.12 (130)	5.12 (130)	5.12 (130)
Brake shoe O.D. Wear limit				
Front	4.96 (126)	4.96 (126)	4.96 (126)	4.17 (106)
Rear	6.14 (156)	4.96 (126)	4.96 (126)	4.96 (126)
Lining thickness Wear limit				
Front and rear	all — 0.08 (2)			
Shoe spring free length (NEW)				
Front	1.38 (35)	1.38 (35)	1.38 (35)	**1.36 (34.5)**
Rear	2.68 (68)	1.38 (35)	1.38 (35)	**1.44 (36.5)**

NOTE: X.XX = inches　　(XX) = millimeters.

CHAPTER ELEVEN

FRAME AND REPAINTING

The frame does not require routine maintenance. However it should be inspected after each trials competition or after a weekend of hard riding. All welds should be inspected immediately after any accident or spill. This chapter describes procedures for completely stripping the frame. In addition, recommendations are provided for repainting the stripped frame.

This chapter also includes procedures for the kickstand and footpegs.

KICKSTAND (SIDE STAND)

Removal/Installation

1. Place the bike on a milk crate or wood blocks to support it securely.
2. Raise the kickstand and disconnect the return spring (A, **Figure 1**) from the pin on the frame with Vise Grips.
3. From under the frame, remove the cotter pin (**Figure 2**) from the bolt.
4. Remove the bolt and nut (B, **Figure 1**) and remove the kickstand from the frame.
5. Install by reversing these removal steps. Apply a light coat of multipurpose grease to the pivot surfaces of the frame tab and the kickstand yoke prior to installation. Install a new cotter pin and bend it over completely.

FOOTPEGS

Replacement

Remove the bolts (**Figure 3**) securing the footpegs to the frame and remove them.

Make sure the spring is in good condition and not broken. Replace as necessary.

Lubricate the pivot points prior to installation. Tighten the bolts securely.

FRAME

The frame does not require routine maintenance. However it should be inspected

FRAME AND REPAINTING

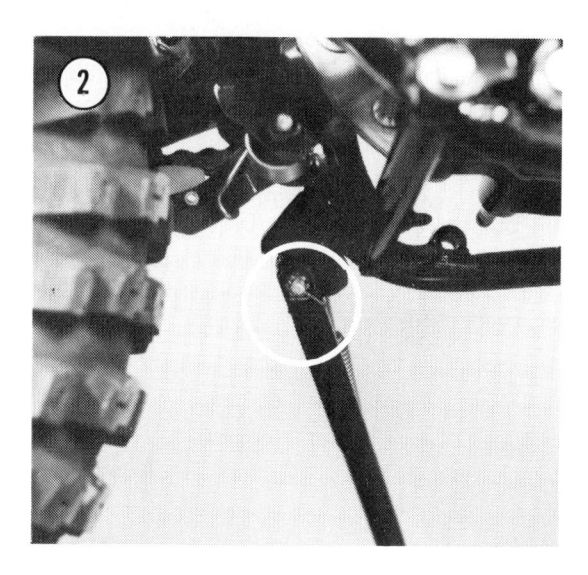

after each trials competition or after a weekend of hard riding. All welds should be inspected immediately after any accident or spill.

Component Removal/Installation

1. Remove the seat, side cover/number panels and fuel tank.
2. Remove the engine as described in Chapter Four.
3. Remove the front wheel, steering and suspension components as described in Chapter Eight.
4. Remove the rear wheel, fender, monoshock and rear swing arm as described in Chapter Nine.
5. Remove the ignition coil and wiring harness as described in Chapter Seven.
6. Remove the kickstand and footpegs as described in this chapter.
7. Remove the steering head races from the steering head tube as described in Chapter Eight.
8. Inspect the frame for bends, cracks or other damage, especially around welded joints and areas that are rusted.
9. Assemble by reversing these removal steps.

Stripping and Painting

Remove all components from the frame. Thoroughly strip off all old paint. The best way is to have it sandblasted down to bare metal. If this is not possible, you can use a liquid paint remover and steel wool and a fine, hard wire brush.

CAUTION
The side cover/number panels, fenders, air box and fuel tank are molded polypropylene which is very slick and flexible plastic (Figure 4). Do not try to paint them as it is very difficult. Do not use any liquid paint remover on these components as it will damage the surface. The color is an integral part of the component and cannot be removed.

When the frame is down to bare metal, have it inspected for hairline and internal cracks. Magnafluxing is the most common and complete process.

Make sure that the primer is compatible with the type of paint you are going to use for the final coat. Spray one or two coats of primer as smoothly as possible. Let it dry thoroughly and use a fine grade of wet sandpaper (400-600 grit) to remove any flaws. Carefully wipe the surface clean and then spray the final coat. Use either lacquer or enamel base paint and follow the manufacturer's instructions.

An alternative to painting is powder coating. The process involves spraying electrically charged particles of pigment and resin on the object to be coated, which is negatively charged. The charged powder particles adhere to the electrically grounded object until heated and fused into a smooth coating in a curing oven.

Powder coated surfaces are more resistant to chipping, scratching, fading and wearing than other finishes. A variety of colors and textures are available. Powder coating also has advantages over paint as no environmentally hazardous solvents are used.

SUPPLEMENT

1981 AND LATER SERVICE INFORMATION

> The following supplement provides additional information for servicing all 1981 and later Yamaha IT models.
>
> The chapter headings in this supplement correspond to those in the main portion of this manual. If a chapter is not included in this supplement, then there are no changes in that chapter for 1981 and later models.
>
> If your bike is covered by this supplement, carefully read the supplement and then read the appropriate chapter in the basic book before beginning any work.

CHAPTER ONE

GENERAL INFORMATION

NEW MODELS

IT465 and IT490

During the 1981 model year, the displacement of the IT425 was increased to 465 cc. During the 1983 model year, the displacement of the IT465 was increased to 490 cc. When information concerning a certain procedure or specification is not found in this supplement for either the IT465 or IT490, refer to model IT425 information in the main book.

IT200

During the 1981 model year, the displacement of the IT175 was increased to 200 cc. When information concerning a certain procedure or specification is not found in this supplement for the IT200, refer to model IT175K information in the main book.

SERIAL NUMBERS

Table 1 lists serial numbers for 1981 and later models.

Table 1 ENGINE AND CHASSIS NUMBERS

Model No.	Engine/chassis serial No.
IT465H	4V6-000101-on
IT465J	4V6-010101-on
IT490K	26A-000101-on
IT490L	26A-100101-on
IT250H	4V5-000101-on
IT250J	4V5-020101-on
IT250K	25Y-000101-on
IT200L	43G-000101-on
IT200N	43G-007101-on
IT200S	43G-015101-on
IT175H	3R6-020101-on
IT175J	5X8-000101-on
IT175K	5X8-050101-on
IT125H*	3R9-050101-on

* Last year model offered.

CHAPTER TWO

TROUBLESHOOTING

DISC BRAKE (IT200S)

Figure 1 lists potential disc brake troubles and checks to make.

WARNING
Whenever refilling brake fluid, use brake fluid clearly marked DOT 3 and specified for disc brakes. Others may vaporize and cause brake failure. Do not intermix different brands of brake fluid as they may not be compatible.

CAUTION
Be careful when handling brake fluid. Do not spill it on painted or plastic surfaces as it will destroy the surface. Wash the area immediately with soapy water and rinse it off thoroughly.

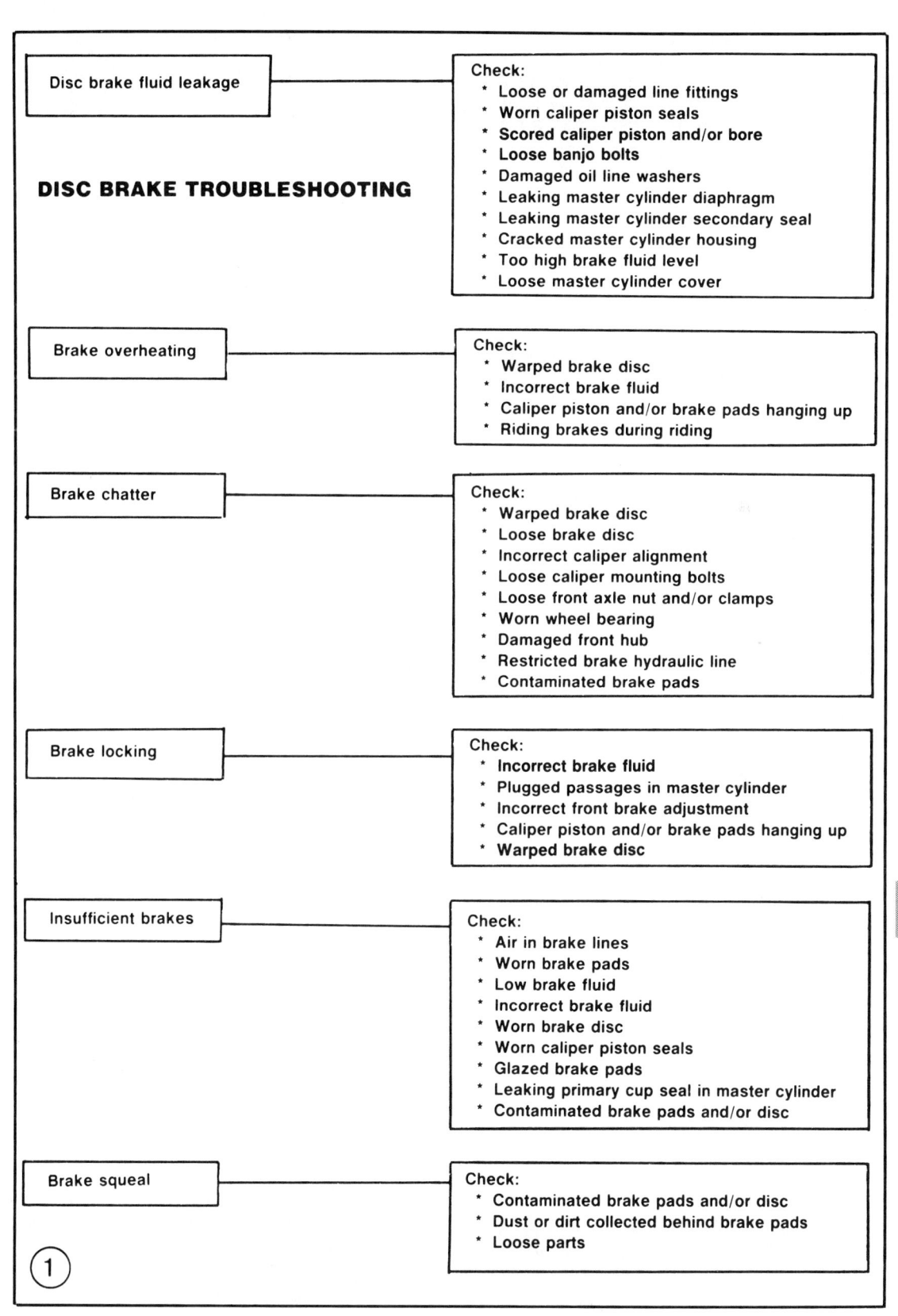

1981 AND LATER INFORMATION

DISC BRAKE TROUBLESHOOTING

Disc brake fluid leakage

Check:
* Loose or damaged line fittings
* Worn caliper piston seals
* Scored caliper piston and/or bore
* Loose banjo bolts
* Damaged oil line washers
* Leaking master cylinder diaphragm
* Leaking master cylinder secondary seal
* Cracked master cylinder housing
* Too high brake fluid level
* Loose master cylinder cover

Brake overheating

Check:
* Warped brake disc
* Incorrect brake fluid
* Caliper piston and/or brake pads hanging up
* Riding brakes during riding

Brake chatter

Check:
* Warped brake disc
* Loose brake disc
* Incorrect caliper alignment
* Loose caliper mounting bolts
* Loose front axle nut and/or clamps
* Worn wheel bearing
* Damaged front hub
* Restricted brake hydraulic line
* Contaminated brake pads

Brake locking

Check:
* Incorrect brake fluid
* Plugged passages in master cylinder
* Incorrect front brake adjustment
* Caliper piston and/or brake pads hanging up
* Warped brake disc

Insufficient brakes

Check:
* Air in brake lines
* Worn brake pads
* Low brake fluid
* Incorrect brake fluid
* Worn brake disc
* Worn caliper piston seals
* Glazed brake pads
* Leaking primary cup seal in master cylinder
* Contaminated brake pads and/or disc

Brake squeal

Check:
* Contaminated brake pads and/or disc
* Dust or dirt collected behind brake pads
* Loose parts

①

OIL LEAK

Some early production IT465H and IT250H models have side stands that are too short. When the bike is supported by the side stand, it leans too far to the left and oil leaks from the crankcase breather pipe. The affected models are:

a. IT465H: 4V6-000101 through 001469.
b. IT250H: 4V5-000101 through 001871.

If oil leakage traced to the crankcase breather pipe is a problem with your IT465H or IT250H model and the serial number falls within the affected models listed above, take your bike to a Yamaha dealer for repair under warranty.

CHAPTER THREE

PERIODIC LUBRICATION

Engine Oil

Table 2 lists new fuel/oil recommendations for 1981 and later models that differ from 1980 models.

Fuel Capacity

Table 3 lists new fuel tank capacities for 1981 and later models that differ from 1980 models.

Transmission Oil

Table 4 lists new transmission oil capacities for 1981 and later models that differ from 1980 models.

NOTE
According to a Yamaha Technical Bulletin, all IT465H and IT250H models have incorrect oil capacity numbers on the clutch cover. Refer to **Table 4** *for the correct transmission oil capacity for these models.*

Front Fork Oil Change/Fork Oil Level

Procedures used to drain and refill the front forks are the same as for 1980 models. Some specifications have changed. See **Table 5**. On some 1981 and later models, Yamaha recommends measuring the oil level and adjusting it so that the level is the same in both fork tubes (see **Table 6**). See *Front Fork Oil Change* in Chapter Three of the main book for service procedures.

Front Fork Air Pressure

Table 7 lists new front fork air pressure specifications for 1981 and later models.

PERIODIC MAINTENANCE

Monoshock Adjustment

Refer to *Monoshock Adjustments* in the Chapter Nine section of this supplement.

Drive Chain Adjustment

Procedures used to check and adjust the drive chain are the same as for 1980 models, except for the following.
1. Drive chain tension specifications have changed for some models. Refer to **Table 8**.
2. When checking the chain tension on 1981 and later IT250, IT465 and IT490 models, the free movement is measured on the *upper run* of the chain.

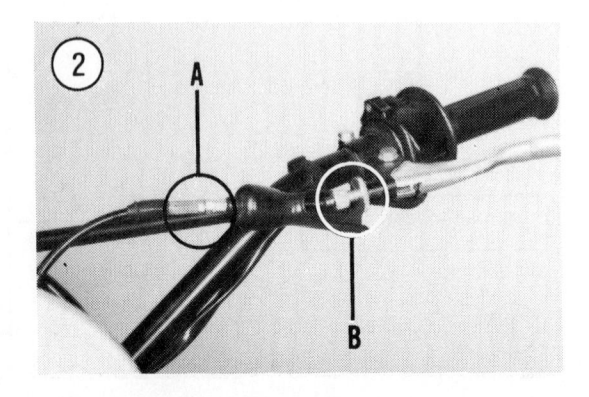

1981 AND LATER INFORMATION

3. Some axle nut tightening torques have changed. Refer to **Table 9**.

Drive Chain Replacement

Some models now use a different size drive chain. These are listed in **Table 10**.

Clutch Mechanism Adjustment

IT175J and K; IT200L and N

1. Remove the clutch cover as describeds under *Clutch Removal/Disassembly* in Chapter Five of the main book.
2. Completely loosen the locknut on the clutch cable inline adjuster and screw in the adjuster (A, **Figure 2**) until tight.
3. Loosen the locknut on the hand lever and screw the adjuster (B, **Figure 2**) in all the way.
4. Loosen the clutch mechanism locknut (A, **Figure 3**).
5. Turn the cable inline adjuster (A, **Figure 2**) until the edge of the push lever and the mark on the crankcase align (**Figure 4**). Tighten the inline adjuster locknut. Then turn the mechanism adjuster (B, **Figure 3**) clockwise until resistance is felt and tighten the adjuster locknut (A, **Figure 3**).
6. Reinstall the clutch cover as described under *Clutch Assembly/Installation* in Chapter Five of the main book.

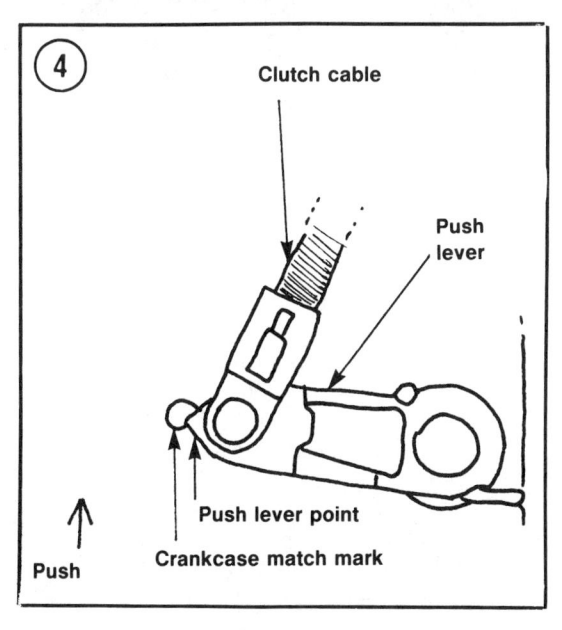

IT200S

1. Remove the clutch cover as described under *Clutch Removal/Disassembly* in Chapter Five of the main book.
2. Loosen the clutch mechanism locknut (A, **Figure 3**).
3. Push the push lever (**Figure 4**) towards the engine until it stops.

> *NOTE*
> *Continue to hold the push lever in this position when performing Step 4.*

4. Turn the mechanism adjuster (B, **Figure 3**) in or out until the edge of the push lever and the mark on the crankcase align (**Figure 4**).
5. Reinstall the clutch cover as described under *Clutch Assembly/Installation* in Chapter Five of the main book.

IT250, IT465 and IT490

1. Remove the clutch cover as described under *Clutch Removal/Disassembly* in Chapter Five of the main book.
2. Completely loosen the locknut on the clutch cable inline adjuster and screw in the adjuster (A, **Figure 2**) until it is tight.
3. Loosen the locknut on the hand lever and screw the adjuster barrel (B, **Figure 2**) in all the way.
4. Loosen the clutch mechanism locknut (A, **Figure 3**).

5. Turn the cable inline adjuster (A, **Figure 2**) by hand until the edge of the push lever and the mark on the crankcase align (**Figure 5**). Then tighten the cable inline adjuster locknut.
6. Tighten the mechanism adjuster (B, **Figure 3**) until resistance is felt, then tighten the locknut.
7. Adjust the clutch cable free play as described in Chapter Three of the main book.

Front Brake Lever Adjustment (IT200S)

Brake pad wear in the caliper is automatically adjusted as the piston moves forward in the caliper. However, the front brake lever free play must be maintained to prevent excessive brake drag. This would cause premature brake pad wear.
1. Slide back the rubber boot.
2. Loosen the locknut (**Figure 6**) and turn the adjuster bolt (**Figure 6**) in or out to achieve 7/16-3/4 in. (10-20 mm) of free play.
3. Tighten the locknut and reposition the rubber boot.

Front Brake Fluid Level Check (IT200S)

The fluid level for the front brake should be above the lower mark on the reservoir. If the brake fluid reaches the lower mark (A, **Figure 7**), the fluid level must be corrected by adding fresh brake fluid.

1. Place the bike on level ground and position the handlebars so the master cylinder reservoir is level.
2. Clean any dirt from the area around the top cover before removing the cover.
3. Remove the top cover and the diaphragm. Add fresh brake fluid (DOT 3) from a sealed container (**Figure 8**).

WARNING
Use brake fluid clearly marked DOT 3 and specified for disc brakes. Others may vaporize and cause brake failure. Do not intermix different brands of brake fluid as they may not be compatible.

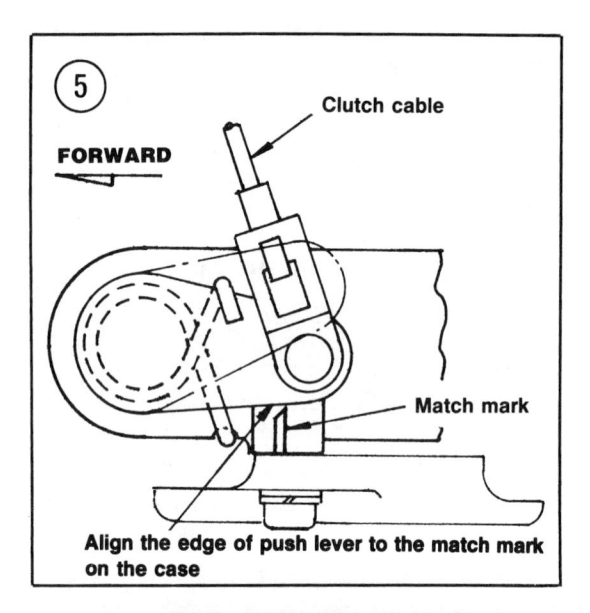

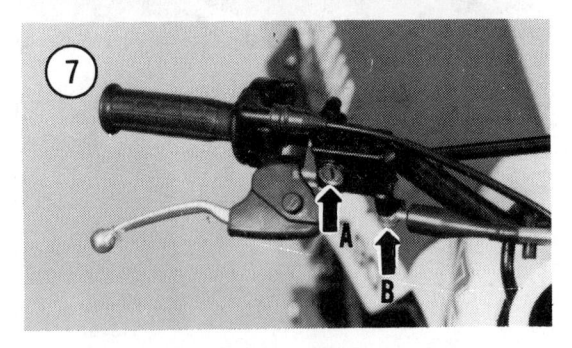

CAUTION
Be careful when handling brake fluid. Do not spill it on painted or plastic surfaces as it will destroy the surface. Wash the area immediately with soapy water and rinse it off thoroughly.

4. Reinstall the diaphragm and top cover. Tighten the screws securely.

1981 AND LATER INFORMATION

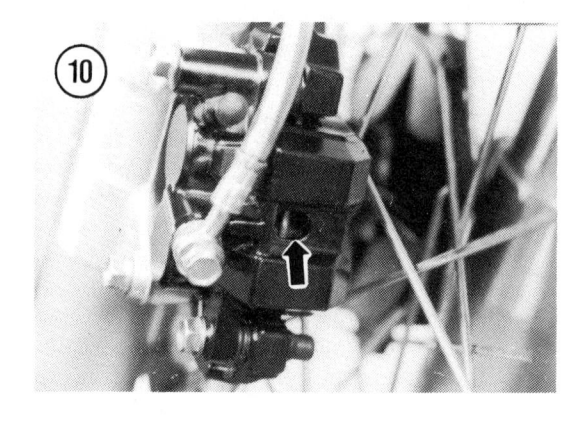

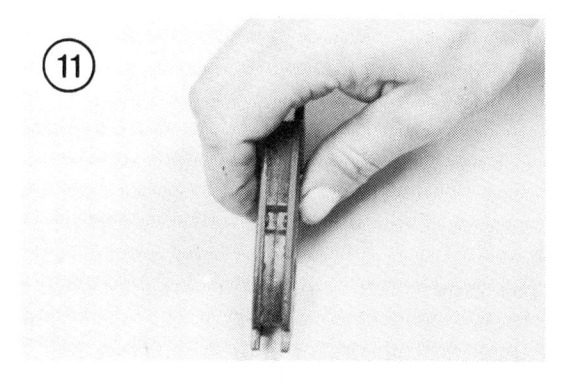

Disc Brake Lines

Check brake lines between the master cylinder and brake caliper. See B, **Figure 7** and **Figure 9**. If there is any leakage, tighten the connections and bleed the brake as described in Chapter Ten of this supplement. If this does not stop the leak or if a brake line is obviously damaged, cracked or chafed, replace the brake line and bleed the system.

Disc Brake Pad Wear

Inspect brake pads for excessive or uneven wear, scoring and oil or grease on the friction surface. Remove the rubber plug and look through the slot in the caliper assembly. If the pads are worn to the wear line (**Figure 10**), they must be replaced. Reinstall the rubber plug.

NOTE
Figure 11 shows the pad wear indicators with the brake pads removed for clarity.

NOTE
Always replace both pads at the same time.

If any of these conditions exist, replace the pads as described in Chapter Ten of this supplement.

Disc Brake Fluid Change

Every time the reservoir cap is removed, a small amount of dirt and moisture enters the brake fluid. The same thing happens if a leak occurs or any part of the hydraulic system is loosened or disconnected. Dirt can clog the system and cause unnecessary war. Water in the brake fluid vaporizers at high temperature, impairing the hydraulic action and reducing the brake's stopping ability.

To maintain peak performance, change the brake fluid once a year. To change brake fluid, follow the *Bleeding the Brake System* procedure in the Chapter Ten section of this supplement.

WARNING
Use brake fluid clearly marked DOT 3 only. Others may vaporize and cause brake failure.

ENGINE TUNE-UP

Correct Spark Plug Heat Range

Table 11 lists new spark plug specifications.

Ignition Timing (IT465H)

Procedures used to check and adjust the ignition timing on IT465H models are the same as for 1980 models, except that when checking the ignition timing with a timing light, the correct engine speed is 2,000 rpm.

Ignition Timing (All 1982-on Except IT200S)

A timing light, tachometer and 6-volt battery are required for this procedure.

1. Remove the timing cover from the left-hand side.
2. Connect the timing light and tachometer to the battery following the manufacturer's instructions.
3. Start the engine and let it reach normal operating temperture.

> **WARNING**
> *The exhaust system is hot; protect yourself and the timing instrument wires accordingly.*

4. Idle the engine at the rpm specified in **Table 12**. Adjust the idle as necessary as described in Chapter Three of the main book.
5. Direct the timing light to the timing marks on the magneto flywheel. See **Figure 12**. The timing is correct if the rotor mark aligns with the fixed mark on the crankcase.
6. If the timing is incorrect, perform the following.
7. Install a dial indicator stand into the cylinder head.
8. Install an extension on the dial indicator and place the indicator assembly into the indicator stand. Do not lock the dial indicator in its stand at this time. See **Figure 13**.

> **CAUTION**
> *If top dead center (TDC) is not correctly determined as described in Step 9, the dial indicator will be damaged.*

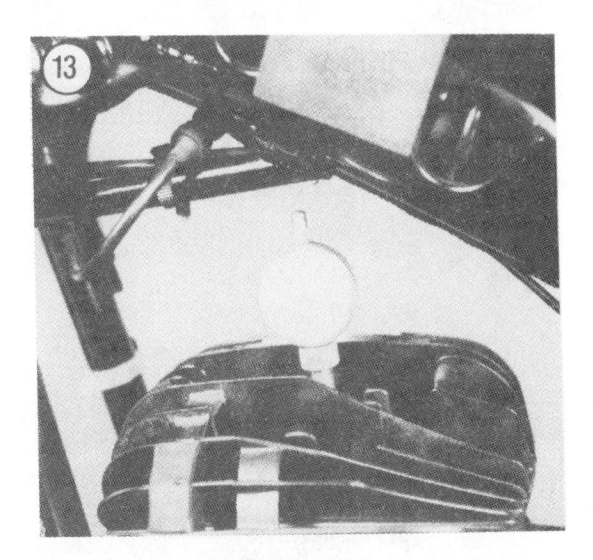

9. Position the dial indicator as follows:
   a. Rotate the magneto rotor (with a wrench on the crankshaft nut) until the dial indicator rises all the way up in its holder (piston is approaching TDC).
   b. Lightly tighten the set screw on the dial indicator holder to secure the dial gauge.
   c. Rotate the magneto rotor until the dial on the gauge stops and reverses direction. This is TDC. Zero the dial gauge by aligning the 0 with the dial.
   d. Tighten the set screw on the dial indicator holder securely.

10. From TDC, rotate the magneto rotor clockwise until the dial reads the dimension given in **Table 13** for your specific model.

1981 AND LATER INFORMATION 283

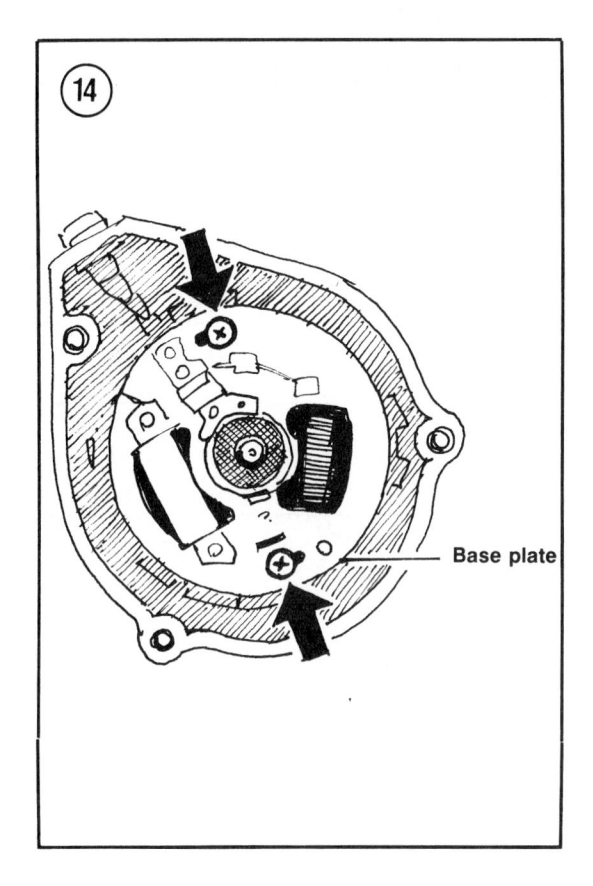

⑭

Base plate

11. Check that the timing mark on the magneto rotor aligns with the fixed mark on the stator plate (**Figure 12**). Interpret results as follows:
   a. If the timing marks are aligned but they were off when checked with the timing light, there may be a problem with the ignition system. Refer to Chapter Two and Chapter Seven in the main book for ignition system troubleshooting.
   b. If the timing marks do not align, proceed to Step 12.
12. Punch a new timing mark on the crankcase that aligns with the magneto rotor timing mark.
13. Remove the magneto rotor as described in Chapter Seven of the main book.
14. Loosen the 2 stator plate screws (**Figure 14**) and rotate the stator plate until its timing mark aligns with the new crankcase timing mark.
15. Tighten the stator plate screws and install the magneto rotor. Recheck the timing mark alignment.

16. Remove the dial indicator assembly and reinstall the spark plug.
17. Complete magneto installation as described in Chapter Seven of the main book.

Ignition Timing (IT200S)

1. Place the bike on the sidestand.
2. Remove the ignition cover.
3. Remove the spark plug.
4. Install a dial indicator stand into the cylinder head.
5. Install an extension on the dial indicator and place the indicator assembly into the indicator stand. Do not lock the dial indicator in its stand at this time. See **Figure 13**.

CAUTION
If top dead center (TDC) is not correctly determined as described in Step 6, the dial indicator will be damaged.

6. Position the dial indicator as follows:
   a. Rotate the magneto rotor (with a wrench on the crankshaft nut) until the dial indicator rises all the way up in its holder (piston is approaching TDC).
   b. Lightly tighten the set screw on the dial indicator holder to secure the dial gauge.
   c. Rotate the magneto rotor until the dial on the gauge stops and reverses direction. This is TDC. Zero the dial gauge by aligning the 0 with the dial.
   d. Tighten the set screw on the dial indicator holder securely.
7. From TDC, rotate the magneto rotor counterclockwise until the dial reads the dimension given in **Table 13**.
8. Check that the timing mark on the magneto rotor aligns with the fixed mark on the stator plate.
9. If the timing is incorrect, loosen the 2 stator plate screws (**Figure 14**) and rotate the stator plate until the timing marks are aligned. Tighten the stator plate screws and recheck the timing mark alignment.
10. Remove the dial indicator assembly and reinstall the spark plug.
11. Install the timing cover.

Table 2 CORRECT FUEL/OIL MIXTURE WITH YAMALUBE "R" *

IT175H	16:1
IT175J,K	24:1
IT200	24:1
IT250H	16:1
IT250J,K	24:1
IT465H	16:1
IT465J	24:1
IT490K	24:1

* Use a 20:1 ratio if the mixture is prepared with Castrol R.

Table 3 FUEL CAPACITIES

Model	U.S. gal.	Liters
IT200	2.9	11
IT250H, J	3.4	13
IT250K	3.6	13.5
IT465H, J	3.4	13
IT490K, L	3.6	13.5

Table 4 TRANSMISSION OIL CAPACITY

Model	Drain/refill	Rebuild
IT200L	700 cc	800 cc
IT200N, S	700 cc	750 cc
IT250H, J, K	750 cc	800 cc
IT465H	650 cc	700 cc
IT465J	750 cc	800 cc
IT490K, L	750 cc	800 cc

Table 5 FRONT FORK OIL CAPACITY

Model	oz.	cc
IT125H	8.7	258
IT175J, K	14.9	440
IT200	18.9	560
IT250H	14.0	415
IT250J	14.3	423
IT250K	19.5	578
IT465H	14.0	415
IT465J	14.3	423
IT490K, L	19.5	578

1981 AND LATER INFORMATION

Table 6 FRONT FORK OIL LEVEL MEASUREMENT

Model	Standard in.	mm	Minimum in.	mm	Maximum in.	mm
IT125H	See note *					
IT175J, K	6.65	169	5.12	130	7.87	200
IT200	7.01	178	5.12	130	8.67	220
IT250H	7.9	200	See note *			
IT250J	7.5	190	See note *			
IT250K	6.7	170	5.90	150	7.87	200
IT465H	7.9	200	See note *			
IT465J	7.5	190	See note *			
IT490K, L	6.7	170	5.90	150	7.87	200

* Dimension does not apply to these models.

Table 7 FRONT FORK AIR PRESSURE*

Model	Standard Psi	Kg/cm²	Maximum Psi	Kg/cm²
IT175H	0	0	35.5	2.5
IT175J, K	0	0	17	1.2
IT200L, N	0	0	17	1.2
IT200S	0	0	35.5	2.5
IT250J	0	0	35.5	2.5
IT250K	0	0	17	1.2
IT465J	0	0	35.5	2.5
IT490K, L	0	0	17	1.2

* Never exceed the maximum air pressure as this will rupture the fork oil seals.

Table 8 DRIVE CHAIN SLACK

Model	in.	mm
IT175J, K	1 3/16-1 3/8	30-35
IT200	1 3/16-1 3/8	30-35
IT250H, J	7/16-5/8	10-15
IT250K	3/4-1 3/16	20-30
IT465H, J	7/16-5/8	10-15
IT490K, L	3/4-1 3/16	20-30

Table 9 REAR AXLE NUT TORQUE SPECIFICATIONS

Model	ft.-lb.	N•m
IT175H, J, K	61	85
IT200	61	85
IT250H, J, K	70	100
IT465H, J	70	100
IT490K, L	70	100

Table 10 DRIVE CHAIN REPLACEMENT NUMBERS

Model	Type	Number of links
IT175J, K	DK520 DS	103
IT200	DK520 DS	105
IT250H	DK520 DS	107
IT250J	DK520 VS	107
IT250K	DK520 VS	111
IT465H, J	DK520 DS	107
IT490K, L	DK520 VS	109

Table 11 SPARK PLUG TYPE AND GAP

Model	Type	in.	mm
IT175H	Champion N-2G	0.028	0.7
IT175J, K	Champion N-86	0.020-0.024	0.5-0.6
IT200	Champion N-86	0.020-0.024	0.5-0.6
IT250K	Champion N-86	0.020-0.024	0.5-0.6
IT490K, L	Champion N-3C	0.028-0.031	0.7-0.8

Table 12 IDLE SPEED WHEN CHECKING IGNITION TIMING

IT175	2,000 rpm
IT250J	5,000 rpm
IT250K	2,000 rpm
IT465J	2,000 rpm
IT490J, K	2,000 rpm

Table 13 TIMING DIMENSIONS

Model	in.*	mm*
IT125H	0.059	1.5
IT175J,K	0.094	2.4
IT200	0.089-0.102	2.25-2.60
IT250H,J,K	0.065	1.65
IT465H,J	0.081	2.05
IT490K, L	0.079	2.00

* All dimensions taken with a dial indicator @ before top dead center (BTDC).

1981 AND LATER INFORMATION

CHAPTER FOUR

ENGINE

⑮

⑯

Engine service specifications for 1981 and later models that differ from 1980 models are listed in **Table 14**. Complete service specifications for the IT200 are listed in **Table 15**.

Engine torque specifications for 1981 and later models that differ from 1980 models are listed in **Table 16**. Complete torque specifications for the IT200 are listed in **Table 17**.

PISTON

Procedures to service the cylinder and piston assembly on 1981 IT175 and IT200 models are the same as for 1980 IT175 models, except for piston measurement location. On all 1981 and later IT175 and IT200 models, the correct measuring height location (**Figure 15**) is 13/32 in. (10 mm).

CRANKCASE

When disassembling the crankcase on 1981 and later IT250, IT465 and IT490 models, follow the procedures in Chapter Four of the main book. However, note that the external shift drum plug, washer and circlip are not used on these 1981 and later models. The early model plug is shown in **Figure 16**.

KICKSTARTER
(IT250, IT465 AND IT490)

Removal/Disassembly

The kickstarter on all 1981 and later IT250, IT465 and IT490 models has been redesigned. It is classified as a Type VI kickstarter and is shown in **Figure 17**.
1. Remove the clutch assembly as described in Chapter Five of the basic book.
2. Remove the idle gear circlip and washers and remove the gear from the shaft.
3. Using a pair of pliers, unhook the kickstarter spring from the pin in the crankcase and allow the spring to unwind and relax. Then rotate the kickstarter assembly counterclockwise and remove from the crankcase.
4. Perform the *Disassembly/Inspection/Assembly (Type I, II, III and V)* procedures in Chapter Four of the main book to inspect the kickstarter assembly. Refer to **Figure 17** to disassemble, inspect and rebuild the kickstarter.

Installation
1. Install the kickstarter shaft into the crankcase housing, making sure the projection on the spring clip is engaged into the notch in the crankcase (**Figure 18**). Then insert the end of the return spring into the opening in the hole in the crankcase (**Figure 19**).
2. Install the idler gear, washer and circlip.
3. Install the clutch assembly as described in Chapter Five of the main book.

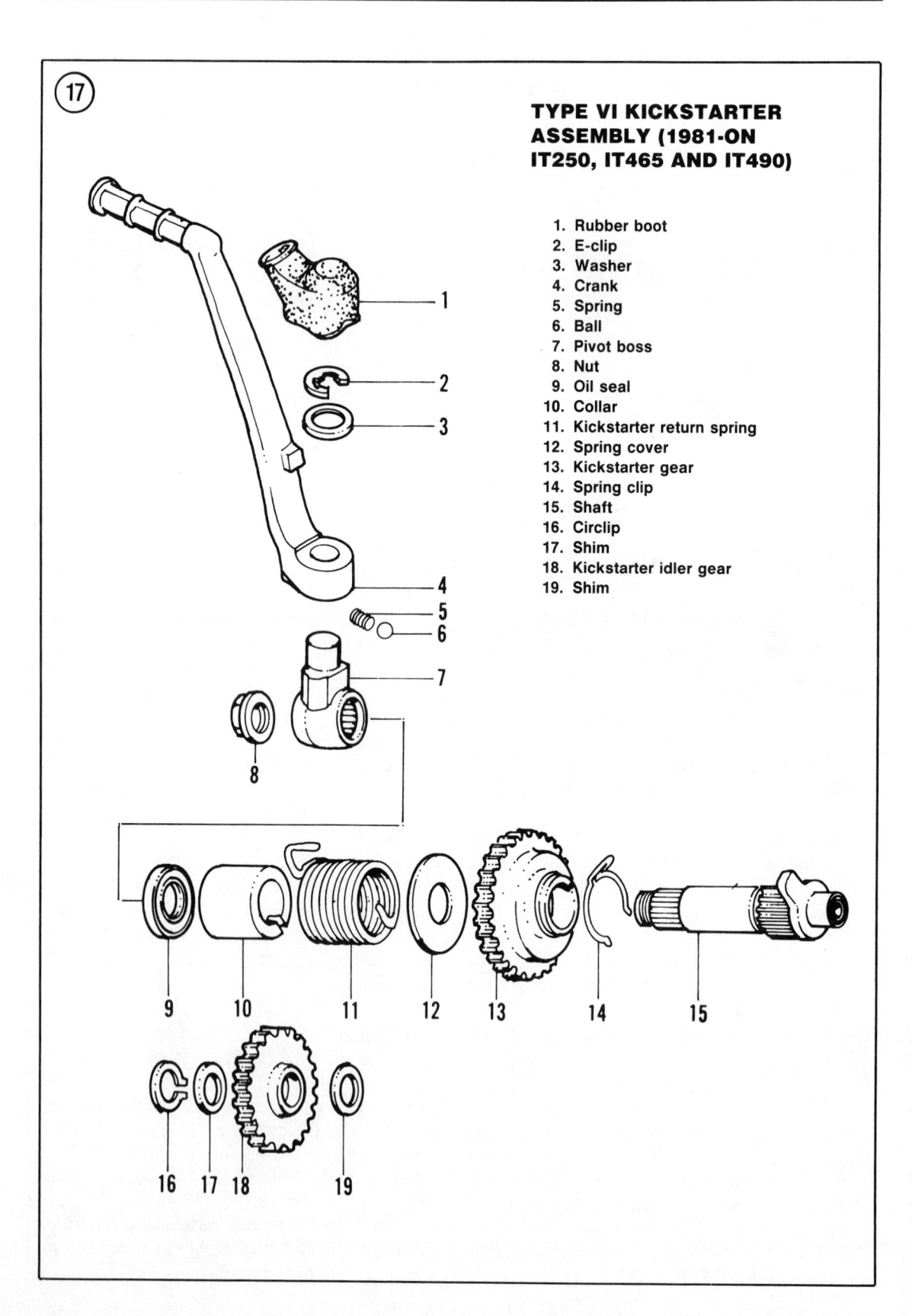

SUPPLEMENT

TYPE VI KICKSTARTER ASSEMBLY (1981-ON IT250, IT465 AND IT490)

1. Rubber boot
2. E-clip
3. Washer
4. Crank
5. Spring
6. Ball
7. Pivot boss
8. Nut
9. Oil seal
10. Collar
11. Kickstarter return spring
12. Spring cover
13. Kickstarter gear
14. Spring clip
15. Shaft
16. Circlip
17. Shim
18. Kickstarter idler gear
19. Shim

1981 AND LATER INFORMATION

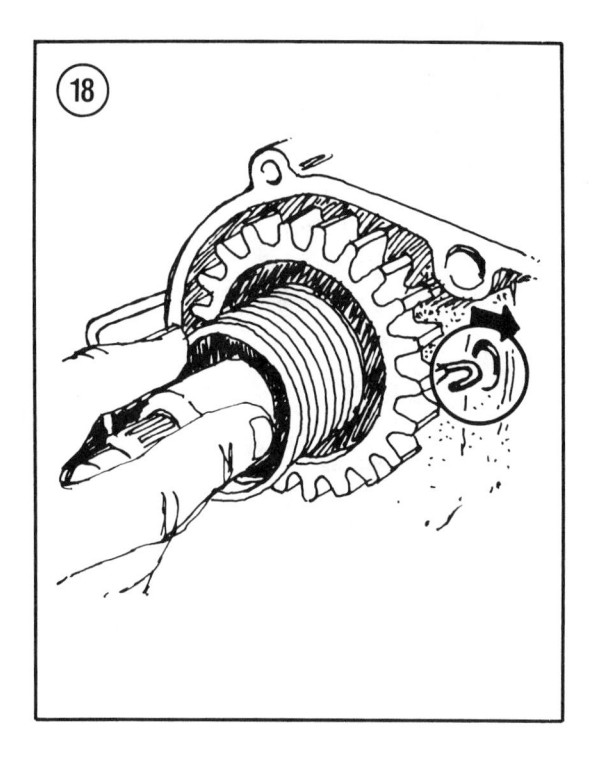

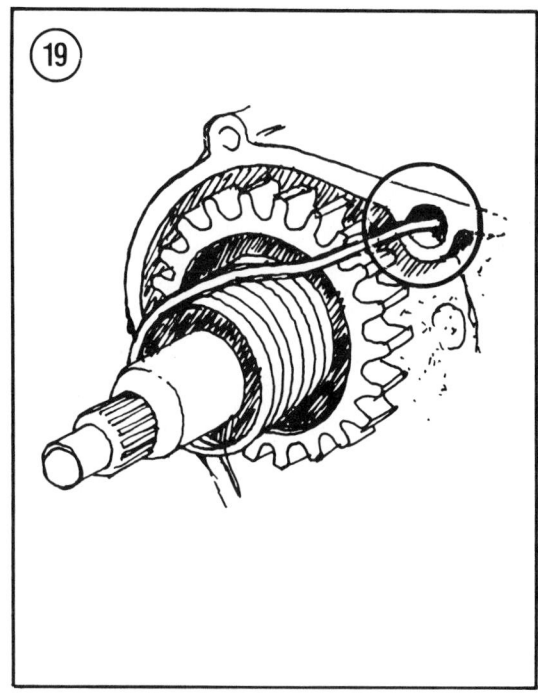

Table 14 ENGINE SPECIFICATIONS (IT175, 250, 465 and 490)

	in.	mm
Service specifications		
Cylinder		
Bore and stroke		
IT465H, J	3.346×3.228	85×82
IT490K, L	3.43×3.228	87×82
Bore		
IT465H, J	3.346	85.00
IT490K, L	3.43	87.00
Piston		
IT465H, J*	0.0028-0.0030	0.070-0.075
IT490K, L	0.0028-0.0030	0.070-0.075
Piston rings		
Ring end gap		
IT175J, K	0.008-0.014	0.2-0.35
IT250K	0.014-0.020	0.35-0.50
IT465H	0.012-0.020	0.3-0.50
IT490K, L	0.014-0.020	0.35-0.50
Side clearance		
IT175J, K (all)	0.0008-0.0024	0.02-0.06
IT250J (all)	0.0012-0.0020	0.03-0.05
IT250K (all)	0.0008-0.0024	0.02-0.06
IT465J		
Top	0.0008-0.0024	0.02-0.06
Second	0.0024-0.0039	0.06-0.1
IT490K, L (all)	0.0008-0.0024	0.02-0.06

* This specification in some Yamaha IT465H owner's service manuals is incorrect. The specification shown here is the correct piston/cylinder clearance as specified by a Yamaha technical service bulletin.

Table 15 ENGINE SPECIFICATIONS (IT200)

	Specifications in. (mm)	Wear limit in. (mm)
Cylinder		
Bore and stroke	2.60×2.24 (66×57)	
Bore	2.598-2.599 (66.00-66.02)	66.00-66.02
Taper		0.002 (0.05)
Out of round		0.0004 (0.01)
Piston		
Diameter	2.5982-2.5984 (65.955-66.00)	
Clearance	0.0020-0.0022) (0.050-0.055)	0.004 (0.1)
Piston rings		
Ring end gap	0.008-0.014 (0.2-0.35)	0.0032 (0.08)
Side clearance	0.0008-0.0024 (0.02-0.06)	0.032 (0.8)
Crankshaft		
Runout		0.0012 (0.03)
Side clearance	0.008-0.028 (0.2-0.7)	
Reed valve		
Thickness	0.017 (0.42)	
Valve stopper height	0.342-0.358 (8.8-9.2)	
Valve bending limit		0.055 (1.4)

Table 16 ENGINE TORQUE SPECIFICATIONS (IT175, 250, 465 and 490)

	ft.-lb.	N·m
Cylinder head		
IT250K, IT490K		
Stud bolt	11	15
Nut	16	22
Cylinder base nuts		
IT175J,K	25	35
IT250H	42	60
IT250K	25	35
IT465H,J	42	60
IT490K, L	25	35
Cylinder studs		
IT175J,K	9	13
IT250K	11	15
IT490K, L	11	15
Drive sprocket		
IT175H,J,K	42	60
IT250J,K	54	75
IT465J,K	54	75
Magneto		
IT175J,K	56	80
IT250J	56	80
IT250K	61	85
IT465J	56	80
IT490K, L	61	85

1981 AND LATER INFORMATION

Table 17 ENGINE TORQUE SPECIFICATIONS (IT200)

	ft.-lb.	N·m
Cylinder head		
Stud bolt	13	18
Nut	18	25
Cylinder		
Stud bolt	13	18
Base nuts	18	25
Oil drain bolt	14	20
Drive sprocket	42	60
Magneto	71	98

CHAPTER FIVE

CLUTCH AND TRANSMISSION

Clutch service specifications for 1981 and later models that differ from 1980 models are listed in **Table 18**. Complete clutch specifications for the IT200 are listed in **Table 19**.

Clutch torque specifications for 1981 and later models that differ from 1980 models are listed in **Table 20**. Clutch torque specifications for the IT200 are listed in **Table 20**.

Procedures used to service the clutch and transmission components are the same as for 1980 models. Some specifications have changed. See **Table 15**.

EXTERNAL SHIFT MECHANISM

The 1981 and later IT250, IT465 and IT490 models use the Type III external shift mechanism as described in Chapter Five of the main book. The procedure in Chapter Five of the main book shows service performed on a model that has the clutch and external shift mechanism on the left-hand side. All 1981 and later IT250, IT465 and IT490 models have these same components on the right-hand side.

TRANSMISSION

Transmission service procedures remain the same as for 1980 models. The following paragraphs describe parts changes on affected 1981 and later models.

Transmission Removal/Installation

IT465H and J; IT490K

These models use the basic 5-speed transmission described in Chapter Five of the main book. However, the location of some circlips and shims has changed. See **Figure 20**.

IT250J and K

These models use the basic 6-speed transmission described in Chapter Five of the mian book. However, the location of some circlips and shims has changed. See **Figure 21**.

Internal Shift Mechanism (IT250, IT465 and IT490)

These models now use the Type III internal shift mechanism described in Chapter Five of the main book. See **Figure 22**.

Internal Shift Mechanism (IT200)

These models use a one-piece shift drum unit (**Figure 23**). Removal and installation is the same as for IT175K models.

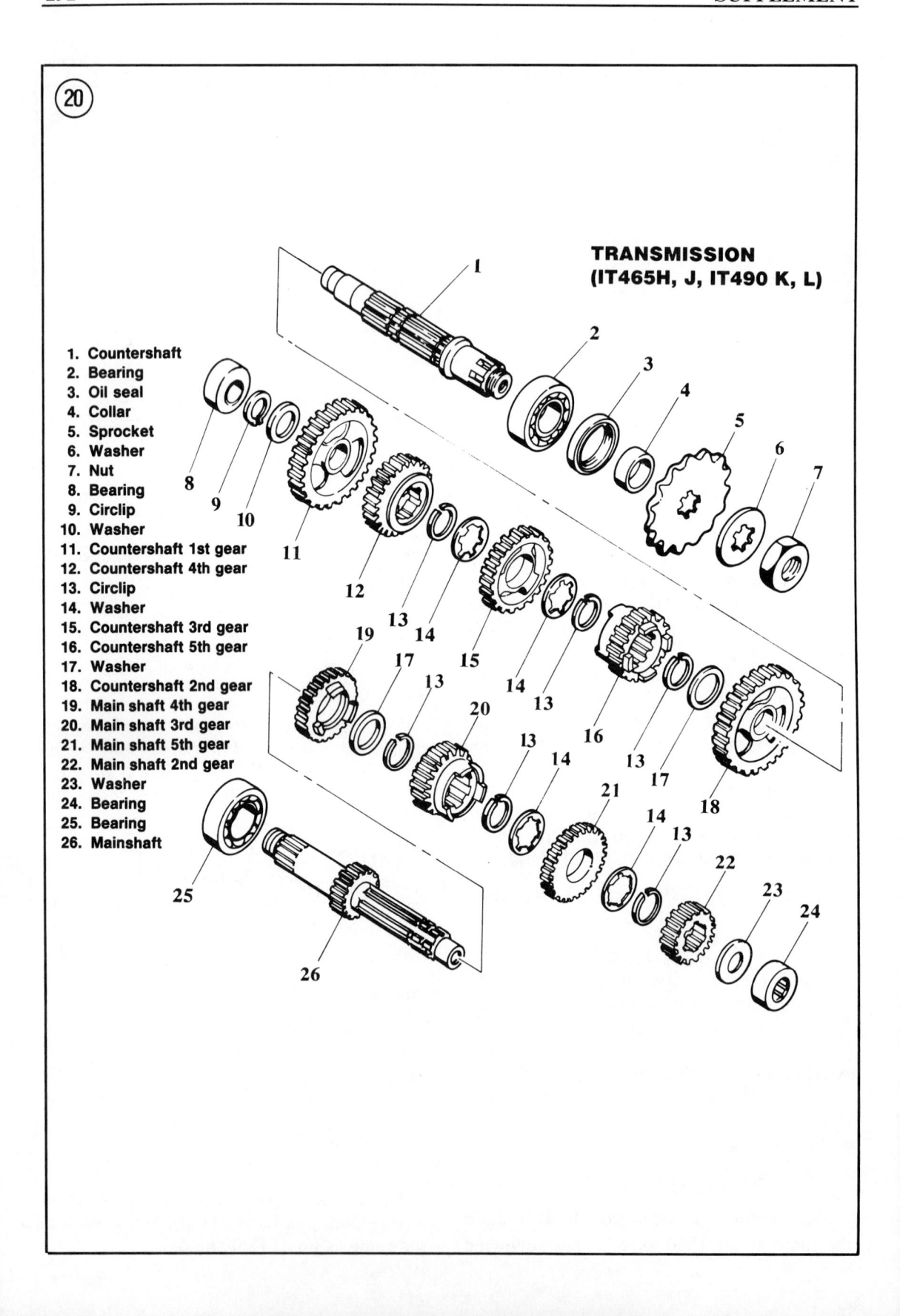

TRANSMISSION (IT465H, J, IT490 K, L)

1. Countershaft
2. Bearing
3. Oil seal
4. Collar
5. Sprocket
6. Washer
7. Nut
8. Bearing
9. Circlip
10. Washer
11. Countershaft 1st gear
12. Countershaft 4th gear
13. Circlip
14. Washer
15. Countershaft 3rd gear
16. Countershaft 5th gear
17. Washer
18. Countershaft 2nd gear
19. Main shaft 4th gear
20. Main shaft 3rd gear
21. Main shaft 5th gear
22. Main shaft 2nd gear
23. Washer
24. Bearing
25. Bearing
26. Mainshaft

1981 AND LATER INFORMATION 293

TRANSMISSION (IT250J and K)

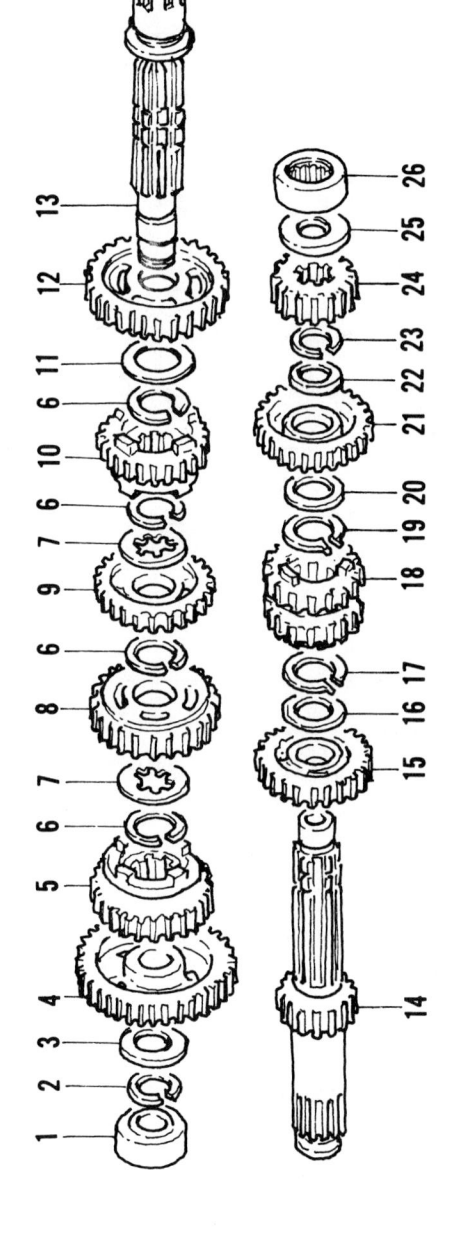

1. Bearing
2. Circlip
3. Thrust washer
4. Countershaft 1st gear
5. Countershaft 5th gear
6. Circlip
7. Splined washer
8. Countershaft 3rd gear
9. Countershaft 4th gear
10. Countershaft 6th gear
11. Shim
12. Countershaft 2nd gear
13. Countershaft
14. Main shaft
15. Main shaft 5th gear
16. Washer
17. Circlip
18. Main shaft 3rd/4th gear
19. Circlip
20. Washer
21. Main shaft 6th gear
22. Washer (IT250J only)
23. Circlip (IT250J only)
24. Main shaft 2nd gear
25. Washer
26. Needle bearing

SUPPLEMENT

22 INTERNAL SHIFT MECHANISM (IT250H, IT465H)

1. Shift fork shaft (long)
2. Shift fork no. 3
3. Shift fork no. 1
4. Cam pin follower
5. Key
6. Shift drum
7. Bearing
8. Stopper plate
9. Washer
10. Screw
11. Shift fork no. 2
12. Shift fork shaft (short)
13. Spring
14. Shift pawl
15. Bolt

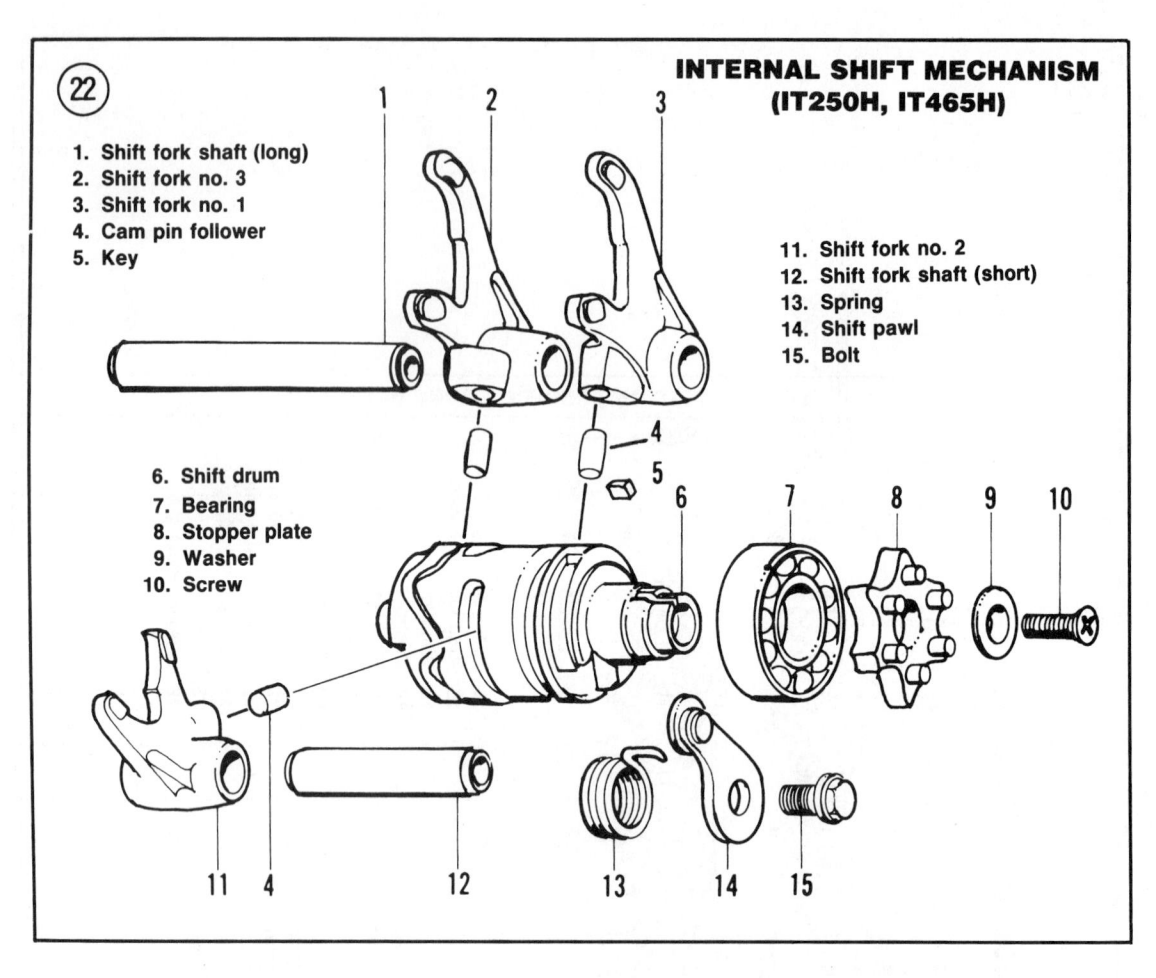

23 INTERNAL SHIFT MECHANISM (IT200)

1. Shaft fork shaft
2. Shift fork No. 3
3. Shift fork No. 1
4. Shift fork No. 2
5. Pin
6. Segment
7. Shift fork shaft
8. Spring
9. Stopper lever
10. Bolt
11. Shift drum

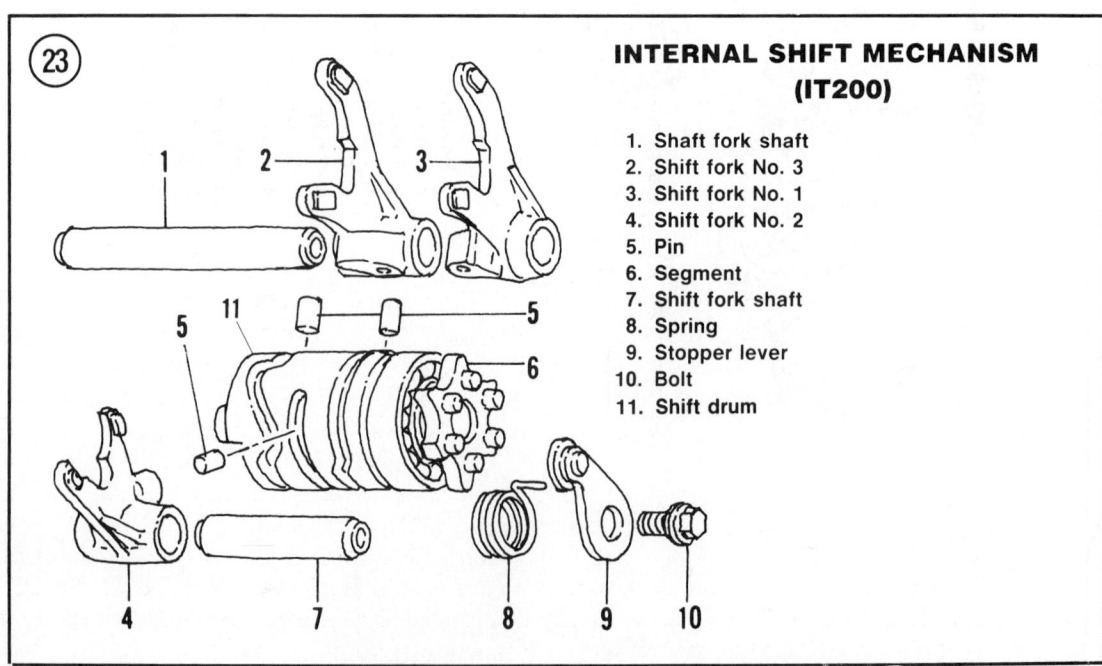

Table 18 CLUTCH SPECIFICATIONS (IT175, IT250 AND IT490)

	Standard in. (mm)	Wear limit in. (mm)	No. of items
Clutch spring free length			
IT250H	1.43 (36.4)	1.39 (35.4)	
IT250K	1.23 (31.2)	1.19 (30.2)	
IT490K, L	1.40 (35.5)	1.36 (34.5)	
IT250H, J, K			
Friction disc			7
Clutch plate			6

Table 19 CLUTCH SPECIFICATIONS (IT200)

	Standard in. (mm)	Wear limit in. (mm)
Friction plate thickness	0.12 (30)	0.11 (2.7)
Clutch plate		
Thickness	0.063 (1.2)	
Warp limit		0.002 (0.05)
Clutch spring free length	1.38 (35.0)	1.34 (34.0)
Pushrod bend limit		0.006 (0.15)

Table 20 CLUTCH TIGHTENING TORQUES

	ft.-lb.	N·m
Clutch nut		
IT175J, K	58	80
IT200	58	80

CHAPTER SIX

FUEL AND EXHAUST SYSTEMS

Changes have been made to all 1981 and later IT250, IT465, IT490 and 1982 IT175 carburetors. Use the procedures in Chapter Six of the main book while referring to **Figures 24-26**. The IT200 carburetor is shown in **Figure 26**. **Table 21** lists carburetor specifications that differ from 1980 models.

YAMAHA ENERGY INDUCTION SYSTEM

The Yamaha energy induction system (YEIS) is installed on all IT490K and L, IT250K, IT175J and K and IT200 models. The YEIS system increases low- and mid-range power while maintaining maximum engine power by reducing air speed fluctuations through the intake tract. By maintaining a smoother flow of air, carburetor jetting is more precise.

The YEIS system consists of a single air chamber connected to the intake manifold by a hose (**Figure 27**). Because the chamber and hose size determine the operating range of the YEIS system, do not tamper with or alter either. The chamber and hose dimensions on the IT models are designed to deliver the greatest effect during low- and mid-range engine operation.

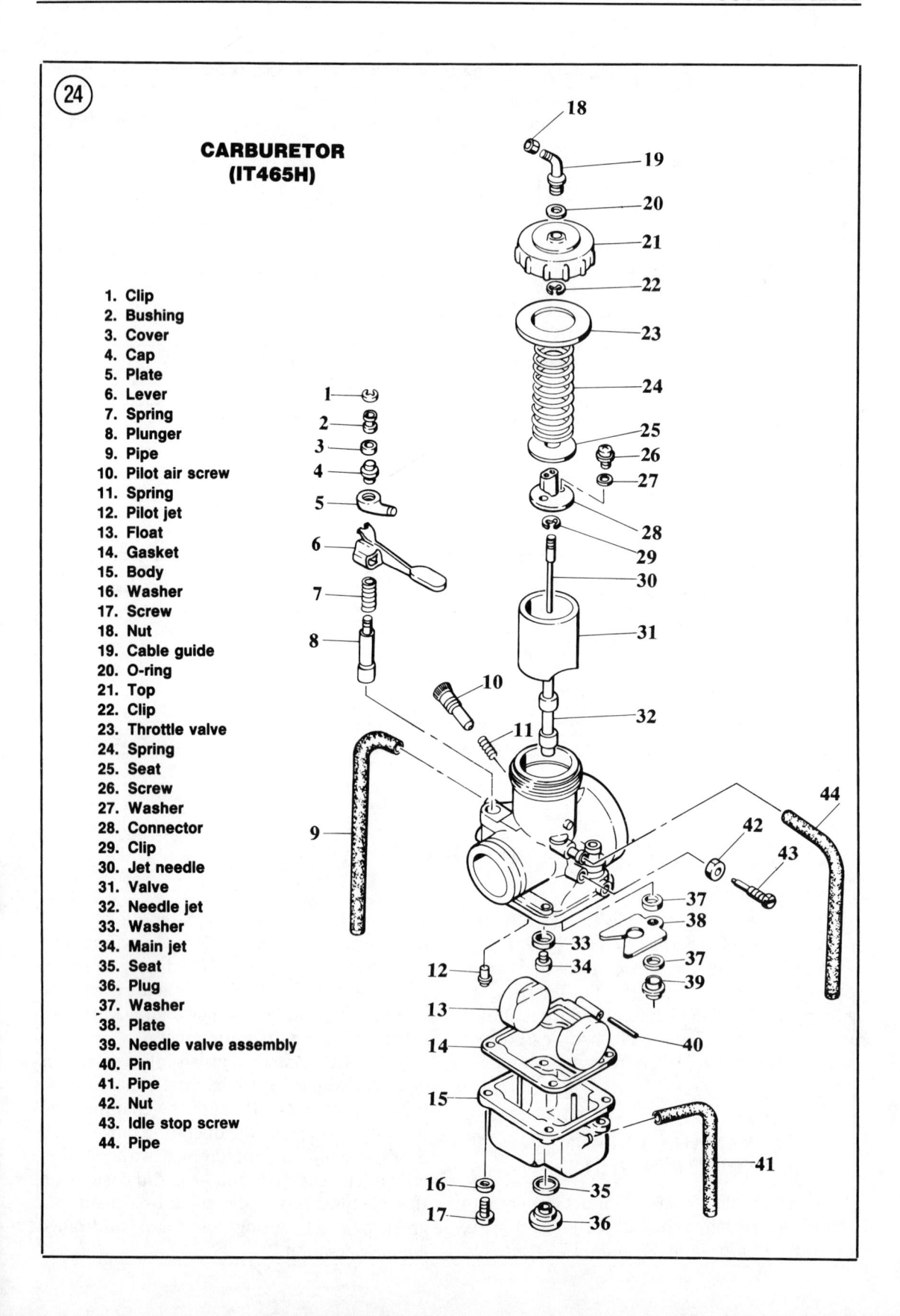

SUPPLEMENT

CARBURETOR (IT465H)

1. Clip
2. Bushing
3. Cover
4. Cap
5. Plate
6. Lever
7. Spring
8. Plunger
9. Pipe
10. Pilot air screw
11. Spring
12. Pilot jet
13. Float
14. Gasket
15. Body
16. Washer
17. Screw
18. Nut
19. Cable guide
20. O-ring
21. Top
22. Clip
23. Throttle valve
24. Spring
25. Seat
26. Screw
27. Washer
28. Connector
29. Clip
30. Jet needle
31. Valve
32. Needle jet
33. Washer
34. Main jet
35. Seat
36. Plug
37. Washer
38. Plate
39. Needle valve assembly
40. Pin
41. Pipe
42. Nut
43. Idle stop screw
44. Pipe

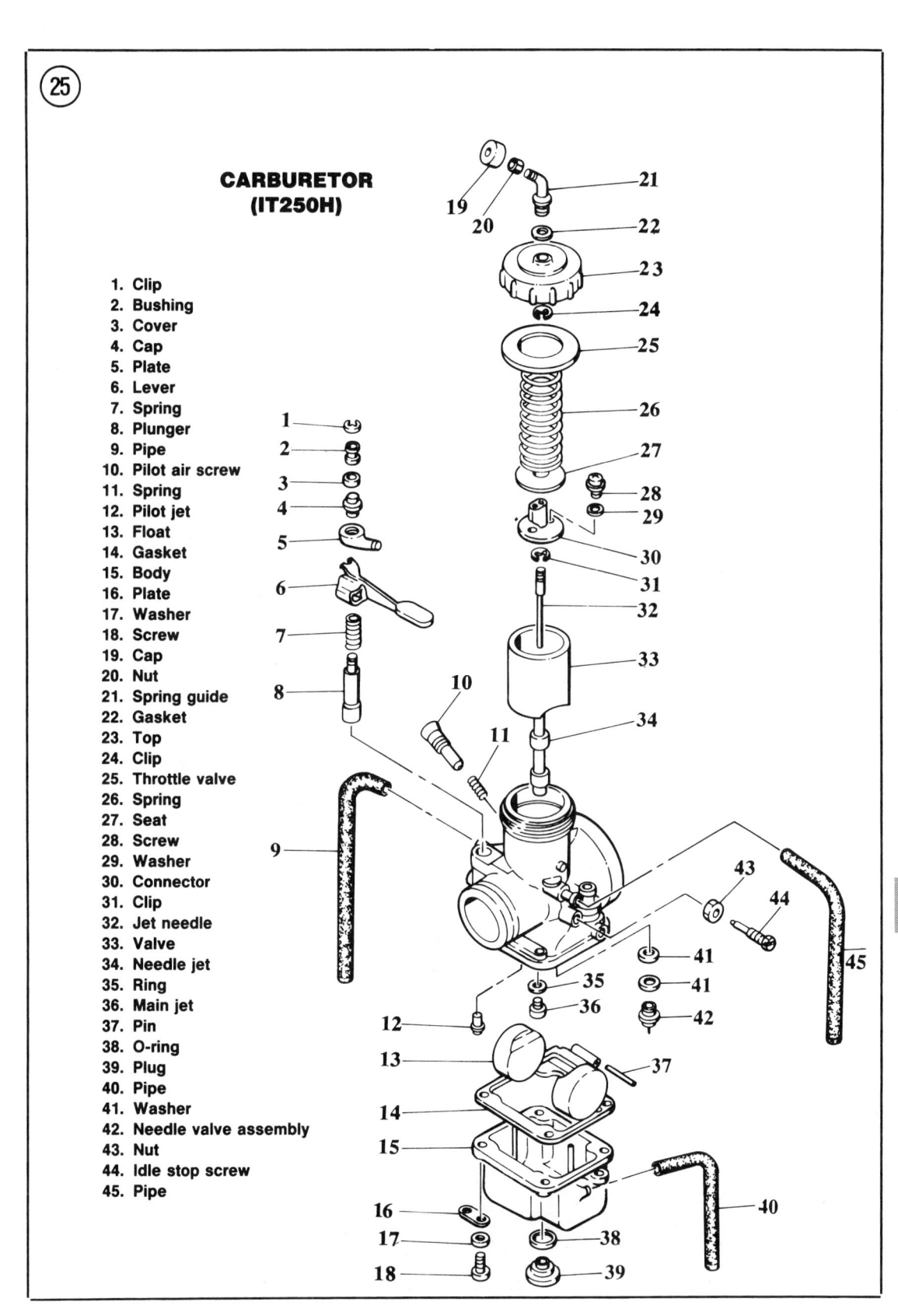

1981 AND LATER INFORMATION

CARBURETOR (IT250H)

1. Clip
2. Bushing
3. Cover
4. Cap
5. Plate
6. Lever
7. Spring
8. Plunger
9. Pipe
10. Pilot air screw
11. Spring
12. Pilot jet
13. Float
14. Gasket
15. Body
16. Plate
17. Washer
18. Screw
19. Cap
20. Nut
21. Spring guide
22. Gasket
23. Top
24. Clip
25. Throttle valve
26. Spring
27. Seat
28. Screw
29. Washer
30. Connector
31. Clip
32. Jet needle
33. Valve
34. Needle jet
35. Ring
36. Main jet
37. Pin
38. O-ring
39. Plug
40. Pipe
41. Washer
42. Needle valve assembly
43. Nut
44. Idle stop screw
45. Pipe

298 SUPPLEMENT

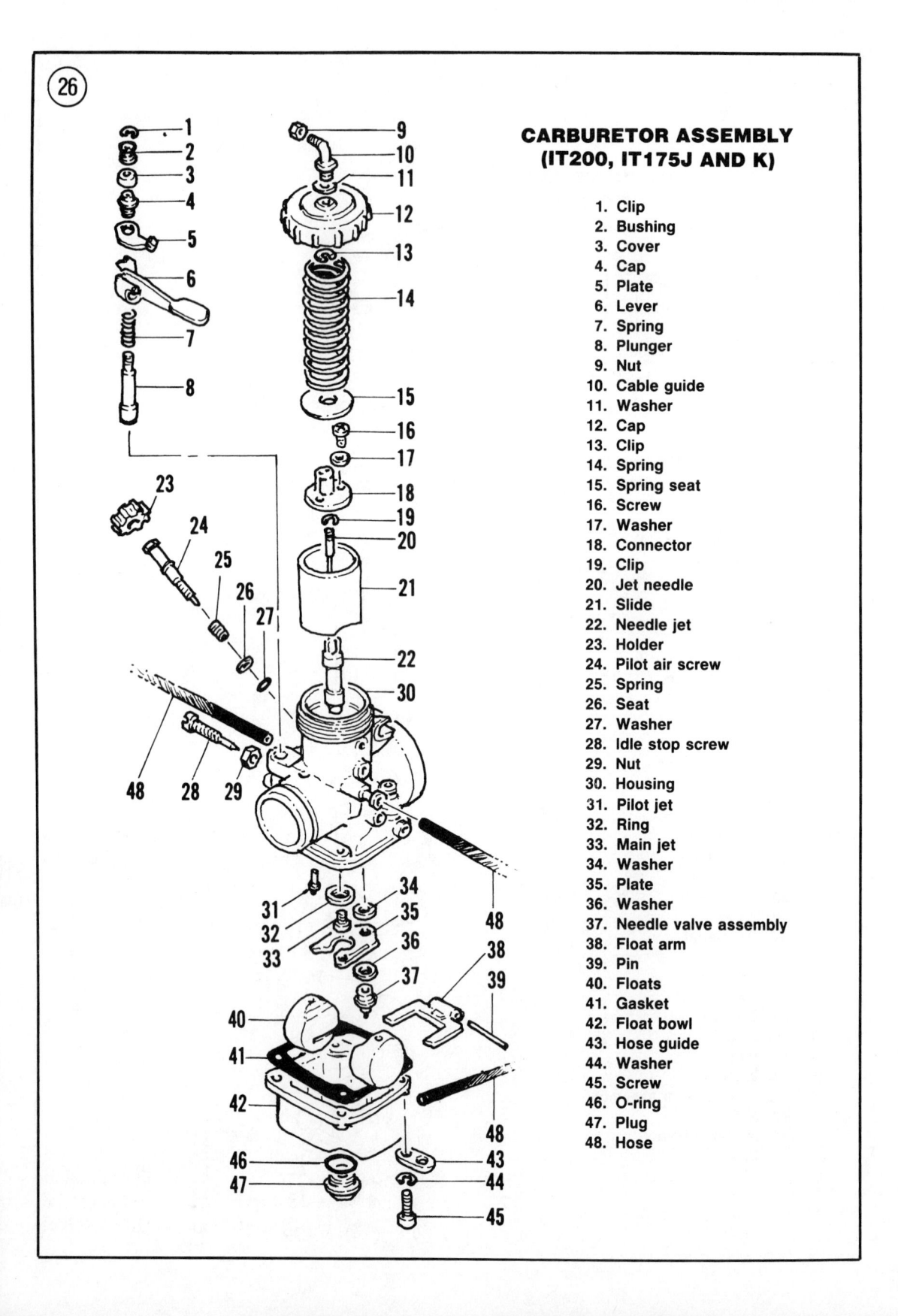

CARBURETOR ASSEMBLY (IT200, IT175J AND K)

1. Clip
2. Bushing
3. Cover
4. Cap
5. Plate
6. Lever
7. Spring
8. Plunger
9. Nut
10. Cable guide
11. Washer
12. Cap
13. Clip
14. Spring
15. Spring seat
16. Screw
17. Washer
18. Connector
19. Clip
20. Jet needle
21. Slide
22. Needle jet
23. Holder
24. Pilot air screw
25. Spring
26. Seat
27. Washer
28. Idle stop screw
29. Nut
30. Housing
31. Pilot jet
32. Ring
33. Main jet
34. Washer
35. Plate
36. Washer
37. Needle valve assembly
38. Float arm
39. Pin
40. Floats
41. Gasket
42. Float bowl
43. Hose guide
44. Washer
45. Screw
46. O-ring
47. Plug
48. Hose

1981 AND LATER INFORMATION

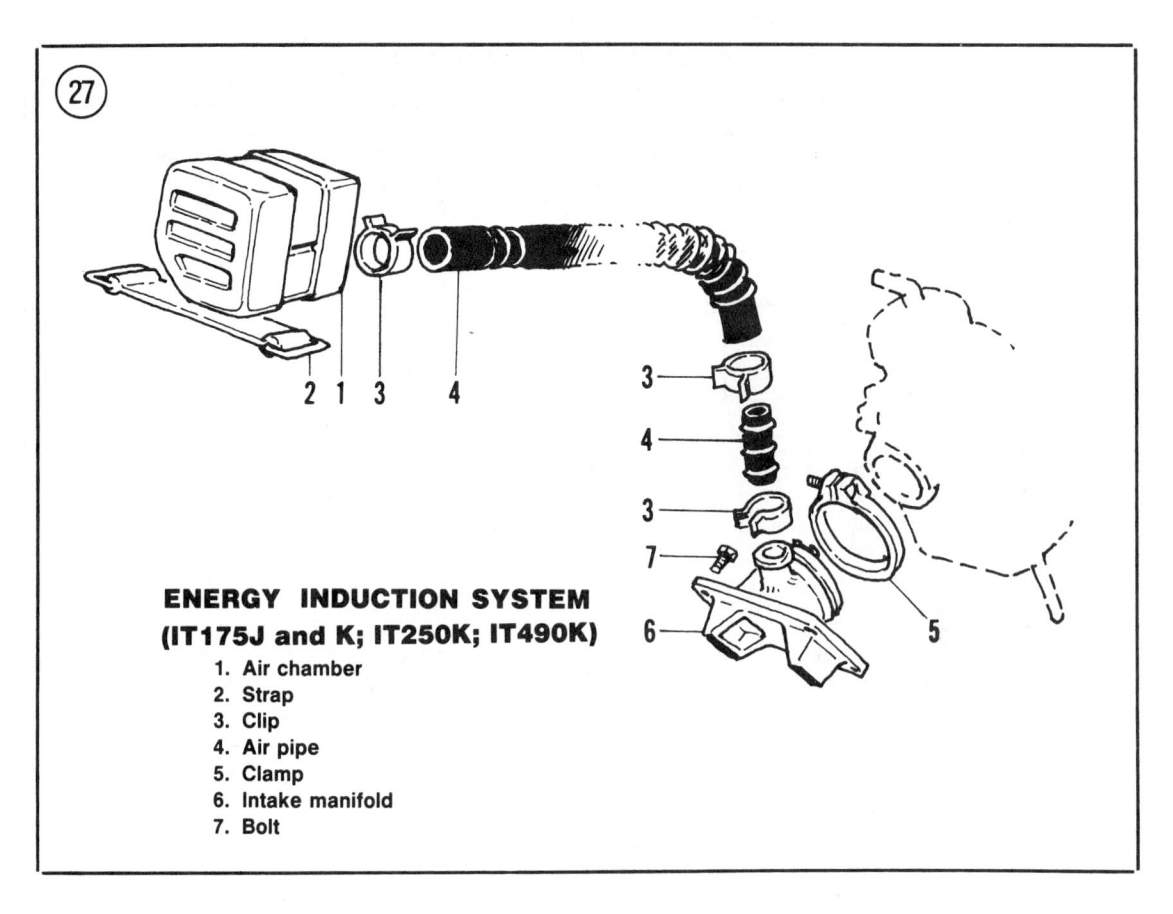

**ENERGY INDUCTION SYSTEM
(IT175J and K; IT250K; IT490K)**
1. Air chamber
2. Strap
3. Clip
4. Air pipe
5. Clamp
6. Intake manifold
7. Bolt

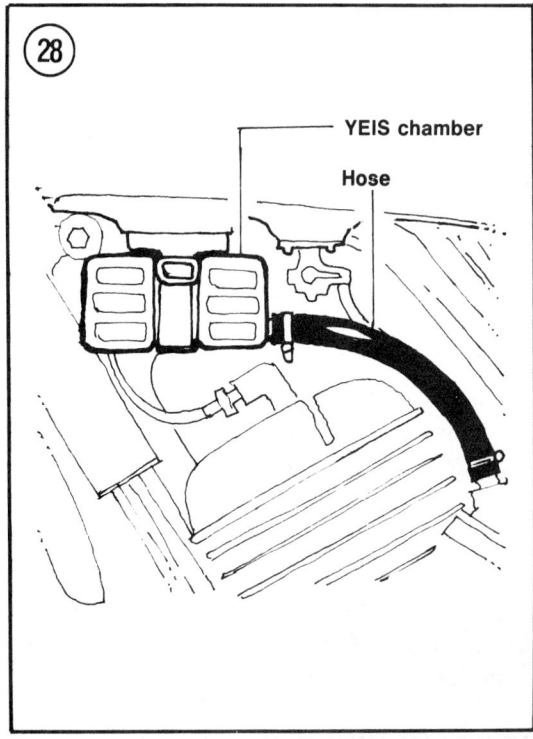

Removal/Installation

1. Disconnect the YEIS chamber hose at the intake manifold (**Figure 28**).

2. Disconnect the YEIS chamber underneath the fuel tank (**Figure 28**) and remove the YEIS chamber and hose.

3. Check the YEIS chamber and hose for any signs of wear or damage. Replace any parts as required.

4. Installation is the reverse of these steps.

FUEL TANK

Removal/Installation

When removing the fuel tank on models equipped with the Yamaha Energy Induction System, it is first necessary to remove the YEIS chamber from its mounting on the fuel tank.

Table 21 CARBURETOR SPECIFICATIONS

	IT175J, K	IT200L, N	IT200S	IT250H
Model No.	VM34SS	VM34SS	VM36SS	VM36SS
I.D. mark	5X810	43G-00	43G-10	4V500
Main jet	320	330	330	400
Needle jet	P-4	P-6	Q-0	N-8
Pilot jet	70	55	70	50
Jet needle	6F21	6F21	6F21	6F34
Clip position	4	4	3	3
Float level	0.93 in. (23.5 mm)	0.93 in. (23.5 mm)	0.93 in. (23.5 mm)	0.7 in. (18.1 mm)

	IT250J	IT250K	IT465H	IT465J
Model No.	VM36SS	VM36SS	VM36SS	VM36SS
I.D. mark	4V500	25Y-00	4V600	4V610
Main jet	400	380	360	390
Needle jet	N-8	N-8	Q-2	Q-2
Pilot jet	50	40	35	40
Jet needle	6F34	6F34	F36	6F39
Clip position	3	4	3	4
Float level	0.94 in. (24 mm)	0.94 in. (24 mm)	1.1 in. (27 mm)	1.1 in. (27 mm)

	IT490K*	IT490L
Model No.	VM38SS	VM38SS
I.D. mark	4V610	26A00
Main jet	370	370
Needle jet	Q-2	Q-2
Pilot jet	50	50
Jet needle	6F39	6F39
Clip position	3	3
Float level	1.1 in. (27 mm)	1.1 in. (27 mm)

* For better performance, carburetor settings on this model have changed from those listed in the Yamaha Owner's Service Manual. The specifications listed in this table are recommended by Yamaha.

CHAPTER SEVEN
ELECTRICAL SYSTEMS

Table 22 lists new electrical specifications for 1981 and later models that differ from 1980 models. Test procedures remain the same for all models.

MAGNETO

Removal/Installation

Table 23 lists new magneto nut torque specifications for 1981 models that differ from 1980 models.

Table 22 ELECTRICAL SPECIFICATIONS

Charge coil resistance	
High speed winding	
IT250H, J, K	14.0 ohms ±10%
IT465H, J	13.6 ohms ±10%
IT490K, L	13.6 ohms ±10%
Low speed winding	
IT250H, J	360 ohms ±10%
IT250K	370 ohms ±10%
IT465H	420 ohms ±10%
IT490K, L	420 ohms ±10%
Pulser coil resistance	
IT200	12.4 ohms ±10%
IT250H	14.0 ohms ±10%
IT250J	9.0 ohms ±10%
IT250K	10.0 ohms ±10%
IT465H	13.6 ohms ±10%
IT465J	12.4 ohms ±10%
IT490K, L	12.4 ohms ±10%
Source coil	
IT200	420 ohms ±10%
Lighting coil resistance	
IT200	0.48 ohms ±10%
IT250H, J, K	0.48 ohms ±10%
IT465H, J	0.48 ohms ±10%
IT490K, L	0.48 ohms ±10%
Ignition coil resistance	
Primary	
IT200	1.0 ohms ±15%
IT250J	0.6 ohms ±10%
IT250K	1.0 ohms ±15%
IT465J	0.6 ohms ±10%
IT490K, L	1.0 ohms ±15%
Secondary	
IT200	5.9K ohms ±15%
Magneto output test	
2,500 rpm	
IT200L	6.0 volts or more
IT200N, S	6.4 volts or more
IT250K	6.4 volts or more
IT490K, L	5.0 volts or more
8,000 rpm	
IT200	8.5 volts or less
IT250K	5.0 volts or less
IT490K, L	7.0 volts or less

Table 23 MAGNETO ROTOR NUT TORQUE SPECIFICATIONS

Model	ft.-lb.	N•m
IT175J, K	58	80
IT200	71	98
IT250H, J	58	80
IT250K	61	85
IT465H, J	58	80
IT490K, L	61	85

CHAPTER EIGHT

FRONT SUSPENSION AND STEERING

FRONT WHEEL (IT490K; IT250K AND L)

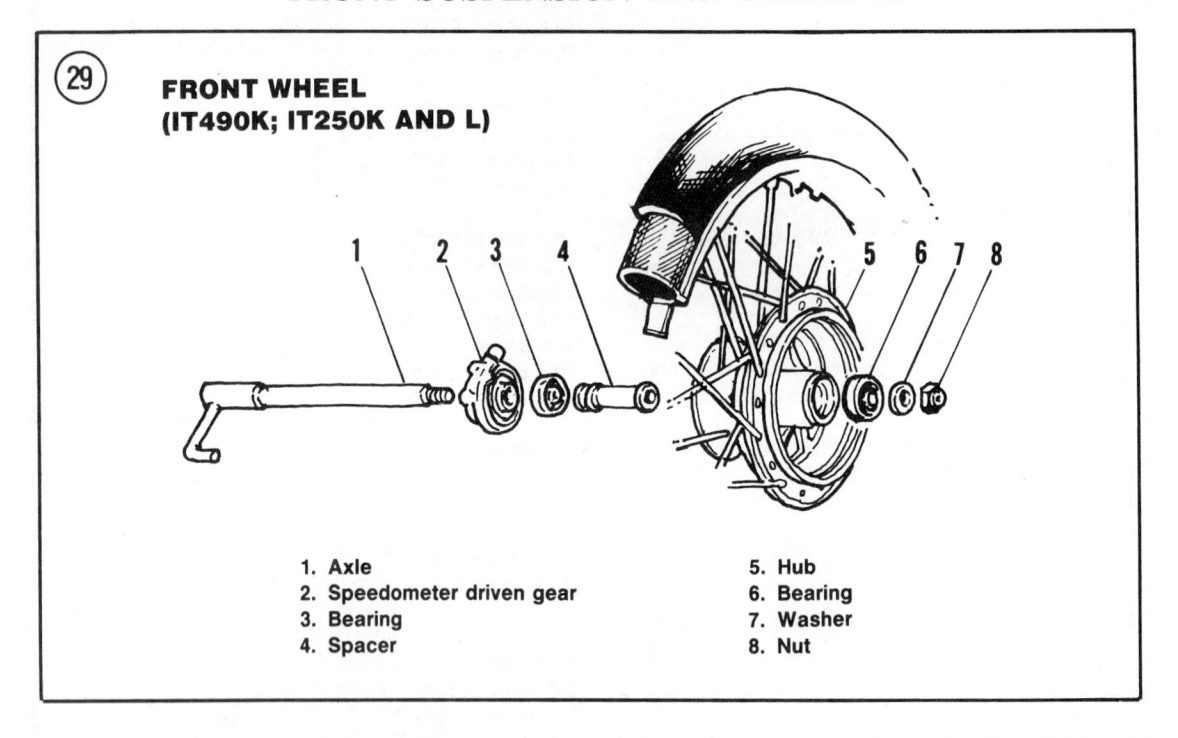

1. Axle
2. Speedometer driven gear
3. Bearing
4. Spacer
5. Hub
6. Bearing
7. Washer
8. Nut

Table 24 lists new front suspension torque specifications. IT200 front suspension torque specifications are listed in **Table 24**.

FRONT WHEEL

Removal/Installation (IT250K and IT490K and L)

A new front wheel bearing and spacer alignment is used on all IT250K and IT490K and L models. See **Figure 29**. Removal and installation remains the same as for 1982 and earlier models, except that when installing the speedometer cable housing, align the 3 projections in the back of the housing with the 3 slots in the wheel hub (**Figure 30**).

Removal/Installation (IT200L and N)

Refer to **Figure 31** for the front wheel assembly and bearing alignment used on IT200L and N models. Service procedures remain the same as for IT175 models.

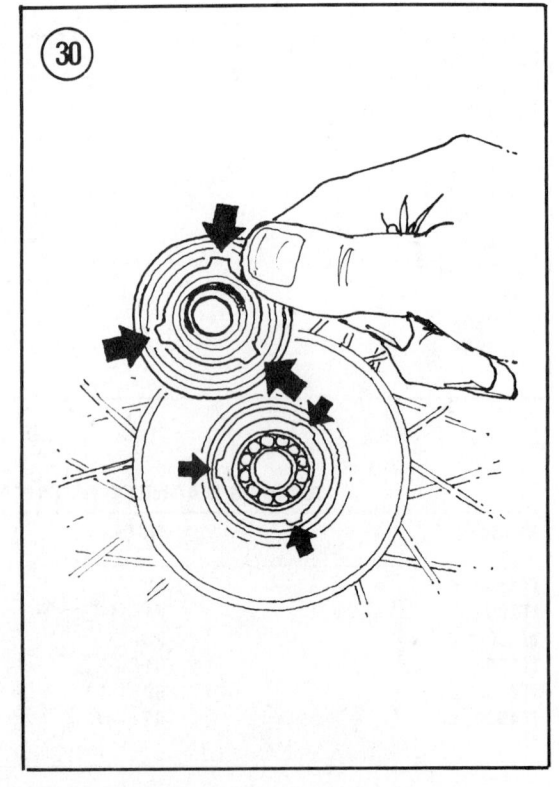

1981 AND LATER INFORMATION

③

FRONT WHEEL (IT200L AND N)

1. Axle
2. Speedometer drive unit
3. Bearing
4. Spacer
5. Rim
6. Front hub
7. Washer
8. Nut

③

FRONT WHEEL (IT200S)

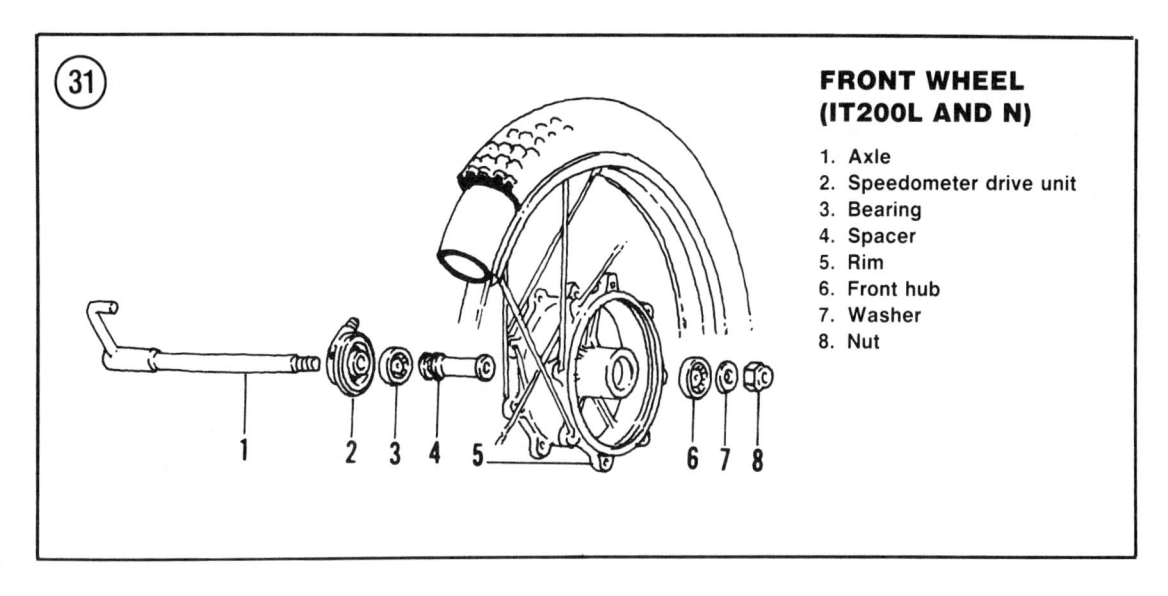

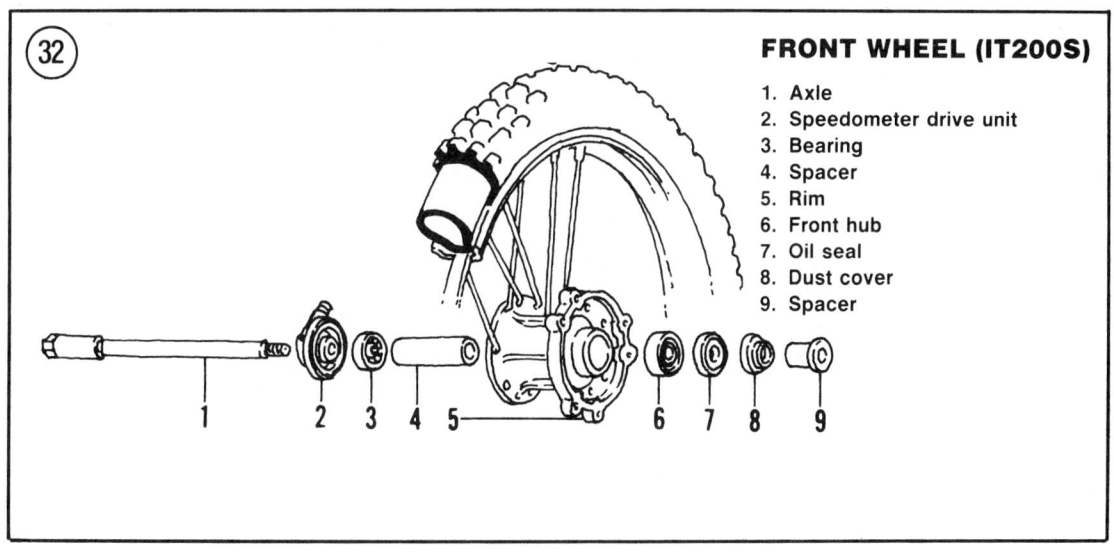

1. Axle
2. Speedometer drive unit
3. Bearing
4. Spacer
5. Rim
6. Front hub
7. Oil seal
8. Dust cover
9. Spacer

③

Removal (IT200S)

Refer to **Figure 32** when performing these procedures.

1. Place a milk crate or wood block(s) under the crankcase to lift the front wheel off the ground.
2. Loosen the front axle holders.
3. Unscrew the axle and remove it.
4. Remove the wheel slightly and remove the speedometer drive from the wheel.
5. Remove the wheel.
6. Remove the left-hand axle spacer (**Figure 33**).

NOTE
*Insert a piece of wood in the caliper (**Figure 34**) in place of the disc. That way, if the brake lever is inadvertently squeezed, the piston will not be forced out of cylinder. If this does happen, the caliper might have to be disassembled to reseat the piston and the system will have to be bled. By using the wood, bleeding the brake should not be necessary when installing the wheel.*

7. Install the axle spacer, washer and axle nut on the axle to prevent their loss when servicing the wheel or brake disc.

Installation (IT200S)

1. Check the fork sliders, axle bearing surfaces to make sure they are free from burrs or nicks. This condition can be repaired with fine grit sand paper or careful work with hand files.
2. Clean the axle in solvent and dry thoroughly. Make sure all axle contact surfaces are clean and free of road dirt and old grease before installation. If these surfaces are not cleaned, the axle may be difficult to remove later on.
3. Install the left-hand axle spacer into the seal (**Figure 33**).
4. Align the wheel through the front forks. Then align the 3 projections in the speedometer cable housing with the 3 slots in the wheel hub (**Figure 30**) and install the housing.
5. Carefully insert the disc between the brake pads when installing the wheel. Make sure the torque stopper on the front fork aligns with the slot in the speedometer housing.

NOTE
When tightening the axle holder nuts in Step 6, first tighten the top and then the bottom nuts.

6. Install the axle from the right-hand side through the wheel hub. Tighten the axle holder nuts and the axle to the specifications in **Table 24**.

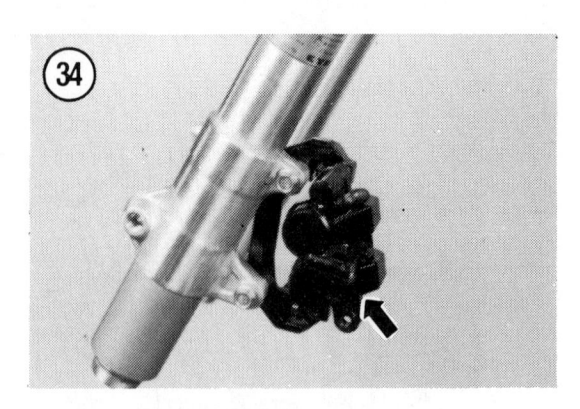

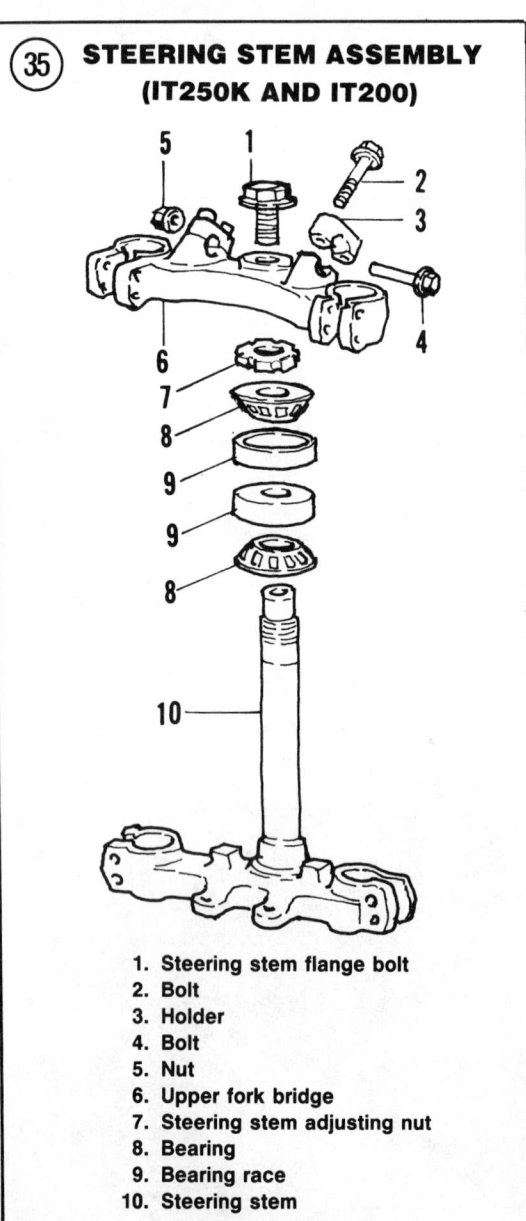

STEERING STEM ASSEMBLY (IT250K AND IT200)

1. Steering stem flange bolt
2. Bolt
3. Holder
4. Bolt
5. Nut
6. Upper fork bridge
7. Steering stem adjusting nut
8. Bearing
9. Bearing race
10. Steering stem

1981 AND LATER INFORMATION

36

STEERING STEM ASSEMBLY (IT250K)

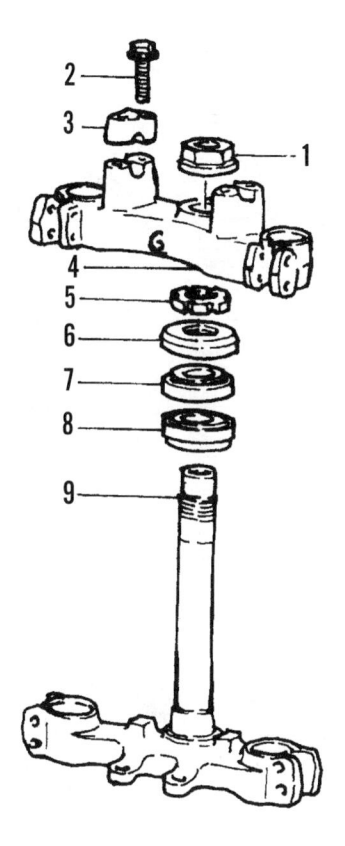

1. Steering stem flange bolt
2. Bolt
3. Holder
4. Upper fork bridge
5. Steering stem adjusting nut
6. Cover
7. Bearing
8. Bearing
9. Steering stem

7. After the wheel is completely installed, rotate the front wheel and apply the brake. Do this a couple of times to make sure the front wheel and brake are operating correctly.

STEERING HEAD

Removal/Installation (IT250, IT465 and IT490)

The procedures used to remove the steering head on 1981 and later IT250, IT465 and IT490 models are the same as for 1980 models, except for the following:

a. IT250, IT465 and IT490 models now use either ball bearing or tapered roller bearings. See **Figures 35-38**.
b. IT465 and IT490 models now use rubber damper design handlebar holders. See **Figure 37** and **Figure 38**. On these models, periodically remove the handlebar (see Chapter Eight of the main book), the handlebar holder and the damper assembly. Examine parts for wear or damage and replace as required. Install new cotter pins during installation.

Removal/Installation (IT200)

Figure 36 shows the steering stem assembly used on all IT200 models. Refer to Chapter Eight of the main book during steering stem service.

FRONT FORK

The front fork on 1981 and later IT250, IT465 and IT490 models and 1982-1983 IT175 models have been redesigned. See **Figure 39** and **40**. **Figure 41** shows the front fork used on all IT200 models.

On these models, front fork service requires a number of special tools and a press for disassembly. Service to these forks is limited to front fork oil replacement (see Chapter Three). For the safe operation of the fork, all service should be referred to a Yamaha dealer.

Spring Length

Refer to **Table 25** for new front fork spring lengths.

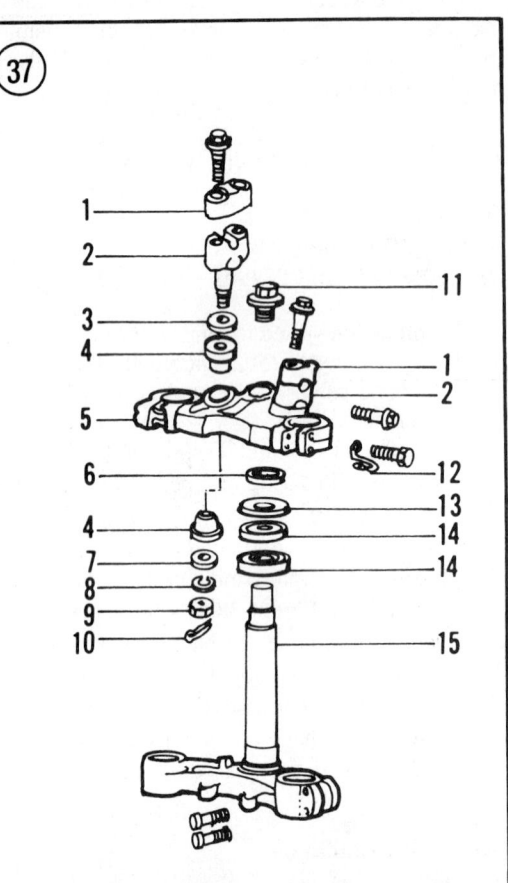

STEERING STEM ASSEMBLY (IT465H AND J)

1. Upper handlebar holder
2. Lower handlebar holder
3. Washer
4. Damper holder
5. Upper fork bridge
6. Steering stem adjusting nut
7. Washer
8. Lockwasher
9. Nut
10. Cotter pin
11. Steering stem flange bolt
12. Cable holder/clip
13. Upper bearing race cover
14. Upper and lower roller bearing assembly
15. Steering stem

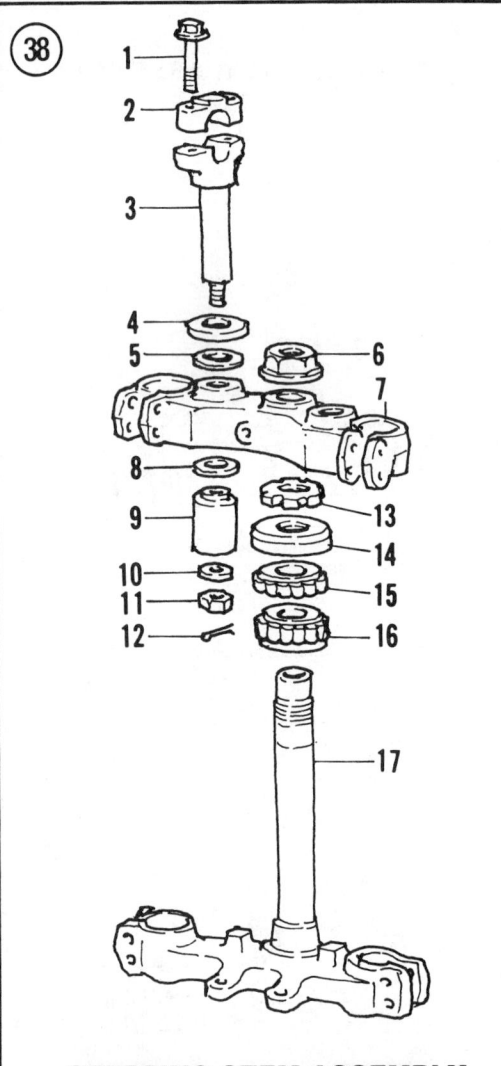

STEERING STEM ASSEMBLY (IT490K)

1. Bolt
2. Holder
3. Holder bracket
4. Washer
5. Washer
6. Steering stem flange nuts
7. Upper fork bridge
8. Washer
9. Bushing
10. Washer
11. Nut
12. Cotter pin
13. Steering stem adjusting nut
14. Washer
15. Bearing
16. Bearing
17. Steering stem

1981 AND LATER INFORMATION

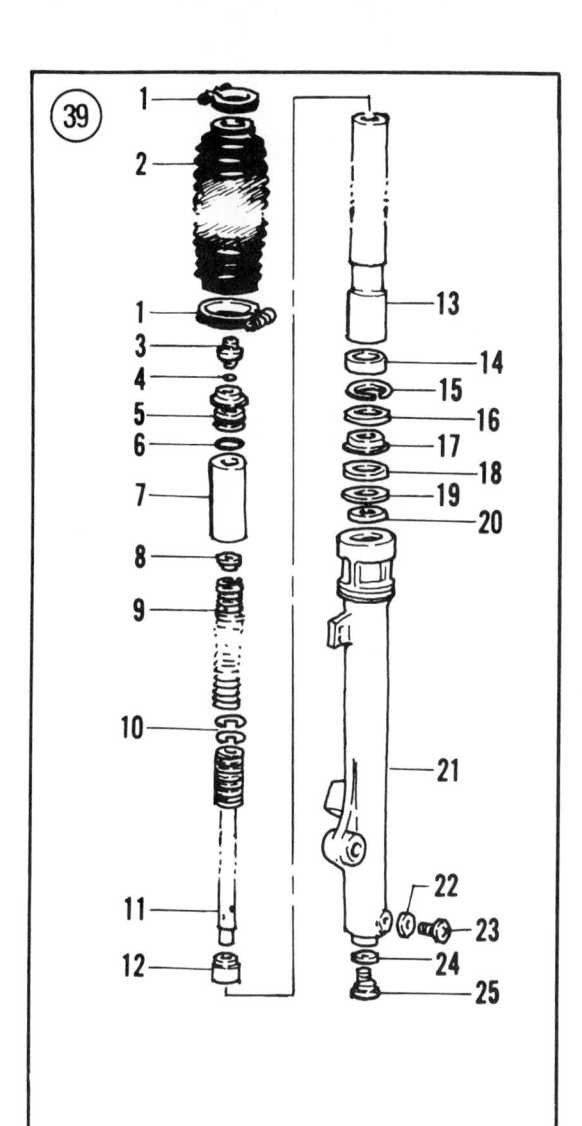

FRONT FORK (IT465H; IT250H AND J; IT200, IT175J AND K)

1. Clamp
2. Boot
3. Air valve
4. O-ring
5. Fork cap
6. O-ring
7. Spacer
8. Spring seat
9. Spring
10. Piston ring
11. Damper rod
12. Oil lock
13. Inner fork tube
14. Piston (IT175 models only)
15. Snap ring
16. Dust cover
17. Dust seal
18. Oil seal
19. Washer
20. Metal slide
21. Lower fork tube
22. Washer
23. Drain screw
24. Washer
25. Bolt

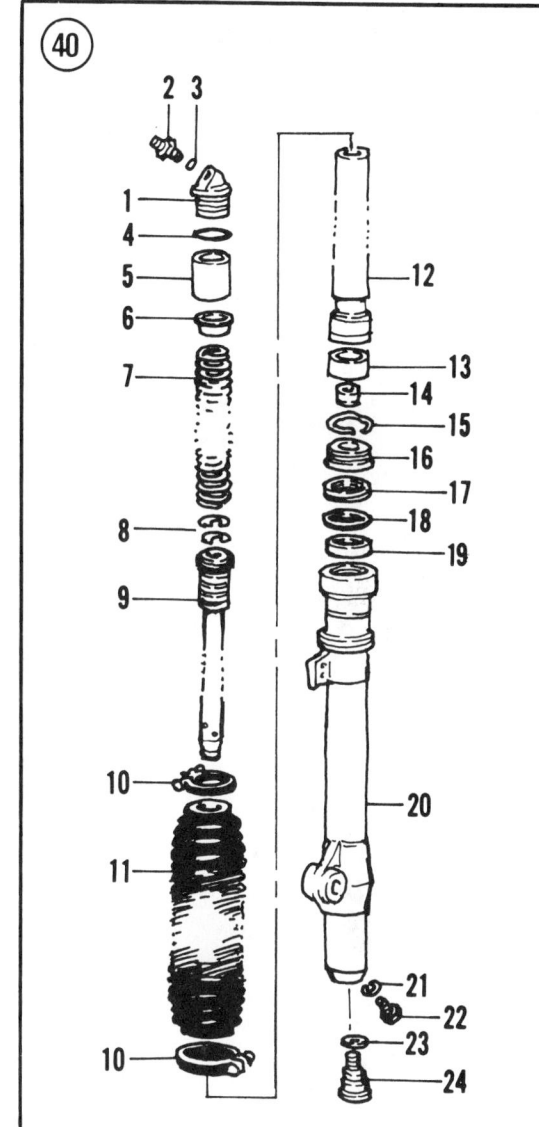

FRONT FORK (IT490K AND L; IT250K)

1. Fork cap
2. Air valve
3. O-ring
4. O-ring
5. Spacer
6. Spring seat
7. Fork spring
8. Piston rings
9. Damper rod
10. Clamp
11. Boot
12. Inner fork tube
13. Metal bushing
14. Oil lock
15. Clip
16. Dust seal
17. Oil seal
18. Washer
19. Metal slide
20. Outer fork tube
21. Washer
22. Drain screw
23. Washer
24. Bolt

SUPPLEMENT

④ FRONT FORK (IT200)

1. Air valve
2. O-ring
3. Fork cap
4. O-ring
5. Spring seat
6. Spacer
7. Screw
8. Clamp
9. Boot
10. Spring seat
11. Spring
12. Piston rings
13. Spring
14. Damper rod
15. Oil lock
16. Inner fork tube
17. Piston (IT200L and N only)
18. Dust seal
19. Snap ring
20. Oil seal
21. Washer
22. Metal slide
23. Lower fork tube
24. Washer
25. Drain screw
26. Washer
27A. Holding bolt and compression damping adjuster (IT200L and N)
27B. Holding bolt (IT200S)
28. Rubber cap (IT200L and N)

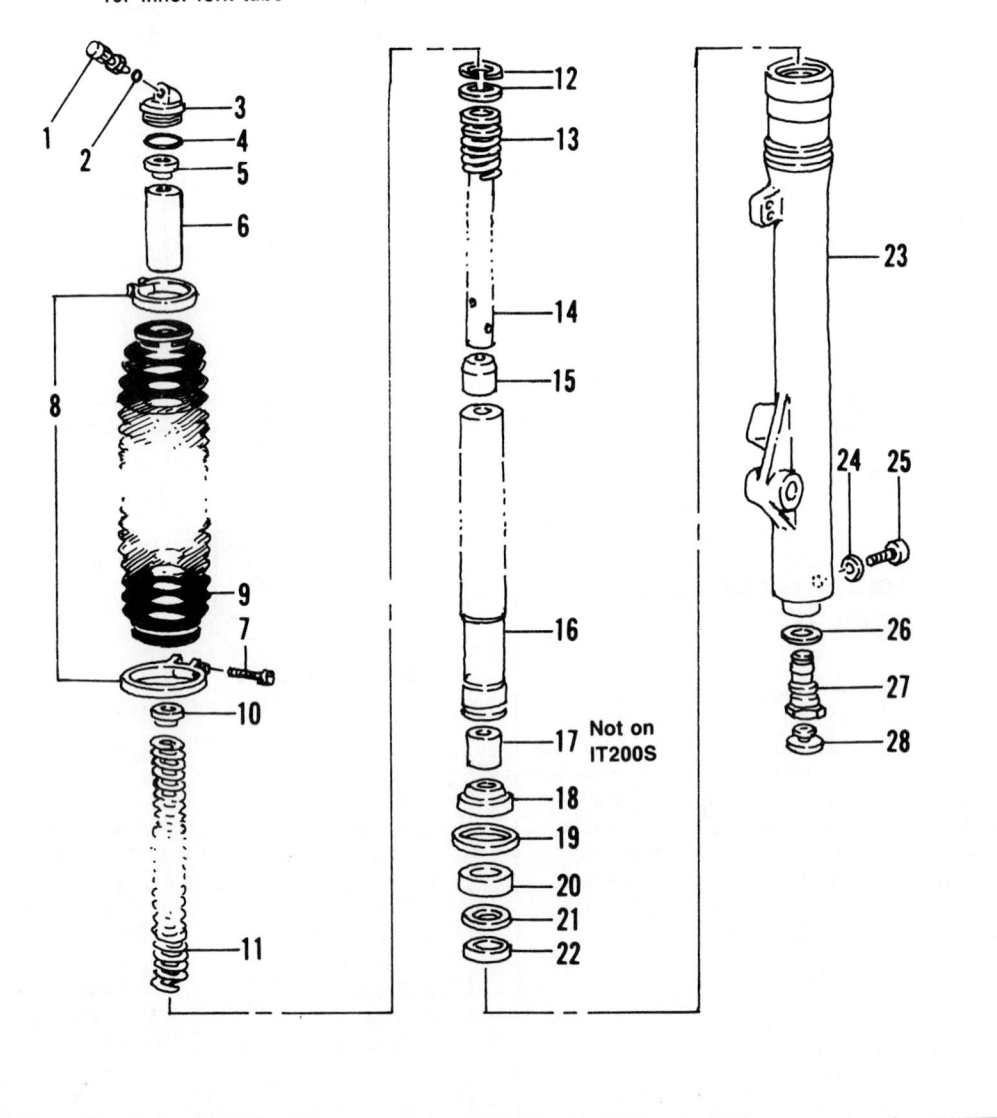

1981 AND LATER INFORMATION

damping adjustments are made by turning the adjuster/fork tube holding bolt at the bottom of the fork tube. See **Figure 42**. Adjust as follows.

1. Remove the rubber cap at the bottom fo the fork tube.

2. To make compression damping stiffer, turn the adjuster bolt *counterclockwise* as seen from the front of the fork tube (**Figure 42**). For softer damping turn the adjuster *clockwise*.

WARNING
Do not turn the adjuster more than the 8 turns (clicks) from the seated position. The adjustment positions are 0 (minimum) to 8 (maximum). The standard setting is 4 clicks. The adjuster bolt also serves as the fork tube holding bolt.

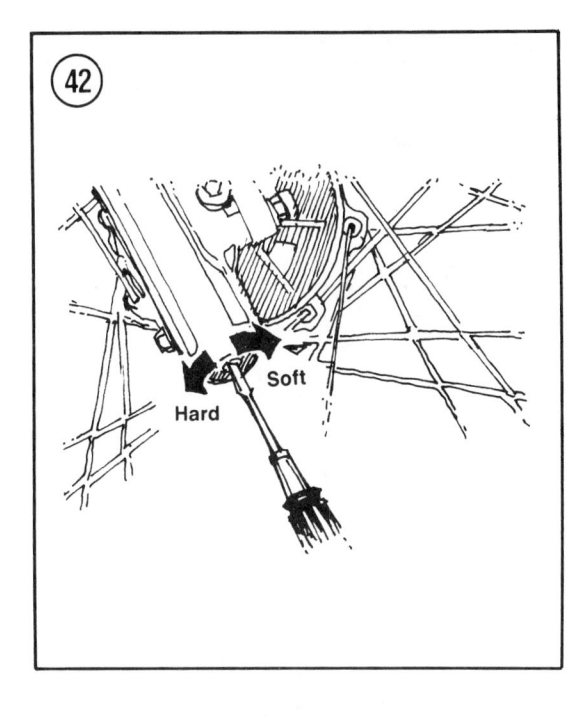

FRONT FORK ADJUSTMENT (IT200)

Compression Damping Adjustment (IT200L and N)

Compression damping adjustments are provided for IT200L and N models. Compression

WARNING
Do not use a torque of more than 10 N•m (7.2 ft.-lb.) when turn the ompression damping adjuster.

3. Install the lower fork tube rubber cap to prevent dirt and other debris from obstructing the adjuster bolt threads.

Table 24 FRONT SUSPENSION TORQUE SPECIFICATIONS

	ft.-lb.	N•m
Front axle nut		
IT175J, K	43	60
IT200	43	60
Front axle pinch bolt		
IT175J, K	7	10
IT200	7	10
IT250J, K	7	10
IT465J	7	10
IT490K, L	7	10
Steering stem bolt		
IT175J, K	36	50
IT200	61	85
IT250K	36	50
IT490K	36	50
Steering nut (IT200)	7	10
Handlebar clamps (IT200)	17	23
Front fork pinch bolts		
IT200	17	23

Table 25 FRONT FORK SPRING FREE LENGTH

Model	in.	mm
IT125H	21.3	541.5
IT175J, K	21.0	533.5
IT200	18.1	459.5
IT250H	23.7	603
IT250J	24.2	615
IT250K	20.8	529
IT465H	23.7	603
IT465J	24.2	615
IT490K, L	20.8	529

CHAPTER NINE

REAR SUSPENSION

Rear suspension torque specifications for 1981 and later models that differ from 1980 models are listed in **Table 26**. Complete torque specifications for the IT200 are listed in **Table 27**. **Table 28** lists new monoshock installed spring lengths for 1981 and later models.

SWING ARM

Removal/Installation

1981-1982 IT250 and IT465

The swing arm service procedures described in Chapter Nine of the main book can be used on these 1981-1982 models. However, a new style chain tensioner assembly is used. See **Figure 43** for an exploded view of the swing arm and chain tensioner assembly.

IT250K, IT490K and L models

Refer to **Figure 44** and **Figure 45** during removal and installation of the swing arm/relay arm assembly. After reassembly, lubricate all grease points with a lithium base grease. Tighten all fasteners to specifications in **Table 26**.

IT175J and K models

Refer to **Figure 46** and **Figure 47** during removal and installation of the swing arm/relay assembly. After reassembly, lubricate all grease points with a lithium base grease. Tighten all fasteners to specifications in **Table 26**.

IT200

Refer to **Figure 48** during removal and installation of the swing arm/relay assembly. After reassembly, lubricate all grease points with a lithium base grease. Tighten all fasteners to specifications in **Table 27**.

REAR SUSPENSION (DECARBON MONOCROSS SYSTEM)

This section provides tuning information for 1981 and later IT models that differ from 1980 models. In addition, consult your Yamaha dealer on the availability of hard and soft springs for your particular model. For some models, Yamaha offers different springs to aid in suspension tuning. When choosing a hard or soft spring, consider the following:

a. Light springs have a lower spring rate; the spring is softer and will rebound more slowly.

b. Heavy springs have a higher spring rate; the spring is stiffer and will rebound more quickly.

1981 AND LATER INFORMATION

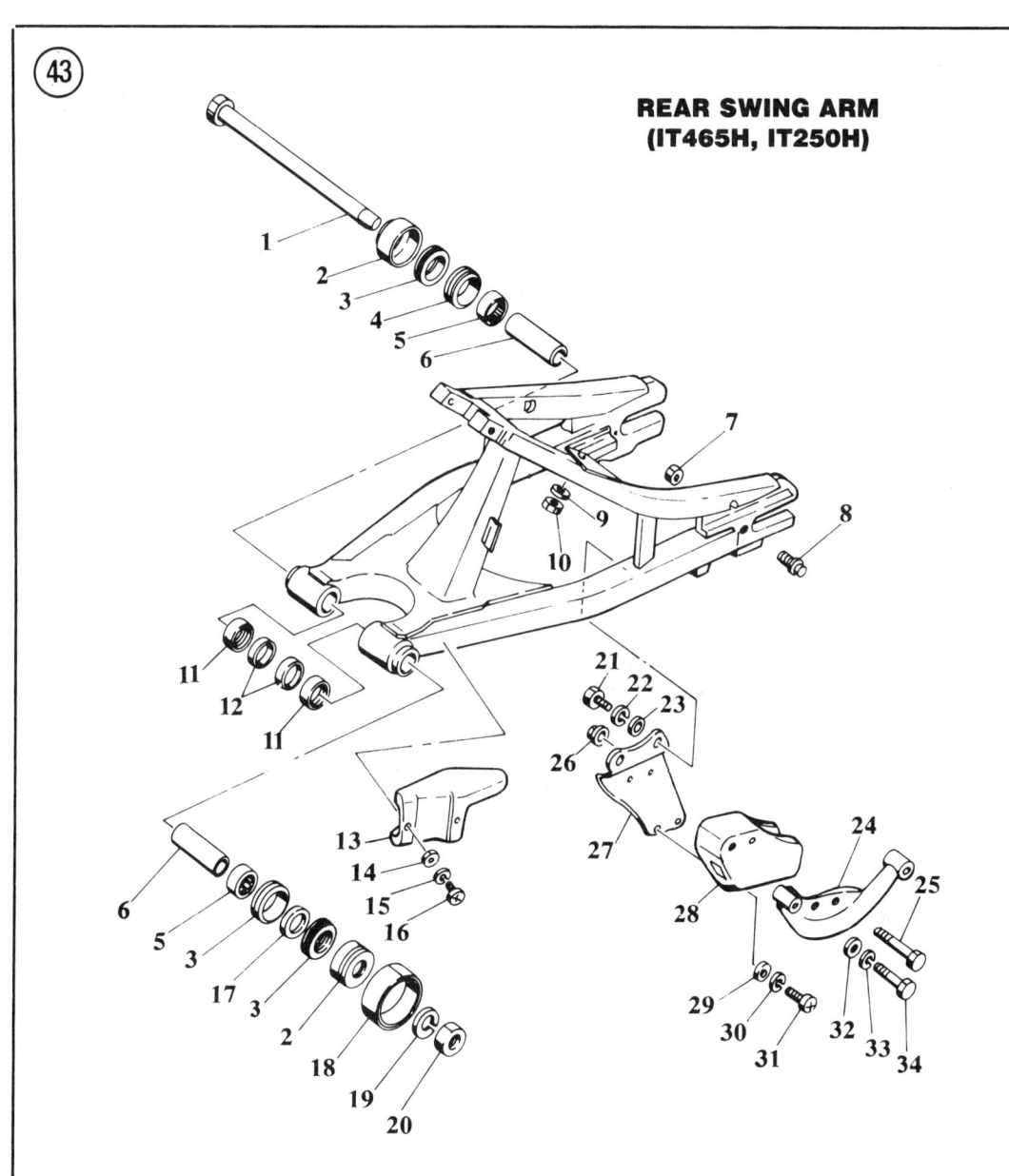

43

REAR SWING ARM (IT465H, IT250H)

1. Pivot shaft
2. Thrust cover
3. Bearing
4. Oil seal
5. Bearing
6. Bushing
7. Nut
8. Bolt
9. Washer
10. Nut
11. Bushing
12. Seal
13. Chain
14. Washer
15. Washer
16. Screw
17. Shim
18. Seal
19. Washer
20. Nut
21. Bolt
22. Washer
23. Washer
24. Chain guard
25. Bolt
26. Nut
27. Tensioner arm
28. Chain support
29. Washer
30. Washer
31. Screw
32. Washer
33. Washer
34. Bolt

SUPPLEMENT

④ REAR SWING ARM (IT490K AND L; IT250K)

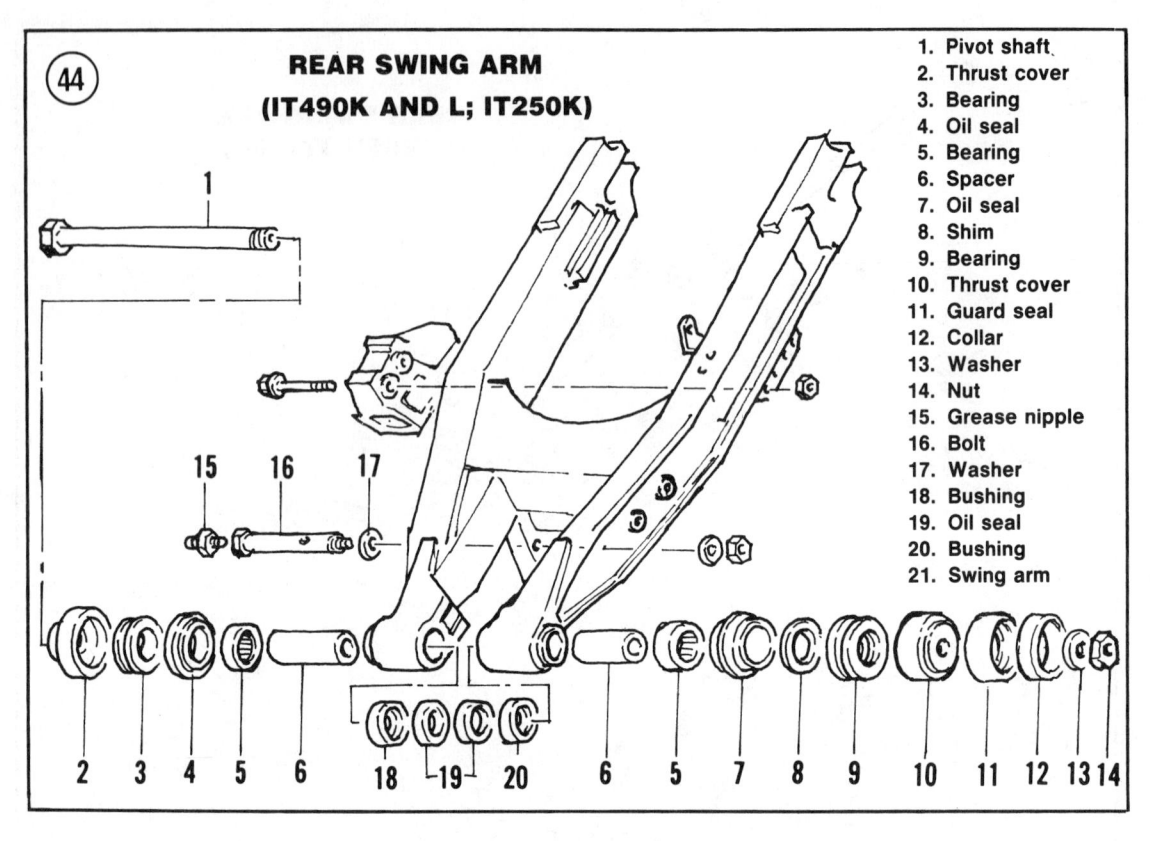

1. Pivot shaft
2. Thrust cover
3. Bearing
4. Oil seal
5. Bearing
6. Spacer
7. Oil seal
8. Shim
9. Bearing
10. Thrust cover
11. Guard seal
12. Collar
13. Washer
14. Nut
15. Grease nipple
16. Bolt
17. Washer
18. Bushing
19. Oil seal
20. Bushing
21. Swing arm

㊺ RELAY ARM (IT490K AND L; IT250K)

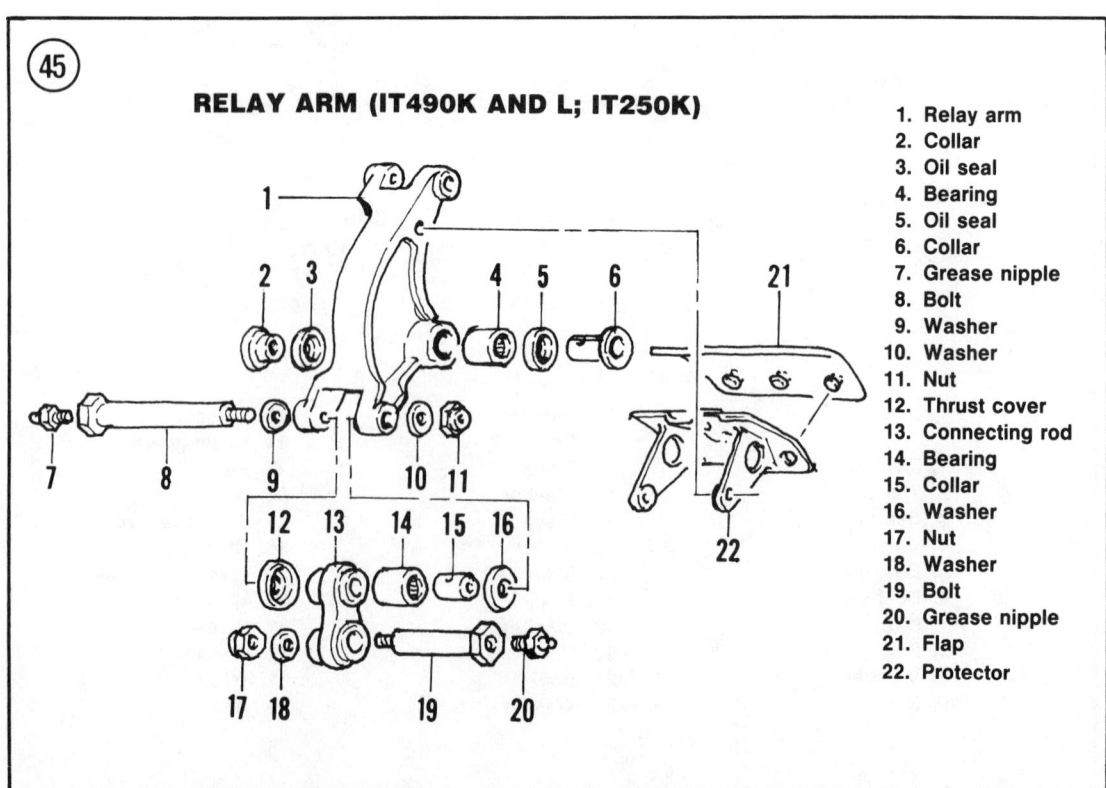

1. Relay arm
2. Collar
3. Oil seal
4. Bearing
5. Oil seal
6. Collar
7. Grease nipple
8. Bolt
9. Washer
10. Washer
11. Nut
12. Thrust cover
13. Connecting rod
14. Bearing
15. Collar
16. Washer
17. Nut
18. Washer
19. Bolt
20. Grease nipple
21. Flap
22. Protector

1981 AND LATER INFORMATION 313

⑯

**SWING ARM
REMOVAL/INSTALLATION
(IT175J AND K)**

1. Pivot shaft
2. Thrust cover
3. Washer
4. Oil seal
5. Collar
6. Guard seal
7. Bearing
8. Bushing
9. Bushing
10. Oil seal
11. Oil seal
12. Washer
13. Shim
14. Thrust cover
15. Washer
16. Nut
17. Chain guard
18. Guard
19. Swing arm
20. Chain guard

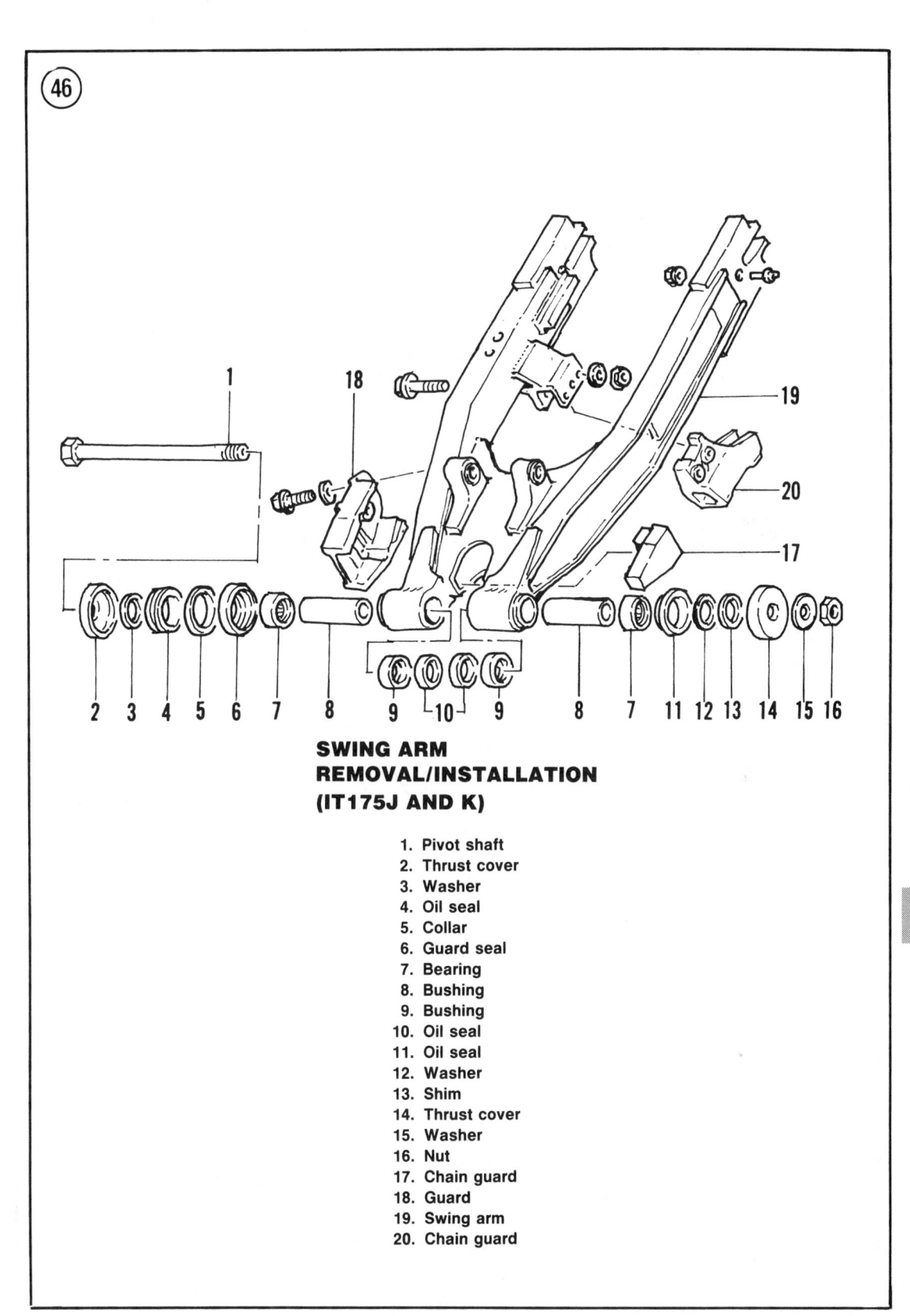

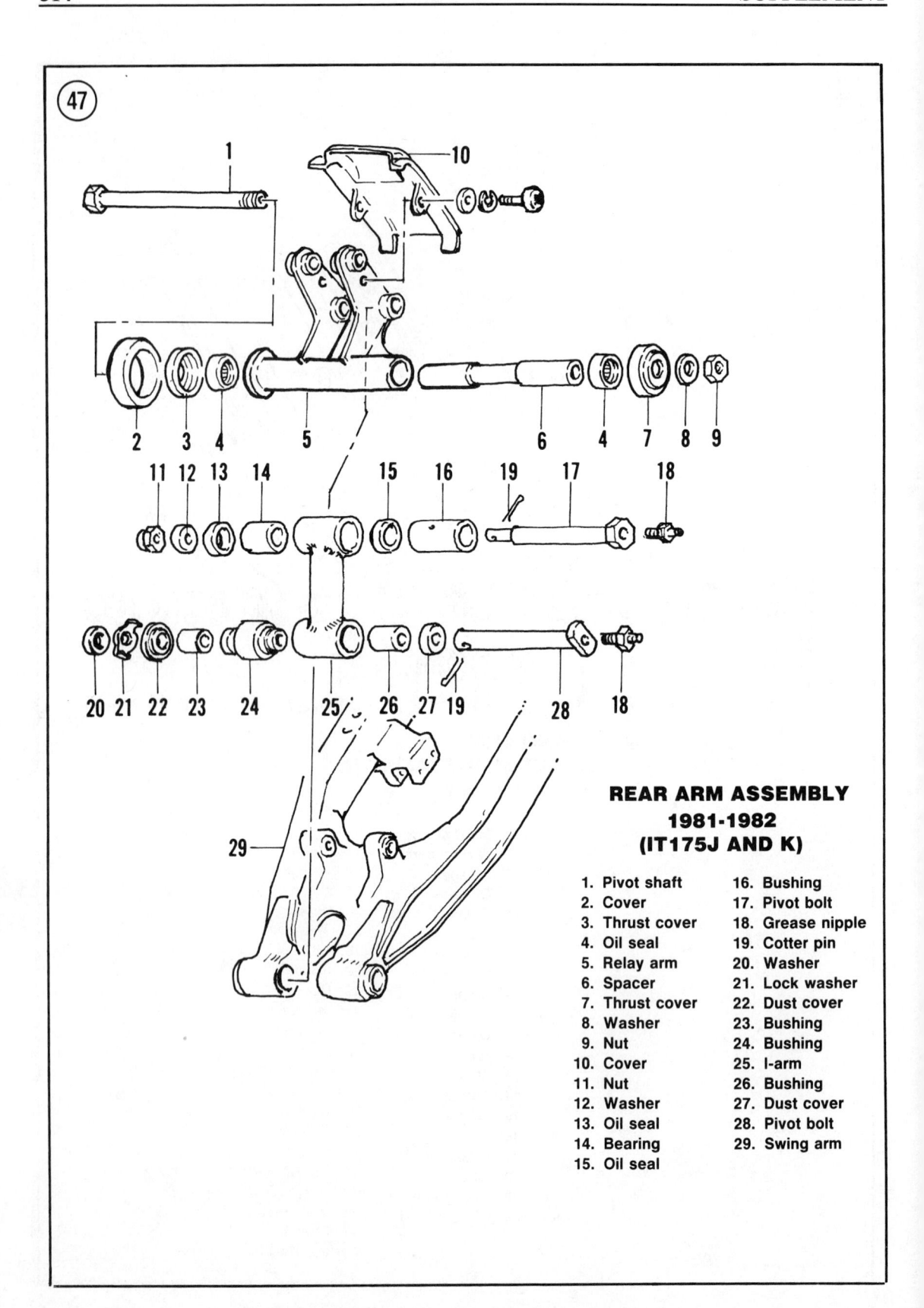

SUPPLEMENT

**REAR ARM ASSEMBLY
1981-1982
(IT175J AND K)**

1. Pivot shaft
2. Cover
3. Thrust cover
4. Oil seal
5. Relay arm
6. Spacer
7. Thrust cover
8. Washer
9. Nut
10. Cover
11. Nut
12. Washer
13. Oil seal
14. Bearing
15. Oil seal
16. Bushing
17. Pivot bolt
18. Grease nipple
19. Cotter pin
20. Washer
21. Lock washer
22. Dust cover
23. Bushing
24. Bushing
25. I-arm
26. Bushing
27. Dust cover
28. Pivot bolt
29. Swing arm

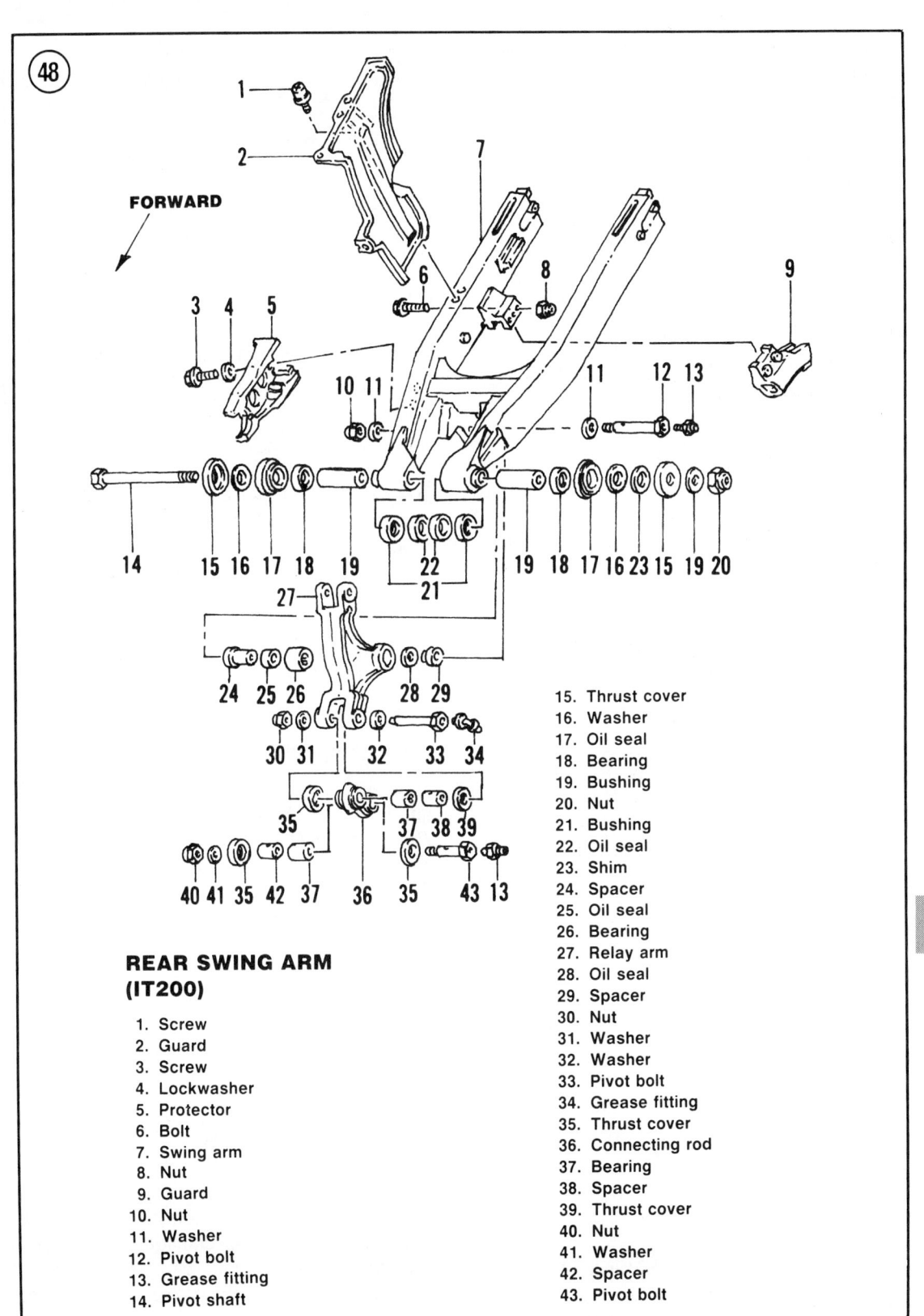

1981 AND LATER INFORMATION 315

REAR SWING ARM (IT200)

1. Screw
2. Guard
3. Screw
4. Lockwasher
5. Protector
6. Bolt
7. Swing arm
8. Nut
9. Guard
10. Nut
11. Washer
12. Pivot bolt
13. Grease fitting
14. Pivot shaft
15. Thrust cover
16. Washer
17. Oil seal
18. Bearing
19. Bushing
20. Nut
21. Bushing
22. Oil seal
23. Shim
24. Spacer
25. Oil seal
26. Bearing
27. Relay arm
28. Oil seal
29. Spacer
30. Nut
31. Washer
32. Washer
33. Pivot bolt
34. Grease fitting
35. Thrust cover
36. Connecting rod
37. Bearing
38. Spacer
39. Thrust cover
40. Nut
41. Washer
42. Spacer
43. Pivot bolt

Damping Adjustment

IT175H

Procedures used to adjust the damping on this model are the same as for 1980 models. On the 1981 IT175H, there are a total of 30 damping selections—20 on the stiffer side and 10 on the softer side. The damping adjuster on the end of the monoshock is marked with punch marks to indicate soft and standard positions. See **Figure 49**.

> *WARNING*
> *Do not turn the adjuster when it becomes either easy or hard to turn.*

IT175J and K and IT200

The following adjustment should be made 2 notches at a time; test ride the bike after each adjustment. Turn the adjuster until it clicks into position. There are a total of 35 click positions on the IT175J and 25 click positions on the IT175K and IT200. The standard setting on IT175 models is 15 clicks out from the fully clockwise positon. On IT200 models it is 8 clicks out from the fully clockwise position.

1. Adjustment is performed by turning the adjusting ring at the shock's rear mount bracket to any of the 35 (IT175J) or 25 (IT175K and IT200) click positions. It is not necessary to remove the shock to perform this adjustment.
2. When making adjustments, turn the adjusting ring all the way clockwise. Then turn the ring counterclockwise to the desired setting.
3. During adjustment, note the following:
   a. Shock rebound is quicker when the adjusting ring is turned counterclockwise.
   b. Shock rebound is slower when the adjusting ring is turned clockwise.

1981 and later IT250, IT465 and IT490

Damping adjustments on these models can be made with the *Damping Adjustment, Models With Remote Nitrogen Gas Tank* procedure in Chapter Nine of the main book. On 1981 and 1982 models, there are 24 possible damping selections—12 on the stiffer side and 10 on the softer side. On 1983 models, there are 25 possible damping selections—7 on the stiffer side and 18 on the softer side. The damping adjuster on the end of the monoshock is marked with punch marks to indicate soft and standard positions. See **Figure 49**.

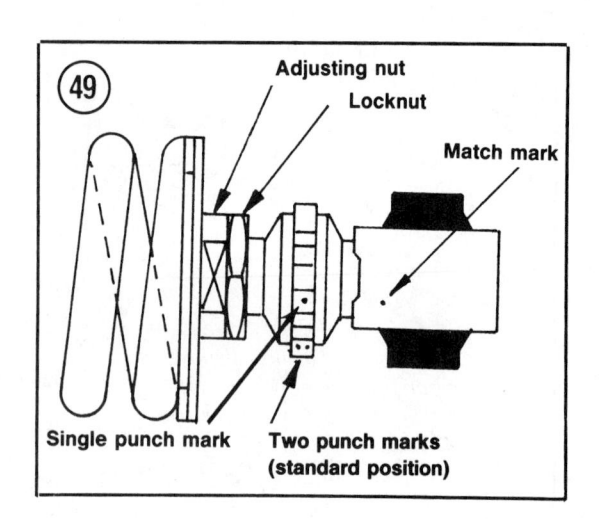

Spring Pre-load

Spring pre-load adjustments on all 1981 and later models can be made with the *Spring Pre-load—1977 and Later Models With Remote Nitrogen Gas Tank* procedures in Chapter Nine of the main book. When making this adjustment, refer to **Table 28** for new spring length specifications.

Nitrogen Gas Pressure Adjustment

The nitrogen pressure on all 1982 and later models can now be adjusted; raising the pressure increases shock stiffness while decreasing the pressure softens the shock. This adjustment is normally performed as a fine-tuning adjustment only. Because this adjustment requires special equipment, only a qualified Yamaha dealer can perform it. Do *not* attempt to adjust the nitrogen gas pressure yourself.

1981 AND LATER INFORMATION

Monoshock Disassembly/Inspection/Assembly

WARNING
The monoshock unit contains highly compressed nitrogen gas. Do not tamper with or attempt to open the damper/cylinder assembly. Do not place it near an open flame or other extreme heat. Do not weld on the frame near it. Do not dispose of the damper subassembly yourself. Take it to a Yamaha dealer where it can be deactivated and disposed of properly. Never attempt to remove the plug or hose on the tank.

Procedures used to service the monoshock are the same as for 1980 and earlier models. Some monoshock units have changed. See **Figure 50** or **Figure 51**. **Figure 52** shows the monoshock unit for the IT200. Use the *Monoshock–1977 and Later (Except IT125) Disassembly/Inspection and Assembly* procedure in Chapter Nine of the main book while referring to **Figure 50** through **Figure 52** to service these monoshock units.

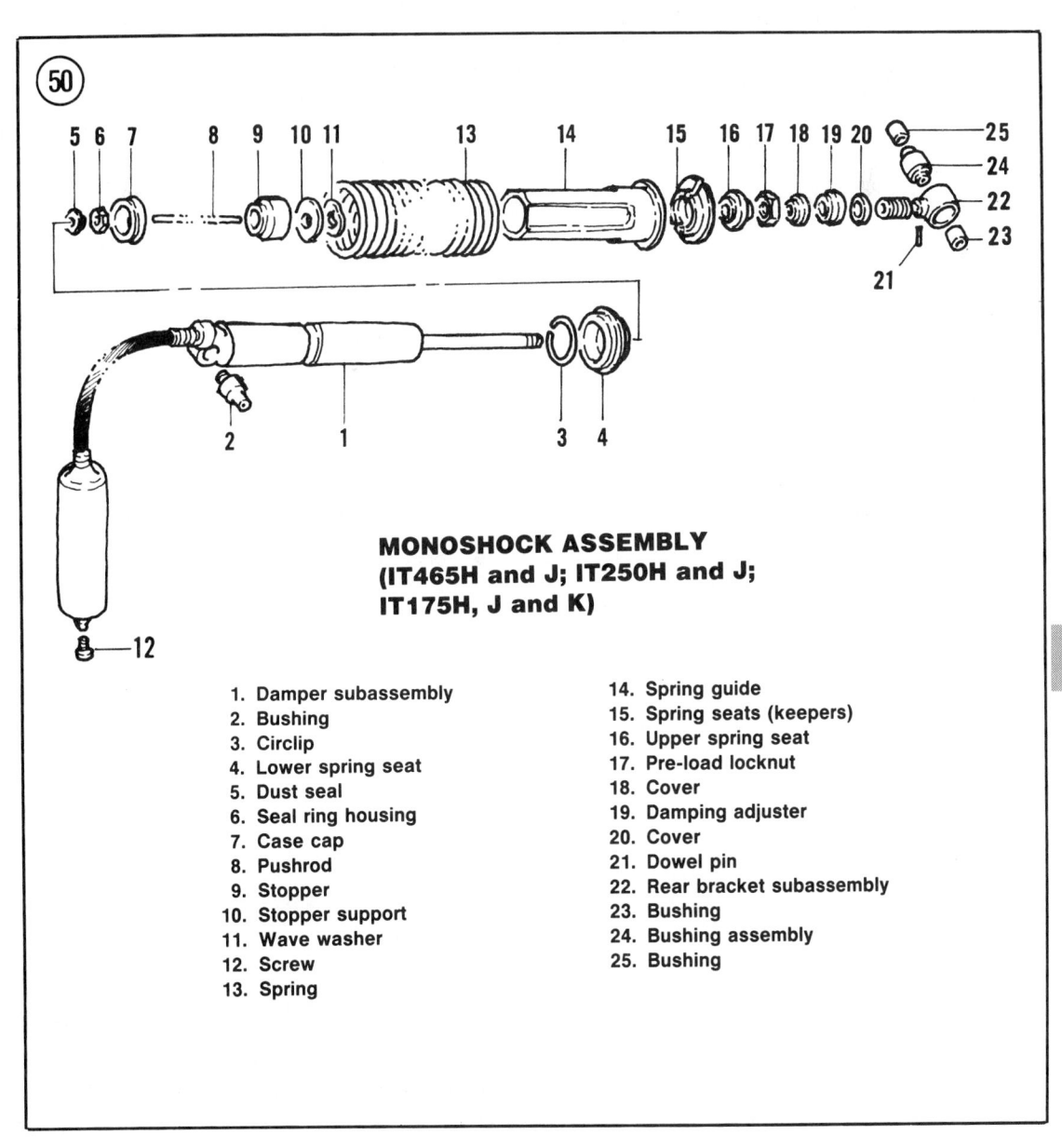

**MONOSHOCK ASSEMBLY
(IT465H and J; IT250H and J;
IT175H, J and K)**

1. Damper subassembly
2. Bushing
3. Circlip
4. Lower spring seat
5. Dust seal
6. Seal ring housing
7. Case cap
8. Pushrod
9. Stopper
10. Stopper support
11. Wave washer
12. Screw
13. Spring
14. Spring guide
15. Spring seats (keepers)
16. Upper spring seat
17. Pre-load locknut
18. Cover
19. Damping adjuster
20. Cover
21. Dowel pin
22. Rear bracket subassembly
23. Bushing
24. Bushing assembly
25. Bushing

SUPPLEMENT

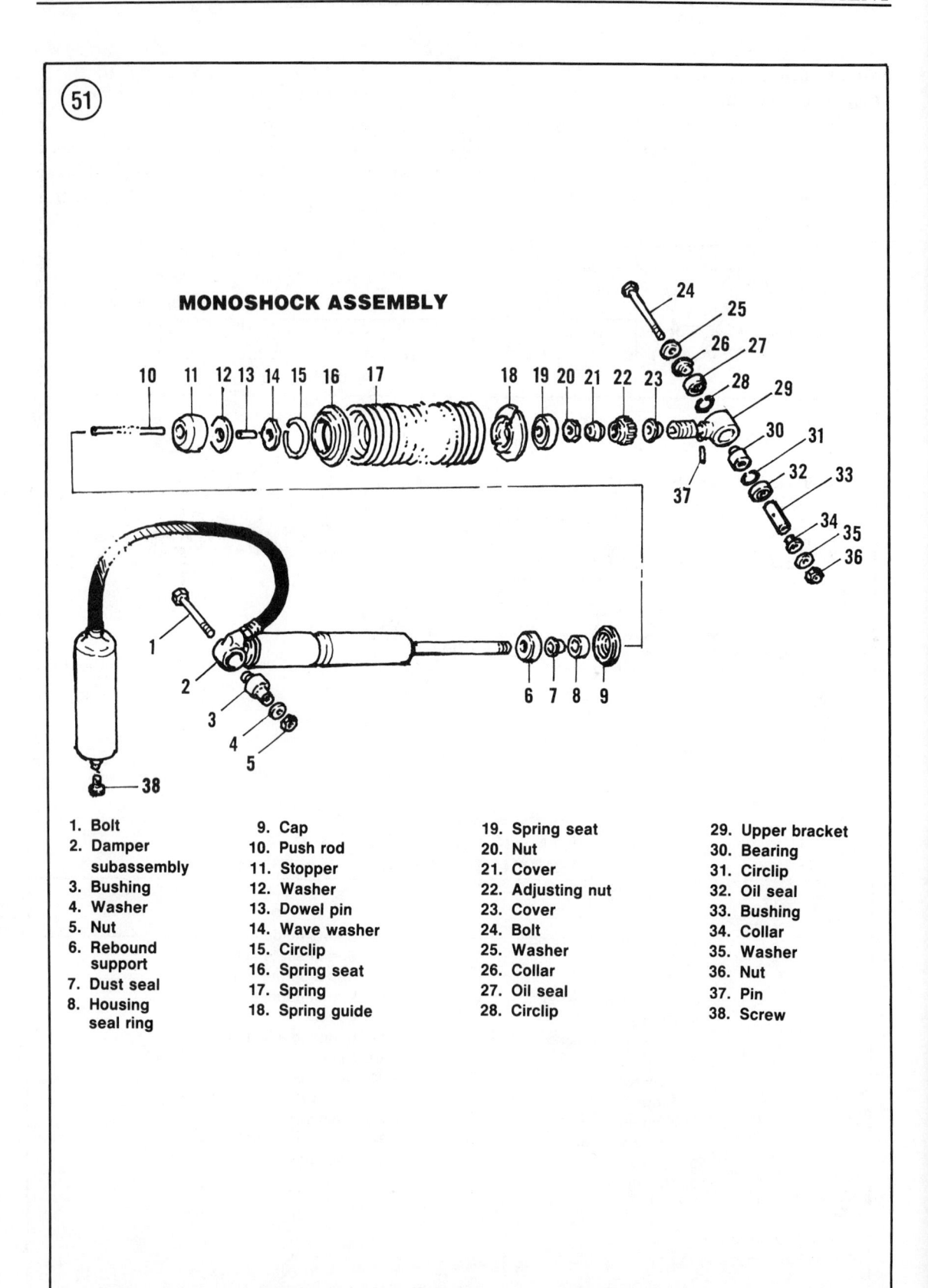

MONOSHOCK ASSEMBLY

1. Bolt
2. Damper subassembly
3. Bushing
4. Washer
5. Nut
6. Rebound support
7. Dust seal
8. Housing seal ring
9. Cap
10. Push rod
11. Stopper
12. Washer
13. Dowel pin
14. Wave washer
15. Circlip
16. Spring seat
17. Spring
18. Spring guide
19. Spring seat
20. Nut
21. Cover
22. Adjusting nut
23. Cover
24. Bolt
25. Washer
26. Collar
27. Oil seal
28. Circlip
29. Upper bracket
30. Bearing
31. Circlip
32. Oil seal
33. Bushing
34. Collar
35. Washer
36. Nut
37. Pin
38. Screw

1981 AND LATER INFORMATION

MONOSHOCK ASSEMBLY (IT200)

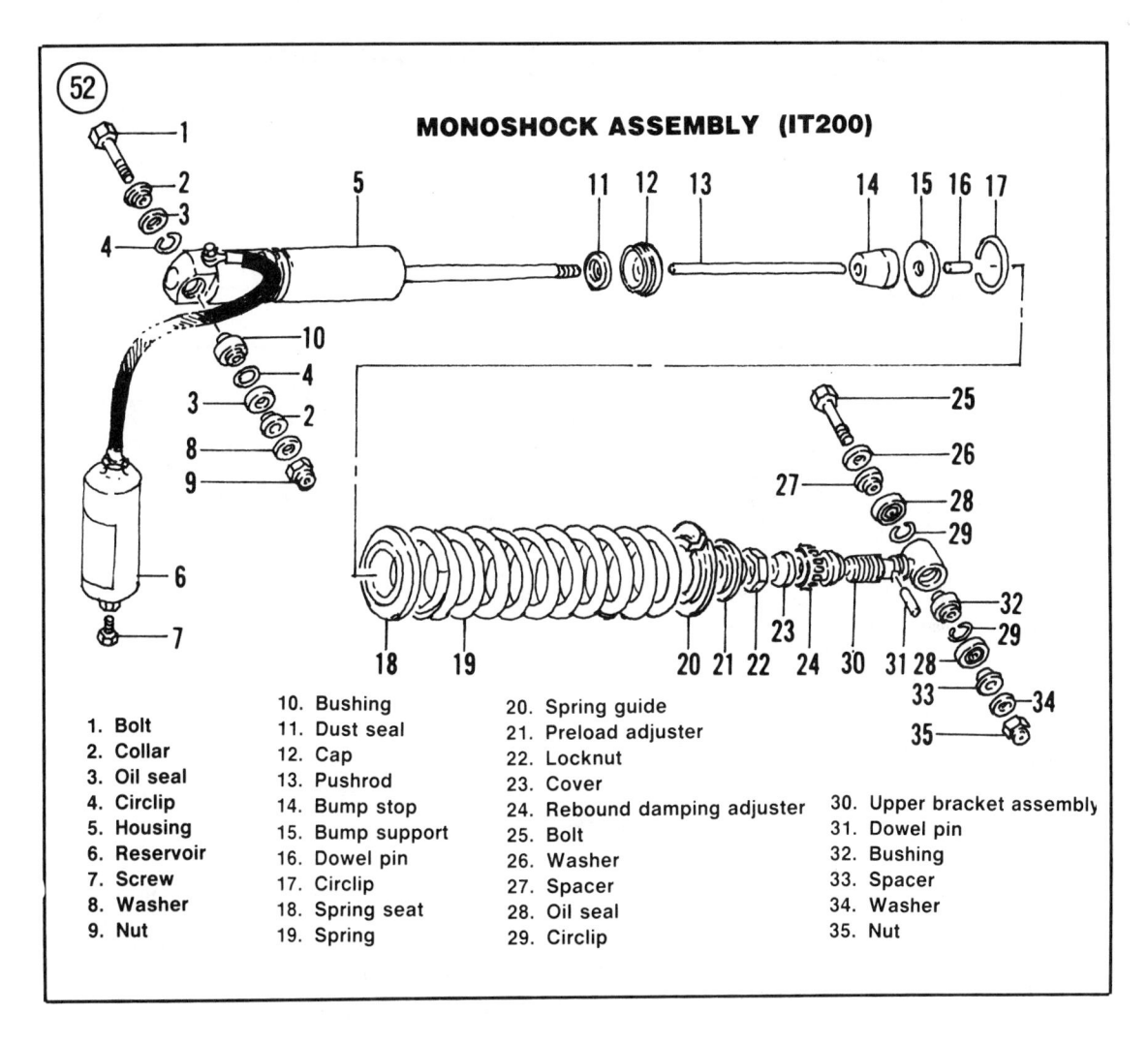

1. Bolt
2. Collar
3. Oil seal
4. Circlip
5. Housing
6. Reservoir
7. Screw
8. Washer
9. Nut
10. Bushing
11. Dust seal
12. Cap
13. Pushrod
14. Bump stop
15. Bump support
16. Dowel pin
17. Circlip
18. Spring seat
19. Spring
20. Spring guide
21. Preload adjuster
22. Locknut
23. Cover
24. Rebound damping adjuster
25. Bolt
26. Washer
27. Spacer
28. Oil seal
29. Circlip
30. Upper bracket assembly
31. Dowel pin
32. Bushing
33. Spacer
34. Washer
35. Nut

Table 26 REAR SUSPENSION TORQUE SPECIFICATIONS

(IT175, IT250, IT465 AND IT490)	ft.-lb.	N•m
Rear axle nut		
IT175H, J, K	61	85
IT250H, J, K	72	100
IT465H, J, K	72	100
IT490K, L	72	100
Rear shock/Relay arm		
IT175J, K		
Frame @ shock	22	30
Relay arm @ shock	22	30
Relay arm @ frame	60	85
Relay arm @ l arm	42	60
IT250K; IT490K, L		
At swing arm	43	60
At rear shock	32	45
At connecting rod	32	45
Frame to connecting rod	43	60

Table 27 REAR SUSPENSION TORQUE SPECIFICATIONS (IT200)

	ft.-lb.	N·m
Rear axle nut	61	86
Sprocket	22	30
Rear shock	22	30
Pivot shaft	61	85
Relay arm @ swing arm	43	60
Relay arm @ connecting rod	22	30
Frame @ connecting rod	43	60

Table 28 MONOSHOCK SPRING LENGTH—INSTALLED

Model	Standard in. (mm)	Maximum in. (mm)	Minimum in. (mm)
IT175J, K	12.32 (313)	12.52 (318)	11.73 (298)
1T200	10.24 (260)	10.59 (269)	9.61 (244)
IT250H, J	13.66 (347)	13.66 (347)	13.07 (332)
IT250K	11.14 (283)	11.61 (295)	10.43 (265)
IT465H, J	13.66 (347)	13.66 (347)	13.07 (332)
IT490K, L	11.14 (283)	11.61 (295)	10.43 (265)

CHAPTER TEN

BRAKES

Table 29 lists new brake specificatons for 1981 and later IT250, IT465 and IT490 models. Table 30 lists brake specifications for IT200L and N models. Table 31 and Table 32 list brake specifications and tightening torques for the IT200S.

FRONT DRUM BRAKE

The IT250K, IT465H and J and IT490K and L models are equipped with a double leading shoe brake unit. See **Figure 53**.

Disassembly/Adjustment

During disassembly of the front brake, punch alignment marks on both the cam lever and the shaft as shown in **Figure 54**. This will help align the brake shoes during installation.

When assembling the brake shoes, the cam levers should be installed so that when the brake is applied, the cams push the brake shoes simultaneously (**Figure 55**). To adjust, loosen the brake adjuster locknuts and turn the adjuster as required. See **Figure 56**.

FRONT DISC BRAKE (IT200S)

All 1986 IT200S models are equipped with a front disc brake. The front disc brake is actuated by hydraulic fluid and controlled by a hand lever on the master cylinder. As the brake pads wear, the brake fluid level drops in the reservoir and automatically adjusts for wear.

When working on hydraulic brake systems, it is necessary that the work area and all tools be absolutely clean. Any tiny particles of foreign matter and grit in the caliper assembly or master cylinder can damage the components.

Specifications for the front disc brake are listed in **Table 31** and **Table 32**.

Consider the following when servicing the front disc brake.
1. Use only DOT 3 brake fluid.
2. Do not allow disc brake fluid to contact any plastic parts or painted surfaces or damage will result.

1981 AND LATER INFORMATION

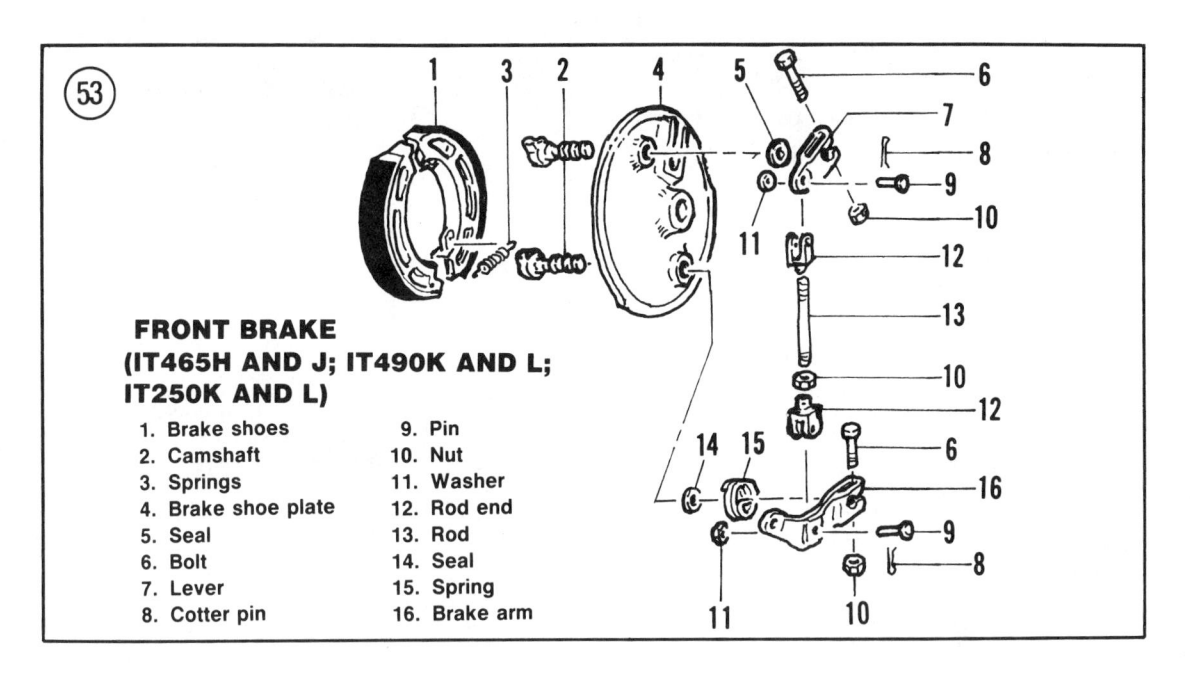

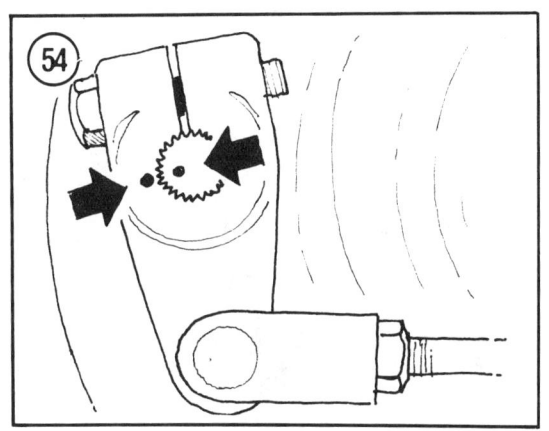

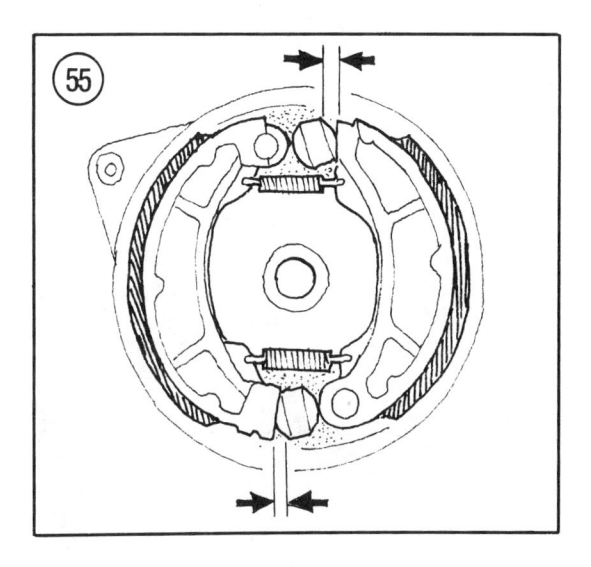

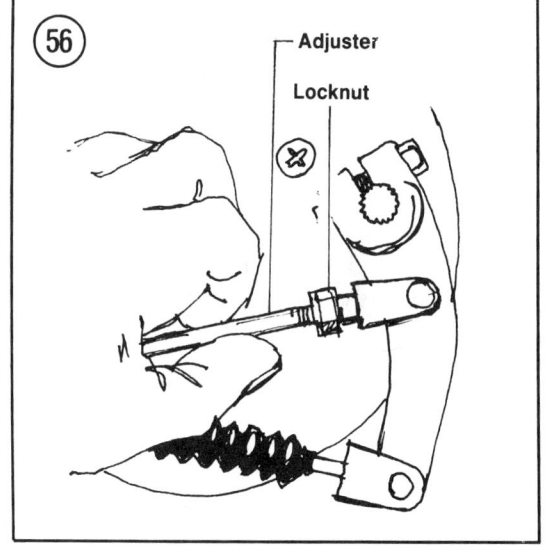

FRONT BRAKE (IT465H AND J; IT490K AND L; IT250K AND L)

1. Brake shoes
2. Camshaft
3. Springs
4. Brake shoe plate
5. Seal
6. Bolt
7. Lever
8. Cotter pin
9. Pin
10. Nut
11. Washer
12. Rod end
13. Rod
14. Seal
15. Spring
16. Brake arm

3. Always keep the master cylinder reservoir and spare cans of brake fluid closed to prevent dust or moisture from entering. This condition would result in brake fluid contamination and brake problems.

4. Use only disc brake fluid (DOT 3) to wash parts. Never clean any internal brake components with solvent or any other petroleum base cleaners.

5. Whenever *any* component has been removed from the brake system, the system is considered "opened" and must be bled to

remove air bubbles. Also, if the brake feels "spongy," this usually means there are air bubbles in the system and it must be bled. For safe brake operation, refer to *Bleeding the System* in this supplement for complete details.

CAUTION
Disc brake components rarely require disassembly. Do not disassemble unless absolutely necessary. Do not use solvents of any kind of the brake system's internal components. Solvents will cause the seals to swell and distort. When disassembling and cleaning brake components (except brake pads) use new brake fluid.

Troubleshooting

Troubleshooting procedures unique to disc brakes are found in the Chapter Two section of this supplement.

FRONT BRAKE CALIPER (IT200S)

1. Pad springs
2. Brake shoes
3. Dust seal
4. Piston seal
5. Piston
6. Boot
7. Cap
8. Bleed screw
9. Inspection cover
10. Brake caliper housing
11. Boot
12. Bolt

FRONT BRAKE PAD REPLACEMENT

There is no recommended time interval for changing the brake pads. The pads should be checked for wear and damage after every race. The brake pads should be replaced when the pad thickness reaches the wear indicator. See *Disc Brake Pad Wear* in Chapter Three of this supplement.

Refer to **Figure 57** for this procedure.
1. Place the bike on a stand so the front wheel clears the ground.
2. Remove the brake caliper bolt (**Figure 58**) and lift the caliper housing up (**Figure 59**).
3. Remove the brake pads (**Figure 60**).
4. Remove the upper and lower (**Figure 61**) pad springs.
5. Clean the pad recess and the end of the pistons with a soft brush. Do not use solvent, wire brush or any hard tool which could damage the cylinders or pistons.

NOTE
Figure 62 shows the caliper housing with pistons removed for clarity.

6. Carefully remove any rust or corrosion from the brake disc.

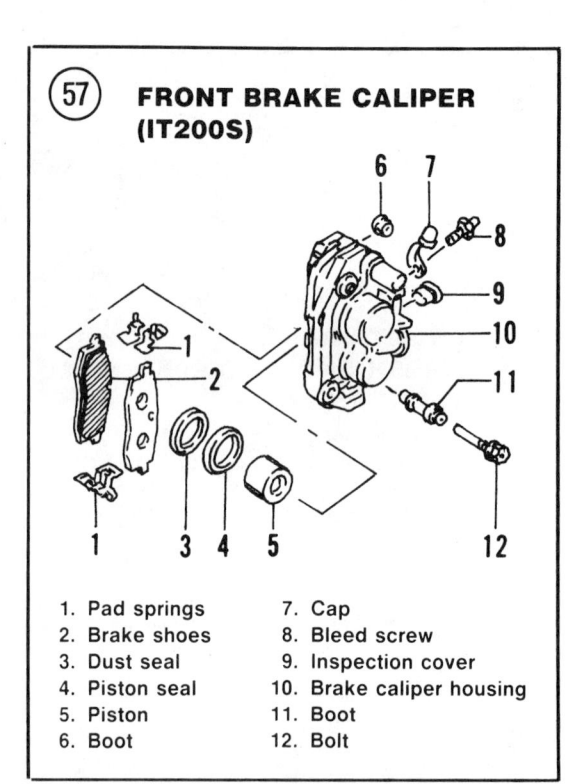

1981 AND LATER INFORMATION

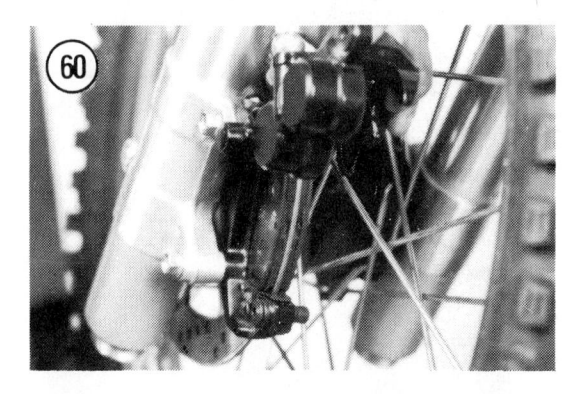

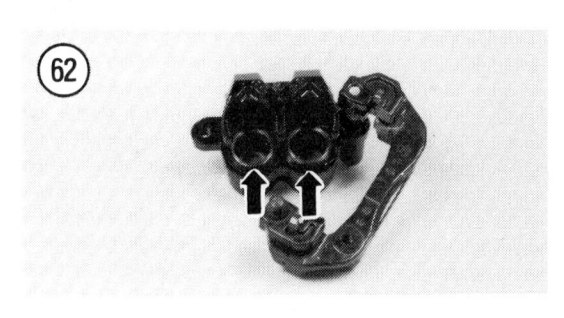

60

61

62

7. When new brake pads are installed in the caliper the master cylinder brake fluid will rise as the caliper pistons are repositioned. Clean the top of the master cylinder of all dirt. Remove the cap (**Figure 63**) and diaphragm from the master cylinder and slowly push the caliper pistons (**Figure 62**) into the caliper. Constantly check the reservoir to make sure brake fluid does not overflow. Remove fluid, if necessary, before it overflows. The pistons should move freely in the caliper bores. If they don't, and there is evidence of them sticking in the caliper, the caliper should be removed and serviced as described under *Front Caliper Disassembly/Inspection/Reassembly* in this supplement.

8. Push the caliper pistons in all the way to allow room for the new pads.

9. Install new anti-rattle springs. **Figure 61** shows the lower spring. The top spring is similar.

10. Place the new brake pads in the caliper bracket (**Figure 60**) and turn the caliper housing clockwise and install it over the brake disc.

11. Install the caliper bolt (**Figure 58**) and tighten to specifications in **Table 32**.

12. Spin the front wheel and activate the brake lever as many times as necessary to refill the cylinder in the caliper and correctly locate the pads.

13. Refill the master cylinder reservoir, if necessary, to maintain the correct brake fluid level. Install the diaphragm and top cover.

WARNING
Use brake fluid clearly marked DOT 3 from a sealed container. Other types may vaporize and cause brake failure. Always use the same brand name; do not intermix as many brands are not compatible.

WARNING
Do not ride the motorcycle until you are sure the brake is operating correctly with full hydraulic advantage. If necessary, bleed the brake system as described in this chapter.

FRONT CALIPER

Removal/Installation

1. Place the bike on a stand so the front wheel clears the ground.

2. Remove the brake pads as described in this chapter.

3. Disconnect the caliper brake hose and washers. See **Figure 64**.

4. Place the end of the brake hose in a clean container. Operate the front brake lever to drain the master cylinder and brake hose of all brake fluid, Dispose of this brake fluid–never reuse brake fluid. To prevent the entry of moisture and dirt, cap the end of the brake line and tie the loose end up to the forks.

5. Remove the caliper bolts (**Figure 65**) and remove the caliper.

6. Install by reversing these removal steps, noting the following.
7. Install the brake hose, with a sealing washer on each side of the fitting, onto the caliper (**Figure 64**). Install the union bolt and tighten to the torque specification listed in **Table 32**.
8. Install the brake pads and tighten the caliper bolt as described under *Front Brake Pad Replacement* in this chapter.
9. Bleed the brake as described in this chapter.

WARNING
Do not ride the motorcycle until you are sure the brake is operating properly.

Disassembly/Inspection/Reassembly

Refer to **Figure 57** for this procedure.
1. Remove the bracket from the caliper housing. See **Figure 66**.

NOTE
Keep track of each piston's position. They must be reinstalled in their original cylinder.

WARNING
Cushion the pistons with a shop rag and wood block. Do not try to cushion the pistons with your fingers, as injury could result.

2. Cushion the caliper pistons with a shop rage and block of wood. Then apply compressed air through the brake line to remove one of the pistons (**Figure 67**).
3. Repeat Step 2 and remove the opposite piston (**Figure 68**).
4. Remove the dust seal and piston seal from each piston bore. See **Figure 69** and **Figure 70**.

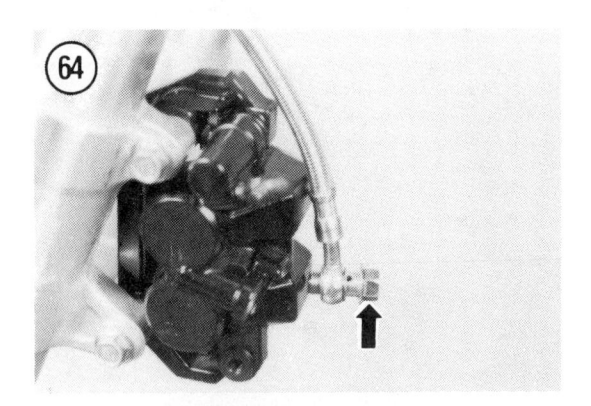

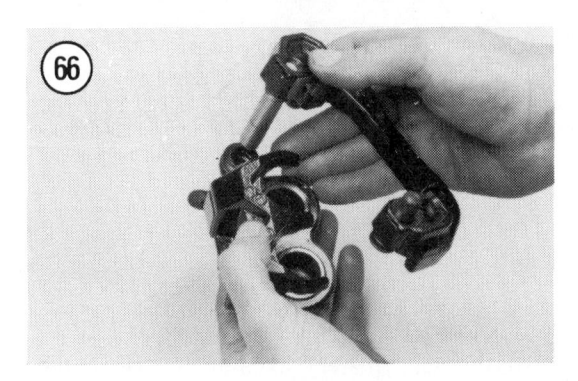

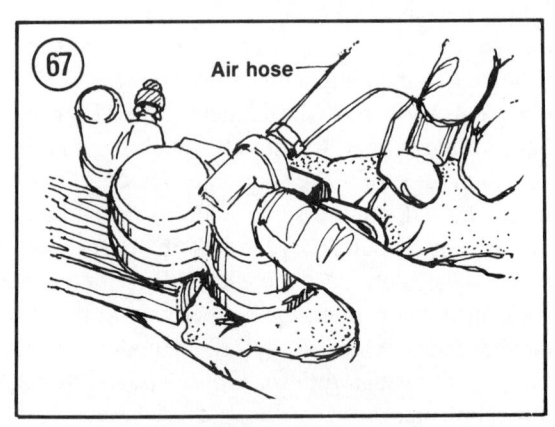

1981 AND LATER INFORMATION

5. Check the pistons and piston bores for deep scratches or other obvious wear marks. If either part is less than perfect, replace it.
6. Check the caliper housing (**Figure 71**) for damage; replace if needed.
7. Remove the bleed screw and check it for wear or damage.
8. Check all threads in the caliper housing for damage.
9. Check the bracket bushings (**Figure 72**) for wear or damage. Check the bracket pivot rod (**Figure 73**) for wear or damage. Replace the bracket if necessary.
10. Clean all parts (except brake pads) with DOT 3 brake fluid.
11. Refer to **Figure 74**. Soak the new dust seals and piston seals in fresh DOT 3 brake fluid. Coat the inside of the cylinder with fresh brake fluid before assembling the parts.
12. Install the pistons in their respective cylinder.
13. Coat the bracket pivot rod (**Figure 73**) with high temperature grease and insert it into the brake caliper housing (**Figure 66**).
14. Install the brake caliper assembly as described in this chapter.

FRONT MASTER CYLINDER

Removal/Installation

Refer to **Figure 75** for this procedure.

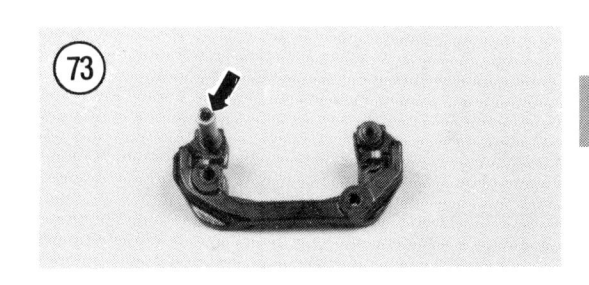

1. Place the bike on a stand so the front wheel clears the ground.
2. Remove the caliper brake hose and washers. See **Figure 76**.
3. Place the end of the brake hose in a clean container. Operate the front brake lever to drain the master cylinder and brake hose of all brake fluid. Dispose of this brake fluid–never reuse brake fluid. To prevent the entry of moisture and dirt, cap the end of the brake line and tie the loose end up to the forks.
4. Remove the master cylinder brake hose and washers. See **Figure 77**.
5. Remove the master cylinder clamp bolts at the handlebar and remove the master cylinder.
6. Install by reversing these removal steps, noting the following.
7. Install the brake hose, with a sealing washer on each side of the fitting, onto the master cylinder and caliper. Install the union bolts and tighten to the torque specifications listed in **Table 32**.
8. Bleed the brake as described in this chapter.

WARNING
Do not ride the motorcycle until you are sure the brake is operating properly.

Disassembly/Inspection/Assembly

Refer to **Figure 75** for this procedure.
1. Remove the master cylinder brake lever.
2. Remove the master cylinder as described in this chapter.
3. Remove the screws securing the cover and remove the cover and diaphragm; pour out the remaining brake fluid and discard it. Never reuse brake fluid.
4. Remove the piston assembly rubber boot.
5. Remove the circlip and remove the piston assembly.
6. Disassemble the parts in the order shown in **Figure 75**.
7. Clean all parts in fresh brake fluid.

NOTE
If any one piston assembly part is worn or damaged, it will be necessary to replace the complete piston assembly.

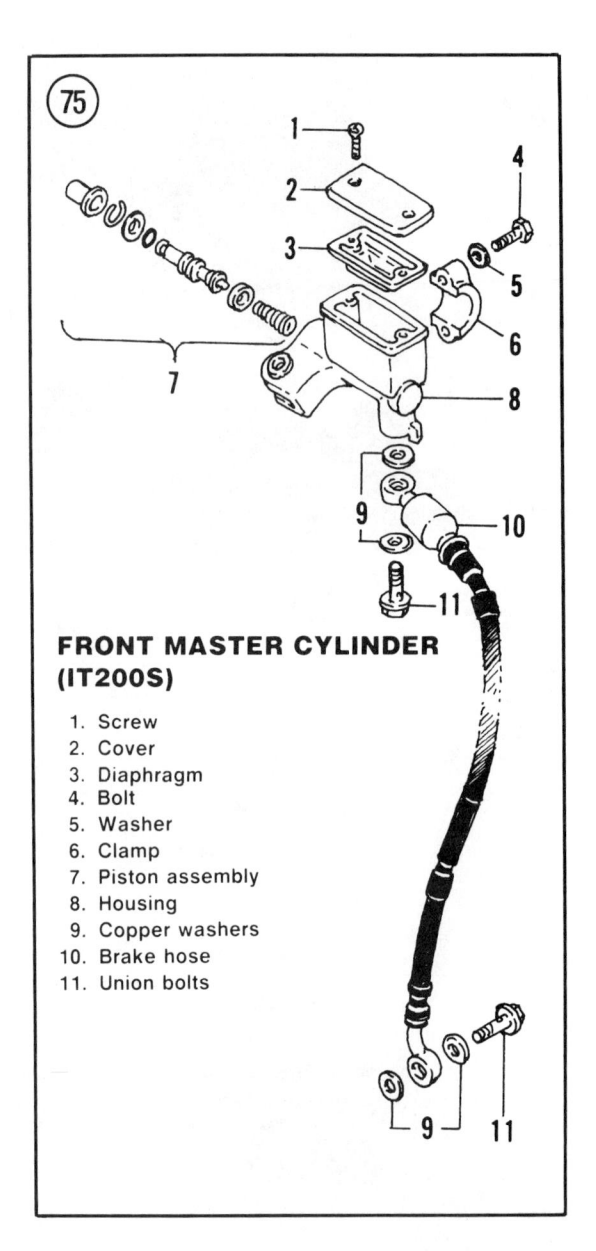

FRONT MASTER CYLINDER (IT200S)

1. Screw
2. Cover
3. Diaphragm
4. Bolt
5. Washer
6. Clamp
7. Piston assembly
8. Housing
9. Copper washers
10. Brake hose
11. Union bolts

1981 AND LATER INFORMATION

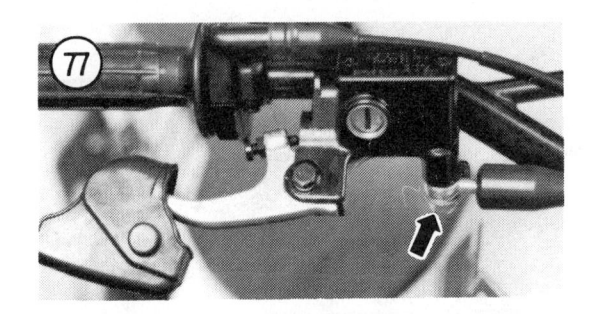

8. Inspect the cylinder bore and piston contact surfaces for signs of wear and damage. If either part is less than perfect, replace it.
9. Check the end of the piston for wear cause by the hand lever. Replace if worn.
10. Check the piston assembly for wear or damage; replace if necessary.
11. Inspect the pivot hole in the hand lever. If worn or elongated it must be replaced.
12. Make sure the passages in the bottom of the brake fluid reservoir are clear. Check the reservoir cap and diaphragm for damge and deterioration and replace as necessary.
13. Inspect the brake line threads; replace if necessary.
14. Assemble the master cylinder as follows.
15. Soak the piston assembly in fresh brake fluid. Coat the inside of the cylinder with fresh DOT 3 brake fluid before assembling the parts.
16. Install the piston assembly in the order shown in **Figure 75**. Secure the assembly with the circlip.
17. Install the piston assembly rubber boot into the master cylinder.
18. Reinstall the master cylinder onto the handlebar.
19. Install the brake lever onto the master cylinder body.

FRONT BRAKE HOSE REPLACEMENT

The brake hose should be replaced whenever it shows signs of wear or damage. Refer to **Figure 75** for this procedure.

1. Place a container under the brake line at the caliper. Remove the union bolt and sealing washer at the caliper assembly (**Figure 76**).
2. Place the end of the brake hose in a clean container. Operate the front brake lever to drain the master cylinder and brake hose of all brake fluid. Dispose of this brake fluid–never reuse brake fluid.
3. Remove the union bolt and sealing washer at the master cylinder (**Figure 77**).
4. Disconnect the brake hose at the front fork.
5. Install a new brake hose in the reverse order of removal. Install new sealing washers and union bolts if necessary.
6. Tighten all union bolts to torque specifications listed in **Table 32**.
7. Refill the master cylinder with fresh brake fluid clearly marked DOT 3. Bleed the brake as described.

WARNING
Do not ride the motorcycle untilyou are sure that the brakes are operating properly.

FRONT BRAKE DISC

Removal/Installation

1. Remove the front wheel as described in Chapter Nine.

NOTE
Place a piece of wood in the caliper in place of the disc. This way, if the brake lever is inadvertently squeezed., the pistons will not be forced out of the cylinder. If this does happen, the caliper might have to be disassembled to reseat the pistons and the system willhave to be bled. By using the wood, bleeding is not necessary when installing the wheel.

2. Remove the bolts securing the disc to the wheel. See **Figure 78**.

3. Install by reversing these removal steps. Tighten bolts to specifications in **Table 32**.
4. Reinstall the front wheel as described in this chapter.

Inspection

It is not necessary to remove the disc from the wheel to inspect it. Small marks on the disc are not important, but radial scratches deep enough to snag a fingernail reduce braking effectiveness and increase brake pad wear. If these grooves are found, the disc should be resurfaced or replaced.

1. Measure the thickness around the disc at several locations with vernier calipers or a micrometer (**Figure 79**). The disc must be replaced if the thickness at any point is less than specified in **Table 31**.
2. Make sure the disc bolts are tight before performing this check. Check the disc runout with a dial indicator as shown in **Figure 80**. Slowly rotate the wheel and watch the dial indicator. If the runout exceeds 0.006 in. (0.15 mm), replace the disc.
3. Clean the disc of any rust or corrosion and wipe clean with lacquer thinner. Never use an oil based solvent that may leave an oil residue on the disc.

BLEEDING THE SYSTEM

This procedure is necessary only when the brakes feel spongy, there is a leak in the hydraulic system, a component has been replaced or the brake fluid has been replaced.

1. Flip off the dust cap from the brake bleeder valve (**Figure 81**).
2. Connect a length of clear tubing to the bleeder valve on the caliper (**Figure 82**). Place the other end of the tube into a clean container. Fill the container with enough fresh brake fluid to keep the end submerge. The tube should be long enough so that a loop can be made higher than the bleeder valve to prevent air from being drawn into the caliper during bleeding. See **Figure 83**.

CAUTION
Cover the front wheel, fender and fuel tank with a heavy cloth or plastic tarp to protect it from the accidental spilling of brake fluid. Wash any spilled brake fluid off of any painted or plated surface immediately, as it will destroy the finish. Use soapy water and rinse completely.

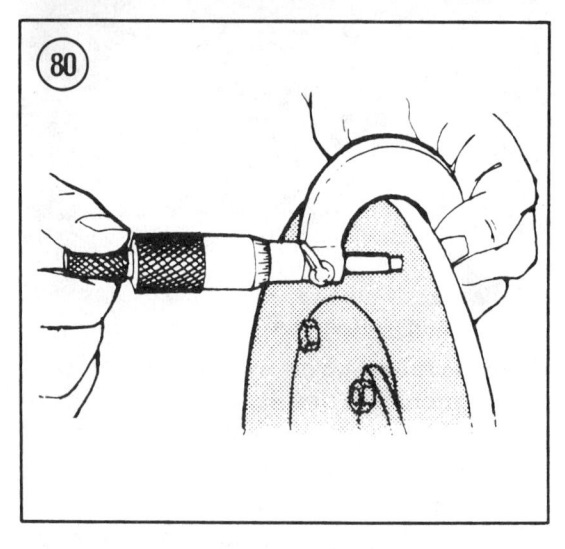

3. Clean the top of the master cylinder of all dirt and foreign matter. Remove the cap and diaphragm. Fill the reservoir to about 3/8 in. (10 mm) from the top. Insert the diaphragm to prevent the entry of dirt and moisture.

WARNING
Use brake fluid clearly marked DOT 3 only. Others may vaporize and cause brake failure. Always use the same brand name; do not intermix the brake fluids, as many brands are not compatible.

4. Slowly apply the brake lever several times. Hold the lever in the applied position and open

1981 AND LATER INFORMATION

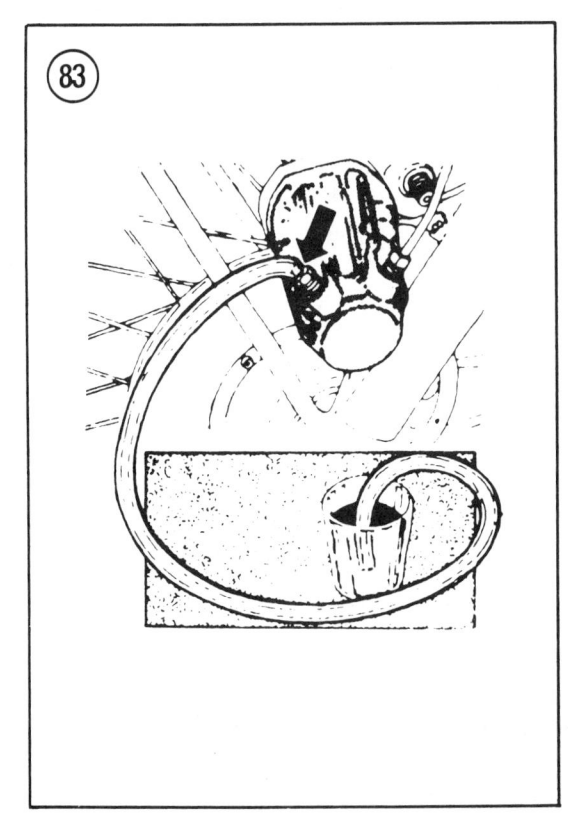

the bleeder valve about 1/2 turn (**Figure 82**). Allow the lever to travel to its limit. When this limit is reached, tighten the bleeder screw. As the brake fluid enters the system, the level will drop in the master cylinder reservoir. Maintain the level at about 10 mm (3.8 in.) from the top of the reservoir to prevent air air from being drawn into the system.

5. Continue to pump the lever and fill the reservoir until the fluid emerging from the hose is completely free of air bubbles. If you are replacing the fluid, continue until the fluid emerging from the hose is clean.

NOTE
If bleeding is difficult, it may be necessary to allow the fluid to stabilize for a few hours. Repeat the bleeding procedure when the tiny bubbles in the system settle out.

6. Hold the lever in the applied position and tighten the bleeder valve. Remove the bleeder tube and install the bleeder valve dust cap (**Figure 81**).

7. If necessary, add fluid to correct the level in the master cylinder reservoir. It must be above the level line.

8. Install the cap and tighten the screws.

9. Test the feel of the brake lever. It should feel firm and should offer the same resistance each time it's operated. If it feels spongy, it is likely that air is still in the system and it must be bled again. When all air has been bled from the system and the brake fluid level is correct in the reservoir, double-check for leaks and tighten all fittings and connections.

WARNING
Before riding the motorcycle make certain that the front brake is operating correctly by operating the lever several times. Then make the rest ride a slow one at first to make sure the brake is operating correctly.

Table 29 BRAKE SPECIFICATIONS (IT250H, J, K; IT465H, J; IT490K, L)

Item	in.	mm
Drum ID (new)		
Rear	5.91	150
Brake shoe wear limit		
Rear	0.08	2
Shoe spring free length (new)		
Front	1.44	36.5
Rear	2.68	68

Table 30 BRAKE SPECIFICATIONS (IT200N AND L)

	Standard in. (mm)	Wear limit in. (mm)
Brake drum inside diameter		
Front and rear	5.12 (130)	5.16 (131)
Brake shoe lining thickness	0.16 (4)	0.08 (2)
Shoe spring free length	1.44 (36.5)	

Table 31 BRAKE SPECIFICATIONS (IT200S)

	Standard in. (mm)	Wear limit in. (mm)
Front disc brake		
Front disc		
Outside diameter	9.06 (230)	
Thickness	0.12 (3.0)	0.1 (2.5)
Front pad thickness	0.16 (4.0)	0.03 (0.8)
Master cylinder inside diameter	0.433 (11.0)	
Caliper inside diameter	1.061 (27.0)	
Rear drum brake		
Brake drum inside diameter	5.12 (130)	5.16 (131)
Lining thickness	0.16 (4)	0.08 (2)
Brake shoe free length	1.44 (36.5)	

Table 32 BRAKE TIGHTENING TORQUES (IT200S)

	ft.-lb.	N·m
Brake disc	9	12
Brake caliper bolt	17	23
Caliper bracket	22	30
Banjo (union) bolts	19	26

INDEX

A
Air cleaner 42, 166

B
Brakes
    Assembly, front 264-265
    Cable 268-269
    Disassembly, front 261-263
    Disassembly, rear 265
    Inspection, front 263-264
    Inspection, rear 265-268
    Maintenance 38, 39
    Pedal assembly 269-271
    Troubleshooting 21
    1981 service information 320-330

C
Capacitor discharge ignition 182
Carburetor adjustments 174-177
Carburetor operation 166
Carburetor service 166-174
    1981 service information 295
Cleaning solvent 24
Clutch
    Assembly/installation 126-129
    Cable 130-131
    Inspection 121-126
    Maintenance 39-42
    Release mechanism 131-132
    Removal/disassembly 118-121
    1981 service information 291-295
Crankcase
    Assembly (type I) 87-90
    Assembly (type II) 92-93
    Assembly (type III) 96-98
    Assembly (type IV) 99-102
    Disassembly (type I) 84-87
    Disassembly (type II) 90-92
    Disassembly (type III) 93-96
    Disassembly (type IV) 98-99
    Inspection 102-105
Crankshaft 83-84, 102-105
Cylinder head 68-69
Cylinder 69-73

D
Decarbon monocross system 242-257
Drive chain 33-37, 233-234

E
Electrical system
    Capacitor discharge ignition 182
    Engine kill switch 191
    Ignition coil 190-191
    Lighting system 192-193
    Magneto 183-190
    Spark plug 183
    Speedometer housing 193
    Wiring diagrams .... end of book
    1981 service information 300
Engine
    Break-in procedure 79
    Compression release (IT400C only) 81-83
    Cooling 65
    Crankcase and crankshaft 83-105
    Cylinder 69-73
    Cylinder head 68-69
    Kickstarter 105-114
    Kill switch 191
    Lubrication 65
    Magneto 79
    Piston, piston pin and
      piston rings 73-79
    Reed valve assembly 79-81
    Removal/installation 65-68
    Service and adjustment 114
    Servicing (in frame) 65
    Specifications 116-117
    Troubleshooting 18-20
    1981 service information 287-290
Exhaust system 178-180

F
Footpegs 272
Frame 272-274

INDEX

Front fork
    Assembly 218-220
    Disassembly 217
    Inspection 217-218
    Periodic maintenance 32
    Removal/installation 215-217
Fuel filter 178
Fuel shutoff valve 177-178
Fuel system
    Air cleaner 42, 166
    Carburetor adjustments 174-177
    Carburetor operation 166
    Carburetor service 166-174
Fuel tank 178

H

Handlebar 206-207
Hub, front 197-200
Hub, rear 227-232

I

Ignition coil 190-191

K

Kickstand (side stand) 272
Kickstarter 105-114

L

Lighting system 192-193
Lubrication 23-24
Lubrication, periodic
    Control cables 31-32
    Drive chain 30-31
    Engine 24, 65
    Front fork 27-30
    Miscellaneous 32
    Transmission 26-27
    1981 service information 302

M

Magneto
    Charge, lighting,
        and pulser coil replacement 188
    Coil testing 188-190
    Removal/installation 79
    Rotor removal/installation 183-186
    Stator assembly
        removal/installation 187-188
Maintenance, general (see also Tune-up)

Maintenance, periodic
    Air cleaner 42
    Clutch 39-42
    Drive chain 33-37
    Front brake lever adjustment 38
    Front fork air pressure 32
    Fuel line inpection 44
    Monoshock adjustment 33
    Nuts, bolts, and other fasteners 46
    Rear brake pedal 39
    Servicing 42-44
    Suspension, front 45
    Suspension, rear 46
    Throttle adjustment and operation 42
    Wheel bearings 45
    Wheel hubs, rims and spokes 45
    1981 service information 278-281

P

Piston 73-79

S

Servicing 42-44
Shift mechanism, external 132-140
Spark plug 183
Special tips 6
Speedometer housing 193
Steering
    Handlebar 206-207
    Steering head 208-214
    Troubleshooting 21
    Wheels 200-202
Storage 55-57
Suspension, front
    Front forks 214-220
    Front hub 197-200
    Front wheel 195-197
    Maintenance 45
    Troubleshooting 21
    1981 service information 302-309
Suspension, rear
    DeCarbon monocross system 242-257
    Drive chain 233-234
    Drive sprocket 232-233
    Maintenance 46
    Monocross type 257-259
    Rear hub 227-232
    Rear swing arm 234-242
    Rear wheel 224-229
    Tire changing and repairs 234
    Wheel balancing 234
    1981 service information 310-318

INDEX

Swing arm, rear
    Aluminum 240-242
    Removal/installation 234-236
    Steel swing arm 236-240

T

Tools 8-12
Transmission and internal shift mechanism
    Countershaft (6-speed) 160-162
    5-speed removal/installation 148-150
    Internal shift mechanism
        inspection 162-165
    Main shaft (5-speed) 152-157
    Main shaft (6-speed) 158-160
    6-speed removal/installation 150-152
    1981 service information 291-294
Troubleshooting
    Brake problems 21
    Emergency 18
    Engine 18-20
    Excessive vibration 20
    Front suspension and steering 21
    Operating requirements 17-18
    Tools and instruments 12, 18
    Two-stroke pressure testing 20-21
    1981 service information 276-278

Tune-up
    Cylinder head nuts 47
    Decarbonizing 54-55
    Idle speed adjustment 53-54
    Ignition timing 49-53
    Spark plugs 47-49
    Tools 12

W

Wheels and tires
    Front wheel 195-196
    Maintenance 45
    Rear wheel 222-227
    Spokes 201-202
    Tire changing 202-204, 234
    Tire repairs 204-206, 234
    Wheel balance 200-201, 234
Wiring diagrams .... 193, end of book

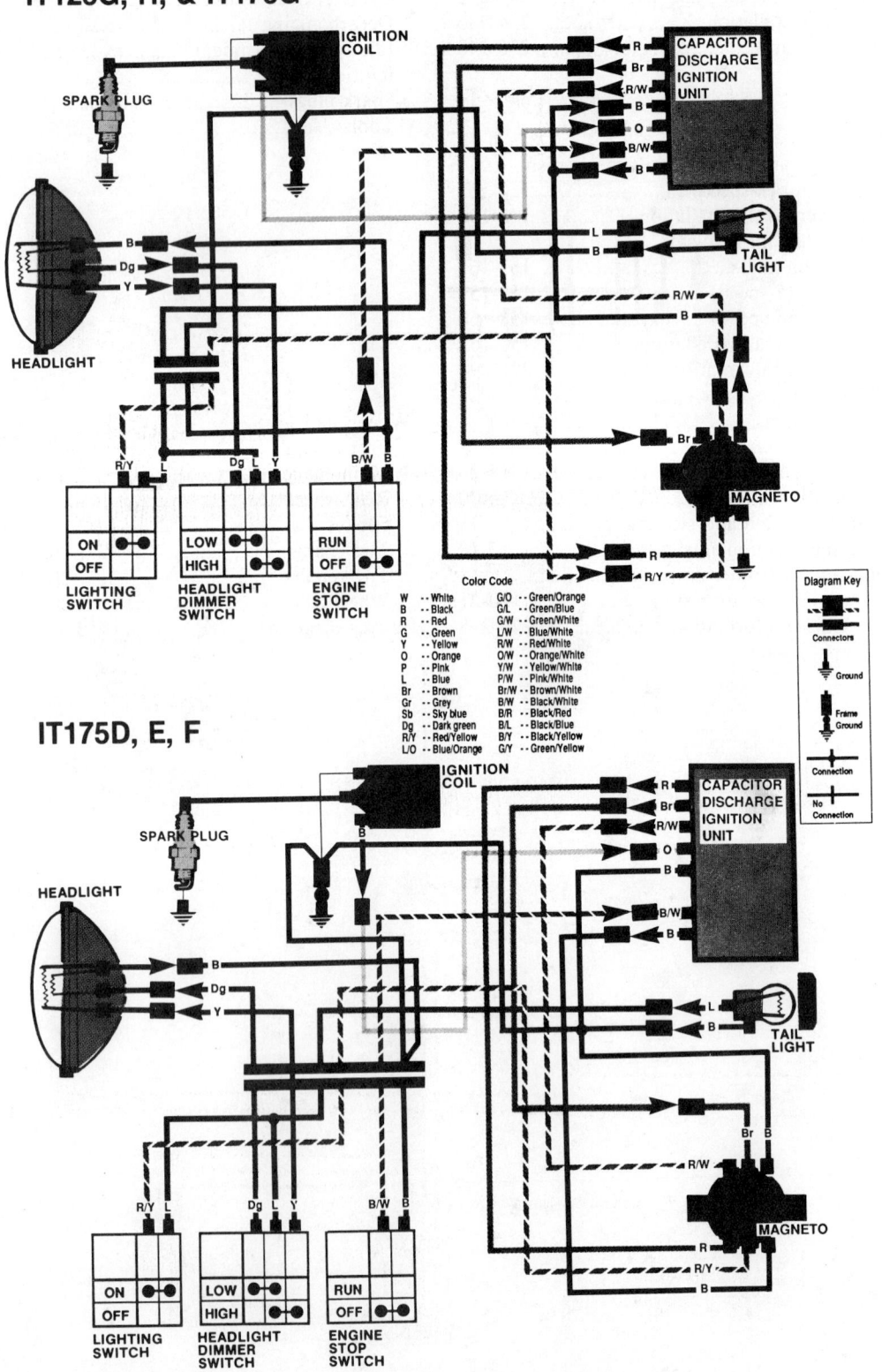

WIRING DIAGRAMS

IT125G, H, & IT175G

IT175D, E, F

Color Code

W	-- White	G/O	-- Green/Orange
B	-- Black	G/L	-- Green/Blue
R	-- Red	G/W	-- Green/White
G	-- Green	L/W	-- Blue/White
Y	-- Yellow	R/W	-- Red/White
O	-- Orange	O/W	-- Orange/White
P	-- Pink	Y/W	-- Yellow/White
L	-- Blue	P/W	-- Pink/White
Br	-- Brown	Br/W	-- Brown/White
Gr	-- Grey	B/W	-- Black/White
Sb	-- Sky blue	B/R	-- Black/Red
Dg	-- Dark green	B/L	-- Black/Blue
R/Y	-- Red/Yellow	B/Y	-- Black/Yellow
L/O	-- Blue/Orange	G/Y	-- Green/Yellow

Diagram Key: Connectors, Ground, Frame Ground, Connection, No Connection

WIRING DIAGRAMS

IT175H

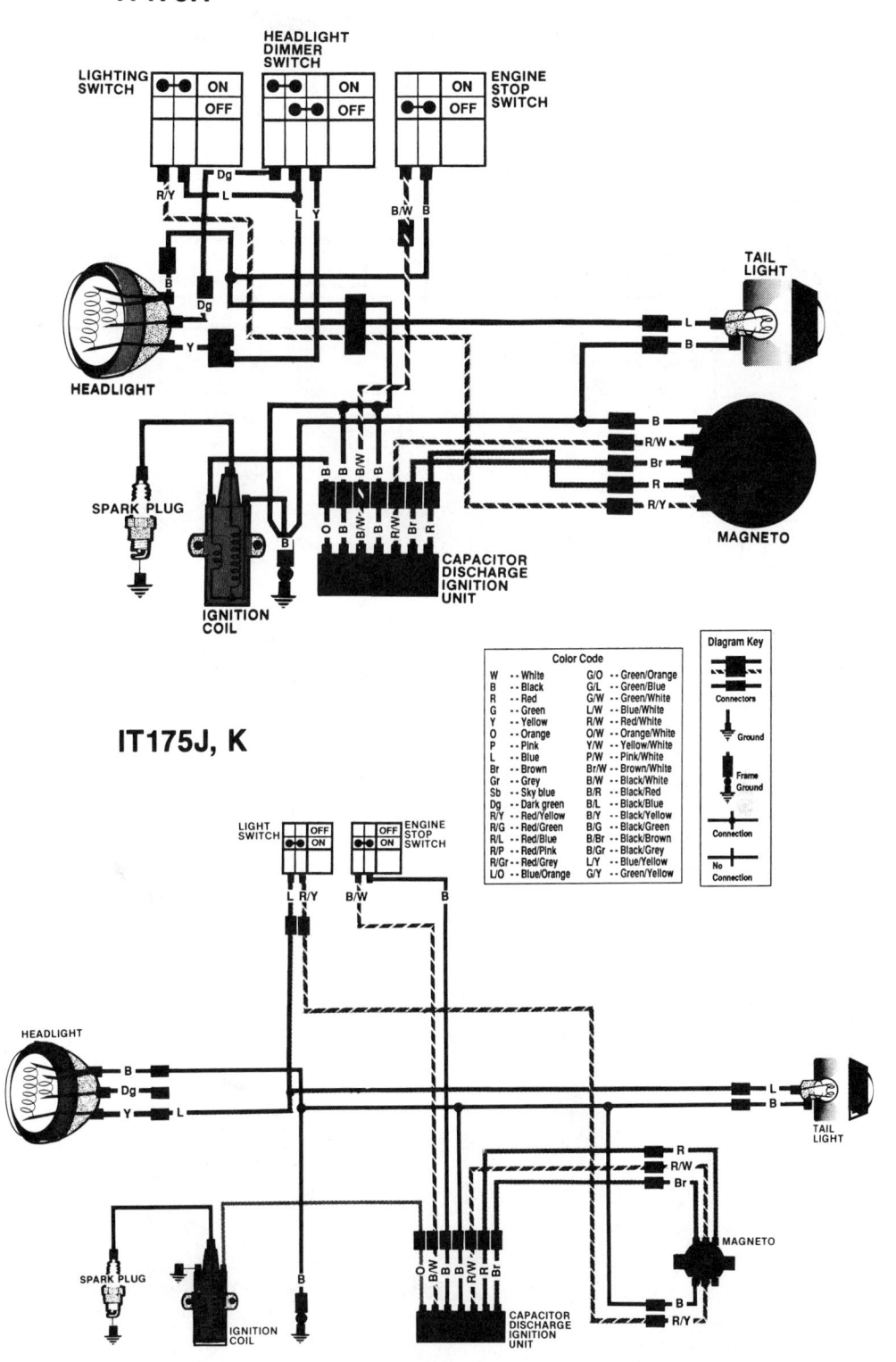

IT175J, K

Color Code

W	White	G/O	Green/Orange
B	Black	G/L	Green/Blue
R	Red	G/W	Green/White
G	Green	L/W	Blue/White
Y	Yellow	R/W	Red/White
O	Orange	O/W	Orange/White
P	Pink	Y/W	Yellow/White
L	Blue	P/W	Pink/White
Br	Brown	Br/W	Brown/White
Gr	Grey	B/W	Black/White
Sb	Sky blue	B/R	Black/Red
Dg	Dark green	B/L	Black/Blue
R/Y	Red/Yellow	B/Y	Black/Yellow
R/G	Red/Green	B/G	Black/Green
R/L	Red/Blue	B/Br	Black/Brown
R/P	Red/Pink	B/Gr	Black/Grey
R/Gr	Red/Grey	L/Y	Blue/Yellow
L/O	Blue/Orange	G/Y	Green/Yellow

Diagram Key: Connectors, Ground, Frame Ground, Connection, No Connection

WIRING DIAGRAMS

IT200N,S

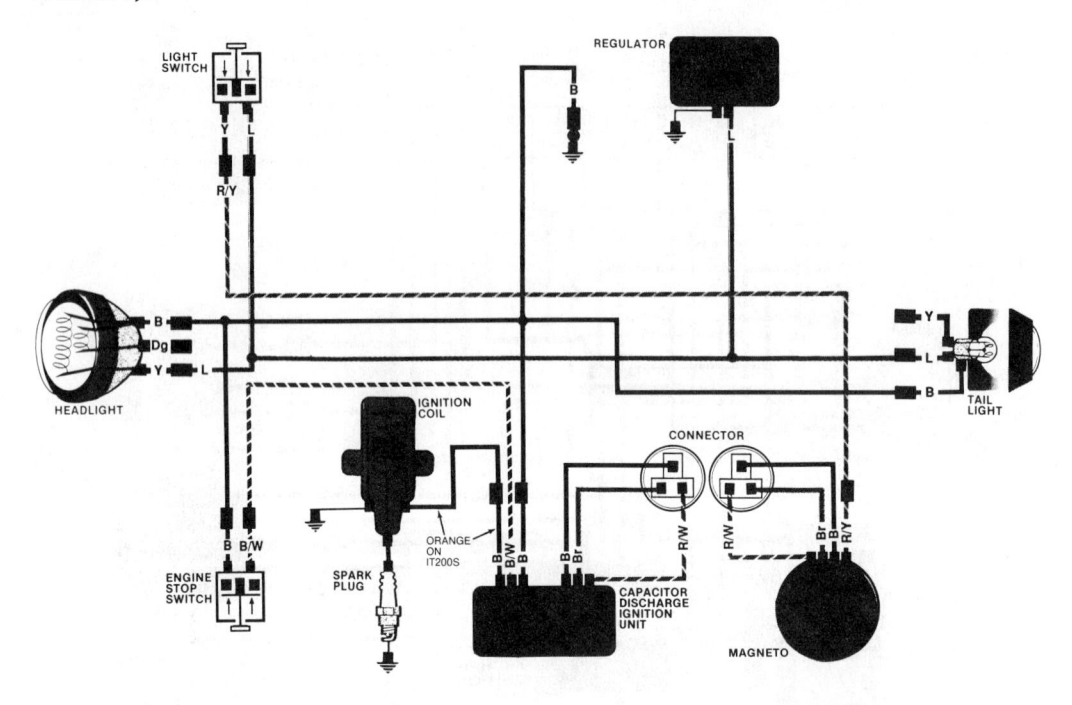

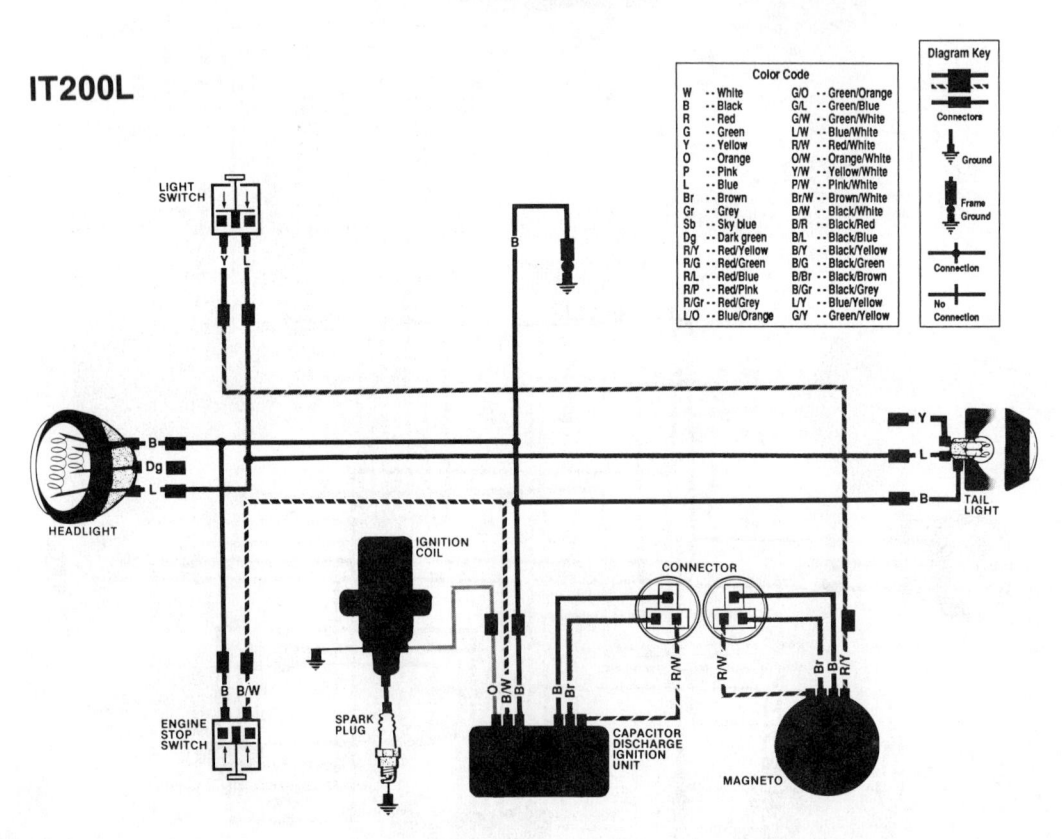

IT200L

Color Code

W	-- White	G/O	-- Green/Orange
B	-- Black	G/L	-- Green/Blue
R	-- Red	G/W	-- Green/White
G	-- Green	L/W	-- Blue/White
Y	-- Yellow	R/W	-- Red/White
O	-- Orange	O/W	-- Orange/White
P	-- Pink	Y/W	-- Yellow/White
L	-- Blue	P/W	-- Pink/White
Br	-- Brown	Br/W	-- Brown/White
Gr	-- Grey	B/W	-- Black/White
Sb	-- Sky blue	B/R	-- Black/Red
Dg	-- Dark green	B/L	-- Black/Blue
R/Y	-- Red/Yellow	B/Y	-- Black/Yellow
R/G	-- Red/Green	B/G	-- Black/Green
R/L	-- Red/Blue	B/Br	-- Black/Brown
R/P	-- Red/Pink	B/Gr	-- Black/Grey
R/Gr	-- Red/Grey	L/Y	-- Blue/Yellow
L/O	-- Blue/Orange	G/Y	-- Green/Yellow

Diagram Key

- Connectors
- Ground
- Frame Ground
- Connection
- No Connection

WIRING DIAGRAMS

IT250D, E, F

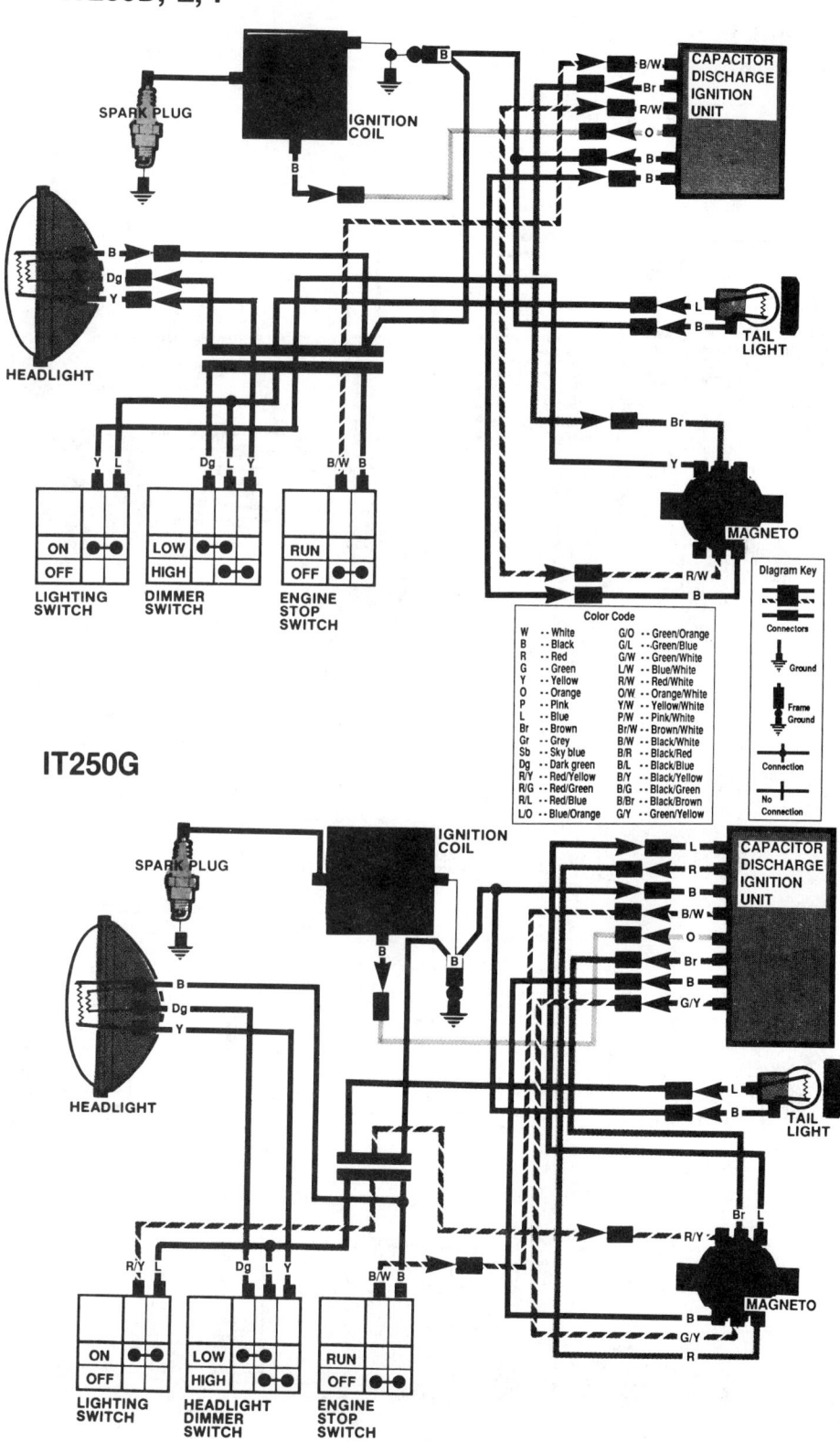

IT250G

Color Code

W	White	G/O	Green/Orange
B	Black	G/L	Green/Blue
R	Red	G/W	Green/White
G	Green	L/W	Blue/White
Y	Yellow	R/W	Red/White
O	Orange	O/W	Orange/White
P	Pink	Y/W	Yellow/White
L	Blue	P/W	Pink/White
Br	Brown	Br/W	Brown/White
Gr	Grey	B/W	Black/White
Sb	Sky blue	B/R	Black/Red
Dg	Dark green	B/L	Black/Blue
R/Y	Red/Yellow	B/Y	Black/Yellow
R/G	Red/Green	B/G	Black/Green
R/L	Red/Blue	B/Br	Black/Brown
L/O	Blue/Orange	G/Y	Green/Yellow

Diagram Key

- Connectors
- Ground
- Frame Ground
- Connection
- No Connection

WIRING DIAGRAMS

IT250H

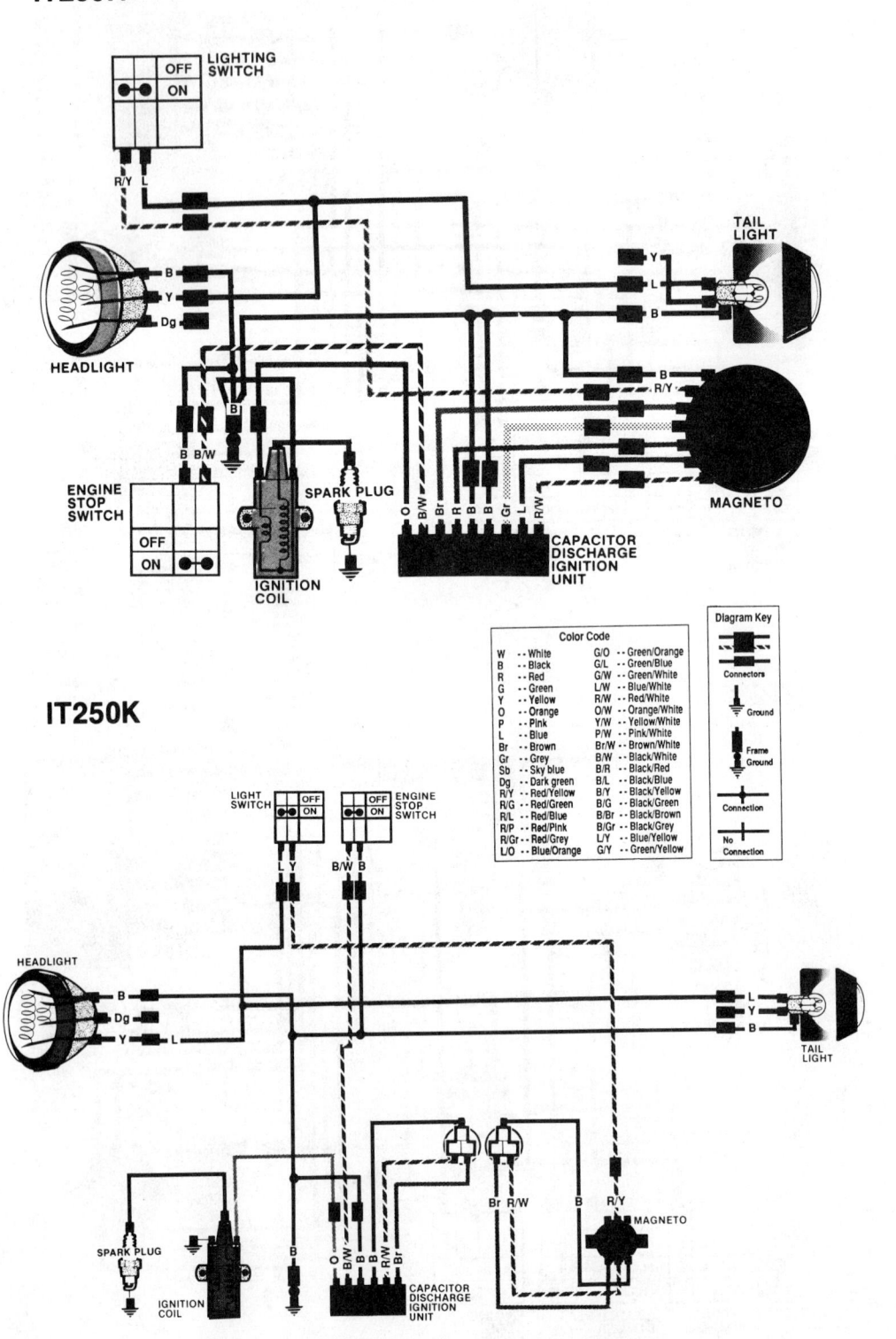

IT250K

WIRING DIAGRAMS

IT400C, D, E, F

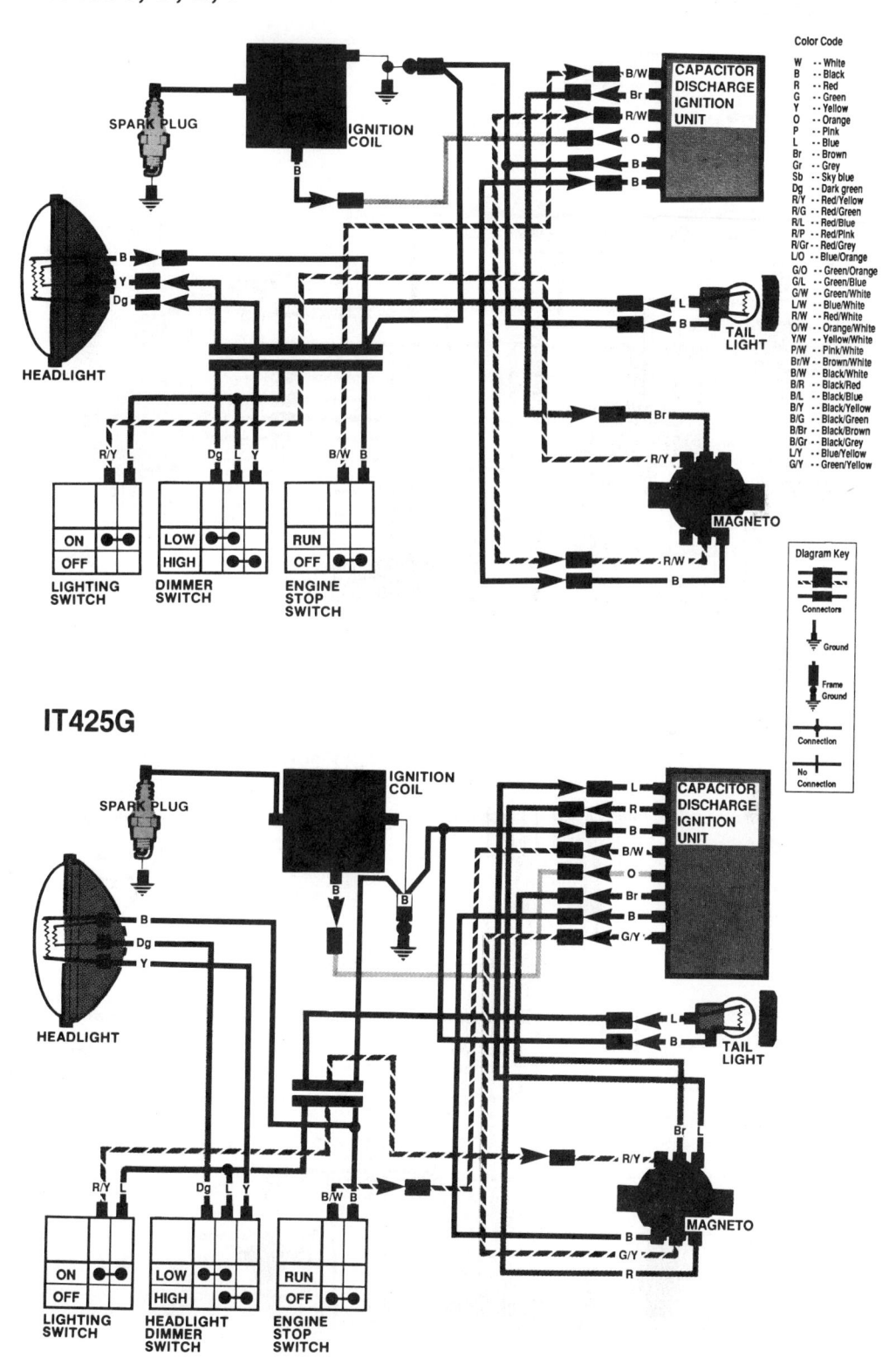

IT425G

Color Code

W	White
B	Black
R	Red
G	Green
Y	Yellow
O	Orange
P	Pink
L	Blue
Br	Brown
Gr	Grey
Sb	Sky blue
Dg	Dark green
R/Y	Red/Yellow
R/G	Red/Green
R/L	Red/Blue
R/P	Red/Pink
R/Gr	Red/Grey
L/O	Blue/Orange
G/O	Green/Orange
G/L	Green/Blue
G/W	Green/White
L/W	Blue/White
R/W	Red/White
O/W	Orange/White
Y/W	Yellow/White
P/W	Pink/White
Br/W	Brown/White
B/W	Black/White
B/R	Black/Red
B/L	Black/Blue
B/Y	Black/Yellow
B/G	Black/Green
B/Br	Black/Brown
B/Gr	Black/Grey
L/Y	Blue/Yellow
G/Y	Green/Yellow

Diagram Key
- Connectors
- Ground
- Frame Ground
- Connection
- No Connection

WIRING DIAGRAMS

IT465H

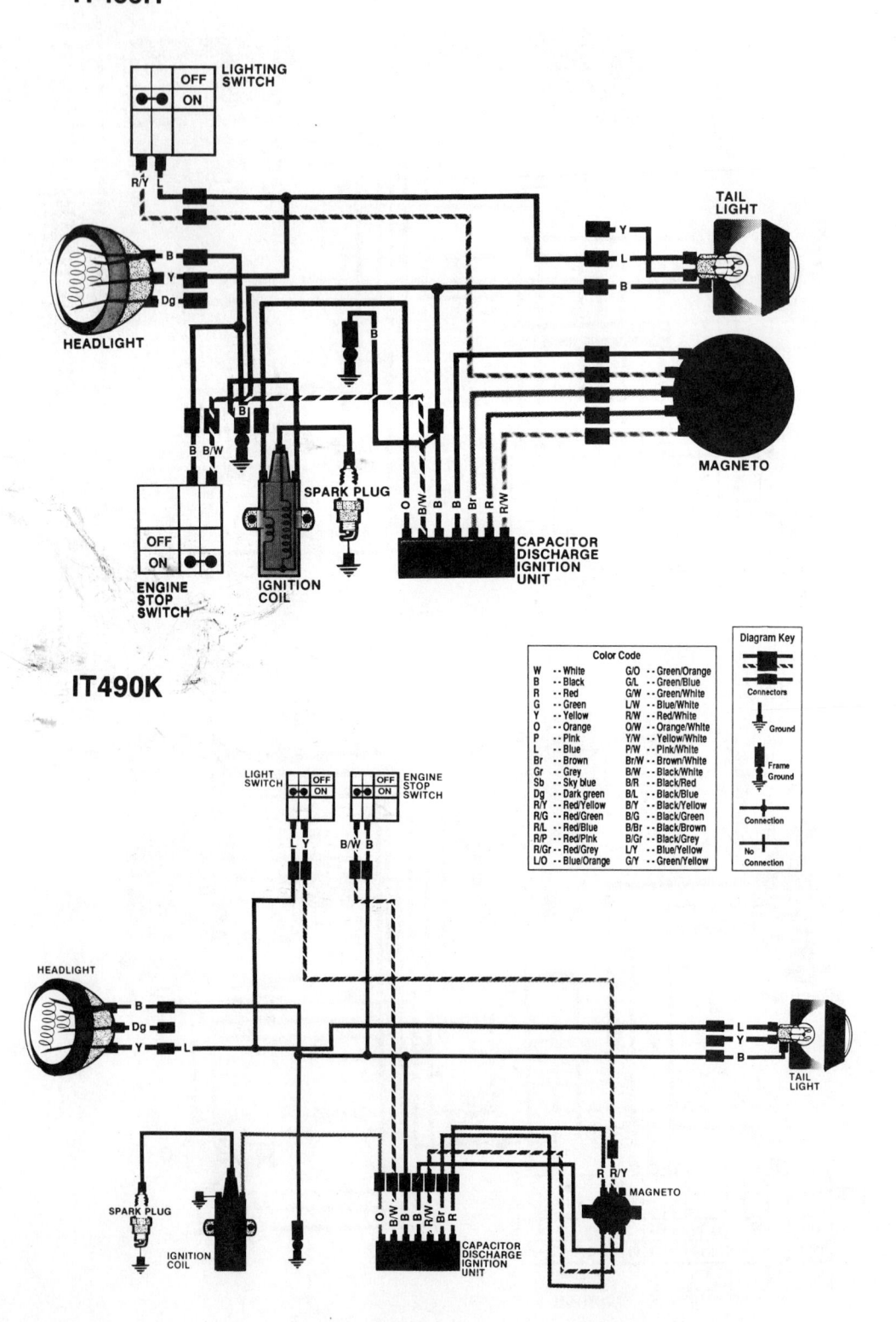

IT490K